Rosemary Stanfield
1978
NYU.

A LITERARY
HISTORY OF PERSIA

IN FOUR VOLUMES

VOLUME II

A PERSIAN POET OF THE LATE THIRTEENTH CENTURY PRESENTING A QAṢÍDA OR PANEGYRIC TO A MONGOL PRINCE OR GOVERNOR.

This miniature is from a Persian Manuscript containing selected poems from the Díwáns of Six Persian poets. The manuscript was transcribed in A.H. 714 (=A.D. 1315), formerly belonged to Sháh Isma'íl the Ṣafawí, and is now in the India Office Library (No. 132 = No. 903 of Ethé's Catalogue). As the artist himself lived in the Mongol Period, the details of costume may be regarded as authoritative; while the difference of physiognomy between the Persian and the six Mongols is clearly apparent.

A LITERARY HISTORY OF PERSIA

VOLUME II

From Firdawsí to Sa'dí

BY

EDWARD G. BROWNE

CAMBRIDGE UNIVERSITY PRESS

CAMBRIDGE

LONDON · NEW YORK · MELBOURNE

Published by the Syndics of the Cambridge University Press
The Pitt Building, Trumpington Street, Cambridge CB2 1RP
Bentley House, 200 Euston Road, London NW1 2DB
32 East 57th Street, New York, NY 10022, USA
296 Beaconsfield Parade, Middle Park, Melbourne 3206, Australia

ISBN 0 521 04345 X

First published by T. Fisher Unwin 1906
Reprinted 1915, 1920
First published by Cambridge University Press 1928
Reprinted 1951, 1956, 1964, 1969, 1977

First printed in Great Britain at the University Press, Cambridge
Reprinted by Lewis Reprints, Tonbridge

DEDICATION

ALTHOUGH this book of mine is all unmeet,
Light of mine eyes, to lay at thy dear feet,
I think that Alchemy which worketh still
Can turn to gold this copper, if it will,
Enlarge its merits and ignore its ill.

Can I forget how, as it neared its end,
A happy chance permitted me to blend
Rare intervals of worship ill-concealed,
Occasions brief of love but half revealed,
Long days of hope deferred, short hours of bliss,
Into a happiness so full as this?
Now come I, Dearest, for my book to claim
Even so great an honour as thy name!

Preface

THE present volume is a continuation of that which I published in the same series four years ago, and carries the Literary History of Persia on from the beginning of the eleventh to the middle of the thirteenth century of our era. This period, comparatively short as it is, includes most of the greatest poets and writers of the Persians, and I hardly anticipate that I shall be accused by any competent critic of discussing it with undue detail. Should I succeed in carrying out my original plan, by continuing the history down to our own times, I believe that the remaining six centuries and a half can be adequately treated in one volume equal in size to this.

Of the defects of this book, now that it is all in type, I am fully sensible. They arise largely from the fact that it was chiefly written during vacations, and that two months or more often elapsed between the completion of one chapter and the beginning of the next. Under present conditions the University of Cambridge is far from being the best place in the world for quiet, steady, regular work; and though the books of reference indispensable for a compilation of this kind were there, leisure was only to be found elsewhere, even as the poet Ṣá'ib says:—

Shigúfa bá thamar hargiz na-gardad jam' dar yak já:
Muḥál-ast ánki bá-ham ni'mat u dindán shavad paydá!

"Never in one place are found the luscious fruit and blossom fine;
Vain it is for one to hope both teeth and dainties to combine!"

In consequence of this, the book, as I am well aware, is

marred not only by occasional repetitions, but by a certain disconnectedness and lack of uniformity for which I crave the reader's indulgence. On the other hand I have throughout endeavoured to use original sources and to form independent views, and in this I have been aided by several rare works, inaccessible or hardly accessible to my predecessors, of which I may specially mention the *Chahár Maqála* ("Four Discourses") of Nidhámí-i-'Arúḍí of Samarqand, the *Lubábu'l-Albáb* of Muḥammad 'Awfí, the *Mu'ajjam* of Shams-i-Qays, and my notes on the *Ráḥatu'ṣ-Ṣudúr* of ar-Ráwandí, the *Jahán-gushá* of 'Aṭá Malik-i-Juwayní, the *Jámi'u't-Tawáríkh* of Rashídu'd-Dín Faḍlu'lláh, and other similar books.

The work itself has had my whole heart, and I would that it could also have had my undivided attention. For Islám and the Perso-Arabian civilisation of Islám I have the deepest admiration; an admiration which it is especially incumbent on me to confess at a time when these are so much misunderstood and misrepresented by Europeans; who appear to imagine that they themselves have a monopoly of civilisation, and a kind of divine mandate to impose on the whole world not only their own political institutions but their own modes of thought. Year by year, almost, the number of independent Muslim States grows less and less, while such as still remain—Persia, Turkey, Arabia, Morocco, and a few others—are ever more and more overshadowed by the menace of European interference. Of course it is in part their own fault, and Asiatic indifference and apathy combine with European "earth-hunger" and lust of conquest to hasten their disintegration. To the unreflecting Western mind the extinction of these States causes no regret, but only exhilarating thoughts of more "openings" for their children and their capital; but those few who know and love the East and its peoples, and realise how deeply we are indebted to it for most of the great spiritual ideas which give meaning and value to life, will feel, with Chesterton's "Man in Green," that with the subsidence of every such State something is lost to the world which can never be replaced. Yet this is not, perhaps, a question which can be settled by argument, any more than it can be settled by argument which is better, a garden planted with one useful vegetable or with a variety of beautiful flowers, each possessing its own distinctive colour and fragrance. But this at least must be admitted by any one who has a real sympathy with and understanding of the Spirit of the East, that it suffers atrophy and finally death under even a good and well-meaning European administration; and that for this reason Constantinople, Damascus, Shíráz and Fez, for all their shortcomings, do possess something of artistic and intellectual, even, perhaps, of moral value, which Cairo, Delhi, Algiers, and Tunis are losing or have lost. Whether Islám is still bleeding to death from the wounds first inflicted on it by the Mongols six hundred and fifty years ago, or whether the proof given by Japan that the Asiatic is not, even on the physical plane, necessarily inferior to the European may lead to some unexpected revival, is a question of supreme interest which cannot here be discussed.

My deepest gratitude is due to my sister, Miss E. M. Browne, and to my friend and colleague, Mr. E. H. Minns, for reading through the proofs of this book, and for making not only minor verbal corrections, but suggestions of a more general character. To Mr. Minns I am also indebted for interpreting to me the monographs of several eminent Russian Orientalists to which I have referred in these pages, and which, but for his generous help, would have been to me sealed books. Of the general criticisms which he was kind enough to make, one, I think, merits a reference in this place. He tells me that in the first chapter, when treating of Persian Prosody, I have not been sufficiently explicit for the reader who is not an Orientalist as to the nature of the *bayt* and the fundamental laws of quantity in scansion.

As regards the first of these points, the *bayt* or verse is, as I have said, always regarded by the Muslims as the unit, and for this reason I consider that it should not, as is often done in European books, be called a "couplet." That it is the unit is clearly shown by the fact that a metre is called *musaddas* (hexameter) or *muthamman* (octameter) when the *bayt* comprises six or eight feet respectively. Unfortunately the *bayt*, which is always written or printed in one line in the East, is generally, when transcribed in Roman characters, too long to be thus treated, and has to be printed in two lines, as occurs, for instance, in the *bayt* printed in the Roman character about the middle of page 15, and again in the *bayt* occupying lines 5 and 6 on the following page. This fashion of printing, and, in the first case, the fact that the *bayt*, being the initial verse of a *ghazal* or ode, has an internal rhyme, is liable to delude the reader into supposing that he has to do with what we understand by a couplet, and not with the unit connoted by the word *bayt*.

As regards the second point, the rules of scansion in Persian are exceedingly simple, and no *gradus* is needed to determine the quantity of the vowels. All long vowels (equally unmistakeable in the written and the spoken word) are, of course, long, and are distinguished in this book by accents. Short vowels are short, unless followed by two consonants, whether both consonants come in the same word, or one at the end of one word and the other at the beginning of the next. All this is easy enough of comprehension to the classical scholar, but what follows is peculiar to Persian. Every word ending in two consonants, or in one consonant (except *n*, which, being reckoned as a nasal, does not count) preceded by a long vowel, is scanned as though it ended with an additional short vowel.[1] This hypothetical vowel (called in the East *ním-fatḥa*, the "half-fatḥa," and, most inappro-

[1] This additional short vowel (the *ním-fatḥa*) is, however, not reckoned at the end of a verse (*bayt*) or half-verse (*miṣrá'*).

priately, by some French writers "*l'izafet metrique*") is actually pronounced by the Indians, but not by the Persians, but it must always be reckoned unless the succeeding word begins with a vowel. The same rule also applies to syllables.

A few examples will best serve to illustrate the above remarks. Words like *bád* (wind), *bíd* (willow), *búd* (was), *kár* (work), *shír* (lion), *múr* (ant) scan as though they were *bád*^{a}, *bíd*^{a}, &c., *i.e.*, | — ⏑ |, not | — |. The same applies to words like *dast* (hand), *band* (bond), *gard* (dust), which scan as though they were *dast*^{a}, *band*^{a} and *gard*^{a}. Similarly, words like *bád-gír* ("wind-catcher," a kind of ventilation-shaft), *shír-mard* (brave man, lit. "lion-man"), *dúr-bín* (telescope), *dast-kash* (glove) scan as though they were *bád*^{a}*-gír*^{a}, *shír*^{a}*-mard*^{a} (— ⏑ — ⏑), *dúr*^{a}*-bín*, *dast*^{a}*-kash* (— ⏑ —). But *jahán* (world), *nigín* (signet), *darún* (inside) scan | ⏑ — |, because they end in *n*. So in the verse on page 16, which is written in the apocopated hexameter *ramal*:—

| — ⏑ — — | — ⏑ — — | — ⏑ — || — ⏑ — — |
— ⏑ — — | — ⏑ — |

the scansion is as follows:—

Áfárínū | *mādḥă sūdă-* | *yād hămí* || *găr bĭ-gănjān-* | *dăr zīyānă-* |
yād hămí ||

There are a few other peculiarities of scansion in Persian verse, as, for example, that monosyllables ending in *-u*, like *tú* (thou), *dú* (two), *chú* (like), &c., may be scanned either short or long, as is the case with the *i* which marks the *iḍáfat*, while the monosyllable connoting the word for "and" may be treated either as a long vowel (*ū*), or a short vowel (*ŭ*), or as a consonant followed by a short vowel (*wă*); but, save in a few exceptional cases, the reader who has familiarised himself with the peculiarities above mentioned will have no difficulty in scanning any Persian verse which he may come across.

The publication of this volume, originally fixed for May 1st of the present year, was inevitably delayed by circumstances into which I need not here enter. This delay I regret, and I desire to offer my apologies for it to my friend Mr. Fisher Unwin, and also my thanks for his readiness to accept an excuse which he was kind enough to regard as valid and sufficient. My thanks are also due to the printers, Messrs. Unwin Brothers, Ltd., of Woking and London, for the singular care with which they have printed a book presenting many typographical difficulties.

EDWARD G. BROWNE.

May 16, 1906.

Contents

CHAPTER I

RETROSPECTIVE AND INTRODUCTORY

Scope of this volume.

In a former volume,[1] intended to serve as an Introduction to this work, and yet to be in a measure independent, I have treated of the History of the Persians, chiefly from the intellectual and literary standpoints, from its first beginnings down to the early Ghaznawí Period, in which, about A.D. 1000, the genius of Firdawsí definitely assured the success of that Renaissance of Persian literature which began rather more than a century before his time. The present volume, therefore, deals not with origins, but with Persian literary history in the narrower sense—that is, the literature of the Persians (including so much of the external and intellectual history of Persia as is necessary for a proper comprehension of this) from the time when their language assumed its present form (that is, from the time of the Arab Conquest and the adoption by the Persians of the religion of Islám in the seventh century of our era) down to the present day. This post-Muhammadan literature (which is what we ordinarily mean when we speak of "Persian Literature") arose gradually after the subjugation of Persia by the Arabs, and the overthrow by Islám of the Zoroastrian creed,

[1] *A Literary History of Persia from the Earliest Times until Firdawsí* (London: T. Fisher Unwin, 1902; pp. xiv and 521). For the sake of brevity I shall henceforth refer to this volume simply as the *Prolegomena*; a title which best indicates its scope, aim, and character.

and may be said to have begun, so far as documentary evidence exists, about a thousand years ago. During the whole of this period the language has undergone changes so slight that the verses of ancient poets like Ḥandhala of Bádghís (A.D. 820–872) and Rúdagí (end of ninth and beginning of tenth centuries) are at least as easily understood by a Persian of the present day as are the works of Shakespear by a modern Englishman. It is important for all students of Persian to apprehend this fact thoroughly, and to realise that that language has changed less in the last thousand years than English has changed in the last three centuries. The most archaic literary monuments of the Persian language (by which term, throughout this volume, post-Muhammadan Persian is intended) are, indeed, characterised by certain peculiarities of style and vocabulary; but I much question whether there exists any Persian scholar, native or foreign, who could assign even an approximate date to a work of unknown authorship written within the last five centuries and containing no historical allusions which might serve to fix the period of its composition.

Scope of the *Prolegomena* contained in the previous volume.

I cannot in this volume repeat what I have elsewhere set forth in detail as to the history of Persia in pre-Muhammadan and early Muhammadan times. This history was in my *Prolegomena* carried down to that period when the great 'Abbásid Caliphate of Baghdád, culminating in the splendid reigns of Hárúnu'r-Rashíd and his son al-Ma'mún (A.D. 786–833), was already on the decline; a decline manifested externally by the gradual detachment from effective central control of one province after another, and continuing steadily, if slowly, until Húlágú's Mongol hordes gave it the *coup de grâce* in A.D. 1258, when Baghdád was sacked and the last real Caliph of the House of 'Abbás cruelly done to death.

For the ordinary student of Persian literature it is sufficient to know, so far as its origins are concerned, that the immediate ancestor of Persian was Pahlawí, the official language of Persia under the Sásánian kings (A.D. 226–651), and, for two or three subsequent centuries, the religious language of the Zoroastrian priests; that the extant literature of Pahlawí has been estimated by Dr. E. W. West (perhaps the greatest European authority on this subject) as roughly equal in bulk to the Old Testament, and that it is chiefly religious and liturgical in character; that there exist, besides this literature, inscriptions on rocks, coins, and gems dating from the middle of the third century; that this Pahlawí language, the ancestor of later Persian, is itself the descendant of the Old Persian tongue known to us only through the inscriptions carved on the rocks of Persepolis, Behistun, and other places by order of Darius the Great and subsequent Achæmenian kings; and that the Avestic (so-called "Zend") language in which the Zoroastrian scriptures are written was a sister-tongue to that last mentioned and to Sanskrit, standing, therefore, out of the direct line of ascent from modern Persian, and represented at the present day by certain provincial dialects of Persia, and, as Darmesteter supposes, by the Pashto or Afghán speech.

Sketch of the origins discussed in the *Prolegomena*.

Arranged in tabular form, the above facts may be expressed as follows:—

I. *Old Persian* of Achæmenian Period (B.C. 550–330), represented only by inscriptions.	*Avestic*, represented by the Avesta, of which the oldest portion is that known as the *Gáthás*, which are generally supposed to date from the time of Zoroaster or his immediate disciples (probably about B.C. 600).

II. The *Invasion of Alexander* (B.C. 333) inaugurates a period of anarchy, devoid of literary monuments, which lasted five centuries and a half, and was terminated by the establishment of—

III. The *Sásánian Dynasty* (A.D. 226–651), under which *Pahlawí* became the official language of the State and of the Zoroastrian Church, this language being the child of Old Persian, and the parent of modern Persian.

IV. The *Arab Conquest* (A.D. 641–651), resulting in the conversion of the great bulk of the Persian nation to the religion of Islám, and in the practical supersession of Persian by Arabic as the official and literary language.

V. The *Persian Renaissance*, with which the period included in this volume may be said to begin, and which, beginning about A.D. 850, gathers strength in proportion as Persia succeeds in emancipating herself more and more from the control of the weakening Caliphate of Baghdád, and in re-asserting her political independence.

Influence of the Arab Conquest on Persia.

Such, in outline, is Persian literary history; but while the ordinary student of Persian may well content himself with a summary and superficial knowledge of all that precedes the Arab Conquest, he cannot thus lightly pass over the consequences of that momentous event. Once again in this volume, as in that which preceded it (p. 6), I am fain to quote Nöldeke's most pregnant saying, "Hellenism never touched more than the surface of Persian life, but Írán was penetrated to the core by Arabian religion and Arabian ways."

The unique position of the Arabic language.

The Arabic language is in a special degree the language of a great religion. To us the Bible is the Bible, whether we read it in the original tongues or in our own; but it is otherwise with the Qur'án amongst the Muslims. To them this Arabic Qur'án is the very Word of God, an objective, not a subjective revelation. When we read therein: "*Qul: Huwa 'lláhu Aḥad*" ("Say: He, God, is One"), God Himself is the speaker, not the Prophet; and therefore the Muslim, in quoting his scripture, employs the formula, "HE says, exalted is HE"; while only in quoting the traditions (*Aḥádíth*) of the Prophet does he say, "He says, upon him be the Blessing of God and His Peace." Hence the Qur'án cannot properly be translated into another tongue, for he who translates by so doing interprets and perchance distorts. It is only by Christian missionaries, so far as my knowledge goes, that translations of the Qur'án have been published detached from the text; amongst Muslims the most that we find is an interlinear rendering of the Arabic text in Persian, Turkish, or Urdú, as the case may be, such rendering being in general slavishly literal.[1] In addition to this, the prayers which every good Muslim should recite five times a day are in Arabic, as are the Confession of Faith and other religious formulæ which are constantly on the tongue of the true believer, be he Persian, Turk, Indian, Afghan, or Malay; so that every Muslim must have some slight acquaintance with the Arabic language, while nothing so greatly raises him in the eyes of his fellows as a more profound knowledge of the sacred tongue of Islám. In addition to all this, the language of every people who embraced Islám was inundated from the first by Arabic words, first the technical terms of Theology and Jurisprudence, then the terminology of all the nascent sciences known to the Muhammadan civilisation, and lastly a mass of ordinary words, which latter have often, as the former have almost always, entirely displaced the native equivalent. To write Persian devoid of any admixture of Arabic is at least as difficult as to write English devoid of any admixture of Greek, Latin, or French derivatives; it can be done within certain limits, but the result is generally incomprehensible without the aid of a dictionary. As I write, there lies before me a specimen of such attempts, to wit a communication of nearly one hundred lines made to the *Akhtar* or "Star" (an excellent Persian newspaper formerly published at Constantinople, but now unfortunately extinct) by certain Zoroastrians or "guebres" of Yazd, and published in the issue of October 27, 1890. The matter is simple, and the abstract ideas requiring expression few; yet the writers have felt themselves compelled to give

[1] This statement needs some qualification, for my colleague and friend, Ḥájji Mírzá 'Abdu'l-Ḥusayn Khán of Káshán, brought back with him to England from the Ḥijáz a very fine manuscript containing a Persian translation of the Qur'án, made by order of Nádir Sháh and unaccompanied by the Arabic original.

footnotes explaining (in every case save two by an Arabic equivalent) the meanings of no less than fourteen words, and many other such glosses would be required to make the article intelligible to the ordinary Persian reader. Thus *áwízha* (pure) must be glossed as *kháṣṣ*, *darad* (form) as *ṣúrat*, *khuhr* (country) as *waṭan*, *farhikht* (courtesy, culture) as *adab*, and so on, the glosses in all these cases and most others being Arabic words. Another more ambitious, but scarcely more successful, attempt of the same kind is Prince Jalál's *Náma-i-Khusrawán* ("Book of Princes"), a short history of the pre-Muhammadan dynasties of Persia published at Vienna in A.H. 1297 (A.D. 1880), and reviewed by Mordtmann in vol. xxviii of the *Zeitschrift der Deutschen Morgenländischen Gesellschaft*, pp. 506–508. Even the *Sháhnáma* of Firdawsí, composed nine centuries ago, and, as I think is shown by a study of contemporary poetry, purposely composed in the most archaic style and speech which the author could command, is far from being so free from Arabic words as is often asserted and imagined.

Arabian Science.

Thus far we have confined ourselves to the consideration of the influence exerted by the Arabs on the Persians in the domain of language only, but this influence is not less perceptible in other fields. Strongest in Theology and Jurisprudence, it extends also to Grammar, Rhetoric, Poetry, and all the sciences known to the Muslims. These sciences were, of course, in many cases of complex origin, being borrowed by the Arabs (chiefly during the early 'Abbásid period, *i.e.*, the latter part of the eighth century of our era) from other more civilised nations, notably the Persians and the Greeks; and indeed they are divided in such works as the *Mafátíḥu'l-'Ulúm* ("Keys of the Sciences")[1] into two groups, the native or indigenous (Jurisprudence, Scholastic Theology, Grammar, Writing, Poetry and Prosody,

[1] Ed. Van Vloten, pp. 5–7. For an account of the contents, see my *Prolegomena*, pp. 382–383.

and History), and the exotic (Philosophy, Logic, Medicine, Arithmetic, Mathematics, Astronomy and Astrology, Music, Mechanics, and Alchemy). All these, however, were thoroughly assimilated into the complex Arabo-Persian culture of the 'Abbásid capital, Baghdád, and in their entirety constitute what is often, but inexactly, styled "Arabian Science" —a science which, drawn from many different sources, forms a synthesis common to all Muhammadan peoples, and which has exercised and continues to exercise an influence second only to that of the religion of Islám itself in bringing about that solidarity of sentiment so conspicuous in the Muslim world.

Fitness of Arabic for scientific purposes.

For a scientific language, indeed, Arabic is eminently fitted by its wealth of roots and by the number of derivative forms, each expressing some particular modification of the root-idea, of which each is susceptible. Let us illustrate this by two examples, the first drawn from the terminology of Medicine, the second formed after a perfectly sound analogy to express a quite modern idea. The primitive verb has in Arabic some dozen derived forms (commonly called "conjugations"), each expressing some definite modification (causative, intensive, reciprocal, middle, &c.) of the meaning connoted by the original verb. Of these ten conjugations, the tenth is commonly desiderative, and, if we substitute the numbers 1, 2, 3, for the first, second, and third letters of the triliteral root the general form of its verbal noun will be (*Isti.* 1. 2. *á.* 3), and of its active participle (*Musta.* 1. 2. *i.* 3). Thus from the simple verb *ghafara*, "he pardoned," we have in the tenth conjugation *istighfár*, "asking for pardon," and *mustaghfir*, "one who asks for pardon"; from *kamala*, "he was perfect," *istikmál*, "seeking perfection," and *mustakmil*, "one who seeks perfection"; and so on. Now the old theory (adopted by the Arabian physicians) as to the ætiology of dropsy was that it was caused by excessive drinking ("*crescit indulgens sibi dirus hydrops*"), and hence it was named by the Arabs (and consequently by all the Muhammadan peoples) *istisqá*, "craving for drink," while the sufferer is called *mustasqí*, both forms belonging to the tenth conjugation of the root *saqá*, "he gave drink to." So in quite modern times a need has arisen for an equivalent in Arabic to the European term "Orientalist," and this has been met by taking the regularly-formed participle of the tenth, or desiderative, conjugation of the root from which comes the word *sharq*, "the East," and coining the derivative *mustashriq*, which can only mean "one who desires" or "is interested in the East." These instances will suffice to show the facility wherewith new ideas can be denoted in Arabic by forms which, hitherto unused, precisely and unmistakeably indicate the idea to be expressed.

Pride of the Arabs in their language.

The Arabs themselves (including, of course, peoples like the Egyptians who have adopted the Arabic speech) are intensely, and justly, proud of their glorious language, and exclaim with the fullest conviction, "*Al-ḥamdu li 'lláhi 'lladhí khalaqa' l-Lisána'l-'Arabiyya aḥsana min kulli lisán*" ("Praise be to God who created the Arabic language the finest of all languages"). Whether or not we are prepared to go as far as this, it is at least certain that no satisfactory knowledge of the languages, literatures, and modes of thought of Persia, Turkey, Muhammadan India, or any other Muslim land is possible without a considerable knowledge of Arabic, and that in particular our appreciation and enjoyment of these literatures grows in direct ratio to this knowledge.

Recapitulation of *Prolegomena*.

In my previous volume on the *Literary History of Persia until the Time of Firdawsí* I discussed at some length what I have called the *Prolegomena* to the history of Persian literature in the narrower sense. I spoke there of the three ancient languages of Persia (the Old Persian, the Avestic, and the Pahlawí), and of some of the dialects by which they are now represented. I sketched in outline the earlier religious systems which prevailed in that country (to wit, Zoroastrianism and the heresies of Manes and

Mazdak), and the history of the last great national dynasty, the Sásánian. Passing, then, to the Arabs, whose conquest of Persia in the seventh century of our era wrought, as we have seen, such deep and lasting changes alike in the religion, the language, the literature, the life, and the thought of the Persians, I spoke briefly of their state in the "Days of Ignorance" (*Ayyámu'l-Jáhiliyyat*) or heathendom, ere the Prophet Muhammad arose, and of their ancient poems, which, dating at least from the end of the fifth century of our era, still remain the classical models which every versifier of Arab speech aspires to imitate when writing in the heroic vein. I then described in a summary manner the advent of the Prophet, the doctrine of al-Islám, the triumph of the Muhammadan arms, the rule of the Four Orthodox Caliphs, and the origin of the great Shí'ite and Khárijite schisms. I endeavoured to depict the semi-pagan Imperialism of the Umayyad Caliphs, and the growing discontent of the subject-races (especially the Persians), culminating in the middle of the eighth century in the great revolt of the Khurásánís under Abú Muslim, the Battle of the Záb, the overthrow and destruction of the Umayyad power in the East, and the establishment of the 'Abbásid Caliphate, which, enduring for some five centuries, was finally destroyed (save for the shadowy existence which it maintained in Egypt until the Ottoman Turkish Sulṭán Selím the First, in A.D. 1517, took from the last scion of this House the titles and insignia which it had hitherto preserved) by the great catastrophe of the Mongol Invasion in the middle of the thirteenth century.

The period included in this volume begins at a time when the glories of "the golden prime of good Haroun Alraschid" had long passed away. The early 'Abbásid Caliphs, though they never obtained possession of Spain, otherwise maintained and extended the vast empire won by the first successors of the Prophet—an empire extending from Morocco to Sind and from Aden to

The period discussed in this volume.

Khwárazm (Khiva), and including, besides North Africa, Egypt, Syria, Arabia, Mesopotamia, Armenia, Persia, Afghánistán, Balúchistán, a large portion of Turkistán, a smaller portion of India, and the islands of Crete and Cyprus. The first step towards the weakening and dissolution of this empire may be said to have been taken when al-Ma'mún, the son of Hárúnu'r-Rashíd, rewarded his general Ṭáhir Dhu'l-Yamínayn ("the Ambidexter"), in A.D. 820, with the permanent government of Khurásán for himself and his heirs, who held this province from father to son till they were displaced by the "Brazier" or Ṣaffárí dynasty in A.D. 872. These Ṭáhirids are generally accounted the first post-Muhammadan Persian dynasty; and, though they never claimed to be in any way independent of the Caliphs of Baghdád, the hereditary character of their power clearly differentiates them from the governors and proconsuls of previous times, who were transferred from province to province by the central Government as it saw fit. The transition from the state of an hereditary governor or satrap to that of a practically independent Amír (for the title of Sultán was first assumed by Maḥmúd of Ghazna at the period with which this volume opens) was very gradual, and was not always continuous. The Ṣaffárí dynasty was, for instance, less obedient and more independent in its earlier days than the Sámánid dynasty which succeeded it; but nominally even the mighty rulers of the Houses of Ghazna and Seljúq accounted themselves the vassals of the Caliph, regarded him as their over-lord and suzerain, and eagerly sought after those titles and honours of which he was the only recognised and legitimate source. Individual instances of overt disobedience and rebellion did, of course, occur—as, for instance, the march of Ya'qúb b. Layth, the Ṣaffárí, on Baghdád, and his battle with the troops of the Caliph al-Mu'tamid in A.H. 262 (A.D. 875–76)[1]; the attempt of the Seljúq Malikshåh to

[1] A very full, but somewhat fanciful, account of this is given by the Niḏẖámu'l-Mulk in his *Siyásat-náma* (ed. Schefer), pp. 11–14.

compel the Caliph al-Muqtadí to transfer his capital from Baghdád to Damascus or the Ḥijáz[1] about A.D. 1080; and the still more serious quarrel between Sanjar and al-Mustarshid in A.D. 1133, which ended in the Caliph being taken prisoner and, during his captivity, assassinated (in A.D. 1135) by the Isma'ílís, who, as al-Bundárí asserts,[2] were instigated to this deed by Sanjar himself. The nominal suzerainty of the Caliph of Baghdád was, however, more or less recognised by all orthodox Muhammadan princes and *amírs* save those of Spain, from the foundation of the 'Abbásid Caliphate, about A.D. 750, till its extinction in A.D. 1258, and during this period of five centuries Baghdád continued to be the metropolis and intellectual centre of Muslim civilisation, and Arabic the language of diplomacy, philosophy, and science, and, to a large extent, of *belles lettres* and polite conversation.

The Shí'ite rivals of the 'Abbásids.

The great religious and political rivals of the 'Abbásids were the heterodox Fáṭimid anti-Caliphs of Egypt. These represented one of the two great divisions of the *Shí'a*, or "Faction," of 'Alí—to wit, the "Sect of the Seven," or Isma'ílís, whose origin and history were fully discussed in the *Prolegomena* to this volume, together with those of the allied party of the Carmathians. The other great division of the *Shí'a*, the "Sect of the Twelve," which is now the State-religion of Persia, only became so generally (though it prevailed for some time in Ṭabaristán, and was professed by the powerful House of Buwayh) on the rise of the Ṣafawí dynasty under Sháh Isma'íl in A.H. 1502, though it always had a strong hold amongst the Persians. Until the Mongol Invasion in the thirteenth century the political power of the Isma'ílís (represented in Persia by the so-called Assassins or Isma'ílís of Alamút) was, however, as we shall presently see, much greater.

[1] See al-Bundárí's *History of the Seljúqs* (vol. ii of Houtsma's *Recueil*), p. 70.

[2] Ibid., p. 178.

The Mongol Invasion of the thirteenth century.

The great dividing line in the Muhammadan period of Asiatic history is the Mongol Invasion, which inflicted on the Muslim civilisation a blow from which it has never recovered, and, by destroying the Caliphate and its metropolis of Baghdád, definitely put an end to the unity of the Muslim empire. This Mongol Invasion, beginning early in the thirteenth century with the conquests of Chingíz Khán, culminated in the sack of Baghdád and murder of al-Musta'ṣim, the last 'Abbásid Caliph, by Húlágú Khán in A.D. 1258. The devastation wrought by it throughout Persia was terrific. The irresistible Mongol hordes were bloodthirsty heathens who respected nothing, but slew, burnt, and destroyed without mercy or compunction. "They came, they uprooted, they burned, they slew, they carried off, they departed" ("*Ámadand, u kandand, u súkhtand, u kushtand, u burdand, u raftand*")[1]—such was the account of their methods and procedure given by one of the few who escaped from the sack of Bukhárá, wherein 30,000 were slain; and there were other cities which fared even worse than Bukhárá. The invasion of Tímúr the Tartar, horrible as it was, was not so terrible in its effects as this, for Tímúr was professedly a Muslim, and had some consideration for mosques, libraries, and men of learning; but Chingíz and Húlágú were bloodthirsty heathens, who, especially when resistance was encountered, and most of all when some Mongol prince was slain in battle, spared neither old nor young, gentle nor simple, learned nor unlearned; who stabled their horses in the mosques, burned the libraries, used priceless manuscripts for fuel, and often razed the conquered city to the ground, destroyed every living thing within it, and sowed the site with salt.

Hence, as it seems to me, there is a gulf between what preceded and what followed this terrific catastrophe, which

[1] *Ta'ríkh-i-Jahán-gushá.*

effected in Muslim civilisation, science, and letters a deterioration never afterwards wholly repaired. So, though less than two centuries and a half of the period which remains to be considered precede the Mongol Invasion, while six centuries and a half succeed it, the former may well claim for their treatment an equal space with the latter.

Irrevocable harm done by Mongol Invasion.

The earliest dawn of the Persian Renaissance, which culminated in Firdawsí and his contemporaries, was fully discussed in the *Prolegomena* to this volume, but a brief recapitulation in this place may not be amiss. According to 'Awfí, the oldest biographer of the Persian poets whose work has been preserved to us, and who wrote early in the thirteenth century, the first Persian *qaṣída* was composed by a certain 'Abbás to celebrate the entry of the 'Abbásid Caliph al-Ma'mún, the son of Hárúnu'r-Rashíd, into Merv, in A.H. 193 (A.D. 808–9). This extract from 'Awfí's work (the *Lubábu'l-Albáb*), including four couplets of the poem in question, was published, with translation, by Dr. H. Ethé in his interesting paper entitled *Rûdagî's Vorlaüfer und Zeitgenossen* (pp. 36–38), but I entirely agree with A. de Biberstein Kazimirski's[1] view as to the spurious character of this poem. One of the oldest Persian verses which has come down to us is probably that which, as we learn from the "Four Discourses" (*Chahár Maqála*) of Nidhámí-i-'Arúḍí-i-Samarqandí (composed about the middle of the twelfth century),[2] inspired Aḥmad al-Khujistání to rebel against the Ṣaffárí dynasty in

The Persian Renaissance.

[1] *Divan de Menoutchehri*, pp. 8–9. Pizzi, I think, takes the same view. See an interesting paper on a *Judæo-Persian Document from Khotan* by Professor Margoliouth in the *J.R.A.S.* for October, 1903, p. 747.

[2] Lithographed at Ṭihrán in A.H. 1305, and translated by me in the *J.R.A.S.* for July and October, 1899. There are two MSS. in the British Museum, and one (of which I have a copy) in Constantinople. The story to which reference is here made occurs on p. 43 of the *tirage-à-part* of my translation. A critical edition of this important work, prepared by Mírzá Muḥammad of Qazwín, is now being printed by the Trustees of the Gibb Memorial.

A.H. 262 (A.D. 875–76), and "stirred within him an impulse which would not suffer him to remain in the condition wherein he was." The verse is as follows:—

Mihtarí gar bi-kám-i-shír dar-ast
Shaw, khaṭar kun, zi kám-i-shír bi-júy,
Yá buzurgí u náz u ni'mat u jáh,
Yá, chú mardán't marg-i-rúy-á-rúy.

"If lordship lies within the lion's jaws,
Go, risk it, and from those dread portals seize
Such straight-confronting death as men desire,
Or riches, greatness, rank, and lasting ease."

These verses are quoted by the author of the "Four Discourses" in support of his proposition that "poetry is that art whereby the poet arranges imaginary propositions, and adapts the deductions, with the result that he can make a little thing appear great and a great thing small, or cause good to appear in the garb of evil and evil in the garb of good. By acting on the imagination, he excites the faculties of anger and concupiscence in such a way that by his suggestion men's temperaments become affected with exaltation or depression; whereby he conduces to the accomplishment of great things in the order of the world."

Wonderful stability of the Persian language.

Persian poetry, then, began to be composed more than a thousand years ago,[1] under the earliest independent or semi-independent rulers who sprung up *pari passu* with the decline, decentralisation, and disintegration of the Caliphate of Baghdád. The Persian language has changed so little during this long period that, save for a few archaic words and spellings, the oldest verses extant hardly present any difficulty, or even uncouthness or unfamiliarity, to the Persian of to-day. In feeling and

[1] In my previous volume, or *Prolegomena*, I have discussed the question whether or not poetry existed in Sásánian times; but, even if it existed, no traces of it have been preserved, and the earliest extant poetry in Persian dates from the Muhammadan period.

sentiment, however, a certain difference is, as it seems to me, perceptible; the older poetry of the Ṣaffárí and Sámání periods is simpler, more natural, more objective, and less ornate and rhetorical. Nothing can be more instructive, as an indication of the change of taste which three and a half centuries effected in Persia, than to compare two criticisms of the same celebrated verses of the poet Rúdagí (by common consent the greatest Persian poet before the epoch of the Kings of Ghazna), the one contained in the *Four Discourses* of Nidhámí-i-'Arúḍí (about A.D. 1150), the other in Dawlatsháh's *Memoirs of the Poets* (A.D. 1487). The poem in question begins:—

Change of taste and canons of criticism.

Bú-yi Jú-yi-Múliyán áyad hamí,
Bú-yi yár-i-mihrabán áyad hamí,

and its translation is as follows:—

"The Jú-yi-Múliyán we call to mind,
We long for those dear friends long left behind.
The sands of Oxus, toilsome though they be,
Beneath my feet were soft as silk to me.
Glad at the friend's return, the Oxus deep
Up to our girths in laughing waves shall leap.
Long live Bukhárá! Be thou of good cheer!
Joyous towards thee hasteth our Amír!
The Moon's the Prince, Bukhárá is the sky;
O sky, the Moon shall light thee by and by!
Bukhárá is the mead, the Cypress he;
Receive at last, O Mead, the Cypress-tree!"[1]

The extraordinary effect produced on the Amír Naṣr ibn Aḥmad the Sámánid by these verses, and the rich reward which Rúdagí earned for them, seemed natural enough to the earlier critic, who considers that "that illustrious man (Rúdagí) was worthy of this splendid equipment, for no one has yet produced a successful imitation of that elegy, nor

[1] For the text of these verses and the whole story connected with them, see the separate reprint of my translation of the *Chahár Maqála* pp. 51–56. The Jú-yi-Múliyán is a stream near Bukhárá.

found means to surmount triumphantly the difficulties [which the subject presents]." In particular he maintains that in the following verse (not generally included in the current text of the poem, but evidently belonging to it) :—

Áfarín u madḥ súd áyad hamí,
Gar bi-ganj andar ziyán áyad hamí.

"Surely are renown and praise a lasting gain,
Even though the royal coffers loss sustain"—

"are seven admirable touches of art: first, the verse is apposite; secondly, antithetical; thirdly, it has a refrain; fourthly, it embodies an enunciation of equivalence; fifthly, it has sweetness; sixthly, style; seventhly, energy." "Every master of the craft," he concludes, "who has deeply considered the poetic art, will admit, after a little reflection, that I am right"; and, so far as a foreigner may be permitted to express a judgement in the matter, I am inclined to agree with him. That the verse is *apposite* cannot be denied: the poet wanted a present from the Amír, and his hint is delicate yet unmistakeable. The *antithesis* between the loss in money and the gain in glory and fame is well brought out. The *refrain*, needed only at the end of the verse, is here naturally and effectively anticipated at the end of the first hemistich. The *equivalent* which the Amír receives for his money is clearly indicated; and the last three "touches," two of which at least can only be judged in the original, are undeniably present.

Degenerate taste of Dawlatsháh.

Now hear how Dawlatsháh, writing about A.D. 1487, judges these same verses, so highly esteemed by Nidhámí-i-'Arúḍí :—

"This poem [of Rúdagí's] is too long to be cited in its entirety in this place. It is said that it so delighted the King's heart that he mounted his horse and set out for Bukhárá without even stopping to put on his boots. To men of sense this appears astonishing, *for the verses are extremely simple, entirely devoid of rhetorical artifices and embellishments, and lacking in strength; and if in these days any one were to produce such a poem in the presence of kings or nobles, it would meet with the reprobation of all.* It is, however, probable that as Master Rúdagí possessed the completest knowledge of music [attainable] in that country, he may have composed some tune or air, and produced this poem of his in the form of a ballad with musical accompaniment, and that it was in this way that it obtained so favourable a reception. In short, we must not lightly esteem Master Rúdagí merely on account of this poem, for assuredly he was expert in all manner of arts and accomplishments, and has produced good poetry of several kinds, both *mathnawís* and *qaṣídas*, for he was a man of great distinction, and admired by high and low."

Persian style not essentially florid.

Many persons are accustomed to think of Persian literature as essentially florid and ornate, abounding in rhetorical embellishments, and overlaid with metaphor, but this is only true of the literature produced at certain periods and in certain circles, especially under the patronage of foreign conquerors of Mongolian or Turkish race. The *History of the Mongol Conquest*, by Waṣṣáf,[1] written about A.D. 1328, is one notable example of this florid style of composition; while the *Rawḍatu'ṣ-Ṣafá*, the *Anwár-i-Suhaylí*, and other contemporary works produced under the patronage of the Tímúrid princes (by whom it was transmitted to India on the foundation by Bábar of the so-called "Moghul" dynasty) about the end of the fifteenth and beginning of the sixteenth centuries afford others of a later date. It is, however, amongst the Turks of the Ottoman Empire that this detestable style finds its highest development in writers like Veysí and Nergisí, of whom a modern Turkish critic says that, though a Persian might recognise the fact that they were not writing Persian, a Turk could hardly divine that they were by way of writing Turkish.

In my previous volume on the literary history of Persia, published in 1902, I gave (pp. 452–471) specimens of the verses

[1] This was his title: "the Panegyrist" [of the Court]. His name was 'Abdu'lláh b. Faḍlu'lláh of Shíráz.

of some seventeen Persian poets of the oldest or pre-Ghaznawí period, an amount sufficient, in my opinion, to entitle us to characterise in general terms this earliest verse. Unfortunately, with the exception of the thousand couplets of Daqíqí incorporated by Firdawsí in his *Sháhnáma*,[1] no *mathnawí* or other long poem of the Sámánid or pre-Sámánid period has come down to us, though we know that such long narrative poems existed, *e.g.*, Rúdagí's version of the well-known tale of *Kalíla and Dimna*, of which sixteen couplets are preserved in Asadí's *Lughat-i-Furs*, or Persian Lexicon, compiled about A.D. 1060, and rendered accessible to students in Dr. Paul Horn's excellent edition. What is preserved to us consists chiefly of short fragments (*muqaṭṭa'át*), quatrains (*rubá'iyyát*), and a few odes (*ghazals*), besides which we know that narrative *mathnawí* poems also existed, as well as *qaṣídas* ("purpose-poems," generally panegyrics). These last, however, reached their full development about the time of Firdawsí (A.D. 1000), with which our history begins. Of these forms, the *qaṣída* (and the *qiṭ'a*, or "fragment" of the *qaṣída*) was borrowed by the Persians from the Arabs, whose ancient pre-Islámic poems (*e.g.*, the celebrated *Mu'allaqát)* are the classical models for this style of composition, which, however, together with the love-poem or *ghazal*, underwent certain modifications in the hands of the Persians. The quatrain, on the other hand, as well as the *mathnawí* (or "couplet" poem, where the rhyme is between the two hemistichs composing the *bayt*, and changes from couplet to couplet), is essentially a Persian invention; and one tradition as to the earliest poem composed in Persian[2] points definitely to the quatrain (first called *dú-baytí* and afterwards *rubá'í*) as the oldest indigenous verse-form produced in Írán. Mystical

Characteristics of early Persian poetry, as regards form and style.

[1] See p. 460 of my previous volume.

[2] This tradition is given in its most familiar version by Dawlatsháh, pp. 30–31 of my edition, and in a more credible and circumstantial form in the rare British Museum MS. of the *Mu'ajjam fí ma'áyíri ash'ári'l-'Ajam* of Shams-i-Qays, ff. 49–50 (pp. 88–89 of my forthcoming edition).

poetry, so common from the twelfth century onwards, is, at the early period which we are now discussing, rare and undeveloped.

Verse-forms and rhetoric of the Persians.

In order to avoid constant digressions and explanations in the following chapters, it may be well to give in this place a general account of the varieties of literary composition recognised by the Persians, the rhetorical figures of which they make such frequent use, and the metres employed in their poetry. Of these and other kindred matters I should have considered it necessary to treat more fully had it not been for the admirable account of them prefixed by my friend the late Mr. E. J. W. Gibb to his monumental *History of Ottoman Poetry*, of which the first volume opens with a general discussion on Oriental thought, taste, poetry, and rhetoric, which applies not only to Turkish, but also to Persian, and, in large measure, to Arabic and other Muhammadan languages also. These *Prolegomena* of Mr. Gibb's (especially ch. ii, treating of Tradition, Philosophy, and Mysticism, and ch. iii, treating of Verse-forms, Prosody, and Rhetoric, pp. 33–124) form one of the best introductions to the study of Muhammadan literature with which I am acquainted, and should be read by every student of this subject. Other excellent treatises are Gladwin's *Dissertations on the Rhetoric, Prosody, and Rhyme of the Persians* (Calcutta, 1801); Rückert's *Grammatik, Poetik, und Rhetorik der Perser* (originally published in 1827–28 in vols. xl-xliv of the *Wiener Jahrbücher*, and re-edited by Pertsch in a separate volume in 1874); Blochmann's *Prosody of the Persians* (Calcutta, 1872); and, for the comparisons used by the erotic poets, Huart's annotated translation of the *Anísu'l-'Ushsháq*, or "Lover's Companion, of Sharafu'd-Dín Rámí. Persian works on these subjects are, of course, numerous: Farrukhí, a contemporary of Firdawsí, composed one (mentioned by Dawlatsháh, pp. 9 and 57 of my edition, and also by Hájjí Khalífa, ed. Flügel, vol. ii, p. 277), entitled *Tarjumánu'l-Balágha* ("The Interpreter of Eloquence"), while Bahrámí of Sarakhs, who lived about the same time, wrote two treatises, strongly recommended by the author of the *Four Discourses* (p. 50 of the *tirage-à-part* of my translation), entitled respectively "The Goal of Prosodists" (*Gháyatu'l-'Arúḍiyyín*) and "The Thesaurus of Rhyme" (*Kanzu'l-Qáfiya*). These works appear to be lost, or at least no copies are known to exist; and of extant Persian treatises on these subjects the "Gardens of Magic" (*Ḥadá'iqu's-Siḥr*)[1] of Rashídu'd-Dín Waṭwáṭ (died A.D. 1182) and the already mentioned *Mu'ajjam* of Shams-i-Qays (the rare old MS. marked Or. 2,814 in the British Museum), which was composed during the thirteenth century (soon after A.H. 614 = A.D. 1217–18), seem to be the oldest.

The Science of Rhetoric.

I shall speak first of Rhetoric (*'Ilmu'l-Badáyi'*), choosing my examples chiefly from the "Gardens of Magic," but sometimes from other sources, and departing from Waṭwáṭ's arrangement where this seems to me to be faulty. I shall also endeavour to illustrate the different rhetorical figures, so far as possible, by English examples, in order that the nature of each figure may be more readily apprehended by the English reader.

1. *Prose.*

Recognised varieties of prose.

Prose (*nathr*) is of three kinds—simple or unornate (*'árí*, "naked"); cadenced (*murajjaz*), which has metre without rhyme; and rhymed (*musajja'*), which has rhyme without metre. Concerning the first variety nothing need be said. The second demands more attention, since its recognition as a separate species of prose depends on what may be described as a theological dogma. Much of the Qur'án is written in rhymed prose, and here and

[1] The edition which I use is that lithographed at Tihrán in A.H. 1302, at the beginning of the works of Qá'ání.

there it happens that a verse falls into one of the recognised metres, as in *súra* ii, 78–79 :—

Thumma aqrartum, wa antum tashhadún,
Thumma antum há'ulá'i taqtulún,

which scans in the *Ramal* metre, *i.e.*, the foot *fá'ilátun* (— ⏑ — —) repeated six times in the *bayt* or verse and apocopated to *fá'ilát* (— ⏑ —) at the end of each *miṣrá'* or hemistich. Now the Prophet's adversaries used to call him a "mad poet," which description he vehemently repudiated; and hence it became necessary for his followers to frame a definition of poetry which would not apply to any verse or portion of the Qur'án. And since, as we have seen, certain verses of the Qur'án have both rhyme and metre, it became necessary to add a third condition, namely, that there must exist an *intention* (*qaṣd*) on the part of the writer or speaker to produce poetry. It is, therefore, spontaneous or involuntary poetry, occurring in the midst of a prose discourse, and reckoned as prose because it is not produced with *intention*, which is called *murajjaz.* The other classical instance, occurring in a traditional saying of the Prophet's, is :—

Al-karímu 'bnu 'l-karími 'bni 'l-karími 'bni 'l-karím,

which also scans in the *Ramal* (octameter) metre. The third variety of prose (*musajja'*, or rhymed) is very common in ornate writing in all the Muhammadan languages. Three kinds are recognised, called respectively *mutawází* ("parallel" or "concordant"), *muṭarraf* ("lop-sided"), and *mutawázin* ("symmetrical"). In the first kind the rhyming words ending two successive clauses agree in measure (*i.e.*, scansion) and number of letters, as, for example, in the tradition of the Prophet: *Allahumma! I'ti kulla munfiqin khalafan, wa kulla mumsikin talafan!* ("O God! give every spender a successor, and every miser destruction"); or, as we might say in English, "Give the spender health, and the lender wealth." In the second kind the rhyming words in two or more successive clauses differ in measure and number of letters, as though we should say in English, "He awakes to reprieve us from the aches which grieve us." In the third kind (common to verse and prose), the words in two or more successive clauses correspond in measure, each to each, but do not rhyme, as in the Qur'án, *súra* xxxvii, 117–118: *Wa átaynáhuma'l-Kitába 'l-mustabín: wa hadaynáhuma 'ṣ-Ṣiráṭa 'l-mustaqím.* An English example would be: "He came uplifted with joy, he went dejected with woe." The best European imitations of rhymed prose which I have seen are in German, and some very ingenious translations of this sort from the *Maqámát*, or "Séances," of Badí'u'z-Zamán al-Hamadhání (died A.D. 1007–8 in Herát) may be seen in vol. ii of Von Kremer's admirable *Culturgeschichte*, pp. 471–475. The following short extract will serve as a specimen:—

> "*Seine Antwort auf diesen Schreibebrief war kalt und schneidend—und ich, jede weitere Berührung vermeidend,—liess ihn in seinem Dünkel schalten—und legte ihn nach seinem Buge in Falten,—sein Andenken aber löschte ich aus dem Gedächtnissschrein,—seinen Namen warf ich in den Strom hinein.*"

George Puttenham, in his *Arte of English Poesie* (1589: Arber's reprint, 1869, p. 184) calls this figure *Omoioteleton*, or "Like loose," and gives the following prose example:—

> "*Mischaunces ought not to be lamented, But rather by wisedome in time prevented: For such mishappes as be remedilesse, To sorrow them it is but foolishnesse: Yet are we all so frayle of nature, As to be greeved with every displeasure.*"

2. *Verse-forms.*

Verse-forms recognised by the Persians.

Eleven different verse-forms, or varieties of poem, are enumerated by Rückert (ed. Pertsch, p. 55) as recognised in Persian by the author of the *Haft Qulzum* or "Seven Seas"; to wit, the *ghazal* or ode, the *qaṣída*, "purpose-poem" or elegy, the *tashbíb*, the *qiṭ'a* or fragment, the *rubá'í* or quatrain, the *fard* or "unit," the *mathnawí* or double-rhyme, the *tarjí'-band* or "return-tie," the *tarkíb-band* or "composite-tie," the *mustazád* or "complemented," and the *musammaṭ*; to which may be added the *murabba'* or "foursome," the *mukhammas* or "fivesome," &c., up to the *mu'ashshar* or "tensome," the "foursome," "fivesome," and "sixsome" being by far the commonest. There is also the *muwashshaḥ*, which was very popular amongst the Moors of Spain and the Maghrib, but is rarely met with in Persian. The *mulamma'*, "patch-work," or "macaronic" poem, composed in alternate lines or couplets in two or more different languages, has no separate form, and will be more suitably considered when we come to speak of *Verse-subjects*, or the classification of poems according to matter.

The classification adopted in the *Haft Qulzum* (and also by Gladwin) is neither clear nor satisfactory. The *tashbíb*, for instance, is merely that part of a *qaṣída* which describes, to quote Gladwin, "the season of youth (*shabáb*) and beauty, being a description of one's own feelings in love; but in common use it implies that praise which is bestowed on anything [other than the person whose praises it is the 'purpose' or object of the poet to celebrate, to which praises the *tashbíb* merely serves as an introduction], and the relation of circumstances, whether in celebration of love or any other subject." The *fard* ("unit" or hemistich) and the *qiṭ'a* ("fragment"), as well as the *bayt* (or couplet, consisting of two hemistichs), have also no right to be reckoned as separate verse-forms, since the first and last are the elements of which every poem consists, and the "fragment" is merely a piece of a *qaṣída*, though it may be that no more of the *qaṣída* was ever written, and, indeed, the productions of some few poets, notably Ibn Yamín (died A.D. 1344–45), consist entirely of such "fragments." Again, the two forms of *band*, or poem in strophes separated either by a recurrent verse, or by verses which, though different, rhyme with one another and not with the verses of the preceding or succeeding *band*, may well be classed together; as may also the "foursome," "fivesome," and other forms of multiple poem. The *muwashshaḥ*, again, like the *musammaṭ* and *muraṣṣa'*, is merely an ornate *qaṣída* or *ghazal* of a particular kind. Before attempting a more scientific and natural classification of the varieties of Persian verse, it is, however, necessary to say a few more words about the elements of which it consists.

The *Bayt* and the *Miṣrá'*.

The unit in every species of poem is the *bayt*, which consists of two symmetrical halves, each called *miṣrá'*, and comprises a certain number of feet, in all save the rarest cases either eight (when the *bayt* is called *muthamman* or "octameter") or six (in which case it is called *musaddas* or "hexameter"). Into the elements composing the foot (*viz.*, the *watad* or "peg," the *sabab* or "cord," and the *fáṣila* or "stay") we need not enter, only pausing to observe that, owing to a fanciful analogy drawn between the *baytu'sh-sha'r*, or "house of hair" (*i.e.*, the tent of the nomad Arabs), and the *baytu'sh-shi'r*, or verse of poetry, they, as well as most of the other technical terms of the Arabian Prosody (substantially identical with the Prosody of the Persians, Turks, and other Muhammadan nations), are named after parts of the tent. Thus the tent, or *baytu'sh-sha'r*, looked at from in front, consists of two flaps (*miṣrá'*) which together constitute the door; and so the word *miṣrá'* is also used in Prosody to denote each of the two half-verses which make up the *baytu'sh-shi'r*. Various reasons (which will be found set forth in detail at pp. 20–21 of Blochmann's *Persian Prosody*) are adduced to account for this curious comparison or analogy, the prettiest being that, as the *baytu'sh-sha'r*, or "house of hair," shelters the beautiful girls of the nomad tribe, so the *baytu'sh-shi'r*, or "verse of poetry," harbours the "virgin thoughts" (*abkár-i-afkár*) of the poet. In English the term *bayt* in poetry is generally rendered by "couplet," and the word *miṣrá'* by "hemistich." This seems to me an unfortunate nomenclature, since it suggests that the *bayt* is two units and the *miṣrá'* half a unit, and consequently that four, instead of two, of the latter go to make up one of the former. It would therefore seem to me much better to render *bayt* by "verse," and *miṣrá'* by "half-verse," though there would be no objection to continuing to call the latter "hemistich" ir we could agree to call the *bayt*, or verse, *stichos;* in which case the *rubá'í*, or quatrain, which consists of four hemistichs, or two *stichoi* (hence more accurately named by many Persians *du-baytí*), would be the distich. In any case it is important to remember that the *bayt* is the unit, and that the terms "hexameter" (*musaddas*) or "octameter" (*muthamman*) denote the number of feet in the *bayt*, and that, since all the *bayts* in a poem must be equal in length, that combination of hexameters and pentameters which is so common in Latin verse is impossible in Persian. In the course of prose works like the *Gulistán* a single *bayt*, or even a single *miṣrá'*, is often introduced to give point to some statement or incident, and such may have been composed for that sole purpose, and not detached from a longer poetical composition. The *miṣrá'* is in this case often called a *fard*, or "unit."

Classification of Persian verse-forms.

So much being clearly understood, we may proceed to the classification of the various verse-forms. The primary division depends on whether the rhyme of the *bayt* is, so to say, internal (the two *miṣrá's* composing each *bayt* rhyming together), or final (the *bayts* throughout the poem rhyming together, but their component *miṣrá's* not rhyming, as a rule, save in the *maṭla'*, or opening verse). These two primary divisions may be called the "many-rhymed" (represented only by the *mathnawí*, or "couplet-poem") and the "one-rhymed" (represented by the *qaṣída*, or "purpose-poem," and its "fragment," the *qiṭ'a;* the *ghazal*, or ode; and the *tarjí'-band* and *tarkíb-band*, or strophe-poems; to which, perhaps, we should add the *rubá'í*, or quatrain). What I have called the "multiple poems" (from the *murabba'* or "foursome" to the *mu'ashshar* or "tensome") must be placed in a separate class.

Concerning the many-rhymed poem, or *mathnawí*, little need be said, since most European poetry which is not written in blank verse belongs to this category. The rhyme, as has been said, is contained in the *bayt*, and changes from *bayt* to *bayt*. Tennyson's *Locksley Hall* furnishes an admirable example in English (taking accent for quantity, which the genius of our language requires), since it represents as closely as is possible what would be technically described in Persian Prosody as a *mathnawí* poem written in the metre called *Ramal-i-muthamman-i-maḥdhúf*, or the "apocopated octameter Ramal," *viz.*:—

The *Mathnawí.*

| — ◡ — — | — ◡ — — | — ◡ — — | — ◡ — |

twice repeated in the *bayt*. Here are the two first *bayts* (four lines of the English) scanned in this Persian fashion:—

"Cómrades, léave mé | hére a líttlé, | whíle as yét 'tís | éarly mórn | :
Léave me hére, ánd | whén you wánt me, | sóund upón thé | búgle hórn. |
'Tís the pláce, ánd | áll aroúnd ít, | ás of óld, thé | cúrlews cáll, |
Dréary gleáms á | bóut the móorlánd | flýing óvér | Lócksley Háll. |"

All long narrative and systematised didactic poems in Persian, like the *Sháhnáma*, or "Epic of Kings," of Firdawsí; the *Panj Ganj*, or "Five Treasures," of Nidhámí of Ganja; the *Haft Awrang*, or "Seven Thrones," of Jámí; and the great Mystical *Mathnawí* of Jalálu'd-Dín Rúmí, are composed in this form, which is of Persian invention, and unknown in classical Arabic poetry, though occasionally employed (under the name of *muzdawaj* or "consorted") in post-classical Arabic verse (late tenth century onwards) by Persian writers.[1]

[1] For an example of Arabic *mathnawí* or *muzdawaj*, see vol. iv of the *Yatímatu'd-Dahr*, p. 23 (Damascus edition).

We now pass to the one-rhymed forms of verse, wherein the same rhyme runs through the whole poem, and comes at the end of each *bayt*, while the two half-verses composing the *bayt* do not, as a rule, rhyme together, save in the *maṭla'*, or opening verse of the poem. The two most important verse-forms included in this class are the *ghazal*, or ode, and the *qaṣída*, or elegy. The same metres are used for both, and in both the first *bayt*, or *maṭla'*, has an internal rhyme, *i.e.*, consists of two rhyming *miṣrá's*, while the remaining rhymes are at the ends of the *bayts* only. The *ghazal* differs from the *qaṣída* mainly in subject and length. The former is generally erotic or mystical, and seldom exceeds ten or a dozen *bayts*; the latter may be a panegyric, or a satire, or it may be didactic, philosophical, or religious. In later days (but not, I think, before the Mongol Invasion) it became customary for the poet to introduce his *takhalluṣ*, *nom de guerre*, or "pen-name," in the last *bayt*, or *maqṭa'*, of the *ghazal*, which is not done in the *qaṣída*. As an example of the *ghazal* I give the following rendering of the very well-known ode from the *Díwán* of Ḥáfidh of Shíráz which begins:—

The Ghazal.

Agar án Turk-i-Shírázi bi-dast árad dil-i-márá
Bi-khál-i-Hinduwash bakhsham Samarqand u Bukhárá-rá.

"If that unkindly Shíráz Turk[1] would take my heart within her hand,
I'd give Bukhárá for the mole upon her cheek, or Samarqand!
Sáqí,[2] what wine is left for me pour, for in Heaven thou wilt not see
Muṣallá's sweet rose-haunted walks, nor Ruknábád's[3] wave-dimpled strand.

[1] The poet calls his sweetheart a "Turk" because the Turks are celebrated both for their beauty and their cruelty.
[2] Cupbearer.
[3] Two suburbs of Shíráz.

Alas! those maids, whose wanton ways such turmoil in our city raise,
Have stolen patience from my heart as spoil is seized by Tartar band.
Our Darling's beauty hath, indeed, of our imperfect love no need;
On paint and pigment, patch and line, a lovely face makes no demand.
Of Wine and Minstrel let us speak, nor Fate's dark riddle's answer seek,
Since none hath guessed and none shall guess enigmas none may understand.
That beauty, waxing day by day, of Joseph needs must lead astray
The fair Zulaykhá from the veils for modest maids' seclusion planned.
Auspicious youths more highly prize the counsels of the old and wise
Than life itself: then take, O Heart, the counsels ready to thy hand!
You spoke me ill; I acquiesced. God pardon you! 'twas for the best;
Yet scarce such bitter answer suits those rubies sugar-sweet and bland!
Your ode you've sung, your pearls you've strung; come, chant it sweetly, Ḥáfidh mine!
That as you sing the sky may fling the Pleiades' bejewelled band!"

The Qaṣída.

The great length of most *qaṣídas* makes it almost impossible to give an English verse-translation which shall preserve the one-rhymed character throughout, though many such translations of Turkish *qaṣídas* may be seen by the curious in such matters in the late Mr. E. J. W. Gibb's great *History of Ottoman Poetry*. To preserve the original form (both as regards metre and rhyme) of whatever poem he translated was with this great scholar an unvarying principle; but I, having less skill in verse-making, have felt myself constrained as a rule to abandon this plan, and translate *qaṣídas*, and sometimes even *ghazals*, as though they were *mathnawís*. I am emboldened to make such changes in rhyme and metre by the example of the Orientals themselves, for, as I have observed at pp. 464–5 of the *Prolegomena* to this volume, at the time when such verse-translations from Arabic into Persian and *vice versâ* were common feats of ingenuity and tests of scholarship in the two languages, it was usual to adopt a different metre in translating, and to change *mathnawí* Persian verses (*e.g.*, in al-Bundárí's Arabic translation of the *Sháhnáma*) into the *qaṣída* form in Arabic, notwithstanding the fact that both languages have a common system of Prosody, which, of course, does not extend to English. If, then, these masters of style and language permitted themselves these liberties, why should we, who are in every way placed at a disadvantage compared with them, deny ourselves a similar freedom?

However, since we are here speaking of verse-forms, I shall give a few specimens from *qaṣídas* in the proper monorhythmic form, which I have not found it possible to maintain in my translations for any complete *qaṣída*, the *qaṣída* being, as I have said, always of considerably greater length than the ode or *ghazal*, and often extending to more than a hundred *bayts*. My first specimen consists of six *bayts* taken from a *marthiya* (threnody, or *qaṣída* of mourning) composed by Shaykh Sa'dí of Shíráz on the sack of Baghdád by the Mongols and the cruel murder of the last 'Abbásid Caliph, al-Musta'ṣim bi'lláh, and his family. The text, which is interesting as showing the effect produced on the mind of a contemporary Muslim by this horrible catastrophe, is taken from vol. i of Ẓiyá Bey's *Kharábát* (Constantinople, A.H. 1291, p. 156). The metre is again the apocopated octameter *Ramal*. I give the six first of the twenty-one *bayts* which the poem comprises—

Specimen of a *Marthiya*, or Threnody.

Asmán-rá ḥaqq buwad gar khún bi-rízad bar zamín
Bar zawál-i-mulk-i-Musta'ṣim, Amíru'l-Mú'minín.

"Well it were if from the heavens tears of blood on earth should flow
For the Ruler of the Faithful, al-Musta'sim, brought so low.

If, Muḥammad, at the Judgement from the dust thy head thou'lt raise,
Raise it now, behold the Judgement fallen on thy folk below!
Waves of blood the dainty thresholds of the Palace-beauties whelm;
While from out my heart the life-blood dyes my sleeve with hues of woe.[1]
Fear vicissitudes of Fortune; fear the Sphere's revolving change;
Who could dream that such a splendour such a fate should overthrow?
Raise your eyes, O ye who once upon that Holy House did gaze,
Watching Kháns and Roman Cæsars cringing to its portals go.
Now upon that self-same threshold where the Kings their foreheads laid,
From the children of the Prophet's Uncle[2] streams of blood do flow!"

The above, however, is far less typical of the classical *qaṣída*, beginning with the *tashbíb* already described, and passing, in the *bayt* known technically as the *guríz-gáh*, or "transition-verse," into the *madíḥa*, or panegyric proper, than a very fine *qaṣída* (No. 29 in Kazimirski's edition, pp. 73–76) by the poet Minúchihrí, a younger contemporary of Firdawsí. This poem comprises seventy-two *bayts*, of which I give only a selection, indicating in each case the position of the translated verses in the complete text by prefixing the number which they bear in it. The metre is the apocopated hexameter *Hazaj* (⏑ — — — | ⏑ — — — | ⏑ — —), which I have been obliged to shorten by one syllable in my translation. It begins—

The typical Qaṣída.

Aláyá khaymagí, khayma firú hil,
Ki písh-áhang birún shud zi manzil.

---

[1] The Muslim poets suppose that when one weeps long and bitterly all the supply of tears is exhausted, and blood comes in their place, whence the red and bloodshot appearance of the eyes of him who has wept much.

[2] Al-'Abbás b. 'Abdu'l-Muṭṭalib, the ancestor of the Caliphs called after him 'Abbásid.

1. "O tentsman, haste, and strike the tent, I pray!
The caravan's already under way;
2. The drummer sounds already the first drum;
The *Tashbíb*, or Exordium.
Their loads the drivers on the camels lay.
3. The evening-prayer is nigh, and lo! to-night
The sun and moon opposed do stand at bay,
4. Save that the moon climbs upwards through the sky,
While sinks the sun o'er Babel's mountains grey,
5. Like to two scales of golden balance, when
One pan doth upwards and one downwards weigh."

The poet next describes his parting with his sweetheart, whom he addresses as follows:—

6. "'O silver cypress! Little did I think
To see so swiftly pass our trysting-day!
7. We are all heedless, but the moon and sun
Are heedful things, whose purposes ne'er stray.
8. My darling, wend thee hence, and weep no more,
For fruitless are the hopes of lovers aye.
9. With parting Time is pregnant; know ye not
Needs must the pregnant bring to birth one day?'
10. When thus my love beheld my state, her eyes
Rained tears like drops which fall when lightnings play.
11. That she crushed pepper held within her hand
And cast it in her eyes thou wouldest say.
12. Drooping and trembling unto me she came
Like throat-cut bird, whose life-blood ebbs away,
13. Around my neck like sword-belt flung her arms,
And on my breast like belt depending lay.
14. 'O cruel,' cried she; 'by my soul I swear
My envious foes rejoice through thee this day!
15. Wilt thou, what time the caravan returns,
Return therewith, or still in exile stay?
16. Perfect I deemed thee once in all thy deeds,
But now in love imperfect, wel-a-way!'"

The poet again endeavours to console his beloved, who finally departs and leaves him alone. He looks round the caravansaray, and sees "neither beast nor man, neither rider nor pedestrian," save his own camel, fretting "like a demon chained hand and foot." Having arranged its harness, he mounts, and it springs forward on the path whereby the caravan has departed, "measuring with its feet the stages like a surveyor measuring the land." He enters the desert—"a desert so cold and rugged that none who enters it comes forth again"—and describes the biting wind "which freezes the blood in the veins," and the silver patches of snow on the golden sand. Then comes the dawn, blinding him with its glare, and causing the snow to melt "as one who wastes of consumption," and the sticky mud to cling to his camel's feet like strings of isinglass. At length the caravan which he has striven to overtake appears encamped before him in the plain; he sees the lances of the escort planted in the ground like ears of wheat in a cornfield, and hears the tinkle of the camel-bells, sweet to his ears as the nightingale's song.

He then continues :—

48. "Then to my gallant beast I cried aloud,
'O friend of talent! Slower now, I pray!
49. Graze, sweet to thee as ambergris the grass!
Walk proudly, thou whom iron thews did stay!
50. Traverse the desert, climb the mountain ridge,
Beat down the stages, cut the miles away!
51. Then set me down at that Wazír's high court

* * * * * *

* * * * *

The *Guriz-gáh*, or *Takhalluṣ*.

52. Whose lofty aims great things and small display.'[1]

* * * * *

56. Mír Mas'úd[2] glories in his glorious time
As did the Prophet in Núshirwán's day.[3]

---

[1] This verse is the *guriz-gáh* or "transition-verse." I have here combined the first *miṣrá'* of 51 and the second of 52 in one *bayt*, to avoid (somewhat pusillanimously, perhaps) an allusion which I do not fully understand to some event in the life of the Arabian poet al-A'shá.

[2] *I.e.* Sultán Mas'úd ibn Maḥmúd of Ghazna, who reigned from A.D. 1030–40.

[3] Khusraw Anúshírwán (Anôshak-rûbân in Pahlawí) the Sásánian (reigned A.D. 531–78). He is still a proverb for justice in the East, and the Prophet is reported to have said, "I was born in the days of the Just King," meaning him.

57. The purse as rich as Korah[1] to him comes,
The beggar comes in suppliant's array;
58. The beggar leaves him gold-lined as a purse,
The purse it is which empty goes away."

The *Madiḥa*, or Panegyric proper.

In conclusion I give the last seven *bayts* of this *qaṣída*, wherein the poet craves his patron's favour and generosity, and prays for his long life. A hint that a reward would be acceptable to the poet (which always comes near the end of the poem), is called, when neatly introduced and expressed, *ḥusn-i-ṭalab*, or "beauty of demand." The last three *bayts* of the poem also illustrate the figure called *ḥusn-i-maqṭa'*, or "beauty of conclusion," which, in Gladwin's words (p. 62), "is when the poet exerts himself in the concluding verses, and ends with something striking, in order that the reader may leave off with satisfaction, and be induced to excuse any inaccuracies which may have occurred in the course of the poem." He adds very truly that "in the *qaṣída* the *husn-i-maqṭa'* is generally used in imploring blessing."

66. "O Master! Hither do I come in hope
To gain some gleanings from thy bounteous sway.
67. To thee come flocking ever men of parts,
For like to like doth surely find the way.
68. Provide me with some place, and thou shalt see
Di'bil and A'shá[2] envious of my lay!
69. But if of serving thee I be deprived,
My pen I'll burn, my fingers hew away.
70. So long as sounds the dove's and woodcock's cry,
And name of hawk and Símurgh[3] with us stay,

---

[1] Korah, or Qárún, is believed by the Muslims to have been immensely rich, and to have been punished by God at the prayer of Moses because he refused to disburse money. "As rich as Qárún" is, therefore, equivalent to "as rich as Crœsus."

[2] Two Arabic poets. The first, who belonged to the Shí'a sect died in A.D. 860. The second, al-A'shá Ma'mún b. Qays, was contemporary with the Prophet.

[3] The *Símurgh* or *'Anqá* is a gigantic mythical bird of great wisdom, supposed to inhabit the Mountain of Qáf.

71. Thy frame be lasting and thine eye be bright,
Thy heart be pure, thy luck increasing aye!
72. God give me Bashshár's[1] talent, and the tongue
Of Ibnu Muqbil, thee to praise alway!"

The *Qiṭ'a* or Fragment.

We now come to the *qiṭ'a*, and for this few words will suffice. Essentially (as its name implies) it is, as has been already said, merely a detached "fragment" of a *qaṣída*, but it may be an uncompleted fragment—a torso, so to speak; or it may be so far complete in itself that the poet never intended to add to it. Nay, in some cases its style and subject-matter are such that it was evidently intended from the first to be an independent poem. The following "fragment" by Anwarí (died A.D. 1191) may suffice as a specimen:—

"'Have patience; patience will perform thy work
Quickly and well,' to me a comrade said;
'The water to the river will return;
Thine aims shall speed as never they have sped.'
I said: 'Suppose the water does return,
What boots it, if the fish meanwhile be dead?'"

This "fragment" is evidently complete in itself, and no addition to it can ever have been contemplated.

The *Rubá'í* or Quatrain.

The *rubá'í* or quatrain, again, is formally two *bayts* (whence called *dú-baytí*) or four hemistichs (whence called *rubá'í*) from the beginning of a *qaṣída* or *ghazal* written in certain varieties of a particular metre, the *Hazaj*; but, like the epigram, it is always complete in itself. FitzGerald's beautiful renderings of the quatrains of 'Umar Khayyám have rendered this verse-form so familiar that it is hardly necessary to say more of it in this place. As I have observed, however, that some admirers of FitzGerald's 'Umar imagine that quatrains can be linked together to form

[1] Bashshár b. Burd, the blind sceptic and poet, who, though excelling in Arabic verse, was of Persian, and, as he boasted, of royal descent. He was put to death in A.D. 783.

a poem, I should perhaps emphasise the fact that the effect of continuity in FitzGerald's version is due to his arrangement and selection of the *rubá'ís* which he translated, and that quatrains are always quite independent and complete in themselves, and, in the collected works of Persian poets, are never arranged otherwise than alphabetically, according to the final letter of the rhyme. The quatrain metres, as we said above, are generally special derivatives of the *Hazaj*, and the first, second, and fourth *misrá's* must rhyme, while the third need not, and generally does not. The two following quatrains extemporised by Mu'izzí for the Seljúq Malikshah (whose Poet-laureate he afterwards became) are not, perhaps, of any special literary merit, but are historically interesting, since we have in the *Four Discourses* (pp. 67–70 of the *tirage-à-part*) the poet's own account, given to the author of that work, of the circumstances under which they were composed. He says:—

Instance of improvisation from the *Chahár Maqála*.

"My father Burhání, the Poet-laureate (may God be merciful to him!) passed away from this transitory to that eternal world in the town of Qazwín in the early part of the reign of Malikshah, entrusting me to the King in this verse, since then become famous:—

Man raftam, u farzand-i-man ámad khalaf-i-ṣidq;
Úrá bi-Khudá ú bi-Khudáwand sipurdam.[1]

'I am flitting, but I leave a son behind me,
And commend him to my God and to my King.'

"So my father's salary and allowances were transferred to me, and I became Malikshah's Court-poet, and spent a year in the King's

[1] This verse, supplemented by several others, which are undoubtedly spurious, is commonly ascribed (*e.g.*, by Dawlatsháh, p. 59 of my edition) to the Nidhámu'l-Mulk, who, as we learn from the next paragraph of this extract, "had no opinion of poets, because he had no skill in their art." One of these spurious verses which gives his age as ninety-four at the time of his death (he being actually eighty at most) is alone enough to discredit the story, apart from the small probability that one who had been mortally wounded by an assassin's knife would be in the humour to compose verses. This is a good example of the universal tendency of mankind to ascribe well-known stories or verses to notable men.

service; yet was I unable to see him save from a distance, nor did I get one *dínár* of my salary or one maund of my allowances, while my expenditure was increased, I became involved in debt, and my brain was perplexed by my affairs. For that great minister, the Nidhámu'l-Mulk (may God be merciful to him!), had no opinion of poets, because he had no skill in their art; nor did he pay any attention to any one of the religious leaders or mystics.

"One day—it was the eve of the day on which the new moon of Ramadán was due to appear, and I had not a farthing to meet all the expenses incidental to that month and the feast which follows it —I went thus sad at heart to the Amír 'Alí Farámarz 'Alá'u'd-Dawla,[1] a man of royal parentage, a lover of poetry, and the intimate companion and son-in-law of the King, with whom he enjoyed the highest honour, and before whom he could speak boldly, since he held high rank under that administration. And he had already been my patron. I said, 'May my lord's life be long! Not all that the father could do can the son do, nor does that which accrued to the father accrue to the son. My father was a bold and energetic man, and was sustained by his art, and the martyred King Alp Arslán, the lord of the world, entertained the highest opinion of him. But what he could do that cannot I, for modesty forbids me. I have served this prince for a year, and have contracted debts to the extent of a thousand *dínárs*, and have not received a farthing. Crave permission, then, for thy servant to go to Níshápúr, and discharge his debts, and live on that which is left over, and express his gratitude to this victorious dynasty.'

"'Thou speakest truly,' replied Amír 'Alí: 'we have all been at fault, but this shall be so no longer. The King, at the time of Evening Prayer, will go up to look for the moon. Thou must be present there, and we will see what Fortune will do.' Thereupon he at once ordered me to receive a hundred *dínárs* to defray my Ramadán expenses, and a purse containing this sum in Níshápúr coinage was forthwith brought and placed before me. So I returned, mightily well pleased, and made my preparations for Ramadán, and at the time of the second prayer went to the King's pavilion. It chanced that 'Alá'u'd-Dawla arrived at the very same moment, and I paid my respects to him. 'Thou hast done exceedingly well,' said he, 'and hast come punctually.' Then he dismounted and went in before the King.

"At sundown the King came forth from his pavilion, with a cross-

---

[1] Probably 'Alí b. Farámarz the Kákwayhid is intended. See Lane's *Muhammadan Dynasties*, p. 145.

bow in his hand and 'Alá'u'd-Dawla on his right hand. I ran
forward to do obeisance. Amír 'Alí continued the kindnesses he
had already shown me, and then busied himself in looking for the
moon. The King, however, was the first to see it, whereat he
was mightily pleased. Then 'Alá'u'd-Dawla said to me, ' O son of
Burhání, say something appropriate,' and I at once recited these
two verses ¹ :—

> *Ay Máh ! chú abruwán-ı-Yárí, gú'í,*
> *Yá nay, chú kamán-i-Shahriyárí gú'í,*
> *Na'lí zada az zar-i-'iyárí, gú'í,*
> *Bar gúsh-i-sipihr gúshwárí, gú'í.*

' Methinks, O Moon, thou art our Prince's bow,
  Or his arched eyebrow, which doth charm us so,
  Or else a horse-shoe wrought of gold refined,
  Or ring from Heaven's ear depending low.'

" When I had submitted these verses, Amír 'Alí applauded, and
the King said : ' Go, loose from the stables whichever horse thou
pleasest.' When I was close to the stable, Amír 'Alí designated a
horse which was brought out and given to my attendants, and which
proved to be worth 300 *dínárs* of Níshápúr. The King then went
to his oratory, and I performed the evening prayer, after which we
sat down to meat. At the table Amír 'Alí said : ' O son of Burhání !
Thou hast not yet said anything about this favour conferred on thee
by the lord of the world. Compose a quatrain at once !' I thereupon sprang to my feet and recited these two verses :—

> *Chún átash-i-khátir-i-mará Sháh bi-did,*
> *Az khák mará bar zabar-i-máh kashid ;*
> *Chún áb yakí tarána az man shunid,*
> *Chán bád yakí markab-ı-khássam bakhshíd.*

' The King beheld the *fire* which in me blazed :
  Me from low *earth* above the moon he raised :
  From me a verse, like *water* fluent, heard,
  And swift as *wind* a noble steed conferred.'

" When I recited these verses 'Alá'u'd-Dawla warmly applauded
me, and by reason of his applause the King gave me a thousand
dínárs. Then 'Alá'u'd-Dawla said : ' He hath not yet received his
salary and allowances. To-morrow I will sit by the Minister until

¹ As has been already said, the quatrain, as consisting of two verses, is
called *dú-baytí*, or, as consisting of four hemistichs, *rubá'í*.

he writes a draft for his salary on Iṣfahán, and orders his allowances to be paid out of the treasury.' Said the King: 'Thou must do it, then, for none else has sufficient boldness. And call this poet after my title.' Now the King's title was *Mu'izzu'd-Dunyá wa'd-Dín*,[1] so Amír 'Alí called me Mu'izzí. '*Amír* Mu'izzí,' said the King [correcting him]. And this noble lord was so zealous for me that next day, by the time of the first prayer, I had received a thousand *dinárs* as a gift, twelve hundred more as allowances, and an order for a thousand maunds of corn. And when the month of Ramaḍán was passed, he summoned me to a private audience, and caused me to become the King's boon-companion. So my fortune began to improve, and thenceforth he made enduring provision for me, and to-day whatever I have I possess by the favour of that Prince. May God, blessed and exalted is He, rejoice his dust with the lights of His Mercy, by His Favour and His Grace!"

Improvisation highly esteemed in early times.

This anecdote further illustrates the importance attached in earlier days to the faculty of improvisation in poets, and several other striking instances are given in this same book, the *Chahár Maqála*. Thus (pp. 56–58) when Sulṭán Maḥmúd of Ghazna had cut off the locks of his favourite Ayáz in a moment of drunken excitement, and, partly from remorse, partly from the after-effects of his drinking-bout, was next day in so evil a temper that none dared approach him, the Poet-laureate 'Unṣurí restored him to good humour by this quatrain:—

Gar 'ayb-i-sar-i-zulf-i-but az kástan-ast,
Chi já-yi bi-gham nishastan u khástan-ast?
Já-yi ṭarab u nisháṭ u may khwástan-ast,
K'árástan-i-sarv zi pírástan-ast.

"Though shame it be a fair one's curls to shear,
Why rise in wrath or sit in sorrow here?
Rather rejoice, make merry, call for wine;
When clipped the cypress[2] doth most trim appear."

---

[1] "The Glorifier of the World and the Faith." Every poet in Persia assumes a "pen-name," *nom de guerre*, or *takhalluṣ*, which is most often derived from his patron's title, *e.g.*, Sa'dí, Anwarí, Nidhámí, &c.

[2] The comparison of a tall and graceful beauty to a cypress is very common in Persian and Turkish poetry.

Another extemporised quatrain of Azraqí's (*Chahár Maqála*, pp. 71–72) had an equally happy effect in calming the dangerous anger of his patron, the young King Ṭughánsháh, whose temper had given way in consequence of his having thrown two ones instead of the two sixes he desired at a critical point in a game of backgammon. This quatrain ran :—

Gar Sháh du shish khwást, du yak zakhm uftád,
Tá ẓan na-barí ki ka'batayn dád na-dád ;
Án zakhm ki kard ray-i-Sháhinshah yád
Dar khidmat-i-Sháh rúy bar khák nihád.

"Reproach not Fortune with discourteous tricks
If by the King, desiring double six,
Two ones were thrown ; for whomsoe'er he calls
Face to the earth before him prostrate falls."[1]

These two last quatrains have two points in common ; first, the four *miṣrá's* all rhyme in both cases, whereas the third is in the quatrain commonly not rhymed ; secondly, both exhibit the rhetorical figure technically called *ḥusn-i-ta'líl* ("poetical ætiology"), where a real effect is explained by an imaginary or fanciful reason.

We must now briefly consider some of the remaining and less important verse-forms, *viz.*, the two kinds of strophe-poem (the *tarjí'-band* and *tarkíb-band*), the various forms of multiple-poem (the *murabba'*, *mukhammas*, &c.), the *musammaṭ*, and the *mustazád*.

The *Tarjí'-band* and *Tarkíb-band.*

The two kinds of strophe-poem both consist of a series of stanzas, each containing a variable, but equal, or nearly equal, number of couplets, all in one rhyme, these stanzas being separated from one another by a series of isolated verses which mark the end of each strophe. If the same verse (which in this case may be best described as a refrain) be repeated at the close of each *band*, or strophe, the poem is called a *tarjí'-band*, or "return-tie" ; if, on the other hand, the verses which

[1] In this translation I have departed from the proper quatrain rhyme.

conclude each strophe be different, each rhyming internally in a rhyme differing from that of the preceding and succeeding strophes, the poem is called a *tarkib-band*, or "composite tie." In both cases the metre is the same throughout.

To translate in its entirety a poem of either of these two classes, having regard to the proper arrangement of the rhymes, is beyond my powers, but I here give a few lines from two successive strophes of a very celebrated and very beautiful *tarjí'-band* by Hátif of Iṣfahán, who flourished towards the end of the eighteenth century:—

"O heart and soul a sacrifice to Thee,
Before Thee all we have an off'ring free!
The heart, Sweetheart, we yield as service meet;
The soul, O Soul, we give right cheerfully.
Scarce from Thy hands may we preserve our hearts,
But at Thy feet surrender life with glee.
The way to Thee is fraught with perils dire,
And Thy love-sickness knows no remedy.
Eyes for Thy gestures, ears for Thy commands,
Servants with lives and hearts in hand are we.
Would'st Thou have peace? Behold, our hearts are here!
Would'st Thou have war? Our lives we offer Thee!

* * * * * *

HE is alone, beside HIM there is none;
No God there is but HE, and HE is One!

* * * * * *

From Thee, O Friend, I cannot break my chain,
Though limb from limb they hew my trunk amain.
In truth, from us a hundred lives were meet;
Half a sweet smile from Thee will ease our pain!
O father, cease to caution me of Love!
This headstrong son will never prudence gain.
Rather 'twere meet they should admonish those
Who 'gainst Thy love admonish me in vain.
Well do I know the way to Safety's street,
But what can I, who long in bonds have lain?

* * * * * *

HE is alone, beside HIM there is none;
No God there is but HE, and HE is one!"

This poem comprises six strophes, separated by the above refrain, and contains in all (including the refrain-verse, five times repeated) about 148 verses, *viz.*, 23 + 1 in the first strophe, 13 + 1 in the second, 17 + 1 in the third, 15 + 1 in the fourth, 18 + 1 in the fifth, and 57 in the sixth. If at the end of the second strophe, instead of having the same verse repeated we had a different verse in a different rhyme, the two half-verses of which rhymed together, the result would be a *tarkíb-band*.[1] It will be observed that each strophe begins like a *qaṣída* or *ghazal*, with a *maṭla'*, or initial verse, of which the two halves rhyme together.

The Musammaṭ

The *musammaṭ*, according to Rückert (p. 85 of Pertsch's edition), is a general term including all the varieties of multiple-poem, while the definition given by Rashídu'd-Dín Waṭwáṭ identifies it with what the Moorish poets called *muwashshaḥ*, where the *miṣrá'* has an internal rhyme, as in the following verses contained in my rendering of a poem ascribed to the Bábí heroine, Qurratu'l-'Ayn :—

"The musk of Cathay might perfume gain from the scent those fragrant tresses rain,
While those eyes demolish a faith in vain attacked by the pagans of Tartary.
With you who despise both Love and wine for the hermit's cell and the zealot's shrine,
What can I do? For our faith divine ye hold as a thing of infamy!"

Of all the early poets Minúchihrí appears to have been fondest of the *musammaṭ*, which has been revived in quite modern times by Mírzá Dáwarí of Shíráz. Two strophes from an unpublished *musammaṭ* of the latter will suffice to illustrate the usual form of this variety of poem :—

[1] The verses which form the *bands* of a *tarkíb-band* must rhyme within themselves, and may, but need not, rhyme with one another.

"O Arab boy, God give you happy n.orn!
The morning wine-cup give, for here's the dawn!
Give to the Pole one draught, and I'll be sworn
'Twill cast you down the crown of Capricorn:
You Ursa makes its ransom, tender fawn,
When sphere-like round the wine-jar you rotate.
Hast thou no wine? Clasp close the wine-skin old,
Then Arab-wise o'er head thy mantle hold,
And, like the Arabs, skirt in girdle fold;
Mantle and wine-skin clasp in hand-grip bold,
By wine-stained robe be wine-skin's bounty told;
And from thy lodging seek the Tavern's gate."

The rhyme of this kind of *musammaṭ*, which is by far the commonest, may therefore be represented by the formula: *a,a,a,a,a,x ; b,b,b,b,b,x ; c,c,c,c,c,x*, &c. Another form used by Minúchihrí consists of a series of strophes each containing six rhyming *miṣra'ṣ*, according to the formula: *a,a,a,a,a,a ; b,b,b,b,b,b*, &c. It will thus be seen that the *musammaṭ* of the former and most usual type is essentially a *mukhammas*, or "fivesome," save that generally in the true *mukhammas* the five lines, or half-verses, composing the opening stanza all rhyme together, after which the rhyme changes, save in the tenth, fifteenth, and twentieth lines or half-verses, which maintain the rhyme of the first stanza. Very often the basis of a multiple-poem is a *ghazal* of some other poet, to each *bayt* of which two more half-verses or *miṣrá'ṣ* are added to make a *murabba'* ("foursome"), three to make a *mukhammas* ("fivesome"), and so on. We can most easily illustrate these forms by taking the opening lines of the translation given at p. 31 *supra* of Minúchihrí's *qaṣída*, as follows:—

(*Murabba'*, or "Foursome.")

The shades of evening mark the close of day;
The sunset fades, the world grows cold and grey;
*"O tentsman, haste, and strike the tents, I pray!
The caravan's already under way."*

In haste the travellers together come;
Their voices rise like swarming bee-hive's hum;
"The drummer sounds already the first drum;
Their loads the drivers on the camels lay."

(*Mukhammas*, or "Fivesome.")

The shades of evening mark the close of day;
The sunset fades, the world grows cold and grey;
Across the plain the length'ning shadows play;
"O tentsman, haste, and strike the tents, I pray!
The caravan's already under way."

In haste the travellers together come;
Some all unready, long expectant some;
Their voices rise like swarming bee-hive's hum;
"The drummer sounds already the first drum;
Their loads the drivers on the camels lay."

The structure of the *musaddas* ("sixsome"), *musabba'* ("sevensome"), and the remaining multiple-poems is precisely similar to these, and need not be further illustrated.

The Mustazád.

The *mustazád*, or "increment-poem," is an ordinary quatrain, ode, or the like, whereof each half-verse is followed by a short metrical line, not required to complete the sense or metre of the poem to which it is appended; these "increment-verses" rhyming and making sense together like a separate poem. We may illustrate this verse-form by means of the poem used to illustrate the *murabba'* and the *mukhammas*.

"O tentsman, haste, and strike the tents, I pray;"	The day grows late;
"The caravan's already under way;"	They will not wait.
"The drummer sounds already the first drum;"	The mule-bells call;
"Their loads the drivers on the camels lay."	Mate cries to mate.
"The evening-prayer is near, and lo! to-night"	The sky is clear;
"The sun and moon opposed do stand at bay,"	Beyond the gate—

and so on. It will be observed that the sense and rhyme of the poem is complete without the increment, and *vice versâ*. It is not, however, necessary that the multiple-poem or the increment-poem should be based upon an earlier poem by some other author, for a poem may be composed originally in one of these forms.[1]

Classification by subject.

Besides the above classification by form, there is another classification (referring especially to the *qaṣída*, whereof the scope is much wider and more varied than that of any other verse-form, except, perhaps, the *qiṭ'a* and the *mathnawí*) according to topic or subject. Thus a *qaṣída* may be a panegyric (*madíḥa*), or a satire (*hajw*), or a death-elegy (*marthiya*), or philosophical (*ḥikamiyya*), or it may contain a description of spring (*rabí'iyya*), or winter (*shitá'iyya*), or autumn (*khizániyya*), or it may consist of a discussion between two personified opposites (*e.g.*, night and day, summer and winter, lance and bow, heaven and earth, Persian and Arab, Muslim and Zoroastrian, heat and cold, or the like), when it is called a *munáḏhara*, "joust," or "strife-poem,"[2] or it may be in the form of a dialogue (*su'ál u jawáb*, "question and answer"), and so on. The "dialogue" also occurs in *ghazals*, of which also sundry other forms exist, such as the *mulamma'*, or "patch-work" poem, where alternate lines or verses are in two (occasionally three) different languages, *e.g.*, Arabic and Persian, or both of these and one of the dialects of Persian ; or we may have poems entirely in dialect, the so-called *Fahlawiyyát*, or "Pahlawí" ballads, which were common down to the thirteenth century of our era, and not rare in later times. In addition to these, there is the *muwash-*

[1] An excellent English *mustazád* composed during the American Revolution will be found at p. 54 of Morgan's *Macaronic Poetry* (New York, 1872). The poem with the increment is pro-English, but if the increment be removed, the sense is reversed, and it becomes strongly pro-American.

[2] See Dr. H. Ethé's very interesting paper, *Ueber persischen Tenzonen*, published in the Acts of the Berlin Oriental Congress of 1881, pp. 48–135.

shah or acrostic,[1] the *mu'ammá* or riddle, the *lughz* or enigma, the *nadhíra* (which may be merely a "parallel," or imitation, or an actual parody), and the *taḍmín*, or quotation (literally, "insertion"), where a poem by another author is taken as the basis, and added to, often in the spirit of parody. The only example of this last I can recollect in English is by Lewis Carroll, and occurs in his *Phantasmagoria*, afterwards re-published under the title of *Rhyme? and Reason?* This is a genuine *taḍmín* of the well-known poem beginning, "I never loved[2] a dear gazelle," and the first verse runs, so far as I can recollect (for I have not the book at hand) :—

> "*I never loved a dear gazelle,*
> Nor anything that cost me much :
> High prices profit those who sell,
> But why should I be fond of such?"

Macaronic verse.

Mention should also be made of the genuine "macaronic" poem, where Persian words are constructed and treated as Arabic, just as, in the absurd schoolboy doggerel beginning :—

> "*Patres conscripti took a boat and went to Philippi,*"

English words are Latinized ; as in the line :—

> "*Omnes drownderunt, quiâ swim-away non potuerunt.*"

Such "macaronic" verses and prose occur in Sa'dí's *facetiæ*, but there is a better instance in Ibn Isfandiyár's *History of Ṭabaristán* (compiled about A.D. 1216) in a long *qaṣída* of seventy-four verses written by the Qáḍí Hishám to satirise

[1] The Arabic *muwashshaḥ* which was so popular in Andalusia and the Maghrib is different, and resembles the Persian *musammaṭ* already mentioned.

[2] "Taught" is, I believe, the correct reading, but of course it would not suit Lewis Carroll's *taḍmín*.

one of his contemporaries. This poem is given in full, with the variants, at pp. 81–85 of my abridged translation of this History, published in 1905 as the second volume of the E. J. W. Gibb Memorial Series. It begins :—

Ay bi-farhang u 'ilm daryá'u ! *Laysa márá bi-juz tu hamtá'u.*
Man-am ú tu ki lá ḥayá laná : *Hazl-rá karda'im iḥyá'u.*

Of European macaronic poems, the best known are, perhaps, the *Macaronicorum poema* of Merlinus Coccaius, published about A.D. 1529, and William Drummond of Hawthornden's *Polemo-Middinia*, printed at Oxford in 1691. The following specimen from the latter may suffice :—

"*Hic aderant Geordy Akinhedius, et little Johnus,*
Et Jamy Richæus, et stout Michel Hendersonus,
Qui gillatis pulchris ante alios dansare solebat,
Et bobbare bene, et lassas kissare bonæas ;
Duncan Olyphantus valde stalvertus, et ejus
Filius eldestus jolyboyus, atque Oldmondus," &c.

There are many other terms used in describing the subject-matter of verses, such as *Kufriyyát* (blasphemous or heretical poems), *Khamriyyát* (wine-poems), &c., which it is unnecessary to enumerate, since the number of these classes is not definite, and the terms employed commonly explain themselves.

In addition to the terms above explained, there are a large number of rhetorical devices and quaint conceits employed by writers of ornate prose and verse which demand some notice from any one desirous of understanding the nature, or appreciating the ingenuity, of Persian (and Arabic or Turkish) literary compositions. Many of these figures, though no longer cultivated in this country, were highly esteemed by the Euphuists and other English writers of the sixteenth century, and a rich store of examples may be gleaned from George Puttenham's *Arte of English Poesie*, published in 1589, and quoted hereinafter from Mr. Arber's reprint of 1869; while most varieties of the *tajnís*, or word-play, may be illustrated from the *Ingoldsby Legends*, the works of Tom Hood, and similar books. The more important of these artifices of the Persian rhetoricians and poets are illustrated in a *qaṣída-i-muṣanna'*, or "artifice-qaṣída," composed by the poet Qiwámí of Ganja, the brother of the celebrated Nidhámí of Ganja, who flourished in the twelfth century of our era. This *qaṣída* comprises 101 *bayts*, or verses, and is given on pp. 198–201 of vol. i of Ẓiyá Pasha's *Kharábát*. I reproduce it here, line by line, with prose translation, and running commentary as to the nature of the rhetorical figures which it is intended to illustrate.

1. *Ay falak-rá hawá-yi qadr-i-tu bár, W'ay malak-rá thaná-yi-ṣadr-i-tu kár!*

"O thou the love of whose worth is the burden of heaven,
And O thou the praise of whose high place [affords] occupation to the angels!"

Ḥusn-i-maṭla' and Tarṣí'.

This verse exemplifies two figures, *ḥusn-i-maṭla'*, ("beauty of exordium"), which is, as Gladwin says, "when the poet exerts himself in the maṭla'" (or opening verse of a *qaṣída* or *ghazal*) "to fix the hearer's attention, and excite his curiosity for the catastrophe"; and *tarṣí'*, which literally means "setting with jewels," but in poetical composition is when the words in two successive *miṣrá's*, or half-verses, correspond, each to each, in measure and rhyme. An English example (but imperfect at two points) would be:—

"O love who liest on my breast so light,
O dove who fliest to thy nest at night!"

An excellent Latin example is given in Morgan's *Macaronic Poetry* (New York, 1872, p. 101):—

> *"Quos anguis tristi diro cum vulnere stravit,*
> *Hos sanguis Christi miro tum munere lavit."*

2. *Tír-i-charkhat zi mihr dída sipar, Tír-i-charkhat zi mihr dída-sipár!*

> "The quarrel of thy cross-bow sees in the sun a shield;
> The [planet] Mercury in heaven lovingly follows thee with its eyes!"

Here we have two figures, the *tarṣí'* explained above, but combined with an elaborate series of "homonymies," or word-plays. Such word-plays (called *tajnís* or *jinás*) are of seven kinds (or, if we include the kindred *ishtiqáq*, eight), all of which seven kinds are exemplified in this and the six following verses. In this verse the words on which the poet plays are identical alike in spelling, pointing, and pronunciation, and illustrate the first kind of *tajnís*, called *támm* ("complete"). Thus *tír* is the name of the planet "Mercury," and also denotes "an arrow" or "quarrel"; *charkh* means "heaven," and also "a cross-bow"; *mihr*, "the sun," and "love"; *dída*, "having seen" or "saw," and "the eye"; *sipar* is a shield, while *sipár* is the root of the verb *sipurdan*, "to entrust," *dída-sipár* being, at the end of the verse, a compound adjective meaning "entrusting," *i.e.*, "fixing the eye."

Tarsí' and Tajnís-i-támm.

3. *Júd-rá burda az miyána miyán, Bukhl-rá dáda az kinára kinár!*

> "Out of a company [of rivals] thou hast caught Generosity in thine embrace:
> Thou hast banished Avarice from thy side!"

The *tajnís* here illustrated is really the third variety, called *zá'id* ("redundant"), though described in the margin of my text as of the last or "complete" kind, and another instance of it occurs in the fifth verse. It is so called because one of each pair of words has a

Tajnís-i-zá'id.

"redundant" letter, which differentiates it from its fellow (*maydn maydna ; kinár, kinára*), and prevents the word-play from being "complete." An English exemplification from Puttenham's *Arte of English Poesie* is the following :—

"The maid that soon married is, soon marred is."

4. ***Sá'id-i-mulk, u Rakhsh-i-Dawlat-rá, Tu siwárí, wa himmat-i-tu sawár.***

Tajnís-i-náqiṣ.

"On the arm of Empire, and the steed of State,
Thou art the bracelet, and thy courage the rider."

Rakhsh (here rendered by "steed") was the name of the legendary hero Rustam's horse. The verse exemplifies the second kind of *tajnís*, called *náqiṣ*, or "defective," when the words on which the writer plays are spelt alike, but pointed differently, *i.e.*, differ in one or more of the short vowels. The following English example is from Puttenham's *Arte of English Poesie* :—

"To pray for you ever I cannot refuse ;
To prey upon you I should you much abuse.'

5. ***Past bá rif'at-i-tu khána-i-khán : Tang bá fusḥat-i-tu shári'-i-Shár.***

Tajnís-i-zá'id.

"Low compared with thine exaltation is the khán's mansion ;
Narrow compared with thy spaciousness is the street of the Shár."[1]

Here again we have the "redundant" (*zá'id*) variety of *tajnís* explained above in the third verse.

6. ***Bí wafá-yi tu mihr-i-ján ná-chíz : Bá wafá-yi tu Mihriján chu bahár.***

[1] *Shár* is the title of the ruler of Gharjistán, a country near Ghúr and Afghánistán.

5

"The love of the soul is naught without thy faithful troth:
With thy faithful troth Mihriján[1] is like Spring."

Tajnís-i-murakkab.

Here we have the kind of *tajnís* called "compound" (*murakkab*), of which the late Mr. E. J. W. Gibb gives the following ingenious exemplification in English in the first volume (p. 118) of his *History of Ottoman Poetry*:—

"Wandering far, they went *astray*,
When fell on the hills the sun's *last ray*."

7. *Ṣubḥ-i-bad-khwáh z'iḥtishám-i-tu shám; Gul-i-bad-gúy z'iftikhár-i-tu khár.*

"The morning of him who wishes thee ill [becomes as] evening through thy pomp;
The rose of him who speaks evil of thee [becomes as] a thorn through thy pride."

Tajnís-i-mukarrar.

Here the *tajnís* is what is called *mukarrar*, or "repeated," *shám* being a repetition of part of *iḥtishám*, and *khár* of *iftikhár*. Here is an example in English:—

"Alas! you did re*late* to us too *late*,
The perils compassing that *agate gate*."

8. *'Adlat áfáq shusta az áfát; Ṭab'at ázád búda az ázár.*

"Thy justice hath cleansed the horizons from calamities;
Thy nature hath been exempted from hurtfulness."

Tajnís-i-muṭarraf.

Here the *tajnís* is of the kind called *muṭarraf* ("partial" or "lateral"), the words *áfaq* and *áfát*, and *ázád* and *ázár* agreeing save for a "partial" or "lateral" (*i.e.*, terminal) difference. Example in English:—

[1] Mihriján (or Mihragán), "the month of Mithra," is the old Persian month corresponding roughly to our September.

"Like Esau lose thy birthright: I instead
Shall eat the pottage and shall *break* the *bread*."

9. *Az tú bímár-i-dhulm-rá dárú, Wa'z tu a'dá-yi mulk-rá tímár.*

"By thee [is effected] the cure of him who is sick with injustice.
By thee [is undertaken] the care of the enemies of the state."

Tajnís-i-khaṭṭí.

Here the *tajnís* is what is called *khaṭṭí* ("linear" or "scriptory"), *i.e.*, the words *bímár* and *tímár* are the same in outline, and differ only in their diacritical points.

10. *Juz ghubár-i-nabard-i-tu nabarad Dída-i-'aql surma-i-dídár.*

"Save the dust of thy battle, the eye of understanding
Will take naught as collyrium for its eyesight."

Isti'ára.

This verse illustrates the *isti'ára* ("trope" or "simile"), the expression "the eye of understanding" meaning "the understanding eye," or simply "the understanding."

11. *Dar gul-i-sharm yáft bí gul-i-tu Shána-i-charkh máh áyina-dár.*

* * * * * *

Murá'át-i-nadhír.

This verse (which is to me unintelligible, and probably corrupt) illustrates the figure called *murá'át-i-nadhír* ("the observance of the similar"), or *tanásub* ("congruity"), and consists in introducing into a verse things which are naturally associated together, such as *bow* and *arrow*, *night* and *day*, *sun* and *moon*. The following English example is from Puttenham's *Arte of English Poesie* (p. 251), from a "Partheniade" composed by him on Queen Elizabeth:—

"Two lips wrought out of *rubie* rocke,
Like leaves to shut and to unlock.
As portall dore in Prince's chamber:
A *golden* tongue in mouth of *amber*."

12. ***Án kunad kúshish-i-tu bá a'dá Ki kunad bakhshish-i-tu bá dínár.***

Madḥ-i-muwajjah.

"Thy striving does to [thy] foes what thy giving does to [thy] money."

This figure is called *madḥ-i-muwajjah*, or simply *muwajjah*, *i.e.*, "implied praise"; for in the above verse the poet intends primarily to praise his patron's prowess on the field of battle; but by the simile which he employs—"thou scatterest thy foes by thy valour *as thou scatterest thy money by thy generosity*"—he also hints at another virtue.

13. *Bá hawá-yi tu kufr báshad dín: Bí-riḍá-yi tu fakhr báshad 'ár.*

Muḥtamalu'l-wajhayn.

This verse illustrates the figure called "ambiguity," or *muḥtamalu'l-wajhayn* ("that which will bear two [opposite] interpretations"), for, the positions of subject and predicate being interchangeable in Persian, we may translate it either :—

"With thy love, infidelity becomes faith: Without thine approval, pride becomes shame,"

or :—

"With thy love, religion becomes infidelity: Without thine approval, shame becomes pride."

Ambiguity or "amphibology" is treated by Puttenham (*Arte of English Poesie*, pp. 266–267) as a vice of style, which it is, unless it be deliberate, as it usually is with the Orientals, who thus outwardly praise one whom they really intend to censure. So in Morier's *Hajji Baba* the poet Asker ('Askar) is made to speak as follows :—

"I wrote a poem, which answered the double purpose of gratifying my revenge for the ill-treatment I had received from the Lord High Treasurer, and of conciliating his good graces; for it had a double meaning all through : what he in his ignorance mistook for praise, was, in fact, satire ; and as he thought that the high-sounding words in which it abounded (which, being mostly Arabic, he did not understand) must contain an eulogium, he did not in the least suspect that they were, in fact, expressions containing the grossest disrespect. In truth, I had so cloaked my meaning that, without my explanation, it would have been difficult for any one to have discovered it."

Rashídu'd-Dín Waṭwáṭ relates, in his *Gardens of Magic*, that a certain wit among the Arabs said to a one-eyed tailor named 'Amr, "If you will make me a garment such that man shall be unable to say whether it is a *qabá* or a *jubba*, I will make for you a verse such that none shall be sure whether it is intended for praise or blame." The tailor fulfilled his part of the bargain, and received from the poet the following verse:—

Kháṭ^{a} *li 'Amr*^{un} *qabá: Layt*^{a} *'aynayh*^{i} *siwá!*

"'Amr made for me a coat : Would that his two eyes were alike!"

This may be taken as meaning: "Would that both his eyes were sound!" or "Would that both his eyes were blind!"

An English example would be :—

"All can appraise your service's extent:
May you receive its full equivalent!"[1]

14. *Hast ráy-at zamána-rá 'ádil, Lík dast-at khizána-rá ghaddár!*

Ta'kídu'l-madḥi bi-má yush-bihu'dh-dhamm.

"Thy judgement deals justly with the Age,
But thy hand plays the traitor with the Treasury!"

The figure exemplified in this verse is called "emphasis of praise by apparent censure" (*ta'kídu'l-madḥi bi-má yushbihu'dh-dhamm*), or "pseudo-criticism," because the second clause,

[1] Similar in character are some of the *palindromes, equivocal verses*, and *serpentines* given by J. A. Morgan at pp. 50–57 of his excellent *Macaronic Poetry*. If the words (not the letters) in these palindromes be read backwards, the sense is reversed, and praise turned to blame."

while appearing at first sight to be a qualification of the praise expressed in the first, in reality implies further praise, namely, in the instance given above, for generosity as well as justice.

Iltifát. 15. *Falak afzún zi tu na-dárad kas: Ay Falak, nik gir u nik-ash dár!*

"Heaven hath none above thee: O Heaven! hold him well and keep him well!"

This simple figure, called *iltifát*, or "turning from one person to another," needs no explanation. It may be from any person (first, second, or third) to any other, and examples of each kind will be found in Gladwin's *Rhetoric . . . of the Persians*, pp. 56–58.

Ihám. 16. *Bakht sú-yi dar-at khazán áyad; Rást chún but-parast sú-yi Bahár.*"

"Fortune comes creeping to thy door, just as does the idolater to Bahár."

This verse contains the ingenious figure called by Mr. Gibb (*History of Ottoman Poetry*, vol. i, pp. 113–114) "amphibological congruity," and depends on the employment in a verse of two or more ambiguous terms, which, from their juxtaposition, appear to be used in one sense, while they are really intended in the other. Thus, in the above verse, *khazán* means "autumn" and also "creeping" (from the verb *khazídan*, "to creep" or "crawl"); while *Bahár* means "spring," but is also the name of a place in Central Asia (whence the celebrated family of Barmak, or Barmecides, came) where there existed a famous idol-temple. The reader, misled by the juxtaposition of these words, imagines at first sight that the former meaning of each is intended, while in reality it is the latter. In English, a good instance occurs in the following verse of "Look at the Clock," in the *Ingoldsby Legends*:—

"Mr. David has since had a 'serious call,'
And never drinks ale, wine, or spirits at all,
And they say he is going to Exeter Hall
To make a grand speech, And to preach and to teach
People that 'they can't brew their malt liquor too small';
That an ancient Welsh poet, one PYNDAR AP TUDOR,
Was right in proclaiming 'ARISTON MEN UDOR'!
Which means 'The pure Element Is for Man's belly meant!'
And that *Gin's* but a *Snare* of Old Nick the deluder!"

The following verse, which I have constructed to illustrate this figure, is defective as regards spelling, but correct as to sound:—

"O *mother*, halt! No *farther* let us roam;
The *sun* has set, and we are far from home."

Tashbíh (eight varieties).

The next eight couplets, which I take together, illustrate eight different kinds of *tashbíh*, or simile, termed respectively *muṭlaq* ("absolute"), *tafḍíl* ("comparative," or "preferential"), *ta'kíd* ("emphatic"), *mashrúṭ* ("conditional"), *iḍmár* ("implicit"), *taswiya* ("equivalent"), *kináya* ("metaphorical"), and *'aks* ("antithetical"), most of which are sufficiently explained by their names, taken in conjunction with the following exemplifications:—

1.—muṭlaq. 17. *Tígh-i-tu hamchu áftáb bi-núr Sír dárad zamána-rá zi nigár.*

2.—tafḍíl. 18. *Charkh u máhí; na, nistí tu, az ánk Níst ín har du-rá qiwám u qarár!*

3.—ta'kíd. 19. *Balki az tust charkh-rá tamkín, Balki az tust máh-rá idhhár!*

4.—mashrúṭ. 20. *Máhí, ar máh náwarad káhish; Charkhí, ar charkh na-shkanad zinhár!*

5.—iḍmár. 21. *Gar tu charkhí, 'adú chirást nigún? Wa'r tu máhí, 'adú chirást nizár?*

6.—taswiya. 22. *Jáy-i khaṣm-at chu jáy-i-tust rafí'; Án-i-tú takht, wa án-i-khaṣmat dár.*

7.—kináya. 23. *Chún tu dar rúz shab kuní paydá, Chún tu az khár gul kuní dídár,*

8. —'aks.

24. *Shám gardad chu ṣubḥ surkh-libás, Ṣubḥ gardad chu shám tíra-shi'ár.*

"Thy sword, like the sun with its light, keep the world replete with pictures.
Thou art heaven and moon; nay, thou art not, for these two have not [thy] subsistence and endurance!
Nay, rather from thee heaven derives its dignity; Nay, rather from thee the moon derives its manifestation!
Thou art the moon, were it not that the moon wanes; thou art heaven, did not heaven break its troth!
If thou art heaven, why is thine enemy inverted?[1] And if thou art the moon, why is thine enemy on the wane?
Thine enemy's position is high, like thine; for thine is the throne, while his is the gibbet!
When thou displayest the night in the day,[2] [And] when thou revealest the rose from the thorn,[3]
Evening becomes clad in scarlet like morning, [And] morning becomes apparelled in black like evening."

Siyáqatu'l-a'dád.

The next figure illustrated is that called *siyáqatu'l-a'dád* ("the proposition of multiples"), where a common quality or action is ascribed to a number of otherwise dissimilar things:—

25. *Dast burda'st, gáh-i-'arḍ-i-hunar, Bi-sakhá, ú wafá wa 'adl u yasár,*

"What time talents are displayed, In generosity, constancy, justice, and opulence,"

Tansíqu'ṣ-ṣifát.

26. *Núr-at az mihr, luṭf-at az náhíd; Birr-at az abr, júd-at az kuhsár.*

---

[1] For the sky is compared to an "inverted bowl," and the same word, *sar-nigún*, literally "head-downwards," as applied to a foe, means "overthrown."

[2] *I.e.*, when the dust stirred up by the hoofs of thy charger hides the sun so that day becomes like night.

[3] The rose here means the blood of the foe, and the thorn the sword of the poet's patron.

"Thy light excels the Sun, thy grace Venus; Thy benevolence the cloud, thy generosity the highlands."[1]

This figure is named *tansíqu'ṣ-ṣifát*, or "the arrangement of attributes," and is when, to quote Gladwin (pp. 46–47), the poet "uses contrary properties, as they occur, without order or regularity."

The next three verses illustrate the figure known as "pleonasm," or *ḥashw* (lit. "stuffing"), *i.e.*, the introduction of a word or words superfluous to the sense, which may be either a downright blemish (when it is called *ḥashw-i-qabíḥ*, or "cacopleonasm"), or an improvement (*ḥashw-i-malíḥ*, or "eupleonasm"), or neither hurtful nor beneficial (*ḥashw-i-mutawassiṭ*, "mediocre" or "indifferent pleonasm"). I find the following example of "cacopleonasm" at p. 264 of Puttenham's *Arte of English Poesie*:—

Ḥashw.

"For ever may my true love live *and never die*,
And that mine eyes may see her crownde a Queene,"

where the words in italics are quite superfluous to the meaning, and do not in any way beautify the form. The pleonasm is italicised in the translation of each of the following verses:—

—qabíḥ. 27. *Qahr-at, ar mujlahid shawad, bi-barad Ásmán-rá bi-sukhra u bigár;*

—mutawassiṭ. 28. *Lík luṭf-i-tu, ay humáyún ráy, Bi-luṭaf dur bar áwarad zi biḥár.*

—malíḥ. 29. *Bágh-i-'umr-at (ki táza bád mudám Chashm-i-bad dúr!) rawḍa'íst bi-bár.*

"Thy power, should it be exerted, would compel Heaven to forced toil *and labour* for thee;
But thy grace, *O thou of royal mind!* Would by its favours bring forth pearls from the seas.

---

[1] The "generosity" of the highlands consists in the abundance of their streams

The garden of thy life (*may it be ever fresh! May the evil eye be remote from it!*) is a garden in fruit."

The next verse illustrates the figure which is generally called *ishtiqáq* ("etymology"), but more correctly, *shibhu'l-ishtiqáq* ("pseudo-etymology"). It is in reality a variety of *tajnís*, or word-play, where the words upon which the poet plays appear to come from one root, but have really no common derivation. Of this figure of Prosonomasia, George Puttenham says, in his *Arte of English Poesie* (p. 212):—

Ishtiqáq.

"Ye have a figure by which ye play with a couple of words or names much resembling, and because the one seemes to answere the other by manner of illusion, and doth, as it were, nick him, I call him the *Nicknamer*. . . . Now when such resemblance happens betweene words of another nature, and not upon men's names, yet doeth the Poet or maker finde prety sport to play with them in his verse, specially the Comicall Poet and the Epigrammatist. Sir Philip Sidney in a dittie plaide very pretily with these two words, *love* and *live*, thus:—

'And all my *life* I will confesse,
The lesse I *love*, I *live* the lesse.'"

Two other examples from the same passage are as follows:—

"They be *lubbers* not *lovers* that so use to say,"

and—

"*Prove* me, madame, ere ye fall to *reprove*,
Meeke mindes should rather *excuse* than *accuse*."[1]

30. *Rúz-i-kúshish, chu zír-i-rán árí Án qadar-paykar-i-qaḍá-paygár,—*

"In the day of battle, when thou bestridest that [war-horse] like Fate in form, and like Destiny in determination,"—

Here *paykar*, "form," and *paygár*, "determination," or "strife," appear to be, but are not, derived from the same root.

[1] In this verse however, the etymology (*ishtiqáq*) is real.

The next three verses illustrate three varieties of *saj'*, "response," or "harmonious cadence" (literally, "the cooing of doves"), called respectively *mutawází*, *muṭarraf*, and *mutawázin*. In the first, the words involved in the figure agree in measure and rhyme; in the second, in rhyme only; and in the third, in measure only, as follows:—

Saj'.

—mutawází. 31. *Dar sujúd-at nawán shawand zi pish, Bar wujúd-at rawán kunand nithár,*

—mutawázin. 32. *Sar-kashán-i-jahán-i-ḥáditha-war, Akhtarán-i-sipihr-i-áyina-dár.*

—muṭarraf. 33. *Árad-at fatḥ dar makán imkán: Dihad-at kúh bar firár qarár.*

"Trembling there advance to do the homage, Before thee cast their souls as an offering,
The proud ones of this fateful world, The stars of the mirror-holding sphere.
Victory brings thee power in space; The mountain [*i.e.*, thy steadfastness] gives thee endurance against flight."

The next four verses exemplify four varieties of anagram (*maqlúb*), viz., the "complete" (*—i-kull*), where one word in the verse is a complete anagram of another (*e.g.*, *karam* and *marg* in the Arabic character); the "partial" (*—i-ba'ḍ*), where the second word consists of the same letters as the first, but reversed otherwise than consecutively (*e.g.*, *rashk* and *shukr*); the "winged" (*mujannaḥ*), where, in the same verse or half verse, words occur at the beginning and end which are "complete" anagrams of one another; and the "even" (*mustawí*), where the sentence or verse may be read backwards or forwards in the same way. This, properly called the Palindrome, is the most difficult and the most perfect form.[1]

Maqlúb.

[1] Many ingenious examples are given of anagrams (pp. 25–44) and palindromes (pp. 45–50) in Morgan's *Macaronic Verse*. One of the most ingenious of the former is an "*Anagramma Quintuplex—De Fide*," in Latin:—

"*Recta* fides, *certa* est, *arcet* mala schismata, non est,
Sicut *Creta*, fides fictilis, arte *caret*."

—ba'd. 34. RASHK-*i-qadr-at barad sipihr u nujúm;* SHUKR-*i-fatḥ-at kunad bilád u diyár.*

—kull. 35. GARM *dárad zi táb-i-dil paygán;* MARG *bárad bi-khaṣm bar súfár.*

—mujannaḥ. 36. GANJ-*i-nuṣrat dihad guzárish-i-*JANG; RAY-*i-dawlat zanad ḥimáyat-i-*YÁR.

—mustawí. 37. RÁMISH-I-MARD GANJ-BÁRÍ U QÚT; TU QAWÍ-RÁ BI-JANG DAR MA-SHUMÁR.

"The sky and the stars envy thy worth; the countries and lands render thanks for thy victory.
He warms the spear-head with the glow of hearts; the nock [of his arrow] rains death on his foe.
[His] exploits of war yield a treasure of victory; [his] protection of friends devises empire.
The pleasure and substance of a man [is] to lavish treasure; do thou reck nothing of the strong in war."

Raddu'l-'ajuz 'ala'ṣ-ṣadr.

The next eight verses illustrate eight different varieties of what is called *raddu'l-'ajuz 'ala'ṣ-ṣadr* (literally "the throwing back of the last word in the verse to the first place in the verse"), a figure less limited than its name would imply, since it consists, as Gladwin (p. 11) says, in using the same word in any two parts of the verse. This figure resembles those called by Puttenham (*Arte of English Poesie*, p. 210) *Epanalepsis* ("Echo sound," or "slow return"), *Epizeuxis* ("Underlay," or "Cuckoo-spell"), and *Ploche* ("the doubler.") [1]

Another:—
"Perspicuâ brevitate nihil magis afficit aures;
In *verbis, ubi res* postulat, esto *brevis.*"

Of true *Palindromes* are:—Νίψον ἀνομήματα μὴ μόναν ὄψιν; "*Ablata, at alba*" (of a lady excluded from the Court by Queen Elizabeth); "*Able was I ere I saw Elba*" (of Napoleon I); and Taylor's "*Lewd did I live, & evil I did dwel.*"

[1] Somewhat similar, again, is the "concatenation," or "chain-verse," described and illustrated on pp. 91, 92 of Morgan's *Macaronic Poetry; e.g.*, the following:—

"Nerve thy soul with doctrines noble, Noble in the walks of time,
Time that leads to an eternal, An eternal life sublime," &c.

38. KÁR-*i-'adl-i-tu mulk dáshtan-ast: 'Adl-rá khud juz in na-báshad* KÁR.
39. *Bi-*YASÁR-*i-tu júd khurd* YAMÍN : *Shud* YAMÍN-*i-zamána bar tu* YASÁR.
40. *Khaṣm* TÍMÁR-*i-dawlat-i-tu kashad: Khaṣm nikú-tar-ast dar* TÍMÁR.
41. *Dar maqámi ki* BÁR-*i-zar bakhshí, Rízish-i-abr-rá nabáshad* BÁR,
42. *Mí-guzárí bi-*RUMḤ WÁM-*i-'adú: Kas na-dídast* RUMḤ WÁM *guzár.*
43. *Charkh az* ÁZÁR-*i-tu* NAYÁZÁRAD: *Bandagán-rá kujá kuni* ÁZÁR?
44. N'ÁRAD *az khidmat-i-tu birún sar, War chi bishgáfiyash bi-níza chú* MÁR.
45. *Dushmanán-rá bi-*DÁWARÍ *wa khiláf, Bá taqáẓá-yi gunbud-i-*DAWWÁR.
46. *Qahr u kín-at bi-bád dáda chu khak, Luṭf u qahr-at bi-áb kushta chu nár.*

"The task of thy justice is to hold the kingdom: Justice, indeed, has no task but this.
Bounty swears by thy wealth; the right hand of Fate became to thee a left hand.[1]
The foeman is filled with anxiety by reason of thy prosperity; it is best that the foeman should be under care.[2]
On the occasion of thy distributing stores of gold, the pouring of the cloud hath no place.[3]
Thou payest with thy spear the foeman's debt: no one has [hitherto] regarded the spear as a payer of debts.
Fortune is not hurt by thy hurting: How should'st thou hurt thy servants?
It will not withdraw its head from thy service, though thou should'st break it like a snake with thy lance.
Thine enemies by antagonism and opposition, at the instigation of the circling vault [of Heaven],
Thy wrath and ire cast to the winds like dust, Thy clemency and wrath extinguish like water extinguishes fire."[4]

---

[1] Here we have also a good instance of *íhám* ("amphibology," or "ambiguity"), for *yasár* means both "wealth" and "the left hand," while *yamín* means both an "oath" and "the right hand."

[2] *Tímár* signifies "care" in both senses, *i.e.*, anxiety and custody.

[3] *I.e.*, "no access," or, in vulgar English, "is not in it."

[4] *I.e.*, "thy clemency extinguishes thy wrath like fire extinguishes water." This figure resembles that called by Puttenham (p. 219) "*Antitheton*, or the renconter."

The last couplet, as well as the next, illustrates the figure called *mutaḍádd*, or "antithesis," and generally consists in bringing together in one verse things antithetical or opposite, such as the four elements (as in the last of the verses cited above, and in another on p. 37 *supra*), or light and darkness, or day and night, and the like.

Mutaḍádd.

The next two couplets exemplify what is called *i'nát*, which means that the poet "takes unnecessary trouble" either by extending beyond what is required the rhyme of the rhyming words, or by undertaking to use a given word or words in each verse. The following English examples from the *Ingoldsby Legends* will serve as illustrations of the former variety :—

I'nát.

"A slight deviation's forgiven ! but *then this is*
Too long, I fear, for a decent *parenthesis*. . ."

Another example :—

"And a tenderer *leveret* Robin had *never ate;*
So, in after times, oft he was wont to *asseverate*."

Another :—

"And the boldest of mortals a danger like *that must fear*,
Rashly protruding beyond our own *atmosphere*."

47. *Ay nikú-khwáh-i-dawlat-i-tu 'azíz, Wa'y bad-andísh-i-ruzgár-i-tu khwár!*

48. *Har-ki zinhár-khwár-i-'ahd-i-tu shud, Bi-sipár-ash bi-'álam-i-khún-khwár.*

"O thou the well-wisher of whose empire is ennobled, and O thou whose fortune's envier is abased,
Whosoever is false to thy covenant, do thou consign him to the blood-drinking world !" [1]

This figure is also called *Luzúmu má la yalzam*, or "the making obligatory on one's self that which is not obligatory." In the second of its two senses (that illustrated in the Persian

[1] *I.e.*, to a violent death.

verses given above) it only becomes difficult when continued throughout a long *qaṣída.*

Muzdawaj.

The next verse illustrates the figure called *muzdawaj*, or "the paired," which consists in the introduction into the verse of rhyming words other than the necessary rhyme:—

49. *Káh-i-*RÍZA *bi-*NÍZA *bi-r'bá'í: Chún kuní* 'AZM-I-RAZM, *ín'í sawár!*

"Thou snatchest fine chaff with thy spear; when thou seekest battle, see what a horseman!"

Mutalawwin.

The next figure, *mutalawwin* ("variegated," or "chameleon") consists in so constructing a verse that it may be read in either of two metres. Thus the following verse may be scanned, like the rest of the poem, in the metre called *Khafíf-i-makhbún-i-maqṣúr* (— ◡ — — | ◡ — ◡ — | ◡ ◡ —), or in that named *sarí'-i-maṭwí* (— ◡ ◡ — | — ◡ ◡ — | — ◡ — |).

50. *Ay buda qidwa-i-waḍí' u sharíf: W'ay shuda qibla-i-sighár u kibár!*

"O thou who art the model of low and high: and O thou who art the shrine of small and great!"

Irsálu'l-mathal.

The next figure is what is called *irsálu'l-mathal*, a term rendered by the late Mr. E. J. W. Gibb "proverbial commission"; of which there is a subordinate variety, *irsálu'l-mathalayn*, which consists in the introduction into the verse of two proverbial sayings, or of two similitudes. This is similar to the "*Gnome*, or director" of Puttenham (p. 243), and the "*Parimia*, or Proverb" (p. 199), concerning the latter of which he says:—

"We dissemble after a sort, when we speake by common proverbs, or, as we use to call them, old said sawes, as thus:—

'As the olde cocke crowes so doeth the chick:
A bad cooke that cannot his own fingers lick.'

Meaning by the first, that the young learne by the olde to be good or evill in their behaviours: by the second, that he is not to be counted a wise man, who, being in authority, and having the administration of many good and great things, will not serve his owne turne and his friends whilest he may, and many such proverbiall speeches: as *totnesse is turned French*, for a strange alteration: *Skarborow warning*, for a sudaine commandement, allowing no respect or delay to bethinke a man of his busines. Note neverthelesse a diversitie, for the two last examples be proverbs, the two first proverbiall speeches."

This love of introducing proverbs into their verses is very characteristic of several Persian poets, notably Ṣá'ib of Iṣfahán (d. A.D. 1677–78), who served as a model to a host of Turkish verse-writers; and, in much earlier times, Abu'l-Faḍl as-Sukkarí, of Merv, who, as ath-Tha'álibi informs us in his *Yatímatu'd-Dahr* (Damascus edition, vol. iv, pp. 23 and 25), written in A.D. 994, "was very fond of translating Persian proverbs into Arabic."

51. *Na-kushad áb-i-khasm átash-i-tu; Nashkinad táb-i-núr muhra-i-már!*

"The water of the enemy extinguishes not thy fire; the snake-stone[1] cannot outshine the light!"

52. *Gar mahí, fárigh az hawá-yi khusúf: Gar mayí, íman az balá-yi-khumár!*

"If thou art a moon, [then it is one] free from anxiety of eclipse: If thou art wine [it is wine] exempt from the plague of wine-headache!"

Lughaz. The next ten verses form a *lughaz*, or riddle:—

53. *Chíst án dúr, wa aṣl-i-ú nazdík? Chíst an fard, wa fi'l-i-ú bisyár?*

54. *Khám-i-ú har-chi 'ilm-rá pukhta: Mast-i-ú har-chi 'aql-rá hushyár.*

55. *Dil-shikan, lík dard-i-dil-paywand: Khush-guzar, lík rúzgár-guzár.*

[1] It is popularly believed in the East of the snake, as in the West of the toad, that it carries in its head a jewel, generally an emerald.

56. *Ranj-i-ú nazd-i-bí-dilán ráḥat: Khwár-ı-ú nazd-i-zírakan dushwár.*
57. *Chún du'á khush-'inán u bí-markab: Chún qaḍá rah-naward u bí-hanjár.*
58. *Anduh-ash hamchu lahw u ráḥat-bakhsh: Átash-ash hamchu áb núsh-guwár.*
59. *Na'ra dar way shikanj-i-músíqí: Nála dar way nawá-yı músíqár.*
60. *'Ishq aṣlíst kaz munáza'at-ash 'Aql ghamgín buwad, rawán ghamkhwár.*
61. *Kháṣṣa 'ishq-i-butí ki dar ghazal-ash Midḥat-i-Sháh mí-kunam takrár.*
62. *Sháyad ar-zán ghazála bi-n'yúshad Zín nawá ín ghazal bi-naghma-i-zár.*

"What is that distant one, whose origin is withal near? What is that unique one, whose deeds are withal many?

Whose rawest [recruit] ripens whatever is knowledge: whose most drunken [dependent] gives sense to whatever is understanding.

A breaker of hearts, but a healer of hearts' ills: living pleasantly, but compelling fortune:

Whose pain is peace to those who have lost their hearts; whose easiest is hard to the intelligent.

Like prayer, light-reined and horseless: like Fate, a swift and unaccountable traveller.

Care for him is like play and a giver of ease; whose fire is like water, sweet to drink.

A cry in whom is a movement of music; a wail in whom is the melody of the shepherd's pipe.

Love is that element by whose struggles reason is rendered sorrowful and the spirit sad;

In particular the love of that idol in my love-songs to whom I repeat the praises of the king.

Therefore it were meet if the sun should listen graciously to the ode in this song set in plaintive strain."

These riddles are generally very obscure, and I regret to say that of the one here given I do not know the answer. Other specimens, with the solutions, will be found on pp. 336–338 of Rückert's work on Persian Poetry and Rhetoric.

Maṭla'-l-Dhú qáfiyatayn.

Next comes what is called a "double-rhymed *maṭla'*," *i.e.*, a fresh opening-verse with an internal double rhyme, or rhyme between the two half-verses :—

63. *Az dil-am súsan-ash bi-burd qarár : bi-saram nargis-ash supurd khumár.*

"Her lily [breast] hath snatched repose from my heart : her narcissus [eye] hath imposed intoxication on my head."

Tajáhulu'l-'Arif.

Then follows the favourite figure, called "the feigned ignorance of one who knows," which is akin to what Puttenham (p. 234) calls *Aporia*, or "the Doubtful" :—

64. *Wayḥak! Án nargis-ast, yá jádú? Yá Rabb, án súsan-ast, yá gulnár?*

"Alas! is that [eye] a narcissus, or a witch? O Lord! Is that [breast] a lily or a pomegranate?"

Su'ál u Jawáb.

The next figure is the simple one called "Question and Answer" (*su'ál u jawáb*) :—

65. *Guftam: 'Az ján bi-'ishq bi-záram!' Guft: ''Áshiq zi ján buwad bízár!'*

"I said : 'Through love I am sick of life!' She said : 'Sick of life must the lover needs be!'"

Muwashshaḥ.

The next verse is a *muwashshaḥ*, or acrostic, of which also, I regret to say, I have not been able to discover the solution.

66. *Dúst mí-dáram-ash ki yár-i-man-ast: Dushman án bih ki khud na-báshad yár!*

"I love her, for she is my friend : it is, indeed, well that a friend should not be a foe!"

Mulamma'.

The *mulamma'*, or "pied verse," illustrated in the next line, has been already mentioned on p. 23 *supra*. Examples in English and Latin are frequent in the *Ingoldsby Legends*, *e.g.* :—

"... I've always considered Sir Christopher Wren,
As an architect, one of the greatest of men;
And, talking of Epitaphs,—much I admire his,
'*Circumspice, si monumentum requiris.*'"

And again (though this, perhaps, rather comes under the figure *tarjuma*, or "translation"):—

"'*Hos ego versiculos feci, tulit alter honores*':
I wrote the lines— * * owned them—he told stories!"

67. *Súkht dar átash-am: chi mí-gúyam? Aḥraqat-ní 'l-hawá bi-ghayri'n-nár!*

"She hath burned me in fire: What do I say? *Sine igne amor me comburit!*"

The next five verses illustrate figures which depend upon the peculiarities of the Arabic letters, in respect to their being joined or unjoined, dotted or undotted respectively; and which cannot, therefore, be represented in English characters. In the first, termed "disjointed" (*muqaṭṭa'*), all the letters are unjoined; in the second (*muwaṣṣal*, all are joined; the third (*mujarrad*) is not mentioned in the books at my disposal, and I do not see wherein its peculiarity consists; in the fourth (*raqṭá*) the letters are alternately dotted and undotted; while in the fifth (*khayfá*) the words consist alternately of dotted and undotted letters.

Muqaṭṭa'. 68. *Zár u zard-am zi dard-i-dúriy-i-ú: Dard-i-dil-dár zard dárad u zár.*

Muwaṣṣal. 69. *Tan-i-'aysh-am naḥíf gasht bi-gham: gul-i-bakht-am nilúfla gasht bi-khár.*

Mujarrad. 70. *Chihra-i-rawshan-ash, ki rúz-i-man-ast, Zír-i-zulf-ash mahíst dar shab-i-tár.*

Raqṭa. 71. *Ghamza-i-shúkh-i-án ṣanam bu-k'shád ashk-i-khún-am zi chashm-i-khún-áthár.*

Khayfá. 72. *Dil shud, u ham na-bínad az way mihr: sar shud, u ham na-píchad az tan kár.*

"I am weak and pale through grieving at her farness [from me]: grief for one's sweetheart keeps [one] pale and weak.

The frame of my life grew weak in sorrow: the flower of my fortune became hidden by thorns.
Her bright face, which is my day, beneath her locks is a moon in a dark night.
The wanton glances of that idol have loosed blood-stained tears from my blood-shot eyes.
My heart is gone, and it does not even see kindness from her: my head is gone, and it does not even turn aside the trouble from the body."

Mu'ammá.

The next line contains an enigma (*mu'ammá*), which again I have not been able to solve:—

73. *Mawj u dúd-i-dil u du dída-i-man burd daryá wa abr-rá miqdár.*

"The waves (of tears) and heart-smoke (*i.e.*, sighs) of my two eyes have lowered the esteem of the sea and the cloud."

Taḍmín.

The next figure illustrated is the *taḍmín*, or "insertion" (*i.e.*, of the verse of another poet in one's own), already mentioned at p. 45 *supra*. It is necessary, however, either that the "inserted" verse should be very well known, or that it should definitely be introduced as a quotation, lest the poet employing it expose himself to a charge of plagiarism. A good instance in English is the following from the *Ingoldsby Legends*:—

"'*One touch to his hand, and one word to his ear,*'—
(That's a line which I've stolen from Sir Walter, I fear)."

The following *taḍmín* is one of the few Persian verses which the author of this work has ventured to compose, and was written at the request of a friend who was enamoured of a young lady named May, which word (pronounced in exactly the same way) means "wine" in Persian. Shaykh Sa'dí, of Shíráz, says in one of his verses in the *Gulistán*:—

Mast-i-may bídár gardad ním-i-shab:
Mast-i-sáqí rúz-i-maḥshar bámdád,

which means—

"He who is intoxicated with the Wine (*May*) will come to his senses at midnight :
He who is intoxicated with the cup-bearer [only] on the Resurrection morning!"

From these verses I made the following *taḍmín*, which also contains a *tajnís-i-támm*, or "perfect word-play," on the word "*may*," and an *ighráq*, or "exaggeration" of the most approved type :—

'Mast-i-may bídár gardad ním-i-shab,' farmúd Shaykh :
Ín, agarchi qawl-i-Shaykh-ast, níst já-yi i'timád :
Man mayí dánam, ki hargah mast-i-án gardad kasí,
Sar zi mastí bar na-dárad 'rúz-i-maḥshar bámdád.'

"'He who is intoxicated with the Wine will come to his senses at midnight,' says the Shaykh :[1]
This, though it is the Shaykh's saying, is not a statement on which one can rely.
I know a certain Wine (or a certain *May*) wherewith should one become intoxicated
He will not raise up his head from his intoxication even 'on the Resurrection-morning.'"

74. *Waṣl khwáham : na-dánam ánki bi-kas ráyagán rukh namí-numáyad yár?*

"I desire union : [but] do I not know this, that the Beloved will not show her face to any one for nothing?"

The deplorable fact that I do not know which part of the verse is the quotation, nor whence it is borrowed, rather lays me open to the charge of ignorance than the poet to that of plagiarism.

The figure termed *ighráq* ("straining") is next illustrated.

Ighráq.

This is one of the three recognised forms of hyperbole (*mubálagha*), *viz.*, *tablígh*, when the assertion made "is possible both to reason and experience"; *ighráq*, "when it is possible, but not probable";

Ghuluww.

and *ghuluww*, "when the assertion is absolutely impossible." A good instance of this last is given by Dawlat-

[1] Sa'dí is always spoken of by the Persians as "the Shaykh" *par excellence.*

sháh (p. 33 of my edition) in the two following verses in praise of Sulṭán Maḥmúd of Ghazna by the poet Ghaḍá'irí (or 'Aḍá'irí), of Ray[1] :—

Ṣawáb kard ki paydá na-kard har du jahán
Yagána Ízad-i-dádar-i-bí-nadhír u hamál:
Wa gar-na har du bi-bakhshídí ú bi-rúz-i-sakhá;
Umíd-i-banda na-mándí bi-Ízad-i-muta'ál!

"Well it was that God, the One, the Judge, Exempt from peer or mate,
Made apparent one alone of those two worlds He did create;
Else the King's unstinted bounty would have given both away;
Nothing then would have been left for which a man to God should pray!"

Another still more extravagant instance of *ghuluww* (in the theological as well as in the rhetorical sense) is the following verse addressed to Bahá'u'lláh, the late Pontiff of the Bábís, by Nabíl of Zarand :—

Khalq gúyand Khudá'í, wa man andar ghaḍab áyam;
Parda bar dáshta ma-p'sand bi-khud nang-i-Khudá'í!

"Men call Thee God, and I am filled with wrath thereat:
Withdraw the veil, and suffer no longer the shame of Godhead [to rest upon Thee]!"[2]

The instance of *ighráq* given in our *qaṣída* is the following :—

75. *War numáyad zi bas ṣafá ki darúst, Ráz-i-man dar rukhash buwad dídár.*

"Or if she shows it [*i.e.*, her cheek], such is its translucency that my secret will be apparent in her face."

---

[1] Dawlatsháh adds that Sulṭan Maḥmúd was so pleased with this extravagant verse that he gave the poet seven purses of gold, containing a sum equivalent to 14,000 *dirhams*.

[2] See my translation of the *New History*, p. 395. I have heard it said that this verse was really addressed originally to the Imám Ḥusayn by some enthusiastic Shí'ite.

Jam' u tafríq u taqsím.

The next seven verses illustrate different combinations of the figures called *jam'* (combination), *tafríq* (separation), and *taqsím* (discrimination), of which the nature will be sufficiently clear from the following lines:—

Jam'.
76. *Bar lab-ash zulf 'áshiq-ast chu man: lá jaram hamchu man 'sh níst qarár.*

Tafríq.
77. *Bád-i-ṣubḥ-ast bú-yi zulf-ash: nay, na-buwad bád-i-ṣubḥ 'anbar-bár!*

Jam' u taqsím.
78. *Man u zulfín-i-ú nigúnsár-ím, lík ú bar gul-ast u man bar khár.*

Jam' u tafríq.
79. *Hast khaṭṭ-ash firáz-i-'álam-i-rú: án yakí abr, u ín yakí gulzár.*

Taqsím u tafríq.
80. *Ghamm-i-du chíz mará du chíz supurd: dída-rá áb, u sína-rá zangár.*

Jam' u tafríq u taqsím.
81. *Hamchu chashm-am tawángar-ast lab-ash: án bi-ashk, ín bi-lu'lu'i-shahwár.*

82. *Áb-i-án tíra, áb-i-ín rawshan; án-i-ín girya, w'án-i-u guftár.*

"Her tresses, like me, are in love with her lips, consequently, like me, they know no rest.
The fragrance of her tresses is [like] the morning breeze; nay, for the morning breeze is not laden with ambergris!
I and her tresses are cast down headlong, but they on the roses[1] and I on the thorns.[2]
The down overshadows the world of her face: that is the cloud, and this the rose-garden.
Sorrow for two things conferred on me two things: tears on my eyes and verjuice on my bosom.
Her lip is as rich as my eye, the latter in tears, the former in royal pearls.[3]
The water of those [tears] is dark, while the water of these [pearls] is bright; the property of those [my eyes] is weeping, and of these [her lips] speech."

[1] *I.e.*, her cheeks. [2] *I.e.*, affliction.

[3] "Pearls" here evidently means pearls of speech, but the teeth are often metaphorically so called.

Tafsír-i-khafí and Tafsír-i-jalí.

The next four verses illustrate the figure called *tafsír* ("explanation"), of which there are two kinds, called respectively *jalí* ("patent") and *khafí* ("latent"), which last is complicated by a kind of *chiasmus*. The following exemplifies the latter:—

83. [1]*Jigar, ú* [2]*ján, u* [3]*chashm, u* [4]*chihr-i-man-ast, dar gham-i-'ishq-i-án but-i-Farkhár,*
84. *Ham bi-gham*[4] *khasta, ham zi-tan*[2] *mahjúr, ham bi-khún*[3] *gharqa, ham zi zakhm*[1] *afgár.*

"My [1]heart, and [2]soul, and [3]eye, and [4]face are, in love-longing for that fair one of Farkhár,
Sick[4] with grief, parted[2] from the body, submerged[3] in blood, weakened[1] by wounds.

The other kind of *tafsír* is exemplified in the next two verses:—

85. *Khurd,*[1] *u khurdam*[2] *bi-'ishq-i-án ná-kám ; hast,*[3] *u hastam*[4] *zi hajr-i-ú ná-chár ;*
86. *Ú mará khún,*[1] *u man wará andúh*[2] *; ú zi man shád,*[3] *u man zi ú gham-khwár.*[4]

"She consumes,[1] and I consume[2] in her love in spite of myself ; she is,[3] and I am,[4] willing or no, through her separation ;
She my blood,[1] and I her grief[2] ; she glad[3] through me, and I sorrowful[4] through her."

Kalám-i-jámi'.

The next two verses give an instance of what is called *kalám-i-jámi'*, which "is when the poet treats on morality, philosophy, or worldly delights" :—

87. *Mú-yam az gham sapíd gasht chu shír : dil zi miḥnat siyáh gasht chú qár,*
88. *Ín zi 'aks-i-balá kashíd khiḍáb, W'án zi ráh-i-jafá girift ghubár.*

"Through grief, my hair hath turned white as milk ; through sorrow my heart hath become black as pitch ;
This derived its tint from the reflection of [dark] affliction, while that was powdered with the dust of sorrow's path."

Ḥusn-i-makhlaṣ, or "apt transition," the figure next illustrated, means that in the *guríz-gáh*, or "transition-verse" (see pp. 30 and 32, n. 1), the poet passes gracefully and skilfully from the exordium of his *qaṣída* to the *qaṣd* or purpose (panegyric or otherwise) which he has in view :—

Ḥusn-i-makhlaṣ.

89. *Gham-i-dil gar bi-bast bázár-am, madḥ-i-shah mí-kusháyad-am bázár.*

"If the heart's sorrow hath closed my market, the praise of the King re-opens it."

The next figure illustrated is *tazalzul* or *mutazalzil*, which means "shaking" or "shaken" to the foundations, as by an earthquake (*zalzala*), and is, as Gladwin says (p. 32), "when there is a word of which, upon changing the vowel-point of one letter only, the sense is altered entirely" :—

Tazalzul.

90. *Shah Qizil Arslán, ki dast u dil-ash hast khaṣm-shumár u khaṣm-i-shumár.*

"King Qizil Arslán,[1] whose hand and heart are [respectively] an accounter for enemies and an enemy to accounts."[2]

Ibdá', the figure next displayed, means in Rhetoric "re-originating," "reconstructing," or "re-creating," that is, expressing in similar but different form the thought of some previous poet or writer, while giving it a new meaning or application; which procedure, though bordering on *sirqat*, or "plagiarism," is not (like other plagiarisms of form or meaning, viz., *intikhál*, *maskh*, and *salkh*: see Rückert, pp. 188–191) reckoned a fault, but a merit. To judge of the comparative value of a verse inspired by another as regards either form or meaning, it is necessary to be ac-

Ibdá'.

[1] Qizil Arslán 'Uthmán, one of the Atábegs of Ádharbayján, reigned from A.D. 1185–91.

[2] This means that while his hand accounted for his foes in battle, his generous heart knew no reckoning in the distribution of its bounty.

quainted with the original, which, unfortunately, I am not in the following instance :—

91. *Ḥazm-ash áwurda bád-rá bi-sukún: 'azm-ash afganda khák-rá bi-madár.*

"His resolve brings the wind to a standstill: his determination casts the dust into a whirl."

Ta'ajjub.

The next verse illustrates the simple figure called *ta'ajjub*, "astonishment" :—

92. *Já-yi dur gar mayána-i-daryást, az chi ma'níst dast-i-ú dur-bár?*

"If the place for pearls is in the midst of the sea, for what reason does his hand rain pearls?"

Ḥusn-i-ta'líl.

The answer to this question contained in the next verse affords an instance of *ḥusn-i-ta'líl*, or "poetical ætiology," which consists in explaining a real fact by a fanciful or poetical cause :—

93. *Raghm-i-daryá, ki bukhl mí-warzad, Ú kunad mál bar jahán ithár.*

"To spite the sea, which practises avarice, he scatters wealth on the world."

Here the king's liberality is ascribed to disgust at the stinginess of the ocean, though this typifies liberality, so that *daryá-dast* ("ocean-handed") is used as a synonym for bountiful.

The following verse, however, strikes me as a much prettier instance of the figure in question :—

Ḥusn-i-mah-rá bá tu sanjidam bi-mízán-i-qiyás:
Palla-i-mah bar falak shud, u tu mándí bar zamín.

"I weighed the beauty of the moon with thine in the balance of judgment:
The pan containing the moon flew up to heaven, whilst thou wert left on the earth."

George Puttenham's definition and examples of ætiology ("reason-rend" or "tell-cause," as he names it in English, pp. 236–237 of Arber's reprint) hardly agree with the Persian figure, since he has in mind real, not imaginary, causes.

Ṭard u 'aks.

The next figure, *ṭard u 'aks*, or "thrust and inversion," simply consists in the transposition in the second *miṣrá'* of the two halves of the first, thus:—

94. *Chi shikár-ast nazd-i-ú, chi maṣáf: chi maṣaf-ast písh-i-ú, chi shikár.*

"Alike to him are chase and battle: battle and chase are alike to him."

Mukarrar.

The two next couplets illustrate the *mukarrar* or "repeated" figure, which resembles those called *Anadiplosis* ("the redouble"), *Epanalepsis* ("echo-sound," or "slow return"), and *Epizeuxis* ("underlay" or "cuckoo-spell") by Puttenham (pp. 210–212), especially the latter, exemplified in the three following verses:—

"It was *Maryne, Maryne* that wrought mine woe."

Again:

"The chiefest staff of mine assured stay,
With no small grief *is gone, is gone* away."

And again, in a verse of Sir Walter Raleigh's:—

"With wisdom's eyes had but blind fortune seene,
Then had *my love, my love* for ever beene."

95. *Badra badra dihad bi-sá'il zar: Dijla Dijla kashad bi-bazm 'uqár.*

96. *Gashta z'an badra badra badra khajil: burda z'án Dijla Dijla Dijla yasár.*

"He gives gold to the beggar, purse-on-purse: he brings wine to the feast, Tigris-on-Tigris.
From that purse-on-purse the purse is ashamed: from that Tigris-on-Tigris the Tigris derives wealth."

The four concluding verses of the poem illustrate the two figures *ḥusn-i-ṭalab*, or "apposite request," and *ḥusn-i-maqṭa'*, or "apposite conclusion":—

Ḥusn-i-ṭalab.

Ḥusn-i-maqṭa'.

97. *Khusrawá! bá zamána dar jang-am: ki bi-gham mí-gudázad-am hamwár:*
98. *Chi buwad gar kaf-i-tu bar girad az mayán-i-man u zamána ghubár?*
99. *Tá 'ayán-ast mihr-rá tábish, tá nihán-ast charkh-rá asrár,*
100. *Rúz u shab juz sakhá ma-bádat shughl; sál u mah juz ṭarab ma-bádat kár!*

"O Prince! I am at war with Fortune: for ever she consumes me with vexation:
How would it be if thy hand should remove the dust (*i.e.*, disagreement) between me and Fortune?
So long as the shining of the sun is apparent, so long as the secrets of the sphere are hidden,
Day and night may thine occupation be naught but generosity: year and month may thy business be naught but enjoyment!"

Nearly all the more important rhetorical figures are contained and illustrated in the above *qaṣída*, or have been mentioned incidentally in connection with it, though many minor embellishments will be found by those desirous of going further into the matter in the works of Gladwin and Rückert. Of those omitted mention need only be made of the following:—

(1) The *ta'ríkh*, or chronogram, where the sum of the letters, according to the *abjad* reckoning, in a verse, sentence, or group of words, gives the date of the event commemorated. The most ingenious paraphrase in English of a Persian chronogram with which I am acquainted is one by Hermann Bicknell ("Ḥájjí 'Abdu'l-Waḥíd"), the admirer and translator of Ḥáfidh, on the well-known chronogram:—

Ta'ríkh.

Chu dar khák-i-Muṣallá sákht manzil,
Bi-jú ta'ríkh ash az KHÁK-I-MUṢALLA.

"Since he made his home in the earth of Muṣallá,[1]
Seek for his date from *THE EARTH OF MUṢALLÁ*."

The letters composing the words *Khák-i-Muṣallá* are :— *Kh* = 600 ; *á* = 1 ; *k* = 20 ; *m* = 40 ; *ṣ* = 90 ; *l* = 30 ; *y* = 10 : Total = 791 (A.H. = 1389). The difficulty in producing a chronogram in English is that only seven letters (C, D, I, L, M, V, and X) have numerical values, nevertheless Bicknell overcame this difficulty and thus paraphrased the above chronogram :—

"Thrice take thou from *MUṢALLÁ'S EARTH*" (M+L+L = 1100)
"*ITS RICHEST GRAIN*" (I + I + C + I = 103 × 3 = 309 : 1100 — 309 = 791).[2]

(2) The *talmíḥ*, or allusion (to a proverb, story, or well-known verse of poetry) is another pretty figure. Here is an English instance from the *Ingoldsby Legends* :—

Talmíḥ.

"Such a tower as a poet of no mean *calibre*
I once knew and loved, poor, dear Reginald Heber,
Assigns to oblivion—a den for a she-bear."

The allusion is to the following verse in Heber's *Palestine* :—

"And cold Oblivion midst the ruin laid,
Folds her dank wing beneath the ivy shade."

A good instance from the *Bústán* of Sa'dí is (ed. Graf, p. 28, l. 2) :—

[1] "The Oratory," a place close to Shíráz, which was a favourite resort of the poet.

[2] For European chronograms see pp. 23–25 of Morgan's *Macaronic Poetry*. One of the simplest and best is that giving the date of Queen Elizabeth's death : "My Day Is Closed In Immortality" (MDCIII = A.D. 1603). So for Martin Luther's death we have : "eCCe nVnC MorItVr IVstVs In paCe ChrIstI eXItV et beatVs," *i.e.*, M.CCCCC.X.VVVVVV.IIIIII = A.D. 1546.

Chi ḥájat ki nuh kursiy-i-ásmán
Nihí zír-i-pá-yi Qizil Arslán?

"What need that thou should'st place the nine thrones (*i.e.*, spheres) of heaven beneath the feet of Qizil Arslán?"

The allusion is to the following verse by Dhahír of Fáryáb :—

Nuh kursi-i-falak nihad andísha zír-i-páy
Tá búsa bar rikáb-i-Qizil Arslán nihad.

"Imagination puts the nine thrones (spheres) of heaven beneath its feet
That it may imprint a kiss on the stirrup of Qizil Arslán."

'Ubayd-i-Zákání, a very bitter satirist who died some twenty years before Ḥáfidh, wrote amongst other poems a little *mathnawí* (still a popular children's book in Persia) named "The Cat and the Mouse" (*Músh u Gurba*), in which an old cat plays the devotee in order to entice the mice within its clutches. The mice report its "conversion" to their king in the following verse :—

"Muzhdagáná! ki gurba záhid shud,
'Ábid, u mu'min, u musulmáná!"

"Good tidings! for the cat has become an ascetic,
A worshipper, a believer, a devout Muslim!"

From this story the phrase "*gurba záhid shud*" ("the cat has become an ascetic") became very common in speaking of an old sinner who shams piety for purely mundane (generally evil) objects; and Ḥáfidh alludes to this in the following verse :—

Ay kabk-i-khush kharám! Kujá mí-rawí? Bi-ist!
Ghirra ma-shaw ki "gurba-i-'ábid" namáz kard!

"O gracefully-walking partridge! Whither goest thou? Stop!
Be not deceived because the 'devout cat' has said its prayers!"

Difficulty of allusions in poetry of the Muslims.

These allusions often constitute one of the most serious difficulties which the European student of Persian, Arabic, Turkish, and other Muslim languages has to encounter, since the common ground of historical and literary knowledge shared by all persons of education in the lands of Islám is quite different from that in which the European and other Christian nations participate. Any allusion to the Qur'án, for instance, is supposed to be intelligible to a well-educated Muslim; yet it may cost the Christian reader an infinity of trouble to identify it and trace it to its source. To take one instance only, which, *se non è vero è ben trovato.* The poet Firdawsí, when suffering from the sore disappointment occasioned by Sulṭán Maḥmúd's niggardly recognition of his great work, the *Sháhnáma*, or Book of Kings, wrote a most bitter satire (now prefixed to most editions of that work), left it in the hands of a friend of his, with instructions to deliver it after the lapse of a certain period, and then made the best of his way to Ṭabaristán, where he sought refuge with the Ispahbad Shírzád (or, according to others, Shahriyár, the son of Sharzín). Sulṭán Maḥmúd, on reading the satire, was filled with fury, and wrote to this Prince demanding the surrender of the poet, and threatening, should his demand not be complied with, to come with his elephants of war (which appear to have been a great feature of his army) and trample him and his army, villages and people under their feet. It is said that the Ispahbad merely wrote on the back of the Sulṭán's missive the three letters "A. L. M." Though Sulṭán Maḥmúd, it is said, did not at once see the allusion, all his courtiers immediately recognised it, and knew that the Ispahbad's intention was to remind them of the fate which overtook Abraha the Abyssinian, who, trusting in his elephants, would have profaned the Holy City of Mecca in the very year of the Prophet Muḥammad's birth, known ever afterwards as "the Year of the Elephant." For concerning these impious "People of the

Elephant" a short chapter (No. CV) of the Qur'án was revealed, known as the *Súratu'l-Fíl*, which begins with the letters "A. L. M.," *i.e.*, *Alam tara kayfa fa'ala Rabbuka bi-Aṣḥábi'l-Fíl?*—"Hast thou not seen how thy Lord dealt with the People of the Elephant? Did HE not cause their device to miscarry? And send against them birds in flocks, which pelted them with stones of baked clay? And make them like leaves of corn eaten [by cattle]?" The allusion was extraordinarily appropriate, and is said to have effectually turned the Sulṭán from his purpose. Nothing, indeed, is so effective or so much admired amongst Muslims as the skilful and apposite application of a passage from their Sacred Book, and to this topic I shall have occasion to revert again at the end of this chapter.

Taṣḥíf.

Taṣḥíf is another ingenious figure depending on the diacritical points which serve to distinguish so many letters of the Arabic alphabet. By changing these points, without interfering with the bodies of the letters, the sense of a sentence may be completely changed, and the sentence or sense so changed is said to be *muṣaḥḥaf*. The expression occurs in the *Bústán* of Sa'dí (ed. Graf, p. 166, l. 4):—

'Mará búsa,' guftá, 'bi-taṣḥíf dih, Ki darwísh-rá túsha az búsa bih.'

"'Give me,' said he, 'kisses with *taṣḥíf*, For to the poor man *túsha* (provisions) are better than *búsa*' (kisses)."

This figure cannot be illustrated or properly explained without the use of Arabic letters, else I should be tempted to cite an ingenious poem, quoted by Rashíd-i-Waṭwáṭ in his *Ḥadá'iqu's-Siḥr*, wherein the sense of each verse is changed from praise to blame by a slight alteration of the diacritical points, so that, for example, *Hast dar aṣl-at bulandí bí-khiláf* ("The nobility in thy stock is indisputable") becomes *Hast dar aṣl-at pallidí bí-khiláf* ("The uncleanness in thy stock is indisputable").

Some few words should, perhaps, be said at this point concerning the satire (*hajw*) and the parody (*jawáb*). Satire was amongst the Arabs, even in pre-Muhammadan days, a powerful weapon, and commonly took the form of what were known as *mathálib*, *i.e.*, poems on the disgraces and scandals attaching to some rival or hostile tribe. In Persian, one of the earliest satires preserved to us is that of Firdawsí on Sulṭán Maḥmúd, to which allusion has already been made. This, though very bitter, is utterly devoid of the coarse invective and innuendo which mar (according to Western ideas) most satirical poems of the Arabs and Persians. The five following verses may serve to give some idea of its style:—

Satire and Parody.

"Long years this Sháhnáma I toiled to complete,
That the King might award me some recompense meet,
But naught save a heart wrung with grief and despair
Did I get from those promises empty as air!
Had the sire of the King been some Prince of renown,
My forehead had surely been graced by a crown!
Were his mother a lady of high pedigree,
In silver and gold had I stood to the knee!
But, being by birth not a prince but a boor,
The praise of the noble he could not endure!"

Any one who wishes to form an idea of the grossness which mars so much of the satirical verse of the Persians should peruse the *crescendo* series of abusive poems which marked the progress of the quarrel between the poet Kháqání (d. A.D. 1199) and his master and teacher, Abu'l-'Ulá, which will be found in full, with translations, in Khanikof's admirable *Mèmoire sur Khâcâni* (Paris, 1865, pp. 14–23). The quatrain with which Abu'l-'Ulá opened the duel is delicacy itself compared to what follows, and will alone bear translation. He says:—

Kháqániyá! Agarchi sukhan ník dániyá,
Yak nukta gúyam-at: bi-shinaw ráyagániyá!
Hajw-i-kasí ma-kun ki zi tu mih buwad bi-sinn:
Báshad ki ú pidar buwad-at, tu na-dániyá!

which may be paraphrased in English :—

"Thy verse, Kháqání, deeply I admire,
Yet one small hint to offer I desire:
Mock not the man whose years outnumber thine:
He may, perchance (thou know'st not), be thy sire!"

The following, however, ascribed to Kamál Isma'íl of Iṣfahán (killed by the Mongols when they sacked that city in A.D. 1237–38), is the most irreproachable specimen of Persian satire with which I have met :—

Gar kwája zi bahr-i-má badí guft
Má chihra zi gham na-mí kharáshím:
Má ghayr-i-nikú'iyash na-gú'ím,
Tá har du durúgh gufta báshím!

which may be paraphrased :—

"My face shall show no traces of despite,
Although my Patron speaketh ill of me:
His praise I'll still continue to recite,
That both of us alike may liars be!"

Parodies and Parallels.

As for the *jawáb* (literally "answer"), it may be either a parody or merely an imitation, this latter being also called a *nadhíra*, or "parallel." The great parodists of Persia were 'Ubayd-i-Zákání, a ribald wit who died about A.D. 1370, and of whose satires in verse and prose a selection was published in Constantinople in A H. 1303 (A.D. 1885–86); and Abú Isḥáq (Busḥaq) of Shíráz, the Poet of Foods; and Nidháma'd-Dín Maḥmúd Qárí of Yazd, the Poet of Clothes, from the works of both of whom selections were published in the same year and place. Each of these was a parodist, but the first-named was by far the greatest as a master of satire, and excelled in prose as well as in verse, as we shall have occasion to remark when we come to speak of his period.

Much more might be said on the Rhetoric of the Muslims, but considerations of space forbid me for the present to enlarge further on this subject, and I must refer such of my readers as desire fuller information to the works of Gladwin, Rückert, Gibb, Blochmann, and the native writers on these topics. A few words, however, must be added on a work of great utility to students of the erotic poetry of the Persians, I mean the "Lover's Companion" (*Anísu'l-'Ushsháq*) of Sharafu'd-Dín Rámí, who flourished in the latter part of the fourteenth century of our era. This book treats of the similes which may be employed in describing the various features of the beloved, and has been translated and annotated in French by M. Clément Huart, Professor of Persian at the École des Langues Orientales Vivantes (Paris, 1875). It contains nineteen chapters, treating respectively of the hair, the forehead, the eyebrows, the eyes, the eyelashes, the face, the down on the lips and cheeks, the mole or beauty-spot, the lips, the teeth, the mouth, the chin, the neck, the bosom, the arm, the fingers, the figure, the waist, and the legs. In each chapter the author first gives the various terms applied by the Arabs and Persians to the part which he is discussing, differentiating them when any difference in meaning exists; then the metaphors used by writers in speaking of them, and the epithets applied to them, the whole copiously illustrated by examples from the poets. Thus the eyebrows (in Persian *abrú*, in Arabic *ḥájib*) may be either joined together above the nose (*muttaṣil*), which is esteemed a great beauty, or separated (*munfaṣil*), and they are spoken of by the Persian poets by thirteen metaphors or metaphorical adjectives. Thus they may be compared to crescent moons; bows; rainbows; arches; *miḥrábs*;[1] the letter *nún*, ن; the letter *káf*,

Conventionality in metaphor and simile.

[1] The *miḥráb* is the niche in every mosque which shows the direction of the Ka'ba of Mecca, towards which the faithful must turn in prayer.

زلف; the curved head of the mall-bat or polo-stick; the *dágh*, or mark of ownership branded on a horse or other domestic animal; and the *ṭughrá*, or royal seal on the letters-patent of beauty. In the case of the hair the number of metaphors and metaphorical adjectives of which the use is sanctioned is much greater: in Persian, according to our author, "these are, properly speaking, sixty; but, since one can make use of a much larger number of terms, the hair is spoken of metaphorically as 'that which possesses a hundred attributes'"; of which attributes a copious list is appended.

From what has been said, it will now be fully apparent how intensely conventional and artificial much Persian poetry is.

Essentially conventional character of Muslim Poetry.

Not only the metres and ordering of the rhymes, but the sequence of subjects, the permissible comparisons, similes, and metaphors, the varieties of rhetorical embellishment, and the like, are all fixed by a convention dating from the eleventh or twelfth century of our era; and this applies most strongly to the *qaṣída*. Hence it is that the European estimate of the greatness of a Persian poet is often very different from that of his own countrymen, since only beauties of thought can be preserved in translation, while beauties of form almost necessarily disappear, however skilful the translator may be. Thus it happens that 'Umar Khayyám, who is not ranked by the Persians as a poet of even the third class, is now, probably, better known in Europe than any of his fellow-countrymen as a writer of verse; while of the *qaṣída*-writers so highly esteemed by the Persians, such as Anwarí, Kháqání, or Dhahír of Fáryáb, the very names are unfamiliar in the West.

The early Arab poets of the classical (*i.e.*, the pre-Muhammadan, early Muhammadan, and Umayyad) periods are natural,

Substance and style as canons of criticism.

unaffected, and perfectly true to their environment, and the difficulty which we often experience in understanding their meaning depends on the unfamiliarity of that environment rather than upon anything far-fetched or fanciful in their comparisons; but, apart from this, they are splendidly direct and spontaneous. Even in Umayyad times, criticism turned rather on the ideas expressed than on the form into which they were cast, as we plainly see from an anecdote related in the charming history of al-Fakhrí (ed. Ahlwardt, pp. 149–150), according to which 'Abdu'l-Malik (reigned A.D. 685–705) one day asked his courtiers what they had to say about the following verse:—

Ahímu bi-Da'din má ḥayaytu, fa-in amut,
Fa-wá-ḥarabá mim-man yahímu bihá ba'dí!

"I shall continue madly in love with Da'd so long as I live; and, if I die,
Alack and alas for him who shall be in love with her after me!"

They replied, "A fine sentiment." "Nay," said 'Abdu'l-Malik, "this is a fellow over-meddlesome after he is dead. This is not a good sentiment." The courtiers agreed. "How then," continued the Caliph, "should he have expressed himself?" Thereupon one of those present suggested for the second line:—

. . . *Uwakkil bi-Da'din man yahímu bihá ba'dí!*

. . . "I will assign to Da'd one who shall love her after me!"

"Nay," said 'Abdu'l-Malik, "this is [the saying of] a dead man who is a procurer and a go-between." "Then how," the courtiers demanded, "should he have expressed himself?" "Why," said the Caliph, "he should have said:—

. . . *Fa-lá ṣaluḥat Da'dun li-dhí khullatin ba'dí!*

. . . ; 'and if I die,
Da'd shall be no good to any lover after me!'"

Here, then, it is wholly a question of the idea expressed, not of the form in which it is cast.

Ibn Khaldún on "Moulds" or Models of Style.

Now see what that greatest philosophical historian of the Arabs, the celebrated Ibn Khaldún (born in Tunis, A.D. 1332; died in Cairo, A.D. 1406) says in chap. xlvii of the sixth section of his masterly *Prolegomena*,[1] which is headed: "That the Art of composing in verse or prose is concerned only with words, not with ideas":—

"Know," he begins, "that the Art of Discourse, whether in verse or prose, lies only in words, not in ideas; for the latter are merely accessories, while the former are the principal concern [of the writer]. So the artist who would practise the faculty of Discourse in verse and prose, exercises it in words only, by storing his memory with models from the speech of the Arabs, so that the use and fluency thereof may increase on his tongue until the faculty [of expressing himself] in the language of Muḍar becomes confirmed in him, and he becomes freed from the foreign idiom wherein he was educated amongst his people. So he should imagine himself as one born and brought up amongst the Arabs, learning their language by oral prompting as the child learns it, until he becomes, as it were, one of them in their language. This is because, as we have already said, language is a faculty [manifested] in speech and acquired by repetition with the tongue until it be fully acquired. Now the tongue and speech deal only with words, while ideas belong to the mind. And, again, ideas are common to all, and are at the disposal of every understanding, to employ as it will, needing [for such employment] no art; it is the construction of speech to express them which needs art, as we have said; this consisting, as it were, of moulds to contain the ideas. So, just as the vessels wherein water is drawn from the sea may be of gold, or silver, or pottery, or glass, or earthenware, whilst the water is in its essence one, in such wise that the respective excellence [of each] varies according to the vessels filled with water, according to the diversity of their species, not according to any difference in the water; just so the excellence and eloquence of language in its use differs according to the different grades of speech in which it is expressed, in respect of its con-

[1] Beyrout ed. of A.D. 1900, p. 577; vol. iii, p. 383, of de Slane's French translation.

formity with the objects [in view], while the ideas are [in each case] invariable in themselves. He, then, who is incapable of framing a discourse and [shaping] its moulds [*i.e.*, its style] according to the requirements of the faculty of speech, and who endeavours to express his thought, but fails to express it well, is like the paralytic who, desiring to rise up, cannot do so, for loss of the power thereunto."

With these "moulds" (*asálíb*, plural of *uslúb*), wherein, as it were, we cast our ideas, and so give them style and distinction, Ibn Khaldún deals at some length, recommending as models of expression the pre-Islámic pagan poets of the Arabs; Abú Tammám, the compiler of the *Ḥamása*, who died about the middle of the ninth century; Kulthúm b. 'Umar al-'Attábí, who flourished in the reign of Hárúnu'r-Rashíd; Ibnu'l-Mu'tazz, whose one day's Caliphate was extinguished in his blood in A.D. 908; Abú Nuwás, the witty and disreputable Court-poet of ar-Rashíd; the Sharíf ar-Raḍí (died A.D. 1015); 'Abdu'lláh b. al-Muqaffa', the apostate Magian, put to death in A.D. 760; Sahl b. Hárún (died A.D. 860), the *wazír* Ibnu'z-Zayyát (put to death in A.D. 847); Badí'u'z-Zamán al-Hamadhání, the author of the first *Maqámát* (died A.D. 1008), and the historian of the House of Buwayh, aṣ-Ṣábí (died A.D. 1056). He who takes these as models, and commits their compositions to memory, will, says Ibn Khaldún, attain a better style than such as imitate later writers of the twelfth and thirteenth centuries of our era, like Ibn Sahl, Ibnu'n-Nabíh, al-Bayṣání, and 'Imádu'd-Dín al-Kátib of Iṣfahán. And so Ibn Khaldún, logically enough from his point of view, defines poetry (Beyrout ed. of A.D. 1900, p. 573) as follows:—

"Poetry is an effective discourse, based on metaphor and descriptions, divided into parts [*i.e.*, verses] agreeing with one another in metre and rhyme, each one of such parts being independent in scope and aim of what precedes and follows it, and *conforming to the moulds* [or styles] *of the Arabs appropriated to it.*"

And about a page further back he compares the writer, whether in prose or verse, to the architect or the weaver, in that he, like them, must work by pattern; for which reason he seems inclined to agree with those who would exclude al-Mutanabbí and Abu'l-'Alá al-Ma'arrí from the Arabian Parnassus *because* they were original, and "did not observe the moulds [or models sanctioned by long usage] of the Arabs."

Turning now to the Persians, we find, as we should naturally expect in these apt pupils of the Arabs, that precisely similar ideas maintain in this field also. "The words of the secretary (or clerk in a Government office) will not," says the author of the *Chahár Maqála*, "attain to this elevation until he becomes familiar with every science, obtains some hint from every master, hears some aphorism from every philosopher, and *borrows some elegance from every man of letters*." To this end the aspirant to literary skill is advised in particular to study, with a view to forming and improving his style, in Arabic the Qur'án, the Traditions, the proverbial sayings of the Arabs, and the writings of the Ṣáḥib Isma'íl b. 'Abbád, aṣ-Ṣábí, Ibn Qudáma, Badí'u'z-Zamán al-Hamadhání, al-Ḥarírí, and other less well-known writers, with the poems of al-Mutanabbí, al-Abíwardí, and al-Ghazzí; and, in Persian, the *Qábús-náma* (composed by Kay-Ká'ús, the Ziyárid ruler of Ṭabaristán, in A.D. 1082–83), the *Sháhnáma* of Firdawsí, and the poems of Rúdagí and 'Unṣurí. This intense conventionality and conservatism in literary matters, broken down in Turkey by the New School led to victory by Ẓiyá Pasha, Kemál Bey, and Shinásí Efendi, maintains an undiminished sway in Persia; and if, on the one hand, it has checked originality and tended to produce a certain monotony of topic, style, and treatment, it has, on the other, guarded the Persian language from that vulgarisation which the triumph of an untrained, untrammelled, and unconventional genius of the barbaric-degenerate type tends to produce in our own and other European tongues.

Conservatism of Persian poetry and prose styles.

Bombast and inflation an accidental, not an essential, quality of Persian literary style.

The models or "moulds" in Persian, as in Arabic, have, it is true, varied from time to time and, to a certain extent, from place to place; for, as we have seen, the canons of criticism adopted by Dawlatsháh at the end of the fifteenth century differ widely from those laid down by the author of the *Chahár Maqála* in the middle of the twelfth; while Ibn Khaldún's severe and classical taste prevented him from approving the rhetorical extravagances which had prevailed amongst his Eastern co-religionists and kinsfolk for nearly three centuries. Yet simplicity and directness is to be found in modern as well as in ancient writers of Persian verse and prose; the *Íqán* ("Assurance") of the Bábís, written by Bahá'u'lláh about A.D. 1859, is as concise and strong in style as the *Chahár Maqála*, composed some seven centuries earlier, and the verse of the contemporary Passion-Play (*ta'ziya*) or of the popular ballad (*taṣníf*) is as simple and natural as one of Rúdagí's songs; while the flabby, inflated, bombastic style familiar to all students of the *Anwár-i-Suhaylí* has always tended to prevail where the patrons of Persian literature have been of Turkish or Mongolian race, and reaches its highest development in the hands of Ottoman writers like Veysí and Nergisí.

CHAPTER II

THE GHAZNAWÍ PERIOD, UNTIL THE DEATH OF SULṬÁN MAḤMÚD

TOWARDS the end of the tenth century of our era Persia, though still nominally subject to the Caliph of Baghdád (at this time al-Qádir bi'lláh, whose long reign lasted from A.D. 991 to 1031), was in fact divided between the Sámánids, whose capital was at Bukhárá, and the Daylamite House of Buwayh, who dominated the southern and south-western provinces and were practically absolute in Baghdád itself, the Caliph being a mere puppet in their hands.[1] Besides these, two small dynasties, the Houses of Ziyár and Ḥasanawayh, ruled respectively in Ṭabaristán (the modern Gílán and Mázandarán, lying between the southern shore of the Caspian and the Elburz Mountains) and Kurdistán. All of these dynasties appear to have been of Íránian (Persian or Kurdish) race, and none of their rulers claimed the title of *Sulṭán*, but contented themselves generally with those of *Amír*, *Ispahbad*, or *Malik*: in other words, they regarded themselves as princes and governors, but not as kings.

State of Persia at the close of the tenth century.

Al-Bírúní, the great chronologist, who flourished about A.D. 1000, and is therefore a contemporary witness for the period of which we are now speaking, discusses at some length the pedigrees of the three more important of the four dynasties

[1] See Stanley Lane-Poole's *Mohammadan Dynasties*, p. 140.

mentioned above.[1] On the pedigree of the Buwayhids, who traced their descent from the Sásánian king Bahrám Gúr, he casts, it is true, some doubt, and adds that certain persons ascribed to them an Arabian origin; but, whether or no they were scions of the ancient Royal House of Persia, there can be no reasonable doubt as to their Persian nationality. Concerning the House of Sámán he declares that "nobody contests the fact" that they were descended from Bahrám Chúbín, the great *marzubán*, or Warden of the Marches, who raised so formidable an insurrection during the reign of the Sásánian king Khusraw Parwíz (A.D. 590–627); whilst of the Ziyárids he similarly traces the pedigree up to the Sásánian king Qubádh (A.D. 488–531). We must, however, bear in mind that personal and political bias may have somewhat influenced al-Bírúní's doubts and assurances in this matter, since he could hardly refrain from professing certainty as to the noble pedigree claimed by his generous and enlightened patron and benefactor Qábús, the son of Washmgír the Ziyárid, entitled *Shamsu'l-Ma'álí*, "the Sun of the Heights," whom also he may have thought to please by his aspersions on the House of Buwayh. Confirmation of this view is afforded by another passage in the same work (p. 131 of Sachau's translation), where al-Bírúní blames the Buwayhids for the high-sounding titles bestowed by them on their ministers, which he stigmatises as "nothing but one great lie," yet a few lines lower lauds his patron *Shamsu'l-Ma'álí* ("the Sun of the Heights") for choosing for himself "a title the full meaning of which did not exceed his merits."

Persian origin of the Houses of Buwayh, Sámán, and Ziyár.

Khurásán, the realm of the Sámánids (which at that time greatly exceeded its modern limits and included much of what is now known as Transcaspia or Central Asia), was, as has been fully explained in the *Prolegomena* to this work, the cradle of "modern," *i.e.*, post-Muhammadan, Persian litera-

[1] See Sachau's translation of the *Chronology of Ancient Nations*, pp. 44–48.

ture. But in spite of the enthusiasm with which ath-Tha'álibí[1] speaks of the galaxy of literary talent assembled at Bukhárá, it is not to be supposed that in culture and science Khurásán had outstripped Fárs, the cradle of Persian greatness, and the south of Persia generally. Ath-Tha'álibí himself (*loc. cit.*, p. 3) cites an Arabic verse by the poet Abú Aḥmad b. Abí Bakr, who flourished about the end of the ninth century of our era at the Sámánid Court, which points very clearly to the intellectual inferiority of Khurásán to 'Iráq; and a doggerel rhyme current in Persia at the present day stigmatises the Khurásánís as "clowns" (*aldang*).[2] Yet in Khurásán undoubtedly it was that the literary revival of the Persian language first began after the Muhammadan conquest; and that because it was the most remote province of the Caliph's domains and the furthest removed from Baghdád, the centre and metropolis of that Islámic culture of which the Arabic language was, from Spain to Samarqand, the recognised medium, until the destruction of the Caliphate by the barbarous Mongols in the middle of the thirteenth century. In Ṭabaristán also, another remote province, which, first under its Zoroastrian *Ispahbads* (who long survived the fall of their Sásánian masters), then under Shí'ite rulers of the House of 'Alí, and lastly under the House of Ziyár, long maintained itself independent of the Caliphs of Baghdád and the Sámánid rulers of Khurásán, a pretty high degree of literary culture is implied by many remarks in the earliest extant history of that province composed by Ibn Isfandiyár (who flourished in the first half of the thirteenth century); for he mentions numerous Arabic works and cites many Arabic verses produced there in the ninth and tenth

Relative degrees of culture in Khurásán, Ṭabaristán, and Southern Persia.

[1] *Yatímatu'd-Dahr*, Damascus edition, vol. iv, pp. 33–4. The passage is translated in the *Prolegomena* of this work, pp. 365–6. See also B. de Meynard's *Tableau Littéraire du Khorassan et de la Transoxiane au IVe siècle de l'Hégire* in the *Journal Asiatique* for March–April, 1854, pp. 293 *et seqq.*

[2] See my *Year amongst the Persians*, p. 232.

centuries of our era, particularly under the Zaydí Imáms (A.D. 864–928),[1] as well as some Persian works and one or two in the peculiar dialect of Ṭabaristán.[2] As regards the House of Buwayh, Shí'ites and Persians as they were, it appears at first sight remarkable that so little of the literature of the Persian Renaissance should have been produced under their auspices, seeing that they were great patrons of learning and that the phrase "more eloquent than the two *Ṣáds*" (*i.e.*, the Ṣáḥib Isma'íl b. 'Abbád and aṣ-Ṣábí, the great minister and the great historian of the House of Buwayh) had become proverbial[3]; but the fact that the literature produced under their auspices was almost entirely Arabic is explained, as already remarked, by the closer relations which they maintained with Baghdád, the seat of the Caliphate and metropolis of Islám. Yet we cannot doubt that Persian poetry as well as Arabic was cultivated at the Buwayhid Courts, and indeed Muḥammad 'Awfí, the oldest biographer of Persian poets whose work (entitled *Lubábu'l-Albáb*) has been preserved to us, mentions at least two poets who wrote in Persian and who enjoyed the patronage of the Ṣáḥib Isma'íl b. 'Abbád, *viz.*, Manṣúr b. 'Alí of Ray, poetically surnamed *Manṭiqí*, and Abú Bakr Muḥam-

[1] See especially Section i, ch. iv (ff. 42ᵇ *et seqq.* of the India Office MS., pp. 42, *et seqq.* of my translation), which treats of the "Kings, nobles, saintly and famous men, scribes, physicians, astronomers, philosophers, and poets of Ṭabaristán." Abú 'Amr (circ. A.D. 870), who is called "the poet of Ṭabaristán" *par excellence*, Abu'l-'Alá as-Sarwí, and the Sayyid al-Utrúsh were all notable poets; while to the Sayyid Abu'l-Ḥusayn a number of Arabic prose works are ascribed, five of the most famous of which are named.

[2] A good many verses in the dialect of Ṭabaristán are cited by Ibn Isfandiyár, including some composed by the Ispahbad Khurshíd b. Abu'l-Qásim of Mámṭír and Bárbad of Jaríd; but the oldest work composed in this dialect of which we have any knowledge appears to have been the *Níkí-náma*, which formed the basis of the Persian *Marzubán-náma* (see Schefer's *Chrestomathie Persane*, vol. ii, p. 195). Ṭabarí verses by 'Alí Pírúza, called Díwárwaz, a contemporary of the Buwayhid 'Aḍudu'd-Dawla (middle of the tenth century), are also cited by Ibn Isfandiyár.

[3] Ibn Isfandiyár, p. 90 of my translation.

mad b. 'Alí of Sarakhs, surnamed *Khusrawí*.[1] The former, as 'Awfí tells us, was greatly honoured by the Ṣáḥib, in whose praise he indited Persian *qaṣídas*, of which specimens are given; and when Badí'u'z-Zamán al-Hamadhání (the author of a celebrated collection of *Maqámát*, which, in the command of all the wealth and subtlety of the Arabic language, is deemed second only to the homonymous work of his more famous successor, al-Ḥarírí) came as a lad of twelve to the Ṣáḥib's reception, his skill in Arabic was tested by bidding him extemporise an Arabic verse-translation of three Persian couplets by this poet.[2] Khusrawí, the second of the two poets abovementioned, composed verses both in Arabic and Persian in praise of Shamsu'l-Ma'álí Qábús b. Washmgír, the Ziyárid ruler of Ṭabaristán, and the Ṣáḥib; while Qumrí of Gurgán, another early poet, sung the praises of the same prince.

Far surpassing in fame and talent the poets above mentioned was that brilliant galaxy of singers which adorned the Court of the great conqueror, Sulṭán Maḥmúd of Ghazna, who succeeded to the throne of his father Subuktigín in A.D. 998. The dynasty which under his energetic and martial rule rose so rapidly to the most commanding position, and after his death so quickly declined before the growing power of the Seljúqs, was actually founded in A.D. 962 by Alptigín, a Turkish slave of the House of Sámán, at Ghazna, in the heart of the Afghan highlands; but its political significance only began some fourteen years later on the accession of Maḥmúd's father Subuktigín, the slave of Alptigín. This great Maḥmúd, therefore, the champion of Islám, the conqueror of India, the ruthless foe of idolatry, "the Right Hand of the Commander of the Faithful" (*Yamínu Amíri'l-Mú'minín*, or *Yamínu'd-Dawla*), was the son of "the slave of a slave"; a fact of which Firdawsí made full

Sulṭán Maḥmúd of Ghazna.

[1] See vol. ii of the *Lubáb*, lately published in my Persian Historical Text Series by Messrs. Brill of Leyden, pp. 16–19.

[2] The verses are given in the *Prolegomena* pp. 463–464.

use in that bitter satire[1] wherein the disappointment of his legitimate hopes of an adequate reward for his thirty years' labour on his immortal epic, the *Sháhnáma*, found full expression, turning, as it were, in a breath into infamy that reputation as a patron of letters which the King so eagerly desired; so that, as Jámí, writing five centuries later, says:—

> *"Guzasht shawkát-i-Maḥmúd, u dar fasána na-mánd*
> *Juz ín qadar, ki na-dánist qadr-i-Firdawsí."*

> "Gone is the greatness of Maḥmúd, departed his glory,
> And shrunk to '*He knew not the worth of Firdawsí*' his story."

Following the plan which we have adopted in the first part of this History, we shall speak but briefly of Sulṭán Maḥmúd himself, and concentrate our attention on the literary and scientific activity of which, by virtue rather of compulsion than attraction, his Court became for a while the focus. Of military genius and of statecraft his achievements afford ample evidence, so that he pushed back the Buwayhids, absorbed the realms of the Ziyárids, overthrew the Sámánids, invaded India in twelve successive campaigns in twice that number of years (A.D. 1001–24), and enlarged the comparatively narrow borders of the kingdom which he had inherited until it extended from Bukhárá and Samarqand to Guzerat and Qinnawj, and included Afghánistán, Transoxiana, Khurásán, Ṭabaristán, Sístán, Kashmír, and a large part of North-Western India. He finally died in A.D. 1030, and within seven years of his death the kingdom which he had built up had practically passed from his House into the hands of the Seljúqid Turks, though the House of Ghazna was not finally extinguished until A.D. 1186, when the kings of Ghúr wrested from them their last Indian possessions and gave them their *coup de grâce*.

Sulṭán Maḥmúd has often been described as a great patron of letters, but he was in fact rather a great kidnapper of

[1] See p. 81 *supra*.

literary men, whom (as we have already seen in the case of Firdawsí) he often treated in the end scurvily enough. Of the scientific writers of that time none were greater than Avicenna (Abú 'Alí ibn Síná), the physician-philosopher who, himself the disciple of Aristotle and Galen, was during the Middle Ages the teacher of Europe, and al-Bírúní, the historian and chronologist. These two men, of whom the former was born about A.D. 980 and the latter about seven years earlier, together with many other scholars and men of letters, such as Abú Sahl Masíḥí the philosopher, Abu'l-Ḥasan Khammár the physician, and Abú Naṣr 'Arráq the mathematician, had found, as we learn from the *Chahár Maqála* (Anecdote xxxv, pp. 118–124 of my translation), a happy and congenial home at the Court of Ma'mún b. Ma'mún, Prince of Khwárazm, whose territories were annexed by Sulṭán Maḥmúd in A.D. 1017.[1] Shortly before this date Sulṭán Maḥmúd sent to Ma'mún by the hand of one of his nobles, Ḥusayn b. 'Alí b. Míká'íl, a letter to the following effect:—

> "I have heard that there are in attendance on Khwárazmsháh several men of learning, each unrivalled in his science, such as So-and-so and So-and-so. You must send them to my Court, so that they may have the honour of being presented thereat. We rely on being enabled to profit by their knowledge and skill, and request this favour on the part of the Prince of Khwárazm."

Avicenna escapes the clutches of Sulṭán Maḥmúd.

Of course this letter, in spite of its comparatively polite tenour, was in reality a command, and as such Ma'mún understood it. Summoning the men of learning referred to in the letter, he addressed them as follows:—"The Sulṭán is strong, and has a large army recruited from Khurásán and India; and he covets 'Iráq [? Khwárazm]. I cannot refuse to obey his order, or be disobedient to his mandate. What say ye on this

[1] See Sachau's translation of al-Bírúní's *Chronology of Ancient Nations*, p. viii.

matter?" Three of them, al-Bírúní, Khammár, and 'Arráq, moved by the accounts they had heard of the Sulṭán's generosity, were willing to go; but Avicenna and Masíḥí were unwilling, and, with the connivance of Ma'mún, privily made their escape. Overtaken by a dust-storm in the desert, Masíḥí perished; while Avicenna, after experiencing terrible hardships, reached Abíward, whence he made his way successively to Ṭús, Níshápúr, and ultimately Gurgán, over which the enlightened and accomplished Qábús b. Washmgír Shamsu'l-Ma'álí (killed in A.D. 1012) then held sway. Now, of the learned men whom Sulṭán Maḥmúd had demanded, it was Avicenna whom he especially desired to secure; so, on learning of his escape, he caused a portrait of him to be circulated through the lands. Avicenna, having succeeded in restoring to health a favourite kinsman of Qábús, was summoned before that Prince, who at once recognised him from the portrait, but, instead of surrendering him to Maḥmúd, maintained him honourably in his service until the philosopher-physician went to Ray and entered the service of 'Alá'u'd-Dawla Muḥammad, whose minister he became. During this period, as we learn from Anecdote xxxvii (pp. 125–128 of my translation) of the *Chahár Maqála*, he managed, in spite of his manifold official duties, to write daily, in the early morning, some two pages of his great philosophical work, the *Shifá*.

Al-Bírúní and Sulṭán Maḥmúd.

Let us turn now for a moment to al-Bírúní's adventures at the Court of Ghazna, as described in Anecdote xxiii (pp. 92-95 of my translation) of the *Chahár Maqála*. One day the Sulṭán, while seated in his four-doored summer-house in the Garden of a Thousand Trees in Ghazna, requested al-Bírúní to forecast, by his knowledge of the stars, by which door the King would leave the building. When al-Bírúní had complied with this command, and had written his answer secretly on a piece of paper which he placed under a quilt, the Sulṭán caused a hole to be made in one of the walls, and by this quitted the summer-house. Then he called for al-Bírúní's prognostication, and found to his disgust that on it was written, "The King will go out by none of these four doors, but an opening will be made in the eastern wall by which he will leave the building." Sulṭán Maḥmúd, who had hoped to turn the laugh against al-Bírúní, was so angry that he ordered him to be cast down from the roof. His fall was, however, broken by a mosquito-curtain; and, on being again brought before the Sulṭán and asked whether he had foreseen this, he produced from his pocket a note-book in which was written, under the date, "To-day I shall be cast down from a high place, but shall reach the earth in safety, and arise sound in body." Thereupon the Sulṭán, still more incensed, caused him to be confined in the citadel, from which he was only released after six months' imprisonment at the intercession of the prime minister, Aḥmad ibn Ḥasan al-Maymandí, who, taking advantage of a favourable moment, said to Maḥmúd, "Poor Abú Rayḥán [al-Bírúní] made two such accurate predictions, and, instead of decorations and a robe of honour, obtained but bonds and imprisonment!" "Know, my lord," replied the Sulṭán, "that this man is said to have no equal in the world save Avicenna, but both his predictions were opposed to my will; and Kings are like little children—in order to receive rewards from them, one should speak in accordance with their opinion. It would have been better for him on that day if one of those two predictions had been wrong. But to-morrow order him to be brought forth, and to be given a horse caparisoned with gold, a royal robe, a satin turban, a thousand *dínárs*, a slave, and a handmaiden." By such tardy reparation, as in the similar case of Firdawsí, did Sulṭán Maḥmúd seek to atone for acts of meanness and injustice committed in a fit of causeless ill-temper or unreasoning suspicion.

Another notable man of letters, Abu'l-Fatḥ al-Bustí, celebrated for his skill in Arabic verse and prose composition, was carried off by Sulṭán Maḥmúd's father Subuktigín when he captured the city of Bust from its ruler Báytúz.

Abu'l-Fatḥ al-Bustí.

This eminent secretary and poet afterwards passed into the service of Maḥmúd, but finally died at Bukhárá in exile in A.H. 400 (A.D. 1009).[1] He was extraordinarily skilled in word-plays and all other artifices of literary composition. His most celebrated poem, which, as al-Manínī informs us, was greatly appreciated and often learned by heart in his time, and which is still recited in Cairo coffee-houses by the *muḥaddithún*, or professional story-tellers, begins :—

Ziyádatu'l-mar'i fí dunyáhu nuqṣánu, *Wa ribḥu-hu ghayru maḥḍi'l-khayri khusránu*.[2]

"A man's increase in worldly wealth doth ofttimes loss betide,
And all his pains, save Virtue's gains, but swell the debit side."

The following Arabic verses by him are also cited by Dawlatsháh :—

"I counsel you, O Kings of Earth, to cease not
Seeking good name for well-doing and right,
Spending your 'white' and 'red' to purchase honour,
Which shall not wane with change of 'black' and 'white':[3]
These are the lasting spoils of Maḥmúd's prowess,
Which spoils we share when we his praise indite."

The date of his death is thus given in a verse by Malik 'Imád-i-Zawzaní :—

[1] See vol. iv of the *Yatímatu'd-Dahr*, pp. 204–231, 'Utbí's *Ta'ríkhu 'l-Yamíní* (Cairo, A.H. 1286), vol. i, pp. 67–72, with al-Maníní's commentary; and Ibn Khallikán (de Slane's translation), vol. ii, pp. 314–315.

[2] This *qaṣída* is given in vol. i of Ẓiyá Bey's *Kharábát*, pp. 271–273.

[3] By "white and red" silver and gold are meant, and by "black and white," night and day.

"Shaykh of lofty worth Abu'l-Fatḥ Majdu'd-Dín, a man who was
Leader of all wits and scholars and of orators the best;
When four centuries and thirty years from Aḥmad's Flight had passed,
Wended in the month of Shawwál hence unto his Home of Rest."

Abundant patronage of men of letters.

It was, indeed, a time when literary men were highly esteemed and eagerly sought after, each more or less independent ruler or local governor striving to emulate his rivals and peers in the intellectual brilliancy of his *entourage*. The main centres of such patronage were, besides Ghazna, Sulṭán Maḥmúd's capital, Níshápúr, the seat of his brother Abu'l-Mudhaffar Naṣr's government in Khurásán, and, till the extinction of the Sámánid dynasty about A.D. 1000, Bukhárá,[1] the various cities in Southern and Western Persia subject to the House of Buwayh, the Courts of the Sayyids and Ziyárid Princes of Ṭabaristán, and the Court of the three Khwárazmsháhs named Ma'mún in Khiva. On the literary luminaries of each of these Courts a monograph might be written, and in each case the materials, though scattered, are abundant, including, for the Arabic-writing poets, the often-cited *Yatímatu'd-Dahr* of Abú Manṣúr ath-Tha'álibí, and its supplement, the hitherto unpublished *Dumyatu'l-Qaṣr* of al-Bákharzí; for the poets and men of letters of Ṭabaristán, the monographs on the history of that most interesting province published by Dorn at St. Petersburg (A.D. 1850–58) and the more ancient history of Ibn Isfandiyár, of which an abridged translation by myself forms the second volume of the Gibb Memorial Series; and, for Iṣfahán, the rare monograph on that city of which I published an abstract in the *Journal of the Royal Asiatic Society* for July and October, 1901; besides the more

[1] For a description of the literary splendour of this city under the Sámánids, see the previous volume of this History, pp. 365–366.

general historical and biographical works of Ibnu'l-Athír, Ibn Khallikán, al-'Utbí, and others.

Most of the literary and scientific men and poets of the time wandered from Court to Court, dedicating a work or a poem to each of their various patrons. Thus the

Abú Manṣúr ath-Tha'álibí.

above-mentioned Abú Manṣúr ath-Tha'álibí of Níshápúr dedicated his *Lațá'ifu'l-Ma'árif* to the Ṣáḥib Isma'íl b. 'Abbád,[1] the great minister of the Buwayhid Prince Fakhru'd-Dawla; the *Mubhij* and the *Tamaththul wa'l-Muḥádara* to Shamsu'l-Ma'álí Qábús b. Washmgír; the *Siḥru'l-Balágha* and *Fiqhu'l-Lugha* to the Amír Abu'l-Faḍl al-Míkálí; the *Niháya fi'l-Kináya*, the *Nathru'n-Nadhm*, and the *Lațá'if wa'dh-Dhará'if* to Ma'mún b. Ma'mún Khwárazmsháh, and so on.[2] So also that great and admirable scholar Abú Rayḥán al-Bírúní (born A.D. 973)

Abú Rayḥán al-Bírúní.

spent the earlier part of his life, as we have already seen, under the protection of the Ma'múní Princes of Khwárazm or Khiva; then visited the Court of that liberal patron of scholars, Shamsu'l-Ma'álí Qábús b. Washmgír in Ṭabaristán, and dedicated to him his *Chronology of Ancient Nations* about A.D. 1000; then returned to Khwárazm, whence, as we have seen, he was carried off to Afghánistán about A.D. 1017, by Sulṭán Maḥmúd of Ghazna, in whose service he remained until the death of that monarch in A.D. 1030, shortly after which event he published the second of his most notable works, the *Indica*, of which the learned editor and translator, Dr. Sachau, remarks (p. xxii of his Preface to the text) that "if in our days a man began studying Sanskrit

[1] See p. 2 of de Jong's edition (Leyden, 1868).

[2] Lists of ath-Tha'álibí's numerous works will be found in Brockelmann's *Gesch. d. Arab. Litt.*, vol. i, pp. 284–286; and on pp. ix *et seqq.* of Zotenberg's Preface to his edition of the *Ghuraru Akhbári Mulúki'l-Furs* ("Histoire des Rois des Perses"), which work is dedicated to the brother of Sulṭán Maḥmúd, Abu'l Mudhaffar Naṣr. For other dedications of this prolific writer's works, see note 2 on p. xi of Zotenberg's above-mentioned Preface.

and Hindú learning with all the help afforded by modern literature and science, many a year would pass before he would be able to do justice to the antiquity of India to such an extent and with such a degree of accuracy as al-Bírúní has done in his *Indica*." And within a few years of this publication, he produced his bi-lingual *Tafhím*[1] on Astronomy, and his *Qánúnu'l-Mas'údí* on the same subject, the former written for the Lady Rayḥána of Khwárazm, and the latter dedicated to Sulṭán Mas'úd b. Maḥmúd b. Subuktigín; while at a later date he dedicated his work on precious stones[2] to this Mas'úd's son and successor, Mawdúd.

The four centres of culture in Persia, apart from Ghazna.

Thus during the earlier Ghaznawí period there were, apart from Ghazna, four separate centres of attraction to men of letters in the wider Persia of those days; to wit, the Buwayhid minister, the Ṣáḥib Isma'íl b. 'Abbád, who resided generally at Iṣfahán or Ray; the Sámánid Court at Bukhárá; the Court of Shamsu'l-Ma'álí Qábús b. Washmgír in Ṭabaristán, not far from the Caspian Sea; and the Court of the Ma'múní Khwárazmsháhs in Khiva. But in the twenty years which elapsed between A.D. 997 and 1017 the Ṣáḥib had died (in A.D. 997); the Sámání dynasty had fallen (A.D. 999); Shamsu'l-Ma'álí had been murdered by his rebellious nobles (A.D. 1012); and Ma'mún II of Khwárazm had also been killed by rebels, and his country annexed by Sulṭán Maḥmúd (A.D. 1017), who thus, by conquest rather than by any innate merit, nobility, or literary talent such as distinguished his rivals above mentioned, became possessed of their men of letters as of their lands. Thus of the Ṣáḥib ath-Tha'álibí says in his *Yatíma*[3]:—

The Ṣáḥib Isma'íl b. 'Abbád.

[1] See Rieu's *Persian Catalogue*, pp. 451–452, where the Persian version (in a MS. dated A.D. 1286) is described.

[2] For a list of his works, see Brockelmann, *op. cit.*, vol. i, pp. 475–476.

[3] Cited by Ibn Khallikán, de Slane's translation, vol. i, pp. 212–213.

"I am unable to find expressions sufficiently strong to satisfy my wishes, so that I may declare to what a height he attained in learning and philological knowledge; how exalted a rank he held by his liberality and generosity; how far he was placed apart by the excellence of his qualities, and how completely he united in himself all the various endowments which are a source of just pride to their possessor; for my words aspire in vain to attain a height which may accord with even the lowest degree of his merit and his glory, and my powers of description are unequal to pourtraying the least of his noble deeds, the lowest of his exalted purposes."

To this Ibn Khallikán adds:—

"The number of poets who flocked to him and celebrated his praises in splendid *qaṣídas* surpassed that which assembled at the Court of any other."

Shamsu'l-Ma'álí.

Shamsu'l-Ma'álí Qábús b. Washmgír, the ruler of Ṭabaristán, was of the noble and ancient house of Qárin (the Qárinwands), one of the seven most honourable stocks of Sásánian Persia, whose members the Arab historians call the *ahlu'l-buyútát*. His pedigree is traced by al-Bírúní[1] up to the Sásánian King Qubádh, the father of Núshirwán. Ibn Isfandiyár, in his History of Ṭabaristán, says that whoever desires to appreciate his greatness and goodness should read what is said of him by Abú Manṣúr ath-Tha'álibí and al-'Utbí in their works.[2] A compilation of his sayings was made by al-Yazdádí, who entitled it *Qará'inu Shamsi'l-Ma'álí wa Kamálu'l-Balágha*. From this last work Ibn Isfandiyár cites some thirty lines, and praises the extraordinary eloquence of Qábús in the Arabic language, his courage and skill in all manly exercises, and his knowledge of philosophy, astronomy, and astrology. He wrote in Arabic a treatise on the astrolabe, on which Abú Isḥáq aṣ-Ṣábí pronounced a most favourable judgement. He maintained, through his chamberlain 'Abdu's-Salám, a regular

[1] *Chronology of Ancient Nations*, Sachau's translation, p. 47.

[2] See vol. iii of the Damascus ed. of the *Yatíma*, p. 288, and vol. ii of al-'Utbí's History (Cairo ed. of A.H. 1286), pp. 14–17 and 172–178.

correspondence with the Ṣáḥib mentioned in the preceding paragraph, and his minister, Abu'l-'Abbás Ghánimí, corresponded with Abú Naṣr al-'Utbí, the historian of Sulṭán Maḥmúd, who also cites (vol. ii, pp. 18–26), with approval and admiration of its style, a short treatise in Arabic composed by Shamsu'l-Ma'álí on the respective merits of the Prophet's Companions.[1] Unfortunately, with all these gifts of mind, birth, and character, he was stern, harsh, suspicious, and at times bloodthirsty. The execution of one of his chamberlains named Ḥájib Na'ím,[2] on the suspicion of embezzlement, was the final cause which drove his nobles into revolt, and impelled them to depose him and put him to death, and to make king over them his son Minúchihr Falaku'l-Ma'álí, chiefly known to Persian scholars as the patron from whom the Persian poet Minúchihrí (author of the *qaṣída* translated in the last chapter, pp. 30–34 *supra*) took his *nom de guerre*.

Character and titles of Sulṭán Maḥmúd.

Of other more distant rulers contemporary with Sulṭán Maḥmúd it is sufficient to say that the 'Abbásid Caliph of Baghdád during the whole of his reign was al-Qádir bi'lláh, while of the Fáṭimid Anti-Caliphs of Egypt, Abú 'Alí Manṣúr was reigning during the first two-thirds and adh-Dháhir during the last third. Maḥmúd is said to have been the first Muslim sovereign who assumed the title of Sulṭán (a word properly meaning "Power" or "Authority"), and appears from al-'Utbí's History (vol. i, p. 21) to have also styled himself, as do the Ottoman Sulṭáns until the present time, "the Shadow of God on His earth" (*Dhillu'lláhi fí arḍihi*). He recognised the supreme spiritual power of his nominal suzerain the Caliph of Baghdád, and was a fanatical Sunní.[3] His full titles ran

[1] *Loc. cit.*, vol. ii, pp. 17–26.

[2] See al-'Utbí's History, Cairo ed. of A.H. 1286, vol. ii, pp. 172–178.

[3] See Ibnu'l-Athír's *Chronicle*, under the year A.H. 420 (A.D. 1029), which shows him, at the very end of his life, crucifying Ismá'ílís, exiling Mu'tazilites, and burning philosophical, scientific, and heretical books.

(al-ʿUtbí, i, p. 31): *Al-Amír as-Sayyid al-Malik al-Mu'ayyad Yamínu'd-Dawla wa Amínu'l-Milla Abu'l-Qásim Maḥmúd b. Náṣiru'd-Dín Abú Manṣúr Subuktigín Maliku'sh-Sharq bi-janbayhi.* His most celebrated minister was Abu'l-Qásim Aḥmad b. al-Ḥasan al-Maymandí, entitled *Shamsu'l-Kufát*, who is said to have interceded on different occasions both for al-Bírúní (see p. 98 *supra*) and for Firdawsí, and to whose praise many fine *qaṣídas* of contemporary poets are devoted.

We must now turn from this short general sketch of the political state of Persia at this epoch to the consideration of a few of the most distinguished writers and poets of the period. And since, should we confine our attention to those who used the Persian language, we should do a great injustice to the genius of Persia, where, as has been already observed, Arabic was at this time, and for another 250 years, generally used not only as the language of science but also of diplomacy, correspondence, and *belles lettres*, we shall begin by briefly mentioning some of the most celebrated Persian writers who chiefly or exclusively made use in their compositions of the Arabic language.

Abú Rayḥán al Bírúní.

Of one of the greatest of these, Abú Rayḥán al-Bírúní, the author of the Chronology of Ancient Nations (*al-Átháru'l-báqiya*), the *Indica*, the Persian *Tafhím*, and many other works (mostly lost) enumerated by his learned editor and translator, Dr. Sachau, I have already spoken. For a just and sympathetic appreciation of his character and attainments, I must refer the reader to Sachau's prefaces to the translations of the first two works mentioned above, especially to pp. vi-vii of the *Indica*. He was a man of vast learning, critical almost in the modern sense, tolerant, and, as Sachau says, "a champion of the truth, a sharply-cut character of a highly individual stamp, full of real courage, and not refraining from dealing hard blows, when anything which is good or right seems to him to be at stake." He was born at Khwárazm in September, A.D. 973, and died, probably at Ghazna, in December, A.D. 1048.

Of Avicenna (Ibn Síná) also, another of the greatest Persian writers and thinkers of this time, who, carrying on the traditions of Aristotle in Philosophy and of Hippocrates and Galen in Medicine, exercised throughout the Middle Ages a dominant influence in both these fields, not only over Asiatic but over European thought, something has been already said. No adequate treatment of his philosophical and medical systems would be possible in a work of this character and scope, even were I competent to discuss them. Of his extant works Brockelmann (*Gesch. d. Arab. Litt.*, i, pp. 452–458) enumerates nearly a hundred, dealing with a variety of theological, philosophical, astronomical, medical, and other scientific subjects. Of these the *Shifá*, treating of physics, metaphysics, and mathematics, and the *Qánún*, or Canon of Medicine, are the most celebrated. The former comprises eighteen volumes.

Avicenna.

For accounts of Avicenna's life and works the reader may refer to Ibn Khallikán's *Biographies* (translation of de Slane, vol. i, pp. 440–446); the above-mentioned work of Brockelmann; Shahristání's *Kitábu'l-Milal wa'n-Niḥal*, either in the Arabic original (Cureton's edition, pp. 348–429) or in Haarbrucker's German translation (vol. ii, pp. 213–332); and the Baron Carra de Vaux' *Avicenne* (Paris, 1900). He was born near Bukhárá in A.D. 980, and died at Hamadán or Iṣfahán in A.D. 1037. "At the age of ten years," says Ibn Khallikán, "he was a perfect master of the Qur'án and general literature, and had obtained a certain degree of information in dogmatic theology, the Indian calculus (arithmetic), and algebra." He then studied with the physician an-Nátilí the Εἰσαγωγή of Porphyry, Logic, Euclid, and the Almagest, and with Isma'íl the Ṣúfí, the theology of the mystics. He then applied himself to natural philosophy, divinity, and other sciences, including medicine, which he studied under the Christian physician 'Ísá b. Yaḥyá. At the age of seventeen his fame

Sketch of Avicenna's life.

as a physician was such that he was summoned to attend the Sámánid Prince Núḥ b. Manṣúr, who, deriving much benefit from his treatment, took him into his favour and permitted him to make use of his very valuable library, which, according to Avicenna's own account, contained "many books the very titles of which were unknown to most persons, and others which I never met with before nor since." Soon after this it unfortunately happened that this precious library was destroyed by fire, and Avicenna's enemies accused him of having purposely set fire to it so that he might be the sole depository of the knowledge which he had gleaned from some of the rare books which it contained. The death of his father, and the final collapse of the Sámánid power about the end of the tenth century, caused him to leave Bukhárá for Khwárazm, where he was favoured by the Ma'múní prince, from whose Court he was obliged to fly, under the circumstances already described from the *Chahár Maqála* a few pages further back, to Nasá, Abíward, Ṭús and ultimately Gurgán, where he was liberally entertained by Shamsu'l-Ma'álí Qábús b. Washmgír. On the deposition and murder of this unfortunate prince, Avicenna left Gurgán for a while, and subsequently went to Ray, Qazwín and Hamadán, and lastly Iṣfahán, where he was in the service of the Buwayhid Prince 'Alá'u'd-Dawla b. Kákúya. Having undergone many vicissitudes of sickness, imprisonment and threatened death, he ultimately died of an intestinal disorder in the summer of A.D. 1037.[1]

[1] Ibnu'l-Athír remarks (end of the year A.H. 428) that there is no doubt as to the unsoundness of 'Alá'u'd-Dawla's religious views, and that it was on this account that Avicenna attached himself to his Court, so that he might be unmolested in the composition of his own heretical works. According to the same authority, when 'Ala'u'd-Dawla was defeated by the troops of Ghazna in A.H. 425, Avicenna's books were carried off by them as part of their plunder, and were placed in one of the libraries of Ghazna, where they remained until they were destroyed by fire in the sack of that city by Ḥusayn, the King of Ghúr, appropriately called *Jahán-súz*, "the World-burner."

Besides the philosophical and scientific works to which allusion has already been made, and certain Arabic and Persian poems of which we shall speak directly, he was the author of the philosophical romances of *Ḥayy b. Yakdhán* (not to be confounded with the more celebrated homonymous treatise by Ibnu'ṭ-Ṭufayl, published at Oxford in 1671 and 1700, with a Latin translation, by Pococke) and *Salámán and Absál*, which latter was afterwards taken by the Persian poet Jámí as the subject of a poem, printed by Falconer in 1850 and translated into English by FitzGerald, who published his translation anonymously, with a dedication to the late Professor Cowell, in 1856.

Avicenna's Persian poems.

As to Avicenna's Persian poems, Dr. Ethé's industry and research have collected from various sources fifteen short pieces (twelve quatrains, one fragment of two *bayts*, and two *ghazals*), comprising in all some forty verses, which he published, with German translation, in the *Göttinger Nachrichten* for 1875, pp. 555–567, under the title *Avicenna als persischer Lyriker*. Of these quatrains it is to be noted that one of the most familiar is commonly ascribed to 'Umar Khayyám (No. 3 in Ethé = No. 303 in Whinfield's edition of the celebrated astronomer-poet's *Quatrains*), and is familiar to all readers of FitzGerald in the following form:—

> "Up from Earth's Centre through the Seventh Gate
> I rose, and on the Throne of Saturn sate,
> And many a Knot unravelled by the Road;
> But not the Master-Knot of Human Fate."

Whinfield's more literal translation is as follows:—

> "I solved all problems, down from Saturn's wreath,
> Unto this lowly sphere of earth beneath,
> And leapt out free from bonds of fraud and lies,
> Yea, every knot was loosed, save that of death!"

Ethé's German translation of the same quatrain, ascribed by

him, on the authority of three separate Persian manuscript authorities, to Avicenna, is as follows:—

"Vom tiefsten Grund des schwarzen Staubes bis zum Saturnus' höchstem Stand
Entwirrt' ich die Probleme alle, die rings im Weltenraum ich fand.
Entsprungen bin ich jeder Fessel, mit der mich List und Trug umwand,
Gelöst war jeglich Band—nur eines blieb ungelöst—des Todes Band!"

The "wandering quatrains" of 'Umar Khayyám.

It is, of course, well known to all Persian scholars that a great number of the quatrains ascribed to 'Umar Khayyám, and included in most editions of his *rubá'iyyát*, are, on other, and equally good or better, authority, ascribed to other poets; and these "wandering quatrains" have been especially studied by Zhukovski in the very important and instructive article on this subject which he communicated to the *Mudhaffariyya* ("Victoria"), a collection of studies in Oriental letters published at St. Petersburg in 1897 to celebrate the twenty-fifth year of Baron Victor Rosen's tenure of his professorship (pp. 325–363). On this subject Whinfield well observes (p. xvii of his Introduction):—

"Another cognate difficulty is this, that many of the quatrains ascribed to 'Umar are also attributed to other poets. I have marked a few of these in the notes, and, doubtless, careful search would bring many more to light. It might be supposed that the character of the language employed would be sufficient to differentiate the work of 'Umar at any rate from that of poets writing two or three centuries after his time, but, as observed by Chodzko, the literary Persian of 800 years ago differs singularly little from that now in use. Again, if, as has been supposed, there were anything exceptional in 'Umar's poetry, it might be possible to identify it by internal evidence; but the fact is that all Persian poetry runs very much in grooves, and 'Umar's is no exception. The poetry of rebellion and revolt from orthodox opinions, which is supposed to be peculiar to him, may be traced in the works of his predecessor Avicenna, as well as in those of Afḍal-i-Káshí, and others of his successors. For these reasons I have not excluded any quatrains on account of their being ascribed to other writers as well as 'Umar. So long as I find fair MS. authority for such quatrains, I include them in the text, not because I am sure 'Umar wrote them, but because it is just as likely they were written by him as by the other claimants."

Of the two longer poems included in Dr. Ethé's abovementioned article, one is in praise of wine, while the other contains sundry moral precepts and reflections. Neither of them appears to me either of sufficiently high merit or of sufficiently certain authenticity to be worth translating here, and I must therefore refer the curious reader to Dr. Ethé's interesting article in the *Göttinger Nachrichten*.

Avicenna's Arabic poem on the Soul.

Much more remarkable and beautiful is Avicenna's celebrated Arabic *qaṣída* on the Human Soul,[1] of which the following translation may serve to convey some idea :—

"It descended upon thee from out of the regions above,
That exalted, ineffable, glorious, heavenly Dove.
'Twas concealed from the eyes of all those who its nature would ken,
Yet it wears not a veil, and is ever apparent to men.[2]
Unwilling it sought thee and joined thee, and yet, though it grieve,
It is like to be still more unwilling thy body to leave.

---

[1] It is cited by Ibn Khallikán (de Slane's translation, vol. i, p. 443 : ed. Wüstenfeld, vol. i, No. 189), in the *Kharábát* of Ẓiyá Bey, vol. i, pp. 283–284, and in many other places. In my translation I follow the latter text, which towards the end differs somewhat from the former.

[2] It would almost seem as though this verse had inspired the well-known verse of Jalálu'd-Dín Rúmí near the beginning of the *Mathnawí*, "*Tan zi ján u ján zi tan mastúr níst, Lík kas-rá díd-i-ján dastúr níst.*" This in the late Professor E. H. Palmer's pretty version, published in the *Song of the Reed*, runs :—

"Though plainly cometh forth my wail,
'Tis never bared to mortal ken ;
As soul from body hath no veil,
Yet is the soul unseen of men."

It resisted and struggled, and would not be taméd in haste,
Yet it joined thee, and slowly grew used to this desolate waste,
Till, forgotten at length, as I ween, were its haunts and its troth
In the heavenly gardens and groves, which to leave it was loath.
Until, when it entered the D of its downward Descent,
And to earth, to the C of its centre, unwillingly went,[1]
The eye (I) of Infirmity[2] smote it, and lo, it was hurled
Midst the sign-posts and ruined abodes of this desolate world.
It weeps, when it thinks of its home and the peace it possessed,
With tears welling forth from its eyes without pausing or rest,
And with plaintive mourning it broodeth like one bereft
O'er such trace of its home as the fourfold winds have left.
Thick nets detain it, and strong is the cage whereby
It is held from seeking the lofty and spacious sky.
Until, when the hour of its homeward flight draws near,
And 'tis time for it to return to its ampler sphere,
It carols with joy, for the veil is raised, and it spies
Such things as cannot be witnessed by waking eyes.
On a lofty height doth it warble its songs of praise
(For even the lowliest being doth knowledge raise).
And so it returneth, aware of all hidden things
In the universe, while no stain to its garment clings.

"Now why from its perch on high was it cast like this
To the lowest Nadir's gloomy and drear abyss?
Was it God who cast it forth for some purpose wise,
Concealed from the keenest seeker's inquiring eyes?
Then is its descent a discipline wise but stern,
That the things that it hath not heard it thus may learn.
So 'tis she whom Fate doth plunder, until her star
Setteth at length in a place from its rising far,
Like a gleam of lightning which over the meadows shone,
And, as though it ne'er had been, in a moment is gone."

---

[1] This verse, of course, I have been compelled to paraphrase. The expression in the original, which is quite similar, is:—"the H of its *Hubúṭ*" (Descent) and "the M of its *Markaz*" (Centre). The shapes of these two Arabic letters include the downward curve, or arc of descent, and the hollow point, respectively.

[2] Here occurs a similar paraphrase of *Thá'i thaqíli-há*, "the defect of its grosser [part]."

Of other distinguished writers of Arabic produced by Persia, mention should be made of the celebrated inventor of that style of composition known as the *Maqáma*, the ingenious Abu'l-Faḍl Aḥmad b. al-Ḥusayn of Hamadán, better known as *Badí'u'z-Zamán*, "the Wonder of the Age," who, as ath-Tha'álibí tells us (*Yatíma*, vol. iv, pp. 168–169), died in A.H. 398 (A.D. 1008) at the comparatively early age of forty. Of his native town he had but a mean opinion, for he says in an often-quoted verse[1] :—

Badí'u'z-Zamán al-Hamadhání.

"Hamadán is my country; its virtues I'm fain to allow,
Yet most hateful of all our cities I find it, I trow:
Its children are ugly as aged men, and all must admit
That its aged men are like children in lack of wit."

In the same sense he quotes in one of his letters (*Yatíma*, vol. iv, p. 179) another similar verse, which runs :—

"Blame me not for my weak understanding, for I am a man
Who was born, as you very well know, in the town Hamadán!"

We find, consequently, that he quitted his little-loved native town in A.D. 990, being then about twenty-two years of age, and first visited that great patron of letters, the Ṣáḥib Isma'íl b. 'Abbád, who, as we have seen,[2] tested his skill in extempore translation by giving him a Persian verse to render into metrical Arabic. Thence he went to Gurgán, where, if ath-Tha'álibí is to be credited, he frequented the society of the Isma'íli heretics, who even at this time, nearly a century before the notorious Ḥasan-i-Ṣabbáḥ made it the centre of his "New Propaganda," appear to have been numerous in this region. In A.H. 382 (A.D. 992–93) he reached Níshápúr, and there composed his "Séances" (*Maqámát*), which, as stated by ath-Tha'álibí

[1] See Preston's translation of the *Maqámát* (London, 1850), pp. 12–13.

[2] See p. 94 *supra*, and the *Prolegomena*, pp. 463–64. That he was in the habit of making such extempore translations from the Persian appears also from the *Yatíma*, vol. iv, p. 167.

(*loc. cit.*), originally amounted to four hundred. After visiting every town of importance in Khurásán, Sístán, and the regions about Ghazna, he finally settled in Herát, and there died. His memory was prodigious, so that he could repeat by heart a *qaṣída* of fifty verses, after hearing it recited only once, without a single mistake; or four or five pages of a prose work which he had subjected to one hasty perusal. The respective merits of him and his imitator al-Ḥaríri in that style of composition which they so especially made their own is a subject which has been repeatedly discussed, and which need not be considered in this place.[1] Attention may, however, be called to an Arabic *qaṣída*, which he composed in glorification of Sulṭán Maḥmúd, which al-'Utbí cites in his *Kitábu'l-Yamíní* (Cairo ed. of A.H. 1286, vol. i, pp. 384–386).

"*Is this*," the poet asks himself (meaning the Sulṭán), "*Afrídhún with the crown, or a second Alexander? Or hath a re-incarnation brought back unto us Solomon? The sun of Maḥmúd hath cast a shadow over the stars of Sámán, and the House of Bahrám*[2] *have become slaves to the son of the Kháqán.*[3] *When he rides the elephant to battle or review, thine eyes behold a Sulṭán on the shoulders of a devil;* [*a Sulṭán whose sway extends*] *from the midst of India to the coasts of Jurján, and from the limits of Sind to the remotest parts of Khurásán.*"

One other Persian poet who wrote in Arabic, viz., Mihyár ad-Daylamí,[4] deserves mention because of the interesting fact that he was born and brought up in the Zoroastrian religion, from which he was converted to Islám in A.D. 1003, by another poet, the Sharíf ar-Raḍí, who for many years before his death (in A.D. 1015–16)

Mihyár the Daylamí.

[1] See, for instance, Preston's translation of the *Maqámát* of al-Ḥaríri, pp. xiii–xiv and 13–14.

[2] As we have already seen, the Sámánids claimed descent from Bahrám Chúbín.

[3] Kháqán is the generic name of the ruler of the Turks, since the time of the legendary Afrásiyáb.

[4] The first half of his *Díwán* has been printed at Cairo, A.H. 1314 (A.D. 1896–97).

held the high position of *Naqíbu'l-'Alawiyyín*, or Dean of the descendants of 'Alí, at Baghdád. The example of Mihyár shows us how considerable a hold Zoroastrianism still had in the Caspian provinces, how readily it was tolerated, and how fully its representatives were permitted to share in the science and culture of which Arabic was the medium of expression. This appears in the frequency of the *nisba* "al-Majúsí" ("the Magian"), in works like the *Dumyatu'l-Qaṣr* of al-Bákharzí, who composed a supplement to ath-Tha'álibí's oft-cited Biography of Poets, the *Yatímatu'd-Dahr*.

Al-Majúsí, the physician.

The best-known bearer of this *nisba* was, however, 'Alí b. al-'Abbás al-Majúsí, the physician of the Buwayhid 'Aḍudu'd-Dawla, and the author of the *Kámilu'ṣ-Ṣaná'at*, or "Complete Practitioner," who died in A.D. 994; but in his case his father had already renounced the ancient religion. An account of one of this physician's cures is given in Anecdote xxxvi of the *Chahár Maqála* (pp. 124–5 of my translation).

To the period immediately preceding that which we are now discussing belong that great work the *Fihrist* (composed about A.D. 988) and the *Mafatíḥu'l-'Ulúm* (composed about A.D. 976), of both of which the contents were pretty fully analysed in the *Prolegomena*. Of local histories also several important monographs deserve mention, *e.g.*, the History of Bukhárá by Narshakhí (composed about A.D. 942), the History of Qum (composed for the Ṣáḥib Isma'íl b. 'Abbád about A.D. 989), and the Histories of Iṣfahán and Ṭabaristán, composed respectively by al-Máfarrúkhí and al-Yazdádí, all of which were composed originally in Arabic, but are now known to us only in Persian translations. Another Arabic-writing Persian, of whose works too little has survived, was the historian 'Alí b. Miskawayhi, who died in A.D. 1029. Al-'Utbí's monograph on Sulṭán Maḥmúd (which is only carried down to A.D. 1018, though the author lived till A.D. 1035–36) has been already mentioned repeatedly, as well as the numerous works of Abú Manṣúr ath-Tha'álibí, the author of the *Yatímatu'd-Dahr*, who died in A.D. 1038. Persian prose works are still few and unimportant: those which belong to the Sámánid period, such as Bal'amí's translation of Ṭabarí's great history (made about A.D. 964), Abú Manṣúr Muwaffaq's Pharmacology (*circa* A.D. 971), a Persian commentary on the Qur'án preserved in a unique MS. at Cambridge, and Bal'amí's translation of Ṭabarí's commentary (about A.D. 981), have been already mentioned in the *Prolegomena.* If to these we add the rare *Dánish-náma-i-'Alá'í* (composed by Avicenna for 'Alá'u'd-Dawla of Iṣfahán, who died in A.H. 1042), and the lost *Khujista-náma* of Bahrámí, and the *Tarjumánu'l-Balágha* of Farrukhí, both of which treat of Prosody and Rhetoric, and both of which were presumably written about A.D. 1058, we shall have nearly completed the list of Persian prose works composed before the middle of the fifth century of the Flight of which any knowledge is preserved to us. Allusion has already been made to the fact that there is evidence of the existence of a literature, both prose (like the *Marzubán-náma*) and verse (like the *Níkí-náma*), in the dialect of Ṭabaristán; and Ibn Isfandiyár's history of that interesting province (founded on the above-mentioned monograph of al-Yazdádí) has preserved to us specimens (much corrupted, it is true, by lapse of time and careless copyists) of Ṭabarí dialect verses by poets entirely ignored by the ordinary Memoir-writers, such as the Ispahbad Khurshíd b. Abu'l-Qásim of Mámṭir, Bárbad-i-Jarídí, Ibráhím Mu'íní, Ustád 'Alí Pírúza (a contemporary of al-Mutanabbí, and panegyrist of 'Aḍudu'd-Dawla the Buwayhid), and Díwárwaz Mastamard, rival of him last named, who also enjoyed the favour of Shamsu'l-Ma'álí Qábús b. Washmgír.

We must now pass to the great Persian poets from whom the literature of this period, and in particular the Court of Ghazna, derived such lustre. Of these Firdawsí, who successfully accomplished the great work begun by Daqíqí (d. A.D. 975), and embodied for all time in immortal verse the legendary history of his country, ranks not only as the greatest poet of his age, but as one of the greatest poets of all ages, so that, as a well-known Persian verse has it:—

The great Persian poets of this period.

"The sphere poetic hath its prophets three,
(Although '*There is no Prophet after me*')[1]
Firdawsí in the epic, in the ode,
Sa'dí, and in *qaṣída* Anwarí."

After him come the panegyrists and *qaṣída*-writers 'Unṣurí (Sulṭán Maḥmúd's poet-laureate), Asadí (Firdawsí's friend and fellow-townsman and the inventor of the *munáḏhara*, or "strife-poem"), 'Asjadí, Farrukhí of Sístán, and the somewhat later Minúchihrí, with a host of less celebrated poets, like Bahrámí (who also composed a work on Prosody, the *Khujista-náma*, no longer extant), 'Uṭáridí, Ráfi'í, Ghaḍá'irí of Ray, Manṣúrí, Yamíní (who is also said to have written a history of Sulṭán Maḥmúd's reign in Persian prose), Sharafu'l-Mulk (to whom is ascribed a Persian Secretary's Manual entitled the *Kitábu'l-Istífá*), Zínatí-i-'Alawí-i-Maḥmúdí, and the poetess Rábi'a bint Kalb of Qusdár or Quzdár, besides many others whose names and verses are recorded in chapter ix of 'Awfí's *Lubábu'l-Albáb* (pp. 28–67 of my edition of the second part of this work). It is neither necessary nor possible in a work of this character to discuss all of these, and we must confine ourselves to a selection of the most typical and the most celebrated. Three other poets of some note belonging to this period differ somewhat in character from the above; namely Kisá'í, who, beginning as a panegyrist, repented in later life of the time-serving and adulation inseparable from the career of a Court-poet, and devoted himself to religious verse; Abú Sa'íd b.

[1] Alluding to a saying of the Prophet Muḥammad: *Lá nabiyya ba'di*, "There is no Prophet after me."

Abi'l-Khayr, the mystic quatrain-writer; and Pindár of Ray, chiefly notable as a dialect-poet, though he wrote also in Arabic and Persian. Another celebrated dialect-poet and quatrain-writer, reckoned by Ethé[1] as belonging to this period, on the strength of the date (A.H. 410 = A.D. 1019) assigned to his death by Riḍá-qulí Khán (in the *Riyáḍu'l-'Árifín*), really belongs more properly to early Seljúq times; since the History of the Seljúqs,[2] entitled the *Ráḥatu'ṣ-Ṣudúr*, composed in A.D. 1202–03 by Najmu'd-Dín Abú Bakr Muḥammad of Ráwand, and preserved in a unique MS. copied in A.D. 1238, which formerly belonged to M. Schefer, and is now in the Bibliothèque Nationale at Paris (Suppl. pers., No. 1314), recounts an anecdote of his meeting with Ṭughril Beg at Hamadán, probably in A.D. 1055–56 or 1058–59.

Before speaking of Sulṭán Maḥmúd's poets, however, it should be mentioned that he himself is said to have been something of a poet, and stands second, after a brief notice of the unfortunate Isma'íl b. Núḥ, the last Sámánid, in 'Awfí's *Lubáb* amongst the kings and princes who wrote incidental verse. Ethé (*op. cit.*, p. 224) says that six *ghazals* are (on doubtful authority, as he thinks) ascribed to him. 'Awfí cites two short fragments only, of which the first, containing but three verses, is a little elegy on the death of a girl named Gulistán ("Rose-garden"), to whom he was attached. The following is a translation of it:—

"Since thou, O Moon, beneath the dust dost lie,
The dust in worth is raised above the sky.
My heart rebels. 'Be patient, Heart,' I cry;
'An All-just Lord doth rule our destiny.
Earthy and of the earth is man: 'tis plain
What springs from dust to dust must turn again.'"

---

[1] In his article on *Neupersische Litteratur*, in vol. ii of the *Grundriss der Iranischen Philologie*, p. 223.

[2] This valuable work I have fully described in the *Journal of the Royal Asiatic Society* for 1902, pp. 567–610, and 849–887.

The second fragment, comprising six verses, is said to have been composed by Maḥmúd when he felt the approach of death. It is well-known, but its authorship is very doubtful, and Dawlatsháh (who cites three verses of it, p. 67 of my edition) ascribes it, with at least equal probability, to Sanjar the Seljúqid. It runs thus:—

"Through fear of my conquering sword, and my mace which no fort can withstand,
As the body is thrall to the mind, so to me was subjected the land.
Now enthroned in glory and power I'd dwell amid gladness at home,
Now, stirred by ambition, in arms from country to country I'd roam.
I deemed I was somebody great when exulting to conquer I came,
But the prince and the peasant, alas! in their end, I have learned, are the same!
At hazard two mouldering skulls should'st thou take from the dust of the grave,
Can'st pretend to distinguish the skull of the king from the skull of the slave?
With one gesture, one turn of the hand, a thousand strong forts I laid low,
And oft with one prick of my spurs have I scattered the ranks of the foe.
But now, when 'tis Death who attacks me, what profits my skill with the sword?
God only endureth unchanging; dominion belongs to the Lord!"

As regards Sulṭán Maḥmúd's character, we naturally find in the verses of his Court-poets (save such as were disappointed of their hopes, like Firdawsí) and in the works of State historians nothing but the most exaggerated praise, but Ibnu'l-Athír (under the year A.H. 421 = A.D. 1030) in his obituary notice of this monarch says, after praising him for his intelligence, devoutness, virtue, patronage of learned men, and strenuousness in waging war on the unbelievers, that his one fault was love of money and a certain lack of scruple in his methods of obtaining it. "There was in him," he says, "nothing which could be blamed, save that he would seek to obtain money in every way. Thus, to give one instance, being informed of a certain man from Níshápúr that he was of great opulence and copious wealth, he summoned him to Ghazna and said to him, 'I have heard that you are a Carmathian heretic.' 'I am no Carmathian,' replied the unfortunate man; 'but I have wealth wherefrom what is desired [by Your Majesty] may be taken, so that I be cleared of this name.' So the Sulṭán took from him some portion of his wealth, and provided him with a document testifying to the soundness of his religious views." In the eyes of most Muslims, so great a champion of the faith, one who was such a scourge to idolaters and so conspicuous an iconoclast, is raised above all criticism; but there is no doubt that Ibnu'l-Athír has laid his finger on a weak spot in the Sulṭán's character, and that, besides being greedy of wealth (which, no doubt, largely explains the persistence with which he prosecuted his Indian campaign), he was fanatical, cruel to Muslim heretics as well as to Hindoos (of whom he slew an incalculable number), fickle and uncertain in temper, and more notable as an irresistible conqueror than as a faithful friend or a magnanimous foe. He was born on Muḥarram 10, A.H. 350 (= November 13, A.D. 970), and died in March, A.D. 1030, at the age of sixty. His favourite Ayáz, concerning whom so many stories are related by Persian writers, was a historical personage, for his death is chronicled by Ibnu'l-Athír under the year A.H. 449 (= A.D. 1057–58), his full name being given as Ayáz, son of Aymáq Abu'n-Najm.

Having spoken of Maḥmúd, it is right that we should next pass to 'Unṣuri, his poet-laureate, who, if less great than Firdawsí, was highly esteemed as a poet long after the glory had departed from the Court of Ghazna, so that Nidhámí-i-'Arúḍí of Samarqand says in the *Chahár Maqála* (p. 48 of my translation):—

"How many a palace did great Maḥmúd raise,
At whose tall towers the Moon did stand at gaze,
Whereof one brick remaineth not in place,
Though still re-echo 'Unṣurí's sweet lays."

Concerning 'Unṣurí's life we know practically nothing, and even the date assigned to his death by various authorities (mostly modern) varies between A.D. 1040 and 1050. 'Awfí, as usual, contents himself with an encomium embellished with a few word-plays. Dawlatsháh is more prodigal of words, and in the notice which he consecrates to this poet, whose full name he, in common with 'Awfí, gives as Abu'l-Qásim Ḥasan b. Aḥmad (a name vouched for also by the contemporary poet Minúchihrí in a *qaṣída*, of which a translation will follow shortly), writes as follows:—

'Unṣurí.

"His merits and talent are plainer than the sun. He was the chief of the poets of Sulṭán Maḥmúd's time, and possessed many virtues beyond the gift of song, so that by some he is styled 'the Sage' (*Ḥakím*). It is said that four hundred eminent poets were in constant attendance on Sulṭán Maḥmúd *Yamínu'd-Dawla*, and that of all those Master 'Unṣurí was the chief and leader, whose disciples they acknowledged themselves. At the Sulṭán's Court he combined the functions of poet and favourite courtier, and was constantly celebrating in verse the wars and prowess of the King. In a long panegyric of some hundred and eighty couplets he has recorded in metre all the Sulṭán's wars, battles, and conquests. Finally the Sulṭán bestowed on him letters-patent investing him with the Laureateship in his dominions, and commanded that wherever, throughout his empire, there might be a poet or writer of elegance, he should submit his productions to 'Unṣurí, who, after examining its merits and defects, should submit it to the Royal Presence. So 'Unṣurí's daily receptions became the goal of all poets, and thereby there accrued to him much influence and wealth.[1] Firdawsí, in his epic the *Sháhnáma*, bestows on him an eloquent encomium, as will

[1] It does not appear why *wealth* should accrue to him from these receptions unless, as is likely enough, weightier arguments than good style and poetic talent could be employed in enlisting his sympathies.

be set forth in its proper place; though God best knows whether it be true!"

This last saving clause applies to a great deal of Dawlatsháh's information, which is more circumstantial than correct in many cases. As a sample of 'Unṣurí's verse he chooses a *qaṣída* of the kind known as "Question and Answer" (*Su'ál u jawáb*), of which, since it serves as well as another to give an idea of his verse, I here append a translation. The poem is in praise of Sulṭán Maḥmúd's brother, the Amír Naṣr b. Subuktigín, Governor of Khurásán, and the text will be found at pp. 45–46 of my edition of Dawlatsháh, or at ff. 3–4 of the edition of 'Unṣurí's poems lithographed at Ṭihrán without date. I have not attempted in my translation to preserve the uniform rhyme proper to the *qaṣída*.

"To each inquiry which my wit could frame
Last night, from those fresh lips an answer came.
Said I, 'One may not see thee save at night;'
'When else,' said she, 'would'st see the Moon's clear light?'
Said I, 'The sun doth fear thy radiant face;'
Said she, 'When thou art here, sleep comes apace!'[1]
Said I, 'With hues of night stain not the day!'[2]
Said she, 'Stain not with blood thy cheeks, I pray!'[3]
Said I, 'This hair of thine right fragrant is!'
Said she, 'Why not? 'tis purest ambergris!'[4]
Said I, 'Who caused thy cheeks like fire to shine?'
Said she, 'That One who grilled[5] that heart of thine.'

[1] Meaning, I suppose, that the poet's conversation is wearisome to her and sends her to sleep, but the line is rather obscure.

[2] "The day" is a metaphor for the face, and "the hues of night" for the antimony (*surma*) used to darken the eyelashes and eyebrows and the black beauty-spots (*khál*) placed on the cheek.

[3] That is, Do not tear thy face in grief at my indifference; or, Do not shed 'blood-stained tears.'

[4] Ambergris is a common metaphor for the hair of the beloved, it being both dark and fragrant.

[5] "Grill" is the literal, if to our taste somewhat unpoetical, meaning of *kabáb kard*, *kabáb* ("kabob") being the name given to morsels of meat toasted or broiled on a skewer, and generally eaten by the Persians as a relish with wine.

Said I, 'Mine eyes I cannot turn from thee!'
'Who from the *miḥráb*[1] turns in prayer?' quoth she.
Said I, 'Thy love torments me! Grant me grace!'
Said she, 'In torment is the lover's place!'
Said I, 'Where lies my way to rest and peace?'
'Serve our young Prince,' said she, 'withouten cease!'[2]
Said I, 'Mír Naṣr, our Faith's support and stay?'
Said she, 'That same, whom despot kings obey!'
Said I, 'What share is his of wit and worth?'
'Nay,' she replied, 'to him these owe their birth!'
Said I, 'His virtues knowest thou, O Friend?'
'Nay,' she replied, 'our knowledge they transcend!'
Said I, 'Who are his messengers of war?'
Said she, 'Anear the spear, the dart afar!'
Said I, 'The age doth need him sore, in sooth!'
Said she, 'Yea, more than we need life or youth!'
Said I, 'Hast ever seen his like before?'
Said she, 'Not even in the books of yore.'
Said I, 'What say'st thou of his hand?' Said she,
'Like a mirage beside it seems the sea!'[3]
Said I, 'He hearkens to the beggars' cries;'
Said she, 'With gold and garments he replies.
Said I, 'What's left for men of gentle birth?'
'Honour,' she answered, 'rank, and power, and worth!'
'What deemest thou his arrows?' questioned I:
'Meteors and shooting stars,' she made reply.
Said I, 'His sword and he who stirs its ire?'
'This quicksilver,' said she, 'and that the fire!'
Said I, 'Lies aught beyond his mandate's calls?'
Said she, 'If aught, what into ruin falls.'
Said I, 'How false his foes!' She answered, 'Yea,
More false than false Musaylima[4] are they!'

---

[1] The arch of a comely eyebrow is commonly likened by Muslim poets to the arch of the *miḥrab*, or niche in the wall of the mosque which indicates the direction of Mecca, towards which the worshipper must turn in prayer. See p. 83 *supra*.

[2] This is the *guríz-gáh* (see pp. 30; 32, n. 1 *supra*) wherein the poet passes from the *tashbíb* (prelude) to the *madíḥa*, or panegyric proper.

[3] The ocean is amongst the poets of Asia one of the commonest metaphors for unstinted bounty.

[4] Musaylima, the first false prophet in Islám.

'What lands,' said I, 'are left, were mine the might,
Were his.' Said she, 'What's *left* can ne'er be *right*.'[1]
Said I, 'Then doth his bounty cause no stint?'
Said she, 'Of time, in cloth-mill and in mint.'[2]
Said I, 'What nobler is than all beside—'
'—Hath God vouchsafed to him,' my friend replied.
Said I, 'This spacious realm where holds the King?'
Said she, 'Beneath his stirrups and his ring.'[3]
Said I, 'From praising him I will not rest.'
Said she, 'So do the brightest and the best.'
Said I, 'What boon for him shall crave my tongue?'
Said she, 'Long life, and Fortune ever young!'"

'Asjadí.

Of 'Asjadí (Abú Nadhar 'Abdu'l-'Azíz b. Manṣúr), whom we should next mention, we know even less than of 'Unṣurí, since even in Dawlatsháh's day "his *díwán* was unobtainable, though some of his verses were to be found recorded in anthologies." Dawlatsháh describes him as one of 'Unṣurí's pupils and a native of Herát, while the earlier 'Awfí calls him a man of Merv. The following quatrain is ascribed to him by the former biographer:—

"I do repent of wine and talk of wine,
Of idols fair with chins like silver fine:
A lip-repentance and a lustful heart—
O God, forgive this penitence of mine!"

[1] This verse is paraphrased, to imitate the word-play in the original, which, literally translated, means: "I said, 'I would give him [all] the horizons;' she said, 'Indeed none would assign Khaṭá (which means the land of Cathay, or Chinese Tartary, and also "a fault") to rectitude.'"

[2] His constant gifts of robes of honour and money keep the cloth-mills and the mint always hard at work.

[3] The signet-ring is, of course, the symbol of authority, while the hard-pressed stirrup typifies endurance in war and the chase. "He made his reins light and his stirrups heavy" is an expression which constantly recurs in describing feats of knightly prowess; and Ibn Isfandiyár tells us that one of the princes of Ṭabaristán used, when he rode forth in the morning, to place a gold coin between each foot and the corresponding stirrup, and not suffer it to fall out till he returned home.

Farrukhí.

Of Farrukhí (Abu'l-Ḥasan 'Ali b. Júlúgh) of Sístán (Dawlatsháh says "of Tirmidh," but this is certainly an error), the third of the triad of poets with whom Firdawsí, according to the popular legend, was confronted on his arrival at the Court of Ghazna, we know somewhat more, thanks to a long anecdote (No. xv) in the *Chahár Maqála* (pp. 58–66 of my translation). His prose work on Prosody, the *Tarjumánu'l-Balághat* ("Interpreter of Eloquence"), of which Rashídu'd-Dín Waṭwáṭ, who describes its author as "being to the Persians what al-Mutanabbí was to the Arabs," appears to have made use in the compilation of his *Ḥadá'iqu's-Siḥr* ("Gardens of Magic"), is, unfortunately, so far as we know, no longer extant; but of his *Díwán*, which Dawlatsháh describes as "enjoying a wide celebrity in Transoxiana, but lost or little known in Khurásán," two manuscripts exist in the British Museum and one in the India Office, while a lithographed edition was published at Ṭihrán in A.H. 1301 and 1302 (A.D. 1883–85). According to the *Chahár Maqála*, his father, Júlúgh, was in the service of the Amír Khalaf, a descendant of the Ṣaffárids, who still preserved some fragment of his House's ancient power, while Farrukhí, on account of his skill in making verses and playing the harp (in which, like Rúdagí, he excelled), was retained in the service of a *dihqán*, or squire, who allowed him a yearly stipend of a hundred silver *dirhams* and two hundred measures of corn, each comprising five maunds. A marriage contracted with one of the ladies of Khalaf's Court made this allowance insufficient; and though at his request the *dihqán* consented to raise it to five hundred *dirhams* with three hundred maunds of corn, Farrukhí, deeming even this inadequate, and hearing glowing reports of the munificence of the Amír Abu'l-Muḏhaffar of Chagháníyán (a place in Transoxiana, between Tirmidh and Qubádiyán), set off to try his fortune with this new patron, as he himself says:—

"In a caravan for Ḥilla bound from Sístán did I start
With fabrics spun within my brain and woven by my heart."

On arriving at his destination, he found that the Amir Abu'l-Mudhaffar was absent in the country, superintending the branding of his colts and mares at the "branding-ground" (*dágh-gáh*), for he was a great lover of horse-flesh, and possessed, if we may credit the author of the *Chahár Maqála*, more than eighteen thousand beasts. In his absence the poet was received by his steward, the 'Amíd As'ad, who, being himself "a man of parts and a poet," at once recognised the merit of the *qaṣída* which Farrukhí recited to him, but could hardly believe that the uncouth, ill-dressed Sístáni, who was "of the most unprepossessing appearance from head to foot," and whose head was crowned "with a huge turban, after the manner of the Sagzís,"[1] could really be its author. So he said—

"The Amír is at the branding-ground, whither I go to wait upon him, and thither I will take thee also, for it is a mighty pleasant spot—

'World within world of verdure wilt thou see'—

full of tents and star-like lamps, and from each tent come the songs of Rúdagí,[2] and friends sit together, drinking wine and making merry, while before the Amír's pavilion a great fire is kindled, in size like a mountain, whereat they brand the colts. And the Amír, goblet in one hand and lassoo in the other, drinks wine and gives away horses. Compose, now, a *qaṣída* describing this branding-ground, so that I may present thee to the Amír."

---

[1] Sístán was originally called Sagistán (Arabicised to Sijistán), "the country of the Sakas," and a native of that province is therefore called either Sagzí (Sijzí) or Sístání.

[2] So the lithographed edition and the British Museum MSS., but my copy of the Constantinople MS. has "*áwáz-i-rúdí*," "the sounds of the harp."

So that night Farrukhí composed the following *qaṣída*, which is reckoned one of his most successful poems[1] :—

"Since the meadow hides its face in satin shot with greens and blues,
And the mountains wrap their brows in silver veils of seven hues,
Earth is teeming like the musk-pod with aromas rich and rare,
Foliage bright as parrot's plumage doth the graceful willow wear.
Yestere'en the midnight breezes brought the tidings of the spring:
Welcome, O ye northern gales, for this glad promise which ye bring!
Up its sleeve the wind, meseemeth, pounded musk hath stored away,
While the garden fills its lap with shining dolls, as though for play.
On the branches of syringa necklaces of pearls we see,
Ruby ear-rings of Badakhshán sparkle on the Judas-tree.
Since the branches of the rose-bush carmine cups and beakers bore
Human-like five-fingered hands reach downwards from the sycamore.
Gardens all chameleon-coated, branches with chameleon whorls,
Pearly-lustrous pools around us, clouds above us raining pearls!
On the gleaming plain this coat of many colours doth appear
Like a robe of honour granted in the Court of our Amír.
For our Prince's Camp of Branding stirreth in these joyful days,
So that all this age of ours in joyful wonder stands a-gaze.
Green within the green you see, like stars within the firmament;
Like a fort within a fortress spreads the army, tent on tent.
Every tent contains a lover resting in his sweetheart's arms,
Every patch of grass revealeth to a friend a favourite's charms.
Harps are sounding midst the verdure, minstrels sing their lays divine,

[1] I have published both text and translation in my rendering of the *Chahár Maqála*, pp. 61–65, and have there indicated other places where the text is preserved.

Tents resound with clink of glasses as the pages pour the wine.
Kisses, claspings from the lovers; coy reproaches from the fair;
Wine-born slumbers for the sleepers, while the minstrels wake the air.
Branding-fires, like suns ablaze, are kindled at the spacious gate
Leading to the state-pavilion of our Prince so fortunate.
Leap the flames like gleaming lances draped with yellow-lined brocade,
Hotter than a young man's passion, yellower than gold assayed.
Branding-tools like coral branches ruby-tinted glow amain
In the fire, as in the ripe pomegranate glows the crimson grain.
Rank on rank of active boys, whose watchful eyes no slumber know;
Steeds which still await the branding, rank on rank and row on row.
On his horse, the river-forder, roams our genial Prince afar,
Ready to his hand the lassoo, like a young Isfandiyár.
Like the locks of pretty children see it how it curls and bends,
Yet be sure its hold is stronger than the covenant of friends.
Bu'l-Mudhaffar Shah, the Upright, circled by a noble band,
King and conqueror of cities, brave defender of the land.
Serpent-coiled in skilful hands his whirling noose fresh forms doth take,
Like unto the rod of Moses metamorphosed to a snake.
Whosoever hath been captured by that noose and circling line,
On the face and flank and shoulder ever bears the Royal sign.
But, though on one side he brandeth, gives he also rich rewards,
Leads his poets with a bridle, binds his guests as though with cords."

"When 'Amíd As'ad heard this *qaṣída*," continues the author of the *Chahár Maqála*, "he was overwhelmed with amazement, for never had the like of it reached his ears. He put aside all his business, mounted Farrukhí on a horse, and set out for the Amír, whose presence he entered about sundown, saying, 'O Sire, I bring thee a poet the like of whom the eye of Time hath not seen since Daqíqí's face was veiled in death.' Then he related what had passed.

"So the Amír accorded Farrukhí an audience, and he, when he was come in, did reverence, and the Amír gave him his hand, and assigned to him an honourable place, inquiring after his health, treating him with kindness, and inspiring him with hopes of favours to come. When the wine had gone round several times, Farrukhí arose, and, in a sweet and plaintive voice, recited his elegy, beginning :—

'In a caravan for Ḥilla bound from Sístán did I start,
With fabrics spun within my brain and woven in my heart.'

When he had finished, the Amír, himself something of a poet, expressed his astonishment at this *qaṣída*. 'Wait,' said Amír As'ad, 'till you see!' Farrukhí was silent until the wine had produced its full effect on the Amír; then he arose and recited this *qaṣída* on the branding-ground. The Amír was amazed, and in his admiration turned to Farrukhí, saying, 'They have brought in a thousand colts, all with white foreheads, fetlocks, and feet. Thou art a cunning rascal, a Sagzí; catch as many as thou art able, and they shall be thine.' Farrukhí, on whom the wine had produced its full effect, came out, took his turban from his head, hurled himself into the midst of the herd, and chased a drove of them before him across the plain; but, though he caused them to gallop hither and thither, he could not catch a single one. At length a ruined rest-house situated on the edge of the camping-ground came into view, and thither the colts fled. Farrukhí, being tired out, placed his turban under his head in the porch of the rest-house, and at once went to sleep by reason of his extreme weariness, and the effects of the wine. When the colts were counted, they were forty-two in number. The Amír, being informed of this, laughed and said: 'He is a lucky fellow, and will come to great things. Look after him, and look after the colts as well. When he awakes, waken me also.' So they obeyed the Prince's orders.

"Next day, after sunrise, Farrukhí arose. The Amír had already risen, and, when he had performed his prayers, he gave Farrukhí an audience, treated him with great consideration, and handed over the colts to his attendants. He also ordered Farrukhí to be given a horse and equipments suitable to a man of rank, as well as a tent, three camels, five slaves, wearing apparel, and carpets. So Farrukhí prospered in his service, and enjoyed the greatest circumstance, and waited upon Sulṭán Maḥmúd, who, seeing him thus magnificently equipped, regarded him with a like regard, and his affairs reached that pitch of prosperity which they reached, so that twenty servants girt with silver girdles rode behind him."

To the three poets just mentioned, 'Unṣurí, 'Asjadí, and Farrukhí, as they sat conversing together one day in Ghazna, came, according to the popular legend,[1] a stranger from Níshápúr, who made as though to join them. 'Unṣurí, not desiring the intrusion of this provincial, said to him, "O brother, we are the King's poets, and none but poets may enter our company. Each one of us will, therefore, compose a verse in the same rhyme, and if thou canst in thy turn supply the fourth verse of the quartette, then will we admit thee into our society." So Firdawsí (for he it was who was the intruder) consented to the test, and 'Unṣurí, purposely choosing a rhyme wherein three verses might easily, but four, as he imagined, by no means be made, began[2]:—

Firdawsí.

"Thine eyes are clear and blue as sunlit ocean"—

'Asjadí continued:—

"Their glance bewitches like a magic potion"—

Farrukhí proceeded:—

"The wounds they cause no balm can heal, nor lotion"—

And Firdawsí, alluding to a little-known episode in the Legend of the Ancient Kings, concluded:—

"Deadly as those Gív's spear dealt out to Pôshan."

---

[1] As given by Dawlatsháh (p. 51 of my edition), and nearly all later biographers, but neither by the author of the *Chahár Maqála* nor by 'Awfí, the two oldest and most respectable authorities.

[2] To preserve the point of the stratagem, I have had to completely change the verses in English. The reference in the last note will direct the Persian student to the original verses, which may be thus rendered into English:—*'Unṣurí:* "The moon is not so radiant as thy brow." *'Asjadí:* "No garden-rose can match thy cheek, I trow." *Farrukhí:* "Thy lashes through the hardest breastplate pierce." *Firdawsí:* "Like spear of Gív in Púshan's duel fierce."

Being called upon to furnish an explanation of the allusion in this verse, Firdawsí displayed so great a knowledge of the ancient legends of Persia that 'Unṣurí told Sultán Maḥmúd that here at length was one competent to complete the work of versifying the national Epic which had been begun by Daqíqí for one of the Sámánid kings some twenty or thirty years before, but interrupted, when only some thousand [1] verses, dealing with King Gushtásp and the advent of Zoroaster, had been written, by the murder of that talented but ill-starred poet at the hands of one of his Turkish favourites.

Such is the account given by Dawlatsháh and most of the later biographists of Firdawsí's first appearance at the Court of Ghazna; but, as already remarked in a note, no trace of it is to be found in the oldest accounts (dating from the middle of the twelfth and the beginning of the thirteenth centuries respectively) which we possess of the poet's life, and Professor Nöldeke is undoubtedly right in rejecting it as purely fictitious. Here, indeed, we suffer not from the usual dearth of biographical details, but from an embarrassing wealth of circumstantial narratives, of which neither the oldest accounts preserved to us of the poet's life, nor the incidental fragments of autobiography which the *Sháhnáma* itself yields, furnish any corroboration, even when they do not stand in actual contradiction. These later accounts, then, belonging chiefly to the latter part of the fifteenth century of our era, we must here ignore, referring such as are curious as to their contents to Ouseley's *Biographies of the Persian Poets*, Jules Mohl's Introduction to his great edition (accompanied by a French translation) of the *Sháhnáma*, and other books of the kind accessible to non-Orientalists.

By common consent of Easterns and Westerns, Firdawsí is so great a poet that, whatever our personal estimate of his *Sháhnáma* may be, he and his work must necessarily be dis-

[1] 'Awfí (p. 33 of my edition) says 20,000, besides the 60,000 contributed by Firdawsí; but Firdawsí himself (Nöldeke's *Iran. Nationalepos*, p. 19, and notes 1 and 2 *ad calc.*) limits Daqíqí's contribution to 1,000 verses.

cussed at some length ; but, on the other hand, since my aim in this volume is, so far as possible, to furnish the European reader with such particulars about the literary history of Persia as he cannot easily find in European books, I shall endeavour to be as brief as seems permissible. The chief primary sources of trustworthy information at our disposal are, *first*, the poet's own works—to wit, the *Sháhnáma*, the later *Yúsuf and Zulaykhá*, and a certain number of short lyric poems, carefully collected, translated, and studied by Dr. Ethé in his excellent monographs[1] ; *secondly*, the account given by Nidhámí-i-'Arúḍí-i-Samarqandí, who visited Firdawsí's grave at Ṭús in A.D. 1116–1117, only about a century after the poet's death, and embodied the traditions which he there collected in his delightful and oft-cited *Chahár Maqála* (Anecdote xx, pp. 77–84 of my translation)[2] ; and *thirdly*, the brief and jejune account given by 'Awfí in Part ii of his *Lubábu'l-Albáb* (pp. 32–33 of my edition). Amongst European scholars (since the time when Turner Macan, Jules Mohl, and Rückert made the *Sháhnáma* generally known in Europe by their editions and translations), by far the most important critical studies on Firdawsí are those of Ethé mentioned in the last note but two, and Nöldeke's masterly article in the *Grundriss d. Iran. Philologie*, entitled *Das Iranische Nationalepos*, cited here accord-

[1] *Firdûsî als Lyriker* in the *Münch. Sitzungsberichte* for 1872 (pp. 275–304) and 1873 (pp. 623–653), and *Firdausî's Yûsuf und Zalîkhâ* in the Acts of the Seventh International Congress of Orientalists (Vienna, 1889), Semitic Section, pp. 20–45. Also Nöldeke's remarks thereon in his *Persische Studien II*, in vol. cxxvi of the *Wiener Sitzungsberichte*. A list of the English writers who have made use of his materials for magazine articles and other popular purposes is given by Dr. Ethé in his excellent article (in vol. ii of the *Grundriss d. Iran. Philologie*, p. 231) entitled *Neupersische Litteratur*.

[2] This anecdote is quoted in full by Ibn Isfandiyár in his *History of Ṭabaristán*, and was first extracted by Ethé (who at that time had not access to the *Chahár Maqála* itself, either in the lithographed edition or in the British Museum MSS.) from that work. His text, originally copied for Professor Nöldeke's use, was based on three MSS., and was published in vol. xlviii of the *Z.D.M.G.*, pp. 89 *et seqq.*

ing to the paging of the separate reprint (Trübner, 1896). To the last-named scholar in particular we owe a careful and critical statement of what may be regarded as certain and what as probable in the life of Firdawsí, derived mainly from the best possible source, to wit, Firdawsí's own statements scattered here and there through his interminable *Sháhnáma*.

Let us first dispose of the very meagre account of Firdawsí given by 'Awfí (*Lubáb*, Part ii, pp. 32–33 of my edition), and of another short account given by the historian Ḥamdu'lláh Mustawfí of Qazwín in his "Select History" (*Táríkh-i-Guzída*) composed in A.D. 1330, before the growth of the legends to which we have referred above. According to the latter authority, Firdawsí's real name (for Firdawsí, of course, was only his *nom de guerre*), which is very variously given, was Abu'l-Qásim (this much is certain) Ḥasan b. 'Alí of Ṭús, and he died in A.H. 416 (A.D. 1025–26). The *Lubáb*, as usual, gives us little beyond extravagant praises, save that its author insists very strongly on the wonderful uniformity of style, diction, and sentiment maintained throughout so vast a work on which the poet was engaged for so many years, and notices with approval an anthology culled from it by the early poet Mas'úd b. Sa'd (flourished about A.D. 1080), which shows how rapidly the *Sháhnáma* grew in popular favour.

Accounts of *Lubáb* and *Guzída*.

According to the *Chahár Maqála* (the most ancient and important of our extraneous sources of information) Firdawsí was a *dihqán*, or small squire, of a village called Bázh,[1] in the Ṭabarán district of Ṭús, the famous city of Khurásán, which occupied the site of the present Mashhad. He was independent, living on the rents derived from his lands, and had an only daughter. To provide for her an adequate dowry was, says our author, Firdawsí's sole object in composing his great poem, and seeking some wealthy patron who would bestow on him an adequate reward for his

Account of *Chahár Maqála*.

[1] Ibn Isfandiyár, in quoting this passage, omits the name of the village.

toil. When he had completed it (after thirty-five, or, according to other authorities, twenty-five years of labour), probably, as Nöldeke (*op. cit.*, p. 22) observes, in the beginning of the year A.D. 999, it was transcribed by 'Alí Daylam and recited by Abú Dulaf, both of whom, together with the Governor of Ṭús, Ḥusayn b. Qutayba, from whom Firdawsí had received substantial help and encouragement, are mentioned in the following passage of the *Sháhnáma*:—

"Of the notables of the city in this book 'Alí Daylam and Abú Dulaf have a share.
From these my portion was naught save 'Well done!' My gall-bladder was like to burst with their 'Well done's.'[1]
Ḥusayn[2] b. Qutayba is one of the nobles who seeks not from me gratuitous verse:
I know naught of the ground-tax, root or branch; I lounge [at ease] in the midst of my quilt."

In explanation of the last line, our author tells us that the above-mentioned Ḥusayn b. Qutayba, who was the revenue collector of Ṭús, took upon himself to remit Firdawsí's taxes; "whence naturally," he adds, "his name will endure till the Resurrection, and Kings will read it."

The *Sháhnáma* having been transcribed in seven volumes by the above-mentioned 'Alí Daylam, Firdawsí set out with it for Ghazna, taking with him his *ráwí*, or "repeater," Abú Dulaf.

[1] The meaning, and, indeed, the true reading of this verse is uncertain, and I am now inclined to prefer Ibn Isfandiyár's reading *az bakhtashán* for *aḥsantashán* in the first half verse, though I am more doubtful as to the propriety of reading, as he does, *iḥsánashán* for *aḥsantashán* in the second. If we adopt both these modifications in the text given at p. 79 of my translation of the *Chahár Maqála*, the meaning will be: "My share [of good fortune] came not to me save from their good fortune; my gall-bladder came near to bursting [*i.e.*, my heart was moved within me] in consequence of their benevolence." This emendation gets over the difficulty alluded to in n. 4 of my translation above mentioned.

[2] *Ḥa'iy* or *Ḥuyayy* is the reading of the two British Museum MSS. of the *Chahár Maqála*, but Ibn Isfandiyár's reading *Ḥusayn* is, in all probability, correct.

He succeeded in interesting the Prime Minister, Abu'l-Qásim Aḥmad b. al-Ḥasan al-Maymandí,[1] in his work, which was, by his instrumentality, brought to the notice of Sulṭán Maḥmúd, who expressed himself as greatly pleased with it. "But the Minister had enemies," continues our author, "who were continually casting the dust of perturbation into the cup of his position, and Maḥmúd consulted with them as to what he should give Firdawsí. They replied, 'Fifty thousand *dirhams*, and even that is too much, seeing that he is in belief a Ráfiḍí (*i.e.*, a Shí'ite) and a Mu'tazilí.' Of his Mu'tazilí views they adduced this verse as a proof:—

'Thy gaze the Creator can never descry;[2]
Then wherefore by gazing dost weary thine eye?'

While to his Ráfiḍí (Shí'ite) proclivities these verses bear witness." (Here the author cites seven couplets in praise of Alí, of which both text and translation will be found on pp. 80–81 of my translation of the *Chahár Maqála*.)

Now if the above account be true (and there seems no reason for doubting its substantial correctness), we are greatly tempted to connect Firdawsí's disappointment with the disgrace and imprisonment of his patron, al-Maymandí, which, as Ibnu'l-Athír informs us (under the year A.H. 421 = A.D. 1030, when the Minister was released and reinstated by Maḥmúd's son and successor, Mas'úd), took place in A.H. 412 (= A.D. 1021–1022). But the objections to this supposition are, I fear, insuperable, for Nöldeke (*op. cit.*, pp. 22–23) shows that Firdawsí was probably born in A.H. 323 or 324 (= A.D. 935–6), and that he

[1] The *Chahár Maqála* has: "the great Minister Aḥmad-i-Ḥasan, the secretary," by which, no doubt, al-Maymandí is meant. Ibn Isfandiyár, however, has "Ḥusayn b. Aḥmad."

[2] The question of "the Vision of God" (*rúyatu'lláh*) has given rise to fierce controversies in Islám. The anthropomorphic Ḥanbalís represent one extreme, the Mu'tazilís the other.

finished the final edition of the *Sháhnáma*[1] in A.H. 400 (= A.D. 1010), being at that time about eighty years of age, and it is about this time that the question of his recompense must have arisen.

"Now Sulṭan Maḥmúd," continues the author of the *Chahár Maqála*, "was a zealot, and he listened to these imputations and caught hold of them, and, to be brief, only twenty thousand[2] *dirhams* were paid to Ḥakím Firdawsí. He was bitterly disappointed, went to the bath, and, on coming out, bought a drink of sherbet,[3] and divided the money between the bath-man and the sherbet-seller. Knowing, however, Maḥmúd's severity, he fled from Ghazna by night, and alighted in Herát at the shop of Azraqí's[4] father, Isma'íl the bookseller (*warráq*), where he remained in hiding for six months, until Maḥmúd's messengers had visited Ṭús and had turned back thence, when Firdawsí, feeling secure, set out from Herát for Ṭús, taking the *Sháhnáma* with him. Thence he came to Ṭabaristán to the Ispahbad Shahriyár b. Shírwín[5] of the House of Báwand, who was King there; and this is a noble House which traces its descent from Yazdigird, the son of Shahriyár.[6]

"Then Firdawsí wrote a satire on Sulṭán Maḥmúd in the Preface, from which he read a hundred couplets to Shír-zád, saying, 'I will dedicate this *Sháhnáma* to thee instead of to Sulṭán Maḥmúd, since this book deals wholly with the legends and deeds of thy forbears.' The Ispahbad treated him with honour and showed him many kindnesses, and said: 'Maḥmúd had no right knowledge of this matter,

---

[1] Nöldeke clearly shows that Firdawsí completed the *Sháhnáma* long before he dedicated it to Sulṭán Maḥmúd, since there exists another dedication to one Aḥmad b. Muḥammad b. Abí Bakr of Khálanján, which was written in A.H. 389 = A.D. 999.

[2] So the two British Museum MSS. and Ibn Isfandiyár, but the lithographed edition has "sixty thousand." In all forms of the story the point lies in the substitution of silver coins (*dirhams*) for gold coins (*dínárs*).

[3] *Fuqá'*, described as a kind of beer.

[4] A well-known poet of whom we shall shortly have to speak.

[5] So Ibn Isfandiyár, but the MSS. of the *Chahár Maqála* substitute the name of *Shír-zád*.

[6] The last Sásánian King, in whose days Persia was conquered by the Arabs. For the words which here follow "Báwand," Ibn Isfandiyár substitutes: "Who was the maternal uncle of Shamsu'l-Ma'álí Qábús [ibn Washmgír], and whose dominion and greatness are recorded in 'Utbí's *Kitáb-i-Yamíní*."

but was induced to act as he did by others, who did not submit your book to him under proper conditions, and who misrepresented you. Moreover you are a Shí'ite, and naught will befall him who loves the Family of the Prophet which did not befall them.[1] Maḥmúd is my liege lord: let the *Sháhnáma* stand in his name, and give me the satire which you have written on him, that I may expunge it, and bestow on thee some little recompense; and Maḥmúd will surely summon thee and seek to satisfy thee fully. Do not, then, throw away the labour spent on such a book.'[2] And next day he sent Firdawsí 100,000 *dirhams*, saying: 'I will buy each couplet of the satire on the Sulṭán at a thousand *dirhams*; give me those hundred couplets and rest satisfied therewith.'[3] So Firdawsí sent him those verses and he ordered them to be expunged; and Firdawsí also destroyed his rough copy of them, so that this satire was done away with, and only these few[4] verses are preserved:

'They said: "This bard of over-fluent song
Hath loved the Prophet and 'Alí for long."[5]
Yea, when I sing my love for them, I could
Protect from harm a thousand like Maḥmúd.
But can we hope for any noble thing
From a slave's son, e'en were his sire a King?

---

[1] For the last part of this sentence Ibn Isfandiyár substitutes: "And such an one hath never prospered in worldly things, even as they never prospered." The allusion in either case is to the calamities which overtook 'Alí, al-Ḥasan, al-Ḥusayn, and nearly all the Imáms of the Shí'ites.

[2] Ibn Isfandiyár substitutes: "For such a book as this will never be lost."

[3] Ibn Isfandiyár adds: "And reconcile thine heart to the Sulṭán." As Nöldeke points out, the number of verses contained in the satire is 101 in Macan's edition, but varies greatly in different MSS., rising as high as 160, and falling as low as 30.

[4] Ibn Isfandiyár has "two," and accordingly omits the first three of the five given in the *Chahár Maqála*. It is difficult to reconcile the statement as to the ultimate fate of the satire made by this oldest authority with the fact that the text of it, which bears every mark of genuineness, exists. Cf. Nöldeke, *op. cit.*, p. 27.

[5] That is, hath loved these only to the exclusion of Abu Bakr, 'Umar, and 'Uthmán, the first three of the four orthodox Caliphs, according to the Ṣunnís. Firdawsí means to say that the only charge brought against him by his enemies, *viz.*, that he was a Shí'ite, in effect amounted only to this, that he entertained an exaggerated love for the House of the Prophet.

For had this King aught of nobility
High-throned in honour should I seated be.
But since his sires were not of gentle birth
He hates to hear me praising names of worth.'

"In truth the Ispahbad rendered a great service to Maḥmúd, who was thereby placed deeply in his debt.

"In the year A.H. 514" (A.D. 1120–21), continues Nidhámí of Samarqand, "when I was in Níshápúr, I heard the Amír Mu'izzí[1] say that he had heard the Amír 'Abdu'r-Razzáq of Ṭús relate as follows: 'Maḥmúd was once in India, returning thence towards Ghazna. It chanced that on his way was a rebellious chief possessed of a strong fortress, and next day Maḥmúd encamped at its gates, and despatched an ambassador to him, bidding him come before him on the morrow to do homage and pay his respects at the Court, when he should receive a robe of honour and return to his place. Next day Maḥmúd rode out with the Prime Minister[2] on his right hand, for the ambassador had turned back and was coming to meet the King. "I wonder," said the latter to the Minister, "what reply he will have given?" The Minister answered:

"'And should the reply with my wish not accord,
Then Afrásiyáb's field, and the mace, and the sword!'"

"'Whose verse,' inquired Maḥmúd, 'is that? For he must have the heart of a man.'[3] 'Poor Abu'l-Qásim Firdawsí composed it,' answered the Minister; 'he who for five-and-twenty years laboured to complete such a work, and reaped from it no advantage.' 'You speak well,' said Maḥmúd; 'I deeply regret that this noble man was disappointed by me. Remind me at Ghazna to send him something.'

"So when the Sulṭán returned to Ghazna, the Minister reminded him; and Maḥmúd ordered that sixty thousand *dinárs'* worth[4] of

---

[1] The celebrated poet-laureate of Malikshâh and Sanjar, the Seljúqids. He was accidentally killed by a stray arrow from his royal patron's bow in A.D. 1147–48.

[2] Dawlatsháh identifies this Minister with al-Maymandí, which is possible, since, as we have seen (p. 134 *supra*) he was disgraced and imprisoned in A.D. 1021–22, and Firdawsí died between this date and A.D. 1025–26.

[3] Ibn Isfandiyár has: "for valour and swords rain down from it."

[4] Ibn Isfandiyár has *dirhams* for *dinárs*, and continues: "and when the *dirhams* were collected he despatched them with camels to the city of Ṭús."

indigo should be given to Firdawsí, and that this indigo should be carried to Ṭús on the King's own camels, and that apologies should be tendered to Firdawsí. For years the Minister had been working for this, and at length he had achieved his work; so now he caused the camels to be loaded, and the indigo safely reached Ṭábarán.[1] But even as the camels entered the Rúdbár Gate, the corpse of Firdawsí was borne forth from the Gate of Razán.[2] Now at that time there was in Ṭábarán a preacher, whose fanaticism was such that he declared that he would not suffer Firdawsí's body to be buried in the Musulmán Cemetery because he was a Ráfiḍí; and nothing that men could say would serve to move him. Now outside the gate there was a garden belonging to Firdawsí,[3] and there they buried him, and there he lies to this day. And I visited his tomb in the year A.H. 510 (A.D. 1116–17).

"They say that Firdawsí left a very high-spirited[5] daughter, to whom they would have given the King's gift; but she would not accept it, declaring that she needed it not. The Postmaster wrote[6] to the Court and represented this to the King, who ordered this doctor[7] to be expelled from Ṭábarán as a punishment for his officiousness, and to be exiled from his home; and that the money

---

[1] Ṭábarán is the name of a portion of the city of Ṭús. See B. de Meynard's *Dict. de la Perse*, pp. 374–375.

[2] Nöldeke (*op. cit.*, p. 28 and n. 2, and p. 14 at end), following Ibn Isfandiyár, has *Razzáq* for *Razán*, but the lithographed edition of the *Chahár Maqála* and all three MSS. (the two London and the Constantinople codices) agree in the latter reading. A *Razán* in Sístán is mentioned by al-Baládhurí (pp. 396–7), and there is a *Radhán* (Razán) near Nasá in Khurásán (*Dict. de la Perse*, p. 259).

[3] Ibn Isfandiyár has: "called Bágh-i-Firdaws ('the Garden of Paradise'), which was his (*i.e.*, Firdawsí's) property."

[4] Dawlatsháh says that the tomb was still known in his time (A.D. 1487) and was still visited by the poet's admirers. He describes it as situated in Ṭús, beside the 'Abbásiyya Mausoleum.

[5] Ibn Isfandiyár has: "very virtuous and noble."

[6] Ibn Isfandiyár has *paywast* ('went,' 'joined himself') for *navisht* ('wrote'). To keep the King fully informed of all matters within his cognisance, including the doings of the Governor of the Province, was (as is fully set forth in the *Siyásat-náma* of the Nidhámu'l-Mulk) one of the chief duties of the Postmaster or *Ṣáḥibu'l-Baríd*.

[7] *I.e.*, the fanatical preacher mentioned above. In Dawlatsháh and other later accounts this doctor is identified with Shaykh Abu'l-Qásim al-Jurjání, who, it is said, refused to read the Burial Service over one who had devoted his life to praising Zoroastrian heroes. But that night (so runs the story) he saw in a dream Firdawsí highly exalted in Paradise,

should be given to the Imám Abú Bakr [ibn] Isḥáq for the repair of the rest-house of Cháha,[1] which stands on the road between Merv and Níshápúr at the confines of Ṭús. When this order reached Ṭús and Níshápúr, it was faithfully executed; and the restoration of the rest-house of Cháha was effected with this money."

Dawlatsháh's account.

Such, then, is the oldest and most authentic account of Firdawsí which we possess; and we may be quite sure that, even though it be not correct in all particulars, it represents what was known and believed by educated men in the poet's own town a century after his death. Its importance is therefore great, and justifies its introduction in this place. Dawlatsháh certainly made use of this account (for he mentions the *Chahár Maqála* as one of his sources) in compiling his own, which is embroidered with many additional and probably fictitious details. Amongst other things he states that the poet's name was Ḥasan b. Isḥáq b. Sharafsháh, and that in some of his verses he styles himself "son of Sharafsháh";[2] that he was from the village of Razán,[3] near Ṭús, and that he took his pen-name from a garden in that district called Firdaws (Paradise), belonging to the 'Amíd of Khurásán, Súrí b. Mughíra, whose servant his father was. He is further represented as a poor man, fleeing from the oppression of the Governor of his native place to Ghazna, and there supporting himself by the precarious crafts of the ballad-monger, until he was able, in the manner mentioned at the beginning

and asked him how he had attained to so high an estate; to which the poet's shade replied that it was on account of this one verse wherein he had celebrated the Divine Unity: "*In the world Thou art all, both above and below; Thine Essence I know not, Thy Being I know.*"

[1] So one MS. and the edition of the *Chahár Maqála*. The other London MS. has *Jáha*, and the Constantinople codex *Jáma*, while Ibn Isfandiyár has *ribáṭ u cháh*, *i.e.*, "the rest-house and well." Dawlatsháh calls it *Ribáṭ-i-'Ishq*, and describes it as by the defile of Shiqqán, on the road between Khurásán and Astarábád.

[2] Cf. Nöldeke, *op. cit.*, p. 22, n. 2, where it is stated that, according to Baysunghur's Preface, the poet's father was called Fakhru'd-Dín Aḥmad b. Farrukh al-Firdawsí.

[3] See n. 2 on the preceding page.

of our notice, to make himself acquainted with 'Unṣurí, who presents him to the Sulṭán, and appears throughout, like the Wazír al-Maymandí, as his patron and protector. The verse—

> "When the lips of the babe are first dried from their food
> They lisp in the cradle the name of Maḥmúd"—

is said to have definitely gained Firdawsí the favour of the Sulṭán, who is represented as lodging him in apartments in the palace and assigning him a regular salary. The King's favourite Ayáz, whom Firdawsí is said in this narrative (for in others[1] these two are represented as firm friends) to have annoyed by his neglect, is represented as poisoning Maḥmúd's mind against him by accusations of heresy, with which he openly charged the poet, saying, "All the great heresiarchs of this (*i.e.*, the Carmathian or Isma'ílí) sect have come from Ṭús; but I forgive you on condition that you renounce this doctrine." The poet is further represented as hiding in Ghazna for several months after his disappointment in order to get back into his hands from the King's librarian the manuscript of his *Sháhnáma*, and the name of the bookseller with whom he afterwards took refuge at Herát is changed from Isma'íl to Abu'l-Ma'álí. Other details and variations of a similar character mark the remainder of Dawlatsháh's narrative, which, however, on the whole follows that already given.

Internal evidence.

The internal evidence afforded by Firdawsí's own works is, of course, so far as the text of them (which is in many places very uncertain and unsatisfactory) can be trusted, the most authoritative source of information concerning his life. This, as already observed, has been exhaustively examined, with admirable patience and acumen, by Professor Nöldeke and Dr. Ethé. It is impossible for me in the scanty space at my disposal to recapitulate here all their conclusions, neither is it necessary, since every serious student of the *Sháhnáma* must needs read the *Iranisches*

[1] Nöldeke, *op. cit.*, p. 26, n. 2.

Nationalepos of the former scholar, and the already-mentioned articles on this subject published by the latter, together with his edition of Firdawsí's *Yúsuf and Zulaykhá*, and the chapters germane to this topic contained in his *Neupersische Litteratur* in vol. ii of the *Grundriss der Iranischen Philologie.* Briefly, however, we appear to be justified in assuming that Firdawsí was a *dihqán* or squire of Ṭús, of respectable position and comfortable means; that he was born about A.D. 920, or a little later; that a taste for antiquarian research and folk-lore, fostered by the perusal of the prose "Book of Kings" compiled in Persian from older sources by Abú Manṣúr al-Ma'marí for Abú Manṣur b. 'Abdu'r-Razzáq, the then Governor of Ṭús, in A.D. 957–8,[1] led him, about A.D. 974, definitely to undertake the versification of the National Epic; that he completed what we may call "the first edition" in A.D. 999, after twenty-five years' labour, and dedicated it to Aḥmad b. Muḥammad b. Abí Bakr of Khálanján; that the "second edition," dedicated to Sulṭán Maḥmúd, was completed in or shortly before A.D. 1010; that his quarrel with the Sulṭán and flight from Ghazna almost immediately succeeded this; and that, having lived for a short time under the protection of one of the Princes of the House of Buwayh (Bahá'u'd-Dawla or his son Sulṭánu'd-Dawla, who succeeded him in A.D. 1012, as Nöldeke thinks; Majdu'd-Dawla Abú Ṭálib Rustam, as Ethé seems to believe), for whom he composed his other great poem, the *Yúsuf and Zulaykhá*, he returned, an old man of ninety or more, to his native town of Ṭús, and there died about A.D. 1020 or 1025.

Firdawsí's work: (1) the *Sháhnáma.*

We must now pass to the brief consideration of Firdawsí's work, which, so far as it is preserved to us, consists of (1) the *Sháhnáma*; (2) the romance of *Yúsuf and Zulaykha*; and (3) a considerable number of lyrical fragments, preserved by various biographers and anthology-makers, and diligently collected, edited, and translated by Dr. Ethé in his articles *Firdausí als Lyriker* already mentioned.

[1] See Nöldeke, *op. cit.*, p. 14, and notes.

It is on the *Sháhnáma*, of course, that Firdawsí's great reputation as a poet rests. In their high estimate of the literary value of this gigantic poem Eastern and Western critics are almost unanimous, and I therefore feel great diffidence in confessing that I have never been able entirely to share this enthusiasm. The *Sháhnáma* cannot, in my opinion, for one moment be placed on the same level as the Arabian *Mu'allaqát;* and though it is the prototype and model of all epic poetry in the lands of Islám, it cannot, as I think, compare for beauty, feeling, and grace with the work of the best didactic, romantic, and lyric poetry of the Persians. It is, of course, almost impossible to argue about matters of taste, especially in literature; and my failure to appreciate the *Sháhnáma* very likely arises partly from a constitutional disability to appreciate epic poetry in general. With such disabilities we are all familiar, most notably in the case of music, where a Wagner will entrance some, while leaving others indifferent or even uncomfortable. Yet, allowing for this, I cannot help feeling that the *Sháhnáma* has certain definite and positive defects. Its inordinate length is, of course, necessitated by the scope of its subject, which is nothing less than the legendary history of Persia from the beginning of time until the Arab Conquest in the seventh century of our era; and the monotony of its metre it shares with most, if not all, other epics. But the similes employed are also, as it seems to me, unnecessarily monotonous: every hero appears as "a fierce, war-seeking lion," a "crocodile," "a raging elephant," and the like; and when he moves swiftly, he moves "like smoke," "like dust," or "like the wind." The beauty of form in any literary work is necessarily lost in translation, though it may be to some extent replaced or imitated in a clever rendering; but beauty and boldness of ideas there should be less difficulty in preserving, so that, for instance, the beauty of 'Umar Khayyám's quatrains may be said to have been wholly rendered by the genius of FitzGerald. But the *Sháhnáma*, as it seems to me, defies satisfactory translation, for the sonorous majesty of the original (and this at least no one who has heard it declaimed by the professional rhapsodists of Persia, known as *Sháhnáma-khwáns*, will deny) is lost, and the nakedness of the underlying ideas stands revealed. I do not profess to be a skilful versifier, but at least many Persian and Arabic poets have suffered equally at my hands in these pages; and I venture to think that few English readers of this book and its *Prolegomena* (which contained numerous translations from the *Sháhnáma* experimentally rendered in various different ways) will put my renderings of the *Sháhnáma* even on a level with my renderings from other poets, though the coefficient of loss is in all cases about the same.

If there be any truth in these views (quite heretical, as I freely allow), to what does the *Sháhnáma* owe its great and, indeed, unrivalled popularity, not only in Persia, but wherever the Persian language is cultivated? So far as Persia is concerned, national pride in such a monument to the national greatness—a greatness dating from a remote antiquity, though now, alas! long on the decline—has certainly always been a most potent factor. The Persian estimate, however formed, has naturally passed on to all students of Persian in other lands, whether in Asia or Europe, and was adopted as an article of faith by the early European Orientalists. In the case of later and more critical European scholars other factors have come into play, such as the undoubted philological interest of a book comparatively so ancient and so notoriously sparing in the use of Arabic words; the Classical or Hellenistic sentiment, which tends to exalt the genius of Aryan at the expense of Semitic peoples; and the importance of the contents of the book from the point of view of Mythology and Folk-lore. Yet, when all is said, the fact remains that amongst his own countrymen (whose verdict in this matter is unquestionably the most weighty) Firdawsí has, on the strength of his *Sháhnáma* alone

Causes to which the *Sháhnáma* owes its popularity.

(for his other poems are little known and still less read), enjoyed from the first till this present day an unchanging and unrivalled popularity against which I would not presume to set my own personal judgment; though I would remind European scholars that, if we are to take the verdict of a poet's countrymen as final, the Arabic poet al-Mutanabbí, Firdawsí's earlier contemporary (born A.D. 905, killed A.D. 965), who has been very severely handled by some of them, has on this ground a claim almost equally strong on our consideration.

In the previous volume, or *Prolegomena*, of this work I gave translations of a good many passages of the *Sháhnáma* connected with the Legend of Ardashír,[1] showing how closely Firdawsí followed his sources, wherever these have been preserved to us; and I discussed at considerable length the scope and character of the Persian epic and the *Sháhnáma* (pp. 110–123). To these matters I have not space to recur here, and I will give but one more specimen in translation, namely, the opening lines of the celebrated Episode of Rustam and Suhráb (rendered familiar to English readers by Matthew Arnold's paraphrase), which is generally reckoned one of the finest passages in the *Sháhnáma*. The original text will be found at pp. 315–316 of the first volume of Turner Macan's edition, and in my rendering I have departed from the plan adopted in the *Prolegomena* of making alliterative blank verse the medium of my translation, and have endeavoured to imitate as closely as possible the rhyme and metre (*mutaqárib*) of the original.

"The story of Suhráb and Rustam now hear:
Other tales thou hast heard: to this also give ear.
A story it is to bring tears to the eyes,
And wrath in the heart against Rustam will rise.
If forth from its ambush should rush the fierce blast
And down in the dust the young orange should cast,

---

[1] Pp. 140–142, 144–145, and 147–150.

Then call we it just, or unkind and unfair,
And say we that virtue or rudeness is there?
What, then, is injustice, if justice be death?
In weeping and wailing why waste we our breath?
Naught knoweth thy soul of this mystery pale;
No path shall conduct thee beyond the dark veil.
All follow their ways to this hungering door,
A door which, once shut, shall release them no more!
Yet perhaps thou shalt win, when from hence thou shalt roam
In that other abode to a happier home.
If Death's clutch did not daily fresh victims enfold
Our earth would be choked with the young and the old.
Is it strange if the flame of the ravenous fire,
Once kindled, should lead to a holocaust dire?
Nay, its burning outbursteth, once grant it a hold,
As tender twigs spring from some root strong but old.
Death's breath doth resemble such pitiless fire,
Consuming alike both the son and the sire.
E'en the young in the joy of their living must pause,
For, apart from old age, Death has many a cause.
Should Death bid thee fare to thy long home with speed,
And constrain thee to mount on pale Destiny's steed,
Think not that for Justice Injustice is sent,
And if Justice, then wherefore bewail and lament?
In Destiny's sight Youth and Age are as one;
Thus know, if ye want not Religion undone.
If thy heart is fulfilled with Faith's light, then I trow
That silence is best, for God's servant art thou.
Be thy business to supplicate, worship, obey,
And order thine acts for the Last Judgement Day.
In thy heart and thy soul hath the demon no lot,
Then to fathom this secret of God's seek thou not.
Seek now in this world of religion a share;
That alone will support thee when hence thou shalt fare.
Now hearken: the story of Suhráb I'll tell,
And the strife which 'twixt him and his father befell."

It is sometimes asserted that the *Sháhnáma* contains practically no Arabic words. This is incorrect: Firdawsí avoided their use as far as possible in his Epic, because he felt them to be unsuitable to the subject of his poem, but even in his time many Arabic words had become so firmly established in the language that it was impossible to avoid their use. The twenty-one verses translated above comprise about 250 words, of which nine (*'ajab*, *tarab*, *sabab*, *qaḍá*, *ajal*, *khalal*, *núr*, *ímán*, and *Islám*) are pure Arabic, and one (*hawl-nák*) half Arabic; and this is about the usual proportion, namely, 4 or 5 per cent.

Passing now to Firdawsí's remaining poetical works, we come next to his *mathnawí* on the romance of *Yúsuf and Zulaykhá* (Joseph and Potiphar's wife). This legend, greatly expanded and idealised from its original basis, has always been a favourite subject with the romantic poets of Persia and Turkey, nor was Firdawsí (as Dr. Ethé has pointed out) the first Persian poet to handle it, Abu'l-Mu'ayyad of Balkh and Bakhtiyárí of Ahwáz having both, according to one manuscript authority, already made it the subject of a poem. These two earlier versions are otherwise quite unknown to us, while our knowledge of Firdawsí's version, which has luckily survived the vicissitudes of time, is largely due to Dr. Ethé's indefatigable industry. Though the book is but rarely met with in the East, a sufficient number of manuscripts (seven at least) exist in the great public libraries of England and France, one unknown to Dr. Ethé having been discovered by Dr. E. Denison Ross amongst Sir William Jones's manuscripts preserved in the India Office. The poem has been thrice lithographed in India and once in Persia, and we now have Dr. Ethé's critical edition, as well as the German metrical translation of Schlechta-Wssehrd (Vienna, 1889). Dr. Ethé, who is our chief authority on this poem, which he has made peculiarly his own, and which he has carefully compared with the much later versions of Jámí (A.D. 1483) and Nádhim of Herát (whereof the former is by far the most celebrated rendering of the Romance), thinks highly of its merit, which has generally been depreciated by Persian critics, who consider that Firdawsí wrote it when he was past his prime, and, moreover, somewhat broken by his disappointment about the

Firdawsí's *Yúsuf and Zulaykhá.*

Sháhnáma, and that the epic style and metre so successfully employed in the last-named poem were but little suited for romantic verse.

Firdawsí's lyric poems.

The value of Firdawsí's lyric poetry, to judge by the specimens preserved to us in anthologies and biographies, appears to me to have been generally underrated. To Dr. Ethé's excellent treatises on this topic I have already alluded in a note (p. 131, n. 1 *supra*). Here I must content myself with two specimens, the first taken from the *Táríkh-i-Guzída*,[1] the second from 'Awfí's *Lubáb*[2]:—

"Were it mine to repose for one night on thy bosom,
My head, thus exalted, would reach to the skies;
In Mercury's fingers the pen I would shatter;
The crown of the Sun I would grasp as my prize.
O'er the ninth sphere of heaven my soul would be flying
And Saturn's proud head 'neath my feet would be lying,
Yet I'd pity poor lovers sore wounded and dying,
Were thy beauty mine own, or thy lips, or thine eyes."

Here is a rendering of the lines cited by 'Awfí:—

"Much toil did I suffer, much writing I pondered,
Books writ in Arabian and Persian of old;
For sixty-two years many arts did I study:
What gain do they bring me in glory or gold?
Save regret for the past and remorse for its failings
Of the days of my youth every token hath fled,
And I mourn for it now, with sore weepings and wailings,
In the words Khusrawání Bú Ṭáhir[3] hath said:

---

[1] The text will be found at p. 49 of the *tirage-à-part* of my article on *Biographies of Persian Poets*, published in the *J.R.A.S.* for October, 1900, and January, 1901.

[2] For the text, see vol. ii, p. 33, of my edition of this work.

[3] Abú Ṭáhir aṭ-Ṭayyib (or *aṭ-Ṭabíb*, "the physician") b. Muḥammad al-Khusrawání was one of the Sámánid poets. He is mentioned by 'Awfí (vol. ii, p. 20 of my edition). Firdawsí here introduces his verse as a *taḍmín*, concerning which figure see pp. 45 and 68 *supra*.

'My youth as a vision of childhood in sooth
I remember : alas and alas for my youth !'"

Asadi the elder.

The next poet claiming our attention is the elder Asadí, Abú Naṣr Aḥmed b. Manṣúr of Ṭús, not to be confounded with his son 'Alí b. Aḥmed al-Asadí, the author of the *Garshásp-náma* and of the oldest extant Persian Lexicon, in whose handwriting is the most ancient Persian manuscript known to exist, transcribed in A.D. 1055–56, now preserved at Vienna, and published by Seligmann. Perhaps, indeed, he should have been placed before Firdawsí, who is said to have been his pupil as well as his friend and fellow-townsman; but I am not concerned within each period to follow a strictly chronological order, and, even if I were, the date of Asadí's death, which was subsequent to Firdawsí's, would justify this order, since, though in this particular case we have reason to believe that Asadí was the older of the two poets, the obituary dates, as a rule, are alone recorded by Muslim biographers.

Dawlatsháh's fictions.

Our knowledge of Asadí's life is meagre in the extreme. 'Awfí and the *Chahár Maqála* ignore him entirely, and his name is merely mentioned (and that in connection with the *Garshasp-náma*, which was the younger Asadí's work) in the *Ta'ríkh-i-Guzída*. Dawlatsháh, as usual, gives plenty of detail; but as it is, so far as I know, unsupported by any respectable authority of earlier times, it must be regarded as worthless. He pretends, for instance, that Asadí was pressed to undertake the composition of the *Sháhnáma*, but excused himself on the ground of his age, and passed on the task to his pupil Firdawsí; but that when the latter lay dying at Ṭús, with the last four thousand couplets of the Epic still unwritten, Asadí finished it for him in a day and a night, and was able to console the dying poet by reading to him on the following day the completion of the poem. These verses are even specified by Dawlatsháh, who says that they extend from the first invasion of Persia by the Arabs to the end of the book, and that "men of letters are of opinion that it is possible to detect by close attention where the verse of Firdawsí ends and that of Asadí begins." One of the Cambridge MSS. of Dawlatsháh (Add. 831) has the following marginal comment on this baseless fiction: "Firdawsí, as will be subsequently mentioned in the notice of his life, himself completed the *Sháhnáma*, whence it is evident that no other person collaborated with him in its versification. For after he had completed it he succeeded, by a stratagem, in recovering possession of it from the King's librarian, and inserted in it the verses of the celebrated satire. What is here stated is plainly incompatible with this." To this sensible comment another hand has added the words *Níkú guftí!* ("Thou sayest well!").

Asadí's chief claim to distinction rests on the fact that he developed and perfected, if he did not invent, the species of poem entitled *munáḏhara*, or "strife-poem;" and Dr. Ethé, who has gone deeply into this matter, has embodied the results of his erudition and industry in an admirable monograph published in the Acts of the Fifth International Congress of Orientalists, held at Berlin in 1882, and entitled *Über persische Tenzonen*. Asadí is known to have composed five such *munáḏharát*, to wit: (1) Arab and Persian, (2) Heaven and Earth, (3) Spear and Bow, (4) Night and Day, and (5) Muslim and Gabr (Zoroastrian). Of these I shall offer the reader, as a specimen of this kind of composition, a complete translation (from the text given by Dawlatsháh) of the fourth, referring such as desire further information as to the contents of the others, and the light they throw on the poet's life and adventures, to Ethé's monograph mentioned above, and to pp. 226–229 of his article *Neupersische Litteratur* in vol. ii of Geiger and Kuhn's *Grundriss*.

The munáḏhara, or "strife-poem."

ASADÍ'S STRIFE-POEM BETWEEN NIGHT AND DAY.

"Hear the fierce dispute and strife which passed between the Night and Day;
'Tis a tale which from the heart will drive all brooding care away.
Thus it chanced, that these disputed as to which stood first in fame,
And between the two were bandied many words of praise and blame.
'Surely Night should take precedence over Day,' began the Night,
'Since at first the Lord Eternal out of Darkness called the Light.
Do not those who pray by daylight stand in God's esteem less high
Than do those who in the night-time unto Him lift up their cry?
In the night it was that Moses unto prayer led forth his throng,
And at night-time Lot departed from the land of sin and wrong.
'Twas at night that by Muḥammad heaven's orb in twain was cleft,
And at night on his ascent to God the Holy House he left.
Thirty days make up the month, and yet, as God's Qur'án doth tell,
In degree the *Night of Merit*[1] doth a thousand months excel.
Night doth draw a kindly curtain, Day our every fault doth show;
Night conferreth rest and peace, while Day increaseth toil and woe.
In the day are certain seasons when to pray is not allowed,
While of night-long prayer the Prophet and his Church were ever proud.
I'm a King whose throne is earth, whose palace is the vaulted blue,
Captained by the Moon, the stars and planets form my retinue.
Thou with thy blue veil of mourning heaven's face dost hide and mar,

[1] The *Laylatu'l Qadr*, or "Night of Merit," is the night on which the Prophet Muḥammad received his first revelation, and is one of the last ten nights of the month of Ramaḍán. In *Súra* xcvii of the Qur'án it is declared to be "better than a thousand months."

Which through me, like Iram's Garden, glows with many a flower-like star.
By this Moon of mine they count the months of the Arabian year,
And the mark of the Archangel's wing doth on its face appear.
On the visage of the Moon the signs of health one clearly sees,
While apparent on the Sun's face are the symptoms of disease.
Less than thirty days sufficeth for the Moon her course to run,
Such a course as in the year is scarce completed by the Sun.'

"When the Day thus long had listened to the Night, its wrath was stirred :
'Cease!' it cried, 'for surely never hath a vainer claim been heard!
Heaven's Lord doth give precedence, in the oath which He hath sworn,
Over Night to Day; and darest thou to hold the Day in scorn?
All the fastings of the people are observed and kept by day,
And at day-time to the Ka'ba do the pilgrims wend their way.
'Arafa and 'Áshúrá, the Friday prayer, the festal glee,
All are proper to the Day, as every thinking mind can see.
From the void of Non-Existence God by day created men,
And 'twill be by day, we know, that all shall rise to life again.
Art thou not a grief to lovers, to the child a terror great,
Of the Devil's power the heart, and on the sick man's heart the weight?
Owls and bats and birds of darkness, ghosts and things of goblin race,
Thieves and burglars, all together witness to the Night's disgrace.
I am born of Heaven's sunshine, thou art of the Pit's dark hole;
I am like the cheerful firelight, thou art like the dusky coal.
These horizons I adorn by thee are rendered dull and drear;
Leaps the light in human eyes for me, for thee springs forth the tear.
Mine Faith's luminous apparel, Unbelief's dark robe for you;
Mine the raiment of rejoicing, thine the mourner's sable hue.
How canst thou make boast of beauty with thy dusky negro face?
Naught can make the negro fair, though gifted with a statue's grace.

What avail thy starry hosts and regiments, which headlong fly
When my Sun sets up his standard in the verdant field of sky?
What if in God's Holy Book my title after thine appears?
Doth not God in Scripture mention first the deaf, then him who hears?
Read the verse '*He Death created*,' where Life holds the second place,
Yet is Life most surely welcomed more than Death in any case.
By thy Moon the months and years in Arab computation run,
But the Persian months and years are still computed by the Sun.
Though the Sun be sallow-faced, 'tis better than the Moon, I ween;
Better is the golden *dinár* than the *dirham's* silver sheen.
From the Sun the Moon derives the light that causeth it to glow;
In allegiance to the Sun it bends its back in homage low.
If the Moon outstrips the Sun, that surely is no wondrous thing:
Wondrous were it if the footman should not run before the King!
Of the five appointed prayers the Night has two, the Day has three;
Thus thy share hath been diminished to be given unto me.
If thou art not yet content with what I urge in this debate,
Choose between us two an umpire just and wise to arbitrate;
Either choose our noble King, in equity without a peer,
Or elect, if you prefer, that Mine of Grace, the Grand Wazír,
Aḥmad's son Khalíl Abú Naṣr, noble, bounteous, filled with zeal,
Crown of rank and state, assurer of his King's and country's weal.'"

It may be mentioned that Asadí incurred Sulṭán Maḥmúd's displeasure by one of his "strife-poems" (that entitled "Arab and Persian"), in consequence of the praise which he bestowed on two princes of the rival House of Buwayh, *viz.*, Shamsu'd-Dawla Abú Táhír of Hamadán (A.D. 997–1021), and Majdu'd-Dawla Abú Ṭalib Rustam (A.D. 997–1029); another instance of the Sulṭán's jealous disposition.

Abu'l Faraj of Sístán, though earlier in time than most of the poets above mentioned, is subordinate in importance to them, and also to his pupil Minúchihrí, of whom we shall speak immediately. His chief patron was Abú Símjúr, one of the victims of Sulṭán Maḥmúd's inordinate ambition, and he is said to have died in A.D. 1002. Of his life and circumstances we know next to nothing, though in Dawlatsháh,[1] as usual, personal details are forthcoming, though only one fragment of his verse is given, of which this is a translation :—

Abu'l Faraj-i-Sagzí.

"Gladness in this age of ours is like the 'Anqá of the West;
Consecrated unto sorrow seems our mortal life's brief span.
Widely o'er the earth I've wandered, much the World of Form explored,
Man I found fore-doomed to sorrow, made to suffer: wretched man!
Each in varying proportion bears his burden of distress;
Unto none they grant exemption from the universal ban."

Of Abu'l-Faraj's pupil Minúchihrí, who survived till A.D. 1041 or later, mention has been already made, and a translation of one of his most celebrated *qaṣídas* is given at pp. 30–34 *supra*. Manuscripts of his *díwán* are not very common, but it has been printed, with a historical Introduction, a full translation, and excellent notes by A. de Biberstein Kazimirski (Paris, 1886), and a lithographed edition was published in Ṭihrán some six years earlier, while Dawlatsháh speaks of it as "well known and famous in Persia." That he was a native of Dámghán (some fifty miles south of Astarábád, on the Ṭihrán-Mashhad road), not of Balkh or Ghazna, as Dawlatsháh asserts, clearly appears from one of his own verses. 'Awfí[2] gives his full name as Abu'n-Najm Ahmad b. Qúṣ (or Ya'qúb, according to Ethé, *op. cit.*, p. 225)

Minúchihrí.

[1] Pp. 39–40 of my edition.
[2] Pp. 53–55 of Part II of my edition.

b. Aḥmad al-Minúchihrí, and vouchsafes little further information, save that he was precociously clever and died young. He is generally said to have borne the sobriquet of *shast galla*, a term variously interpreted,[1] but generally as meaning "sixty herds," in allusion to his wealth. 'Awfí says nothing of this, and a passage in the unique history of the Seljúqs entitled *Ráḥatu's-Ṣudúr*, to which I called attention in my account of this important work in the *Journal of the Royal Asiatic Society* for 1902, pp. 580–581, inclines me to believe that two different poets have been confounded together by later writers: to wit, Abu'n-Najm Aḥmad *Minúchihrí*, who flourished in the first half of the eleventh century of our era, and Shamsu'd-Dín Aḥmad *Minúchihr*, who lived in the latter part of the twelfth century, and to whom the sobriquet of *shast galla* really belonged. Of this latter poet's verses nothing, so far as I know, has been preserved, and we only know that he wrote a *qaṣída* called (probably from its rhyme) *qaṣída-i-titmáj*.

The "Candle-*qaṣída*."

Here is a translation of another celebrated *qaṣída* by the real Minúchihrí, describing the Candle, and ending with praises of 'Unṣurí. It is given both by 'Awfí and Dawlatsháh, and of course in the editions of the *Díwán*:—

"Thou whose soul upon thy forehead glitters like an aureole,
By our souls our flesh subsists, while by thy flesh subsists thy soul.
Why, if not a star, dost waken only when all others sleep?
Why, if not a lover, ever o'er thyself forlorn dost weep?
Yes, thou art indeed a star, but shinest in a waxen sphere!
Yes, thou art a lover, but thy sweetheart is the chandelier!
O'er thy shirt[2] thou wear'st thy body: strange, indeed; for all the rest
Wear the vest upon the skin, but thou the skin upon the vest!
Thou revivest if upon thee falls the fire when thou art dead,[3]

---

[1] See p. 3 of the Persian text of Kazimirski's edition.

[2] The "shirt" of the candle is its wick, and its "body" is the wax.

[3] "Dead" or "silent" means extinguished, as applied to a fire or light. So the Persians say, "Kill the candle," or "Silence the candle."

And when thou art sick they cure thee best by cutting off thy head![1]
Even midst thy smiles thou weepest,[2] and moreover strange to tell,
Thou art of thyself the lover, and the well-beloved as well!
Thou without the Spring dost blossom, and without the Autumn die,[3]
Laughing now without a mouth, and weeping now without an eye![2]
Me most nearly thou resemblest; closely I resemble thee;
Kindly friends of all the world, but foes unto ourselves are we.
Both of us consume and spend ourselves to make our comrades glad,
And by us our friends are rendered happy while ourselves are sad.
Both are weeping, both are wasting, both are pale and weary-eyed,
Both are burned in isolation, both are spurned and sorely tried.
I behold upon thy head what in my heart doth hidden rest;
Thou upon thy head dost carry what I hide within my breast.
Both our visages resemble yellow flowers of *shanbalíd*,
Mine the bud unopened, thine the bloom which beautifies the mead.
From thy face when I am parted hateful is the sunshine bright,
And when thou art taken from me, sad and sorrowful the night.
All my other friends I've tested, great and little, low and high;
Found not one with kindly feeling, found not two with loyalty.
Thou, O Candle, art my friend; to thee my secrets I consign;
Thou art my familiar comrade, I am thine and thou art mine.
Like a beacon light thou shinest, while with eager eyes I scan
Every night till dawn the *Díwán* of Abu'l-Qásim Ḥasan,[5]
'Unṣurí, the greatest master of the day in this our art,
Soul of faith, of stainless honour, great in wisdom, pure in heart,

---

[1] Alluding to the snuffing of the wick.
[2] The candle "smiles" when it shines, and "weeps" when it gutters.
[3] See n. 3 on previous page.
[4] Viz., fire.
[5] This is 'Unṣurí's name, and this verse is the *gurízgáh*, or transition from the prelude (*tashbíb*) to the panegyric (*madíḥa*).

He whose voice is like his wit, alike original and free;
While his wit is like his verse in grace and spontaneity.
Art in verse surpassing his to claim were but an idle boast;
Others have at best one talent; he of talents owns a host.
In the crow will ne'er appear the virtues of the horse, I trow,
Though the neighing of the horse be like the cawing of the crow.
Whilst his poems you're reciting sugar-plums you seem to eat,
And the fragrance of his verses than the jasmine is more sweet."

Minúchihrí, it may be added, took his pen-name from the Ziyárid Prince of Ṭabaristán, Minúchihr b. Qábús b. Washmgír, entitled *Falaku'l-Ma'álí* ("The Heaven of High Qualities"), who succeeded his murdered father in A.D. 1012–13, and died in A.D. 1028–29.

Ghaḍá'irí.

Ghaḍá'irí of Ray has been already mentioned (pp. 69–70 *supra*) as the author of an *ighráq*, or hyperbolic praise, of Sulṭán Maḥmúd, which is said to have been rewarded with seven purses of gold, equivalent in value to 14,000 *dirhams*. The *qaṣída* in which these two verses occur begins:—

"If in rank be satisfaction, if in wealth be high degree,
Look on me, that so the Beauty of Perfection thou may'st see!
I am one in whom shall glory, even till the end of days,
Every scribe who o'er a couplet writes the customary 'says.'"[1]

Both 'Awfí and Dawlatsháh give brief notices of this poet, of whose life we know practically nothing, save that he excelled in "strife-poems" and poetical duels as well as in panegyric.

Bahrámí.

Bahrámí of Sarakhs has been already mentioned (p. 115 *supra*) as the author of a prose work on Prosody entitled *Khujasta-náma*. Two other similar works of his, the *Gháyatu'l-'Arúḍiyyín* ("Goal of Prosodists"), and the *Kanzu'l-Qáfiya* ("Thesaurus of Rhyme"), are mentioned with high approval in the *Chahár Maqála* (p. 50 of my translation)

[1] In Arabic *qála*, "says," followed by the name of the poet cited.

as invaluable to the aspiring poet. It seems to be implied that he composed other prose works on subjects connected with Rhetoric and the Poetic Art, none of which, unfortunately, have escaped the ravages of time. Dawlatsháh does not mention him, but the earlier 'Awfí accords him (pp. 55–57 of vol. ii) a brief notice, and quotes six or seven short pieces of his verse.

Other minor poets.

Our list of the poets of this period might be greatly extended, for 'Awfí enumerates more than two dozen, and others are mentioned in the *Chahár Maqála*; poetesses like Rábi'a the daughter of Ka'b; poets like Labíbí, Amíní, Abu'l-Faḍl Ṭálaqání, Manshúrí, 'Uṭáridí, and Zínatí-i-'Alawí-i-Maḥmúdí, who, from the opening verses of one of his *qaṣídas*:—

Zinatí.

"Sire, whose protecting strength is sought by all,
Summon the minstrels, for the wine-cup call;
That we with molten ruby may wash out
From palate parched the march's dust and drought"—

would seem to have accompanied Sulṭán Maḥmúd on some of his endless campaigns, in allusion to which he says, in another fragment cited by 'Awfí:—

"With foeman's blood sedition thou dost stay;
Heresy's stain thy falchion wipes away.
Hast thou a vow that each new month shall show
A fortress opened and a firm-bound foe?
Art pledged like Alexander every hour
Before Earth's monarchs to display thy power?"

But only three poets of those still unnoticed in this chapter imperatively demand mention, to wit the dialect-poet Pindár of Ray, Kisá'í of Merv, and the mystic quatrain-writer Abú Sa'íd ibn Abi'l-Khayr. The last-named, whose long life (A.D. 968–1049) bridges over the period separating the Sámánids from the Seljúqids, is by far the most important of the three, and will be more conveniently considered in the next chapter, in which we shall have to say more of religious and didactic and less of epic and panegyric verse; so it only remains here to speak briefly of Pindár and Kisá'í.

Of Pindár of Ray, said to have been called Kamálu'd-Dín, hardly anything is known, save that he was patronised by Majdu'd-Dawla Abú Ṭálib Rustam the Bu-wayhid prince of Ray, and earlier by the great Ṣáḥib Isma'íl b. 'Abbád. He is said to have died in A.D. 1010, and to have composed poetry in Arabic, Persian, and the "Daylamite" dialect. I can find no earlier mention of him than that of Dawlatsháh (pp. 42–44 of my edition), for 'Awfí and Ibn Isfandiyár, from whom we might have expected some light, are both silent; while even Dawlatsháh is unusually sparing of detail, and cites only two of Pindár's verses, one in Persian and one in dialect. The latter, addressed to an acquaintance who advised him to take to himself a wife, is only intelligible enough to make it clear that it could not be translated; the former, "very well known, and ascribed to many well-known poets," may be thus rendered:—

Pindár of Ray.

"Two days there are whereon to flee from Death thou hast no need,
The day when thou art not to die, the day when death's decreed;
For on the day assigned by Fate thy striving naught avails,
And if the day bears not thy doom, from fear of death be freed!"

Dawlatsháh also cites the following verse of the later poet Dhahíru'd-Dín Fáryábí as containing "an (implied) encomium on Pindár":—

Through the depths unrevealed of my genius a glance should'st thou fling,
Behold, out of every corner a Pindár I'll bring."

I doubt, however, if the word *Pindár* in this line is a proper name; it is probable the common noun meaning "thought," "fancy."[1]

For the scantiness of his information about Pindár, Dawlatsháh endeavours to compensate by an anecdote about Majdu'd-Dawla's mother, who, during her lifetime, acted as Regent, which, whether true or not, is pretty enough. When Majdu'd-Dawla came to the throne, in A.D. 997, he was but a boy, and, as above mentioned, the actual control of affairs was in the capable hands of his mother. From her, it is said, Sulṭán Maḥmúd demanded tax and tribute, and the sending of her son with his ambassador to Ghazna; failing her compliance, he threatened "to send two thousand war-elephants to carry the dust of Ray to Ghazna." The Queen-Regent received the ambassador with honour, and placed in his hands the following letter for transmission to the Sulṭán :—

"Sulṭán Maḥmúd is a mighty champion of the Faith and a most puissant Prince, to whom the greater part of Persia and the land of India have submitted. For twelve years, so long as my husband Fakhru'd-Dawla was alive, I feared his ravages and his hostility; but now, ever since my husband attained to God's Paradise, that anxiety has been obliterated from my heart. For Sulṭán Maḥmúd is a great king and also a man of honour, and will not lead his army against an old woman. Should he do so and make war, it is certain that I too would give battle. Should the victory be mine, it would be for me a triumph till the Day of Judgement; while, should he be victorious, men would say, 'He hath only defeated an old woman!' What proclamations of victory could he frame for publication through his dominions?

'*Who is less than a woman is hardly a man!*'

I know, however, that the Sulṭán is wise and prudent, and will never embark on such an enterprise; therefore have I no anxiety as to the issue of this matter, but recline on the couch of tranquillity and confidence."

---

[1] Since writing this I have discovered the preceding verse in the *Majálisu'l-Mú'minín*, and this leaves no doubt that the poet (whose name here appears as *Bundár*) is really meant.

The letter, adds our biographer, had the desired effect, and so long as she lived the Sulṭán made no attack on her son's dominions. Some colour is given to this tale by the fact, recorded by Ibnu'l-Athír, that Ray was seized by Sulṭán Maḥmúd, and Majdu'd-Dawla dethroned, in A.D. 420 (A.D. 1029), the year succeeding that in which the mother of the latter died. It was in the spring of that year that Maḥmúd entered Ray, and took from it a million *dínárs* in money, and half that value in jewelry, with six thousand suits of clothes and innumerable other spoils. He summoned Majdu'd-Dawla before him and said to him, "Hast thou not read the *Sháhnáma* (which is the history of the Persians) and the history of Ṭabarí (which is the history of the Muslims)?" "Yes," answered Majdu'd-Dawla. "Thy conduct," continued Maḥmúd, "is not as of one who has read them. Dost thou not play chess?" "Yes," replied the other. "Didst thou ever see a king approach a king?" the Sulṭán went on. "No," answered the unfortunate prince. "Then," asked Maḥmúd, "what induced thee to surrender thyself to one who is stronger than thee?" And he ordered him to be exiled to Khurásán. It was on this occasion also that Sulṭán Maḥmúd crucified a number of the heretical Báṭinís ("Esoterics") or Isma'ílís, banished the Mu'tazilites, and burned their books, together with the books of the philosophers and astronomers; while of such books as remained after this act of wanton vandalism, he transported a hundred loads to Ghazna.[1]

Kisá'í.

In conclusion, we must say a few words about Kisá'í, not so much for his own sake (though he was a noted poet in his day) as on account of his relations with a much greater man and poet, Náṣir-i-Khusraw, of whom we shall speak at length in the next chapter. Unlike Pindár, Kisá'í is more fully noticed by ancient than by modern writers. 'Awfí devotes to him more than five pages (pp. 33–39 of vol. ii), and the *Chahár Maqála* (which calls him Abu'l-Ḥasan, not,

[1] Ibnu'l-Athír (Cairo ed.), vol. ix, p. 128.

like Ethé, Abú Isḥáq) reckons him as one of the great Sámánid poets (p. 45), while Dawlatsháh ignores him entirely. He was born, according to a statement made by himself in a poem which 'Awfí, who cites it (pp. 38–39), says that he composed "at the end of his life, the time of farewell, and the hour of departure," being at that time, as he twice declares, fifty years of age, on Wednesday, March 16, A.D. 953. Dr. Ethé, in the monograph which he has devoted to this poet,[1] assumed from the above data that Kisá'í died about A.D. 1002; but he has since, in his article *Neupersische Litteratur* in the *Grundriss*, p. 281, modified his views, and supposes that the poet lived to an advanced age, and came into personal conflict with Náṣir-i-Khusraw, who was born, as he himself declares, in A.D. 1003–4 (A.H. 394). Ethé considers that Náṣir's disparagement of Kisá'í was due partly to jealousy, partly to religious differences, which he depicts in a way with which I cannot agree, for he represents the former as objecting to the latter's repudiation of the three great Caliphs. In other words, he considers that Kisá'í's Shí'ite proclivities were offensive to Náṣir, himself (as his poems abundantly show) an extreme Shí'ite, and (as history tells us) for a time the head of the Isma'ílí propaganda in Khurásán. The real ground, as I think, of whatever dislike or contempt Náṣir entertained for Kisá'í was that, though both were Shí'ites, the former belonged to the Isma'ílís, or "Sect of the Seven," and the latter to the "Sect of the Twelve," which sects, however kindred in origin, were entirely at variance as to the more recent objects of their allegiance, and in their actual policy and aspirations. Moreover, Náṣir naturally entertained an intense dislike to Sulṭán Maḥmúd, who was, as we have seen, a bigoted and dangerous foe to the Isma'ílís and other heretics; while Kisá'í, though a Shí'ite, devoted his talents to praising that sovereign. Here, as it seems

[1] *Die Lieder des Kisá'í*, in the *Sitzungsb. der bayr. Akad., philos.-philol. Klasse*, 1874, pp. 133–153.

to me, we have an ample explanation of whatever hostility may have existed between the two poets.

As a matter of fact, however, in the *Díwán* of Náṣir-i-Khusraw I find in all only seven references to Kisá'í (Tabríz lithographed ed. of A.H. 1280, pp. 19, 28, 38, 51, 133, 247, and 251), of which the translation is as follows :—

1 (p. 19).

"If Kisá'í should see in a dream this brocade of mine" (meaning his fine robe of song), "shame and confusion would fret the robe (*kisá*) of Kisá'í."

2 (p. 28).

"If there were poems of Kisá'í, they are old and weak, [while] the verse of *Ḥujjat*[1] is strong, and fresh, and young."

3 (p. 38).

"His (*i.e.*, Náṣir's) verses are like brocade of Rúm, if the verse of Kisá'í's town (*i.e.*, Merv) is a garment (*kisá*)."

4 (p. 51).

"For my verses are brocade of Rúm, if the verse of the accomplished Kisá'í is a garment (*kisá*)."

5 (p. 133).

"The robe (*kisá*) of Kisá'í would become hair (*sha'r*) on his back in shame if he should hear thy (*i.e.*, Náṣir's) verse (*shi'r*)."

6 (p. 247).

"So long as thou art in heart the servant of the Imám of the Age (*i.e.*, the Fáṭimid Caliph al-Mustanṣir), the poetry of Kisá'í will be the slave of thy poetry."

7 (p. 251).

"Beside his (*i.e.*, Náṣir's) fresh verses, that famous discourse of Kisá'í hath grown stale."

I have not, unfortunately, all Dr. Ethé's materials at my disposal, but in the above allusions, and so far as the *Díwán* of Náṣir-i-Khusraw is concerned, I see no particular disparagement

[1] *I.e.*, "the Proof" (*sc.* of Khurásán), which was at once Náṣir's title in the Isma'ílí hierarchy and his pen-name or *nom de guerre.*

of Kisá'í, but rather the reverse; for when a poet is indulging in this style of boasting, so popular with the Eastern poets, he naturally declares himself superior to the greatest, not the least, of his predecessors and contemporaries. Any other method would result in bathos.

Kisá'í, then, was without doubt a noted poet in his day. He was, as already remarked, a Shí'ite, and in many of his poems hymned the praises of 'Alí and the Holy Family. This did not, however, prevent him from celebrating the glories and the generosity of Sulṭán Maḥmúd, or even from praising wine, which was certainly not the metaphorical wine of the mystics. It seems likely enough, however, as suggested by Ethé, that the poem already mentioned which he composed in his fiftieth year marks the date of a change in his life and mind, and an abandonment of sinful pleasures for ascetic exercises. In this poem he says:—

"The turn of the years had reached three hundred and forty one,
A Wednesday, and three days still remaining of [the month of] Shawwál,
[When] I came into the world [to see] how I should say and what I should do,
To sing songs and rejoice in luxury and wealth.
In such fashion, beast-like, have I passed all my life,
For I am become the slave of my offspring and the captive of my household.
What hold I in my hand [of gain] from this full-told tale of fifty [years]?
An account-book [marred] with a hundred thousand losses!
How can I at last resolve this reckoning,
Whose beginning is a lie, and whose end is shame?
I am the bought slave of desire, the victim of greed's tyranny,
The target of vicissitude, a prey to the meanness of begging.
Alas for the glory of youth, alas for pleasant life,
Alas for the comely form, alas for beauty and grace!
Whither hath gone all that beauty and whither all that love?
Whither hath gone all that strength and whither all that circumstance?
My head is [now] the colour of milk, my heart the colour of pitch,

My cheek the colour of indigo, my body the colour of the reed.
Night and day the fear of death makes me tremble
As does fear of the strap children who are slow at their lessons.
We passed [our days] and passed on, and all that was to be took
place ;
We depart, and our verse becomes but rhymes for children.
O Kisá'í, fifty (*panjáh*) hath set its clutch (*panja*) on thee ;
The stroke and the claws of fifty have plucked thy wings!
If thou no longer carest for wealth and ambition,
Separate thyself from ambition, and rub thine ears[1] in time!"

Only one other verse of Kisá'í's will I quote here, and that because it seems to be the prototype of 'Umar Khayyám's—

"I often wonder what the vintners buy
One half so precious as the stuff they sell,"

so familiar to all admirers of FitzGerald's beautiful version of his quatrains. Kisá'í's verse, however, is not in the quatrain form :—

Gul ni'mati 'st hidya firistáda az bihisht,
Mardum karím-tar shavad andar na'ím-i-gul;
Ay gul-furúsh! gul chi firúshí baráyi sím?
Wa'z gul 'azíz-tar chi sitání bi-sím-i-gul?

"A heaven-sent gift and blessing is the rose,
Its grace inspireth aspirations high.
O flower-girl, why the rose for silver sell,
For what more precious with its price canst buy?"

[1] *I.e.*, be admonished and awake from the sleep of heedlessness.

CHAPTER III

THE EARLY SELJÚQ PERIOD, FROM THE RISE OF ṬUGHRIL BEG TILL THE DEATH OF MALIKSHÁH, INCLUDING THE ORIGIN OF THE ORDER OF THE ASSASSINS

"THE advent of the Seljúqian Turks," says Stanley Lane-Poole, in his excellent *Mohammadan Dynasties* (p. 149), "forms a notable epoch in Mohammadan history. At the time of their appearance the Empire of the Caliphate had vanished. What had once been a realm united under a sole Mohammadan ruler was now a collection of scattered dynasties, not one of which, save perhaps the Fáṭimids of Egypt (and they were schismatics) was capable of imperial sway. Spain and Africa, including the important province of Egypt, had long been lost to the Caliphs of Baghdád; Northern Syria and Mesopotamia were in the hands of turbulent Arab chiefs, some of whom had founded dynasties; Persia was split up into the numerous governments of the Buwayhid princes (whose Shí'ite opinions left little respect for the puppet Caliphs of their time), or was held by sundry insignificant dynasts, each ready to attack the other, and thus contribute to the general weakness. The prevalence of schism increased the disunion of the various provinces of the vanished Empire. A drastic remedy was needed, and it was found in the invasion of the Turks. These rude nomads, unspoilt by town life and civilised indifference to religion, embraced Islám with all the fervour of their uncouth souls. They came to the rescue of a dying State, and revived it. They swarmed over Persia, Mesopotamia, Syria, and Asia Minor, devastating the country, and exterminating every dynasty that existed there; and, as the result, they once more united Mohammadan Asia, from the western frontier of Afghánistán to the Mediterranean, under one sovereign; they put a new life into the expiring zeal of the Muslims. drove back the re-encroaching

Byzantines, and bred up a generation of fanatical Mohammadan warriors, to whom, more than to anything else, the Crusaders owed their repeated failure. This it is that gives the Seljúqs so important a place in Mohammadan history."

To this we may add that they were the progenitors of the Ottoman Turks, the foundation of whose Empire in Asia Minor, and afterwards in Syria, Egypt, the Mediterranean, Europe, and North Africa, was laid by the Seljúq kingdoms of Rúm—the so-called Decarchy—and actually determined by the Mongol Invasion, which drove westwards by its storm-blast the Turkish band of Ertoghrul and 'Osmán, whose descendant is the present Sultan of Turkey.

The rise of the Seljúq power, then, constitutes the historical, as opposed to the purely literary, portion of this chapter. For the necessarily brief account of this which I shall here give the chief authorities which I shall use are: (1) Ibnu'l-Athír's Chronicle (Cairo edition, vol. x, and concluding portion of vol. ix); (2) 'Imádu'd-Dín's edition of al-Bundárí's recension of the Arabic monograph on the Seljúqs composed by the Wazír Anúshirwán b. Khálid (died A.D. 1137–38), forming vol. ii of Professor Houtsma's *Recueil de textes relatifs à l'Histoire des Seldjoucides* (Leyden, 1889), with occasional reference to the History of the Seljúqs of Kirmán contained in vol. i of the same; (3) the unique manuscript Persian monograph on Seljúq history, entitled *Ráḥatu'ṣ-Ṣudúr*, and composed in A.D. 1202–3, described by me in the *Journal of the Royal Asiatic Society* for 1902, pp. 567–610 and 849–887. To save space, I shall henceforth refer to these respectively as *Ibnu'l-Athír*, with a reference to the year in his Annals where the matter in question is mentioned (or more rarely the page in the above-mentioned edition); *Bundárí* and *Seljúqs of Kirmán* (Houtsma's ed.); and *Ráḥatu'ṣ-Ṣudúr* ("*f.*" followed by a number meaning leaf so-and-so of the unique Schefer Codex, "*p.*" meaning page so-and-so of my description).

The rise of this dynasty was as swift or swifter than that of the House of Ghazna, and its permanence and power were much greater. They were a branch of the Ghuzz Turks who in A.D. 1029 began to overrun the north and east of Persia, and to cause serious anxiety to Sulṭán Maḥmúd. Of this particular branch the first ancestor was, according to Ibnu'l-Athír, Tuqáq (a name explained as meaning "bow"), the father of Seljúq, who was the first to adopt the religion of Islám; and they came originally from Turkistán to Transoxiana, where they chose as their winter-quarters Núr of Bukhárá, and as their summer pasture-grounds Sughd and Samarqand. The main divisions of Seljúq's descendants are shown in the following tree, wherein the more important names are printed in capitals:—

Origin of the Seljúqs.

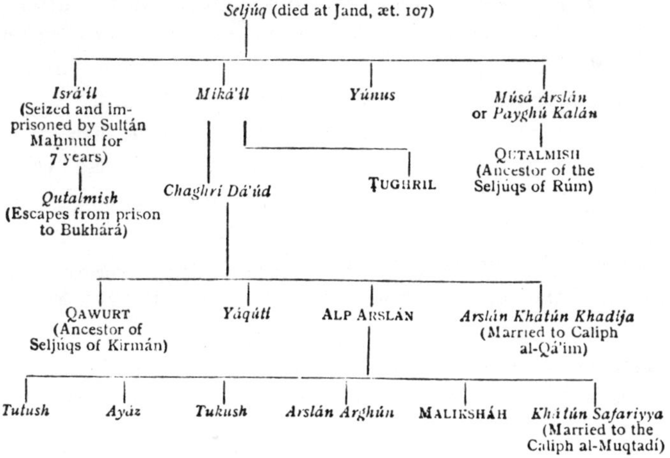

The period covered in this chapter embraces the reigns of Ṭughril (proclaimed king in Merv, A.D. 1037, died Sept. 4, A.D. 1063), Alp Arslán (born A.D. 1032–33, succeeded to the throne 1063, killed Nov. 24, A.D. 1072), and Malikshāh (succeeded A.D. 1072, died Nov. 19, A.D. 1092). During nearly the whole of this period of fifty-five years the control of affairs was committed to the charge of one of the most celebrated Ministers of State whom Persia has produced, the wise and prudent Nidhámu'l-Mulk, whose violent death preceded the decease of his third royal master, Malikshåh, by only thirty-five days, and with whom the most brilliant period of Seljúq rule came to an end. The period with which we are here dealing may, in short, most briefly and suitably be defined as the period of the Nidhámu'l-Mulk.

Like nearly all Turks, the Seljúqids were, as soon as they embraced Islám, rigidly orthodox. The author of the *Ráḥatu'ṣ-Ṣudúr* relates that the Imám Abú Ḥanífa, the founder of the most widely-spread of the four orthodox schools, once prayed to God that his doctrine might endure, and that from the Unseen World the answer came to him, "Thy doctrine shall not wane so long as the sword continues in the hands of the Turks"; whereon the aforesaid author exultantly exclaims that "in Arabia, Persia, Rúm (Turkey in Asia), and Russia the sword is indeed in their hands" (he wrote in A.D. 1202–3); that religion, learning, and piety flourish under their protection, especially in Khurásán; that irreligion, heresy, schism, philosophy, and the doctrines of materialism and metempsychosis have been stamped out, so that "all paths are closed save the Path of Muḥammad." Under Malikshåh, the Seljúq Empire extended, as Ibnu'l-Athír says (vol. x, p. 73) "from the frontiers of China to the confines of Syria, and from the utmost parts of the lands of Islám to the north unto the limits of Arabia Felix; while the Emperors of Rúm (*i.e.*, of the Eastern Empire) brought him tribute."

The Fáṭimid Anti-Caliphs.

Yet orthodoxy did not rule unchallenged in the lands of Islám, for Egypt and much of North Africa and Syria were held by the Fáṭimid or Isma'ílí Anti-Caliphs, whose power and glory may be said to have reached their summit in the long reign of al-Mustanṣir (A.D. 1035–94), which just covers the period discussed in this chapter. And far beyond the limits of their territories, most of all in Persia, these champions of the Báṭiní or "Esoteric" Shí'ite doctrine exercised, by means of their *dá'ís*, or missionaries, a profound and tremendous influence, with some of the most interesting manifestations of which we shall come into contact in this and the following chapters; while two of their chief propagandists, Náṣir-i-Khusraw the poet, and Ḥasan-i-Ṣabbáḥ, the originator of the "New Propaganda" and the founder of the notorious order of the Assassins, are inseparably connected with the greatest events and names of this supremely interesting age.

Of other dynasties besides these two—the Seljúqs and the Fáṭimids—we need hardly speak in this chapter. On Sulṭán Maḥmúd's death the House of Ghazna was rent by a fratricidal struggle, out of which Mas'úd emerged victorious, and carried on for a time the Indian campaigns in which his father so rejoiced, besides taking Ṭabaristán and Gurgán from the Ziyárid prince Dárá b. Minúchihr in A.D. 1034–35. Three years later the Seljúq hordes routed his troops at Balkh and carried off his elephants of war. The year A.D. 1040 saw his deposition and murder, and the accessions first of his brother Muḥammad and then of his son Mawdúd. Ṭabaristán submitted to the Seljúqs in the following year, and in A.D. 1043–44 they defeated Mawdúd in Khurásán, though he succeeded in expelling the Ghuzz Turks from Bust, which they had overrun, and was even able to continue the Indian campaigns. This, so far as Persia was concerned, put an end to the power of the Ghaznawís, though they maintained themselves in their own kingdom of Ghazna until A.D. 1161, when they were expelled by the House of Ghúr, after which their fortunes concern India only.

Decline of the House of Ghazna.

As for the House of Buwayh, the great rivals in former days of the House of Ghazna, their power ended when Ṭughril entered Baghdád on December 18, A.D. 1055, and practically took the 'Abbásid Caliph entirely under his tutelage. Three years

The House of Buwayh.

later died the last prince of this noble house, called al-Maliku'r-Raḥím ("the Merciful King"), at Ray.

To return now to the Seljúqs. They were originally, according to al-Bundárí and the *Ráḥatu'ṣ-Ṣudúr*, invited by Sulṭán Maḥmúd to settle in the region about Bukhárá, but their rapidly increasing power soon alarmed the Sulṭán, who, about A.D. 1029,[1] seized one of Seljúq's sons (Músá Arslán Payghú, according to Ibnu'l-Athír, Isrá'íl according to the other authorities) and interned him in a fortress in India called Kálanjar, where, after languishing in captivity for seven years, he died. According to a well-known story (given by the *Ráḥatu'ṣ-Ṣudúr*) the cause of Sulṭán Maḥmúd's uneasiness was that one day in the course of a conversation he asked Isrá'íl how many armed men he could summon to his standard in case of need, to which the other replied that if he should send to his people an arrow from his quiver, 100,000 would respond to the call, and if he sent his bow, 200,000 more. The Sulṭán, who, as our author says, had forgotten the proverb: "Do not open a door which thou shalt find it hard to shut, nor fire an arrow which thou canst not recall," was so much alarmed at this boast that he decided on the harsh measure mentioned above.

Southward migration of the Seljúqs.

On the death of Isrá'íl b. Seljúq in exile and bonds, his son Qutalmish[2] escaped, and made his way to Bukhárá, where he joined his kinsmen, swearing vengeance against the treacherous Sulṭán. About A.D. 1034–35, having suffered further treachery at the hands of the King of Khwárazm, Hárún b. Altúntásh, they moved southwards to the region between Nasá and Báward. This migration is placed earlier by the author of the *Ráḥatu'ṣ-Ṣudúr*, who says that it took place in Sulṭán Maḥmúd's time and by his permission—a permission which Arslán Jádhib, the Governor

[1] This was also the year in which, according to Ibnu'l-Athír, Alp Arslán was born.

[2] So pointed in the *Ráḥatu'ṣ-Ṣudúr*.

of Ṭús, strongly advised him not to accord to such powerful neighbours, his recommendation being to cut off the thumbs of every one of them whom they could catch, so that they should be unable to use the bow, wherein lay their special skill.[1]

It was after Mas'úd had succeeded in overthrowing his brother and establishing himself on the throne of his father Maḥmúd that the real trouble began. Once, apparently about A.D. 1035, during the time of his invasion of Ṭabaristán, he seems to have had the advantage, but shortly afterwards, at the conclusion of that campaign, his soldiers being weary and their weapons rusted with the damp of that humid climate, he suffered defeat at their hands;[2] and, instead of listening to his advisers, who warned him not to make light of the matter or neglect Khurásán for foreign adventures, he made speedy terms with them in order that he might indulge in another expedition against India. The result of this neglect was that on his return matters had passed far beyond his control, and that in the summer of A.D. 1038 Ṭughril b. Míká'íl b. Seljúq was declared king, by the insertion of his name in the *khuṭba*, or public homily, at Merv, and soon afterwards at Níshápúr. In connection with the occupation of the latter city (A.D. 1039–1040) we read in Ibnu'l-Athír (x, 167) the same story as to the simple-minded conquerors mistaking camphor for common salt as is related in the History of al-Fakhrí in connection with the capture of Ctesiphon by the early Muslims.[3]

Mas'úd and the Seljúqs.

The deposition and murder of Mas'úd (A.D. 1040) and the

[1] From this it appears that in shooting they used what is known as "the Mongol loose," to which allusion will be made in a later chapter, in connection with the murder of the poet Kamálu'd-Dín Isma'íl.

[2] Some details of the battle, showing Mas'úd's valour and skill as a swordsman, and his negligence as a general, will be found in the *Ráḥatu'ṣ-Ṣudúr*, f. 44.

[3] See al-Fakhrí, ed. Ahlwardt, p. 100, and the *Prolegomena* to this volume, p. 199.

fresh distractions caused by this at Ghazna served still further to confirm the power of the Seljúqs, who in the following year reduced Ṭabaristán. Three years later they defeated Mawdúd, the son of Mas'úd, in Khurásán, and then indited a letter to the Caliph al-Qá'im, detailing their grievances against the House of Ghazna, assuring him of their loyalty to himself, and craving his recognition. Then they proceeded to divide the vast territories which had so quickly passed under their sway. Bust, Herát, and Sístán fell to Seljúq's son Músá Arslán Payghú, whose nephews, Chaghrí Beg Dá'úd and Ṭughril, took Merv and 'Iráq respectively; of Chaghrí's sons, Qáwurt took Kirmán, Tún, and Ṭabas, and Yáqútí Ádharbayján, Abhar and Zanján, while the third son, Alp Arslán, elected to remain with his uncle Ṭughril, who selected Ray as his capital. Hamadán was given to Ibráhím b. Ínál[1] b. Seljúq, while Músá's son Qutalmish received Gurgán and Dámghán.

Establishment of Seljúq power.

The Caliph al-Qá'im, on receiving the letter above mentioned, despatched as an ambassador Hibatu'llah b. Muḥammad al-Ma'múní to Ṭughril, who was then at Ray, with a gracious reply, and shortly afterwards caused his name to be inserted in the *khuṭba* and placed on the coins before that of the Buwayhid Amír al-Maliku'r-Raḥím. Finally, in December, A.D. 1055, Ṭughril entered Baghdád in state, and was loaded with honours by the Caliph, who seated him on a throne, clothed him with a robe of honour, and conversed with him through Muḥammad b. Manṣúr al-Kundurí, who acted as interpreter.[2] Shortly afterwards Ṭughril's niece, Arslán Khátún Khadíja, the sister of Alp Arslán, was married to the Caliph with great pomp, and Ṭughril, warned in a dream by the Prophet, left Baghdád after a sojourn of thirteen

Recognition of Ṭughril by the Caliph al-Qá'im.

[1] He was killed by Ṭughril on suspicion of treachery shortly afterwards (A.D. 1057–58).

[2] Bundárí, p. 14.

months, partly in consequence of serious disorders caused by the presence of his Turkish troops in the metropolis of Islám, partly in order to subdue Mawṣil, Diyár Bakr, Sinjár, and other lands to the west.[1] Shortly afterwards Ṭughril returned to Baghdád, where the Caliph thanked him for his services to religion, exhorted him to use well and wisely the great power committed to his hands, and conferred on him the title of "King of the East and of the West" (*Maliku'l-Mashriq wa'l-Maghrib*).

But Ṭughril's ambitions were not yet satisfied, and, on the death of his wife in A.D. 1061–62, he demanded the hand of the Caliph's daughter (or sister, according to the *Ráḥatu'ṣ-Ṣudúr*) in marriage. The Caliph was most unwilling, and only yielded at length to importunities in which a minatory note became ever more dominant. The bride-elect was sent with the circumstance befitting her condition to Tabríz, but ere Ray (where it was intended that the marriage should be celebrated) was reached, Ṭughril fell sick and died, on September 4, A.D. 1063, at the village of Ṭájrisht, and his intended bride was restored to Baghdád. He was seventy years old at the time of his death, and is described by Ibnu'l-Athír (x, 9–10) as being possessed of extraordinary self-control, strict in the performance of his religious duties, secretive, harsh and stern when occasion arose, but at other times very generous, even towards his Byzantine foes.

Death of Ṭughril.

Ṭughril was succeeded by his nephew Alp Arslán, though an attempt was made by the late King's minister, the already-mentioned al-Kundurí, generally known as the 'Amídu'l-Mulk, to proclaim Alp Arslán's brother Sulaymán. This false step proved fatal to al-Kundurí, who was sent a prisoner to Merv, where, after a

Accession of Alp Arslán.

[1] One incident of this campaign was the capture of a monastery containing 400 monks, of whom 120 were put to the sword, while the rest were allowed to ransom their lives by a heavy payment.

year's captivity, he was put to death in the most deliberate and cold-blooded manner by two servants sent by Alp Arslán for that purpose. Having commended himself to God, bidden farewell to his family, and asked to die by the sword, not by strangling, he sent to Alp Arslán and his Minister the Nidhámu'l-Mulk the following celebrated message[1]: "Say to the King, 'Lo, a fortunate service hath your service been to me; for thy uncle gave me this world to rule over, whilst thou, giving me the martyr's portion, hast given me the other world; so, by your service, have I gained this world and that!' And to the Wazír (*i.e.*, the Nidhámu'l-Mulk) say: 'An evil innovation and an ugly practice hast thou introduced into the world by putting to death [dismissed] ministers! I pray that thou may'st experience the same in thine own person and in the persons of thy descendants!'" The unfortunate minister was a little over forty at the time of his death. He was a fine Arabic scholar, and was originally recommended on this ground as secretary to Ṭughril by al-Muwaffaq of Níshápúr[2]; and he composed graceful verses in Arabic, of which Ibnu'l-Athír gives specimens. He was a fanatical adherent of the Sháfi'í school, and instituted the public cursing of the Ráfiḍís (or Shí'ites) and of the Ash'arís[3] in the mosques. The former was continued, but the latter abolished by the Nidhámu'l-Mulk, to the satisfaction of several distinguished theologians like al-Qushayrí, the author of a well-known hagiology of Ṣúfí saints, and Abu'l-Ma'álí al-Juwayní. Al-Kundurí had been made a eunuch in early life at Khwárazm; his blood

Al-Kundurí put to death.

[1] Ibnu'l-Athír, *sub anno* 456 (x, 11); *Ráḥatu'ṣ-Ṣudúr*, f. 51*a*.

[2] The story of the Nidhámu'l-Mulk's connection with this Imám Muwaffaq very probably grew out of this, just as verses which we now know to be by Burhání are by later writers commonly ascribed to him. See p. 35, n. 1 *supra*.

[3] The author of the *Ráḥatu'ṣ-Ṣudúr* (p. 573 of my article) classes these two antagonistic sects together as "heretics who ought to be taxed and mulcted like Jews."

was shed at Merv, his body was buried at his native place, Kundur, and his head at Níshápúr, save part of the cranium, which was sent to Kirmán to the Nidhámu'l-Mulk.

The Nidhámu'l-Mulk.

It is sad that so great, and, on the whole, so good a Minister as Abú 'Alí al-Ḥasan b. Isḥáq, better known by his title Nidhámu'l-Mulk, should first appear prominently in history in connection with this deed of violence, and, as though the curse of his dying predecessor had a real efficacy, should, after a career of usefulness hardly rivalled by any Eastern statesman, come to a bloody and violent end. He was born in A.D. 1017–18, of a family of *dihqáns*, or small landed gentry, in Ṭús. His mother died ere yet he was weaned, and at the same time his father was beset by financial difficulties and losses. Notwithstanding these unpromising circumstances, he obtained a good education, learned Arabic, and studied the theological sciences, until he obtained some secretarial post at Balkh under 'Alí b. Shádhán, the Governor placed over that town by Alp Arslán's father, Chaghrí Beg, who on his death recommended him most strongly to the young prince.[1] So he became Alp Arslán's adviser and minister, and, on the accession of his master to the throne, Prime Minister over the vast realm which acknowledged the Seljúqs' sway. He was a most capable administrator, an acute statesman, a devout and orthodox Sunní, harsh towards heretics, especially the Shí'ites and Isma'ílís, a liberal patron of letters, a sincere friend to men of virtue and learning ('Umar Khayyám, of whom we shall shortly have to speak, being one of the most celebrated of his *protégés*), and unremitting in his efforts to secure public order and prosperity and to promote religion and education. One of his first acts on becoming Prime Minister

[1] Ibnu'l-Athír (x, 71–2) gives, besides this account of his early days, another narrative, which equally places the opening of his career at Balkh, but under a different master. This second account agrees with what al-Bundárí says in the lengthy passage (pp. 55–59) which he devotes to the Nidhámu'l-Mulk's praises.

was to found and endow the celebrated Nidhámiyya College (so called after him) in Baghdád, of which the building was begun in A.D. 1065 and finished in 1067, and which afterwards numbered amongst its professors some of the most eminent men of learning of the time, including (A.D. 1091–95) the great theologian Abú Ḥámid Muḥammad al-Ghazálí, of whom as-Suyúṭí said: "Could there have been a prophet after Muhammad, it would assuredly have been al-Ghazálí."

Alp Arslán.

As regards Alp Arslán, his birth is variously placed in A.H. 420 and 424 (= A.D. 1029, 1033)[1] by Ibnu'l-Athír, and at the beginning of A.H. 431 (September 23, A.D. 1039) by the *Ráḥatu'ṣ-Ṣudúr*, which says (f. 50) that "he reigned twelve years after the death of his uncle, Ṭughril Bey, in A.H. 455 (= A.D. 1063), and two years before that over Khurásán, on the death of his father, Chaghrí Beg Dá'úd"; and that he was thirty-four years of age at the time of his death. "In appearance," continues this history, "he was tall, with moustaches so long that he used to tie up their ends when he wished to shoot; and never did his arrows miss the mark.[2] He used to wear a very high *kuláh* on his head, and men were wont to say that from the top of this *kuláh* to the ends of his moustaches was a distance of two yards. He was a strong and just ruler, generally magnanimous, swift to punish acts of tyranny, especially of extortion and exaction, and so charitable to the poor that at the end of the fast of Ramaḍán he was wont to distribute 15,000 *dínárs* in alms, while many needy and deserving persons in all parts of his vast kingdom (which, as Ibnu'l-Athír[3] says, "stretched from the remotest parts of Transoxiana to the remotest parts of Syria") were provided with pensions. He was also devoted to the study of history, listening with great pleasure and interest to the reading of the chronicles of former kings, and

[1] A.H. 424 (= A.D. 1033) is also the date given by Bundárí (p. 47).

[2] Yet, as we shall see, it was a miss which cost him his life.

[3] Ibnu'l-Athír, x, 26; Bundárí, pp. 45 and 47.

of works which threw light on their characters, institutes, and methods of administration. He left at least five sons and three daughters. Of the former, he married Malikshâh (who succeeded him) to the daughter of the Turkish Khátún, and Arslán Arghún to one of the princesses of the House of Ghazna, while one of his daughters, Khátún Safariyya, was wedded to the Caliph al-Muqtadí.

Alp Arslán's reign, though short (September, A.D. 1063 to November, 1072), was filled with glorious deeds. In the first year of his reign he subdued Khatlán, Herát, and Ṣighániyán in the north-east, and drove back the "Romans" (*i.e.*, the Byzantines) in Asia Minor. A little later (A.D. 1065) he subdued Jand (which, since his great-grandfather Seljúq was buried there, probably had a special importance in his eyes), and put down a rebellion in Fárs and Kirmán. He also checked the power of the Fáṭimid Anti-Caliphs, from whose sway he recovered Aleppo and the holy cities of Mecca and Medína; and last, but not least, in the summer of A.D. 1071, he, at the head of 15,000 picked troops,[1] inflicted a crushing defeat at Malázgird (near Akhláṭ, in Western Asia Minor) on a Byzantine army numbering, at the lowest estimate, 200,000 men (Greeks, Russians, Turks of various kinds, Georgians, and other Caucasian tribes, Franks and Armenians), and took captive the Byzantine Emperor Diogenes Romanus.

Achievements of his reign.

Concerning this last achievement a curious story is told by most of the Muslim historians.[2] Sa'du'd-Dín *Gawhar-Á'ín*, one of Alp Arslán's nobles, had a certain slave so mean and insignificant in appearance that the Nidhámu'l-Mulk was at first unwilling to let him accompany the Muslim army, and said in jest, "What

Capture of Romanus IV.

[1] The *Ráḥatu'ṣ-Ṣudúr* says 12,000, while it raises the strength of the Byzantine army to 600,000. The latter number is reduced by Bundárí to 300,000, and by Ibnu'l-Athír to 200,000.

[2] Ibnu'l-Athír, x, 23; Bundárí, p. 43; *Ráḥatu'ṣ-Ṣudúr*, f. 51.

13

can be expected of him? Will he then bring captive to us the Roman Emperor?" By the strangest of coincidences this actually happened, though the slave, not recognising the rank and importance of his prisoner, would have killed him had not an attendant disclosed his identity. When the captive Emperor was brought before Alp Arslán, the latter struck him thrice with his hand and said, "Did I not offer thee peace, and thou didst refuse?" "Spare me your reproaches," answered the unfortunate Emperor, "and I will do what thou wilt." "And what," continued the Sulṭán, "didst thou intend to do with me hadst thou taken me captive?" "I would have dealt harshly with thee," replied the Greek. "And what," said Alp Arslán, "do you think I shall do with thee?" "Either thou wilt slay me," answered Romanus, "or thou wilt parade me as a spectacle through the Muslim lands; for the third alternative, namely, thy forgiveness, and the acceptance of a ransom, and my employment as thy vassal, is hardly to be hoped for." "Yet this last," said the victor, "is that whereon I am resolved." The ransom was fixed at a million and a half of *dínárs*, peace was to be observed for fifty years, and the Byzantine troops were to be at Alp Arslán's disposal at such times and in such numbers as he might require, while all Muslim prisoners in the hands of the Greeks were to be liberated. These terms having been accepted, Romanus was invested with a robe of honour and given a tent for himself and 15,000 *dínárs* for his expenses, and a number of his nobles and officers were also set free. The Sulṭán sent with them an escort to bring them safely to their own marches, and himself rode with them a parasang. This humiliating defeat, however, proved fatal to the supremacy of Romanus, whose subjects, as al-Bundárí says, "cast aside his name and erased his record from the kingdom, saying, 'he is fallen from the roll of kings,' and supposing that Christ was angered against him."

Two years later, in November, A.D. 1072, Alp Arslán was engaged at the other extremity of his empire in a campaign against the Turks. He reached the Oxus at the head of 200,000 men,[1] whose transport across the river occupied more than three weeks. And while he was halting there, there was brought before him as a prisoner a certain Yúsuf Narzamí (or Barzamí, or Khwárazmí),[2] the warden of a fortress which had withstood his troops and had now fallen before their prowess. Alp Arslán, exasperated, as some historians assert, by the prisoner's evasive answers, ordered him to be brought close to his throne and extended on the ground by being bound by his wrists and ankles to four pegs driven into the earth, so to suffer death. On hearing this sentence the prisoner, hurling at the Sulṭán a term of the foulest abuse, cried out, "Shall one like me die a death like this?" Alp Arslán, filled with fury, waved aside those who guarded the prisoner, and, seizing his bow, fired an arrow at him. The skill for which he was so famous, however, failed him at this supreme moment, and the prisoner, no longer held, rushed in, ere one of the two thousand attendants who were present could interfere, and mortally wounded him in the groin with a dagger which he had concealed about him. Gawhar-Á'ín, who rushed to his master's assistance, was also wounded in several places before a *farrásh* (an Armenian, according to al-Bundárí) succeeded in slaying the desperate man by a blow on the head with his club. Long afterwards the son of this *farrásh* was killed at Baghdád in a quarrel with one of the Caliph's servants, who then sought sanctuary in the Caliph's private apartments, whence none dared drag him forth. But the *farrásh* came before Maliksháh crying for vengeance, and saying, "O Sire! deal with the murderer of my son as did I with thy father's murderer!" And though the Caliph offered a ransom of ten thousand

Death of Alp Arslán.

[1] Bundárí, p. 45; Ibnu'l-Athír, x, 25.

[2] The first is the reading of the *Ráḥatu'ṣ-Ṣudúr*, the second of the *History of the Seljúqs of Kirmán* (p. 12), and the third of Ibnu'l-Athír and al-Bundárí.

dinárs to save his house from such violation, Malikshán was obdurate until the murderer had been given up and put to death.

Alp Arslán's dying words and dispositions.

Alp Arslán lingered on for a day or two after he had received his death-blow, long enough to give to his faithful minister, the Nidhámu'l-Mulk, his dying instructions. His son Malikshán was to succeed him on his throne; Ayáz, another son, was to have Balkh, save the citadel, which was to be held by one of Malikshán's officers; and his brother, Qáwurt, was to continue to hold Kirmán and Fárs.[1] He died with the utmost resignation. "Never," said he, "did I advance on a country or march against a foe without asking help of God in mine adventure; but yesterday, when I stood on a hill, and the earth shook beneath me from the greatness of my army and the host of my soldiers, I said to myself, 'I am the King of the World, and none can prevail against me': wherefore God Almighty hath brought me low by one of the weakest of His creatures. I ask pardon of Him and repent of this my thought."[2] He was buried at Merv, and some poet composed on him the famous epitaph:—

Sar-i Alp Arslán dídí zi rif'at rafta bar gardún:
Bi-Marw á, tá bi-khák andar sar-i-Alp Arslán bíní!

"Thou hast seen Alp Arslán's head in pride exalted to the sky;
Come to Merv, and see how lowly in the dust that head doth lie!"

Accession of Malikshán.

Malikshán was only seventeen or eighteen years of age when he was called upon to assume control of the mighty empire which his great-uncle and his father had built up, and his reign opened with threats of trouble. Altigín, the Khán of Samarqand, seized Tirmidh and routed the troops of Ayáz, the King's brother;

[1] Al-Bundárí, p. 47.
[2] Ibnu'l-Athír, x, 25.

Ibráhím, the Sulṭán of Ghazna, took prisoner his uncle 'Uthmán, and carried him and his treasures off to Afghánistán, but was pursued and routed by the Amír Gumushtigín and his retainer Anúshtigín, the ancestor of the new dynasty of Khwárazmsháhs, whereof we shall have to speak in another chapter; and, worst of all, another of Malikshāh's uncles, Qáwurt Beg, the first Seljúq king of Kirmán, marched on Ray to contest the crown with his nephew. The two armies met near Hamadán, at Karaj, and a fierce fight ensued, which lasted three days and nights. Finally Qáwurt's army was routed, and he himself was taken captive and put to death, while his sons Amíránsháh and Sulṭánsháh, who were taken with him, were blinded, but the latter not sufficiently to prevent him from succeeding his father as ruler of Kirmán. The Nidhámu'l-Mulk, for his many and signal services at this crisis, received the high, though afterwards common, title of Atábek.[1]

The following year saw the death of the Caliph al-Qá'im and the succession of his grandson al-Muqtadí. A year later his Fáṭimid rival succeeded in re-establishing his authority in Mecca, but only for a twelvemonth, while as a set-off to this he lost Damascus. In the same year (A.D. 1074–75) Malikshāh established the observatory in which the celebated 'Umar Khayyám ('Umar ibn Ibráhím al-Khayyámí) was employed with other eminent men of science[2] to compute the new Jalálí Era which the Sulṭán desired to inaugurate, and which dates from the *Naw-rúz*, or New Year's Day (March 15th) of the year A.D. 1079. About two years later Malikshāh gave his daughter in marriage to the Caliph al-Muqtadí, and

[1] This title, which means literally "Father-lord," was lately revived and bestowed on the *Amínu's-Sulṭán*, who was for some time Prime Minister to Náṣiru'd-Dín (the late) Sháh and his son, the present King of Persia, Mudhaffaru'd-Dín Sháh. A year or two ago he was deprived of his office, and is now in exile.

[2] Ibnu'l-Athír, x, 34. Two of 'Umar's colleagues are named Abu'l-Mudhaffar al-Isfizárí and Maymún ibn Najíb al-Wásiṭí.

in the same year lost his son Dá'úd, whose death so afflicted him that he would scarcely suffer the body to be removed for burial, and could hardly be restrained from taking his own life. Time, however, and the birth of another son (Sanjar, so called in allusion to his birthplace, Sinjár, near Mawṣil) three years later, gradually mitigated his grief. About this time (A.D. 1082–83) the curse uttered against the Nidhámu'l-Mulk and his sons bore, as it might seem, its first fruits. Jamálu'l-Mulk, the Premier's eldest son, was of a proud and vindictive disposition, and hearing that Ja'farak, the King's jester, had ridiculed his father, he hastened from Balkh, where he was governor, to the Court, dragged the unfortunate jester from the King's presence, and caused his tongue to be torn out through an incision in his neck, which cruel punishment proved instantly fatal. Maliksh※h said nothing at the time, but shortly afterwards secretly ordered Abú 'Alí, the 'Amíd of Khurásán, on pain of death, to poison Jamálu'l-Mulk, which, through a servant of the doomed man, he succeeded in doing.

Maliksh※h twice visited Baghdád during his reign. The first visit was in A.H. 479 (March, 1087), when, in company with the Nidhámu'l-Mulk, he visited the tombs of the Imám Músá (the seventh Imám of the Shí'a), the Ṣúfí saint Ma'rúf al-Karkhí, Aḥmad b. Ḥanbal, and Abú Ḥanífa. He also sent costly presents to the Caliph al-Muqtadí, and, on the day after his arrival, played in a polo match. About the same time he gave his sister Zulaykhá Khátún in marriage to Muḥammad b. Sharafu'd-Dawla (on whom he bestowed ar-Raḥba, Ḥarrán, Sarúj, Raqqa, and Khábúr in fief), and his daughter to the Caliph; while his wife, Turkán Khátún, bore him a son named Maḥmúd, who was destined to play a brief part in the troublous times which followed his father's death; for Aḥmad, another son whom Maliksh※h designed to succeed him, died at Merv at the age of eleven, a year after Maḥmúd's birth, about the same time that an alliance was concluded with the House of Ghazna by the marriage of another of Malikshâh's daughters to the young King Mas'úd II.

Extent and splendour of Malikshâh's Empire.

Malikshâh's second visit to Baghdád took place in October, 1091, only a year before his death. Since his last visit he had conquered Bukhárá, Samarqand, and other cities of Transoxiana, and had received at distant Káshghar the tribute sent to him by the Emperor of Constantinople. Never did the affairs of the Seljúq Empire seem more prosperous. The boatmen who had ferried Malikshâh and his troops across the Oxus were paid by the Nidhámu'l-Mulk in drafts on Antioch, in order that they might realise the immense extent of their sovereign's dominions; and at Latakia, on the Syrian coast, Malikshâh had ridden his horse into the waters of the Mediterranean and thanked God for the vastness of his empire. He rewarded his retainers with fiefs in Syria and Asia Minor, while his army, numbering 46,000 regular troops whose names were registered at the War Office, pushed forward his frontiers into Chinese Tartary,[1] and captured Aden on the Red Sea. He supervised in person the administration of justice, and was always accessible to such as deemed themselves oppressed or wronged. His care for religion was attested by the wells which he caused to be made along the pilgrim route, and the composition which he effected to relieve the pilgrims from the dues hitherto levied on them by the Warden of the Sacred Cities (*Amíru'l-Ḥaramayn*); while his skill in the chase was commemorated by minarets built of the skulls and horns of the beasts which he had slain. His love of the chase was, indeed, one of his ruling passions, and he caused a register to be kept of each day's bag, which sometimes included as many as seventy gazelles. The author of the *Ráḥatu'ṣ-Ṣudúr* (ff. 56-57) had himself seen one of these registers (called *Shikár-náma*) in the handwriting of the poet Abú Ṭáhir al-Khátúní, who composed in Persian one of the oldest biographies of Persian poets

[1] *Ráḥatu'ṣ-Ṣudúr*, f. 56.

(now, unfortunately, as it would appear, no longer extant) entitled *Manáqibu'sh-Shu'ará*. Yet, as Ibnu'l-Athír tells us (x, 74), he felt some scruples about his right to slay so many innocent creatures. "Once," says this historian, "he slew in the chase a mighty bag, and when he ordered it to be counted it came to ten thousand head of game. And he ordered that ten thousand *dínárs* should be distributed in alms, saying, 'I fear God Almighty, for what right had I to destroy the lives of these animals without necessity or need of them for food?' And he divided amongst his companions of robes and other valuable things a quantity surpassing computation; and thereafter, whenever he indulged in the chase, he would distribute in alms as many *dínárs* as he had slain head of game." Of the many cities of his empire, Iṣfahán was his favourite residence,[1] and he adorned it with many fine buildings and gardens, including the fortress of Dizh-Kúh, which a few years later fell into the hands of a notorious leader of the Assassins, Ibn 'Aṭṭásh.

The Nidhamu'l-Mulk's fall.

During all these prosperous years the wise old Nidhámu'l-Mulk, now nearly eighty years of age, was ever at the young King's elbow to advise and direct him. In his leisure moments he was occupied in superintending or visiting the colleges which he had founded at Baghdád and Iṣfahán, conversing with learned doctors (whom he ever received with the greatest honour), and composing, at the request of Malikshâh, his great *Treatise on the History and Art of Government* (properly entitled *Siyásat-náma*, but often referred to by Persian writers as the *Siyaru'l-Mulúk* or "Biographies of Kings"), one of the most remarkable and instructive prose works which Persian literature can boast, now rendered accessible to all Persian scholars in the late M. Schefer's edition, and to a wider circle by his French translation. Of his twelve sons, all, or nearly all, held high

[1] *Ráḥatu'ṣ-Ṣudúr*, f. 57. Compare my *Account of a Rare Manuscript History of Iṣfahán*, p. 61.

positions in the State, and the achievements of himself and his family seemed to recall and rival the Barmecides[1] of old. But the same cause—Royal jealousy excited by envious rivals—which brought about the fall of the House of Barmak (and which has caused, and will probably continue to cause, the fall of every great Minister whom Persia has produced) was at work to compass the overthrow of the Nidhámu'l-Mulk. His chief enemy was Turkán Khátún, the favourite wife of Malikshláh, over whom she exercised a great influence. Her chief ambition (in which she was seconded by her Minister the Táju'l-Mulk) was to secure to her little son Maḥmúd the succession to the throne, while the Nidhámu'l-Mulk was known to be in favour of the elder Barkiyáruq, then a boy of twelve or thirteen. The immediate cause of the catastrophe was the arrogant conduct of one of the Minister's grandsons (son of that Jamálu'd-Dín who had been poisoned some ten years before by the Sulṭán's orders), who was Governor of Merv. One who had suffered at his hands laid a complaint before Malikshláh, who sent an angry message to the Nidhámu'l-Mulk, asking him ironically whether he was his partner in the throne or his Minister, and complaining that his relations not only held the richest posts under Government, but, not content with this, displayed an arrogance which was intolerable. The aged Minister, angered and hurt by these harsh and ungrateful reproaches from one who owed him so much, answered rashly, "He who gave thee the Crown placed on my head the Turban, and these two are inseparably connected and bound together," with other words of like purport,[2] which he would hardly have employed in calmer moments, and which were reported, probably with exaggerations, to the Sulṭán. The Nidhámu'l-Mulk was dismissed in favour of Abu'l-Gha-

[1] See pp. 257–8 of the *Prolegomena* to this volume.

[2] Ibnu'l-Athír (x, 70–71) gives the most circumstantial account of this transaction, but the words I have quoted (from the *Ráḥatu'ṣ-Ṣudúr*, f. 58) have struck the imagination of nearly all writers who have had occasion to touch on this event.

ná'im Táju'l-Mulk, the *protégé* of Turkán Khátún above mentioned, and this was accompanied by other ministerial changes not less unwise and unpopular, Kamálu'd-Dín Abu'r-Riḍá being replaced by Sadídu'l-Mulk Abu'l-Ma'álí, and Sharafu'l-Mulk Abú Sa'd by Majdu'l-Mulk Abu'l-Faḍl of Qum, who is coarsely satirised for his miserliness in one of the few Persian verses of Abú Ṭáhir al-Khátúní which time has left to us.[1] Another contemporary poet, 'Bu'l-Ma'álí Naḥḥás, condemns these changes of Ministers in the following lines[2]:—

"It was through Abú 'Alí and Abú Riḍá and Abu Sa'd,
O King, that the lion came before thee like the lamb.
At that time every one who came to thy Court
Came as a harbinger of triumph with news of victory.
Through Abu'l-Ghaná'im and Abu'l-Faḍl and Abu'l-Ma'álí
[Even] the grass of thy kingdom's soil grows up as stings.
If thou wast tired of Nidhám and Kamál and Sharaf,
See what hath been done to thee by Táj and Majd and Sadíd!"

Assassination of the Nidhámu'l-Mulk.

The Nidhámu'l-Mulk, however, did not long survive his disgrace. While accompanying Malikshâh from Iṣfahán to Baghdád, he halted on the 10th of Ramaḍán, A.H. 485 (=October 14, 1092), near Naháwand, a place memorable for the final and crushing defeat there sustained by the Zoroastrian soldiers of the last Sásánian monarch at the hands of the followers of the Arabian Prophet, about the middle of the seventh century. The sun had set, and, having broken his fast, he was proceeding to visit the tents of his wife and family, when a youth of Daylam, approaching him in the guise of a sup-

[1] See p. 600 of the *J.R.A.S.* for 1902. A good many more verses of this poet are, however, preserved in the *Mu'ajjam* of Shams-i-Qays, which is now being printed at Beyrout for the Trustees of the Gibb Memorial Fund.

[2] Ibid., and also p. 4 of Schefer's translation of the *Siyásat-náma*. Al-Bundárí also gives their purport in Arabic, p. 63.

pliant, suddenly drew a knife and inflicted on him a mortal wound. The supposed suppliant was, in fact, a member of the redoubtable order of the *Fidá'ís* or Assassins, at this time newly instituted by Ḥasan-i-Ṣabbáḥ and other chiefs of the "New Propaganda"[1] of the Ismaʿílí sect ; and this, it is generally said, was their first bold stroke of terror, though Ibnu'l-Athír (x, 108–9)[2] mentions the earlier assassination of a *muʾadhdhin* at Iṣfahán, and supposes that the execution of a carpenter suspected of being an accomplice in this murder by the Niḏhámu'l-Mulk exposed him to the vengeance of the Order. Apart from this, however, or of that personal animosity which, according to the well-known and oft-told tale, Ḥasan-i-Ṣabbáḥ bore against the Minister, the openly expressed detestation in which the latter held all Ráfiḍís or Shíʿites, and most of all the "Sect of the Seven," those formidable champions of the Ismaʿílí or Fáṭimid Anti-Caliphs of Egypt, would sufficiently account for his assassination. Nor were there wanting some who expressed the belief that the Táju'l-Mulk, the rival who had supplanted the Niḏhámu'l-Mulk, was the real instigator of a crime which, while calculated to perpetuate his power, actually led to his own murder some four months later.[3]

The Niḏhámu'l-Mulk was deeply mourned by the vast majority of those whom he had ruled so wisely for thirty years, and though a fallen Minister is seldom praised by Eastern poets, many, as Ibnu'l-Athír (x, 71) tells us, were

---

[1] Ibnu'l-Athír, x, 108, calls it *ad-Daʿwatu'l-Akhíra*, "the Later Propaganda." It should be borne in mind that there is always a tendency in the East to ascribe the assassination of a great man to a heretical sect whom the orthodox are eager to persecute. Thus the late Náṣiru'd-Dín Sháh's assassination was at first ascribed to the Bábís, whose innocence of all complicity therein was afterwards fully proved.

[2] This author, however, under the year A.H. 440 (= A.D. 1048–49) says that Aq Sunqur was assassinated by the Báṭinís or Ismaʿílís.

[3] He was assassinated by the Niḏhámu'l-Mulk's servants in February, A.D. 1093 (Ibnu'l-Athír, x, 75).

the elegies composed on him, of which the following graceful Arabic verses by Shiblu'd-Dawla [1] are cited :—

"The Minister Nid͟hámu'l-Mulk was a peerless pearl, which the
All-Merciful God esteemed as of great price,
But, precious as it was, the age knew not its value, so in
jealousy He replaced it in its shell."

The author of the *Chahár Maqála* [2] says that an astrologer called Ḥakím-i-Mawṣilí, in whom the Minister had a great belief, had told him that his patron's death would follow his own within six months. This astrologer died in the spring of A.D. 1092, and when news of this was brought to the Minister from Níshápúr, he was greatly perturbed, and at once began to make all his preparations and dispositions for the death which actually befell him in the following autumn.

Ibnu'l-Athír (x, 72) alludes to the numerous stories about the Nid͟hámu'l-Mulk which were current even in his time (the thirteenth century), and of which later writers, as we shall see, are yet more prolific. One of these apocryphal narratives, which too often pass current as history, relates that as the Minister lay dying of his wound he wrote and sent to the Sulṭán Maliksháh the following verses [3] :—

"Thanks to thy luck, for thirty [4] years, O Prince of lucky birth,
From stain of tyranny and wrong I cleansed the face of earth.
Now to the Angel of the Throne I go, and take with me
As witness of my stainless name a warrant signed by thee.
And now of life when four times four and four-score years have
fled
Hard by Naháwand doth the hand of violence strike me dead.

---

[1] He it was who, according to Dawlatsháh (p. 9 of my edition) composed an Arabic *qaṣída* of forty verses in praise of Mukrim b. al-'Alá of Kírmán, beginning :—"Let the tawny camels measure out the desert, if their way leads to Ibnu'l-'Alá's Court : if otherwise, then bid them stay." For this he received a purse of gold, the donor remarking that, had he been rich enough, it should have been a purse of gold for each verse.

[2] Anecdote xxvi, pp. 98–100 of my translation.

[3] Dawlatsháh, p. 59 of my edition ; *Ta'ríkh-i-Guzída*, ed. Gantin, vol. i, p. 230.

[4] *Viz.*, A.D. 1063–92. Dawlatsháh has "forty."

I fain would leave this service long, which now for me doth end,
Unto my son, whom unto thee and God I now commend!"

I have elsewhere pointed out [1] that the last of these verses, in a slightly different form, was undoubtedly written by Burhání, Malikshâh's poet-laureate, to recommend his son Mu'izzí, who succeeded him in this office, to the Royal favour, and that the three first verses are obviously spurious. For firstly, we know, on the authority of the *Chahár Maqála*, that the Nidhámu'l-Mulk "had no opinion of poets, because he had no skill in their art"; secondly, that he was only about seventy-five years old at the time of his death, not ninety-six; and thirdly, that his numerous sons, as previously mentioned, had already obtained more lucrative posts in Malikshâh's domains than most people outside their family deemed at all necessary or desirable. I wish to emphasise this because it well illustrates the remarkable tendency of all peoples, but especially the Persians, to ascribe well-known anecdotes, verses, sayings, and adventures to well-known persons; so that, as already pointed out, the quatrains of a score of less notable poets have been attributed to 'Umar Khayyám, and, as we shall shortly see, stories are told about Náṣir-i-Khusraw and Ḥasan-i-Ṣabbáḥ which are borrowed from the biographies of other less notable or less notorious men.

Malikshâh only survived about a month the Minister whose long and faithful service he had rewarded with such ingratitude. On November 6, A.D. 1092, less than three weeks after the Nidhámu'l-Mulk's death, he went out hunting, and either caught a chill or ate something which disagreed with him, and, though he was bled, a fever supervened which proved fatal on November 19th. On this the poet Mu'izzí has the following well-known verse:—

Death of Malikshâh.

[1] In my translation of the *Chahár Maqála*, p. 67, footnote.

"One month the aged Minister to heaven did translate;
The young King followed him next month, o'erwhelmed by equal Fate.
For such a Minister alas! Alas! for such a King!
What impotence the Power of God on earthly power doth bring!"

On the dismissal of the Nidhámu'l-Mulk in favour of his rival the Táju'l-Mulk, the same poet had already composed these lines:—

"The King, alas! ignored that lucky fate
Which granted him a Minister so great;
O'er his domains he set the cursed Táj,
And jeopardised for him both Crown and State!"[1]

Malikshāh was born in A.H. 445 (A.D. 1053–54) according to the *Ráhatu'ṣ-Ṣudúr*, two years later according to Ibnu'l-Athír, and was in either case under forty years of age at the time of his death.

The legend of the Nidhámu'l-Mulk, Ḥasan-i-Ṣabbáḥ, and 'Umar Khayyám.

Thus far we have spoken of such facts in the life of the Nidhámu'l-Mulk as are recorded by the earliest and most sober historians, but some of the "many legends" concerning him to which Ibnu'l-Athír alludes are so celebrated and have in later times obtained so general a credence, both in Asia and Europe, that they cannot be altogether ignored in a work like the present. Of these legends at once the most dramatic and the most widely-spread is that which connects his earliest days with the formidable organiser of the "New Propaganda,"[2]

[1] The original of these verses will be found on p. 59 of my edition of Dawlatsháh, and the preceding ones on p. 60. *Táj* means "crown," and *al-Mulk* "the State," but the play on the words is lost in the translation, unless we say "For *Táju'l-Mulk* he jeopardised both *Táj* and *Mulk*."

[2] See, besides Ibnu'l-Athír and the other authorities already quoted, al-Bundárí, p. 67.

Ḥasan-i-Ṣabbáḥ, who is on more solid grounds associated with his violent death. This legend, familiar to every admirer of 'Umar Khayyám,[1] involves chronological difficulties so serious that, so long as the chief authority which could be quoted in its favour was the admittedly spurious *Waṣáyá*,[2] or "Testamentary Instructions," of the Nidhámu'l-Mulk, it was unhesitatingly repudiated by all critical scholars, since its fundamental assumption is that two eminent persons (Ḥasan-i-Ṣabbáḥ and 'Umar Khayyám) who died at an unknown age between A.H. 517 and 518 (A.D. 1123-24) were in their youth fellow-students of the Nidhámu'l-Mulk, who was born in A.H. 408 (A.D. 1017). Now, the chances against two given persons living to be a hundred years of age are very great; and, even if we assume this to have been the case, they would still have been considerably younger than the Nidhámu'l-Mulk, who, moreover, appears to have finished his education and entered public life at an early age.[3] This objection has been forcibly urged by Houtsma in his preface to al-Bundárí (p. xiv, n. 2); and he very acutely suggests that it was not the famous Nidhámu'l-Mulk who was the fellow-student of the Astronomer-Poet and of the first Grand Master of the Assassins, but Anúshirwán b. Khálid, the less famous and later Minister of the Seljúqid Prince Maḥmúd b. Muḥammad b. Maliksháh (reigned A.D. 1117–31), who, in speaking of the first appearance of the Assassins or *Maláḥida* in his chronicle (which forms the basis of al-Bundárí), distinctly

Chronological difficulties involved.

Probable origin of the legend.

[1] It is given in the preface of almost every edition of FitzGerald's rendering of the quatrains, and also by Whinfield in his edition and translation of the same.

[2] Ethé, however (*Neupers. Litt.*, in vol. ii of *Grundriss*, p. 348), while admitting that this book was not compiled before the fifteenth century, is of opinion that it rests on a real basis of tradition, and has a greater authority than Rieu (*Persian Catalogue*, p. 446) would allow it.

[3] There is, however, good reason to believe that the Nidhámu'l-Mulk was acquainted with Ḥasan-i-Ṣabbáḥ before the latter went to Egypt See Ibnu'l-Athír, *sub anno* 494 (vol. x, p. 110).

implies (pp. 66–67) that he had been acquainted in his youth and had studied with some of their chief leaders, especially "a man of Ray, who travelled through the world, and whose profession was that of a secretary," in whom we can hardly be mistaken in recognising Ḥasan-i-Ṣabbáḥ himself. If this ingenious conjecture be correct, it would afford another instance of a phenomenon already noticed more than once, namely, the transference of remarkable adventures to remarkable men. The dates, at any rate, agree very much better; for Abú Naṣr Anúshirwán b. Khálid b. Muḥammad al-Káshání (-Qásání), as we learn from the *'Uyúnu'l-Akhbár*,[1] was born at Ray (of which city Ḥasan-i-Ṣabbáḥ was also a native[2]) in A.H. 459 (A.D. 1066–67), became *wazír* to Maḥmúd the Seljúq, whom he accompanied to Baghdád, in A.H. 517 (A.D. 1123–24), and later, in A.H. 526–28 (A.D. 1132–33) to the Caliph al-Mustarshid; and died in A.H. 532 or 533 (A.D. 1138–39); so that he may very well, as his own words suggest, have been the fellow-student of his notorious fellow-townsman.

Oldest occurrence of the legend.

But the legend which we are discussing does, as a matter of fact, rest on older and more respectable authority than the *Waṣáyá*, the *Rawḍatu'ṣ-Ṣafá*, the *Ta'ríkh-i-Alfí*, or other comparatively late works; for, as I pointed out in an article entitled "Yet More Light on 'Umar Khayyám," in the *Journal of the Royal Asiatic Society* for April, 1899 (pp. 409–420), it is given by the great historian Rashídu'd-Dín Faḍlu'lláh (put to death in A.D. 1318) in his valuable *Jámi'u't-Tawáríkh*. The text of this passage, taken from the British Museum Manuscript Add. 7,628, f. 292^{b}, together with a translation, will be found in the article above mentioned. The authority adduced by Rashídu'd-Dín for the story is an Isma'ílí work entitled *Sar-guzasht-i-Sayyid-ná*,

[1] Cambridge Manuscript Add. 2,922, f. 126^{a}. Houtsma, not having knowledge of this MS., says, "l'année de sa naissance ne nous est pas connue."

[2] See *Ta'ríkh-i-Guzída*, ed. Gantin, p. 489.

"The Adventures of our Master" (*i.e.*, Ḥasan-i-Ṣabbáḥ), which was amongst the heretical books found in the Assassin stronghold of Alamút when it was captured by Hulágú Khán's Mongols in the middle of the thirteenth century, and examined by 'Aṭá Malik Juwayní (as he himself tells us in his *Ta'ríkh-i-Jahán-gushá*, or "History of the World-Conqueror," *i.e.*, Chingíz Khán) ere it was committed to the flames with all else savouring of heresy. But, curiously enough, though the author of the *Jahán-gushá* draws largely on this biography of Ḥasan-i-ṣabbáḥ in that portion (the third and last volume) of his great history of the Mongol Invasion which deals with the history of the Isma'ílís and Assassins, he does not allude to this picturesque narrative.

Origin of the Assassins.

The Assassins play so prominent a part in the history of this period and of the two succeeding centuries, and, by the achievements of their Syrian offshoot during the Crusades, made their name so notorious even in Europe, that it is necessary to describe their origin and tenets somewhat fully in this place, in order that the repeated references to them which will occur in future chapters may be understood. In the *Prolegomena*[1] to this volume I have discussed very fully the origin and nature of the Shí'a heresy, and of its two chief divisions, the "Sect of the Seven," or Isma'ílís, and the "Sect of the Twelve," which last is to-day the national religion of Persia. A brief recapitulation of the facts there elaborated may, however, be convenient for such of my readers as have not the earlier volume at hand.

The Shí'a.

The word *Shí'a* means a faction or party, and, *par excellence*, the Faction or Party of 'Alí (*Shí'atu 'Aliyyin*), the Prophet's cousin, the husband of the Prophet's daughter, the father of al-Ḥasan and al-Ḥusayn, and the ancestor of all the other Imáms recognised by the Shí'ites or

[1] *A Literary History of Persia from the Earliest Times until Firdawsí*, pp. 220–247, 295–296, 310 *et seqq.*, and especially ch. xii, on "The Isma'ílís and Carmathians, or the Sect of the Seven," pp. 391–415.

people of the Shí'a. To the "orthodox" Muhammadan (whether Ḥanafite, Sháfi'ite, Málikite, or Ḥanbalite) 'Alí was only the fourth and last of the four orthodox Caliphs (*al-Khulafá'u'r-Ráshidún*), and neither greater nor less than his predecessors, Abú Bakr, 'Umar, and 'Uthman. But to the Shí'a he was, by virtue alike of his kinship and his marriage connection, the sole rightful successor of the Prophet; and this right descended to his sons and their offspring. From a very early time there was a tendency to magnify 'Alí's nature until it assumed a divine character, and even at the present day the 'Alí-Iláhís, who, as their name implies, regard 'Alí as neither more nor less than an Incarnation or "Manifestation" of God, are a numerous sect in Persia. From the earliest times the idea of Divine Right has strongly possessed the Persians, while the idea of popular and democratic election, natural to the Arabs, has always been extremely distasteful to them. It was natural, therefore, that from the first the Persians should have formed the backbone of the Shí'ite party; and their allegiance to the fourth Imám, 'Alí Zaynu'l-'Ábidín, and his descendants was undoubtedly strengthened by the belief that his mother was a princess of the old Royal House of Sásán.[1]

Sects of the Shí'a: the "Sect of the Seven" and the "Sect of the Twelve."

Agreeing, then, in maintaining that 'Alí and his descendants alone were the lawful Vicars of the Prophet and exponents of his doctrines, the Shí'ites differed from one another both as to the actual number and succession of Imáms and as to their nature. The two sects with which we are chiefly concerned, that of the Seven (*Sab'iyya*) and that of the Twelve (*Ithna 'ashariyya*), agreed as to the succession down to Ja'far aṣ-Ṣádiq, the sixth Imám; but at this point they diverged, the former recognising Isma'íl, Ja'far's eldest son, as the seventh and last Imám, the latter recognising Isma'íl's younger brother Músá and his descendants down to the twelfth Imám, or Imám Mahdi,

[1] *Prolegomena*, pp. 130 *et seqq.*

whom they supposed to have disappeared from earth at Sámarrá (Surra man ra'a) in A.H. 260 (A.D. 873–74) into a miraculous seclusion whence he will emerge at "the end of Time" to "fill the earth with justice after that it has been filled with iniquity." And still the Persian Shí'ite, when he mentions this twelfth Imám, adds the formula, "May God hasten his joyful Advent!"

Moderates and Extremists (*Ghulát*).

The moderate Shí'ites confined themselves to maintaining the paramount right of 'Alí and his offspring to succeed the Prophet as the Pontiffs of Islám, and hence were disliked by the Caliphs of Damascus and Baghdád (whom they naturally regarded as usurpers) mainly on political grounds, though on other doctrinal questions besides the succession they differed considerably from the Sunnís, or orthodox Muslims. Hence in biographical and historical works written by Sunnís we constantly meet with the phrase, "*Tashayya'a, wa ḥasuna tashayyu'uhu*" ("He was a Shí'ite, but moderate in his Shí'ite opinions"). But there was another class of Shí'ites, the *Ghulát*, or "Extremists," who not only regarded 'Alí and the Imáms as practically Incarnations of God, but also held a number of other doctrines, like Metempsychosis or "Return," Incarnation, and the like, utterly opposed to the whole teaching of Islám; and the vast majority of these extremists gradually passed into the "Sect of the Seven," or partisans of the Imám Isma'íl.

The Isma'ílís.

The political importance of the Isma'ílís began in the tenth century of our era with the foundation of the Fáṭimid dynasty, so called, as the author of the *Jámi'u't-Tawáríkh* says, because they based their claims [to both temporal and spiritual authority] "on the nobility of their descent from Fáṭima," the Prophet's daughter. Hence they are called indifferently *'Alawí* (descended from 'Alí), *Fáṭimí* (descended from Fáṭima), or *Isma'ílí* (descended from Isma'íl, the seventh Imám), though, as a matter of fact, the pedigree by which they endeavoured to make good this lofty claim was repeatedly challenged, *e.g.*, in A.H. 402 (A.D. 1011–12) and A.H. 444 (A.D. 1052–53), by their rivals, the 'Abbásid Caliphs of Baghdád, who declared that they were really descended from the Persian heretic 'Abdu'llah b. Maymún al-Qaddáḥ,[1] who saw in the hitherto unaggressive sect of the Isma'ílís a suitable instrument for the propagation of his transcendental and eclectic doctrines, and for the achievement of his ambitious political aspirations.

The Fáṭimid dynasty.

This Fáṭimid dynasty—the Anti-Caliphs of North Africa and Egypt—attained and maintained their political power (which endured from A.D. 909 until A.D. 1171, when the fourteenth and last Fáṭimid Caliph was removed by Ṣaláhu'd-Dín, or Saladin, from the throne of Egypt) by a religious propaganda conducted throughout the lands of Islám, and especially in Persia, by numbers of skilful and devoted *dá'ís* (plural *du'át*) or missionaries, men with a profound knowledge of the human heart and of the methods whereby their peculiar doctrines might best be insinuated into minds of the most diverse character. These, if we wish to seek European analogies, may be best described as the Jesuits, and their Isma'ílí Pontiffs as the "Black Popes," of the Eastern World at this epoch. They taught, so far as they deemed it expedient in any particular case, a Doctrine (*Ta'lím*) based on Allegorical Interpretation (*Ta'wíl*) of the Scripture and Law of Islám, of which, as they asserted, their Imáms were the sole inheritors and guardians; hence they were sometimes called *Ta'límís;* and this Doctrine was an esoteric doctrine, whence they were also called *Báṭinís* or "Esoterics." More commonly, especially after the institution of the "New Propaganda," they were simply called, *par excellence*, "the Heretics" (*Maláḥida*).

[1] He died in A.H. 261 (A.D. 874–75) about the same time that the twelfth Imám of the "Sect of the Twelve" disappeared. See pp. 394 *et seqq.* of the *Prolegomena*.

Their Doctrine, which is intricate and ingenious, I have described at some length in the *Prolegomena* (pp. 405–415) to this volume, and it could be illustrated by an abundance of material, much of which may be found set forth with learning and discrimination in the admirable works of de Sacy,[1] Guyard,[2] de Goeje,[3] &c., while much more (*e.g.*, the full accounts given in the *Jahán-gushá* and the *Jámi'u't-Tawárikh*) is still unpublished. In essence, their Inner Doctrine (reserved for those fully initiated) was philosophical and eclectic, borrowing much from old Íránian and Semitic systems, and something from Neo-Platonist and Neo-Pythagorean ideas. It was dominated throughout by the mystic number *Seven*: there were Seven Prophetic Periods (those of Adam, Noah, Abraham, Moses, Jesus, Muḥammad, and Muḥammad b. Isma'íl), and each of these Seven great Prophets was succeeded by Seven Imáms, of whom the first was in each case the trusted ally and intimate, though "Silent" (*Ṣámit*), confidant of his "Speaking" (*Náṭiq*) chief, and his "Foundation" (*Asás*) or "Root" (*Sús*). The last of these Seven Imáms in each cycle was invariably followed by Twelve Apostles (*Naqíb*), with the last of whom that Prophetic Cycle came to an end and a new one began. The sixth of the Seven Prophetic Cycles, that of the Prophet Muḥammad, ended with the Seventh Imám, Isma'íl, and his *naqíbs*; and Isma'íl's son Muḥammad (whose grandson the first Fáṭimid Caliph, 'Ubaydu'lláh the Mahdí, claimed to be) inaugurated the seventh and last cycle. This great principle of the Seven Prophetic Cycles corresponded on the one hand with the Five Grades or Emanations of Being,[4] which, with

Isma'íli Doctrine.

[1] *Exposé de la Religion des Druzes* (Paris, 1838, 2 vols.).

[2] *Fragments relatifs à la Doctrine des Ismaélîs . . . avec traduction et notes* (Paris, 1874); *Un Grand Maître des Assassins* (Paris, 1877).

[3] *Mémoires sur les Carmathes du Bahraïn et les Fatimides* (Leyden, 1886).

[4] These are (1) the Universal Reason; (2) the Universal Soul; (3) Primal Matter; (4) Space; and (5) Time (or the Pleroma and the Kenoma). See the *Prolegomena*, pp. 409–410.

God and Man, made up the Sevenfold Universe, and was typified on the other in the Seven Degrees of Initiation through which the proselyte advanced to the Innermost Doctrine.[1] Every ceremony of religion and every object of the natural universe was but a type or symbol of these Esoteric Mysteries; a wonderful Sacrament, meaningless to the profane formalist and man of science, but to the initiated believer fraught with beauty and marvel. And, as we know from de Sacy's researches, it was the first business of the *dá'í*, or propagandist, to arouse the curiosity of the neophyte as to this esoteric significance of all things by such questions as: "Why did God create the Universe in Seven Days?" "Why are there Seven Heavens, Seven Earths (or Climes), Seven Seas, and Seven Verses in the Opening Chapter of the Qur'án?" "Why does the Vertebral Column contain Seven Cervical and Twelve Dorsal Vertebræ?"[2] The objection that neither this doctrine nor anything greatly resembling it had been taught by any of the Prophets whom they enumerated was met by the explanation that, according to a universal Law, while the Prophet was revealed, the Doctrine was concealed, and that it only became patent when he was latent. In every case the practical aim of the Isma'ílí *dá'í* or missionary was to induce the neophyte to take an oath of allegiance to himself and the Imám whom he represented, and to pay the Imám's money (a sort of "Peter's-pence"), which was at once the symbol of his obedience and his contribution to the material strength of the Church with which he had cast in his lot.

At the epoch of which we are now speaking al-Mustanṣir (Abú Tamím Ma'add), the eighth Fáṭimid Caliph (reigned

[1] These Degrees, with the Doctrine successively revealed in each, are fully described by de Sacy (*Exposé*, vol. i, pp. lxxiv–cxxxviii), and briefly on pp. 411–415 of the *Prolegomena*.

[2] Typifying the Seven Imáms supporting the Head or Chief of their Cycle and supported by the Twelve Naqíbs.

A.D. 1035–94), was the supreme head of all the Isma'ílís, whom the rival claims of his sons, Musta'lí and Nizár, divided after his death into two rival groups, a Western (Egyptian, Syrian, and North African) and an Eastern (Persian), of which the latter (afterwards extended to Syria) constituted the Assassins properly so-called. Al-Mustanṣir's predecessor, the probably insane al-Ḥákim bi amri'lláh ("He who rules according to God's command"), had concluded a reign of eccentric and capricious tyranny, culminating in a claim to receive Divine honours, by a "disappearance" which was almost certainly due to the murderous hand of some outraged victim of his caprice or cruelty, though some of his admirers and followers, the ancestors of the Syrian Druzes of to-day (who derive their name from al-Ḥákim's minister ad-Duruzí, who encouraged him in his pretensions), pretended and believed that he had merely withdrawn himself from the gaze of eyes unworthy to behold his sacred person.[1] The confusion caused by this event had subsided when al-Mustanṣir came to the throne in A.D. 1035, and his long reign of nearly sixty years may justly be regarded as the culminating point of the power and glory of the Isma'ílí or Fáṭimid dynasty, whose empire, in spite of the then recent loss of Morocco, Algiers, and Tunis, still included the rest of North Africa, Egypt, Sicily, Malta, and varying portions of Syria, Asia Minor, and the shores of the Red Sea. Indeed, in A.D. 1056 Wásiṭ, and two years later Baghdád itself, acknowledged al-Mustanṣir the Fáṭimid as their lord, while the allegiance of the Holy Cities of Mecca and Medina, lost for a while to him in A.D. 1070–71, was regained for a time in 1075; and, though Damascus was lost

Al-Mustanṣír, the eighth Fáṭimid Caliph.

[1] Ibnu'l-Athír (*sub anno* 434 = A.D. 1042–43) mentions the appearance in Cairo of a pretender who announced that he was al-Ḥákim returned to earth, and drew after himself many people, at the head of whom he attacked the palace of al-Mustanṣir. He was, however, taken prisoner, and, with many of his adherents, crucified and then shot to death with arrows. His name was Sikkín.

in the same year, Tyre, Sidon, and Acre were occupied by his troops in 1089.

Naṣir-i-Khusraw.

A description of al-Mustanṣir's Court, of his just and wise rule, and of the security and prosperity of his subjects, has been left to us by one of the most remarkable and original men whom Persia produced at this, or, indeed, at any other epoch—to wit, the celebrated poet, traveller, and Isma'ílí missionary, Náṣir-i-Khusraw, called by his fellow-religionists "the Proof" (*Ḥujjat*) of Khurásán. He is briefly mentioned in two places (ff. 286ª and 290^a of the British Museum Manuscript Add. 7,628) of the *Jámi'u't-Tawáríkh*, in connection with the successor to his see,[1] Ḥasan-i-Ṣabbáḥ. The first of these passages runs as follows:—

"Náṣir-i-Khusraw, attracted by the fame of al-Mustanṣir, came from Khurásán to Egypt,[2] where he abode seven years,[3] performing the Pilgrimage and returning to Egypt every year. Finally he came, after performing the [seventh] Pilgrimage, to Baṣra,[4] and so returned to Khurásán, where he carried on a propaganda for the 'Alawís [*i.e.*, Fáṭimid Caliphs] of Egypt in Balkh. His enemies attempted to destroy him, and he became a fugitive in the highlands of Simingán, where he remained for twenty years, content to subsist on water and herbs. Ḥasan-i-Ṣabbáḥ, the Ḥimyarite, of Yaman,[5]

---

[1] The Isma'ílís called each of the regions assigned to a Grand-*Dá'í*, or arch-propagandist, a "Sea" (*Baḥr*), and I have found the word-play, unfortunately, quite irresistible.

[2] In August, A.D. 1047, as we learn from his own record of his travels, the *Safar-náma*.

[3] He was only in Egypt for four years and a half, but he performed the Pilgrimage to Mecca seven times, and was absent from home for exactly seven lunar years (Jumáda II, A.H. 437, till Jumáda II, A.H. 444; *i.e.*, January, A.D. 1046, till October, A.D. 1052.

[4] In Sha'bán, A.H. 443 = December, A.D. 1051.

[5] He claimed to be descended from the old Himyarite Kings of Yaman, but he himself was born at Ray in Persia (near the modern Ṭihrán), and his ancestors had probably been settled in Persia for many generations. According to the *Jámi'u't-Tawáríkh*, however, his father came to Persia from Kúfa, and he was born at Qum.

came from Persia to al-Mustanṣir bi'lláh[1] disguised as a carpenter, and asked his permission to carry on a propaganda in the Persian lands. This permission having been accorded to him, he secretly inquired of al-Mustanṣir in whose name the propaganda should be conducted after his death; to which the Caliph [al-Mustanṣir] replied, 'In the name of my elder son, Nizár'; wherefore the Isma'ílís [of Persia] maintain the Imâmate of Nizár.[2] And 'Our Master' [*Sayyid-ná, i.e.*, Ḥasan-i-Ṣabbáḥ] chose [as the centres of his propaganda] the castles of Quhistán, as we shall presently relate."

Ḥasan-i-Ṣabbáḥ.

The second reference (f. 290^a) is too long to translate in full, and is cited, in what profess to be the *ipsissima verba* of Ḥasan-i-Ṣabbáḥ, from the already-mentioned *Sar-guzasht-i-Sayyid-ná.* According to this passage, Ḥasan-i-Ṣabbáḥ's full name was al-Ḥasan b. 'Alí b. Muḥammad b. Ja'far b. al-Ḥusayn b. aṣ-Ṣabbáḥ al-Ḥimyarí, but he would not allow his followers to record his pedigree, saying, "I would rather be the Imám's chosen servant than his unworthy son." His father came from Kúfa to Qum, where Ḥasan was born. From the age of seven he was passionately fond of study, and till the age of seventeen he read widely and voraciously.[3] Hitherto, like his father, he had belonged to the Sect of the Twelve; but about this time he fell under the influence of a Fáṭimid *dá'í* named Amír Ḍarráb, "and before him," he adds, "of Náṣir-i-Khusraw, the 'Proof' of Khurásán."[4] The pro-

[1] This was, according to Ibnu'l-Athír (vol. ix, p. 154, *sub anno* A.H. 427), in A.H. 479 (=A.D. 1086–87), but according to the *Jámi'u'l-Tawáríkh* (f. 290^b) on Wednesday, Ṣafar 18, A.H. 471 (= August 30, A.D. 1078).

[2] In opposition to those of Egypt, who accepted Nizár's brother Musta'lí. This latter sect is represented at this present day by the *Bahúras* in India, while the Ághá Khán and his followers represent the Persian branch.

[3] Ibnu'l-Athír (x, 110, *sub anno* 494) also describes him as "able, courageous, and learned in mathematics, arithmetic, astronomy (including, of course, astrology), and magic."

[4] The text is rather ambiguous, so that I am not sure whether we should understand before "Náṣir" the words "under the influence of," or simply "was." I incline to the first supposition, for Náṣir-i-Khusraw returned to Persia in A.D. 1052, and Ḥasan-i-Ṣabbáḥ, who was, as we learn from Ibnu'l-Athír (x, 110), suspected of frequenting the assemblies of the

paganda, he adds, had not met with much success in the time of Sulṭán Maḥmúd of Ghazna,[1] though previously Abú 'Alí b. Símjúr and the Sámánid Prince Naṣr b. Aḥmad,[2] with many persons of humbler condition, had embraced the Isma'ílí doctrine in Persia. After many long conferences and discussions with Amír Ḍarráb, Ḥasan remained unconvinced, though shaken ; but a severe illness, from which he scarcely expected to recover, seems to have inclined him still further to belief. On his recovery he sought out other Isma'ílí *dá'ís*, 'Bú Najm-i-Sarráj ("the Saddler"), and a certain Mú'min, who had been authorised to engage in the propaganda by Shaykh [Aḥmad b.] 'Abdu'l-Malik [b.] 'Aṭṭásh, a prominent leader of the Isma'ílís in Persia, mentioned both by al-Bundárí[3] and Ibnu'l-Athír.[4] This man was subsequently captured and crucified on the reduction of the Isma'ílí stronghold of Sháh-dizh or Dizh-kúh, near Iṣfahán, about A.H. 499 (= A.D. 1105–6). Mú'min ultimately, with some diffidence (for he recognised in Ḥasan-i-Ṣabbáḥ a superior in intelligence and force of character), received from the distinguished proselyte the *bí'at*, or oath of allegiance to the Fáṭimid Caliph. In Ramaḍán, A.H. 464 (May–June, 1072) Ibn 'Aṭṭásh, whose proper sphere of activity or "see" was Iṣfahán and Ádharbayján, came to Ray,

"Egyptian Propagandists" (*Du'átu'l-Miṣriyyín*) in Ray (on account of which suspicion he was compelled to flee from thence), may very well have met him. Judging by the modern analogy of the Bábís, it is quite certain to me that a young and promising proselyte would without fail be presented to an eminent and able propagandist just arrived from the centre of the movement with full credentials to the faithful in Persia.

[1] An emissary of the Fáṭimids called at-Táhartí (from Táhart, a town in Morocco) came to Sulṭán Maḥmúd about A.H. 393 (A.D. 1003). See the Cairo ed. of al-'Utbí, vol. ii, pp. 238–251.

[2] The Nidhámu'l-Mulk in his *Siyásat-náma* (ed. Schefer, pp. 188–193) accuses Nasr II of being a "Báṭiní," or Isma'ílí, and describes how his heresy cost him his life and his throne. See also pp. 455–6 of my *Prolegomena* to this volume.

[3] Pp. 90 and 92, where he is called "the chief (*ra'ís*) of the Báṭinís."

[4] Vol. x, pp. 109–110, where it is said that the Báṭinís crowned him with a crown of gold. Ḥasan-i-Ṣabbáḥ is there (p. 110) also described as "one of his pupils."

saw and approved Ḥasan b. Ṣabbáḥ, and bade him go to Egypt, to Cairo, the Fáṭimid capital. Accordingly, in A.H. 467 (A.D. 1074–75) he went to Iṣfahán, whence, after acting for two years as Ibn 'Aṭṭásh's vicar or deputy, he proceeded to Egypt by way of Ádharbayján, Mayáfáriqín, Mawṣil, Sinjár, Raḥba, Damascus, Sidon, Tyre, Acre, and thence by sea. On his arrival at his destination on August 30, A.D. 1078, he was honourably received by the Chief Dá'í (*Dá'í'd-Du'át*) Bú Dá'úd and other notables, and was the object of special favours on the part of al-Mustanṣir, whom, however, he was not privileged to see in person, though he remained at Cairo for eighteen months. At the end of this period he was compelled —by the jealousy of Musta'lí and his partisans, especially Badr, the commander-in-chief, as we are informed—to leave Egypt; and he embarked at Alexandria in Rajab, A.H. 472 (January, A.D. 1080), was wrecked on the Syrian coast, and returned by way of Aleppo, Baghdád, and Khúzistán to Iṣfahán, which he reached at the end of Dhu'l-Ḥijja, A.H. 473 (June, 1081). Thence he extended his propaganda in favour of Nizár, the elder son of al-Mustanṣir, to Yazd, Kirmán, Ṭabaristán, Dámghán, and other parts of Persia, though he avoided Ray, for fear of the Nidhámu'l-Mulk, who was eager to effect his capture, and had given special instructions to that effect to his son-in-law Abú Muslim, the Governor of Ray.[1] Finally he reached Qazwín, and, by a bold stratagem, fully described in the *Ta'ríkh-i-Guzída*,[2] obtained possession of the strong mountain fortress of Alamút, originally *Áluh-ámú't*, a name correctly explained by Ibnu'l-Athír (x, 110) as *ta'límu'l-'aqáb*, "the Eagle's Teaching"; more often, but, as I think, less correctly, as "the Eagle's Nest."[3] As noticed by most historians, by an extra-

[1] Cf. Ibnu'l-Athír, x, 110.

[2] Pp. 488–491 of Gantin's edition (vol. i); also in the *Jámi'u't-Tawáríkh*, f. 291[a].

[3] *Aluh* is a good Persian (and Pahlawí) word for "an eagle," and *ámú't* is provincial for *ámúkht*, "taught," but I know of no word the least resembling this which means "nest.

ordinary coincidence the sum of the numerical values of the letters comprised in the name of this castle (1 + 30 + 5 + 1 + 40 + 6 + 400 = 483) gives the date (A.H. 483 = A.D. 1090–91) of its capture by Ḥasan-i-Ṣabbáḥ.

Other strongholds of the Assassins in Persia.

The capture of Alamút, which was rapidly followed by the seizure of many other similar strongholds,[1] like Sháh-Dizh and Khálanján, near Iṣfahán; Ṭabas, Tún, Qá'in, Zawzan, Khúr and Khúsaf, in Quhistán; Washmkúh, near Abhar; Ustúnáwand, in Mázandarán; Ardahán; Gird-i-Kúh; Qal'atu'n-Nádhir, in Khúzistán; Qal'atu'ṭ-Ṭanbúr, near Arraján; and Qal'atu Khallád Khán, in Fárs, marks the beginning of the political power of the followers of Ḥasan-i-Ṣabbáḥ, who, on the death of al-Mustanṣir, became definitely separated in their aims from the Isma'ílís of Egypt, since they espoused the cause of Nizár, while al-Musta'lí, another son of al-Mustanṣir, succeeded to the Fáṭimid Caliphate of Cairo. Hence, in nearly all Persian histories, such as the *Jámi'u't-Tawáríkh* and the *Ta'ríkh-i-Guzída*, separate sections are generally assigned to the "Isma'ílís of Egypt and the West" and the "Isma'ílís of Persia," "Nizárís," or, to give them the name by which they are best known, "Assassins."

Etymology of the word "Assassin."

The etymology of the name "Assassin" was long disputed, and many absurd derivations were suggested. Some supposed it to be a corruption of *Hasaniyyún* (*-yín*), or "followers of Ḥasan"; Caseneuve proposed to connect it with the Anglo-Saxon word *seâx*, "a knife"; and Gébélin wished to derive it from *Sháhinsháh* (for *Sháhán-sháh*), "King of kings," while many equally impossible theories were advanced. It was reserved for that great scholar Sylvestre de Sacy to show that the word, variously corrupted by the Crusaders (through whom it came into Europe) into Assassini, Assessini, Assissini, and Heissessini, was more closely

[1] Ibnu'l-Athír (x, 109–111) devotes a section of his chronicle for the year A.H. 494 to their enumeration and description.

represented by the Greek chroniclers as *χασισίοι*, and most accurately of all by the *Ḥashishin* of Rabbi Benjamin of Tudela; and that it stood for the Arabic *Ḥashíshí* (in the plural *Ḥashíshiyyún* or *Ḥashíshiyya*),[1] a name given to the sect because of the use which they made of the drug *Ḥashísh*, otherwise known to us as "Indian hemp," "bang," or *Cannabis Indica*. This drug is widely used in most Muhammadan countries from Morocco to India at the present day, and allusions to it in Jalálu'd-Dín Rúmí, Ḥáfidh, and other poets show that it has been familiar to the Persians since, at any rate, the thirteenth century of our era. But, at the epoch of which we are speaking, the secret of its properties seems to have been known in Persia only to a few—in fact, to Ḥasan-i-Ṣabbáḥ and his chief confederates, amongst whom, we may recollect, was at least one physician, the already-mentioned Aḥmad b. 'Abdu'l-Malik b. 'Aṭṭásh.

Ill repute of *Ḥashísh.*

I have elsewhere[2] discussed at greater length than is possible here the use and peculiarities of this drug, and I there emphasised the evil repute, as compared with opium and other narcotics, which it bears in Persia, where it is seldom mentioned save in some metaphorical way, as "the Green Parrot," "the Mysteries," "Master Sayyid," and so on; and I ascribed this ill repute less to the harmfulness of the drug than to its close association with a heretical and terrifying sect. It must not, however, be imagined that the *habitual* use of *ḥashísh* was encouraged, or even permitted, amongst his followers by the "Old Man of the Mountain," for its habitual use causes a lethargy, negligence, and mental weakness which would have fatally disqualified those to whom it was administered from the effective

[1] By Persian historians this term is much more rarely employed than *Mulḥid* (pl. *Maláḥida*), but it is used by al-Bundárí, p. 169.

[2] In the Mid-sessional Address delivered before the Abernethian Society on January 14, 1897, and entitled *A Chapter from the History of Cannabis Indica*; published in the *St. Bartholomew's Hospital Journal* for March, 1897.

performance of the delicate tasks with which they were charged; and its use was confined to one of the Grades or Degrees into which the Isma'ílí organisation was divided. These Grades of Initiation existed, as we have seen, from an early period in the Isma'ílí sect, but after the "New Propaganda" they were in some degree rearranged by Ḥasan-i-Ṣabbáḥ as follows. At the head of the Order (subject at this time to the Imám, who, after the death of al-Mustanṣir, was no longer the Fáṭimid Caliph, but a son of his disinherited and murdered brother Nizár) stood the *Dá'í'd-Du'át*, Chief-Propagandist, or Grand Master, commonly called outside the circle of his followers *Shaykhu'l-Jabal*, "the Mountain Chief," a term which the Crusaders, owing to a misunderstanding, rendered "le Vieux," "the Old One," or "the Old Man of the Mountain." Next came the Grand Priors, or Superior Propagandists (*Dá'í-i-Kabír*), who formed a kind of episcopacy, and to each of whom was probably committed the charge of a particular district or "see."[1] After these came the ordinary propagandists, or *dá'ís*. These formed the higher grades, and were pretty fully initiated into the real doctrines, aims, and politics of the Order. The lower grades comprised the *Rafíqs*, or "Companions" of the Order, who were partly initiated; the *Láṣiqs*, or "Adherents," who had yielded the oath of allegiance without much comprehension of what it involved; and, lastly, the *Fidá'ís*, or "Self-devoted Ones," the "Destroying Angels" and ministers of vengeance of the Order, and the cause of that far-reaching terror which it inspired—a terror which made kings tremble on their thrones and checked the angry anathemas of outraged orthodoxy.

Degrees or Grades in the Order of the Assassins.

In this connection I cannot refrain from again quoting the graphic and entertaining account of the initiation of these *Fidá'ís* given by Marco Polo in the thirteenth century of our era, at a time when the power of the Assassins in Persia (for in Syria they continued to hold their own, and, though quite

[1] See p. 200, n. 1, *supra*.

innocuous, continue to exist there even at the present day) had been just destroyed, or was just about to be destroyed, by the devastating Mongols of Hulágú Khán :—

Marco Polo's description.

"The Old Man," says he, "was called in their language Aloadin.[1] He had caused a certain valley between two mountains to be enclosed, and had turned it into a garden, the largest and most beautiful that ever was seen, filled with every variety of fruit. In it were well-erected pavilions and palaces, the most elegant that can be imagined, all covered with gilding and exquisite painting. And there were runnels, too, flowing freely with wine and milk, and honey and water, and numbers of ladies, and of the most beautiful damsels in the world, who could play on all manner of instruments, and sing most sweetly, and dance in a manner that was most charming to behold. For the Old Man desired to make his people believe that this was actually Paradise. So he fashioned it after the description that Mahomet gave of his Paradise—to wit, that it should be a beautiful garden running with conduits of wine and milk and honey and water, and full of lovely women for the delectation of all its inmates. And, sure enough, the Saracens of those parts believed that it *was* Paradise!

"Now no man was allowed to enter the garden save those whom he intended to be his *Ashishin*.[2] There was a fortress at the entrance of the garden strong enough to resist all the world, and there was no other way to get in. He kept at his Court a number of the youths of the country, from twelve to twenty years of age, such as had a taste for soldiering, and to these he used to tell tales about Paradise, just as Mahomet had been wont to do; and they believed in him, just as the Saracens believe in Mahomet. Then he would introduce them into his garden, some four or six or ten at a time, having made them drink a certain potion[3] which cast them into a deep sleep, and then causing them to be lifted and carried in. So when they awoke they found themselves in the garden.

---

[1] He is speaking, apparently, of the seventh Grand Master of Alamút, 'Alá'u'd-Dín Muḥammad b. al-Ḥasan, who succeeded his father Jalálu'd-Dín in Ramaḍán, A.H. 618 (= November, A.D. 1221), and whose son, Ruknu'd-Dín Khursháh, the last Grand Master of Alamút, was captured and put to death by the Mongols.

[2] *I.e.*, the *Fidá'ís*, to whom alone, as we have seen, the term *Assassin* is really applicable.

[3] This was the decoction of *Ḥashísh;* and hence the "Old Man," the provider of this potion, is sometimes called *Ṣáḥibu'l-Ḥashísh.*

"When, therefore, they awoke and found themselves in a place so charming, they deemed that it was Paradise in very truth. And the ladies and damsels dallied with them to their heart's content, so that they had what young men would have; and with their own good will would they never have quitted the place.

"Now this Prince, whom we call the Old One, kept his Court in grand and noble style, and made those simple hill-folks about him believe firmly that he was a great prophet. And when he wanted any of his *Ashishin* to send on any mission, he would cause that potion whereof I spoke to be given to one of the youths in the garden, and then had him carried into his palace. So when the young man awoke he found himself in the castle, and no longer in that Paradise, whereat he was not over-well pleased. He was then conducted to the Old Man's presence, and bowed before him with great veneration, as believing himself to be in the presence of a true prophet. The Prince would then ask whence he came, and he would reply that he came from Paradise, and that it was exactly such as Mahomet has described it in the law. This, of course, gave the others who stood by, and who had not been admitted, the greatest desire to enter therein.

"So when the Old Man would have any prince slain, he would say to such a youth, 'Go thou and slay So-and-so, and when thou returnest my angels shall bear thee into Paradise. And shouldst thou die, natheless even so will I send my angels to carry thee back into Paradise.' So he caused them to believe, and thus there was no order of his that he would not affront any peril to execute, for the great desire that they had to get back into that Paradise of his. And in this manner the Old One got his people to murder any one whom he desired to get rid of. Thus, too, the great dread that he inspired all princes withal made them become his tributaries, in order that he might abide at peace and amity with them."

Blind obedience of the Fidá'is.

The blind obedience of these *Fidá'is*, who, as will have been gathered from the above quotation, were chosen with special regard to this quality, combined with courage and adroitness, and were not initiated into the philosophical conceptions of the higher degrees of the Order, is well illustrated by an anecdote preserved to us by Fra Pipino and Marino Sanuto :—

"When, during a period of truce, Henry, Count of Champagne (titular King of Jerusalem), was on a visit to the Old Man of Syria, one day, as they walked together, they saw some lads in white sitting on the top of a high tower. The *Shaykh*, turning to the Count, asked if he had any subjects as obedient as his own; and, without waiting for a reply, made a sign to two of the boys, who immediately leaped from the tower and were killed on the spot."

The *Fidá'ís*, though unlearned in the esoteric mysteries of their religion, were carefully trained not only in the use of arms, the endurance of fatigue, and the arts of disguise, but also, in some cases at any rate, in foreign and even European languages; for those deputed to assassinate Conrad, Marquis of Montferrat, were sufficiently conversant with the Frankish language and customs to pass as Christian monks during the six months which they spent in the Crusaders' camp awaiting an opportunity for the accomplishment of their deadly errand. It was seldom, of course, that they survived their victims, especially as they were fond of doing their work in the most dramatic style, striking down the Muslim *Amír* on a Friday in the mosque, and the Christian Prince or Duke on a Sunday in the church, in sight of the assembled congregation. Yet so honourable a death and so sure a way to future happiness was it deemed by the followers of Ḥasan-i-Ṣabbáḥ to die on one of the "Old One's" quests, that we read of the mothers of *Fidá'ís* who wept to see their sons return alive.

Sometimes they only threatened, if thus they could compass their end. The leader who marched to attack one of their strongholds would wake up some morning in his tent to find stuck in the earth beside him a dagger, on which was transfixed a note of warning which might well turn him back from his expedition; as is said (but not, I think, on good authority) to have happened to Malikshāh, and later to Saladin. And a theological professor, confronted by a quasi-student, whose diligent attendance and close attention to his lectures had favourably attracted his notice, with a choice between a purse of gold and a dagger as alternative inducements to him to cease reviling the "heretics" of Alamút, wisely chose the former; and thereafter, when rallied on his avoidance of all disrespectful allusion to them, was wont to reply, with some humour, that he had been "convinced by arguments both *weighty* and *trenchant*" that he had been wrong to indulge in such uncharitable utterances.

Until the final destruction of their strongholds in Persia, and the capture and execution of their eighth and last Grand Master, Ruknu'd-Dín Khursháh, by the Mongols in the middle of the thirteenth century, about the same time that the Caliphate of Baghdád was also extinguished, the Assassins were very active, and will be repeatedly mentioned in these pages, so that it is essential that the reader should have a clear idea of their principles, their organisation, and their relation to the parent sect of the Isma'ílís of Egypt, in the history of which the "New Propaganda" instituted by Ḥasan-i-Ṣabbáḥ, with the new element of physical violence and terrorism which it involved, marks an important epoch. Of the Syrian branch, which made the Order famous in Europe and enriched our language with a new word, and whose political power dates from the seizure of the Castle of Banias about A.D. 1126, we shall not have much occasion to speak; but no one interested in their history should fail to read Stanislas Guyard's most fascinating paper in the *Journal Asiatique* for 1877, *Un Grand Maître des Assassins.* This true and judicious account of the remarkable Shaykh Ráshidu'd-Dín Sinán, who for a while rendered the Syrian branch of the Order independent of the Persian, rivals in interest the most thrilling romance, and supplies a mass of detail concerning the history, achievements, and methods of the sect which I am compelled to omit in this place. Even at the present day the remnants of this once powerful body are widely, though sparsely, scattered through the East, in Syria, Persia, East Africa, Central Asia, and India, where the Ághá Khán—a lineal descendant of Ruknu'd-Dín Khúrsháh, the last Grand Master of Alamút, who himself claimed descent through Nizár, the son of al-Mustanṣir, the Fáṭimid Caliph, from Isma'íl, the Seventh Imám, and great-great-great-grandson of the Prophet's cousin and son-in-law, 'Alí b. Abí Ṭálib—is still honoured as the titular head of this branch of the Isma'ílís.

In following the career and examining the achievements of Ḥasan-i-Ṣabbáḥ we have wandered away from his earlier co-religionist, Náṣir-i-Khusraw, who, from the purely literary point of view, is of greater importance; since, while of the writings of the former we possess no thing (so far as is at present known) except the extracts from the *Sar-guzasht-i-Sayyidná* cited in the *Jahán-gushá* and the *Jámi'u't-Tawáríkh*, of the latter we possess numerous works of the highest value and interest, both in verse and prose, several of which have been the objects of very careful study by Bland, Dorn, Ethé, Fagnan, Nöldeke, Pertsch, Rieu, Schefer, and other eminent scholars. With these and with their author—one of the most attractive and remarkable personalities in Persian literary history—we shall deal in the next chapter, which will be devoted to the literature of the same period whereof we have sketched in this chapter the outward political aspect.

Náṣir-i-Khusraw.

CHAPTER IV

THE LITERATURE OF THE EARLY SELJÚQ PERIOD: THE NIDHÁMU'L-MULK AND HIS CONTEMPORARIES

The Nidhámu'l-Mulk's *Siyásat-náma.*

It seems proper to the perspective of this most interesting and important period that we should begin by considering briefly the literary work of the Nidhámu'l-Mulk himself, who is its dominant figure. This, so far as we know (for the *Waṣáyá*, or "Testament," is notoriously spurious), consists of one work, the *Siyásat-náma*, or "Treatise on the Art of Government," of which the Persian text was published by the late M. Charles Schefer in 1891, and the translation into French, with valuable historical notes, in 1893; while a *Supplement*, containing notices bearing on the life and times of the Nidhámu'l-Mulk extracted from various Persian and Arabic works, was published in 1897. Before the appearance of this edition the book was hardly accessible, manuscripts of it being rare. M. Schefer used three (his own, now in the Bibliothèque Nationale, the British Museum Codex, and another from Berlin, with partial collation of the two St. Petersburg manuscripts). A sixth is to be found in the Pote Collection preserved in the library of King's College, Cambridge, and this, though modern, has been of great service to me in making much-needed corrections in the published text.

The *Siyásat-náma* comprises fifty sections or chapters treating of nearly every royal duty and prerogative and every department of administration. It was written in A.H. 484 (= A.D. 1091–92), only a year before the author's assassination, in response to a request addressed by Malikshāh to his most able and experienced advisers,[1] that each of them should compose a treatise on government, pointing out what defects existed in the organisation and administration of his realms, what evil innovations had been suffered to creep in, and what good customs of former times had been allowed to fall into desuetude. Of the treatises composed in response to this request that of the Nidhámu'l-Mulk was most highly approved by Malikshāh, who said: "All these topics he has treated as my heart desired; there is nothing to be added to his book, which I adopt as my guide, and by which I will walk." It was concluded in A.H. 485 (A.D. 1092–93), only a very short time before the author's assassination, as appears from the following strangely prophetic words occurring in the conclusion: "This is the Book of Government which hath been written. The Lord of the World had commanded his servant to make a compilation on this subject, which was done according to his command. Thirty-nine sections[2] I wrote at once *extempore*, and submitted them to that exalted Court, where they met with approval. This was a very brief [outline], but afterwards I added to it, supplementing each chapter with such observations as were appropriate to it, and explaining all in lucid language. And in the year A.H. 485, when we were about to set out for Baghdád, I gave it to the private copyist of the Royal Library, Muḥammad Maghribí, and ordered him to transcribe it in a fair hand; *so that should I not be destined to return from this journey*, he may lay this book before the Lord of the World. . . ." The book, therefore, was not published until after the author's death, and probably its appearance was

[1] Besides the Nidhámu'l-Mulk, those specially mentioned are Sharafu'l-Mulk, Táju'l-Mulk, and Majdu'l-Mulk.

[2] The remaining eleven chapters appear to have been added at the time of revision.

further delayed by the troubles and civil wars which immediately supervened on Malikshâh's decease.[1]

The *Siyásat-náma* is, in my opinion, one of the most valuable and interesting prose works which exist in Persian, both because of the quantity of historical anecdotes which it contains and because it embodies the views on government of one of the greatest Prime Ministers whom the East has produced—a Minister whose strength and wisdom is in no way better proved than by the chaos and internecine strife which succeeded his death. It is written in a style extraordinarily simple and unadorned, devoid of any kind of rhetorical artifice, at times almost colloquial and even careless, and marked by a good many archaic forms characteristic of this early period. A book so extensive in scope cannot be adequately reviewed in a work like this; and as it is accessible to European readers in M. Schefer's excellent French translation, such review, even were it possible, would be unnecessary. Attention should also be directed to a review of it from the pen of Professor Nöldeke, of Strassburg, which appeared in vol. xlvi (pp. 761–768) of the *Zeitschrift der Deutschen Morgenländischen Gesellschaft* for 1892.

Seven chapters (xli–xlvii, pp. 138–205) are devoted to the denunciation of heretics, especially the Isma'ílís and Báṭinís. The author complains bitterly (p. 139) that Jews, Christians, Fire-worshippers (*gabrs*), and Carmathians are employed by the Government, and praises the greater stringency in this matter observed in Alp Arslán's reign. He argues hotly against the Shí'ites in general and the "Sect of the Seven" in particular, and endeavours to prove that their doctrines are in their essence originally derived from the communist pseudo-prophet Mazdak, whom Anúshirwán the Sásánian slew in the sixth century of the Christian era.[2] Of Mazdak he gives a long

[1] See the Persian editor's note at the end of the Table of Contents, p. 5 of the text.

[2] A full account of Mazdak is given in the *Prolegomena* to this volume, pp. 166–172.

and detailed account (pp. 166–181), and describes how, after the massacre of him and his followers, his doctrine was carried on and revived successively by the Khurramís or Khurram-dínán,[1] Sindbád the Gabr,[2] and 'Abdu'lláh b. Maymún al-Qaddáḥ,[3] who first made the Isma'ílí sect powerful and formidable, and from whom, as their opponents declared, the Fáṭimí, or 'Alawí, Caliphs of Egypt were descended. This portion of the book also comprises a dissertation on the evils wrought by the interference of women in affairs of State, and on the hereditary character of the qualities essential to a great Minister, and there is a good deal of information about the activity of the Isma'ílí propagandists in Sámánid times, especially as to their brief ascendancy during the reign of the ill-starred Naṣr b. Aḥmad (A.D. 913–942),[4] but little or nothing about the "New Propaganda," and no explicit allusion to its originator, Ḥasan-i-Ṣabbáḥ. Implicit references to the growing power of the Báṭinís are, however, numerous, and there is no doubt that the whole of this portion of the book is levelled against Ḥasan-i-Ṣabbáḥ and his followers, as appears pretty clearly from the opening paragraphs of chap. xliii,[5] which begins thus :—

"*Setting forth the character of the heretics who are the foes of Church and State.*

"I desire to devote a few chapters to the rebellions of schismatics, so that all men may know what compassion for this Dynasty doth inspire me, and what loyalty and zeal I bear towards the Seljúq Kingdom, especially towards the Lord of the World (may God make his kingdom eternal !) and his children and household (may the Evil Eye be remote from his reign !).

---

[1] *Prolegomena*, pp. 312–313 and 323 *et seqq.*

[2] Ibid., pp. 313–314.

[3] Ibid., pp. 393–398.

[4] Ibid., p. 456.

[5] This chapter is really xliv, and is so numbered in the translation (p. 242), but in the text, by an oversight, chap. xl and chap. xli are both numbered xl, so that all the succeeding chapters of the text have numbers one short of those they should bear.

"Schismatics have existed at all times, and in every region of the world, from the time of Adam until now, they have revolted against kings and prophets. There is no faction more accursed, more unsound in their religion, or more evil in their deeds than these people. Let [the King] know that behind their walls they meditate evil to this Kingdom, and seek to corrupt religion: their ears are straining for a sound and their eyes for an occasion of ill-doing. If (which God forbid!) any calamitous event (from which God be our refuge!) should befall this victorious dynasty (may God Almighty confirm its endurance!), or if any reverse should happen, these dogs will emerge from their hiding-places, and rise against this Empire to carry out their Shí'ite propaganda. Their power exceeds that of the Ráfiḍís and Khurram-dínís, and all that can be done will be done [by them], nor will they spare aught of sedition, slander or schism. Ostensibly they claim to be Muslims, but in reality their deeds are those of unbelievers, for their hearts (God curse them!) are contrary to their appearance, and their words to their deeds. The religion of Muḥammad the Elect (*Muṣṭafá*) hath, indeed, no more malignant and accursed foe than these, nor the Empire of the Lord of the World any worse enemy; and those persons who to-day have no power in this Empire, and claim to be Shí'ites are [in reality] of this faction, working to accomplish their aims, and strengthening them and carrying on their propaganda. Therefore they seek to persuade the Lord of the World to overthrow the House of the 'Abbásids; and should I remove the lid from this cauldron, how many disgraceful things would come forth therefrom! *But since a certain wealth hath accrued to the Lord of the World through their activities, therefore he is prone to take some step in this direction, by reason of the increased revenue whereof they hold out hopes, making the King eager for wealth. They represent me as a prejudiced advocate, so that my advice on this matter is unlikely to prove acceptable; and their seditious cunning will only become apparent when I shall have departed hence. Then will the King know how great was my loyalty to this victorious Dynasty, and that I was not unacquainted with the character and designs of this faction, which I constantly presented to the Royal judgement* (may God exalt it!), *and did not conceal; though, seeing that my remarks on this subject were not acceptable, I did not again repeat them.*"

The implication contained in the beginning of the italicised portion of the above extract is in striking agreement with a passage (f. 14^a) in the manuscript of the *Ráḥatu'ṣ-Ṣudúr*, where the author complains that "heretic myrmidons" abound and give rise to the distress and heavy taxation against which he protests. These heretics, he adds, come for the most part from the towns of Qum, Káshán, Ray, Ába, and Faráhán, and *gain office by promising the King an increased revenue* (*tawfír*, the very word used by the Nidhámu'l-Mulk in the passage above cited), "under which expression they cloak their exactions." Some confirmation is hereby afforded to an incident in what I may call the classical legend of the counter-intrigues of the Nidhámu'l-Mulk and Ḥasan-i-Ṣabbáḥ, where the latter is represented as recommending himself to the King's favour by a fiscal optimism wherein was implied a disparagement of the Nidhámu'l-Mulk's finance.[1]

In concluding this too brief notice of a most interesting and valuable work, I feel bound to add that, though there is no Persian prose work on which I have lectured with so much pleasure and profit to myself—and I hope also to my hearers—as this, yet the historical anecdotes must be accepted with a certain reserve, while serious anachronisms are of constant occurrence. Thus, on p. 12 of the text, Ya'qúb b. Layth is represented as threatening to bring the Fáṭimid rival of the 'Abbásid Caliph al-Mu'tamid (who reigned from A.D. 870 until 892) from Mahdiyya, which was not founded until A.D. 910 at the earliest computation, and perhaps not till ten years later, and similar errors are common, especially in what concerns the "heretics," with whom, as though by some prophetic instinct of his doom, the author seems to have been so painfully preoccupied as almost to lose his sense of historical proportion and perspective. Indeed, it seems by no means unlikely that his vehement denunciations of their doctrines, practices, and aims may have supplied them with the strongest incentive to his assassination.

I have already briefly alluded in the previous chapter to one

[1] The story will be found in its typical form in the *Ta'ríkh-i-Guzída*, Jules Gantin's text and translation, vol. i, pp. 208–211.

of the most remarkable men of this epoch whose literary work we must now consider. I mean Náṣir-i-Khusraw, the poet, traveller, and Isma'ílí propagandist. About his personality there has grown up a mass of legend mainly derived from the spurious autobiography prefixed to the Tabríz edition of his *Díwán*. This tissue of fables, mingled, apparently, with details drawn from the lives of other eminent persons, and concluding with an account, put in the mouth of Náṣir's brother, of his death at the age of 140 and his supernatural burial by the *Jinn*, occurs, as Ethé has pointed out,[1] in three recensions, of which the longest and most detailed occurs in Taqí Káshí's *Khuláṣatu'l-ash'ár*, and the shortest in the *Haft Iqlím* and the *Safína*, while that given by Luṭf 'Alí Beg in his *Átash-kada* stands midway between the two. A translation of the recension last mentioned was published by N. Bland in vol. vii of the *Journal of the Royal Asiatic Society*, pp. 360 *et seqq*., and the substance of it (omitting the marvels) is given by Schefer in the Introduction to his edition and translation of the *Safar-náma* (pp. viii–xvii). As it stands it is probably, as Ethé supposes, a product of the ninth or tenth century of the *hijra* (fifteenth or sixteenth of the Christian era); for the *Haft Iqlím* is apparently the earliest work in which it occurs, and this was written in A.H. 1002 (A.D. 1593–94). But at a much earlier date many legends gathered round Náṣir-i-Khusraw, as we see from the account of him contained in al-Qazwíní's *Átháru'l-Biláa* (pp. 328–9, *s.v.* Yumgán), a geographical work composed about A.D. 1276. Here he is represented as a King of Balkh, driven out by his subjects, who took refuge in Yumgán, which he adorned with wonderful baths, gardens, and talismanic figures, whereon none might gaze without fear of losing his reason. The bath in particular, which, as the

Náṣir-i-Khusraw.

[1] See his very interesting article on the *Rawshaná'í-náma* in vol. xxiii of the *Z.D.M.G.* for 1879, pp. 645–665.

author declares, was still existing in his time, is described in great detail.

Here is one of the picturesque incidents with which the Pseudo-Autobiography is adorned, and which, in all its essentials, occurs in a manuscript dated A.H. 714 (= A.D. 1314–15) preserved in the India Office Library[1] :—

Specimen of the Pseudo-Autobiography.

"After much trouble we reached the city of Níshápúr, there being with us a pupil of mine, an expert and learned metaphysician. Now in the whole city of Níshápúr there was no one who knew us, so we came and took up our abode in a mosque. As we walked through the city, at the door of every mosque by which we passed men were cursing me, and accusing me of heresy and atheism; but the disciple knew nothing of their opinion concerning me. One day, as I was passing through the *bázár*, a man from Egypt saw and recognised me, saying, 'Art thou not Náṣir-i-Khusraw, and is not this thy brother Abú Sa'íd?' In terror I seized his hand, and, engaging him in conversation, led him to my lodging. Then I said, 'Take thirty thousand *mithqáls* of gold, and refrain from divulging the secret.' When he had consented, I at once bade my familiar spirit produce that sum, gave it to him, and thrust him forth from my lodging. Then I went with Abú Sa'íd to the *bázár*, halted at the shop of a cobbler, and gave him my shoes to repair, that we might go forth from the city, when suddenly a clamour made itself heard near at hand, and the cobbler hurried off in the direction whence the sounds proceeded. After a while he returned with a piece of flesh on the point of his bradawl. 'What,' inquired I, 'was the disturbance, and what is this piece of flesh?' 'Why,' replied the cobbler, 'it seems that one of Náṣir-i-Khusraw's disciples appeared in the city and began to dispute with its doctors, who repudiated his assertions, each adducing some respectable authority, while he continued to quote in support of his views verses of Náṣir-i-Khusraw. So the clergy as a meritorious action tore him in pieces, and I too, to earn some merit, cut off a portion of his flesh.' When I learned what had befallen my disciple, I could no longer control myself, and said to the cobbler, 'Give me

[1] Selections from the *Díwáns* of six old Persian poets, No. 132 (the same manuscript from which the frontispiece of this volume is taken). My translation is from the Tabríz edition of the *Díwán*, pp. 6–7, and was published in my *Year amongst the Persians*, pp. 479–480.

my shoes, for one should not tarry in a city where the verses of Náṣir-i-Khusraw are recited.' So I took my shoes, and with my brother came forth from the city of Níshápúr."

Another fictitious episode in the Pseudo-Autobiography describes how Náṣir-i-Khusraw, having fled from Egypt to Baghdád, is made *wazír* to the 'Abbásid Caliph al-Qádir bi'lláh, and sent by him as an ambassador to the *Maláḥida*, or "Heretics" (*i.e.*, Assassins), of Gílán, who discover his identity with the philosopher whose works they admire, load him with unwelcome honours, and refuse to let him depart until, to secure his release, he compasses the death of their king by magical means, and afterwards, by the invocation of the planet Mars, destroys the army of his pursuers. One knows not which to admire the more, the supernatural features of this episode, or the gross anachronisms which it involves, for the Caliph al-Qádir died in A.D. 1031, while, as we have seen, the Assassins first established themselves in Gílán in A.D. 1090. One feature of this legend, however, seems to be a misplaced reminiscence of an incident which really belongs to the life of another later philosopher, Naṣíru'd-Dín of Ṭús, who, as is well known, actually did dedicate the original, or first edition, of his celebrated Ethics (the *Akhláq-i-Náṣirí*) to the Isma'ílí governor of Quhistán, Naṣíru'd-Dín 'Abdu'r-Raḥím b. Abí Manṣúr. Similarity of names, combined with a vague knowledge ot Náṣir-i-Khusraw's connection with the Isma'ílí sect, no doubt suggested to the compiler of the Pseudo-Autobiography the idea of making Náṣir-i-Khusraw write a commentary on the Qur'án explaining the sacred text according to the heretical views of his host, which unfortunate undertaking is represented as the cause of the disaster at Níshápúr mentioned above.

Another fiction of the Pseudo-Autobiography.

Leaving the Pseudo-Autobiography, we must now proceed to consider Náṣir-i-Khusraw's genuine works, the prose *Safar-náma*, or Narrative of his Travels (edited and translated by

Schefer, Paris, 1881); the *Díwán*, or collected poems (lithographed at Tabríz in A.H. 1280 = A.D. 1864); the *Rawshaná'l-náma*, or Book of Light (published, with translation and commentary, by Dr. Ethé in the *Z.D.M.G.* for 1879–1880, vol. xxxiii, pp. 645–665, vol. xxxiv, pp. 428–468 and 617–642); and the *Sa'ádat-náma*, or Book of Felicity (published by Fagnan in the volume of the *Z.D.M.G.* last mentioned, pp. 643–674). Besides these, another work of this writer, the *Zádu'l-Musáfirín*, or Pilgrims' Provision, is preserved to us in a manuscript formerly belonging to M. Schefer, and now in the Bibliothèque Nationale at Paris. Of these, we shall speak first of the *Safar-náma*, or "Book of Travels," since this furnishes us with the surest basis for an outline of the poet's life.

Extant works of Náṣir-i-Khusraw.

The *Safar-náma* is written in the same simple and unadorned style as the *Siyásat-náma*. The author, who gives his full name as Abú Mu'íni'd-Dín Náṣir-i-Khusraw al-Qubádiyání al-Marwazí,[1] says that he was employed for some while in Khurásán as a secretary and revenue-officer under Government, in the time of Chaghrí Beg Dá'úd the Seljúqid. In the autumn of A.D. 1045, being warned by a dream, he determined to renounce the use of wine, to which he had hitherto been much addicted, as being "the only thing capable of lessening the sorrow of the world," and to undertake the pilgrimage to Mecca. At this time he was about forty years of age. He performed a complete ablution, repaired to the Mosque of Júzjánán, where he then happened to be, registered a solemn vow of repentance, and set out on his journey on Thursday, the sixth of Jumáda II, A.H. 437 (= December 19, A.D. 1045). He travelled by way of Shábурqán to Merv, where he tendered his resignation. Thence he proceeded to Níshápúr, which he quitted in the company of Khwája Muwaffaq (the same, prob-

The *Safar-náma*.

[1] *I.e.*, of Merv (Marw) and Qubádiyán, the latter being the name of a town and canton near Tirmidh and the Oxus.

ably, who appears in the 'Umar Khayyám legend as the tutor of the three companions), and, visiting the tomb of the Ṣúfí saint Báyazíd of Bisṭám at Qúmis, came, by way of Dámghán, to Samnán. Here he met a certain Ustád 'Alí Nisá'í, a pupil of Avicenna and a lecturer on arithmetic, geometry, and medicine, of whom he seems to have formed an unfavourable opinion. Passing onwards through Qazwín, he reached Tabríz on Ṣafar 20, A.H. 438 (= August 26, A.D. 1046), and there made the acquaintance of the poet Qaṭrán, to whom he explained certain difficult passages in the poems of Daqíqí and Manjík. From Tabríz he made his way successively to Ván, Akhláṭ, Bitlis, Arzan, Mayáfáraqín, Ámid, Aleppo, and Ma'arratu'n-Nu'mán, where he met the great Arabic philosophical poet Abu'l-'Alá al-Ma'arrí, of whose character and attainments he speaks in the warmest terms. Thence he came to Ḥamá, Tripoli, Beyrout, Sidon, Tyre, Acre, and Ḥayfá. After spending some time in Syria in visiting the tombs of prophets and other holy places, including Jerusalem and Bethlehem, he made his first pilgrimage to Mecca in the late spring of A.D. 1047. From Mecca he returned by way of Damascus to Jerusalem, whence, finding the weather unfavourable for a sea voyage, he decided to proceed by land to Egypt, and finally arrived in Cairo on Sunday, Ṣafar 7, A.H. 439 (= August 3, A.D. 1047).

Náṣir-i-Khusraw in Egypt.

In Egypt Náṣir-i-Khusraw remained two or three years, and this marks an epoch in his life, for here it was that he became acquainted with the splendour, justice, and wise administration of the Fáṭimid Caliph, al-Mustanṣir bi'lláh, and here it was that he was initiated into the esoteric doctrines of the Isma'ílí creed, and received the commission to carry on their propaganda and to be their "Proof" (*Ḥujjat*) in Khurásán. In the *Safar-náma*, which would seem to have been written for the general public, he is reticent on religious matters; but from two passages (pp. 40 and 42 of the text) it is evident that he had no doubt as to the legitimacy of the Fáṭimid pedigree, while as to the excellence of their administration, and the wealth, contentment, and security of their subjects, he is enthusiastic. His description of Cairo, its mosques (including al-Azhar), its ten quarters (*ḥára*), its gardens, and its buildings and suburbs is admirable; while the details which he gives of the Fáṭimid administration are most valuable. He seems to have been much impressed with the discipline of the army, and the regularity with which the troops were paid, in consequence of which the people stood in no fear of unlawful exactions on their part. The army comprised some 215,000 troops; *viz.*, of cavalry, 20,000 Qayruwánís, 15,000 Bátilís (from North-west Africa), 50,000 Bedouin from al-Ḥijáz, and 30,000 mixed mercenaries; and of infantry 20,000 black Maṣmúdís (also from North-west Africa), 10,000 Orientals (*Masháriqa*), Turks and Persians, 30,000 slaves (*'abídu'sh-shirá*), a Foreign Legion of 10,000 Palace Guards (*Sará'ís*) under a separate commander-in-chief, and lastly 30,000 *Zanj* or Æthiopians. The wealth of the *bázárs* filled him with wonder, and withal, he says, such was the high degree of public safety that the merchants did not deem it necessary to lock up their shops and warehouses.

"While I was there," he says (p. 53), "in the year A.H. 439 (=1047–48), a son was born to the King, and he ordered public rejoicings. The city and *bázárs* were decorated in such wise that, should I describe it, some men would probably decline to believe me or to credit it. The shops of the cloth-sellers, money-changers, etc., were so [filled with precious things], gold, jewels, money, stuffs, gold-embroidery, and satin garments, that there was no place for one to sit down. And all feel secure in the [justice of the] King, and have no fear of myrmidons or spies, by reason of their confidence in him that he will oppress no one and covet no one's wealth.

"There I saw wealth belonging to private individuals, which, should I speak about it or describe it, would seem incredible to the people of Persia; for I could not estimate or compute their wealth, while the well-being which I saw there I have seen in no other place. I saw there, for example, a Christian who was one of the richest men in Cairo, so that it was said to be impossible to compute his ships, wealth, and estates. Now one year, owing to the failure of the Nile, grain waxed dear; and the King's Prime Minister sent for this Christian and said, 'The year is not good, and the King's heart is oppressed on account of his subjects. How much corn canst thou give me either for cash or on loan?' 'By the blessing of the King and his minister,' replied the Christian, 'I have ready so much corn that I could supply Cairo with bread for six years.' Now at this time there were assuredly in Cairo so many inhabitants that those of Níshápúr, at the highest computation, would equal but one-fifth of them, and whoever can judge of quantities will know how wealthy one must be to possess corn to this amount, and how great must be the security of the subject and the justice of the sovereign in order that such conditions and such fortunes may be possible in their days, so that neither doth the King wrong or oppress any man, nor doth the subject hide or conceal anything."

Náṣir-i-Khusraw's journey, from the time that he quitted his country until the time when he returned, lasted exactly seven years (from Thursday, 6 Jumáda II, A.H. 437, until Saturday, 26 Jumáda II, A.H. 444 = December 19, 1045, until October 23, 1052), and during this time he performed the Pilgrimage five times. He finally returned to his country from the Ḥijáz by way of Tiháma, al-Yaman, Laḥsá, and Qaṭíf to Baṣra, where he remained about two months; and thence by Arraján, Iṣfahán, Ná'in, Ṭabas, Tún, and Sarakhs to Merv.

We must now leave the *Safar-náma* and pass on to the *Díwán*. Before doing so, however, it is necessary to advert to a theory which, though championed by so great a scholar as the late Dr. Rieu,[1] and also by Pertsch[2] and Fagnan,[3] must, I think, in the light of further investigations, especially those of Schefer and Ethé, be definitely abandoned.[4] According to this theory,

Disproof of the Dual Theory.

[1] *Persian Catalogue*, pp. 379–381.

[2] *Berlin Persian Catalogue*, pp. 741–42.

[3] *Z.D.M.G.*, vol. xxxiv (1880), pp. 643–674, and *Journal Asiatique*, sér. vii, vol. 13 (1879), pp. 164–168.

[4] See my remarks in the *J.R.A.S.* for 1899, pp. 416–420.

there were two distinct persons called Náṣir-i-Khusraw, both bearing the *kunya* Abú Mu'ín, one the poet, philosopher, and magician; the other the traveller.

"A few facts," says Dr. Rieu, who puts the case most clearly "will show that we have to do with two distinct persons. Ḥakím Náṣir, as the poet is generally called, was born in Iṣfahán, traced his pedigree to the great Imám 'Alí b. Músá Riḍá, and was known as a poet before the composition of the present work (*i.e.*, the *Safar-náma*); his poem, the *Rawshandí-náma*, is dated A.H. 420 (see Pertsch, *Gotha Catalogue*, p. 13; the date A.H. 343, assigned to the same work in the Leyden copy, *Catalogue*, vol. ii, p. 108, is probably erroneous). Our author, on the contrary, designates himself by two *nisbas* which point to Qubádiyán, a town near Balkh, and to Merv, as the places of his birth and of his usual residence, and lays no claim either to noble extraction, or to any fame but that of a skilled accountant. Ḥakím Náṣir was born, according to the *Ḥabíbu's-Siyar*, Bombay edition, vol. ii, *juz* 4, p. 67, in A.H. 358, or, as stated in the *Dabistán*, vol. ii, p. 419, in A.H. 359, while our author appears from his own statement to have been forty years old in A.H. 437."

Other difficulties are raised as to the identification of the poet and the traveller, but most of them arise from the inaccuracies of late writers, and are at once resolved by an attentive perusal of the *Safar-náma* and the *Díwán* side by side. Thus the traveller seems to have been entitled Ḥakím; for the voice which reproaches him in his dream (*Safar-náma*, p. 3) says to him, when he defends his indulgence in wine, "Insensibility and intoxication are not refreshment; one cannot call him *Ḥakím* (wise) who leads men to lose their senses." The notoriously inaccurate Dawlatsháh is responsible for the statement that the poet was a native of Iṣfáhan, a statement conclusively disproved by the following verse from his *Díwán* (p. 241):—

Garchi mará aṣl Khurásániyast, Az pas-i-píriyy u mihiyy u sarí
Dústiy-i-'itrat u khána[-i-]Rasúl Kard mará Yumgí u Mázandarí.

"Although I am originally of Khurásán, after [enjoying] spiritual leadership, authority and supremacy,
Love for the Family and House of the Prophet have made me a dweller in Yumgán and Mázandarán."

And lastly, as regards the date of the poet's birth, we again have his own explicit statement (*Díwán*, p. 110) that he was born in A.H. 394 (= A.D. 1003–4), and in the same poem, on the same page, four lines lower down, he says that he was forty-two years of age when his "reasonable soul began to seek after wisdom," while elsewhere (*e.g.*, p. 217), using round numbers, he says, as in the *Safar-náma*, that he was forty years of age at this turning-point in his life. Nothing, in short, can be more complete than the agreement between the data derived from the *Safar-náma* and those derived from the *Díwán*, and the identity of authorship becomes clearer and clearer the more closely we study them. Forty, as we have said, is a round number, elsewhere appearing as forty-two, and in fact the poet must have been nearly forty-three (437 − 394 = 43) when he set out on his travels. He was just fifty when he returned from Egypt to Khurásán, and nearly all the poems which compose his *Díwán* must have been written after that date. Besides the two allusions to his age at the time of his conversion, to which we have already referred, I have notes of some seventeen passages in which he mentions his age at the time of writing. These are: age 50 (pp. 20, 219, 230, 263); age 50 and odd years (p. 78); age 60 (pp. 24, 79, 102, 164, 173, 179, 199, 207, 244); age 60 and odd years (p. 70); and age 62 (pp. 166, 171). In other passages he speaks of his increasing feebleness (p. 5), and of feeling the approach of death (pp. 6, 7), but we have no data wherewith to determine the date of his decease.

Some two years ago I carefully read through the whole *Díwán* in the Tabríz edition (which comprises 277 pages and, so far as I can reckon, about 7,425 verses), with a view to writing a monograph on the author, taking notes on peculiarities of grammar, vocabulary, and diction; allusions to places, persons, and events; and passages throwing light on the author's religious and metaphysical views, especially as regards his relations to the Isma'ílí sect and the Fáṭimid Caliphs. Some of these results, since I have not yet found time to elaborate them elsewhere, may perhaps with advantage be briefly recorded here.[1]

Study of the *Díwán*.

As regards the diction, it is too technical a matter to be discussed at length in a work not exclusively addressed to Persian scholars, but the language and grammatical peculiarities are thoroughly archaic, and bear an extraordinary resemblance to those of the Old Persian Commentary which I described at great length in the *J.R.A.S.* for July, 1894 (pp. 417–524), and which, as I there endeavoured to show, was written in Khurásán during the Sámánid period. Some forty rare words, or words used in peculiar senses, and numerous remarkable grammatical forms and constructions, are common to both works.

Diction.

The places mentioned include Baghdád, Balkh, Egypt, Gurgán, Ghazna, India, the mythical cities of Jábulqá and Jábulsá, Kháwarán, Khatlán, Khurásán, Mázandarán, the Oxus, the Plain of Qipcháq, Ray, Sind, Sístán, Sipáhán (*i.e.*, Iṣfahán), Shushtar, Sodom, Ṭiráz, Tún, Yumgán, and Zábulistán. Of these, Khurásán, the poet's native place (pp. 33, 241), to which he was sent in later life as the "Proof" (*Ḥujjat*, pp. 169, 178, 181, 221, 232, 247, 256), and wherein he was as "the Ark of Noah" (p. 169) amidst the "beasts" (p. 266) who constituted its ill-ruled (p. 243) and evil (pp. 225, 233, 241) population, is most often addressed, generally with censure (pp. 48,

Places mentioned.

[1] Since writing this passage, however, I have published in the *J.R.A.S.* for 1905 (pp. 313–352) an article entitled, "Náṣir-i-Khusraw, Poet, Traveller and Propagandist," in which are embodied some of these observations, besides some of the translations reprinted in this chapter.

49), as a spiritual salt-desert (203), wherein the writer was compelled to remain in hiding (p. 185). The name of Yumgán, the place of his final retirement, comes next in frequency; he speaks of a sojourn of fifteen years therein (p. 167), and of his loneliness and exile (pp. 161, 170, 227), but while at one time he speaks of himself as a prisoner there (p. 243), at another he calls himself a king (*Shahriyár*, pp. 159, 161). Most of the other places are mentioned only once, save Balkh, which is mentioned seven times, and Baghdád, which is mentioned four times. Allusion is also made to the Turks and the Ghuzz (p. 7).

Persons mentioned.

The persons referred to are much more numerous. Of Old Testament patriarchs, prophets, &c., we find mention of Adam and Eve, Noah, Shem, Ham, Abraham and Sarah, Moses and Aaron, Joshua the son of Nun, and Daniel. Christ is mentioned (p. 178) with the utmost respect as "that fatherless son, the brother of Simon," who by the Water of God restored the dead to life. Of the Greeks, Socrates, Plato, Euclid, and Constantine are mentioned; of the old legendary kings of Persia, Jamshíd, Ḍaḥḥák (Azhidaháka), and Ferídún; of the Sásánians, Shápúr II, the son of Ardashír, and the noble Qáren; of Arab poets and orators, an-Nábigha, Saḥbán b. Wá'il, Ḥassán b. Thábit, and al-Buḥturi; and of Persian poets, Rúdagí (p. 273), 'Unṣurí (pp. 11, 12, 172), Kisá'í (pp. 19, 28, 38, 51, 133, 247, 251), Ahwází (p. 249), and the *Sháhnáma* of Firdawsí (pp. 183, 190).

I do not know on what Dr. Ethé bases his assertion[1] that Náṣir-i-Khusraw "does not share Kisá'í's hatred for the three first Caliphs, but identifies 'Alí with his predecessors Abú Bakr, 'Umar and 'Uthmán, through whom the Divine Incarnation was, as it were, transmitted to him." In the *Díwán* I find six allusions to 'Umar, two of which couple his name

[1] In his article *Neupersische Litteratur* in vol. ii of the *Grundriss d. Iran. Philol.*, p. 281.

with that of Abú Bakr, while 'Uthmán seems not to be mentioned at all. Some of these, indeed, imply no condemnation, but surely this can hardly be said of the following :—

"Without doubt 'Umar will give thee a place in Hell if thou followest the path of those who are the friends of 'Umar" (p. 62).
"Be not sad at heart because in Yumgán thou art left alone and art become a prisoner ;
'Umar drove Salmán from his home : to-day thou art Salmán in this land" (p. 263).

And in another place (p. 262) he says : "How dost thou contend so much with me for 'Umar ?"

Similarly of 'Á'isha and Fáṭima he says (p. 241) :—

"'Á'isha was step-mother to Fáṭima, therefore art thou to me of the faction (*Shí'at*) of the step-mother ;
O ill-starred one ! Thou art of the faction of the step-mother ; it is natural that thou should'st be the enemy of the step-daughter !"

'Alí, Fáṭima, the Imáms, the Fáṭimid Caliphs (especially al Mustanṣir), Salmán the Persian, Mukhtár the Avenger of Kerbelá, and the Shí'ites are, on the other hand, constantly mentioned in terms of warmest praise and commendation ; while the 'Abbásid Caliph is termed *dív-i-'Abbásí*, "the 'Abbásid devil" (p. 261) ; the Sunnís or "Násibís" are vehemently denounced ; Abú Ḥanífa, Málik and ash-Sháfi'í, the founders of three of the four orthodox schools, are represented (pp. 115, 119, 209) as sanctioning dice, wine-drinking, and graver crimes ; and the orthodox jurisconsults (*fuqahá*) are mentioned with contempt (pp. 58, 82, 181). Three of the great Ṣúfí Shaykhs—Báyazíd of Bisṭám, Dhu'n-Nún of Egypt, and Ibráhím Adham—are incidentally mentioned (pp. 237, 195, 264) in a manner which implies commendation. Of Muhammadan rulers there is one reference to the Sámánids (p. 191), combined with a scornful allusion to "the servile crew" (*qawmí zír-dastán*)—presumably the

Ghaznawí slave-kings—who succeeded them in Khurásán. The Faríghúniyán, or first dynasty of Khwárazmsháhs, are once mentioned (p. 7), as is Ṭughril the Seljúq (p. 143), and Sulṭán Maḥmúd of Ghazna, the latter four or five times; and there is one allusion to the Sámánid minister Abu'l-Faḍl al-Bal'amí, the translator into Persian of Ṭabarí's history (p. 263).

Mention of other religions.

Of other religions than Islám, Náṣir-i-Khusraw mentions the Jews (pp. 53, 83, 92, 95, 138), Christians (pp. 14, 15, 67, 242), Magians (pp. 52, 70, 79), Hindús (pp. 33, 204), Dualists (pp. 28, 275), Manichæans (pp. 111, 269), Sabæans (p. 111), Zindíqs (p. 58), and Philosophers (pp. 111, 216); and of Muhammadan sects, besides the Ḥanafís, Málikís, Sháfi'ís, and others already mentioned, the Ḥarúrís, Kirámís, Liyálís (p. 239), and the Carmathians (p. 254). The term Báṭiní ("Esoteric") is used in a favourable sense, and contrasted with Dháhirí ("Exoteric," *i.e.*, Formalist), while of Mulḥid (Heretic) the poet says (p. 118) that whoever seeks to understand the principles of religion is called by this name. From several passages it would appear that the poet had some knowledge of the contents of the Bible; at least the expressions "casting pearls before swine" (p. 11), "answer a fool according to his folly" (p. 67), "thou hast no oil in thy lamp" (p. 138), "I go to the Father" (p. 139), "naked shalt thou depart as thou didst come" (p. 145), and the like, seem to point to this conclusion.

Autobiographical allusions.

A good deal of autobiography, besides what has been already noticed, may be gleaned from the *Díwán*, and the 76th *qaṣída* (pp. 109–113), in which occurs the mention of the year of his birth, is especially rich in such material. He speaks of his eager desire to know the esoteric meaning of the ordinances of religion (p. 112), thanks God for having directed him to the Truth (p. 5), and implies that his conversion to the Isma'ílí doctrine took place at a comparatively late period of his life (p. 91). He describes his Initiation (p. 182) and oath of silence and allegiance (pp. 111–112), and how he becomes notorious, on account of his love for the Holy Family (*Ahlu'l-Bayt*, p. 6), as a Shí'ite (p. 223), Ráfiḍí (p. 115), and Mulḥid, in consequence of which he is persecuted by the Sunnís (pp. 22, 127, 227) and cursed from the pulpit (p. 223), so that no man dares breathe his name. He speaks of himself as "the Proof" (*Ḥujjat*), "the Proof of Khurásán" (p. 33), and "the Proof of Mustanṣir" (p. 239), alluding incidentally to other "Proofs," and calls himself one of the Twelve Isma'ílí *Naqíbs* or Apostles (p. 209), the Chosen one of 'Alí (p. 159), and the Chosen Instrument of the Imám (pp. 158, 162). He vaunts his chaste and pious life (pp. 9, 252), and his attainments in science (pp. 5, 10, 127, 158), as well as in literature and poetry (pp. 22, 80). He alludes to his numerous writings (pp. 5, 9, 233), to his poems in Arabic and Persian (p. 171), and to his work the *Zádu'l-Musáfirín*, or "Pilgrim's Provision" (p. 195). Of his relations he says little, but we find passing allusions to his son (pp. 6, 185), father, mother, and brother (p. 219).

Religious views.

His religious and philosophical views are abundantly illustrated, and, indeed, form the main subject of his verse. Speaking generally, they are, as we have seen, typically Isma'ílí or Báṭiní. The favourite doctrine of *ta'wíl*, or allegorical interpretation, is strongly insisted on; without it the letter of Scripture is bitter as brine (p. 3) and misleading as water running under straw. Paradise, Hell, the Resurrection, the Torment of the Tomb, Antichrist (*Dajjál*), and the Rising of the Sun from the West, are all allegorically explained. This interpretation is the very Spirit of Religion p. 33), and is necessary (p. 39), but the key to it has been committed by God to the representatives of the Prophet's House (pp. 12, 30, 60, 64, 124, 142), who are its sole custodians (p. 4). Revelation is necessary (p. 29), and the nobility of the

Arabic language is due solely to the fact that it was the medium of this revelation (p. 249), but mere parrot-like reading of the Qur'án is useless (p. 214). Piety without knowledge and understanding avails nothing (p. 37), but Knowledge, great as is its honour, is but the handmaid of Religion (pp. 150, 235), which is the fragrance of the world (p. 188). There exists naught but God (p. 193), who can neither be called Eternal nor Temporal (p. 166); phenomena are but an illusory reflection of Him (p. 106), yet are full of significance (p. 197), because the Universal Intelligence is immanent in them (p. 14), and man is the microcosm (p. 232). Space and Time are infinite and unbounded, and the heavens will not perish (p. 4), yet is the world not eternal (pp. 12, 39, 40). The doctrine of Free Will is supported against that of Fatalism by the following amongst other passages:—

"Though God creates the mother, and the breast, and the milk, the children must draw for themselves the mother's milk" (p. 56).

"Thy soul is a book, thy deeds are like the writing: write not on thy soul aught else than a fair inscription:
Write what is wholly good in the book, O brother, for the pen is in thine own hand!" (p. 149).

The Fáṭimid Caliphs are the only lawful rulers (p. 210), and the keepers of the Garden of God (p. 213), and a Gate (*Báb*) to the Imám is to be found in every country (p. 87). Allusions also occur to the mystical number Seven (pp. 88, 131), and to the characteristic Isma'ílí doctrine of the *Asás* (pp. 176–178).

Lastly we may notice, before giving translations of some of his poems, his profound contempt for Royal Courts (p. 6), courtiers (pp. 151, 230), panegyrists (pp. 7, 11, 80, 141, 144), elegant writers and literary triflers (p. 228), and writers of *ghazals* and erotic poetry (pp. 108, 141, 145, 171).

Translations from the Díwán.

The following hundred verses are selected from the first five poems (ten pages) of the *Díwán*, and in each poem the omission of verses, wherever it occurs, is signified by asterisks:—

I (pp. 2–4 of Tabríz edition).

"God's gracious Word in truth is an Ocean of speech, I ween,
Teeming with gems and jewels, and pearls of luminous sheen.
Bitter to outward seeming, like the Sea, is the Scripture's page,
But precious as pearls of price is the Inward Sense to the sage.
Down in the depths of the Ocean are gems and pearls galore;
Seek then a skilful diver, and bid farewell to the shore.
Wherefore hath God bestowed in the depths of the Ocean's brine
All these pearls of price, and jewels so rare and fine?
Wherefore if not for the Prophet, who made the Inward Sense
The portion of Wisdom's children, but the Letter a Rock of Offence?
A handful of salt-stained clay hath the Diver offered to thee
Because in thine heart he beheld but envy and enmity.
Strive from the Outward Form to the Inward Sense to win
Like a man, nor rest content like an ass with a senseless din.

* * * * * *

Darius, for all his thousands of servants and thanes, alone
Had to depart and abandon the chattels he deemed his own.
For the world is a thievish game, from which no man may save
Himself, be he Sultan or subject; his goods, be he master or slave.
That is the day when all men the guerdon they've earned shall win;

The just the fruits of his justice, the tyrant his wage of sin.
In the sight of the Holy Martyrs, in the midst of that fierce dismay,
Will I grasp the robe of Zahrá[1] on that fearful Judgement Day,
And God, the Judge Almighty, shall avenge to the full the woes
I have suffered so long at the hands of the House of the Prophet's foes.'

II (pp. 4–5).

"How can the Heavens rest on thee bestow,
When they themselves nor pause nor peace may know?
This world's the ladder to that world, O Friend;
To mount, thou needs must climb it to the end.
In these two roofs, one whirling and one still,[2]
Behold that Secret-knowing Power and Skill;
How, unconstrained, in one harmonious whole
He blended Matter gross and subtle Soul;
How He did poise this dark stupendous Sphere
In Heaven's hollow dome of emerald clear.
What say'st thou? 'Endlessly recurring day
And month at last shall wear that dome away!'
Nay, for he hath exempted from such wear
The circling Sky, the Water, and the Air.
The canvas of His Art are Time and Place;
Hence Time is infinite, and boundless Space.[3]
Should'st thou object, 'Not thus the Scriptures tell,
I answer that thou hast not conned them well.
And o'er the Scriptures is a Guardian set
From whom both man and *jinn* must knowledge get.
God and His Prophet thus desired: but No!
You 'much prefer the views of So-and-so.'
Thy meat in man begetteth human power;
To dog-flesh turns the meat that dogs devour."

---

[1] *I.e.*, "The Bright One," a title of the Prophet's daughter Fáṭima, the wife of 'Alí and mother of the Imáms.

[2] He means, I suppose, the planetary heavens and the eighth heaven, or Heaven of the Fixed Stars.

[3] *I.e.*, Infinite power demands an infinite field for its activity.

III (pp. 5–7).

"Were the turns of the Wheel of Fortune proportioned to worth alone
O'er the Vault of the Lunar Heaven would have been my abode and throne.
But no! For the worth of Wisdom is lightly esteemed in sooth,
By fickle Fate and Fortune, as my father warned me in youth.
Yet knowledge is more than farms, and estates, and rank, and gold;
Thus my dauntless spirit, whispering, me consoled:
'With a heart more brightly illumined than ever the Moon can be
What were a throne of glory o'er the Sphere of the Moon to thee?'
To meet the foeman's falchion and Fate's close-serried field
Enough for me are Wisdom and Faith as defence and shield.

*   *   *   *   *   *

30. My mind with its meditations is a fair and fruitful tree,
Which yieldeth its fruit and blossom of knowledge and chastity.
Would'st thou see me whole and completed? Then look, as beseems the wise,
At my essence and not my seeming, with keen and discerning eyes.
This feeble frame regard not; remember rather that I
Am the author of works which outnumber and outshine the stars in the sky.
God, to whose name be glory! me hath exempted and freed
In this troubled life of transit from the things that most men need.
I thank the Lord Almighty, who plainly for me did trace
The way to Faith and Wisdom, and opened the Door of Grace,
And who, in His boundless mercy, in this world hath made me one
Whose love for the Holy Household is clear as the noonday sun.

*   *   *   *   *   *

O dark and ignoble body, never on earth have I seen
A fellow-lodger so hurtful as thee, or a mate so mean!
Once on a time my lover and friend I accounted thee,
And thou wast my chosen comrade in travel by land and sea.
But fellest of foes I found thee, spreading thy deadly snare
To entrap me, whilst I of thy scheming was heedless and unaware,
Till finding me all unguarded, and free from all fear of guile,
You strove to take me captive by treachery base and vile.
And surely, but for the Mercy of God and His Gracious Will,
Thy rascally schemes had wrought me a great and enduring ill.
But not the sweetest nectar could tempt me now, for I know
What to expect at the hands of so fierce and deadly a foe.
Sleep, O senseless body, and food are thy only care,
But to me than these is Wisdom better beyond compare!
'Tis the life of a brute, say the sages, to dream but of water and grass,
And shall I, who am dowered with reason, live the life of a soulless ass?
I will not dwell, O Body, with thee in this World of Sense;
To another abode God calls me, and bids me arise from hence.
There are talent and virtue esteemed, not food and sleep;
Then enjoy thy food and slumber, and let me my virtue keep!
Ere me from their earthly casings uncounted spirits have fled,
And I, though long I linger, may be counted already dead.
Through the lofty vault of Ether with the wings of obedience I
One day shall soar to the heavens as the sky-lark soars to the sky.
Fearful of God's Fore-knowledge, quaking at God's Decree,
Is the mass of my fellow-creatures, yet these are as guides to me:
'Speak of the first as "Reason," call the latter "the Word"'—
Such was the explanation that I from a wise man heard.

50. Being myself in essence a rational, logical soul,
Why should I fear myself? Shall the Part be in fear of the Whole?
O man who dost rest contented to claim the Determinist's view,
Though you lack a brute's discernment, must I lack discernment too?"

IV (pp. 7–8).

"Bear from me to Khurásán, Zephyr, a kindly word,
To its scholars and men of learning, not to the witless herd,
And having faithfully carried the message I bid thee bear,
Bring me news of their doings, and tell me how they fare.
I, who was once as the cypress, now upon Fortune's wheel
Am broken and bent, you may tell them; for thus doth Fortune deal.
Let not her specious promise you to destruction lure:
Ne'er was her covenant faithful; ne'er was her pact secure.

* * * * * *

Look at Khurásán only: she is crushed and trodden still
By this one and then by that one, as corn is crushed in the mill.
60. You boast of your Turkish rulers:[1] remember the power and sway
Of the Záwulí Sulṭán Maḥmúd[2] were greater far in their day.
The Royal House of Faríghún[3] before his might did bow,
And abandon the land of Júzján;[4] but where is Maḥmúd now?

---

[1] *I.e.*, the Seljúqs.

[2] *I.e.*, Sulṭán Maḥmúd of Ghazna, who reigned A.D. 998–1030.

[3] *I.e.*, the first dynasty of Khwárazmsháhs. "Faríghún," says Riḍá-qulí Khán in his *Farhang-i-Náṣirí*, "rhyming with Farídún, was the name of a man who attained to the rule of Khwárazm, and whose children and grandchildren are called 'the House of Faríghún.' These were the absolute rulers of Khwárazm, such as 'Alí b. Ma'mún Faríghúní, who was the contemporary of Sulṭán Maḥmúd of Ghazna (to whom he was related by marriage) and who was murdered by his own slaves. Sulṭán Maḥmúd came to Khwárazm and put the murderers to death." See also the Cairo ed. of al-'Utbí (A.H. 1286), vol. ii, pp. 101–105.

[4] The text has Gúrgánán (or Kúrkánán): the emendation is based on al-'Utbí (*loc. cit.*).

'Neath the hoofs of his Turkish squadrons the glory of India lay,
While his elephants proudly trampled the deserts of far Cathay.

* * * * * *

And ye, deceived and deluded, before his throne did sing:
'More than a thousand summers be the life of our Lord the King!
Who, on his might relying, an anvil of steel attacks,
Findeth the anvil crumble under his teeth like wax!'
The goal of the best was Záwul, as it seems, but yesterday,
Whither they turned, as the faithful turn to Mecca to pray.
Where is the power and empire of that King who had deemed it meet
If the heavenly Sign of Cancer had served as a stool for his feet?
Alas! Grim Death did sharpen against him tooth and claw,
And his talons are fallen from him, and his teeth devour no more!

* * * * * *

Be ever fearful of trouble when all seems fair and clear,
For the easy is soon made grievous by the swift-transforming sphere.
Forth will it drive, remorseless, when it deemeth the time at hand,
The King from his Court and Castle, the lord from his house and land.
70. Ne'er was exemption granted, since the Spheres began to run,
From the shadow of dark eclipses to the radiant Moon and Sun.
Whate'er seems cheap and humble and low of the things of earth
Reckon it dear and precious, for Time shall lend it worth.
Seek for the mean in all things, nor strive to fulfil your gain,
For the Moon when the full it reacheth is already about to wane.

* * * * * *

Though the heady wine of success should all men drug and deceive,

Pass thou by and leave them, as the sober the drunkards
leave.
For the sake of the gaudy plumage which the flying pea-
cocks wear,
See how their death is compassed by many a springe and
snare!

* * * * * *

Thy body to thee is a fetter, and the world a prison-cell:
To reckon as home this prison and chains do you deem
it well?
Thy soul is weak in wisdom, and naked of works beside:
Seek for the strength of wisdom: thy nakedness strive to
hide.

* * * * * *

Thy words are the seed; thy soul is the farmer, the world
thy field:
Let the farmer look to the sowing, that the soil may abundance yield.

* * * * * *

Yet dost thou not endeavour, now that the Spring is here,
To garner a little loaflet for the Winter which creepeth
near.
The only use and profit which life for me doth hold
Is to weave a metrical chaplet of coral and pearls and
gold!"

V (pp. 8–10).

80. "Though the courts of earthly rulers have shut their doors
in my face,
Shall I grieve, while I still have access to the Court of the
Lord of Grace?
In truth I desire no longer to deal with the mighty and
proud,
Beneath whose burden of favour my back would be bent
and bowed.

* * * * * *

To con the Holy Scriptures, to renounce, to strive, to
know—
These are the four companions who ever beside me go.
The Eye, the Heart, and the Ear through the long night-
watches speak,

And with their counsels strengthen my body so frail and weak.
'Guard me well, I pray thee, and prison me close,' saith the Eye,
'From gazing on things forbidden, and the lust that comes thereby.'
'Close the road against me, and close it well,' saith the Ear,
'To every lying slander, to gossip and spiteful sneer.'
What saith the Heart within me? 'From Passion's curse and ban
Keep me pure and unsullied, as befits an upright man.'
Then crieth the Voice of Reason, 'To me was the watch and ward
Over the Soul and Body given by God the Lord.
Hold thou nor speech nor commerce with the armies of Hate and Lust,
For I am there to confront them, and to fight them, if fight they must.'
Against the commands of Reason can I rebel and revolt,
When I am preferred through Reason alone to the senseless dolt?
For the Fiend had caught and constrained me to walk in his captives' train,
And 'twas Reason who came and saved me, and gave me freedom again.
'Twas Reason who seized my halter and forced me out of the road
Whereby the Fiend would have led me at last to his own abode.
Though this Cave of the World is truly a tenement dark and dire,
If my 'Friend of the Cave'[1] be Reason, what more can my heart desire?
Deem not the World, O son, a thing to hate and to flee,
For a hundred thousand blessings it hath yielded even to me.

---

[1] The allusion is to the Cave of Thawr, where the Prophet, accompanied only by Abú Bakr, took refuge from his pursuers after his Flight from Mecca. The faithful Abú Bakr is called "the Companion of the Cave," and the term is thence borrowed for any loyal friend in adversity.

Therein is my walk and achievement, my tongue and my gift of speech ;
It yields me a ground of action, and offers me scope for each.
And ever it cries in warning, 'I am hastening fast away,
So clasp me close to your bosom, and cherish me whilst you may!'

* * * * * *

Reason was ever my leader, leading me on by the hand,
Till it made me famed for Wisdom through the length and breadth of the land.
Reason it was which gave me the Crown of Faith, I say,
And Faith hath given me virtue, and strength to endure and obey.

* * * * * *

Since Faith at the Last Great Judgement can make my reckoning light,
Shall I fear, if Faith require it, to lose my life outright?
So the World is now my quarry, and the hunter who hunts am I,
Though I was once the quarry, in the days that are now gone by.
Though others it hunt and capture, I stand from its dangers clear:
My Soul is higher than Fortune: then why should I Fortune fear?"

I should like, did space allow, to quote other extracts from Náṣir-i-Khusraw's *Díwán*, which reveals throughout a combination of originality, learning, sincerity, enthusiastic faith, fearlessness, contempt for time-servers and flatterers, and courage hardly to be found, so far as I know, in any other Persian poet. In particular I would like to call the attention of Persian students to a very remarkable poem (No. 102, pp. 146–7), which is, unfortunately, too full of technical terms connected with the Pilgrimage to be easily translated or rendered intelligible without a disproportionate amount of commentary. In this poem Náṣir-i-Khusraw describes how he goes out to meet the pilgrims returning from Mecca, and in particular to welcome a friend who had accompanied the Pilgrimage. After the interchange of greetings, he says to his friend: "Tell me, how didst thou honour that noble Sanctuary? When thou didst array thyself in the *iḥrám*,[1] what resolve didst thou make in that consecration (*taḥrím*)? Didst thou make wholly unlawful (*ḥarám*) to thyself wrong-doing, and whatever stands between thee and God the Gracious?" "No," replies his friend. "Didst thou," continues Náṣir, "when thou didst cry *Labbík!*[2] with reverence and understanding, hear the echo of God's Voice, and didst thou answer as Moses answered?" "No," replies his friend. "And when," continues Náṣir, "thou didst stand on Mount 'Arafát, and wert permitted to advance, didst thou become a knower (*'árif*) of God and a denier of self, and did some breath of Divine Wisdom (*ma'rifat*) reach thee?" "No," replies his friend. Point by point Náṣir questions him as to his comprehension of the symbolic meanings of the ritual acts he has performed, and finally, having received a negative reply to every question, concludes: "O Friend, then thou hast not [truly] performed the Pilgrimage, nor stood in the station of self-obliteration; thou hast gone, seen Mecca, and come back, having bought the fatigues of the desert for silver. Hereafter, shouldst thou desire to perform the Pilgrimage, do even as I have taught thee!" Here we see in its best light the application of the characteristic Isma'ílí doctrine of *ta'wíl*, or allegorical interpretation.

Blasphemous verses ascribed to Náṣir-i-Khusraw.

In strong contrast to the essentially devout spirit which pervades the poems included in the lithographed edition and in most manuscripts of the *Díwán*, are certain free-thinking and almost blasphemous verses ascribed to Náṣir-i-Khusraw, which are widely known in Persia even at the present day, and are contained in a few manuscripts of his poetical works. Of two of the

[1] The simple garment worn by the pilgrims during certain parts of the ceremonies.

[2] The cry of acquiescence used by the pilgrims, meaning, "Here am I: command me!"

most celebrated of these pieces I published translations at p. 480 of my *Year amongst the Persians*, and I reproduce them here. The first is given by Jámí in his *Bahâristân* in the short notice consecrated to Náṣir-i-Khusraw. Its purport is as follows :—

"O God, although through fear I hardly dare
To hint it, all this trouble springs from Thee!
Hadst Thou no sand or gravel in Thy shoes
What made Thee suffer Satan willingly?
'Twere well if Thou hadst made the lips and teeth
Of Tartar beauties not so fair to see.
With cries of 'On!' Thou bid'st the hound pursue;
With cries of 'On!' Thou bid'st the quarry flee!"

The second is cynical rather than blasphemous:

"Dead drunk, not like a common sot, one day
Náṣir-i-Khusraw went to take the air.
Hard by a dung-heap he espied a grave
And straightway cried, 'O ye who stand and stare,
Behold the world! Behold its luxuries!
Its dainties here—the fools who ate them there!'"

A third piece scoffing at the resurrection of the body is given by Schefer in his Introduction to the *Safar-náma*, together with the two couplets in which Naṣíru'd-Dín Ṭúsí is said to have replied to it. The sense of this third piece (which I have also heard quoted in Persia) is as follows :—

"Some luckless wretch wolves in the plain devour;
His bones are picked by vulture and by crow.
This casts his remnants on the hills above;
That voids its portion in the wells below.
Shall this man's body rise to life again?
Defile the beards of fools who fancy so!"

Naṣíru'd-Dín's reply is as follows :—

"Shall this man's body rise to life again
When thus resolved to elements? I trow
God can remake as easily as make:
Defile the beard of Náṣir-i-Khusraw!"

We must now speak briefly of Náṣir-i-Khusraw's remaining works. Those which Time has spared to us are three, two of which—the *Rawshaná'l-náma* and the *Sa'ádat-náma*—have been printed, while one—the *Zádu'l-Musáfirín*—exists, so far as I know, only in the MS. formerly belonging to M. Schefer, and now preserved in the Bibliothèque Nationale at Paris. Another, the *Iksír-i-A'dham*, is mentioned by Ḥájji Khalífa. Less reliable authors, such as Dawlatsháh and the *Átash-kada*, mention a *Kanzu'l-Ḥaqá'iq* ("Treasury of Verities"), a *Qánún-i-A'dham* ("Greatest Law"), a work on the Science of the Greeks, a treatise on Magic, two works entitled *Dastúr-i-A'dham* and *al-Mustawfí*, and the Commentary on the Qur'án stated in the Pseudo-Autobiography to have been composed for the *Maláḥida*, or "Heretics" of the Isma'ílí sect. It is doubtful how many of the last-mentioned works ever really existed,[1] since no mention of them occurs in any book written within four centuries or so of Náṣir's death.

Náṣir-i-Khusraw's remaining works.

The *Rawshaná'l-náma*, or "Book of Light," is a *mathnawí* poem containing (in Ethé's edition) 579 verses, and written in the hexameter *hazaj* metre. There are two manuscripts in the Bibliothèque Nationale at Paris (one formerly in the possession of M. Schefer), one at Leyden, one at Gotha, and one in the India Office. A line in this poem (l. 555 in Ethé's edition) giving the date of its composition forms the basis of the most serious (indeed, the only serious) argument in favour of the view already discussed that there were two separate Náṣir-i-Khusraws. The reading adopted by Ethé gives the date A.H. 440 (= A.D. 1048–49), and this most plausible conjecture (for it does not occur in any known manuscript) he supports by many strong arguments (*Z.D.M.G.*, xxxiii, pp. 646–649, and xxxiv, p. 638, n. 5). But the date is

The *Rawshaná'l-náma*.

[1] See M. Fagnan's *Note sur Nâçir ibn Khosroû* in the *Journal Asiatique*, ser. vii, vol. 13, pp. 164–168, especially the last page.

variously given in the different MSS. The Leyden and the two Paris MSS. give A.H. 343 (= A.D. 954–55), the Gotha MS. A.H. 420 (= A.D. 1029), and the India Office MS. A.H. 323 (= A.D. 934–35). The lines giving the first two dates do not scan, and may therefore be rejected on metrical grounds, and the latter is entirely at variance with all the facts known to us about Náṣir-i-Khusraw. For it is quite certain that the *Safar-náma* and the *Díwán* are by the same author, of whose life the main outline and principal dates are perfectly well known; and as he was born, as stated explicitly in the *Díwán* and by implication in the *Safar-náma*, in A.H. 394 (= A.D. 1003–4), he evidently cannot have written the *Rawshaná'í-náma* either in A.H. 323 or 343. And to suppose that there were two poets with the same name—Náṣir—the same *kunya*—Abú Mu'ín—the same pen-name—Ḥujjat—and the same patronymic, both of whom were connected with Yumgán in Khurásán, and both of whom wrote moral and didactic verse in exactly the same style, is a hypothesis which hardly any one will venture to maintain. I have therefore no doubt that Dr. Ethé's ingenious conjecture is correct, and that, as he supposes, the *Rawshaná'í-náma* was concluded in Cairo on the Feast of Bayrám, A.H. 440 (= March 9, A.D. 1049). For the fuller discussion of this matter, I must refer the reader to Dr. Ethé's exhaustive monograph.

So much space has already been devoted to Náṣir-i-Khusraw, and so much remains to be said of other important writers of this period, that I cannot discuss either the *Rawshaná'í-náma* or the *Sa'ádat-náma* in this place as I should wish, but this is of less importance, since the European reader has at his disposal Dr. Ethé's metrical German translation of the first and M. Fagnan's French prose translation of the second. Both are didactic and ethical *mathnawí* poems written in the same *hazaj* metre; and both appear to me far inferior in poetic merit to the *Díwán*. The *Sa'ádat-náma* is divided into thirty short chapters, and comprises 287 verses, and deals almost exclusively with practical ethics, while the *Rawshaná'l-náma* discusses also various metaphysical and teleological matters, and includes a very characteristic section (ll. 513–523) in reprobation of secular poets "whose verses have no other object than to gain silver and gold."

Leaving Náṣir-i-Khusraw, we must now pass to the consideration of four poets, all of whom achieved celebrity in one special form of verse—a form, as we have seen, typically Persian—the *rubá'í* or quatrain. These four are, first, the famous Astronomer-Poet of Níshápúr, 'Umar Khayyám; secondly, the dialect-poet—the Persian Burns, as he may be termed—Bábá Ṭáhir of Hamadán; thirdly, the celebrated Ṣúfí, or mystic, Abú Sa'íd b. Abi'l-Khayr; and lastly the pious Shaykh al-Anṣárí, or Pír-i-Anṣár, who, as Ethé says (*Neupers. Litt.*, p. 282), "through his numerous half-mystical, half-ethical writings, which are composed sometimes in rhymed prose, sometimes in prose mingled with actual *ghazals* and *rubá'ís*, contributed more than any one else to the gradual fusion of mystical and didactic poetry, and prepared the way for the great Saná'í."

The four quatrain-writers of this period.

Let us begin first with 'Umar Khayyám (or al-Khayyámí, as he is called in Arabic), who, thanks to the genius of Fitz-Gerald, enjoys a celebrity in Europe, especially in England and America, far greater than that which he has attained in his own country, where his fame rests rather on his mathematical and astronomical than on his poetical achievements. The oldest accounts which we possess of him are contained in the *Chahár Maqála*, or "Four Discourses," of Nidhámí-i-'Arúḍí of Samarqand, and, be it noted, not in that section of the work which treats of Poets, but that which treats of Astrologers and Astronomers. This Nidhámí (not to be confounded with the later and more celebrated Nidhámí of Ganja) wrote his "Four Discourses" in the latter half of the twelfth century of our era, and in Anecdote xxvii (pp. 100–101 of my translation) relates as follows:—

'Umar Khayyám.

"In the year A.H. 506 (= A.D. 1112–13) Khwája Imám 'Umar Khayyám and Khwája Imám Mudhaffar-i-Isfizárí had alighted in the city of Balkh, in the Street of the Slave-sellers, in the house of Amír Abú Sa'd, and I had joined that assembly. In the midst of that friendly gathering I heard that Proof of the Truth (*Ḥujjat-i-Ḥaqq*) 'Umar say, 'My grave will be in a spot where the trees will shed their blossoms on me twice a year.' This thing seemed to me impossible, though I knew that one such as he would not speak idle words.

Account of 'Umar Khayyám from the *Chahár Maqála*.

"When I arrived at Níshápúr in the year A.H. 530 (= A.D. 1135–36), it being then some years[1] since that great man had veiled his countenance in the dust, and this lower world had been bereaved of him, I went to visit his grave on the eve of a certain Friday[2] (seeing that he had the claim of a master on me), taking with me a guide to point out his tomb. So he brought me out to the Ḥíra (or Ḥírí) Cemetery; I turned to the left, and his tomb lay at the foot of a garden-wall, over which pear-trees and peach-trees thrust their heads, and on his grave had fallen so many flower-leaves that his dust was hidden beneath the flowers. Then I remembered that saying which I had heard from him in the city of Balkh, and I fell to weeping, because on the face of the earth, and in all the regions of the habitable globe, I nowhere saw one like unto him. May God (blessed and exalted is He) have mercy upon him, by His Grace and His Favour! Yet although I witnessed this prognostication on the part of that Proof of the Truth 'Umar, I did not observe that he had any great belief in astrological predictions; nor have I seen or heard of any of the great [scientists] who had such belief."

The next anecdote in the *Chahár Maqála* (No. xxviii) also refers to 'Umar, and runs as follows:—

"In the winter of A.H. 508 (= A.D. 1114–15) the King[3] sent a messenger to Merv to the Prime Minister Ṣadru'd-Dín Muḥammad b. al-Mudhaffar (on whom be God's Mercy), bidding him tell Khwája Imám 'Umar to select a favourable time for him to go hunting, such

---

[1] Thirteen years, for 'Umar Khayyám died in A.H. 517 (= A.D. 1123).

[2] *I.e.*, what we call "Thursday night," for with the Muhammadans the day begins at sunset. "The eve of Friday" (*Shab-i-Jum'a*) is especially set apart in Persia for visiting the graves of deceased friends.

[3] Presumably Sulṭán Muḥammad the Seljúq, or his brother Sanjar.

that therein should be no snowy or rainy days. For Khwája Imám 'Umar was in the Minister's company, and used to lodge at his house.

"So the Minister sent a message to summon him, and told him what had happened. The Khwája went and looked into the matter for two days, and made a careful choice; and he himself went and superintended the mounting of the King at the auspicious moment. When the King was mounted and had gone but a short distance, the sky became overcast with clouds, a wind arose, and snow and mist supervened. All present fell to laughing, and the King desired to turn back; but Khwája Imám ['Umar] said: 'Have no anxiety, for this very hour the clouds will clear away, and during these five days there will be not a drop of moisture.' So the King rode on, and the clouds opened, and during those five days there was no wet, and no cloud was seen.

"But prognostication by the stars, though a recognised art, is not to be relied on, and whatever the astrologer predicts, he must leave [its fulfilment] to Fate."

These earliest notices of 'Umar show us that he was alive and well in A.H. 508 [A.D. 1114–15], that his grave was at Níshápúr, and that the idea prevalent in the 'Umar Khayyám Society that he was buried under a rose-bush is a delusion based on the double meaning of the word *gul*, which means a flower in general as well as the rose in particular, the context in the full form of the original anecdote, as here given, showing clearly that not rose-leaves, but the blossoms of peach-trees and pear-trees, are here meant.

Recent researches into 'Umar's biography.

Until the year 1897 the numerous biographical notices of 'Umar published in Europe were, almost without exception, derived from late Persian works of little or no authority, whose object was rather to weave romantic tales than to set forth historical facts. An epoch was marked by the appearance in that year of Professor Valentin Zhukovski's able and original article on *'Umar Khayyám and the "Wandering" Quatrains.* This article, written in Russian, appeared in the *Festschrift* published to commemorate the twenty-fifth anniversary of Baron Victor Rosen's tenure of the Arabic Professorship at the University of St. Petersburg, and was entitled, in allusion to his Christian name, *al-Mudhaffariyya* ("the Victorious"). Seeing that in Western Europe Russian is even less read than Persian, it is a most fortunate circumstance that that talented Orientalist Dr. E. Denison Ross, now Principal of the Muhammadan Madrasa at Calcutta, translated this very important article in the *Journal of the Royal Asiatic Society* for 1898 (vol. xxx, pp. 349–366); and subsequently reproduced its most important results in a more popular form in the Introduction ("on the Life and Times of 'Umar Khayyám") which he prefixed to Messrs. Methuen's edition of FitzGerald's rendering of the *Rubá'iyyát*, with a commentary by Mrs. H. M. Batson, published in 1900.

The notices of 'Umar given by Zhukovski in the original, with Russian translation, and by Ross in English, are, four from books composed in the thirteenth century of our era, one of the fourteenth, and one of the fifteenth and one of the late sixteenth or early seventeenth, the two latter being inserted, in spite of their late date, on account of their intrinsic interest. Many others from late biographers might be added to this list, but most of them do but repeat, and generally embellish or distort, their sources. It is worth remarking, however, that 'Awfí, the author of the oldest biography of Persian poets, the *Lubábu'l-Albáb* (early thirteenth century), does not so much as mention 'Umar Khayyám; while even Dawlatsháh (who completed his book in A.D. 1487) does not accord him a separate notice, but merely mentions him incidentally (p. 138 of my edition) in speaking of his descendant, Sháhfúr-i-Ashharí.

The oldest reference to him, after the two cited from the *Chahár Maqála* on pp. 247–8 *supra*, appears to be that contained in the *Mirṣádu'l-'Ibád*, or "Observatory of God's Servants," composed in A.D. 1223 by Najmu'd-Dín Rází (Zhukovski, *loc. cit.*, pp. 341–2; Ross, *loc. cit.*, pp. 361–2), and its importance, as Zhukovski points

The *Mirṣádu'l-'Ibád.*

out, lies in the fact that the author, a fervent Ṣúfí mystic, speaks of 'Umar as "an unhappy philosopher, atheist and materialist," adducing in proof of this assertion two of his quatrains, the first expressing his complete agnosticism, the second reproaching the Creator for suffering His imperfect creatures to exist, or His perfect creatures to perish (Whinfield, No. 126), which quatrains, says Najmu'd-Dín, demonstrate "the height of confusion and error."

Al-Qifṭí's *Ta'rí-khu'l-Ḥukamá.*

The next notice occurs in al-Qifṭí's *History of the Philosophers* (pp. 243–4 of Dr. Julius Lippert's recent edition, Leipzig, 1903), a work composed in Arabic in the second quarter of the thirteenth century. This notice was published, with a French translation, by Woepcke in his *L'Algèbre d'Omar Alkhayyámí* (Paris, 1851, pp. v–vi of Preface and 52 of text); and again by Zhukovski (*loc. cit.*, pp. 333–335) with a Russian translation; while an English rendering is given by Ross (*loc. cit.*, pp. 354–5). 'Umar is here represented as a champion of Greek learning, *i.e.*, Philosophy, of which the great mystic, Jalálu'd-Dín Rúmí says in his *Mathnawí*:—

"How long, how long [will ye talk of] the Philosophy of the Greeks?
Study also the Philosophy of those of the Faith."

"The later Ṣúfís," says al-Qifṭí, "have found themselves in agreement with some part of the apparent sense of his verse, and have transferred it to their system, and discussed it in their assemblies and private gatherings; though its inward meanings are to the [Ecclesiastical] Law stinging serpents, and combinations rife with malice." Here also, in short, he is represented as "without an equal in astronomy and philosophy," but as an advanced freethinker, constrained only by prudential motives to bridle his tongue. The notice concludes with the citation of four of 'Umar's Arabic verses from a poem of which six verses (three of these four and three others) are quoted in the work next to be mentioned.

ash-Shahrazúrí's *Nuzhatu'l-Arwáḥ.*

The *Nuzhatu'l-Arwáḥ* ("Recreation of Souls") of ash-Shahrazúrí was also compiled in the thirteenth century, and exists both in an Arabic and a Persian version. The notice of 'Umar which it contains is printed in both versions at pp. 327–329 of Zhukovski's article. He translates the Persian into Russian, while Ross in his English translation follows the Arabic. Each version quotes verses by him in the language in which it is written. The Persian version cites the quatrains numbered 193 and 230 in Whinfield, while the Arabic cites three fragments of his Arabic verse, the first containing four, the second six, and the third three couplets. The second of these three pieces is the same from which a shorter extract is given in the work last mentioned. Shahrazúrí's account is a good deal fuller than Al-Qifṭí's. It describes 'Umar as a follower of Avicenna, but ill-tempered and inhospitable, and mentions the titles of two of his philosophical works otherwise unknown. His memory is stated to have been so good that, having read a certain book seven times through at Iṣfahán, he afterwards wrote it out almost word for word at Níshápúr. His knowledge of Arabic philology and the seven readings of the Qur'án was remarkable. He was disliked by the great theologian Abú Ḥámid Muḥammad al-Ghazálí, who conversed with him on at least one occasion, and, it is said, by Sanjar, but was held in high honour by Malikshàh. Immediately before his death he was reading in the *Shifá* of Avicenna the chapter treating of the One and the Many, and his last words were: "O God! Verily I have striven to know Thee according to the range of my powers, therefore forgive me, for indeed such knowledge of Thee as I possess is my [only] means of approach to Thee."

The next notice in point of time is that occurring in al-Qazwíní's *Átháru'l-Bilád* ("Monuments of Countries"), *s.v.*

Níshápúr, p. 318 of Wüstenfeld's edition. Here also 'Umar is described as "versed in all kinds of philosophy, especially mathematics," and as favoured by Sulṭán Malik-shah. He is also credited with the invention of clay scare-crows, and an account is given of the method which he once adopted to cover with shame and confusion a certain theologian who, while denouncing him from the pulpit as a freethinker and atheist, used privately to come to him early in the morning to take lessons in philosophy.

Al-Qazwíní's *Átháru'l Bilád.*

We have now come to the end of the thirteenth century authorities, and before passing on to those of a later date we may note that these earlier records consistently represent 'Umar Khayyám as essentially a philosopher, astronomer, and mathematician, and that, so far from his being represented as a mystic, he is denounced by the Ṣúfí Najmu'd-Dín Rází as the arch-freethinker of his time, while al-Qifṭí speaks of the later Ṣúfís being deceived by the outward appearance of some of his words and adapting them to their own ideas.

Character of 'Umar as it appears in thirteenth-century writings.

Our one fourteenth-century authority of weight is the *Jámi'u't-Tawáríkh* of Rashídu'd-Dín Faḍul'lláh, a great history of the Mongols, including a section on General History, composed in the first quarter of the fourteenth century, and still, unfortunately, in spite of its vast importance, unpublished.[1] In this book we first find what is now generally known as the Story of the Three Friends, already discussed on pp. 190–193 *supra*. Part of this I published in the *Journal of the Royal Asiatic Society* for April, 1899 (pp. 409–411), in a short article entitled *Yet more Light on 'Umar Khayyám*, and, since this is the oldest form of a legend which has attracted a good deal of attention amongst

The *Jámi'u't-Tawáríkh.*

[1] A small portion dealing with the history of Hulágú Khán was published by Quatremère (Paris, 1836), and the trustees of the Gibb Memorial Fund are now making arrangements for the gradual publication of other portions.

the admirers of the Astronomer-Poet and his interpreter Fitz-Gerald, it seems to me desirable to reprint this translation here, so far as it concerns 'Umar. This narrative runs as follows[1] :—

"Now the cause of the enmity and mistrust which existed between the Nidhámu'l-Mulk and Ḥasan-i-Ṣabbáḥ was that they and 'Umar Khayyám were at school together in Níshápúr, and there, in boyish fashion, conceived for one another a devoted friendship which culminated in their partaking of each other's blood and registering a solemn vow that whichever of them should attain to high rank and lofty degree should protect and help the others.

"Now it happened, by a train of circumstances fully set forth in the *History of the House of Seljúq*, that the Nidhámu'l-Mulk attained to the position of Prime Minister. 'Umar Khayyám waited upon him and reminded him of the vows and covenants of their boyish days. The Nidhámu'l-Mulk, recognising these old claims, said, 'I give thee the government of Níshápúr and its dependencies.' But 'Umar, who was a great man, and withal a philosopher and a man of sense, replied, 'I have no desire to administer a province or to exercise authority over the people. Rather assign to me a stipend or pension.' So the Nidhámu'l-Mulk assigned him an allowance of ten thousand *dínárs* from the treasury of Níshápúr, to be paid over to him annually without deduction or tax."

The narrative continues with the arrival of Ḥasan-i-Ṣabbáh to claim his share of the Nidhámu'l-Mulk's favours, and describes how he refuses the government of Ray or Iṣfahán, and will be satisfied with nothing less than a high post at Court, which position he abuses by trying to compass the downfall of his benefactor, whom he hopes to succeed as Prime Minister. How he failed in his attempt, was covered with disgrace, and, fleeing from Khurásán, made his way to Iṣfahán and thence to the Court of the Fáṭimid Caliph al-Mustanṣir at Cairo, where he espoused the cause of Nizár, and returned to Persia to carry on the "New Propaganda" in his name, are matters which have been already discussed in the last chapter, and will be found set forth with many embellishments in the

[1] While omitting nothing essential, I have made this translation a little freer than it is in my article.

Ta'ríkh-i-Guzída (ed. and trans. Gantin, pp. 486–497), Dawlatsháh's *Memoirs* (pp. 138–141 of my edition) and other later writers.

The next notice of 'Umar Khayyám cited by Zhukovski is from the *Firdawsu't-Tawáríkh*, or "Paradise of Histories," composed about A.D. 1405–6. This quotes two of his quatrains, describes a discussion between him and Abu'l-Ḥasan al-Bayhaqí (in which the latter took by far the greater part) as to the meaning of an Arabic verse in the Ḥamása, and repeats the story of his death, which essentially agrees with that given by Shahrazúrí in the *Nuzhatu'l-Arwáḥ*.

Firdawsu't-Tawáríkh.

The last notice which Zhukovski gives is from a very modern work, the *Ta'ríkh-i-Alfí*, or "Millennial History," so called because it was meant to be carried down to the year A.H. 1000 (= A.D. 1591–92), though it actually ends with the year A.H. 997. This account for the most part reproduces the statements of Shahrazúrí in an abridged form, but ends with the following curious passage:—

Ta'ríkh-i-Alfí.

"It appears from numerous books that he (*i.e.*, 'Umar Khayyám) held the doctrine of Metempsychosis. It is related that there was in Níshápúr an old College, for the repairing of which donkeys were bringing bricks. One day, while the Sage (*Ḥakím*, *i.e.*, 'Umar) was walking with a group of students, one of the donkeys would on no account enter (the College). When 'Umar saw this, he smiled, went up to the donkey, and extemporised [the following quatrain]:—

Ay rafta, wa báz ámada "Bal hum" *gashta,*
Nám-at zi mayán-i-nám-há gum gashta,
Nákhun hama jam' ámada, u sum gashta
Rísh uz pas-i-kún dar amáda dum gashta.

"O lost and now returned '*yet more astray*,'[1]
Thy name from men's remembrance passed away,
Thy nails have now combined to form thy hoofs,
Thy tail's a beard turned round the other way!"

[1] This verse has caused great trouble to European scholars, but the explanation of the words *bal hum* will be found in the Qur'án, vii, 178

The donkey then entered, and they asked 'Umar the reason of this. He replied, 'The spirit which has now attached itself to the body of this ass [formerly] inhabited the body of a lecturer in this college, therefore it would not come in until now, when, perceiving that its colleagues had recognised it, it was obliged to step inside.' "

It is impossible here to enumerate all the late accounts of 'Umar Khayyám, many of which contain anecdotes obviously invented to explain the production of certain quatrains. He is strangely ignored by the great biographer Ibn Khallikán, and by Ibn Shákir, who strove in his *Fawátu'l-Wafayát* to supply the omissions of his predecessor. Ḥájji Khalífa, the great Turkish bibliographer, mentions him three times (ii, 584; iii, 570; vi, 273), once in connection with the science of Algebra, once in connection with Malikshâh's reformed Calendar, and once as contemporary with another author whom he is discussing, but omits to mention the year of his death, which was therefore presumably unknown to him. The date ordinarily given for his decease[1] is A.H. 517 (= A.D. 1123–24), but I cannot find any strong authority for it. It is, however, certain from the *Chahár Maqála* that he died between A.D. 1115 and 1135, and "some years" before the latter date, and that his father's name was Ibráhím. Although described as indolent and averse from writing or teaching, Ross[2] has compiled a list of ten books (including the Persian quatrains, and the *Zíj-i-Malikshâhí*, for which he was only in part responsible) ascribed to him by various authorities. Most of these were scientific or philosophical treatises in Arabic, one of which, his *Treatise on Algebra*, was edited by Woepcke with a French translation in 1851, while another, containing some observa-

and xxv, 46, in the words "*Ka'l-an'ámi, bal hum aḍallu*," "like cattle, nay, they are yet more misguided." To a Muhammadan reasonably conversant with his Qur'án the allusion is evident. Whinfield (No. 423) has quite misunderstood the verse.

[1] See Rieu's *Persian Catalogue*, p. 546, and also Ross's Introductory Sketch to Messrs. Methuen's edition of FitzGerald's version of the *Rubá'iyyát* (London, 1900), pp. 71–72.

[2] *Loc. cit.*, pp. 72–73.

tions on Euclid's definitions, exists in manuscript in the Leyden Library.

"Omarian" literature.

It is, of course, in the Quatrains that the interest of most readers centres, but with the appalling mass of literature which the popularity of FitzGerald's rendering has produced in Europe and America it is quite impossible to deal in a book like the present. This literature contains some of the best and some of the worst literary work which I have ever seen, and the judicious bibliography which forms Appendix xlix (pp. 438–594) of Nathan Haskell Dole's beautiful "Multi-variorum edition" (Boston and London, 1898) should suffice to satisfy the most insatiable "Omarian," though at the end the diligent compiler is fain to admit (p. 594) that "certainly all the extant references to Omar in all languages would require a lifetime [to elucidate], and make a library in itself." With every desire for brevity, however, we must add a few more words on Zhukovski's researches as to the "wandering quatrains" (*i.e.*, quatrains commonly attributed to 'Umar, but ascribed on older and better authority to other poets), and Heron Allen's careful and exhaustive analysis of the relation existing between FitzGerald's rendering and the originals on which it was based.

The "wandering quatrains."

Of the quatrains of 'Umar Khayyám included in M. Nicolas' edition, no fewer than eighty-two were found by Zhukovski ascribed on at least equally good authority to one or other of the following poets: 'Abdu'lláh Anṣárí, Abú Sa'íd b. Abi'l-Khayr, Afḍal-i-Káshí, 'Ákif, 'Alá'u'd-Dawla Simnání, Anwarí, 'Asjadí, Athíru'd-Dín, 'Aṭṭár, Avicenna (Ibn Síná), Awḥadí-i-Kirmání, Badíhí-i-Sajáwandí, Bákharzí (Sayfu'd-Dín), Fakhru'd-Dín Rází, Firdawsí, Ghazálí (Aḥmad), Ḥáfidh-i-Shírází, Jalálu'd-Dín Rúmí, Jamálu'd-Dín Qazwíní, Kháqání, Kamálu'd-Dín Isma'íl, Majdu'd-Dín Hamkar, Maghribí, Malik Shamsu'd-Dín, Najmu'd-Dín Rází, Naṣíru'd-Dín Ṭúsí, Ni'matu'lláh-i-Kirmání, Riḍá'u'd-Dín, Sa'du'd-Dín Ḥamawí, Salmán-i-

Sáwají, Sháhí, Siráju'd-Dín Qumrí, and Ṭálib-i-Ámulí. This list could, with a little trouble, be greatly increased. I have myself noticed (without searching for) a few more instances. Thus the quatrains ascribed by Whinfield (Nos. 144 and 197) and by Nicolas (Nos. 116 and 182) to 'Umar, and by Zhukovski (Nos. 26 and 27) to Naṣíru'd-Dín Ṭúsí and Ṭálib-i-Ámulí, are attributed in the *Ta'ríkh-i-Guzída* (composed in A.D. 1330) to Siráju'd-Dín Qumrí and 'Izzu'd-Dín Karachí respectively;[1] and, since they represent diametrically opposite points of view, it is at least certain that they are not by the same author. A useful tabulated concordance of these quatrains, showing their correspondence with the editions of Whinfield and Nicolas, and the Bodleian manuscript, is appended by Ross to his translation of Zhukovski's article. The upshot of the whole inquiry is that, while it is certain that 'Umar Khayyám wrote many quatrains, it is hardly possible, save in a few exceptional cases, to assert positively that he wrote any particular one of those ascribed to him. The oldest known manuscript of 'Umar's *Rubá'iyyát* (Bodleian, No. 525) dates from the year A.H. 865 (= A.D. 1460–1461), and was therefore transcribed nearly three centuries and a half after his death. It contains only 158 quatrains, and has been published in *fac-simile*, with literal prose translation, Introduction, and other matter, by Mr. Edward Heron Allen (London, 1898), who in a later publication on the same subject (*Edward FitzGerald's Rubá'iyyát of 'Omar Khayyám with their Original Persian Sources*, London, 1899), enumerates, on pp. xv–xvi, the manuscripts and editions known to him, with the number of quatrains contained in each. This varies from 76 in one of the older Paris MSS. (dated A.H. 937 = A.D. 1530–1531) to 604 in the Bankipúr MS., 770 in the edition lithographed at Lucknow in A.H. 1312

[1] See my *Biographies of Persian Poets contained in . . . the Ta'ríkh-i-Guzída*, in the *J.R.A.S.* for October, 1900, and January, 1901, Nos. 38 and 50.

(= A.D. 1894–95), and 845 in John Payne's metrical translation, while Miss Jessie E. Cadell succeeded in collecting from all available sources over twelve hundred quatrains attributed to 'Umar Khayyám. It is, of course, always possible that an ancient and authoritative manuscript may some day be discovered in one of the unexplored libraries of Asia, but, failing this, it must, save in a few isolated cases, remain uncertain which of the many quatrains ascribed to 'Umar are really his. Both external and internal evidence fail us; the former because we possess no manuscript which even approaches the poet's time, the latter because nearly all quatrains are so similar in form, metre, style, and diction, so brief in extent, so much more prone to treat of the Universal than of the Particular, and so easy to make or paraphrase, that not even the most accomplished Persian man of letters could seriously pretend to decide by their style as to their authorship, which, indeed, if I may be pardoned the somewhat irreverent comparison, is often as uncertain as that of an English "Limerick."

As regards the relations between FitzGerald's translation or paraphrase and the original, this point has been exhaustively and conscientiously worked out by Mr. Edward Heron Allen in the second of the two books mentioned on the preceding page, and it is sufficient here to quote in his own words the final conclusion at which, after much labour, he arrived (pp. xi–xii of his Preface):—

"Of Edward FitzGerald's quatrains, forty-nine are faithful and beautiful paraphrases of single quatrains to be found in the Ouseley or Calcutta MSS., or both.

"Forty-four are traceable to more than one quatrain, and may therefore be termed the 'composite' quatrains.

"Two are inspired by quatrains found by FitzGerald only in Nicolas' text.

"Two are quatrains reflecting the whole spirit of the original poem.

"Two are traceable exclusively to the influence of the *Manṭiqu'ṭ-Ṭayr* of Farídu'd-Dín 'Aṭṭár.

"Two quatrains primarily inspired by 'Umar were influenced by the Odes of Ḥáfidh.

"And three, which appeared only in the first and second editions, and were afterwards suppressed by Edward FitzGerald himself, are not—so far as a careful search enables me to judge—attributable to any lines of the original texts. Other authors may have inspired them, but their identification is not useful in this case."

Only the veriest tyros need to be reminded that in Persian the quatrain is always an absolutely complete and isolated unit, that there is no such thing as a poem composed of a number of quatrains, and that in collections of quatrains the only order observed or recognised is the alphabetical, according to the final letter of the three rhyming half-verses.

Báb á Ṭáhir 'Uryán of Hamadán.

Of Bábá Ṭáhir, of Hamadán, nick-named "the Naked" (*'Uryán*), the second of the four famous quatrain-writers of this period, I shall speak but briefly, since his quatrains have been published by M. Clément Huart in the *Journal Asiatique* for Nov.–Dec., 1885 (ser. viii, vol. 6), with a French translation and notes, and again by Mr. Edward Heron Allen in his *Lament of Bábá Ṭáhir* (Quaritch, 1902), with Introduction, literal prose translation and notes, to which is added an English verse-translation by Mrs. Elizabeth Curtis Brenton. I have also devoted several pages (83–87) in the *Prolegomena* to this volume to a discussion of the dialects and dialect-poetry of Persia in general, and Bábá Ṭáhir in particular, and gave the text and metrical translations of three of his most popular quatrains.[1] These, and most other dialect-quatrains, are written not in the usual *rubá'í* metres but in the apocopated hexameter *hazaj*, *i.e.*, the foot (⏑ — — —) six times repeated in the *bayt*, but "docked" to (⏑ — —) in

[1] Of less use to the ordinary English reader, because written in Russian, is Zhukovski's article in vol. xiii. (pp. 104–108) of the *Zapiski* of the Oriental Section of the Imperial Russian Archæological Society for 1901.

the third and sixth feet. They are naturally, as being the work of simple and provincial men, usually of a less introspective and philosophical character than those of quatrain-writers like 'Umar Khayyám.

Of Bábá Ṭáhir's life we know but little, and very various dates, ranging from the beginning of the eleventh to the latter part of the thirteenth century of our era, have been assigned to him by different Persian writers. By far the oldest mention of him which I have met with occurs in the already-mentioned *Ráḥatu'ṣ-Ṣudúr*,[1] on f. 43 of the unique Paris MS., and runs as follows:—

Oldest notice of Bábá Ṭáhir, written in A.D. 1202–3.

"I have heard that when Sulṭán Ṭughril Beg came to Hamadán, there were three elders of the saints (*i.e.*, the Ṣúfís), Bábá Ṭáhir, Bábá Ja'far, and Shaykh Ḥamshá. Now there is by the gate of Hamadán a little mountain called Khiḍr, and there they were standing. The Sulṭán's eyes fell upon them; he halted the vanguard of his army, alighted, approached, and kissed their hands. Bábá Ṭáhir, who was somewhat crazy in his manner, said to him, 'O Turk, what wilt thou do with God's people?' 'Whatever thou biddest me,' replied the Sulṭán. 'Do [rather] that which God biddeth thee,' replied Bábá; '"*Verily God enjoineth Justice and Well-doing.*"'[2] The Sulṭán wept and said, 'I will do so.' Bábá took his hand and said, 'Dost thou accept this from me?' 'Yes,' replied the Sulṭán. Bábá had on his finger the top of a broken *ibríq*[3] wherewith he had for many years performed his ablutions. This he took off and placed on the Sulṭán's finger, saying, 'Thus do I place on thy hand the empire of the world: be thou just!' The Sulṭán used to keep this amongst his amulets, and, when a battle was impending, used to put it on his finger. Such was his pure faith and sincere belief; for in the Muhammadan religion there was none more devout or watchful than he."

The meeting here described probably took place about A.H. 447 or 450 (A.D. 1055–58), so that we may safely reject

[1] See pp. 117 and 166 *supra*. [2] Qur'an, xvi, 92.

[3] A pitcher with a long, narrow neck used for the ablutions prescribed by Islám. A ring-shaped fragment had in this case resulted from a horizontal fracture of the neck.

the date (A.H. 410 = A.D. 1019–20) assigned to Bábá Ṭáhir's death by Riḍá-qulí Khán in the *Riyáḍu'l-'Árifín*, while the statement cited by Zhukovski in the article alluded to in a preceding footnote, that Bábá Ṭáhir conversed with Avicenna (who died in A.D. 1036) contains no inherent improbability. The anecdote cited above is quite in character both with the little we know of Bábá Ṭáhir from other sources, and with the consideration and respect still shown by the highest and noblest in Muhammadan countries to half-crazy (*majdhúb*) dervishes with a reputation for sanctity. Such I have myself seen wander at will into Turkish Government offices, where they always met with a kind and even deferential reception.

Abú Sa'íd b. Abi'l-Khayr.

We now pass on to the third great quatrain-writer, Abú Sa'íd b. Abi'l-Khayr (born at Mahna, in the district of Kháwarán, on December 7, A.D. 967, died on January 12, A.D. 1049), whom Ethé describes as the first master of theosophic verse, the first to popularise the quatrain as a vehicle of religious, mystic, and philosophic thought, and to make it "the focus of all mystic-pantheistic irradiations," and the first "to give the presentations and forms of the Ṣúfí doctrine those fantastic and gorgeous hues which thenceforth remained typical of this kind of poetry." Like Bábá Ṭáhir, Abú Sa'íd is said to have come into personal relations with Avicenna, and when they separated after their first interview, according to the popular story, the mystic said, "What I see he knows," while the philosopher said, "What I know he sees."[1] But Ethé has shown that (as, indeed, was to be expected) they were on important points of belief

[1] This story is given, amongst other places, in the *Akhláq-i-Jalálí* (composed in the second half of the fifteenth century), p. 28 of the edition lithographed at Lucknow in A.H. 1283 (A.D. 1866–67). According to another account given in the *Ta'ríkh-i-Guzída* and cited by Ethé (*loc. cit.*, p. 151), Avicenna said, "All that I know he also sees," while Abú Sa'íd said, "All that I do not see he knows."

(*e.g.*, the efficacy of faith without works) in direct antagonism (pp. 52–53 of the article mentioned in n. 1 *ad calc*).

Materials for his biography unusually copious.

The materials for Abú Sa'íd's biography are exceptionally complete, for, besides the usual hagiologies and anthologies, we have first of all two monographs compiled by Ethé with his usual diligence and scholarship,[1] and subsequently the publication by Zhukovski in 1899 of two volumes of rare texts dealing wholly or chiefly with his life, words, and verses. These two volumes are so important that they merit a somewhat detailed notice.

The first volume contains the texts of two Persian works, the *Asráru't-Tawḥíd fí Maqámáti'sh-Shaykh Abí Sa'íd* ("Mysteries of the Divine Unity, treating of the Stations of Shaykh Abú Sa'íd"), and the short *Risála-i-Ḥawrá'iyya* ("Treatise of the Houri"). The former, a lengthy work of 485 pages, was compiled by the Saint's great-great-grandson, Muḥammad b. al-Munawwar b. Abí's-Sa'íd b. Abí Ṭáhir b. Abí Sa'íd b. Abi'l-Khayr of Mayhana,[2] and, as Zhukovski has shown in his learned preface, between the years A.H. 552 and 599 (A.D. 1157 and 1203), for it alludes to the death of Sanjar the Seljúq, which took place in the former year, and is dedicated to Ghiyáthu'd-Dín Muḥammad b. Sám, King of Ghúr, who died in the latter year. Zhukovski's text is based on two MSS., those of St. Petersburg and Copenhagen, and the importance of the work lies, as he points out, in the fact that it is one of the original sources used by 'Aṭṭár, Jámí, and other later compilers, and that it rests almost entirely on the statement of contemporaries transmitted either orally or in the form of notes and memoranda. Besides being one of the oldest monographs on Súfí saints, and giving a very clear

[1] In the *Sitzungsb. d. bayr. Akad.*, *philos.-philolog. Klasse*, 1875, pp. 145–168, and 1878, pp. 38–70. In these articles Dr. Ethé published ninety-two of Abú Sa'íd's quatrains with metrical translations and copious explanations and commentary.

[2] So pointed in the *Asráru't-Tawḥíd*, p. 3, l. 17.

picture of the dervish life of that period, it is also of considerable philological interest, and the editor has wisely preserved unchanged the archaic forms in which it abounds. Both manuscripts date from the eighth century of the Flight (fourteenth of our era).

The *Risála-i-Ḥawrá'iyya* is a short treatise of five pages written by 'Abdu'lláh b. Maḥmúd of Shásh (or Chách) in Transoxiana to explain one of Shaykh Abú Sa'íd's quatrains.

The second volume published by Zhukovski comprises the text of an ancient and unique manuscript in the British Museum (dated A.D. 1299) whereof the greater part treats of "the spiritual teachings and supernatural powers" of Shaykh Abú Sa'íd. The author of this work, which amounts to seventy-eight pages of printed text, and was written somewhat earlier than the *Asráru't-Tawḥíd*, was also a great-great-grandson of the Saint, and a son, as Zhukovski conjectures, of Abú Rawḥ Luṭfu'lláh.

Besides these ample materials, to do justice to which would require in itself a volume, we have numerous notices of the Saint's life in later biographical works like the *Haft Iqlím* (cited by Ethé), *Ta'ríkh-i-Guzída*, *Nafaḥátu'l-Uns* (ed. Nassau Lees, pp. 339–347), &c., as well as Oriental editions of his *Rubá'iyyát*, which are sometimes combined in one volume with those of 'Umar Khayyám and Bábá Ṭáhir, and other kindred matter. His life, however, seems to have been uneventful, his experiences lying, to make use of the idiom of the Persian mystics, rather in the "World of Souls" than in the "World of Horizons." In this respect he differs essentially from the writers and poets to whom the first part of this chapter was devoted.

To Dr. Ethé, I think, belongs the credit of establishing Shaykh Abú Sa'íd's pre-eminent importance in the history of Persian Mysticism—an importance hardly recognised even by his own countrymen, who, following the well-known saying of their greatest theosophical writer, Jalálu'd-Dín Rúmí, commonly reckon Saná'í and 'Aṭṭár, both of whom were subsequent to Abú Sa'íd, as the first and second of their three arch-mystagogues. Yet, as Dr. Ethé has amply shown in the selection of the Saint's quatrains which he published (and the same holds good of his sayings, whereof an abundance is recorded by his biographers), all the characteristics of Persian mystical thought and diction now for the first time present themselves in a combination which has ever since remained typical of Persian, Turkish, and Indian Ṣúfí poets. The following quatrains, selected from Dr. Ethé's monograph, and numbered with the numbers which he there assigns to them, will, I think, suffice to prove the truth of this assertion :—

(1)

"To gladden one poor heart of man is more,
Be sure, than fanes a thousand to restore :
And one free man by kindness to enslave
Is better than to free of slaves a score."

(2)

"O Thou whose Visage makes our world so fair,
Whose union, night and day, is all man's prayer,
Art kinder unto others? Woe is me!
But woe to them if they my anguish share!"

(5)

"In search of martyrdom the *Ghâzis* go[1]
To fight Faith's battles : do they then not know
That martyred lovers higher rank, as slain
By hand of Friend, and not by hand of Foe?"

(6)

"Let no one of Thy boundless Grace despair;
Thine own elect shall ever upward fare :
The mote, if once illumined by Thy Sun,
The brightness of a thousand suns shall share."

---

[1] Those who engage in the *ghazw*, or religious war.

(10)

"Till Mosque and College fall 'neath Ruin's ban,
And Doubt and Faith be interchanged in man,
How can the Order of the *Qalandars*[1]
Prevail, and raise up one true Musulmán?"

(13)

"Sir, blame me not if wine I drink, or spend
My life in striving Wine and Love to blend;
When sober, I with rivals sit; but when
Beside myself, I am beside the Friend."

(17)

"Said I, 'To whom belongs thy Beauty!' He
Replied, 'Since I alone exist, to Me;
Lover, Beloved and Love am I in one,
Beauty, and Mirror, and the Eyes which see!'"

(18)

"I sought the Leech and told my inward Pain:
Said he, 'From speech of all but Him refrain;
As for thy diet, Heart's-blood shall it be,
And from both Worlds thy thoughts shalt thou restrain."

(19)

"Those men who lavish on me titles fair
Know not my heart, nor what is hidden there;
But, if they once could turn me inside out,
They'd doom me to the Burning, that I'll swear!"

(20)

"Thou bid'st me love, and midst Thy lovers pine,
Of Sense and Reason strip'st this Heart of mine;
Devout and much revered was I, but now
Toper, and gad-about, and libertine."

(21)

"That Moon in Beauty rich and Constancy,
Beauty's high Zenith is His least Degree;
Gaze on His Sun-bright Face; or, can'st thou not,
On those dark curls which bear it company."

---

[1] A *Qalandar* is a kind of dervish who disregards all appearances and is heedless of men's opinion.

(27)

"My countenance is blanched of Islám's hue;
More honour to a Frankish dog is due!
So black with shame's my visage that of me
Hell is ashamed, and Hell's despairing crew."

(28)

"When me at length Thy Love's Embrace shall claim
To glance at Paradise I'd deem it shame,
While to a Thee-less Heaven were I called,
Such Heaven and Hell to me would seem the same."

(30)

"What time nor Stars nor Skies existent were,
Nor Fire nor Water was, nor Earth, nor Air,
Nor Form, nor Voice, nor Understanding, I
The Secrets of God's One-ness did declare."

(32)

"Brahmin, before that cheek rose-tinted bow
Of fourteen-year-old beauty, for I vow
That, failing eyes God-seeing, to adore
Fire is more fit than to adore a cow!"[1]

(33)

"O God, I crave Thy Grace for hapless me!
For hapless me enough Thy Clemency!
Each some protector, some defender claims;
But I, poor friendless I, have none but Thee!"

(38)

"By whatsoever Path, blessèd the Feet
Which seek Thee; blessèd He who strives to meet
Thy Beauty; blessèd they who on it gaze,
And blessed every tongue which Thee doth greet!"

---

[1] "Cow-worshippers" (*gáv-parast*), or "calf-worshippers" (*gúsála-parast*), is a term not unfrequently applied by the Persian to the Hindús. The ruddy glow on beauty's cheeks is compared to the sun or to fire, and hence the lover is metaphorically termed a Fire-worshipper or Sun-worshipper.

(54)

"The Gnostic, who hath known the Mystery,
Is one with God, and from his Self-hood free:
Affirm God's Being and deny thine own:
This is the meaning of '*no god but HE.*'"

(55)

"Last night I passed in converse with the Friend,
Who strove to break the vows which I would mend:
The long Night passed: the Tale was scarce begun:
Blame not the Night, the Tale hath ne'er an end!"

(61)

"Since first I was, ne'er far from Thee I've been;
My lucky star hath served me well, I ween;
Extinguished in Thine Essence, if extinct,
And if existent, by Thy Light I'm seen."

And here, to conclude, is the quatrain ascribed to Avicenna, with the reply of Shaykh Abú Sa'íd. The former runs:—

"'Tis we who on God's Grace do most rely,
Who put our vices and our virtues by,
For where Thy Grace exists, the undone done
Is reckoned, and the done undone thereby."

This is Abú Sa'íd's reply:—

"O steeped in sin and void of good, dost try
To save thyself, and thy misdeeds deny?
Can sins be cancelled, or neglect made good?
Vainly on Grace Divine dost thou rely!"

The verses above cited illustrate most of the salient peculiarities of Ṣúfí thought and diction. There is the fundamental conception of God as not only Almighty and All-good, but as the sole source of Being and Beauty, and, indeed, the one Beauty and the one Being, "in Whom is submerged whatever becomes non-apparent, and by Whose light whatever is apparent is made manifest." Closely connected with this is the symbolic language so characteristic of these, and, indeed, of nearly all mystics, to whom God is essentially "the Friend," "the Beloved," and "the Darling"; the ecstasy of meditating on Him "the Wine" and "the Intoxication"; His self-revelations and Occultations, "the Face" and "the Night-black Tresses," and so forth. There is also the exaltation of the Subjective and Ideal over the Objective and Formal, and the spiritualisation of religious obligations and formulæ, which has been already noticed amongst the Isma'ílís, from whom, though otherwise strongly divergent, the Ṣúfís probably borrowed it. Last, but not least, is the broad tolerance which sees Truth in greater or less measure in all Creeds; recognises that "the Ways unto God are as the number of the souls of men";[1] and, with the later Ḥáfidh, declares that "any shrine is better than self-worship."[2]

Innumerable sayings and anecdotes of Abú Sa'íd are recorded by his diligent biographers. A very few examples of these must suffice. Being once asked to define Ṣúfíism, he said, "To lay aside what thou hast in thy head (such as desires and ambitions), and to give away what thou hast in thy hand, and not to flinch from whatever befalls thee." "The veil between God and His servant," he observed on another occasion, "is neither earth nor heaven, nor the Throne nor the Footstool: thy selfhood and illusions are the veil, and when thou removest these thou hast attained unto God." They described to him how one holy man could walk on the water, how another could fly in the air, and how a third could in the twinkling of an eye transport himself from one city to another. "The frog can swim and the swallow skim the water," he replied; "the crow and the fly can traverse the air, and the Devil can pass in a moment from East to West. These things are of no great account: he is a man who dwells amongst mankind, buys and

[1] *Ṭuruqu'lláhi ka-'adadi nufúsi Bani Ádam.* The Ṣúfís ascribe this saying to the Prophet, but there can be little doubt that it is spurious.
[2] *Har qibla'í ki báshad bihtar zi khud-parastí.*

sells, marries, and associates with his fellow-creatures, yet is never for a single moment forgetful of God."

It is said that one of Abú Sa'íd's favourite verses, forming part of an Arabic poem addressed by Kuthayyir to his beloved 'Azza, was this :—

"I would answer thy voice did'st thou call me, though over my body lay
Heavy the earth of the grave-yard, and my bones were crumbled away" ;

a verse which strongly recalls Tennyson's beautiful lines in *Maud* :—

"She is coming, my own, my sweet;
Were it ever so airy a tread,
My heart would hear her and beat,
Were it earth in an earthy bed;
My dust would hear her and beat,
Had I lain for a century dead;
Would start and tremble under her feet,
And blossom in purple and red."

On his tombstone was engraved the following verse in Arabic :—

"I ask thee, nay, command thee, when comes my time to die,
To carve upon my tombstone, 'Here doth a lover lie.'
That perchance some other lover, who Passion's laws doth know,
May halt his feet at my grave, and greet the lover who lies below." [1]

Shaykh 'Abdu-'lláh Anṣárí.

Of Shaykh Abú Isma'íl 'Abdu'lláh Anṣárí of Herát, chiefly known for his *Munáját*, or Supplications, and his *Rubá'iyyát*, or Quatrains, I shall say but little. He claimed, as his *nisba* implies, an Arabian origin, being descended from the Prophet's companion Abú Ayyúb; he was born at Herát on May 4, A.D. 1006, and died

[1] For the Arabic text, see the last page (p. 78) of Zhukovski's *Ḥálát u Sukhanán*, &c.

in 1088. Two works named "The Stages of the Pilgrims" (*Manázilu's-Sá'irín*) and "The Lights of Verification" (*Anwáru't-Taḥqíq*) are also ascribed to him. The following is from his *Munáját*:—

From the *Munáját*.

"O God! Two pieces of iron are taken from one spot, one becomes a horse-shoe and one a King's mirror. O God! Since Thou hadst the Fire of Separation, why didst Thou raise up the Fire of Hell? O God! I fancied that I knew Thee, but now I have cast my fancies into the water. O God! I am helpless and dizzy; I neither know what I have, nor have what I know!"

Quatrains.

This well-known quatrain is attributed to him:—

"Great shame it is to deem of high degree
Thyself, or over others reckon thee:
Strive to be like the pupil of thine eye—
To see all else, but not thyself to see."

The following is also typical:—

"I need nor wine nor cup: I'm drunk with Thee;
Thy quarry I, from other snares set free:
In Ka'ba and Pagoda Thee I seek:
Ka'ba, Pagoda, what are these to me?"

Other works of Shaykh-i-Anṣárí.

Ethé (*loc. cit.*, p. 282) enumerates the following works of Shaykh 'Abdu'lláh Anṣárí: the *Naṣíḥat*, or "Advice," dedicated to the Nidhámu'l-Mulk; the *Iláhí-náma*, or "Divine Book"; the *Zádu'l-'Árifín*, or "Gnostics' Provision"; the *Kitáb-i-Asrár*, or "Book of Mysteries"; a new and enlarged redaction of Sullamí's *Ṭabaqát-i-Ṣúfíyya*, or Biographies of Ṣúfí Saints; and a prose Romance of Yúsuf and Zulaykhá entitled *Anísu'l-Muríaín wa Shamsu'l-Majális*, or "The Companion of Disciples and Sun of Assemblies."

We must now pass on to some of the chief non-mystical poets of this period, of whom four at least deserve mention, *viz.*, the younger Asadí of Ṭús, the two poets of Jurján, Fakhru'd-Dín As'ad and Faṣíḥí, and Qaṭrán of Tabríz. Let us begin with the latter, whom Náṣir-i-Khusraw met and conversed with during his halt at Tabríz (August 26 to September 18, 1046), and of whom he speaks as follows in his *Safar-náma* (p. 6 of the text):—

Qaṭrán of Tabríz.

"In Tabríz I saw a poet named Qaṭrán. He wrote good poetry, but did not know Persian well. He came to me bringing the *Diwáns* of Manjík and Daqíqí, which he read with me, questioning me about every passage in which he found difficulty. Then I explained, and he wrote down the explanation. He also recited to me some of his own poems."

Both 'Awfí (*Lubáb*, vol. ii of my edition, pp. 214–221) and Dawlatsháh (pp. 67–69) consecrate separate notices to Qaṭrán, but both are meagre in biographical details. According to the former he was a native of Tabríz, according to the latter, of Tirmidh, while Schefer conjectures that he was born in the mountains of Daylam, between Qazwín and the Caspian Sea. Dawlatsháh speaks of him as the founder of a school of poetry which included such distinguished poets as Anwarí, Rashídí of Samarqand, Rúḥí of Walwálaj, Shams-i-Símkash, 'Adnání, and *Pisar-i-khum-kháná* ("the Son of the Tavern"), and adds that the eminent secretary and poet, Rashídu'd-Dín Waṭwáṭ, used to say: "I consider Qaṭrán as incontestably the Master of Poetry in our time, and regard the other poets as being so rather by natural genius than by artistic training." And it is certainly true that with him poetry becomes infinitely more artificial and rhetorical than with most of his predecessors, while, as Dawlatsháh adds, he especially cultivated the more difficult verse-forms, such as the *murabba'* (foursome), *mukhammas* (fivesome), and double rhyme (*dhu'l-qáfiyatayn*). In this latter device he is especially skilful, and, though imitated by some later poets, is surpassed by few. Amongst his imitators in this respect was Sanjar's Poet-Laureate Mu'izzí, who has a celebrated poem in double rhyme [1] beginning :—

"Fresh as rose-leaves freshly fallen dost thou on my breast rest;
Didst thou erst in Heaven's embraces as a nursling pressed rest?"

This ingenious artifice is very difficult to imitate in English, and as it is the special characteristic of nearly all his verse,[2] which depends for its beauty rather on form than idea, it must be left to those who can read it in the original to judge of its merit. The above attempt to reproduce this artifice in a single verse of English is, indeed, inadequate; each line should end with a word which in spelling and pronunciation exactly corresponds with the last syllable of the preceding word, like *farsang* (parasang) and *sang* (stone), *nárang* (orange) and *rang* (colour), *Ámúy* (the Oxus) and *múy* (hair), and so on; and to produce the effect in English it would be necessary to compose verses of which each line should, besides observing the ordinary laws of rhyme and metre, end with pairs of words like "recoil, coil," "efface, face," "refuse, use," and the like. But in Persian the figure, though very artificial, is pretty enough when skilfully handled.

Asadí the younger, of Ṭús.

Asadí the younger, named 'Alí, who concluded his heroic poem, the *Garshásp-náma* (one of the numerous imitations of the *Sháhnáma*), in A.D. 1066, must be carefully distinguished from his father Abú Naṣr Aḥmad, the teacher of Firdawsí and author of the "strife-poems" (*munáḏharát*) discussed at pp. 149–152 *supra*, who died in the reign of Sulṭán Mas'úd, *i.e.*, before A.D. 1041. One point

[1] See my edition of Dawlatsháh, p. 58.

[2] Many instances of it will be found in 'Awfí's notice of him in the *Lubáb*. See pp. 214–221 of my edition of vol. ii of that work.

of great interest connected with the younger Asadí is that we possess a complete manuscript—and that the oldest known Persian manuscript, dated Shawwál, A.H. 447 (= December, 1055, or January, 1056)—entirely written in his own handwriting. This manuscript is in the Vienna Library, and has been beautifully edited by Dr. Seligmann (Vienna, 1859), while a German translation by 'Abdu'l-Khálíq ("Abdul Chalig Achundow") was printed, without date, at Halle. It is a copy of a work on Pharmacology, entitled *Kitábu'l-abniya 'an ḥaqá'iqi'l-adwiya* ("The Book of Principles on the True Nature of Drugs"), composed by Abú Manṣúr Muwaffaq b. 'Alí of Herát, and the copyist in the colophon calls himself "'Alí b. Aḥmad al-Asadí of Ṭús, the Poet."

Asadí's *Garshásp-náma*, an epic poem describing the adventures and achievements of Garshásp, an old legendary hero of Sístán, contains some nine or ten thousand verses. It is very similar in style to its prototype, the *Sháhnáma*, but as I have not had access to any one of the ten manuscripts enumerated by Ethé,[1] and have only at my disposal the portions published by Turner Macan in vol. iv of his edition of the *Sháhnáma* (pp. 2099 *et seqq.*), I am unable to say anything more about it

The *Garshásp-náma.*

Of greater interest and importance is his Persian Lexicon (*Lughat-i-Furs*), preserved in the Vatican MS., the publication of which in Göttingen in 1897 is, perhaps, the greatest of the many services rendered to Persian letters by Dr. Paul Horn. Ethé has since that time discovered another MS. in the India Office (No. 2,516 = No. 2,455 of his *Catalogue*), and has indicated the most important variants. The Vatican MS. is an ancient one, bearing a date equivalent to September 30, A.D. 1332. The Lexicon appears to have been composed by Asadí towards the

The *Lughat-i-Furs.*

[1] See his article in vol. ii of the *Grundriss d. Iranisch. Philolog.*, pp. 233–235; and also his article *Über persische Tenzonen* in vol. ii (pp. 62–66) of the *Transactions of the Fifth International Congress of Orientalists* (Berlin, 1882).

end of his life (p. 31 of Horn's Preface), but at what precise epoch is not certain. It only explains rare and archaic Persian words, but its great value lies in the fact that each word is illustrated and vouched for by a citation from one of the old poets, including many otherwise unknown to us. The total number of poets thus cited is seventy-six, and the citations include passages from Rúdagí's lost *Kalíla and Dimna*, and other poems hitherto known to us either not at all, or only by name. One of the most remarkable omissions is the name of Náṣir-i-Khusraw, whom, as we have seen, 'Awfí also ignores. The explanation of this lies, I have no doubt, in the hatred and terror inspired in the minds of the orthodox by the Isma'ílís.

Fakhru'd-Dín As'ad of Gurgán.

Fakhru'd-Dín As'ad of Jurján (or Gurgán) is scarcely known to us except as the author of the romantic poem of *Wís and Rámín*, a romance said to be based on an old Pahlawí original,[1] and compared by Ethé (*op. cit.*, p. 240) to that of Tristan and Iseult. Even 'Awfí (vol. ii, p. 240) says that, apart from this poem, he had only met with five verses by this poet. These verses, which he cites, contain an expression of the poet's disappointment at the lack of appreciation shown by his patron, Thiqatu'l-Mulk Shahriyár, in spite of the "much poetry" which he had composed and recited to him; and, with two very abusive lines, in which, after observing that he "had never seen or heard of a man who was more of a cow than him," he loads him with coarse invective. Dawlatsháh makes no mention of this poet, and ascribes the poem of *Wís and Rámín* to Nidhámí-i-'Arúḍí of Samarqand (p. 60), adding (p. 130) that others attribute it to Nidhámí of Ganja. It was composed about A.D. 1048, after Ṭughril's victory over the "Romans," and is dedicated to his Minister, 'Amídu'd-Dín Abu'l-Fatḥ Mudhaffar of Níshápúr, and was published (from a manuscript unfortunately defective)

[1] See p. 11, l. 8, of the edition published by Nassau Lees in the Bibliotheca Indica Series (Calcutta, 1865).

in the Bibliotheca Indica Series in 1865. Its importance, as Dr. Ethé points out, lies in the fact that with it begins the differentiation of the romantic from the heroic variety of *mathnawí*, and the consecration of the *hazaj* metre to the former as of the *mutaqárib* to the latter. The following slightly expanded translation of four verses of the Song of Rámín (p. 142, ll. 11–14) may suffice as a specimen :—

"O happy, happy Wísa, who dost lie
At Rámín's feet, and with bewitchéd eye
Gazest on him, as partridge doomed to die
Its gaze upon the hawk doth concentrate!

"O happy, happy Wísa, who dost hold
Clasped in thy hand the jewelled cup of gold,
Filled to the brim with nectar rare and old,
Which like thy beauty doth intoxicate!

"O happy Wísa, whose red lips confess
With smiles their love, ere Rámín's lips they press,
Whom with desire's fulfilment Heaven doth bless,
And Múbad's fruitless passion doth frustrate!"

The Romance of *Wámiq* and *'Adhrá*.

The Romance of *Wámiq and 'Adhrá*, first versified in Persian by 'Unsurí, and later (after A.D. 1049) by Faṣíḥí of Jurján, is also said to be based on a Pahlawí original, concerning which Dawlatsháh (p. 30, ll. 3–12) writes as follows :—

"They likewise relate that the Amír 'Abdu'lláh b. Ṭáhir (A.D. 828–844), who was Governor of Khurásán in the time of the 'Abbásid Caliphs, was residing at Níshápúr when one day a man brought a book and offered it to him as a present. He inquired what book it was. The man replied that it was the Romance of Wámiq and 'Adhrá, a pleasant tale which wise men had compiled for King Núshirwán. The Amír said: 'We are men who read the Qur'án, and we need nothing beside the Qur'án and the Traditions of the Prophet. Of such books as this we have no need, for they are compilations of the Magians, and are objectionable in our eyes.' Then he ordered the book to be thrown into the water, and issued orders that wherever in his dominions there should be any books composed by the Persians and Magians, they should all be burned. Hence till the time of the House of Sámán, no Persian poems were seen, and if now and then poetry was composed [in Persian], it was not collected."

All the six versions of this poem enumerated by Ethé (p. 240) as having been composed in Persian seem to be lost, and its contents are only known from the Turkish version by Lámi'í of 'Unṣurí's redaction, which latter (the earliest) is merely mentioned by 'Awfí (vol. ii, p. 32, l. 9). Dawlatsháh (p. 69), in his brief notice of Faṣíḥí of Jurján, says that he had seen a few mutilated leaves of the version made by that poet, from which he quotes one verse, written in the same metre as the *Sháhnáma* (the hexameter *mutaqárib*), and endeavours to make up for the scantiness of his information concerning the poet by giving a short account of his patron, 'Unṣuru'l-Ma'álí Kay-ká'ús, the grandson of Qábús b. Washmgír, Prince of Ṭabaristán, himself a man of high literary attainments, and author of the *Qábús-náma*, which we must now briefly consider.

The *Qábús-náma*.

The *Qábús-náma* is a book of moral precepts and rules of conduct, composed in A.D. 1082–83 by the above-mentioned Kay-ká'ús, then sixty-three years of age, for his son Gílánsháh. Manuscripts of it exist in the British Museum (Or. 3,252), Leyden, and Berlin; the text has been lithographed in Ṭihrán by Riḍá-qulí Khán in A.H. 1285 (= A.D. 1868–69); and there is a French translation by Querry (Paris, 1886), and three Turkish versions (the oldest apparently lost), discussed by Dr. Rieu at p. 116 of his *Turkish Catalogue*. The book, therefore, has enjoyed a pretty wide popularity, which it unquestionably deserves; for it is full of wit and wisdom, rich in anecdote and illustration, and withal a royal book, written with a frank directness out of a ripe experience; and, in this respect, comparable to the *Siyásat-náma* already discussed in this chapter.

The *Qábús-náma* contains forty-four chapters, preceded by a preface, in which the royal author laments the decline of filial obedience, and exhorts his son to live virtuously, remembering that on his father's side he is descended from the old Persian King of Gílán, Arghash Farhádwand, who is mentioned in the *Sháhnáma* of Abu'l-Mu'ayyad of Balkh, and, through his father's grandmother, from Marzubán b. Rustam b. Sharwín, author of the *Marzubán-náma*, whose thirteenth ancestor was Kay-ká'ús b. Qubád, the brother of Núshirwán, the Sásánian King, while his mother was the daughter of Sulṭán Maḥmúd of Ghazna, and his great-grand-mother on his father's side the daughter of Ḥasan b. Fírúzán, King of Daylam. The preface is followed by the table of contents. The first four chapters deal with God, creation, and religious duties; the fifth with duty towards parents; the sixth and seventh with the cultivation of the mind and the powers of expression; and the eighth with the maxims inscribed in Pahlawí on the tomb of Núshirwán. Then follow chapters on age and youth (ix); self-restraint in eating (x); wine-drinking (xi); entertaining (xii); chess, backgammon, and light jesting (xiii); love (xiv); enjoyment of life (xv); the use of the hot bath (xvi); sleeping and resting (xvii); hunting (xviii); polo (xix); war (xx); accumulation of wealth (xxi); keeping faith in trusts (xxii); buying slaves (xxiii); buying immovable property (xxiv); buying quadrupeds (xxv); marriage (xxvi); education of children (xxvii); choice of friends (xxviii); precautions against enemies (xxix); pardon, punishment, and granting of favours (xxx); study and legal functions (xxxi); mercantile pursuits (xxxii); the Science of Medicine (xxxiii); Astrology and Mathematics (xxxiv); the Poetic Art (xxxv); the Minstrel's Art (xxxvi); on the service of kings (xxxvii); on the qualities of the courtier (xxxviii); on Secretaries of State and the Secretarial Art (xxxix); on the qualities and duties of a *wazír* (xl); on the qualities and duties of a general (xli); on the qualities and duties of the King (xlii); on farmers and agriculture (xliii): and, lastly, on generosity.

Contents of the *Qábús-náma.*

Incidentally the *Qábús-náma* contains, like the *Siyásat-náma*, numerous (about fifty) anecdotes, introduced to illustrate his counsels, and largely drawn from his personal recollections. A good many of these commonly found in collections of Persian stories (such as that contained in Forbes' *Persian Grammar*) in a vague and impersonal form are here ascribed to definite persons, and *vice versâ*, some here told indefinitely having been appropriated by later writers to some famous man. Of the first class I will only mention the anecdote (pp. 143–146 of the Ṭihrán lithograph) of the Qáḍí Abu'l-'Abbás Rúyání's sagacity, and how he cites a tree as witness, which occurs also, told of the same personage, in Ibn Isfandiyár's *History of Ṭabaristán* (India Office MS. No. 1,134, f. 59[a]), and, in an impersonal and garbled form, in Forbes' Grammar (No. 71 of the Persian stories, pp. 28–29 of the texts). Of the second class, I may cite the allusion (p. 210) to an alleged rule adopted by the Greeks that none might strike one whom their King had smitten, out of respect for the subject of such royal chastisement, which practice Dawlatsháh (p. 7 of my edition) attributes to the Court of Sulṭán Maḥmúd of Ghazna. Dawlatsháh is, indeed, without doubt considerably indebted to the *Qábús-náma*, though he only mentions it once (p. 69), for he has evidently taken from it (*Qábús-náma*, pp. 87–88) his account of the deposition and murder of Qábús b. Washmgír (pp. 48–49), and of the bold answer whereby the Sayyida, the mother of Majdu'd-Dawla, succeeded in preventing Sulṭán Maḥmúd from attacking her capital, Ray (see pp. 159–160 *supra*, and *Qábús-náma*, pp. 128–129 = Dawlatsháh, pp. 43–44). The celebrated story of Sulṭán Maḥmúd's threat which was answered by the letters "A.L.M." (see pp. 79–80 *supra*) also occurs on pp. 185–187 of the *Qábús-náma*, but the returner of this answer is here stated to have been the Caliph al-Qádir bi'lláh instead of the King of Ṭabaristán, the solution of the enigma is credited to Abú Bakr Kuhistání, who thereby gained promotion, and Firdawsí's name is not connected with the matter at all.

It may, I think, be interesting or useful to some of my readers if I append here a list of the Anecdotes occurring in the *Qábús-náma*, with a reference to the chapter and page in the Ṭihrán lithograph of A.H. 1285 in which they occur.

1. Brutal rejoinder of a rich pilgrim to a poor one (ch. iv, p. 20).
2. How the Caliph al-Mutawakkil's favourite slave Fatḥ was saved from drowning (ch. vi, p. 28).
3. Anecdote of Plato, and his grief at being praised by a fool (ch. vi, p. 34).
4. Muḥammad b. Zakariyyá ar-Rází, the physician, is alarmed because a madman smiles at him (ch. vi, p. 45).
5. Anecdote of Núshirwán and his Minister Buzurjmihr (ch. vi, p. 37).
6. Autobiographical, on the inexpediency of making improbable statements, even if they be true, unless they are susceptible of speedy proof (ch. vii, p. 39).
7. On the importance of phraseology: Hárúnu'r-Rashíd's dream and the two interpreters thereof (ch. vii, p. 42).
8. On the same subject: remonstrance of a favourite slave to a libertine master (ch. vii, p. 42).
9. Repartee of Buzurjmihr to an old woman who blamed him for not being able to answer her question (ch. vii, p. 43).
10. How a young 'Alawí of Zanján is discomfited by an old Sunní (ch. vii, p. 45).
11. The tailor and his jar (ch. ix, p. 52).
12. The old hunchback's reply to a youth who mocked him (ch. ix, p. 53).
13. The old chamberlain and the horse (ch. ix, p. 56).
14. The Ṣáḥib Isma'íl b. 'Abbád and his guest (ch. x, p. 59).
15. Anecdote of Ibn Muqla and Naṣr b. Manṣúr at-Tamímí (ch. xii, p. 65).
16. How a criminal condemned to death by al-Mu'taṣim saves his life by means of a cup of water (ch. xii, p. 67). (The same story is commonly told of the Persian Hurmuzán and the Caliph 'Umar. See Ṭabarí's Annals, Ser. i, vol. 5, pp. 2558–9.)
17. The Prophet and the old woman (ch. xiii, p. 70).
18. Anecdote of Shamsu'l-Ma'álí Qábús b. Washmgír, the author's grandfather (ch. xiv, p. 74).
19. Anecdote of Sulṭán Mas'úd of Ghazna (ch. xiv, p. 75).

20. Anecdote of 'Amr b. Layth (ch. xx, p. 85).
21. The deposition and murder of Qábús b. Washmgír (ch. xx, p. 87).
22. Instance of honour in thieves (ch. xxii, p. 94).
23. Anecdote of Aḥmad-i-Faríghún (ch. xxv, p. 111).
24. Autobiographical, on the advantages of swimming (ch. xxvii, p. 115).
25. Anecdote of Gushtásp (ch. xxvii, p. 118).
26. Anecdote of Shahrbánúya and al-Ḥusayn (ch. xxvii, p. 120).
27. The death of Socrates (ch. xxviii, p. 125).
28. Anecdote of al-Muhallab (ch. xxix, p. 127).
29. Sayyida, the mother of Majdu'l-Mulk, and Sulṭán Maḥmúd (ch. xxix, p. 128).
30. Dhu'l-Qarnayn's instructions as to his burial (ch. xxix, p. 131).
31. Anecdote of Mu'áwiya (ch. xxx, p. 135).
32. How the Qáḍí Abu'l-'Abbás Rúyání cites a tree as witness (ch. xxxi, p. 143).
33. Anecdote of a merchant and a dealer (ch. xxxii, p. 150).
34. How retribution overtakes a dishonest milkman (ch. xxxii, p. 154).
35. Anecdote of Faḍlún, King of Ganja (ch. xxxvii, p. 177).
36. Another anecdote of Faḍlún (ch. xxxvii, p. 179).
37. Anecdote of al-Ma'mún and the Qáḍí 'Abdu'l-Malik of 'Abkara (ch. xxxix, p. 184).
38. Anecdote of the Ṣáḥib Isma'íl b. 'Abbád (ch. xxxix, p. 184).
39. Reply of the Caliph al-Qádir bi'lláh to Sulṭán Maḥmúd's threats (ch. xxxix, p. 185).
40. Anecdote of Abú 'Alí Símjúr's discerning secretary 'Abdu'l-Jabbár Khújání (ch. xxxix, p. 187).
41. Anecdote of Rabí' b. al-Muṭahhar al-Qaṣrí (ch. xxxix, p. 191).
42. Anecdote of a Persian King and his Minister (ch. xl, p. 193).
43. Anecdote of Fakhru'd-Dawla and Isma'íl b. 'Abbád (ch. xl, p. 195).
44. Anecdote of Abu'l-Faḍl al-Bal'amí and Sahl of Khujand (ch. xl, p. 197).
45. Anecdote of Ṭughril the Seljúq (ch. xlii, p. 204).
46. Anecdote of Sulṭán Maḥmúd and Abu'l-Faraj al-Bustí (ch. xlii, p. 206).
47. Anecdote of Sulṭán Mas'úd of Ghazna (ch. xlii, p. 207).
48. Anecdote of Fakhru'd-Dawla and 'Aḍudu'd-Dawla (ch. xlii, p. 210).
49. Anecdote of Alexander the Great (ch. xlii, p. 213).
50. A problem for thieves (ch. xliv, p. 220).
51. Anecdote of two Ṣúfís (ch. xliv, p. 223).

Besides these anecdotes, many of which are at once apposite, original, and entertaining, the *Qábús-náma* contains many verses of poetry, most of which are quatrains composed by the author. Amongst the other poets cited are Abú Sa'íd b. Abi'l-Khayr, Abú Shukúr of Balkh, Abú Salík (of Gurgán, who is cited as the inventor of a certain musical air or mode), 'Asjadí, Farrukhí, Labíbí, and Qumrí of Gurgán. One verse in the Ṭabarí dialect is also quoted (p. 86), with a Persian rendering by the author.

Verses cited in *Qábús-náma.*

The persons mentioned in the anecdotes include the ancient Greek sages Pythagoras, Socrates, Plato, Aristotle, Hippocrates, Galen, Alexander the Great; of the Sásánian Royal Family and ministers, Núshirwán, Buzurjmihr, and Shahrbánú, daughter of Yazdigird III, who was taken captive by the Arabs and married to al-Ḥusayn; of the House of the Prophet, besides al-Ḥusayn, 'Alí, and al-Ḥasan; of the Umayyads, Mu'áwiya; of the 'Abbásid Caliphs, Hárúnu'r-Rashíd, al-Ma'mún, al-Mutawakkil, and al-Qá'im; of past Muhammadan rulers and ministers of Persia, 'Amr b. Layth, Sulṭán Maḥmúd and Sultán Mas'úd of Ghazna, Abu'l-Faḍl al-Bal'amí, the Ṣáḥib Isma'íl b. 'Abbád, Abú 'Alí Símjúr, Ṭughril the Seljúq, Núshtigín, Ḥasan-i-Pírúzán the Daylamí, Shamsu'l-Ma'álí-Qa'bús, Sharafu'l-Ma'álí, and many persons of less note. Of himself the author does not tell us very much. His genealogy, which he traces up to Núshirwán, is, of course, known from other sources, and we also learn that he made the Pilgrimage to Mecca in the Caliphate of al-Qá'im, and that he had engaged in wars for the Faith both in India and in Georgia and Armenia. He also tells us incidentally a good deal about his ancestors and kinsmen of the House of Ziyár, giving, for example, a very full narrative of the deposition and murder of his grandfather Qábús, and mentioning how two of his predecessors, Washmgír and Sharafu'l-Ma'álí, were accidentally killed while hunting.

Persons mentioned.

Style of the *Qábús-náma.*

The style of the *Qábús-náma* affords an excellent example of simple, straightforward Persian prose, being less rugged and unpolished than the *Siyásat-náma*, but much less ornate than books like the *Gulistán*. It has a good deal of character and humour, and abounds in pithy proverbial sayings, of which the following may serve as specimens: "Every bird flies with its like" (p. 45); "A man within his own four walls is like a king in his own dominion" (p. 61); "A daughter is best unborn; if she be born, either give her to a husband or to the grave" (p. 120: this proverb is still current); "The house with two mistresses is unswept"; "A sparrow in the hand is better than a peacock on promise"; "No man dies till his time is come, but till his time is come he does not go to Barda'[1] in summer" (p. 179); "It is a very shameful thing if the watcher should need a watcher" (p. 199); "Into whatever affair thou desirest to enter, look first how thou may'st emerge therefrom" (p. 202); "One cannot all at once trust the cat with the fat" (p. 204). The author's ideas display a curious mixture of craft and simplicity, of scepticism and piety. Thus he dwells on the ethical, as apart from the spiritual, value of prayer, fasting, and other religious exercises as means to cleanliness, humility, and temperance; and advocates conformity with the laws of Islám "because there is no State stronger than the Commonwealth of Islám." The prescription of the Pilgrimage to the rich seems to him a valuable method of compelling persons of condition to see the world, and in concluding his observations on religious observances he recommends his son not to inquire too deeply into the fundamental doctrines of the faith, "for," says he, "with the why and wherefore thou hast nothing to do." Excellent also is his advice to consider one's poor rather than one's rich neigh-

[1] Also called Barda'a, or Bardha'a, a town in Ádharbayján. See Barbier de Meynard's *Dictionnaire Géographique, etc. . . . de la Perse*, pp. 91–93. I cannot find any evidence that it was generally considered especially unhealthy.

bours, since this will conduce to thankfulness to God instead of breeding envy.

Worldly wisdom of the author.

His worldly maxims are shrewd, and wonderfully modern at times. He expatiates on the advantages of a smooth tongue, bids his son learn wisdom from fools, and cautions him against over-modesty, "for," says he, "many men fail of their objects through bashfulness." His remarks on truthfulness are delightful. "But do thou, O son," says he, "be specious, but not a liar: make thyself famous as a speaker of truth, so that, if at some time thou shouldst tell a lie, men may accept it as true from thee." He also cautions his son against making statements which, though true, are likely to be disbelieved, and cannot be easily proved; for, says he, "why should one make a statement, even if it be true, which it needs four months and the testimony of two hundred respectable witnesses to prove?"

Social maxims.

His social maxims are generally sound. A host, says he, should never apologise to his guests for the entertainment which he offers them, as it only makes them ill at ease; nor should he ever find fault with his servants in their presence. He bids his son avoid playing games of chance for money, or with notorious gamblers; confirming his words with an oath; or lending money to friends, unless he is prepared to make the loan a gift. His advice as to drinking wine is tinged with a delicate irony. He admits that to drink wine at all is contrary to religion, "but I know," he continues, "that you will not refrain from it for any words of mine, or hearken to what I say." Therefore he confines himself to recommending his son not to drink in the morning, or at least not often, for thereby he will be tempted to omit his prayers, and will fill his head with fresh fumes of wine ere those of the previous evening's debauch be dissipated. He also counsels him to get drunk in his own house, so as to avoid scandal; not to drink on the eve of Friday, out of respect for the day, so that men, seeing this, may forgive his drinking on other evenings; and not to behave, when drunk, in a riotous and offensive manner. "To drink wine," says he, "is a sin, and if you must sin, let it at least be pleasantly and gracefully. So let the wine which you drink be of the best, and likewise the music to which you listen; and if you jest with any one, do it well, so that, if you are to be punished in the next world, you may at least not be blamed and censured in this." He also recommends that favours should be asked of stingy and avaricious persons only when they are drunk, and therefore in a more generous humour.

After interesting chapters on the purchase of slaves and horses, and the good and bad points of different kinds of each, and on hunting and falconry, the author passes to marriage. Love at first sight he considers to be absurd and impossible. He discusses the qualities which go to the making of a good wife, and emphasises the importance of allying oneself by marriage with powerful and influential families. Girls, in his opinion, should not be taught to read and write, but should not be "sold" to rich but undesirable suitors. Children should be beaten if they are idle or naughty, and liberally rewarded with pocket-money if they are industrious and well-behaved; and on no account should boys omit to learn the art of swimming. The wise man will be outwardly friendly and polite even to persons he dislikes, and will avoid putting himself in the power of a friend, lest his friend should become hostile to him, and should use this power against him. He will refrain also from rejoicing over the death of an enemy, since only the assurance that he himself is secure against death could justify such exultation. Honesty is the merchant's best policy. Poets should be discriminating in their praise, and, even if they exaggerate, should not say that one who has never even had a knife in his belt "overthrows lions with his sword, and overturns Mount Bísitún [1] with his spear"; or that the steed

[1] The ancient Bagastâna, or Behistûn, celebrated for the Achæmenian inscriptions carved on it, situated near Kirmánsháh.

of one who has never even ridden a donkey "resembles Duldul, Buráq, or Rakhsh."[1] Satire should be indulged in but sparingly, "for the pitcher does not always return unscathed from the water"; and the poet "should not lie overmuch in his verse." A flying foe should not be pursued or too hotly pressed, lest he turn at bay in desperation. If letters be written in Persian, they should be written with an admixture of Arabic, "for unmixed Persian is distasteful." One should not be over-eager for the service of kings, and should avoid the society of soldiers.

Specimens of the *Qábús-náma.*

In conclusion, I give the following extracts from the ninth chapter, "on Old Age and Youth," as a specimen of the style of this interesting book.

"O son, though thou art young, be old in understanding. I do not bid thee not to play the youth, but be a youth self-controlled, not one of those worn-out[2] youths; for the young are ever high-spirited, as Aristotle says: '*Youth is a kind of madness.*' Moreover, be not one of the foolish youths, for harm comes of folly, not of high spirits. Take thy pleasure of life, for when thou art old, thou wilt assuredly be unable so to do, even as a certain aged man said, 'For many years I vainly sorrowed because, when I should grow old, the pretty ones would not care for me; but now that I am old, I do not care about them.' And indeed, even though he be capable thereof, such dalliance ill beseems an old man. And even though thou art young, never forget God Almighty, nor deem thyself secure against Death for Death regards neither youth nor age, as 'Asjadí says:—

'*Gar bi-juwání u bi-píristi,*
Pír bi-murdí u juwán zisti.'

'In youth or age did the question lie,
The young would live and the old would die.

[1] These three names belong to the mule of 'Alí, the celestial steed of the Prophet, and the horse of Rustam respectively.

[2] Literally "faded," "withered," to wit, by debauchery and excess.

Anecdote.

"I have heard that in a certain city lived a tailor, who had a shop hard by the city gate; and he had hung a pitcher on a nail, because it pleased his fancy to cast therein a pebble for every corpse which was borne forth from the city. And once a month he used to count these stones, to see how many had thus been borne forth, after which he would empty the pitcher and again hang it on the nail, and continue to cast stones into it until another month had elapsed. When some while had thus elapsed, it happened that the tailor died. And a certain man, who had not heard of the tailor's death, came to look for him, and, finding his shop closed, inquired of a neighbour where he was, since he was not there. 'The tailor,' replied the neighbour, 'hath gone into the pitcher!'

"But do thou, O my son, be watchful: be not deceived by thy youth. In obedience or disobedience, wherever thou art, remember God, and seek forgiveness, and fear Death, lest thou fall suddenly into the pitcher! . . . Respect the aged, and address them not with mockery, lest their answer silence thee.

Anecdote.

"I have heard that an old man, whose back was bent double with the weight of a hundred years, was going along leaning on a staff, when a young man, wishing to mock him, said, 'Aged sir, for how much didst thou buy this pretty bow [meaning his back] for I too would buy one for myself?' 'If thou livest,' answered the old man, 'and art patient, it will be given to thee for nothing!' . . . Be more careful to observe a virtuous old age than a virtuous youth, for youths have hope of old age, but the aged have naught to hope for save death, and it is impossible for them to look for aught else. For when the corn is white, if it be not reaped, it will fall of itself, and so likewise fruit which is mature, if it be not gathered, will of itself drop from the tree, without its being shaken. . . . They say in Arabic:—

'Idhá tamm^{a} amr^{un} daná naqṣuhu:
Tawaqqá' zawál^{an} idhá qíl^{a}, "tamm!"'

'When aught is completed, its waning is nigh:
When they say, "'Tis completed!" then look for decline.'

"Know, then, that they will not let thee be when thy senses have declined from their use. When the doors of speech, sight, hearing, touch, and taste are all shut on thee, neither wilt thou be able to enjoy life, nor can thy life give enjoyment to others. Thou wilt become a trouble to all, therefore death is better than such a life. But when thou art old, avoid the extravagances of youth, for the nearer one comes to death, the further should he be from extravagance. Man's life is like the sun, and thou mayest regard the sun which is on the western horizon as already set; as I say :—

'In Age's clutch Kay-Ká'ús helpless see:
Prepare to go, for years three-score and three
Press hard. Thy day to Vesper-time draws nigh,
And after Vespers Night comes suddenly.'

Therefore an old man should not be in intelligence and actions as are the young. But be thou ever compassionate towards the old, for age is a sickness cheered by no visits, and a disease which no physician can heal save Death alone; seeing that the old man can find no relief from the troubles of age till he dies. For whatever sickness befalleth man, if he dieth not, he hath each day some hope of improvement; save in the case of the sickness of age, since herein he waxeth ever older, and hath no hope of betterment. Thus I have read in some book that up to thirty-four years man waxeth daily in strength and robustness. After thirty-four years he remains the same, neither waxing nor waning, just as when the sun stands in the midst of heaven, it moveth slowly until it begins to sink. From forty to fifty years, every year he sees in himself some decrease which he did not notice the year before. From fifty to sixty years, every month he sees in himself some decrease which he did not notice in the previous month. From sixty to seventy years, every week he sees in himself some decrease which he did not notice in the previous week. From seventy to eighty years, every day he sees in himself some decrease which he did not see in himself the day before. And if he outlives eighty, every hour he is sensible of some pain or ache which he did not perceive the previous hour. The pleasure of life is until forty years of age: when thou hast ascended forty rungs of the ladder, thou shalt without doubt descend, and must needs come to that place whence thou didst set out. So he must needs be dissatisfied who is hourly afflicted with some pain or ache which had not befallen him in the previous hour. Therefore, O my son, and the Delight of mine Eyes, I have complained to thee at length of old age, because I have against it a grievous indictment; nor is this strange, for old age is an enemy, and of enemies do we make complaint."

Other prose works of this period.

Before bidding farewell to the Persian writers of this period, mention must be made of one or two other prose works, which are either not at present accessible to me, or, being accessible, must for lack of space be dismissed with a very brief notice. Amongst these is the *Nuzhat-náma-i-'Alá'í*, an encyclopædia composed by Shahmardán b. Abi'l-Khayr towards the end of the eleventh century for 'Alá'u'd-Dawla Kháṣṣ-beg, Prince of Ṭabaristán, of which the contents are fully described by Pertsch at pp. 30–36 of the Gotha Persian Catalogue, and more briefly by Ethé in columns 906–908 of the Bodleian Persian Catalogue. The similar but earlier *Dánish-náma-i-'Alá'í*, composed by Avicenna, has been already mentioned (p. 115 *supra*). The *Bayánu'l-Adyán*, or account of different religions, written by Abu'l-Ma'álí Muḥammad 'Ubaydu'lláh in A.D. 1092, has been made known by Schefer in vol. i of his *Chrestomathie persane*, pp. 132–189 (pp. 132–171 of the text). A very important historical work, especially in what concerns Khurásán, is Kardízí's *Zaynu'l-Akhbár*, composed about the middle of the eleventh century of our era, of which the only known manuscript (and even this is defective) is described by Ethé in columns 9–11 of the Bodleian Persian Catalogue. Equally important is the rare and unpublished *Kashfu'l-Maḥjúb* ("Revelation of the Occult"), a work treating of the lives and doctrines of the Ṣúfís, and composed by 'Alí b. 'Uthmán al-Jullábí al-Hujwírí in the latter part of the eleventh century. In connection with this, mention should also be made of the Treatise (*Risála*) on Ṣufiism compiled in Arabic in A.D. 1046–47 by Abu'l-Qásim 'Abdu'l-Karím b. Hawázin al-Qushayrí (died A.D. 1072–73), a work containing fifty-four chapters, which has been printed twice at least at Buláq, and of which there exists in the British Museum a Persian translation (Or. 4,118) made at an unknown but certainly early epoch, this manuscript being dated A.D. 1205

Three more writers of greater importance remain to be

mentioned, though it is, unfortunately, impossible in this place to accord them anything approaching adequate treatment. Of these, Abu'l-Ḥasan 'Alí al-Máwardí (died A.D. 1058) may be taken first, since he can be most briefly dismissed. Nine of his works (all of which are in Arabic) are enumerated by Brockelmann (*Gesch. d. Arab. Litt.*, i, p. 386), but only two of these are so celebrated as to need mention here. The first is the *Kitábu'l-Aḥkámi's-Sulṭániyya*, or "Constitutiones politicæ" (printed at Bonn and Cairo), which "depicts the ideal of Muslim Public Law, as it certainly can never have really existed, or at least not in the author's time." The second is the *Adabu'd-Dunyá wa'd-Dín*, an ethical work still widely studied in the higher schools of Turkey and Egypt.

Al-Máwardí.

The second of the three, though he has nothing to do with Persia, is too great a figure in the world of Muslim thought and literature to be passed over in silence. This is the blind[1] poet, sceptic and philosopher, Abu'l-'Ala al-Ma'arrí, so called from the little Syrian town of Ma'arratu'n-Nu'mán, where he was born, and in which he spent the greater part of his life. Náṣir-i-Khusraw visited him there during the three days which he spent in Ma'arra (January 12–15, A.D. 1047), and thus speaks of him in his *Safar-náma* (pp. 10–11 of Schefer's edition):—

Abu'l-'Alá al-Ma'arrí.

"There dwelt a man called Abu'l-'Alá al-Ma'arrí, the chief man of the city, but blind. He was very wealthy, and had many servants and workmen; indeed all the town's folk were as servants to him. But he had adopted the ascetic life, wearing a coarse cloak, sitting in his house, and allowing himself half a maund of bread daily, beyond which he ate nothing. I heard that he kept open house, and that his agents and stewards managed the affairs of the town, save in matters involving a general principle, which they referred to him.

[1] He lost the sight of one eye in A.D. 997, when only four years old, in consequence of small-pox, and of the other somewhat later.

20

He refuses his beneficence to none, but himself observes perpetual fast and nightly vigils, and occupies himself with no worldly business. And in poetry and literature he holds so high a rank that the greatest scholars of Syria, the Maghrib (*i.e.*, the Moorish States and Spain) and 'Iráq admit that in this age no one hath been or is of like degree. He had composed a book entitled *al-Fuṣúl wa'l-Gháyát*, wherein he set forth, in eloquent and wondrous words, riddles and parables which men cannot understand, save a little here and there, even such as had studied it with him. And they found fault with him for writing this book, declaring that he had intended therein to travesty the Qur'án.[1] There are always at least some two hundred persons who have come from all parts of the world to study poetry and literature with him. I heard that he had composed more than a hundred thousand verses of poetry. A certain person asked him why, seeing that God had bestowed on him all this wealth and riches, he gave it all away to other people, and did not enjoy it himself, to which he replied, 'I can take possession of no more than what I eat.' And when I arrived there (*i.e.*, at Ma'arratu'n-Nu'mán) this man was still alive."[2]

To Baron A. von Kremer chiefly belongs the credit of bringing home to European scholars the greatness and originality of al-Ma'arrí, to whom he devotes nine pages (pp. 386–394) in the second volume of his admirable *Culturgeschichte des Orients*, and on whom he has also published a series of excellent monographs.[3] The three following specimens of al-Ma'arrí's verse are cited by Dawlatsháh in the short notice which he consecrates to the poet (p. 25 of my edition) :—

[1] A sample of this mock Qur'án has been preserved to us, and was published by Goldziher in vol. xxix (1875) of the *Z.D.M.G.*, with some very interesting remarks on al-Ma'arrí, pp. 637–641. See also the same periodical, vol. xxxii, p. 383, and xxxi, p. 176, and Goldziher's *Muhammedanische Studien*, vol. ii, p. 403.

[2] He died ten years later, in A.D. 1057, being then eighty years old.

[3] The longest of these is in the *Sitzungsberichte d. Wiener Akad.* (*philos.-philol.-Klass.*) for 1888, vol. cxvii. His earlier monographs appeared in the *Z.D.M.G.* for 1875, 1876, 1877, and 1884, vol. xxix, pp. 304–312 ; vol. xxx, pp. 40–52 ; vol. xxxi, pp. 471 *et seqq.* ; and vol. xxxviii, pp. 499–529.

"O thou Abu'l-'Alá, Sulaymán's son,
Surely thy blindness hath been good to thee;
For, wert thou able to behold mankind,
No man amongst them would thy pupil[1] see!"

Here is the second specimen :—

"The days are but one parent's progeny,
The nights are sisters of one family:
Then seek not, either from the days or nights,
For aught that hath not been in years gone by!"

And here is the third :—

"Who is he whom aught can fright or startle,
Any marvel fill with doubts or fears?
I at least have never seen a marvel,
Though I've watched and waited eighty years:
Still Time's Time, men men, the days one pattern;
Still the World's success to strength adheres!"

The following is from Goldziher's article (*Z.D.M.G.*, xxix, pp. 637–8) :—

"Within Jerusalem was rife 'Twixt Christ and Aḥmed bitter strife:
This with *adhán* and that with blare Of bell doth summon men to prayer:
Each seeks to prove his doctrine true; But which is right? Ah, would I knew!"

According to Muhammadan law a theft exceeding a quarter of a *dínár* is punished by amputation of the thief's hand, while the compensation for the loss of a hand under other circumstances is fixed at five hundred *dínárs*. On this al-Ma'arrí says (Goldziher, *loc. cit.*, p. 639) :—

[1] The pupil of the eye is called by the Arabs *insánu'l-'ayn*, "the man of the eye," as it is called by the Persians *mardumak*, "the mannikin," and by the Turks *bebek*, "the infant." I have endeavoured to preserve the word-play.

'Why for a quarter do they amputate A hand five hundred serve to compensate?
Such contradictions silent awe compel. Lord God, deliver us from Fires of Hell!"

The next specimen is given by Von Kremer (*Z.D.M.G.*, xxix, p. 305 *ad calc.*) :—

"We laugh, but foolish is our joyless mirth;
Tears best befit all dwellers upon earth!
'Neath Fortune's Wheel we break like brittle glass,
Which no fresh mould shall e'er restore, alas!"

Al-Ma'arrí, as I have said, had no connection with Persia, either by birth or residence, and I have only mentioned him because he is so great and original a poet and thinker, and because further researches may very probably show that he was not without influence on the pessimist and sceptic poets of that country. In his peculiar line of thought he somewhat recalls 'Umar Khayyám, but is incomparably greater and more systematic, both as a poet and as an agnostic. His best-known works are the *Siqṭu'z-Zand*, which comprises his earlier poems; the *Luzúmiyyát*, or *Luzúmu má la yalzam*, which embodies his later philosophical and pessimistic verse; his *Letters*, admirably edited and translated by Professor Margoliouth of Oxford, and published in the *Anecdota Oxoniensia* (1898); and his *Risálatu'l-Ghufrán*, a sort of prose *Paradiso* and *Inferno*, in which the author describes an imaginary visit to the World of Shades, and the conversations which he held with various heathen and other poets of the Arabs. Some account of this last, with extracts, has been published by Mr. R. A. Nicholson, in the *Journal of the Royal Asiatic Society* for 1900 (pp. 637–720) and 1902 (pp. 75–101; 337–362; 813–847). This last-mentioned work also is of equal interest and difficulty, especially the latter portion, which deals with the heretics and *Zindíqs*, with whom the author, however much he may have felt by expediency compelled to censure them, must be supposed to have had considerable sympathy. His most impious work, from the Muslim point of view, was probably the parody of the Qur'án which, like al-Mutanabbí, he composed. This he named *Kitábu'l-Fuṣúl wa'l-Ghāyát*, and a specimen of it was published by Goldziher in the article entitled *Abu'l-'Alá al-Ma'arrí als Freidenker* in vol. xxix (1875) of the *Z.D.M.G.*, pp. 637–641. An excellent sketch of his life will be found prefixed by Professor Margoliouth to his above-mentioned edition of al-Ma'arrí's *Letters* (pp. xi–xliii), while Von Kremer's numerous notices, which contain many of his poems with German verse renderings, will afford the European reader abundant material for further study of this original and powerful thinker.

Al-Ghazálí.

I have left till the last in this chapter one of the most influential, if not one of the greatest, thinkers of this period, the Imám Abú Ḥámid Muḥammad al-Ghazálí (according to some al-Ghazzálí[1]), the theologian who did more than any one else to bring to an end the reign of Philosophy in Islám, and to set up in its stead a devotional mysticism which is at once the highest expression and the clearest limitation of the orthodox Muhammadan doctrine. "Ever since his time," says Dr. T. J. de Boer, in his *History of Philosophy in Islám* (English translation, p. 155), "Mysticism both sustains and crowns the Temple of Learning in Orthodox Islám." The admirable account of al-Ghazálí and his doctrine given in Dr. de Boer's lucid and learned work (pp. 154–168) renders it unnecessary that I should discuss at any great length this eminent theologian, whose services to Religion earned for him the title of *Ḥujjatu'l-Islám* ("The Proof of Islám"), by which he is generally known.

[1] I have been censured by so great an authority as Goldziher for writing "al-Ghazzálí" in a previous work, but at any rate this orthography was widely adopted by Muslim writers as early as the thirteenth century of our era. See *al-Fakhrí*, ed. Ahlwardt, p. 181. Cf., however, Brockelmann's *Gesch. d. arab. Litt.*, vol. i, p. 419 *ad calc.*

Al-Ghazálí was born at Ṭús in Khurásán in A.H. 450 (= A.D. 1058–59) or A.H. 451 (= A.D. 1059–60), about the time of Alp Arslán's accession to the Seljúq throne, and, being left an orphan at a comparatively early age, was, together with his brother, educated first by a Ṣúfí friend of his father's, and afterwards at one of the colleges of his native city. "We sought knowledge," he used afterwards to say, "otherwise than for God, but it refused to be otherwise than for God." He also studied for a while in Gurgán with the Imám Abú Naṣr al-Isma'ílí, and, while returning thence, was, it is said, robbed by highwaymen of all his possessions. He followed them to crave the return of his lecture-notes, "for which," said he, "I left my home, and which contain my knowledge." Thereat the chief robber laughed and said, "How dost thou pretend to have learned the knowledge contained in them, for, we having taken them from thee, thou art robbed of thy knowledge and left knowledgeless?" And thereafter al-Ghazálí, having recovered his note-books, did not rest till all their contents had been learned and digested, "so that," as he said, "should I again be robbed, I should not be deprived of my knowledge."

Thereafter al-Ghazálí went to Níshápúr, where he continued his studies and began to attract attention by his writings, which finally brought him to the notice of the great minister, Nidhámu'l-Mulk, who, in A.H. 484 (= A.D. 1091–92), appointed him a Professor in the Nidhámiyya College which he had founded and endowed twenty-five years before at Baghdád. After he had held this post with all distinction and honour for four years, "his soul soared above the mean things of the world, . . . and he cast all this behind his back"; and, appointing his brother as his deputy, he made the Pilgrimage to Mecca, and thence visited Syria, where he composed his great work, the *Iḥyá'u 'ulúmi'd-Dín*, or "Revivification of the Religious Sciences." This work, written in Arabic, was subsequently epitomised in a more popular form in Persian, under the title of *Kímiyá-yi-Sa'ádat*, "The Alchemy of Happiness"; and it served as the text for a series of sermons which the author preached on his return to Baghdád. Thence al-Ghazálí returned to Níshápúr and taught for a while in the Nidhámiyya College in that city, but ere long came back once more to his native Ṭús, where he died on Monday, 14 Jumáda II, A.H. 505 (= December 18, A.D. 1111). His writings were numerous (some seventy are enumerated by Brockelmann), and include, besides those already mentioned, a refutation of the Báṭinís or Isma'ílís, the "Saviour from Error" (*al-Munqidh mina'ḍ-Ḍalál*), and the celebrated "Destruction of the Philosophers" (*Taháfutu'l-Falásifa*), which at a later date called forth the "Destruction of the 'Destruction'" (*Taháfutu't-Taháfut*) of Averroes (Ibn Rushd) of Cordova.

The following passage from the *Munqidh* is interesting as showing how deeply al-Ghazálí had tasted that religious experience which he so highly valued ere he attained to the spiritual peace and conviction whereunto he finally won.

"In the prime of my youth," says he, "when, ere I was yet twenty years of age, I attained to discretion, until now, when my age approaches fifty, I ceased not to dare the depths of this deep sea, and to plunge into its midst as plunges the bold, not the fearful and cautious, diver, and to penetrate into its every dark recess, and to confront its every difficulty, and to breast its every eddy; investigating the creed of every sect, and discovering the secrets of every creed, that I might distinguish between the holders of true and false doctrine, and between the orthodox and the heretical. Therefore I never left an Esoteric [*Báṭini, i.e.*, an Isma'ílí, Carmathian, or "Assassin"] without desiring to acquaint myself with his Esotericism; nor an Exoteric [*Dháhiri*, or Formalist] without wishing to know the outcome of his Exotericism; nor a Philosopher without aiming at a comprehension of the essence of his Philosophy; nor a Scholastic Theologian without striving to understand the aim of his Scholasticism and his dialectic; nor a Ṣúfí without longing to stumble on the secret of his Ṣúfiism; nor a devotee without wishing to ascertain in what his devotion resulted; nor an infidel [*Zindíq*, properly a Manichæan] or atheist without spying through him to discern the causes which had emboldened him to profess his atheism or infidelity. For a thirst to comprehend the true essences of all things was, from my earliest days and the prime of my life, my characteristic idiosyncrasy, a natural gift of God and a disposition which He had implanted in my nature, by no choice or devising of mine own; until there was loosed from me the bond of conformity, and my inherited beliefs were broken down when I was yet but little more than a lad."

From such early strugglings after truth and dark accesses of doubt did al-Ghazálí win to a bright faith, a sure conviction, and a power of leading others to the haven reached by himself, which not only earned for him the illustrious title of "The Proof of Islám," but caused the learned Suyúṭí to exclaim, "Could there be another Prophet after Muḥammad, surely it would have been al-Ghazálí!"

CHAPTER V

THE PERIOD OF SANJAR AND HIS BROTHERS

(A.H. 485–552 = A.D 1092–1157)

THE period of sixty-five years which we are now about to consider begins with the death of Malikshāh, described at the end of chap. iii, and ends with the death of his son Sanjar, who, though he reigned supreme in the Seljúq Empire only from A.D. 1117 to 1157, had ruled over Khurásán, and been the dominant figure in the House of Seljúq, from A.D. 1096. From the fratricidal wars which troubled this Empire before his succession, Khurásán, thanks to his wise and firm government, stood in large measure aloof, and only towards the end of his reign did it suffer at the hands of the Ghuzz Turks devastations which, frightful as they were, were eclipsed some seventy years later by the horrors of the Mongol invasion. The period which we are now considering may, therefore, fairly be called "the Period of Sanjar," and with his death the epoch of the "Great Seljúqs" came to an end. Alike in length of life and brilliant achievements, according to ar-Ráwandí's *Ráḥatu'ṣ-Ṣudúr*,[1] Sanjar surpassed all the other Seljúq monarchs. From the time he was made king of Khurásán by Barkiyáruq, he effected, during a period of forty years, nineteen conquests. He took Ghazna and made Bahrámsháh king over it, on con-

[1] See my *Account of a rare . . . Manuscript History of the Seljúqs*, in the *J.R.A.S.* for 1902, p. 849.

dition that he should pay him a tribute of one thousand *dínárs* a day. He also took captive the king of Samarqand, Aḥmad Khán, who had rebelled on Barkiyáruq's death, in A.D. 1130, and subdued Sístán and Khwárazm. Yet from the political point of view the Seljúq power was no longer what it had been in the days of Alp Arslán and Maliksháh; for, apart from the fratricidal wars which marked the beginning of this period, the catastrophe of the Ghuzz invasion with which it ended, and the revolts of various turbulent *amírs*, which were of constant occurrence, two or three rival powers, even in Persia, were always ready to contest the supremacy of the "Great Seljúqs." Of these the most important were, in the north-east the "Kings of the mountains" of Ghúr, whose rising power gave to the House of Ghazna the *coup de grâce*; and the new dynasty of Khwárazm-sháhs, or rulers of Khiva, which, with the accession of Atsiz in A.D. 1127, became a formidable rival to the Seljúqs; while in the south-east the independent Seljúqs of Kirmán held sway. Almost more dangerous, because ubiquitous, was the sect of the Isma'ílís or "Heretics" (*Maláḥida*) of Alamút, whose achievements, notwithstanding numerous and violent repressive measures, maintained and extended the terror which they had already established, and who became a formidable force not only in Persia but also in Syria.

Rivals of the Seljúqs.

In literature and science this period was as brilliant as any which preceded or followed it; the number of Persian writers, both in prose and verse, vastly increased, while much important Arabic work continued to be produced in Persia. In the reign of Sanjar, of the great Persian poets Shaykh Farídu'd-Dín 'Aṭṭár (A.D. 1120) and Nidhámí of Ganja (A.D. 1140) were born; 'Umar Khayyám (A.D. 1121–22), Azraqí (A.D. 1130), Mas'úd b. Sa'd (A.D. 1131), Adíb Ṣábir (A.D. 1143–44), Mu'izzí (A.D. 1147–48), and 'Am'aq of Bukhárá (A.D. 1148–49), died; and Saná'í, Nidhámí-i-'Arúḍí of Samarqand, the great Anwarí,

Literary and scientific character of the period.

Rashídu'd-Dín Waṭwáṭ, the satirist Súzaní, and a host of less famous singers, flourished. Of contemporary Persian prose works, the great medical Encyclopædia entitled *Dhakhira-i-Khwárazmsháhí* (A.D. 1110), the translation of *Kalíla and Dimna* by Naṣru'lláh b. 'Abdu'l-Ḥamíd (A.D. 1143–44), the *Maqámát* of the Qáḍí Ḥamídu'd-Dín Abú Bakr of Balkh (circâ A.D. 1160), and the *Chahár Maqála* of Nidhímí of Samarqand (about the same date), which will be cited at least as frequently in this chapter as in the preceding ones, are the most important. Of writers who wrote chiefly or wholly in Arabic, the great al-Ghazálí, whose death falls within this period (A.D. 1111–12), has been already mentioned; other notable persons are the philologists az-Zawzaní, at-Tabrízí, and al-Jawálíqí; the geographer al-Bakrí; the poets al-Abíwardí and aṭ-Ṭughrá'í (the author of the well-known *Lámiyyatu'l-'Ajam*, or "L-poem of the Persians"); Ibn Manda, the historian of Iṣfahán; al-Qushayrí, the hagiologist and mystic; al-Ḥarírí, the author of the celebrated *Maqámát* (which were composed at the request of the minister and historian of the Seljúqs, Khálid b. Anúshirwán); al-Farrá al-Baghawí, and the greater az-Zamakhsharí, the commentators; al-Maydání, the author of the celebrated collection of Arabic proverbs; and ash-Shahristání, the author of the *Kitábu'l-Milal wa'n-Niḥal*, or "Book of Sects and Schools," besides many others whom it would take too long to enumerate.

Following the plan hitherto adopted, we shall first take a general view of the political history of Persia and the neighbouring countries during this period, and shall then pass to the literary and other intellectual manifestations to which it gave birth.

Maliksháh left behind him on his death four sons—Barkiyáruq, aged eleven or twelve, Muḥammad, who was six months younger; Sanjar, aged eight; and Maḥmúd, a child of four. Of these the first, whose mother, Zubayda, was of the

House of Seljúq, was at Iṣfahán, his native place, when his father's death took place. Maḥmúd's mother, the astute and ambitious Turkán Khátún, who was with her infant son at Baghdád, took advantage of her position to secure his accession to the throne. The Caliph al-Muqtadí was at first unwilling to consent, on account of Maḥmúd's tender years; but the influence of the Amír Ja'far, the Caliph's son by Máh-Malik, the sister of Maliksháh, secured, it is said, by bribes and flattery, finally enabled Turkán Khátún to gain her point. No sooner had she done so than she despatched Amír Búghá post-haste to Iṣfahán (which he reached in a week from Baghdád) to secure the person of Barkiyáruq, whom, however, some of the sons of the late Nidhámu'l-Mulk secretly carried off under cover of the darkness of night to Sáwa, Ába and Ray, where he was proclaimed King. At the time of his coronation he was under thirteen years of age, and the great jewelled crown had to be suspended over the young head still too weak to bear its weight.[1] Abú Muslim, the Governor of Ray, presided over the coronation, and some twenty thousand soldiers assembled at the gates of the city to support the claims of the young King.

Reign of Maḥmúd b. Maliksháh.

Meanwhile Turkán Khátún, aided by her advisers Majdu'l-Mulk of Qum, Táju'l-Mulk Abu'l-Ghaná'im, Amír Unrú Bulká, and others, the rivals and destroyers of the great Nidhámu'l-Mulk, had occupied Iṣfahán, against which Barkiyáruq now marched; but for a sum of 500,000 *dínárs* he consented to refrain from besieging it, and turned aside to Hamadán. Thereupon Turkán Khátún again began to intrigue against him, and, by a promise of marriage, induced his maternal uncle, Malik Isma'íl, to attack him (A.D. 1093) at Karach. Malik Isma'íl was defeated, and, on February 3rd, A.D. 1094, Barkiyáruq was formally proclaimed King at

[1] Cf. Ibn Hishám's Biography of the Prophet, ed. Wüstenfeld, p. 42, and the translation of this passage on pp. 128–9 of the *Prolegomena* to this volume.

Baghdád; but soon afterwards Tutush, one of his paternal uncles, raised a much more formidable rebellion, defeated and took him prisoner, and brought him to Iṣfahán, where, though received with apparent kindness by his younger brother Maḥmúd, he was imprisoned in the Kúshk-i-Maydán by Unrú Bulká, who decided to disqualify him from again aspiring to the throne by putting out his eyes.

Reign of Barkiyáruq b. Malikshah.

Fortunately for him, ere this cruel intention had been carried out his brother Maḥmúd sickened with the small-pox and died within the week, whereupon the Amírs placed Barkiyáruq once more upon the throne, and the disappearance of Turkán Khátún, who had been put to death in the autumn of A.D. 1094, doubtless tended to simplify matters. Barkiyáruq was in turn attacked by the disease which had proved fatal to his brother, but recovered, though his life was despaired of, and in the following year defeated and killed his uncle Tutush. Arslán Arghún, another rebellious uncle, was assassinated by one of his pages at Merv, and Barkiyáruq himself hardly escaped a similar fate at the hands of one of the "heretics" of Alamút. Shortly afterwards, having made his brother Sanjar king of Khurásán (A.D. 1096), Barkiyáruq returned to 'Iráq, but in A.D. 1099 his power was more seriously threatened by the rebellion of his brother Muḥammad, who was aided by the Mu'ayyidu'l-Mulk, the ablest of the late Nidhámu'l-Mulk's sons, whom Barkiyáruq had, by dismissing him from his service, converted into an irreconcilable foe. This unnatural war lasted with little intermission, and with varying fortune, till A.D. 1103–4, and five pitched battles were fought ere a truce was patched up a year or two before Barkiyáruq's death. During this period many fierce and cruel deeds were done; Barkiyáruq's mother, Zubayda, was taken prisoner and strangled by Muḥammad in her forty-third year (A.D. 1099); Majdu'l-Mulk of Qum, who had succeeded Mu'ayyidu'l-Mulk as Barkiyáruq's Prime Minister, was torn to pieces, notwithstanding his master's attempt to save him, by the infuriated soldiers, who suspected him of leaning towards the doctrines of the heretical Assassins; and Mu'ayyidu'l-Mulk was taken prisoner and decapitated in cold blood by Barkiyáruq. Peace was finally concluded between the two brothers in A.D. 1103–4, but towards the end of the latter year Barkiyáruq, being then but twenty-five years of age, sickened and died at Burújird, having nominated to succeed him his little son MalikSháh II, then a child under five years of age, who, after a nominal reign of a few weeks or months, was deposed, and, after the cruel fashion of the time, deprived of his eyesight.

Reign of Malikháh II. b. Barkiyáruq.

Muḥammad b. Malikháh, entitled Ghiyáthu'd-Dín, who now became the practically undisputed ruler of the Persian dominions of the Seljúq Empire, reigned rather more than thirteen years (A.D. 1105–18), during which time he sedulously strove to suppress the growing power of the Assassins, of whose development during this period we shall speak presently. Otherwise his reign was comparatively uneventful, save for his successful campaign, in A.D. 1108, against the noble Arabian Amír Ṣadaqa b. Mazyad, lord of Ḥilla and "King of the Arabs," concerning which, *à propos* of astrologers, Nidhámí-i-'Arúḍí of Samarqand has a curious anecdote.[1] Muḥammad was succeeded by his son Maḥmúd, a boy of fourteen, who, after a brief period of misrule,[2] had the folly to give battle to his uncle Sanjar, the powerful ruler of Khurásán, in August, A.D. 1119, at Sáwa. The defeat which he suffered cost him less dear than was usual in those days, for Sanjar, at the intercession of his mother, received his vanquished nephew with kindness, pardoned his rash folly, delegated to him the

Reign of Muḥammad b. Malikháh.

Reign of Maḥmúd b. Muḥammad.

[1] See Anecdote xxix (pp. 102–104) of my translation of the *Chahár Maqála*, and also the *J.R.A.S.* for 1902, p. 605.

[2] Cf. Houtsma's edition of al-Bundárí, pp. 121–124, where a list of ten of the chief abuses of his short reign are enumerated.

government of 'Iráq,[1] over which he continued to reign for some fourteen years, and bestowed on him the hand of his daughter Máh-Malik Khátún. She died soon afterwards, and her father Sanjar, whose love for her was deep and sincere, is said to have been for some time inconsolable, and to have expressly summoned the aged poet 'Am'aq of Bukhárá to compose a brief elegy[2] on her death.

Sanjar was formally proclaimed King at Baghdád on the 4th of September, A.D. 1119, having already, as stated above, exercised sovereign sway over Khurásán for some twenty-four years. His reign, in spite of the dark clouds which overshadowed its latter days, was on the whole brilliant and prosperous, and with him and his Court were associated Anwarí, Mu'izzí, Adíb Ṣábir, and other great names amongst the Persian poets of this period. He was born in A.H. 479 (= A.D. 1086–87),[3] at Sinjár in Asia Minor (after which he was named),[4] and died in A.H. 551 or 552 (= A.D. 1156–57), at the age of seventy-two lunar years, having reigned, as ar-Ráwandi says, "61 years, 20 years over his own appanage of Khurásán, and 41 years over the world," *i.e.*, the whole Seljúq Empire. The troubles which darkened his later days began with the overt rebellion of Atsiz Khwárazmsháh, who declared his independence in A.D. 1140–41. In the following year he was defeated by heathen Turks, his wife was taken captive, and he lost a

Reign of Sanjar.

[1] See Dawlatsháh's *Memoirs*, p. 130 of my edition, where a graphic, but probably fanciful, account of this event is given under a date which is four years too early.

[2] See my edition of Dawlatsháh, p. 65, ll. 1–4.

[3] So Ibnu'l-Athír and the *Ráḥatu'ṣ-Ṣudúr*. See *J.R.A.S.* for 1902, p. 856. Bundárí (ed. Houtsma, p. 255) gives an earlier date, corresponding to February 1, A.D. 1079.

[4] To speak more accurately, he was given the Turkish name which most closely resembled the name of his birth-place. *Sanjar* in Turkish means some kind of hawk or other bird of prey. Names of animals were very commonly taken as proper names by the Seljúqs and other Turks, *e.g. Arslán* ("Lion"), *Tughril* ("Falcon"), etc.

hundred thousand of his troops, and for a while Merv, Sarakhs, Níshápúr and Bayhaq. His disastrous defeat by the Ghuzz took place in the summer of A.D. 1153, when Ṭús and Níshápúr were sacked, and many of their inhabitants, including some of those most celebrated for their learning and piety, were slain. He was practically a prisoner in the hands of the Ghuzz, outwardly treated with some respect, but unable to go where he would, or to protect his unfortunate people, till the autumn of A.D. 1156, when Mu'ayyidá and a few others of his old retainers succeeded, by bribing some of his Ghuzz custodians, in effecting his deliverance, and in bringing him safely to Merv, where he began to collect an army; but grief at the ruin and desolation of his country, combined with old age, caused his death a few months later. He was buried, like his grandfather, Alp Arslán, at Merv, in the building called Dawlat-Khána, which he had erected there.

Seljúqs of Kirmán.

Of the Seljúqs of Kirmán, four, Túránsháh (d. A.D. 1097), his son, Iránsháh (murdered in A.D. 1101 on the suspicion of leaning towards the doctrines of the Isma'ílí heretics), Arslánsháh (cousin of him last-named, d. A.D. 1142), and Mughíthu'd-Dín Muḥammad, son of Arslánsháh, who inaugurated his reign by blinding some twenty of his brothers and nephews (d. A.D. 1156), are included in the period covered by the present chapter.

Contemporary Caliphs of Baghdád.

Of the 'Abbásid Caliphs of Baghdád, al-Muqtadí died about the beginning of this period (A.D. 1094), and al-Muqtafí about the end (A.D. 1160); while of the three intervening Caliphs, al-Mustadhhir died in A.D. 1118, and al-Mustarshid and his son ar-Ráshid were both assassinated by the Isma'ílís, the former (by the instigation of Sanjar, it is said) at Marágha, where he was a captive in the hands of Sulṭán Mas'úd the Seljúq, on Sunday, August 29, 1135; the latter, two years after he had been deposed by the same Sulṭán, at Iṣfahán, on Tuesday, June 7, 1138. The Caliphs were, indeed, at this epoch, little more than puppets in the hands of the Seljúqs, so that al-Mustarshid said in a homily which he delivered at Kirmánsháh while on his way to make against their power that vain effort which cost him his life: "We entrusted our affairs to the House of Seljúq, but they rebelled against us, and time lengthened over them, and their hearts were hardened, and many of them were sinners."[1]

The Houses of Ghúr and Ghazna.

The star of the House of Ghazna had long been on the wane, and the latter part of the period which now occupies our attention saw its final extinction at the hands of the "Kings of the Mountains of Ghúr," those fierce and hardy Afgháns of Fírúzkúh. The King of Ghazna at the time when this period opens was Ibráhím, who, to judge by an anecdote contained in the *Siyásat-náma* (ed. Schefer, p. 42), seems to have been a prince of some force of character. There was a dearth of bread in Ghazna, the bakers closed their shops, and the poor, in great distress, appealed to the King, who summoned the bakers before him and inquired as to the cause of this scarcity. They informed him that the Royal Baker had made a "corner" in flour in order to raise the price. Thereupon the Sulṭán caused the offender to be trampled to death by an elephant; his mangled body was then attached to its tusks and paraded through the city; and proclamation was made that the same fate would befall any baker who closed his shop. "That evening," says the author, "at the door of every shop were fifty maunds of bread which no one would buy."

Sulṭán Ibráhím of Ghazna died in A.D. 1099, and was succeeded by his son Mas'úd III, who died in A.D. 1114, and was followed in succession by his three sons, Shírzád (d. A.D. 1115), Arslán, and Bahrámsháh, who strangled his brother and possessed himself of the throne in A.D. 1118, and reigned till near the end of our present period (A.D. 1152). His name is associated with that of the first great mystic poet of Persia, Saná'í, who composed his *Ḥadíqatu'l-Ḥaqíqat*, or

[1] See my translation of the *Chahár Maqála*, Anecdote viii, pp. 37–38.

"Garden of Truth," in A.D. 1131. His reign closed in disaster. In the autumn of A.D. 1135 Sanjar, suspecting him of disloyalty to his engagements, marched against him, and exacted an apology and a fine, and, after remaining at Ghazna for some months, returned to Balkh in July of the following year.[1] Some twelve years later Bahrámsháh saw fit to put to death his son-in-law, Quṭbu'd-Dín Muḥammad, a prince of the House of Ghúr, whose brothers, 'Alá'u'd-Dín Ḥusayn and Sayfu'd-Dín Súrí avenged this deed in A.D. 1148, by driving Bahrámsháh out of Ghazna, where Sayfu'd-Dín established himself as Governor for his brother, 'Alá'u'd-Dín. A conspiracy was formed against him, however, in the following winter. When the roads were blocked with snow, Bahrámsháh was invited back, and Sayfu'd-Dín, seized unawares, was paraded through the city with blackened face, mounted on a mule, and then hanged or crucified. For this outrage a terrible retribution was exacted by 'Alá'u'd-Dín Ḥusayn in A.D. 1155, three years after Bahrámsháh had died and been succeeded by his son Khusrawsháh. The title "*Jahán-súz*" ("the World-consumer"), gained by the fierce Ghúrí is sufficiently significant of what befell the proud city of Ghazna during his three days' vengeance; but it is notable, as indicating the respect in which literature was held, that, as we are informed in the *Chahár Maqála* (p. 48 of my translation), while "he sacked Ghazna and destroyed the buildings raised by Maḥmúd, Mas'úd, and Ibráhím, he bought with gold the poems written in their praise, and placed them in his library. In that army and in that city none dared call them king, yet he himself would read that *Sháh-náma* wherein Firdawsí says :—

'Of the child in its cot, ere its lips yet are dry
From the milk of its mother, "Maḥmúd" is the cry!
Maḥmúd, the Great King, who such order doth keep
That in peace from one pool drink the wolf and the sheep!'"

[1] According to the *Jahán-gushá* of Juwayní, Bahrámsháh fled before the Seljúq, who remarked to his staff, "There is a back whose face one will not be able to see again!"

More important in the history of Persia than the dynasties of Ghazna and Ghúr were the Khwárazmsháhs, or Kings of Khiva, who began with a favourite cup-bearer of Maliksháh named Anúshtigín in A.D. 1077,[1] and, after completely displacing the Seljúqs, their former masters and suzerains, ended with the gallant Jalálu'd-Dín Mankoburní, the last bulwark of Islám against the devastating hordes of heathen Mongols (A.D. 1220–31). The power of this dynasty began in A.D. 1127 with the accession of the crafty and ambitious Atsiz, rumours of whose intentions reached Sanjar in the summer of A.D. 1138, and prompted him to march against Khwárazm. Atsiz was on this occasion defeated with heavy losses, which included his son,[2] over whom he mourned most bitterly, and Khwárazm was taken and given in fief by Sanjar to his nephew, Ghiyáthu'd-Dín Sulaymán Sháh. But no sooner had Sanjar retired to Merv than Atsiz returned, regained possession of his capital, and sought to avenge himself by inciting the heathen of Cathay (Khaṭá) to attack Sanjar, whom they utterly routed in the summer of A.D. 1141, killing 100,000 of his soldiers, taking captive his wife, and driving the Seljúq King back on Tirmidh and Balkh, while Atsiz himself, having declared his independence, occupied Merv and killed or carried away captive a number of its leading men, including the theologian Abu'l-Faḍl al-Kirmání.[3] This was, according to Ibnu'l-Athír, the first defeat sustained by Sanjar, and, as we have seen, was but the prelude to far worse disasters. In Níshápúr,

The Khwárazmsháhs.

[1] According to the *Jahán-gushá* of Juwayní, it was a common practice of the Seljúqs to reward with such fiefs the services of their cup-bearers, keepers of the wardrobe, and the like.

[2] According to the *Jahán-gushá* of Juwayní, his name was Ílígh, and he was taken prisoner, brought before Sanjar, and, by his orders, sawn in two.

[3] It appears, however, from Ibnu'l-Athír's account (*sub anno* 536) that Atsiz originally intended to spare Merv, as he had already spared Sarakhs, but that the murder of some of his followers prompted him to this act of vengeance, which took place at the end of October, A.D. 1141.

which was occupied for a while, but otherwise unmolested, by Atsiz, Sanjar's name was suppressed in the *khuṭba* from May 28 till July 27, A.D. 1142. About a year after this, Sanjar again besieged Khwárazm, but, failing to take it, concluded a treaty of peace with Atsiz, whose death took place on July 30, A.D. 1156, only a short time before his rival's.

Four poets specially associated with Sanjar and Atsiz.

With the names of Sanjar and Atsiz[1] are inseparably associated the names of four great Persian poets—Mu'izzí, Anwarí, Adíb Ṣábir, and Rashídu'd-Dín Waṭwáṭ, whose work will be considered in detail presently. The first of these was Sanjar's poet-laureate, and his father, Burhání, held the same position.[2] The high honour in which he was held by his sovereign enhanced the tragedy of his death, which was caused by a stray arrow fired by Sanjar's hand in A.D. 1147–48.

Mu'izzí, Sanjar's poet-laureate.

The death of Adíb Ṣábir was yet more tragic. According to Dawlatsháh (p. 93 of my edition), he was sent by Sanjar to Khwárazm to keep a watch on Atsiz, nominally, as it would appear from Juwayní's *Jahán-gushá*, as an ambassador. Atsiz hired two assassins to go to Merv and murder Sanjar. Adíb Ṣábir wrote private information of this to Sanjar, enclosing portraits or descriptions of the two assassins, and his missive was carried to Merv by an old woman in her shoe. The assassins were identified and put to death, and Atsiz, on receiving news of this, caused Adíb Ṣábir to be bound hand and foot and drowned in the Oxus. The date of this event is given by Dawlatsháh as A.H. 546 (= A.D. 1151–52), but according to the *Jahán-gushá*, a much better authority, it took place in or before A.H. 542 (A.D. 1147), and A.H. 538 (= A.D. 1143–44), the date given by Dr. Ethé, is still more probable.

Adíb Ṣábir.

[1] The author of the *Jahán-gushá* states that Atsiz was a very accomplished prince, and himself composed many quatrains and other verses in Persian.

[2] See pp. 35–38 *supra*, and Anecdote xvi in the *Chahár Maqála* (pp. 66–70 of my translation).

Concerning Anwarí and Rashídu'd-Dín "Waṭwáṭ" ("the Swallow," so called from his small stature and insignificant appearance) I shall only mention in this place their connection with the campaigns discussed above. Waṭwáṭ, who was the secretary and Court-poet of Atsiz, had aroused the anger of Sanjar in the first instance by writing a *qaṣída*, which began—

Anwarí and Rashídu'd-Dín Waṭwáṭ.

Chún Malik Atsiz bi-takht-i-mulk bar ámad,
Dawlat-i-Saljúq u ál-i-ú bi-sar ámad.

"When King Atsiz on the throne of power ascended,
The luck of Seljúq and his House was ended."

Later, while Sanjar was besieging Atsiz in the fortress of Hazár-asp (a name which, being interpreted, means "a thousand horses") in the autumn of A.D. 1147, he ordered Anwarí, who had accompanied him on the campaign, to compose a taunting verse, which, inscribed on an arrow, should be shot into the besieged town. Anwarí accordingly wrote:—

Ay Sháh! hama mulk-i-zamín ḥasb turást;
Wa'z dawlat u iqbál jahán kasb turást:
Imrúz bi-yak ḥamla Hazárasp bi-gír!
Fardá Khwárazm u ṣad hazár asp turást!

There is little point, except the play on the name Hazárasp, in this verse, which means:—

"O King! all the dominion of earth is accounted thine;
By fortune and good luck the world is thine acquisition:
Take Hazárasp to-day with a single assault,
And to-morrow Khwárazm and a hundred thousand horses (*ṣad hazár asp*) shall be thine!'

The following reply from Waṭwáṭ's pen was shot back on another arrow[1]:—

[1] The shooting of arrows inscribed with messages into or out of a besieged town seems to have been an ancient practice in Persia. See

Gar khiṣm-ı-tu, ay Sháh, shawad Rustam-ı-gurd,
Yak khar zı Hazárasp-i-tu na-t'wánad burd!

"If thine enemy, O King, were Knight Rustam himself,
He could not carry off from thy Hazárasp (or thy thousand horses) a single ass!"

Thereafter Sanjar sought eagerly to capture Waṭwáṭ, and, having at length succeeded, ordered him to be cut into seven pieces. Muntakhabu'd-Dín Badí'u 'l-Kátib,[1] an ancestor of the author of the *Jahán-gushá*, who relates the story, succeeded in appeasing the King by making him laugh. "O King," he said, "I have a request to prefer. Waṭwáṭ" ("the Swallow") "is a feeble little bird, and cannot bear to be divided into seven pieces: order him, then, to be merely cut in two!" So Waṭwáṭ was pardoned because he had enabled Sanjar to enjoy a laugh.

The Isma'ílís of Alamút, or Assassins.

To complete our brief survey of the political state of Persia at this period, it remains to consider that power which, though not a kingdom, was more than Seljúq, Ghaznawí, Ghúrí, or Khwárazmsháh in the wide influence which it wielded and the terror it inspired—to wit, the Assassins, or Isma'ílís of Alamút. The circumstances which led to the establishment of that power in Persia, and the change in its character wrought by the "New Propaganda" of Ḥasan-i-Ṣabbáḥ, have been already described in a previous chapter. That redoubtable heresiarch was still flourishing in the reign of Sanjar, for he did not die until the year A.D. 1124. For many years he had never stirred from the Castle of Alamút—hardly, indeed, from his own house—though his power reached to Syria, and his name was a terror throughout Western Asia. Austere in his way of living, he put to death his two sons on the suspicion of forni-

Nöldeke's *Geschichte des Artachšîr-i-Pâpakân*, p. 53 of the Separat-Abdruck (Göttingen, 1879).

[1] His life is given in vol. i of 'Awfí's *Lubábu'l-Albáb*, pp. 78–9 of my edition.

cation and wine-bibbing, and named as his successor his associate, Kiyá Buzurg-Ummíd, who died in A.D. 1137–38, and was followed by his son Muḥammad, who died in A.D. 1162.

Achievements of the Assassins.

It would be impossible in a work like the present to follow in detail the history of the Assassins or Isma'ílís of Alamút during the period which we are now considering, but the sect is so interesting and characteristic a feature of the times that certain manifestations of their activity must needs be recorded in order to present a true picture of the age. Under almost every year in the great chronicle of Ibnu'l-Athír mention occurs of the name of this redoubtable organisation, which, on the death of the Fáṭimid Caliph al-Mustanṣir, definitely severed its connection with the parent sect of Egypt and North Africa. Their political power began with the seizure of the mountain-stronghold of Alamút ("the Eagle's teaching," *áluh-ámú't*) in A.H. 483 (= A.D. 1090–91), which date, by a curious coincidence noticed by most Persian historians of the period, is exactly given by the sum of the numerical values of the letters composing this word. Their first great achievement was the assassination, two years later, of the Nidhámu'l-Mulk, which was followed at short intervals by the assassination of Barkiyáruq's mother's *wazír*, 'Abdu'r-Raḥmán as-Sumayramí (A.D. 1097);[1] Unrú Bulká (A.D. 1100); Janáḥu'd-Dawla, in the mosque at Ḥims (A.D. 1102); the Qáḍí Abu'l-'Alá Sa'íd of Níshápúr (A.D. 1105–6); Fakhru'l-Mulk, one of the sons of the Nidhámu'l-Mulk (A.D. 1106–7); the *qáḍís*, or judges, of Iṣfahán and Níshápúr, and 'Abdu'l-Wáḥid of Rúyán in Ṭabaristán (A.D. 1108–9); Mawdúd, in the Mosque of Damascus (A.D. 1113–14); Aḥmadíl b. Wahsúdán, in Baghdád (A.D. 1116–17); the Qáḍí Sa'd al-Hirawí at Hamadán (A.D. 1125–26); 'Abdu'l-Laṭíf b. al-Khujandí (A.D. 1129); the Fáṭimid Caliph al-Ámir bi'amri'lláh (A.D. 1130); Abú

[1] There is some doubt about this date, the event being otherwise referred to the years 1122–23.

'Alí b. Afdal, the *wazír* of his successor and cousin, al-Ḥáfidh (A.D. 1132); the 'Abbásid Caliph al-Mustarshid (A.D. 1135); his son and successor, ar-Ráshid (A.D. 1137–38); Jawhar, a favourite courtier of Sanjar (A.D. 1139–40), and many other persons of lesser note. Of course there were savage reprisals on the part of the orthodox: thus we read of a persecution of "heretics and free-thinkers" at Níshápúr in A.D. 1096; of a massacre of Báṭinís ordered by Barkiyáruq in June, A.D. 1101; of the crucifixion of Sa'du'l-Mulk, the *wazír*, with four Báṭinís, and of the notorious Ibn 'Aṭṭásh and some of his followers in A.D. 1106–7; of a massacre of seven hundred Báṭinís at Ámid in A.D. 1124; of a yet greater slaughter of them by Sanjar in A.D. 1127, to avenge the death of the minister Mu'ínu'l-Mulk; and of 'Abbás of Ray, one of their most relentless foes, killed in A.D. 1146–47, who used to build pyramids of their skulls.

As has been already said, the civil wars which prevailed during the earlier part of this period enabled the Assassins to establish and consolidate their power in a way which would otherwise have been impossible. Barkiyáruq, indeed, was accused of being in sympathy with them, or at least of allowing them a large measure of toleration in return for their support or benevolent neutrality. Under the year A.H. 494 (A.D. 1100–1) Ibnu'l-Athír tells us that, having taken prisoner Mu'ayyidu'l-Mulk, one of the sons of the Nidhámu'l-Mulk, Barkiyáruq reviled him for having made this assertion, and then slew him with his own hand.[1] In the same year, when he marched against his brothers Sanjar and Muḥammad at Baghdád, and the two armies confronted one another across the Tigris, the enemy taunted him and his soldiers with cries of "*Yá Báṭiniyya!*" ("O Báṭinís!"). The massacre of Báṭinís which he ordered about this time was probably intended to dispel from the minds of his subjects this

[1] For a somewhat different account, given in the *Ráḥatu'ṣ-Ṣudúr*, see the *J.R.A.S.* for 1902, pp. 603–604.

dangerous belief, a belief which might easily have led to his murder or deposition, as happened in the case of Aḥmad Khán, the ruler of Samarqand, and Íránsháh, the Seljúq prince of Kirmán, both of whom, not to mention numerous ministers and statesmen, like the Majdu'l-Mulk, suffered this fate because they were suspected of sympathy with the heretics. Such fear prevailed that it was not uncommon for those who had reason to dread the vengeance of the Assassins to wear a shirt of mail under their clothes, as was the custom of Bulká; but one day he omitted this precaution, and paid for his negligence with his life. Even when captured and put to death—often with torture—the *fidá'ís* of the Assassins often managed to wreak a further vengeance on their foes, as did the murderer of Fakhru'l-Mulk, who, being brought before Sanjar and interrogated, denounced as confederates of his order a number of prominent *amírs* and officers of the Court, who, though probably innocent, shared his fate.

Episode in the history of the Assassins at Isfahán.

One of the most curious episodes connected with the history of these formidable heretics is very fully described by the author of the *Ráḥatu'ṣ-Ṣudúr* (see *J.R.A.S.* for 1902, pp. 606–609) and by Ibnu'l-Athír; I mean the events which culminated in the destruction of the Assassin stronghold of Sháh Dizh or Dizh-i-Kúh near Iṣfahán, the crucifixion of Ibn 'Aṭṭásh and the slaughter of a great number of his followers, which occurred in the spring of A.D. 1107. 'Abdu'l-Malik 'Aṭṭásh, the father of the above-mentioned Aḥmad b. 'Aṭṭásh, was a man of letters resident in Iṣfahán, who, being persecuted there on account of his Shí'ite sympathies, fled to Ray, came under the influence of Ḥasan-i-Ṣabbáḥ, and embraced his doctrines.[1] "I have fallen in with the Grey Falcon," he wrote to one of his friends, "and this hath compensated me for what I have left behind." His son, who was a linen merchant, professed

[1] According to Ibnu'l-Athír and other authorities, 'Abdu'l-Malik 'Aṭṭásh was the teacher, not the pupil, of Ḥasan-i-Ṣabbáḥ.

the greatest detestation for the father's heretical doctrines, and was consequently suffered to remain unmolested.

Ibn 'Aṭṭásh.

Close to Iṣfahán stood the Castle of Dizh-i-Kúh, built by Maliksháh and named therefore Sháh-dizh, "the King's Fortress." In it were stored arms and treasure, and there dwelt certain of the royal pages and girls attached to the Court, guarded by a company of Daylamí soldiers. Thither Ibn 'Aṭṭásh, under the pretence of giving lessons to these young people, used to repair, and gradually, by means of fair words and presents, he succeeded in bringing over the garrison to his allegiance.

He next established a mission-house in the Dasht-i-gúr, hard by the gates of the city; and such was his success that the number of his converts and adherents ultimately reached thirty thousand, according to the statement of our historian. About this time the people of Iṣfahán began to be alarmed by repeated mysterious disappearances of their fellow-citizens. The mystery was ultimately solved by a poor beggar-woman, who, craving an alms from a certain house, and hearing from within a lamentable groaning and wailing, exclaimed, "May God heal your sick!" But when an attempt was made by the inmates of the house to induce her to enter, on the pretext of giving her food, she became suspicious, fled, and gave the alarm. A crowd soon surrounded the house, broke open the door, and found within in the cellars a horrible sight; for there against the walls and on the floor they beheld some four or five hundred unfortunate victims—some slain, some crucified, of whom a few still breathed—amongst whom many of those who had lately been missed by their friends were identified. The house in question belonged to a blind man named 'Alawí Madaní, and was a meeting-place of the Assassins. This man, staff in hand, used, about nightfall, to take his stand at the end of the long, dark lane which led to the house, and cry out, "May God pardon him who will take the hand of this poor blind man and lead him to the door of his dwelling in this lane!" So the unsuspecting victim who charitably complied with this request was lured to his destruction, for when he had come to the end of the lane he was seized by a number of the blind man's confederates, cast into the cellars, and there done to death. And this had been going on for several months ere the terrible discovery above mentioned was made. Vengeance swiftly followed, 'Alawí Madání, his wife, and some of his accomplices being burned to death in the market-place. Suspicion was rife, and fell, amongst others, upon the minister Sa'du'l-Mulk, but the King, whose confidence he enjoyed, refused at first to believe in his guilt. The Castle of Dizh-i-Kúh had at this period been besieged for some time, and Ibn 'Aṭṭásh, being nearly at the end of his resources, sent a secret message to Sa'du'l-Mulk to the effect that he could hold out no longer and desired to surrender. "Be patient for a week," Sa'du'l-Mulk replied, "until I destroy this dog" (meaning the King). His plan was to take advantage of the King's habit of being bled every month to destroy him by poisoning the lancet used by the surgeon-barber, whom he succeeded in bribing to his purpose. The plot, however, was communicated by his chamberlain, who shared all his secrets, to his beautiful wife, who told her paramour, who told an officer of Sharafu'l-Mulk, who told the King. So the King summoned the surgeon-barber, and, on his arrival, caused him to be scratched with his own knife, whereupon, as the poison took effect, he turned black and soon expired in great agony.

Then the King was convinced of the guilt of his minister, whom he hanged or crucified together with four of his accomplices, including one Abu'l-'Alá al-Mufaḍḍal. Two days after this Ibn 'Aṭṭásh surrendered the Castle of Dizh-i-Kúh. He was paraded on a camel through the streets of Iṣfahán, a spectacle for thousands, pelted with mud and dirt, and mocked in derisive verses, of which a specimen (in dialect) is given in the *Ráḥatu'ṣ-Ṣudúr*; afterwards he was crucified, and hung on the cross for seven days. Arrows were fired at him as he hung there, helpless and tormented, and finally his body was burned to ashes. He pretended to have some considerable skill in astrology, and as he hung on the cross one of the bystanders asked him whether he had, by virtue of his science, been able to foresee this fate. He replied, "I perceived from my horoscope that I should traverse the streets of Iṣfahán with pomp and parade more than royal, but I did not know that it would be in such fashion."[1]

Sulṭán Muḥammad, now thoroughly aroused and alarmed, began to take measures for the systematic extirpation of the Assassins and the reduction of the many mountain strongholds of which they had gained possession, but his death in A.D. 1118 put an end to these projects and gave the heretics a fresh chance, of which they were not slow to avail themselves, so that within the next ten or fifteen years they had, by force, stratagem, or bribery, added the Syrian fastnesses of Qadmús, Bániyás, and Maṣyáth to their possessions, which included in Persia, besides Alamút, Gird-i-kúh, and Shir-kúh, Ṭabas, Khúr, Khúsaf, Zawzan, Qá'in, Tún, Washm-kúh near Abhar, Khálanján near Isfahán, Ustunáwand in Mázandarán, Qal'atu'n-Nádhir in Khúzistán, Qal'atu'ṭ-Ṭanbúr near Arraján, Khalládkhán, and many other strongholds in almost every part of Persia.

Having thus briefly sketched in broad outline the political

[1] This anecdote, with some slight modification and suppression of the names, is often met with in Arabic and Persian story-books, such as 'Awfí's *Jawámi'u'l-Ḥikáyát*. The poet Anwarí evidently alludes to Ibn 'Aṭṭásh in the following verse :—

Dar khwáb dída khiṣm-i-tu khud-rá bulandí'í :
Ta'bír-i-án bi-dída-i-bídár dár yáft.

"Thine enemy saw in a dream exaltation for himself :
With his waking eyes he found it to be the gibbet."

condition of Persia during the period of Sanjar and his brothers, we may turn to the literature of this epoch. The great increase in the number of Persian poets, and the growing employment of Persian instead of Arabic as the literary language of Írán, will, on the one hand, oblige us to confine our attention to the most celebrated poets, and, on the other, will permit us to concern ourselves less and less with Arabic writings. Let us first consider the most notable Persian poets, arranging them approximately in chronological order.

Literary History of the Period.

Persian poets.

Sanáʼí of Ghazna or Balkh,[1] whose proper name was Abu'l-Majd Majdúd b. Ádam, is the first of the three great mystical *mathnawí*-writers of Persia, the second being Shaykh Farídu'd-Dín ʻAṭṭár, and the third Jalálu'd-Dín Rúmí, who, though by far the greatest, had the humility to write:—

Sanáʼí.

ʻAṭṭár rúḥ búd, u Sanáʼí du chashm-i-ú;
Má az pay-i-Sanáʼí u ʻAṭṭár ámadim.

"ʻAṭṭár was the Spirit, and Sanáʼí its two eyes;
We come after Sanáʼí and ʻAṭṭár."

Of Sanáʼí's life we know very little, save that he was attached, at any rate during its earlier period, to the Court of Bahrám-sháh; for the account of his conversion from the worldly state of a Court-poet to the higher life of the mystic given by Dawlatsháh (pp. 95–97), and reproduced by Ouseley in his *Lives of the Persian Poets* (pp. 184–187), is not deserving of much attention, while neither his own preface to the *Ḥadíqa*, nor that of his disciple Muḥammad b. ʻAlí Raqqám[2] throw much light on his circumstances, save that they tend to confirm, as Rieu points out, the statement made by Jámí that the

[1] On p. 81 of the Persian lithographed edition of his *Díwán* Sanáʼí speaks of Balkh as glorying in his fame.

[2] The contents of these prefaces are briefly described by Rieu in his *Persian Catalogue*, p. 550.

poet wrote the *Ḥadíqa*, his best-known work, in his old age, and died almost immediately after its completion in A.D. 1131. 'Awfí in his *Lubábu'l-Albáb* (vol. ii, p. 252 of my edition) gives, as usual, no biographical information whatever; while certain facts to which Ethé has called attention [1] are in contradiction with the chronological data deducible from the prefaces to the *Ḥadíqa*, and tend to show that the poet survived Mu'izzí and did not die much before A.D. 1150.

Saná'í's work, so far as it has come down to us, consists of seven *mathnawís* and a *díwán*. Of the former the *Ḥadíqatu'l-Ḥaqíqat* ("Garden of Truth") is the only one which is at all celebrated; the other six, *viz.*, the *Ṭaríqu't-Taḥqíq* ("Path of Verification"), *Gharíb-náma* ("Book of the Stranger"), *Sayru'l-'ibád ila'l-Ma'ád* ("Pilgrimage of [God's] servants to the Hereafter"), *Kár-náma* ("Book of Deeds"), *'Ishq-náma* ("Book of Love"), and *'Aql-náma* ("Book of Reason"), are very rare, and I have never seen them.[2] Manuscripts of the *Díwán* are not common, but it has been lithographed at Ṭihrán in A.H. 1274 (= A.D. 1857–58). This edition comprises 271 pages, each containing some 45 couplets—in all, perhaps, some twelve thousand *bayts* distributed amongst the *qaṣídas*, *tarjí'-bands*, *tarkíb-bands*, *ghazals*, and *quatrains* which compose the whole. The *Ḥadíqa* is much the most frequently met with of all Saná'í's works, and there exists a very fair Oriental edition, lithographed at Bombay in A.H. 1275 (= A.D. 1859). We shall confine our remarks to it and the *Díwán*.

The *Ḥadíqa*, dedicated to Bahrámsháh, Sulṭán of Ghazna, is a moral and ethical rather than a purely mystical poem of about eleven thousand verses, divided into ten books, the first in praise of God, the second in praise of the Prophet,

[1] *Catalogue of Persian MSS. of Bodleian Library*, col. 463; *Catalogue of India Office Library*, col. 571.

[2] They are all contained in No. 3,346 of the India Office Persian MSS. (Ethé, No. 914), and other copies of all save the *Gharíb-náma* exist in the same collection.

the third on Reason, the fourth on the excellence of Knowledge, the fifth on Carelessness, the sixth on the Heavens and Zodiacal Signs, the seventh on Philosophy, the eighth on Love, the ninth on the poet's own condition and circumstances, and the tenth in praise of Bahrámsháh, Sulṭán of Ghazna. The poem is written in a halting and unattractive metre, and is in my opinion one of the dullest books in Persian, seldom rising to the level of Martin Tupper's *Proverbial Philosophy*, filled with fatuous truisms and pointless anecdotes, and as far inferior to the *Mathnawí* of Jalálu'd-Dín Rúmí as is Robert Montgomery's *Satan* to Milton's *Paradise Lost*. The following parable, illustrating the impossibility that man should be able to form more than a partial and distorted conception of God, may be taken as, on the whole, a favourable specimen :—

The *Ḥadíqatu'l-Ḥaqíqat.*

ABOUT THE COMPANY OF BLIND MEN AND THE CHARACTERISTICS OF THE ELEPHANT.[1]

"Not far from Ghúr once stood a city tall
Whose denizens were sightless one and all.
A certain Sultan once, when passing nigh,
Had pitched his camp upon the plain hard by,
Wherein, to prove his splendour, rank and state,
Was kept an elephant most huge and great.
Then in the townsmen's minds arose desire
To know the nature of this creature dire.
Blind delegates by blind electorate
Were therefore chosen to investigate
The beast, and each, by feeling trunk or limb,
Strove to acquire an image clear of him.
Thus each conceived a visionary whole,
And to the phantom clung with heart and soul.

When to the city they were come again,
The eager townsmen flocked to them amain.

[1] For the text see pp. 9–10 of the Bombay lithographed edition of A.H. 1275.

Each one of them—wrong and misguided all—
Was eager his impressions to recall.
Asked to describe the creature's size and shape,
They spoke, while round about them, all agape,
Stamping impatiently, their comrades swarm
To hear about the monster's shape and form.

Now, for his knowledge each inquiring wight
Must trust to touch, being devoid of sight,
So he who'd only felt the creature's ear,
On being asked, 'How doth its heart appear?'
'Mighty and terrible,' at once replied,
'Like to a carpet, hard and flat and wide!'

Then he who on its trunk had laid his hand
Broke in: 'Nay: nay! I better understand!
'Tis like a water-pipe, I tell you true,
Hollow, yet deadly and destructive too";
While he who'd had but leisure to explore
The sturdy limbs which the great beast upbore,
Exclaimed, 'No, no! To all men be it known
'Tis like a column tapered to a cone!'

Each had but known one part, and no man all;
Hence into deadly error each did fall.
No way to know the All man's heart can find:
Can knowledge e'er accompany the blind?
Fancies and phantoms vain as these, alack!
What else can you expect from fool in sack?
Naught of Almighty God can creatures learn,
Nor e'en the wise such mysteries discern."

The *Díwán*, in my judgment, contains poetry of a far higher order than the *Ḥadíqa*; so much higher that one might almost be tempted to doubt whether the same author composed both, were it not for the unquestionable fact that Persian poets seldom excel in all forms of verse, so that, to take one instance only, the *qaṣídas* of Anwarí excel those of Ḥáfidh by as much as the *ghazals* of Ḥáfidh excel those of Anwarí. The following specimens from the *Díwán* of Sanáʼí must suffice, though his work in this field well deserves a closer and more extended examination:—

"Boast not[1] dervish-hood unless the store of storelessness[2] be thine:
Neither rogue-like deck thy visage, nor like craven-heart repine.
Either woman-like adopt the toilet-tricks of paint and scent,
Or like men approach the field, and cast the ball across the line.[3]
All thou see'st beyond thy lusts is Heaven; clasp it to thy soul:
All thou findest short of God's an idol; break it, crush it fine!
Dance when like the headsman's carpet heart and soul lie 'neath thy feet:
Clap thy hands when earth and heaven in thy grasp thou dost confine!
From the bowers of meditation raise thy head, that thou may'st see
Those who still, though slain, are living,[4] rank on rank and line on line.
There are those who, like Ḥusayn, have fallen by the tyrant's sword;
Here are these who, like Ḥasan, by poison met their fate malign.
Wondrous is the zeal of Faith, wherein, like candle, waxing faint,
By removal of thy head thy radiance doth brighter shine.[5]
For the Jew in this arena fearless casts himself amain,
And the Brahmin in this temple burns his idol at the shrine.

* * * * * *

Years are needed ere the sunshine, working on the primal rock,
Yemen's blood-stone or Badakhshán's rubies can incarnadine.
Months are needed ere, by earth and water fed, the cotton-seed
Can provide the martyr's shroud, or clothe the fair with raiment fine.
Days are needed ere a handful of the wool from back of sheep
Can provide the ass's halter, or the hermit's gabardine.

---

[1] The text of this poem, of which only a portion is here given, will be found on p. 80 of the lithographed edition.

[2] That is, the treasure of poverty for God's sake.

[3] Allusion is here made to the game of polo.

[4] Alluding, probably, to *Qur'án*, iii, 163: "And deem not dead those slain in God's way; nay, they are living, provided for by their Lord."

[5] *Cf.* p. 155 *supra*, and n. 1 *ad calc.*

Lives are needed ere, by Nature's kindly fostering, the child
Can become a famous poet, or a scholar ripe and fine.
Ages needs must pass before a Bu'l-Wafá or an Uways [1]
Can arise from Adam's loins to glorify the Might Divine."

The following little *ghazal*, or ode, is also his (p. 168 of the lithographed edition) :—

"That heart which stands aloof from pain and woe
No seal or signature of Love can show:
Thy Love, thy Love I chose, and as for wealth,
If wealth be not my portion, be it so!
For wealth, I ween, pertaineth to the World;
Ne'er can the World and Love together go!
So long as Thou dost dwell within my heart
Ne'er can my heart become the thrall of Woe."

Here is another specimen of Saná'í's lyrical verse (p. 206) :—

"Darling, my heart I gave to thee— Good-night! I go.
Thou know'st my heartfelt sympathy— Good-night! I go.
Should I behold thee ne'er again 'Tis right, 'tis right;
I clasp this Hour of Parting tight— Good-night! I go.
With raven tress and visage clear, Enchantress dear,
Hast made my daylight dark and drear: Good-night! I go.
O Light of Faith thy Face, thy hair Like Doubt's Despair
Both this and that yield torment rare— Good-night! I go.
Therefore 'twixt Fire and Water me Thou thus dost see,
Lips parched and dry, tear-raining eye: Good-night! I go."

These specimens, selected almost at random, display both grace and originality; and there are probably few unexplored mines of Persian poetry which would yield to the diligent seeker a richer store of gems.

[1] Uways al-Qaraní was a well-known saint and mystic, whose biography stands second in Shaykh Farídu'd-Dín 'Aṭṭár's "Memoirs of the Saints" (*Tadhkiratu'l-Awliyá*, pp. 15–24 of Mr. R. A. Nicholson's forthcoming edition). Abu'l-Wafá the Kurd is no doubt another Ṣúfí saint, but I have not been able to identify him.

Abú Bakr (or Abu'l-Maḥásin) Azraqí, son of Isma'íl the bookseller of Herát, in whose house Firdawsí is stated by the author of the *Chahár Maqála* [1] to have concealed himself for six months after he had incurred the anger of Sulṭán Maḥmúd of Ghazna, is best known (thanks to Jámí and Dawlatsháh) for the somewhat dubious literary performance [2] which, in conjunction with the happily-improvised quatrain given in chapter i (p. 39 *supra*), is said to have secured him the favour and patronage of the Seljúq Prince Ṭughánsháh. He was famous in his own day as a *qaṣída*-writer and panegyrist, and is placed by 'Awfí (vol. ii, p. 88 of my edition) only a little below the younger but more eminent Mu'izzí. Panegyrics, however grateful they may be to those whose praises they celebrate, and however much they may enrich their authors, for obvious reasons seldom interest posterity to the same extent as verse which appeals to the human heart for all time; and so it happens that Azraqí, like many of his more famous rivals, is to most Persian readers little more than a name, and that copies of his collected poems are exceedingly rare. Dawlatsháh, though he consecrates to Azraqí a separate notice (pp. 72–73 of my edition), cites of his verse only the quatrain to which allusion has been already made; but 'Awfí (vol. ii, pp. 86–104) quotes several long poems of his in full; and another long *qaṣída* which he composed in praise of Amíránsháh, one of the Seljúq Princes of Kirmán, will be found in Muḥammad Ibráhím's History of that dynasty (ed. Houtsma, pp. 14–16). As we possess hardly anything of Azraqí's work except *qaṣídas*, and as these are very difficult to translate, and, as a rule, unreadable when translated, I shall follow Dawlatsháh's example and pass on to another poet.

Azraqí.

[1] See p. 81 of the separate reprint of my translation.

[2] Viz., the *Alfiyya Shalfiyya*, of which the nature is sufficiently indicated by 'Awfí (*Lubáb*, vol. ii, p. 87 of my edition) as well as by the authorities mentioned in the texts. I give the title as it occurs in the texts, but I believe it should be *Alfiyya-i-Shalaqiyya*.

Mas'úd-i-Sa'd-i-Salmán[1] (*i.e.*, Mas'úd the son of Sa'd the son of Salmán) deserves to be remembered, if for no other reason, for some original and pathetic verses which he wrote while imprisoned in the Castle of Náy by command of Sulṭán Ibráhím of Ghazna, who suspected him of intriguing with the Seljúq King Malikshá h. Of these verses the author of the *Chahár Maqála*, who records the story (pp. 72–75 of the separate reprint of my translation), says that, whenever he read them, his skin would creep and his eyes fill with tears at their eloquence and pathos. He quotes two of these *Ḥabsiyyát*, or "Songs of Captivity," of which the first, a quatrain, is as follows:—

Mas'úd-i-Sa'd-i-Salmán.

"O King, 'tis Malikshah should wear thy chain,
That royal limbs might fret with captive's pain,
But Sa'd-i-Salmán's offspring could not hurt,
Though venomous as poison, thy domain!"

The second fragment runs thus:—

"Naught served the ends of statesmen save that I,
A helpless exile, should in fetters lie,
Nor do they deem me safe within their cells
Unless surrounded by ten sentinels,
Which ten sit ever by the gates and walls,
While ever one unto his comrade calls:
'Ho, there! On guard! This cunning rogue is one
To fashion bridge and steps from shade and sun!'[2]
Why, grant I stood arrayed for such a fight,
And suddenly sprang forth, attempting flight,
Could elephant or raging lion hope,
Thus cramped in prison-cage, with ten to cope?
Can I, bereft of weapons, take the field,
Or make of back or bosom bow and shield?"

[1] Since writing this, I have published in the *J.R.A.S.* for October, 1905 (pp. 693–740), and January, 1906 (pp. 11–51), a translation of an excellent monograph on this poet written in Persian by my learned friend Mírzá Muḥammad b. 'Abdu'l-Wahháb of Qazwín. To this the more studious reader should refer, since it not only supplements, but in some cases corrects, the account here given.

[2] *I.e.*, bridges of the shadows and ladders of the sunbeams.

The King, however, remained obdurate till his death, and Mas'úd languished in captivity for twelve years.

The following poem by Mas'úd is given by Dawlatsháh (pp. 47–48 of my edition):—

"When I saw with eyes discerning that this World's the Home of Woe,
And that o'er the best and noblest Death his cerement doth throw,
And that Fate, false friend, to cheat me and to rob me did propose,
Then from off Ambition's sick-bed wholly cured, thank God, I rose;
To the drug-shop of Repentance hastened, and did there beseech
Tonic medicines to give me strength to practise what I preach.
Therefore now this tongue, which lately sang the praise of earthly Kings,
Unto God, the King Eternal, humble praise as tribute brings;
And my voice, retuned, melodious with a newer, nobler tale,
In the Garden of the Prophet hath become a nightingale;
And the glorious apparel, and the silken robes of yore,
Now a wider-seeing wisdom puts away for evermore.

Five yards of wool or cotton are sufficient to contain
A body free from vain desires, a calm untroubled brain.
Long while the praise and service of princes was my care;
To God I now will offer my service and my prayer!"

Dawlatsháh adds that Mas'úd was a native of Gurgán, and his father Sa'd, according to Dr. Ethé (p. 256 of his article in the *Grundriss*) was in the service of the Ziyárid princes of that little kingdom. "Men of letters and poets of distinction," adds the Persian biographer, "have a high opinion of his verse, so that Falakí [of Shírwán], while lauding his own genius, thus alludes to Mas'úd's poetry:—

"Had Mas'úd such cunning in verse as is mine, from the Land of the Dead
Sa'd-i-Salmán, his father, would come, and blessings invoke on his head.'"

The poet's death took place either in A.D. 1121, or, more probably, in A.D. 1131.

Abu Táhir al-Khátúní.

Abú Ṭáhir al-Khátúní is chiefly remarkable as the author of what must at present be regarded as the oldest Biography of Persian poets of which we possess any definite record, though unhappily the work itself is no longer known to exist. It is twice referred to by Dawlatsháh (pp. 29 and 58 of my edition), who cites it as authority for two of his statements, but if he really had access to the book it is surprising that he did not make greater use of it, and it seems probable that he only quotes it at second hand. Ḥájji Khalífa also mentions it in his great bibliography (ed. Flügel, vol. vi, p. 152, No. 13,026), adding that it was written in Persian, but omitting the date of the author's death, which he was presumably unable to discover. Mention is also made of al-Khátúní in several places in al-Bundárí's *History of the Seljúqs* (ed. Houtsma, pp. 89, 105–108, 110, 113). Thence we learn that he wrote against one of Muḥammad b. Malikshâh's Ministers a diatribe entitled *Tanzíru'l-Wazíri 'z-zíri'l-khinzír*, and that he was one of the most eminent men and wittiest writers of his time.[1] Several of his satirical verses are quoted, but unfortunately those which he composed in Persian have been turned into Arabic. He flourished in the early part of the twelfth century of our era (A.H. 500), and seems to have derived the title of al-Khátúní from the fact that he was in the service of Gawhar Khátún, the Sulṭán's wife. One of his Persian verses is cited in Asadí's *Lughat* (ed. Horn, p. 31), but the editor's conversion of Khátúní into Ḥánútí is indefensible.[2] The largest number of his Persian verses is, so far as I know, contained in the very

[1] According to Riḍá-qulí Khán's statement in vol. i of the *Majma'u'l-Fuṣaḥá* (p. 66), where some of his verses are cited, he also composed a History of the Seljúqs, which is, perhaps, the *Ta'ríkh-i-Saláfiqa* referred to by Dawlatsháh.

[2] See p. 23 of Horn's Preface.

rare Persian work on Prosody and Poetry by Shams-i-Qays (Or. 2,814 of the British Museum).[1] Mention is also made of him in ar-Ráwandí's *Ráḥatu'ṣ-Ṣudúr* (*J.R.A.S.* for 1902, p. 598) as keeping the register of the game killed in the chase by Maliksháh. That he was in his time eminent in several ways is very clear from the older authorities, and it is curious that so little mention is made of him in more modern works, while the loss of his *Manáqibu'sh-Shu'ará*, or Biographies of the Poets, can only be described as a literary catastrophe. A somewhat coarse Persian epigram of two *bayts*, in which he satirises the stinginess of the Minister Majdu'l-Mulk of Qum, is also given in the *Ráḥatu'ṣ-Ṣudúr* (*J.R.A.S.* for 1902, p. 600).

Amír Mu'izzí, the poet-laureate of Sanjar, had already established his reputation as a poet in the reign of Malikshásh, from whose title *Mu'izzu'd-Dín* ("the Glorifier of Religion") he derived his *nom-de-guerre*, as he himself relates in an anecdote contained in the *Chahár Maqála* and already cited in full in chapter i (pp. 35–38) of this volume. He is called by the author of that work (p. 55 of my translation) "one of the sweetest singers and most graceful wits in Persia, whose poetry reaches the highest level in freshness and sweetness, and excels in fluency and charm." 'Awfí says (*Lubáb*, vol. ii, p. 69) that three Persian poets attained, under three different dynasties, to a consideration and wealth beyond compare, namely, Rúdagí under the Sámánids, 'Unṣurí under the Sulṭáns of Ghazna, and Mu'izzí under the House of Seljúq. But Mu'izzí's end was a sad one, for he was accidentally shot by Sanjar while the latter was practising archery. Such, at least, is the ordinarily accepted story; but others say that he was only wounded, and recovered from his

Mu'izzí.

[1] This work, of which the full title is *al-Mu'ajjam fí Ma'áyíri Ash'ári'l-'Ajam*, is now in process of publication for the Gibb Memorial Series at Beyrout.

wound, in support of which view Riḍá-qulí Khán (*Majma'u'l-Fuṣaḥá*, vol. i, p. 571) cites the following verse, which, if genuine, certainly seems to bear out this view:—

"*Minnat Khudáy-rá, ki bi-tír-i Khudáyagán*
Man banda bi-gunah na-shudam kushta ráyagán!"

"Thanks be to God that by the arrow of His Majesty
I the innocent servant was not slain to no purpose!"

The same authority gives A.H. 542 (=A.D. 1147–48) as the year of his death, and quotes a few verses in which Saná'í mourns his loss. He adds that in the *ghazal* he follows the style of Farrukhí, and in the *qaṣída* that of 'Unṣurí. Here is a fairly typical fragment from one of Mu'izzí's *ghazals*:—

"Her face were a moon, if o'er the moon could a cloud of musk blow free;
And her stature a cypress, if cypresses bore flowers of anemone.
For if to the crown of the cypress-tree could anemone-clusters cling,
Perchance it might be accounted right such musk o'er the moon to fling.
For her rounded chin and her curved tress, alack! her lovers all
Lend bended backs for her polo-sticks, and a heart for the polo-ball!
Yet if hearts should ache through the witchery of the Hárút-spells of her eye,
Her rubies twain are ever fain to offer the remedy."

When 'Awfí remarks (p. 69 of vol. ii of my edition of the *Lubábu'l-Albáb*) that with Mu'izzí "the child of Rhetoric reached maturity," he probably means that in his verse for the first time we find in constant use all the once original and striking, but now hackneyed, similes with which every student of Persian poetry is familiar. Thus in the four couplets cited above we have the familiar comparison of a beautiful face to the moon, of a mass of black and fragrant hair to musk, of a tall and graceful figure to the cypress, of red cheeks to the anemone (*lála*),[1] of the chin and the heart respectively to a ball, of the back of one bent down by age or sorrow to a polo-stick, of the lips to rubies, and of witching eyes to Hárút, the fallen angel, who teaches magic to such as seek him in the pit where he is imprisoned at Babylon.

Here is another of his odes (*Lubáb*, vol. ii, p. 73) :—

"Since that sugar-raining ruby made my heart its thrall,
Hath mine eye become a shell to harbour pearls withal.
Yea, as oysters filled with pearls must surely be the eyes
Of each lover who for those sweet sugar-liplets sighs.
Yet the shafts of thy narcissus-eye blood-drinking fail
To transfix my heart protected by thy tresses' mail.
Picture fair, by whose belovéd presence by me here
Seems my chamber now like Farkhár, now like far Cashmere,
If thy darkling tresses have not sinned against thy face
Wherefore hang they, head-dependent, downward in disgrace?
Yet, if sin be theirs, then why do they in heaven dwell,
Since the sinner's portion is not Paradise, but Hell?"

Again we are met by a whole string of the conventional similes of Persian erotic verse: the tearful eye is the pearl-yielding oyster-shell; sugar-raining rubies are sweet red lips; the narcissus is the eye, called "blood-drinking" or "blood-thirsty" because it wounds the hearts of lovers; plaited hair is curiously likened to chain armour; the beloved is a "picture" or "idol" more beautiful than the Manichæan pictures (*Arzhang-i-Mání*) of Transoxiana or the idols of India; and the sweet face of the beloved is Paradise. In short, it would not surprise me to learn that almost every simile employed by the later love-poets of Western Asia had been

[1] *Lála*, often translated "tulip," is really the scarlet anemone which gives such beauty to the Persian hills in spring-time. *Lála-rukh*, "with cheeks like the red anemone" (whence Moore's familiar "Lalla Rookh"), is one of the commonest attributes of beauty with the Persian poets.

employed by Mu'izzí, and that most of them were first invented and brought into use by him. This perhaps, if true, accounts in some measure for his high reputation in his own country, for to us, who are sufficiently familiar with Ḥáfidh and other comparatively modern poets, Mu'izzí, unless we keep constantly in mind the epoch at which he flourished, does not appear as a poet of striking power or originality. Let us therefore turn to another poet whom we have already had occasion to mention in this chapter, Rashídu'd-Dín *Waṭwáṭ* ("the Swallow").

Rashídu'd-Dín Waṭwáṭ.

Rashíd-i-Waṭwáṭ, whose proper name was Muḥammad b. 'Abdu'l-Jalíl al-'Umarí (so-called because he claimed descent from the Caliph 'Umar), was by profession a scribe or secretary (whence he is often called *al-Kátib*), and, besides his poetry, was the author of several prose works, of which the most celebrated are the *Ṣad Kalima*, or "Hundred Sayings," of the Four Caliphs,[1] paraphrased and explained in Persian, and a well-known work on Rhetoric and Poetry entitled *Ḥadá'iqu's-Siḥr*, or "Gardens of Magic," which latter, based, I believe, on the lost *Tarjumánu'l-Balághat* ("Interpreter of Eloquence") of Farrukhí, has been lithographed in Persia, and is one of the most useful manuals on the *Ars Poetica* of the Persians. He was nicknamed "the Swallow" (*Waṭwáṭ*) on account of his small size and insignificant appearance, but, according to Dawlatsháh, his tongue was as sharp as it was active, and made him many enemies. Once, according to this biographer, he was disputing in an assembly at which his sovereign and patron Atsiz Khwárazmsháh was present. It chanced that an ink-bottle stood before him, and Atsiz, amused at the violent torrent of words which issued from so small a body, exclaimed in jest, "Take

[1] Manuscripts of the complete work exist at Leyden and Cambridge (Add. 264), but the last of the four parts into which the work is divided, containing the "Hundred Sayings" of 'Alí, is naturally most popular in Persia, and is often found alone.

away that ink-bottle that we may see who is behind it!" Rashíd-i-Waṭwáṭ at once rose to his feet and quoted the Arabic proverb: "A man is a man by virtue of his two smallest parts, his heart and his tongue!" Dawlatsháh adds that Waṭwáṭ lived to a great age and died in Khwárazm, or Khiva, in A.H. 578 (=A.D. 1182–83). In A.H. 551 (= A.D. 1156–57) his patron Atsiz died, and the poet, with tears in his eyes, addressed his dead patron in the following quatrain [1]:—

"O King, the heavens before thy power did quake,
And humbly like a slave thine orders take:
Where is a man of judgement to decide
If *this* be bearable for kingship's sake?"

Seventeen years later, in A.H. 568 (=A.D. 1172), Sulṭán Sháh Maḥmúd, the grandson of Atsiz, succeeded to the throne of Khwárazm, and desired to see the now infirm and aged poet, who, being brought before him in a litter, apostrophised him in the following quatrain [2]:—

"From tyranny thy grandsire cleared the ground;
Thy father's justice made the broken sound:
'Tis now thy turn: what, therefore, wilt thou do
While Empire's robe still compasseth thee round?"

A good deal of incidental information about Rashíd-i-Waṭwáṭ is contained in al-Juwayní's great unpublished history of the Mongols, the *Jahán-gushá*, in the second volume, which deals with the history of the Khwárazmsháhs. Quite at the beginning of this volume, immediately after the account of Sanjar's defeat in his campaign against Khitá, and the sack of Merv by Atsiz, in A.H. 536 (= A.D. 1141–42), is inserted a long letter in Arabic from Waṭwáṭ to a certain Ḥakím Ḥasan Qaṭṭán (?), who, it appears, suspected the poet

[1] It is given not only by Dawlatsháh, but in the *Ta'ríkh-i-Jahán-gushá* of Juwayní. By "*this*," in the concluding line, Death is meant.

[2] This quatrain is also given by Juwayní, who was one of Dawlatsháh's sources.

of having appropriated certain books of his which had been lost at Merv. In this letter the poet defends himself vigorously against a charge which he regards as particularly odious, inasmuch as he had, as he says, presented to various public libraries some thousand fine manuscripts and rare books "so that the Muslims might profit thereby," in spite of which he is suspected without reasonable cause of stooping to lay hands on the little library of an eminent scholar, which, he disparagingly observes, if sold, bindings and all, in the market, would only realise an insignificant sum of money. Here follows the account of the siege of Hazár-asp, the execution of the poet Adíb-i-Ṣábir by Atsiz, and the narrow escape of Waṭwáṭ from Sanjar, whose anger he had aroused by verses already cited. A few pages further on we learn that about A.H. 547 (= A.D. 1152–53) Waṭwáṭ, together with his friend Kamálu'd-Dín b. Arslán Khán Maḥmúd, the Governor of Jand, incurred the anger of Atsiz, and was banished from the court of Khwárazm in disgrace, but succeeded in winning his pardon by sundry contrite verses, of which the following are cited by al-Juwayní :—

> "*Sí sál shud ki banda bi-ṣaff-i-ni'ál dar*
> *Búdast madḥ-khwán, u tu bar takht madḥ-khwáh.*
> *Dánad Khudáy-i-'arsh ki hargiz na istád*
> *Chún banda madḥ-khwání dar hích bárgáh.*
> *Aknún dil-at zi banda-i-sí-sála shud malúl;*
> *Dar dil bi-ṭúl-i-muddat yábad malál ráh.*
> *Líkin malhal zanand ki 'makhdúm shud malúl,*
> *Júyad gunáh, u banda-i-bí-chára bí-gunáh'.*"

> "For thirty years thy servant, standing meek
> In shoe-rank,[1] sang the praises thou didst seek:
> Such praise, God wotteth well, as none before
> Hath ever laid before a patron's door.

[1] The "shoe-rank" (*Ṣaffu'n-ni'ál* in Arabic, *pá-máchán* in Persian) is the place by the door where those who enter kick off their shoes, and where servants and humble visitors take their stand.

Thou'rt tired of him who served thee thirty years :[1]
Such lengthy service bores thee, it appears.
'The master seeks some fault' (the saw runs so),
'And the poor servant hath no fault to show.'"

Dawlatsháh says that Waṭwáṭ's *Díwán* comprises nearly fifteen thousand verses, remarkable for their ornate and rhetorical style and elaborate tropes. He was particularly fond of the artifice called *tarṣí'* (see pp. 47–48 *supra*), and boasted that before him no one had ever composed an entire *qaṣída* in which this figure had been observed in every single line. His *qaṣídas* are of the boastful and exaggerated type usually affected by Persian panegyrists at this period, and he owes his immortality less to them than to his treatise on the Poetic Art (the *Ḥadá'iqu's-Siḥr*), and a few occasional verses, such as those above cited, which are connected with historical events.

Amongst the rivals of Rashíd-i-Waṭwáṭ was the unfortunate Adíb-i-Ṣábir, whose tragic fate has been already mentioned.[2]

Adíb-i-Ṣábir b. Isma'íl.

According to Dawlatsháh (p. 92 of my edition) these two poets attacked one another in satires of such coarseness that he did not feel justified in quoting them in his Memoirs. Each had his admirers, Anwarí and Kháqání being the most eminent of Adíb-i-Ṣábir's partisans; while Anwarí even sets him above the far more celebrated Saná'í, for he says [3] :—

[1] From this double allusion to "thirty years' service" it would appear that Waṭwáṭ must have been attached to the Court of Khwárazm since about A.H. 517 (= A.D. 1123–24). As we have seen, he was an old and infirm man in A.H. 568 (= A.D. 1172), and, according to Dawlatsháh, survived till A.H. 578 (= A.D. 1182). Juwayní says specifically that at the former date his age already exceeded eighty, in which case we may place his birth about A.H. 488 (= A.D. 1095). I know not on what authority Brockelmann, in his *Arabische Litteraturgeschichte* (vol. i, p. 275) places his death in A.H. 509.

[2] He was drowned in the Oxus by order of Atsiz in Jumáda I, A.H. 542 (= October, A.D. 1147). Dawlatsháh gives A.H. 546 as the date.

[3] The verse is cited in vol. ii of 'Awfí's *Lubáb*, p. 117 of my edition.

"Chún Saná'í hastam ákhir, gar na hamchún Ṣábir-am."

("At any rate I am like Saná'í, even though I be not like Ṣábir.")

Of Adíb-í-Ṣábir's life we have few particulars, save what can be gleaned from his verse. He was a native of Tirmidh, and, though, according to Dawlatsháh, he spent most of his life in Khurásán, especially at Merv, the following fragment, quoted by 'Awfí (vol. ii, p. 123), composed by him on the death of a tyrannical noble of Tirmidh, named Akhtí, who choked himself with wine at a drinking-bout, and, to make use of 'Awfí's graceful expression, "took the aqueous road to hell-fire," shows that his own town was not wholly deprived of his talents :—

"O Akhṭí, the day thou drankest wine was the day thou didst hie thee to hell;
A hundred thousand blessings rest on the day of thy drinking wine!
Since thy departure once more the world is alive and all goes well:
Cursed thou art, yet may mercy rest on this sudden death of thine!"

He was entitled Shihábu'd-Dín ("the Meteor of the Faith"), and must evidently have been for a time on good terms with Atsiz, at whose hands he ultimately suffered death, since he has *qaṣídas* in his praise. He also appears to have been in relations, friendly or otherwise, with several poets besides Waṭwaṭ; thus we find in 'Awfí's *Lubáb* complimentary verses addressed by him to 'Imádí and Futúḥí, and recriminations addressed to Shimálí. The following lines were written by him to a man of position who had been attacked in an anonymous lampoon of which some persons declared Ṣábir to be the author :—

"They say, 'Why hast thou spoken ill
Of him whom all the world doth praise?'

> Such deed was never done by me;
> Such word ne'er marred my noble lays.
> What dirty scoundrel tells this tale?
> This trick on me what blackguard plays?"

'Am'aq of Bukhárá and Rashídí.

This violently personal style is, unfortunately, common enough with the poets, especially the Court-poets, of Persia, but only the mildest examples of it, and those rather toned down, can well be offered to the modern European reader. Contemporary princes, however, appear to have derived great entertainment from these outbursts of spite or jealousy, and even strove at times to provoke them, as we see from one of the anecdotes (No. xix, pp. 75–77 of my translation) in the *Chahár Maqála* concerning two other poets of this period, 'Am'aq of Bukhárá and Rashídí, of whom the former was poet-laureate to Khiḍr Khán, one of the Ílak Kháns of Transoxiana. This prince, says the author of the *Chahár Maqála*,

"was a great patron of poets, and in his service were Amír 'Am'aq, Master Rashídí, Najjár-i-Ságharchí, 'Alí Pánídhí, Bishr of Darghúsh, Bishr of Isfará'in,[1] 'Alí Sipihrí, and Wajíbí of Farghána, all of whom obtained rich rewards and ample honours. The Poet-Laureate was Amír 'Am'aq, who had profited abundantly by that dynasty and obtained the most ample circumstance, comprising fair damsels, well-paced horses, golden vessels, sumptuous apparel, and servants, biped and quadruped, innumerable. He was greatly honoured at the King's Court, so that the other poets must needs do him reverence. Such homage as he obtained from the others he desired also from Master Rashídí, but herein he was disappointed, for Rashídí, though still young, was nevertheless learned in his art. The Lady Zaynab was the special object of his panegyrics, and he enjoyed the fullest favour of the King, who was constantly praising him and proclaiming his merits, so that Rashídí's affairs

[1] This name is doubtful. In my translation of the *Chahár Maqála* I read *pisar-i-* for *Bishr*, and accordingly translated "the son of." But *Isfará'iní* at least is too common a *nisba* to be distinctive, and I now incline to think that the preceding word must be a name, and *Bishr* is the only name which in the Arabic script looks like *pisar*.

prospered, the title of 'Prince of Poets' (*Sayyidu'sh-Shu'ará* was conferred upon him, and he continued to rise ever higher in the King's favour and to receive from him gifts of great value.

"One day, in Rashídí's absence, the King asked 'Am'aq, 'What sayest thou of the verse of Rashídí, the Prince of Poets?' 'His verse,' replied the other, 'is excellent, being both chaste and correct, but it wants salt.'[1]

"When some time had elapsed, Rashídí entered, and, having made obeisance, was about to sit down when the King called him forward, and, teasing him as is the way of Kings, said, 'I asked the Poet-Laureate just now what he thought of Rashídí's poetry, and he replied that it was good, but wanted spice. Now you must compose a quatrain on this topic.' Rashídí, with a bow, sat down in his place and improvised the following fragment:—

> 'You stigmatize my verse as "wanting salt,"
> And possibly, my friend, you may be right.
> My verse is honey-flavoured, sugar-sweet,
> And salt with sweetmeats cannot give delight.
> Salt is for you, you blackguard, not for me,
> For beans and turnips is the stuff you write!'"

Khiḍr Khán was so delighted with this rude but spirited retort to the Poet-Laureate's criticism that, according to the *Chahár Maqála*, he bestowed on Rashídí a thousand gold *dínárs*, which were set out in his audience-hall on four trays, as was the practice of the princes of Transoxiana.

Nidhámí-i-'Arúḍí of Samarqand.

It is now time to say something more about the author of this *Chahár Maqála*, or "Four Discourses," which has been so freely quoted in this and the preceding chapters, and which is, in my opinion, one of the most interesting and remarkable prose works in Persian, and one which throws a far fuller light than any other book with which I am acquainted on the intimate life of Persian and Central Asian Courts in the twelfth century of our era. The author was essentially a Court-poet attached to the service of the House of Ghúr, or "Kings of the Mountains," with

[1] *Bí-namak*, "salt-less" or insipid, is the expression in the original.

which, when he wrote the *Chahár Maqála*, he had been connected for forty-five years, as he himself tells us. His name, according to his own statement (*Chahár Maqála*, p. 10 of my translation) was Aḥmad b. ʿUmar b. ʿAlí, and his title (*laqab*), Najmu'd-Dín, but he is always known by his pen-name (*takhalluṣ*) of Niḏhámí. Even amongst his contemporaries, however, there were, as will directly appear, several Niḏhámís more celebrated than himself, not to mention his later, greater namesake, Niḏhámí of Ganja, who is *the* Niḏhámí *par excellence* of Persian literature ; so the poet with whom we are now concerned is always spoken of as Niḏhámí-i-ʿArúḍí (*i.e.*, "the Prosodist") of Samarqand. Little of his verse has come down to us : Dawlatsháh (pp. 60–61 of my edition) quotes only one couplet from the *Wísa and Rámín*, which, unfortunately, appears not to be his work. ʿAwfí, who gives him a notice of two pages (vol. ii, pp. 207–8), quotes five fragments, all of which are *vers d'occasion*, mostly of the personal and vituperative kind just spoken of, and adds that he was the author of several *mathnawí* poems, of which not even the names are preserved. All that we know of him is what he himself tells us in his "Four Discourses," from which we are able to fix the following dates in his career. In A.H. 504 (= A.D. 1110–11) he was at Samarqand, hearing traditions about the early poet Rúdagí ; in A.H. 506 (= 1112–13) he was at Níshápúr, enjoying the society of the celebrated astronomer-poet, ʿUmar Khayyám ; three years later he was at Herát ; next year (A.H. 510 = A.D. 1116–17) he was at Níshápúr again, and also at Ṭús, where he collected traditions about the great Firdawsí, and visited his grave. About this time, it would appear, he succeeded, encouraged and assisted by Muʿizzí, Sanjar's Poet-Laureate, in bringing himself to the notice of the King, from which period his fortune and fame may be supposed to date. In A.H. 512 and 530 (= A.D. 1118–19 and 1135–36) we again find him at Níshápúr, and it was in the latter year that he paid that pious visit to the tomb of 'Umar Khayyám which has indirectly afforded so much occupation to members of the "Omar Khayyám Club," who, because they have not read their *Chahár Maqála*, bestow on the rose a worship to which the peach-tree and pear-tree have a better claim. In A.H. 547 (= A.D. 1152–53) he was in hiding at Herát, after the defeat of the army of Ghúr by Sanjar the Seljúq. His *Chahár Maqála* was written sometime within the next nine years, since he alludes to Ḥusayn "the World-consumer" (*Jahán-súz*), who died in A.D. 1161, as still living. For a knowledge of his later life we have no data, and even the date of his death is, so far as I am aware, quite unknown. His claim to immortality rests entirely on this one book, the *Chahár Maqála*, of which the unique value has hitherto met with the most inadequate recognition, though it is now accessible to Persian scholars in the lithographed edition published at Tihrán in A.H. 1305 (= A.D. 1887–88), and to English readers in the translation which I published in 1899 in the *Journal of the Royal Asiatic Society*, as well as in a separate reprint. The whole book is worth reading, and though I have quoted from it very largely in these pages, considerations of space have compelled me to omit much which I should like to have included. I will content myself with quoting here an autobiographical anecdote (No. xxi) with which the second of the "Four Discourses" (on poets) ends:—

"At the period when I was in the service of that martyred prince, the King of the Mountains (may God illuminate his tomb and exalt his station in Paradise!), that august personage had a high opinion of me, and showed himself towards me a most generous patron. Now on the Festival of the breaking of the Fast, one of the nobles of the city of Balkh (may God maintain its prosperity!), the Amír 'Amíd Ṣafiyyu'd-Dín Abú Bakr Muḥammad b. al-Ḥusayn Rawánsháhí, came to the Court. Though young, he was an expert writer, a capable Secretary of State, richly dowered with culture and its fruits, and popular with all, so that his praises were on every tongue. At the moment [of his arrival] I was not in attendance.

"Now at a reception the King chanced to say, 'Call Nidhámí.' 'Is Nidhámí here?' inquired the Amír 'Amíd Ṣafiyyu'd-Dín. They replied that he was. But he supposed that it was Nidhámí-i-Muniri.[1] 'Ah,' said he, 'a fine poet, and a man of wide celebrity!'

"When the messenger came to summon me, I put on my shoes, and, as I entered, did obeisance, and sat down in my place. When the wine had gone round several times, Amír 'Amíd said, 'Nidhámí has not yet come.' 'Nay,' replied the King, 'he is come; see, there he is, seated in such-and-such a place.' 'I am not speaking of this Nidhámí,' said Amír 'Amíd; 'the Nidhámí of whom I speak is another, and as for this one, I am not even acquainted with him.' Thereat I saw that the King was vexed; and, turning to me, he straightway asked, 'Is there another Nidhámí besides thee?' 'Yes, sire,' I replied, 'two others, one of Samarqand, whom they call Nidhámí-i-Munírí, and another of Níshápúr, whom they call Nidhámí-i-Athírí; while me they call Nidhámí-i-'Arúḍí.' 'Art thou better, or they?' demanded he.

"Then Amír 'Amíd, perceiving that he had made an unfortunate remark, and that the King was vexed, said, 'Sire, those two Nidhámís are quarrelsome fellows, apt to break up social gatherings by their brawls, and to cause trouble and do mischief.' 'Wait a while,' said the King jestingly, 'till you see this one drain a bumper and break up the meeting. But tell me, of these three Nidhámís, which is the best poet?' 'Of those two,' answered the Amír 'Amíd, 'I have personal knowledge, having seen them; but this one I have not previously seen, nor have I heard his poetry. If he will compose a couple of verses on this topic which we have been discussing, so that I may see his talents and hear his verse, I will tell you which of the three is the best.' Then the King turned to me, saying, 'Now, O Nidhámí, do not put us to shame, and say what the 'Amíd desires.'

"Now at the time when I was in the service of this prince I possessed copious talents and a brilliant wit, while the favours and gifts of my patron had so stimulated me that my improvisations came fluent as running water. So I took up a pen, and, ere the wine-cup had gone twice round, composed these five couplets, which I then submitted to the King:—

---

[1] The reading of this last word is very doubtful; in some of the texts it appears to read *Minbari.*

'O Sire, there be Nidhámís three, and the world with their fame doth ring;
Two are in Merv at the Sultan's Court, one here before the King.
All are the pride of Khurásán wide in song, and I tell you true
That as water fluent, as wisdom wise, is the verse of the other two.
But I am the wine, the headstrong wine, and so, when I them o'ertake,
Their song they cease, they rest in peace, and the making of verse forsake.'

"When I submitted these verses, the Amír 'Amíd Ṣafiyyu'd-Dín bowed and said, 'O King, I know of no poet, let alone the Nidhámís, in all Transoxiana, 'Iráq, and Khurásán, able to improvise five such verses, particularly having regard to their strength, energy, and sweetness, combined with such grace of diction and containing ideas so original. Be of good cheer, O Nidhámí, for thou hast no rival on the face of the earth! O Sire, he hath a pretty wit, a mind swift to conceive, and a finished art. By the good fortune of the King of the age, he hath developed into a unique genius, and will even improve upon this, seeing that he is young and hath many days before him.'

"Thereat the countenance of my lord the King brightened mightily, and a great cheerfulness showed itself in his gracious temperament, and he applauded me, saying, 'I give thee the lead-mine of Warsá from this Festival until the Festival of Sacrifice.[1] Send thine agent thither.' So I sent Isaac the Jew. It was then the middle of summer, and while they were working the mine they smelted so much ore that in the seventy days twelve thousand maunds of lead accrued to me, while the King's opinion of me was increased a thousand-fold. May God (blessed and exalted is He) illuminate his august ashes with the light of His approbation, and gladden his noble spirit with all riches, by His Favour and Grace!"

Our poet, it will be seen, was not modest as to his attainments; but the frank delight in his cleverness here and elsewhere revealed is such as to disarm hostile criticism. Modesty, indeed, has seldom characterised the Persian poets.

[1] *I.e.*, from the first of Shawwál till the tenth of Dhu'l-Ḥijja, or two months and ten days. Mining concessions, it will be seen, are not so modern as some persons may be tempted to suppose

Before we proceed to speak of Anwarí, the most celebrated of the poets associated with the Court of Sanjar, a few words must be said about two or three of his fellow-craftsmen, who, though less illustrious than he, or than those already mentioned in this chapter, are sufficiently conspicuous amidst the almost innumerable writers of elegant verse who flourished at this epoch to deserve at least a passing notice.

'Abdu'l-Wási' al-Jabalí.

'Abdu'l-Wási' al-Jabalí was, as his *nisba* "al-Jabalí" ("the Highlander") implies, originally from the mountainous district of Gharjistán. Thence he came to Herát and Ghazna, where he was for a while attached to the Court of Sulṭán Bahrámsháh b. Mas'úd. When Sanjar marched against this ruler in A.D. 1135,[1] the poet, according to Dawlatsháh (p. 74 of my edition), won the victor's favour by a rather graceful and original *qaṣída*, in which the following eight couplets occur:—

"Through the King's unswerving justice, through the Sultan's catholic care,
Is the pheasant, the ant, the partridge, and the wild ass in its lair,
The first the falcon's neighbour, the next to the serpent dear,
The third the hawk's bed-fellow, and the last the lion's fere.
The Lord of the World King Sanjar, with whom for evermore
In standard, policy, forehead and face are signals four;
In the first the pride of empire, in the second the people's weal,
In the third all worldly splendour, in the fourth all godly zeal.
His fingers are in bounty, his lance where foes cry 'Yield!'
His presence in festal banquet, his flag on the hard-fought field,
The first a giver of guerdons, the next a seizer of souls,
The third joy's source, while the last-named attesteth Victory's scrolls.
Null in his glorious epoch, void in his golden prime,
Found in his days of splendour, dimmed in his lustrous time,
Is, first, Kay-Khusraw's glory; second, Sikandar's fame;
Third, the renown of Ferídún; and, last, Núshirwán's name."

[1] See p. 306 *supra*.

Dawlatsháh repudiates, on grounds that do not in themselves appear very adequate, the well known, though possibly fictitious, anecdote[1] (given by Sir Gore Ouseley in his *Biographies of Persian Poets*, p. 108) that 'Abdu'l-Wási' Jabalí, then a humble peasant lad, first attracted the attention of a rich and powerful patron by the following extemporised verses, wherein, unconscious of a human audience, he was apostrophising some camels which were trespassing on a cotton-field entrusted to his care:

"Flasked-necked camels, hence! Get out!
Well I know what you're about!
Those long necks which forward crane
Shall not touch my cotton-grain!"

Súzaní.

Súzaní of Nasaf (or Samarqand, according to Dawlatsháh), whose proper name was Muḥammad b. 'Alí, is chiefly famous for the ribald and satirical verses to which in earlier life he mainly devoted his talent. These verses must have been exceptionally vitriolic,[2] even for the time and place in which he lived, since Dawlatsháh, who is not, as his notices of Abu'l-'Alá of Ganja and Kháqání abundantly show, particularly squeamish, excuses himself from giving specimens; while 'Awfí, though regarding his *facetiæ* as full of talent, considers it best "to draw in the reins of utterance from putting forward such things," and adds a pious hope that, in consideration of a few serious and penitential poems composed in old age, God may pardon the erring poet. His pen-name, Súzaní, is stated by 'Awfí to have been adopted

[1] In spite of Dawlatsháh's assertion that he has found this story in no reputable history, it is given in the *Ta'ríkh-i-Guzída*, one of the sources he used in compiling his *Memoirs of the Poets*, and a work which enjoys a much higher credit than his own.

[2] The author of the *Ta'ríkh-i-Guzída* gives one specimen, consisting of three couplets, which amply justifies his assertion that "he carried ribaldry to excess." The lines in question, which show no sign of repentance, were written when the poet was fifty-one years of age. His proper name is given by this writer as Abú Bakr ibnu's-Salmání of Kalásh, near Samarqand.

by, or given to, him in consequence of an attachment which he formed to the apprentice of a manufacturer of needles (*súzan*). One of his rivals, between whom and himself many a duel of words seems to have been waged, was, according to 'Awfí (vol. ii, pp. 208–9), Ḥamídu'd-Dín al-Jawharí. Dawlatsháh says that Súzaní died in A.H. 569 (= A.D. 1173–74). The author of the *Ta'ríkh-i-Guzída* says that God pardoned him at last for this verse :—

"Four things I bring, O Lord, to Thee, which exist not Thy treasure within ;
Need I bring, and nothingness, and my crimes, and my deadly sin."

Súzaní's own words sufficiently show that his life, to put it mildly, was open to criticism. Thus, in a fine poem quoted by Dawlatsháh (p. 100), he says :—

"I trod in the path of the Devil, I was snared in the Devil's gin,
Till my evil conduct made me surpass the Devil in sin.
Unstained by sin in my lifetime I scarcely recall a day ;
That I reckoned innocence sinful 'twere almost just to say.
From each of my limbs and members a crop of sins had birth,
As weeds of every species will flourish in humid earth.
At To-morrow's great Uprising, which men to-day deny,
Each limb of my sinful body my shame will loudly cry."

'Alí Shaṭranjí, the author of the "Stork qaṣída" (*Qaṣída-i-Laklak*, 'Awfí's *Lubáb*, vol. ii, pp. 199–200), Jannatí of Nakhshab, and Lámi'í of Bukhárá were, according to Dawlatsháh, amongst the pupils and imitators of Súzaní.

Minor poets of this period.

It would be useless to attempt an enumeration of all the poets of this period who achieved some celebrity in their day, but whose very names are now almost forgotten, and must be sought in the older histories and biographies. 'Awfí, for example, in the tenth chapter of his *Lubáb*, which deals with the poets of the earlier

Seljúq period—that is, the period ending with the death of Sanjar, which we are considering in this chapter—enumerates fifty-two, not including those who, being princes, ministers, or doctors, as well as poets, are discussed in the first half of his Anthology. Some of these—like Jawharí of Herát; Samá'í and Athíru'd-Dín of Merv; Sayfí of Níshápúr; Rúḥí-i-Walwálají; Rashídí of Samarqand; Athíru'd-Dín of Akhsíkat; Abu'l-Ma'álí and Qiwámí of Ray; Abu'l-Faraj of Rúna; Kúhyárí of Ṭabaristán; Sayyid Ḥasan, 'Imadu'd-Dín and 'Alí b. Abi Rijá of Ghazna; and Faríd-i-*Kátib* (or *Dabír*, both words meaning "the scribe" or "secretary")—might claim a brief mention in a more exhaustive work than this, but I cannot claim to have a sufficiently clear idea of their personalities or the distinctive character of their work to make it worth while discussing them at greater length. It would, however, be unchivalrous to pass over in silence the first Persian poetess whom we have yet come across.

Mahsatí.

Of Mahsatí we know but little, and even the correct pronunciation and derivation of her name (also given as Mihsití, Mahastí and Mihastí) are uncertain.[1] She seems to have been, not to speak harshly, of a somewhat gay disposition, and to have chiefly employed the *rubá'í*, or quatrain, as the vehicle of her expression. She is said[2] to have attracted the notice and gained the favour of Sanjar by the following verse, which she extemporised one evening when the King, on going out from his audience-hall to mount his horse, found that a sudden fall of snow had covered the ground:—

"For thee hath Heaven saddled Fortune's steed,
O King, and chosen thee from all who lead;
Now o'er the Earth it spreads a silver sheet
To guard from mud thy gold-shod charger's feet."

[1] See my *Biographies of Persian Poets* from the *Taríkh-i-Guzída*, reprinted from the *Journal of the Royal Asiatic Society* for 1900–1901, p. 16 *ad calc.*

[2] Dawlatsháh, p. 65 of my edition.

She is said to have been the mistress of the poet Táju'd-Dín Aḥmad ibn Khaṭíb of Ganja, and quatrains interchanged between these two are quoted in the *Ta'ríkh-i-Guzída*,[1] which also gives two quatrains addressed by her to a butcher-boy of whom she was enamoured.[2] The brief notice of her contained in vol. iii of the I'timádu's-Salṭana's *Khayrát^un Ḥisán^un*, or Biographies of Eminent Women (pp. 103–4), adds little to our knowledge of her life and work, but it is worth noticing that the last but one of the quatrains there ascribed to her is in the *Ta'ríkh-i-Guzída*[3] attributed to another poetess named Bintu'n-Najjáriyya.

Faríd-i-Katib, 'Imád-i Zawzaní, and Ḥasan of Ghazna.

Of the innumerable minor poets of this period Faríd-*i-Kátib* (or *-i-Dabír*, both words, as stated above, meaning "the scribe"), 'Imád-i-Zawzaní, and Sayyid Ḥasan of Ghazna are, perhaps, the most celebrated. The following quatrain composed by the first-named of these poets on the occasion of Sanjar's defeat by the Ghuzz about A.H. 535 (= A.D. 1140–41) is sufficiently celebrated to make it worth quoting :—

> "O King, thy spear hath set the whole world straight;
> Thy foes for forty years thy sword did sate :
> If now ill luck befalls, Fate willed it so,
> For God alone remaineth in one state!"

Anwarí, Kháqání, Nidhámí, and Dhahír of Fáryáb.

The most celebrated of all the poets whose names are associated with Sanjar's Court is without doubt Anwarí, whose work will be considered, along with that of his younger contemporaries, Kháqání, Nidhámí of Ganja, and Dhahír of Fáryáb, in the following chapter, since their importance demands that they should be discussed at considerable length.

[1] See the *Biographies* above mentioned, pp. 15–16
[2] Ibid., pp. 71–2.
[3] Ibid., p. 73.

Persian prose works of this period.

Of the most important Persian prose works of this period, two, the *Ḥadá'iqu's-Siḥr* ("Gardens of Magic") of Waṭwáṭ and the *Chahár Maqála* ("Four Discourses") of Nidhamí-i-'Arúḍí of Samarqand, have been already discussed, the latter very fully. Al-Ghazálí's work and influence have likewise been noticed, and it is sufficient to mention here the most celebrated of his Persian works, the *Kímiyá-yi-Sa'ádat* ("Alchemy of Happiness"), which is essentially an abridgement of the much fuller *Iḥyá'u'l-'Ulúm*, or "Quickening of the Sciences" [of Religion], composed by him in Arabic. Three other prose works of this period deserve at least a brief mention, *viz.*, the great medical Encyclopædia known as the *Dhakhíra-i-Khwárazmsháhí*; the Persian *Maqámát* of Ḥamídí; and the version of *Kalíla and Dimna* made by Abu'l-Ma'álí Naṣru'lláh.

The *Dhakhíra-i-Khwárazmsháhí.*

The *Thesaurus*, or Encyclopædia of Medical Science, composed early in the sixth century of the *hijra* (twelfth of our era) by Zaynu'd-Dín Abú Ibráhím Isma'íl al-Jurjání, and dedicated to Quṭbu'd-Dín Khwárazmsháh, the father of Atsiz, need not detain us, as it does not fall into the category of Belles Lettres, and is, so far as I know, a mere *résumé* or digest of the medical theories and practice of Avicenna (Ibn Síná) and his successors, set forth in Persian for the benefit of laymen unskilled either in the healing art or in the Arabic language.[1]

The *Maqámát-i-Ḥamídí.*

The *Maqámát*, or Séances, of the Qáḍí Ḥamídu'd-Dín Abú Bakr of Balkh (a contemporary of Anwarí, who has eulogised him in several of his poems) is an imitation in Persian of the similar but much more celebrated Arabic *Maqámát* of Badí'u'z-Zamán al-Hamadhání and of al-Ḥarírí, to whom this style of ornate writing owes its origin and popularity. The composition of the Persian *Maqámát-i-Ḥamídí* was begun in the summer of

[1] For description of contents see Rieu's *Catalogue of the Persian Manuscripts in the British Museum*, pp. 466–468.

A.D. 1156, and it is especially mentioned by the author of the *Chahár Maqála* (p. 25 of my translation) as a model of style. It contains twenty-three (or, in the Ṭihrán and Cawnpore lithographed editions, twenty-four) *Maqámát*, and its author died in A.D. 1164. Its contents are fully stated by Rieu.[1] Inferior though it be, alike in scope, finish, and ingenuity, to its Arabic prototypes, it is nevertheless highly esteemed amongst the Persians, as the following verses of Anwarí[2] clearly show :—

"Every discourse which is not the Qur'án or the Traditions of Muṣṭafá[3]
Hath now, by the *Maqámát* of Ḥamídu'd-Dín, become as vain words.
Regard as blind men's tears the *Maqámát* of Ḥaríri and Badí'[4]
Compared with that Ocean fulfilled of the Water of Life.
Rejoice, O thou who art the Spirit [animating] the elemental form of the followers of Maḥmúd![5]
Go [onwards], for thou art the Maḥmúd of the age, and we [but] the idols of Somnáth![6]
Should I read a chapter of thy *Maqámát* over the numbers,
At once the 'Surds' would find deliverance from their speechlessness.
The Universal Intelligence meditated on a line thereof, and exclaimed, 'O Wonderful!
Does this most learned judge [Ḥamídu'd-Dín, the author] possess the Science of the Transmutation of Speech?'
Live long, O powerful judgement, for in the World of Divine Talent
Thou art an undeclining Sun and an enduring Heaven!"

The arrangement, as well as the nomenclature, of the *Maqámát* in the Ṭihrán edition differs considerably from that

[1] *Persian Catalogue*, p. 747.

[2] These verses will be found on p. 251 of the Tabríz edition of A.H. 1266, and on p. 602 of the Lucknow edition of A.H. 1297

[3] *I.e.*, "the Elect One," the Prophet Muḥammad.

[4] *I.e.*, Badí'u'z-Zamán al-Hamadhání.

[5] By *Maḥmúdiyán* Anwarí means the great poets (such as Firdawsí) of Sulṭán Maḥmúd's time.

[6] *I.e.*, thou hast broken and destroyed our fame and self-esteem as Sulṭán Maḥmúd of Ghazna broke the idols in the Hindoo temples of Somnáth.

which obtains in the manuscript described by Dr. Rieu. Several of them are of the nature of *munáẓarát*, or disputations, as, for example, between Youth and Old Age, between an orthodox Sunní and a "heretical" Shí'í, or between a Physician and an Astronomer. Others deal with such things as Spring, Love, Autumn, and Madness. Others, again, contain enigmas, riddles, or acrostics, or deal with legal questions or mystical speculations. Two of the descriptive *Maqámát*, on the cities of Balkh and Samarqand, inspire hopes of more definite and tangible information, and even of autobiographical particulars, but the form ever prevails over the matter of the discourse, and we find our hopes doomed to disappointment. The laboured and artificial style of these *Maqámát* does not readily lend itself to translation, and, since the form is everything and the substance entirely subordinate, to give any idea of the original it is necessary to paraphrase rather than to translate. The following attempt, taken from the description of Balkh[1] before and after it had been harried and looted by the barbarous Ghuzz in A.H. 548 (A.D. 1153), may serve as a sufficient sample of the whole :—

"But when to the confines of that country I at length drew near —and to those journeying from Balkh did lend my ear—far otherwise did things appear.

'Who news of absent friends doth seek to know,
Must needs hear tidings both of joy and woe.'

"Thus spake informants credible :—'Haste thee not, for thy goal and aim—is no more the same—as that of days which are past—and a season which did not last :—those fragrant breezes now are changed to the desert's deadly gale—and that sugar-sweetness is transformed to draughts of lethal bale ;—of those sweet beds of basil only thorns remain—and of those cups of pleasure naught save an aching pain.—What boots it to behold thy fair-faced fere—in

[1] This is the twentieth *Maqáma* in the Ṭihrán edition, and the passage I have rendered occurs on p. 165.

weeds of woe and garments dark and drear—or to witness the spring-land of thy mays—a prey to dispraise—withered and sere?

'Can these dumb remnants mark Umm Awfá's home?'[1]

"Said I:—'What overlooker's evil eye did light—on those fair gardens bright?—And what dread poisoned desert-blast—of desolation drear hath past—to wreck their order, and their beauty to the winds to cast?'

"Then they, 'O youth!—such evil change, in sooth—awaking in us boundless grief and ruth—too often hath accrued—from Fortune rude—and fickle Fate's undreamed vicissitude.—Heaven is harsh, I ween—yet is not what is heard as what is seen.—Haste thee, and onwards go—that thou may'st see and know;—for to attempt to picture the unseen—is vain, I ween.'"

I turn now to the last of the three Persian prose works of this period which I propose to discuss, I mean the translation made by Nidhámu'd-Dín Abu'l-Ma'álí Naṣru'lláh b. Muḥammad b. 'Abdu'l-Ḥamíd of 'Abdu'lláh ibnu'l-Muqaffa''s Arabic version of the celebrated *Book of Kalíla and Dimna*. This translation was made for and dedicated to Bahrám-Sháh of Ghazna, who reigned from A.H. 512 until A.H. 544 or 547 or 548 (= A.D. 1118–50 or 1153–54),[2] and, as Rieu has shown,[3] probably after A.H. 539 (A.D. 1144–45). It also, as Rieu points out, is so highly esteemed in Persia that Waṣṣáf, the historian and panegyrist of the Mongols, praises it as a model of eloquence, while the author of the *Haft Iqlím* says that no Persian prose work was ever so much admired. An excellent lithographed edition appeared at Ṭihrán in A.H. 1305 (end of A.D. 1887 or beginning of 1888), and to this I shall refer when need arises.[4]

The *Kalíla and Dimna* of Naṣru'lláh b. al-Ḥamíd.

[1] *'A min Ummi Awfá dimnatun lam takallami?'* This is the opening of the celebrated *Mu'allaqa* of Zuhayr ibn Abí Sulmá al-Muzaní.

[2] The earlier date is that of the *Ta'ríkh-i-Guzída*, the second that of the *Rawḍatu'ṣ-Ṣafá*, and the last that of Ibnu'l-Athír.

[3] *Catalogue of Persian MSS. in British Museum*, pp. 745–746.

[4] The editor, Muḥammad Kádhim aṭ-Ṭabáṭabá'í, mentions two earlier Ṭihrán editions, published in A.H. 1282 and 1304 respectively.

Few books in the world have achieved so great a success as that of *Kalíla and Dimna*, or have been translated into so many languages. Originally of Indian origin, it was brought to Persia in the sixth century of our era, in the reign of Kisrá Anúshirwán, and translated into Pahlawí; from the Pahlawí version sprung immediately the earlier Syriac and the Arabic versions; and from the Arabic it was rendered into numerous other languages, Eastern and Western. The literary history of *Kalílah and Dimnah, or the Fables of Bidpai*, is fully given in Keith-Falconer's work, published under this title in 1885 by the University Press, Cambridge; and a table showing the affiliation of the different versions, with their dates, is given on p. lxxxv. All these versions, except the Tibetan, which came immediately from the Sanskrit, are descended from the lost Pahlawí, from which the old Syriac version was made about A.D. 570 and the Arabic version of Ibnu'l-Muqaffa' about A.D. 750. The remaining known versions, including the later Syriac (tenth or eleventh century of our era),[1] are all derived from the Arabic of Ibnu'l-Muqaffa', and comprise Greek, Persian, Hebrew,[2] Latin,[3] Spanish, Italian, Slavonic, Turkish, German, English, Danish, Dutch, and French renderings, of which the last, begun by Galland and completed by Cardonne in A.D. 1778, is the latest in point of time. Of the Persian versions, that which we are about to discuss is the oldest extant, though, as we have already seen, the tale had at a much earlier date been versified by the poet Rúdagí. By far the best known Persian version, however, is that made about the end of the fifteenth century

[1] This later Syriac version was edited by the late Professor W. Wright (Oxford, 1884).

[2] See I. Derenbourg's *Deux versions hébraïques du livre de Kalîlâh et Dimnâh* (Paris, 1881).

[3] John of Capua's Latin version, called *Directorium Vitæ Humanæ*, has been published in full in the Bibliothèque de l'École des Hautes Études (Paris, 1887–89). It was made about A.D. 1270 from the older Hebrew version, which derives directly from the Arabic of Ibnu'l-Muqaffa'.

of our era by Ḥusayn Wá'idh-i-Káshifí, and entitled *Anwár-i-Suhaylí*; from which in turn were derived the third Persian version, known as the *'Iyár-i-Dánish*, or "Touchstone of Wisdom," made by Abu'l-Faḍl for Akbar, and the Turkish *Humáyún-náma*, or "Royal Book," made by 'Alí Chelebi for Sulṭán Sulaymán I, both in the sixteenth century of our era.

Although the author of the *Anwár-i-Suhaylí* ostensibly aimed at simplifying and popularising Naṣru'lláh's earlier version, his style is in fact much more bombastic and florid. For purposes of comparison, let us take the short apologue of the Fox and the Drum which occurs near the beginning of the chapter of the Lion and the Ox, beginning with a translation of Ibnu'l-Muqaffa''s Arabic text of this tale (p. 106 of the Beyrout edition of 1884):—

"Said Dimna: 'They allege that a certain fox came to a wood in which was a drum suspended on a tree; and whenever the wind blew on the branches of this tree, it stirred them so that they beat the drum, and there became audible in it a loud and sonorous sound. So the fox directed his steps towards it, because of what he heard of the loudness of its sound. And when he came to it, he found it bulky, and made sure within himself of an abundance of fat and meat. Wherefore he struggled with it until he had split it asunder; but when he perceived it to be hollow, containing naught within it, he said: "I know not whether perchance the feeblest of things be not the loudest in outcry and the greatest in bulk."'"

Let us now take Naṣru'lláh's version of the same (p. 79 of the Ṭihrán lithographed edition of A.H. 1305):—

"He [Dimna] said: 'They relate that a fox entered a thicket. There he saw a drum cast down by the side of a tree, and whenever the wind stirred, the branches of the tree reached the drum, and a terrific noise assailed the fox's ears. When the fox saw the bulkiness of its carcase and heard the majesty of its voice, he greedily imagined that its flesh and skin would prove worthy of the voice. He strove until he had rent it asunder. In fact he found nothing more than skin. Urging the steed of remorse into its course, he said: "I did not realise that wherever there is the greater bulk and the more terrible noise, there is the less profit."'"

Turning now to the *Anwár-i-Suhaylí*, we find the story considerably expanded and padded, as follows (pp. 58–59 of the lithographed edition of A.H. 1270):—

"Dimna said: 'They relate that a fox was passing through a thicket, and was wandering in every direction in hopes of food. [He came at length] to the foot of a tree by the side of which they had hung a drum; and whenever a wind blew, a branch of that tree was stirred and reached the surface of the drum, from which a frightful noise arose. The fox saw beneath the tree a hen, which was driving its beak into the ground in search of food. Crouching in ambush, it prepared to seize it, when suddenly the sound of the drum reached its ears. Looking up, it beheld a very stout body, while its voice sounded terrible. The greed of the fox was stirred, and it reflected within itself that the flesh and skin of this thing should be worthy of its voice. Quitting the ambush of the hen, it turned its face towards the tree. The hen, warned of the [impending] catastrophe, fled; while the fox, with a hundred toils, came up to the tree. Much it strove until it had rent asunder the drum, but naught did it find save a skin and a piece of wood. The fire of remorse fell into its heart, and the tears of regret began to pour from its eyes, and it said, "Alas, that for the sake of this bulky carcase, which was all wind, that lawful quarry [*i.e.*, the hen] hath escaped from my hands, while from this form without sense no profit hath accrued to me.

"'"The drum ever cries, but what good doth it do,
Since its carcase is hollow and empty within?
If wisdom be thine, then the Real pursue,
And be not deceived by a flatulent skin."'"

In this particular instance the *Anwár-i-Suhaylí* version, though considerably expanded, not to say inflated, is comparatively faithful to its original; but in general it is full of absurd exaggerations, recondite words, vain epithets, far-fetched comparisons, and tasteless bombast, and represents to perfection the worst style of those florid writers who flourished under the patronage of the Tímúrids in North-Eastern Persia and Transoxiana during the fifteenth and sixteenth centuries of our era, and who, unfortunately, passing with Bábar into India, became models and exemplars to the bombast-loving people of that country. This is one and perhaps the chief reason why good and chaste Persian has very rarely been produced or admired in Hindustán, where we find a Baboo Persian precisely similar to the Baboo English which, in the immortal pages of the *Biography of Honble. Chief Justice Mookerjee*, has afforded us such exquisite material for mirth.

For purposes of comparison I here reproduce the above apologue of the Fox and the Drum from the Latin version of John of Capua, which was made about A.D. 1270 from the earlier Hebrew rendering of the Arabic [1] :—

"Ait Dimna : 'Fuit vulpes quidam ambulans versus flumen, circa quod suspensum erat cimbalum in arbore; ventus autem ramos arboris agitabat et propulsabatur cimbalum. Et cum vulpes videret, estimavit esse aliquod pingue animal et plenum carnibus ; que cum scinderet ipsum, invenit ipsum concavum et vacuum. Et ait: "Nolo credere res magni corporis et fortis vocis in se habere potentiam," et abiit in viam suam.'"

It remains now to notice briefly some of the most epoch-making Arabic works composed at this period. To make a selection of those most deserving of mention is by no means easy, and in doing so I have chosen rather what I deem valuable to the Persian student for purposes of reference than what enjoys the greatest celebrity.

Important Arabic works composed at this period.

The most notable Arabic authors and scholars whose deaths took place during the period which we are now discussing are, in chronological order, as follows: az-Zawzaní († A.D. 1093), a philologist chiefly known for his commentary on the seven *Mu'allaqát*, who also compiled two

az-Zawzaní.

[1] P. 50 of Derenbourg's text.

Arabic-Persian dictionaries, one, the *Tarjumánu'l-Qur'án*, especially for the reading of the Muslim Scriptures; at-Tabrízí († A.D. 1109), another philologist, whose commentaries on the *Ḥamása* and the *Mu'allaqát* are the most celebrated of his works, and who was a pupil of the great 'Abu'l-'Alá al-Ma'arrí; al-Ghazálí, "the Proof of Islám" († A.D. 1111), whose life and work we have already considered in the last chapter; 'Abdu'l-Wáḥid-i-Rúyání, murdered by one of the Assassins at Ámul whilst he was lecturing (A.D. 1108); aṭ-Ṭughrá'í, author of the celebrated *Lámiyyatu'l-'Ajam*, or "L-poem of the Persians," and Minister to the Seljúq Sulṭán Mas'úd, put to death in or about A.D. 1120; al-Ḥarírí († A.D. 1122), author of the celebrated *Maqámát*, which he composed for the Minister Anúshirwán b. Khálid († A.D. 1138), himself the author of an excellent historical monograph on the Seljúqs, edited in the later recension of al-Bundárí by Houtsma (Leyden, 1889); al-Farrá al-Baghawí († A.D. 1122), a theologian and traditionist, whose best-known work is a commentary on the *Qur'án* entitled the *Ma'álimu't-Tanzíl;* al-Maydání of Níshápúr († A.D. 1124), chiefly famous for his classical work on Arabian Proverbs; Ibn 'Abdún († A.D. 1126), the Andalusian, whose great historical *qaṣída* was afterwards commentated by his countryman, Ibn Badrún († *circâ* A.D. 1184); az-Zamakhsharí († A.D. 1143), the Mu'tazilite author of the great commentary on the *Qur'án* known as the *Kashsháf*, and of several Arabic-Persian lexicographical works; al-Jawálíqí († A.D. 1145), another philologist, author of the *Mu'arrab*, a dictionary of foreign loan-words adopted into Arabic; ash-Shahristání († A.D. 1153), author of the *Kitábu'l-Milal wa'n-Niḥal*, or Book of Sects

at-Tabrízí. al-Ghazálí. ar-Rúyání. aṭ-Ṭughrá'í. al-Ḥarírí. Anúshirwán b. Khálid. al-Farrá al-Baghawí. al-Maydání. Ibn 'Abdún. az-Zamakhsharí. al-Jawálíqí. ash-Shahristání.

an-Nasafí.

at-Túsí and at-Tabarsí.

and Schools; Najmu'd-Dín Abú Ḥafs 'Umar of Nasaf or Nakhshab († A.D. 1142), "one of the greatest Ḥanafite jurisconsults of his time"; and the Shí'ite theologians aṭ-Ṭúsí († A.D. 1067) and aṭ-Ṭabarsí († A.D. 1153), to the former of whom we owe the *List* (or *Index*) *of Shí'ite Books* (edited by Sprenger at Calcutta, A.D. 1853–55).

The fuller consideration of these authors (although, as will be seen, most of them were Persians by birth) belongs rather to the history of Arabic Literature, and would be out of place here, even did space admit of it; but the serious student of Persian literary history will from time to time have occasion to consult the works of most of them, for, as has been already pointed out, till the Mongol Invasion and Fall of Baghdád in the middle of the thirteenth century of our era Arabic continued to hold its place in Persia as the language of science and literature, and in it the bulk of the most indispensable works of reference are composed. A few words may, however, be added about some of the authors above mentioned. I begin with one who, since he met his death in A.D. 1075, should properly have been mentioned in an earlier chapter, from which he was omitted by an oversight, I mean al-Bákharzí.

al-Bákharzí.

Abu'l-Qásim 'Alí b. al-Ḥasan b. Abí Ṭayyib al-Bákharzí was notable both as a poet and as a biographer of poets. In the former capacity he is noticed at some length in vol. i of 'Awfí's *Lubábu'l-Albáb* (pp. 68–71 of my forthcoming edition). In the latter he continued the work begun by ath-Tha'álibí in the *Yatímatu'd-Dahr*, and wrote a most comprehensive work entitled the *Dumyatu'l-Qaṣr*, which contains notices of about 225 more or less contemporary poets and 20 notable men of letters of whom no poetry is recorded.[1] Unfortunately, however, he confines his attention to those who wrote in Arabic, and entirely ignores the Persian poets

[1] This important work has unfortunately not been published. There are two MSS. (Add. 9,994 and Add. 22,374) in the British Museum.

concerning whom he might have given us such valuable and authentic information. His own verse is partly in Arabic and partly in Persian; as 'Awfí puts it, "he became a signal in the world in both writings, and snatched the prize of pre-eminence from the literary men of his age in both languages." In his youth he was one of the secretaries of the Seljúq Sulṭán Ṭughril, but afterwards, preferring lettered ease, resigned that position, and ended a gay and apparently somewhat dissolute life by a violent death, resulting, as it would seem, from a drinking bout. Besides his other verses, he is stated by 'Awfí (*loc. cit.*, p. 70) and Riḍá-qulí Khán (*Majma'u'l-Fuṣaḥá*, vol. i, pp. 343–4) to have written a *Ṭarab-náma*, or "Book of Delight," consisting of Persian quatrains arranged alphabetically.

The following verses (*Lubáb*, vol. i, p. 69) form part of an Arabic *qaṣída* composed in praise of Ṭughril:—

"When we first set out, the Mirror of Time[1] was a disc of silvery sheen,
But now it is darkened, hath suffered eclipse, and can be no longer seen.[2]
Our camels haste to cross the waste, nor halt to let us view
The ash-strewn site of our sweetheart's camp, and revive her image anew.
They shake their sides, and with eager strides they press and they labour still
To bring us straight to the palace-gate of the glorious Prince Ṭughril."

Here is a translation of one of his Persian quatrains:—

"Night black as pitch she bids bright day bestride;[3]
Two sugar-plums stars two-and-thirty hide;[4]

[1] *I.e.*, the Moon.

[2] *I.e.*, we set out when the moon was full, and now we are close on the new moon; in other words, we have been two weeks on our journey.

[3] The black night is the hair, the bright day the face of the beloved.

[4] He means the lips and the teeth of his sweetheart.

O'er the red rose a musky scorpion strays,[1]
For which she keeps two antidotes well tried."[2]

Here is another of his quatrains in praise of wine (*Lubáb*, vol. i, p. 70):—

"That wine which causeth joy do I desire;
Red as the jujube-fruit, the grape its sire;
Named wine, entitled 'Alchemy of Joy'—
Strange water this, which sets the cheeks on fire!"

Lastly, here is the quatrain which (*Lubáb*, i, 71) he is said to have written at the moment of his death:—

"I go; come, cast on me a last long gaze:
Behold me tortured in ten thousand ways!
A stone above, my pleading hand beneath,
And there my friend, and there the sword which slays!"

A poet named 'Ayyáḍí commemorated his death in these lines (*Lubáb*, i, 71):—

"Poor Ḥasan 'Alí in this luckless strife
Faultless, like 'Alí's Ḥusayn,[3] lost his life:
A lion he, who dwelt in Culture's glen:
Small wonder for a lion slain of men!"

ar-Rúyání.

The most interesting thing about 'Abdu'l-Wáḥid b. Isma'íl ar-Rúyání, an eminent jurisconsult of the Sháfi'ite school, entitled during his life *Fakhru'l-Islám* ("the Glory of Islám"), and after his death *Imám-i-shahíd* ("the martyred Imám"), is the manner of his death, concerning which Ibn Isfandiyár in his *History of Ṭabaristán* writes as follows[4]:—

[1] The red rose is the cheek, on which lies one of her black fragrant curls, which he compares to a "musky scorpion."

[2] These are, of course, the two sweet lips which bring balm to the lover whose heart has been wounded by her scorpion-like tresses.

[3] *I.e.*, the Imám Ḥusayn ibn 'Alí, "the Martyr of Kerbelá."

[4] See pp. 75–76 of my abridged translation of this work, forming vol. ii of the Gibb Memorial Series, where the Persian text of this passage is given in full.

"His discernment reached such a point that in his time the accursed heretics[1] sought for a decision (*fatwá*[2]) on the following case which they had committed to writing: 'What say the leaders of Religion as to a case where both plaintiff and defendant are content to abide by what is just and right, when a witness appears and bears testimony opposed alike to the claim of the plaintiff and the admission of the defendant? Can such testimony be lawfully heard, or not?' This question, written on a piece of paper, they sent to the two Sacred Cities (Mecca and al-Madína); and the leading theologians of the Sacred Cities, Muḥammad Juwayní and Muḥammad Ghazálí, together with the Imáms of Baghdád and Syria, all wrote in reply that such testimony could not be adduced or heard. But he [*i.e.*, ar-Rúyání], having glanced at the paper, turned his face towards the man [who had brought it], and exclaimed, 'O ill-starred wretch! So much thankless labour will bring calamity upon thee!' Then he ordered him to be detained, and assembled all the judges and religious leaders. 'This enquiry,' said he, 'was written by the Heretics. The plaintiff and defendant are respectively the Jews and the Christians, and the witness they mean is our Apostle (Muḥammad, on whom be the Blessings of God and His Peace; for the glorious Qu'rán bears testimony as follows: "*And they neither slew Him* [*i.e.*, Jesus Christ] *nor crucified Him, but it was made so to appear to them.*"'[3] They then enquired of the heretic, who admitted that for a whole year he had been sent hither and thither through the world to seek an answer to this enquiry. He was then stoned to death by the people of Ámul, and Fakhru'l-Islám [ar-Rúyání] enjoined the cursing of the progeny of the Heretics, until they sent [*Fidá'ís*, or Assassins] who treacherously slew that martyred Imám with blows of their knives at the door of one of the chapels of the Great Mosque of Ámul, on that side where stands the minaret. The knife is still preserved in his rooms in the College, where I have repeatedly seen it."

The object of the Assassins evidently was to stultify the orthodox doctors of Islám by proving their law to be in contradiction with their theology. The Christians, who are the plaintiffs in the case, accuse the Jews, who are the defendants, of crucifying Jesus Christ. The Jews admit this,

[1] *Maláḥida*, the name commonly applied in Persia to the Assassins.

[2] *I.e.*, a formal legal opinion based on the *Sharí'at*, or Sacred Law of Islám.

[3] Qur'án, iv, 156.

and are therefore agreed as to the facts, and are prepared to abide by the consequences. The Prophet Muḥammad, here following certain Gnostic sects, denies that Christ was really crucified by the Jews, and so "bears testimony opposed alike to the claim of the plaintiff and the admission of the defendant"; but, though all Muhammadans accept his testimony on this as on all other matters, they have, according to the decision of their own chief theologians and doctors, no justification for so doing. Ar-Rúyání's quickness in detecting the trap set by the "Heretics" for the moment confounded them, and ultimately led to his own death.

We have already sufficiently discussed that very artificial and ingenious style of composition which characterises all *Maqámát*, whether written in Arabic, as by Badí'u'z-Zamán al-Hamadhání and al-Ḥarírí, or in Persian, as by Ḥamídu'd-Dín of Balkh, and need not stop here to consider the work of al-Ḥarírí, who, by common consent, is the King, as Badí'u'z-Zamán al-Hamadhání is the Pioneer of all those who devoted themselves to this species of exaggerated euphuism. Moreover, al-Ḥarírí's work has been so much discussed, commentated, and translated, both in the East and in Europe, that only an account thereof far lengthier than this volume could afford to give would dispense the reader who desires to look into the matter from having recourse to such materials as are given by de Sacy in his monumental edition (Paris, 1822); or by Chenery in the hundred pages of Introduction which he prefixed to the first volume of his Translation of the "Assemblies" or *Maqámát* (London, 1867); or to the excellent German paraphrases of the *Maqáma* style which will be found in Von Kremer's *Culturgeschichte des Orients* (vol. ii, pp. 470–476),[1] and other works specially devoted to Arabic literature. Zamakhsharí, of whom we shall speak very shortly, solemnly asseverates, in a verse which de Sacy cites on

al-Ḥarírí.

[1] Cf. p. 22 *supra*.

the title-page of his edition, that al-Ḥaríri's *Maqámát* deserve to be written in gold, and this is the general opinion of his countrymen and co-religionists, though not of several distinguished European Orientalists. For better or worse, however, the materials available for the study of these *Maqámát* are singularly copious As to their author, it is sufficient to say that he was born at Baṣra in A.D. 1054–55, and died there in A.D. 1121–22; that he was of insignificant and even displeasing appearance, and had an unpleasant trick of plucking hairs from his beard when he was engaged in thought; and that he enjoyed the friendship and patronage of the amiable and talented *wazír* Anúshirwán b. Khálid, at whose instigation the *Maqámát* were written, and to whom they were dedicated.[1]

Anúshirwán b. Khálid.

This *Wazír*, on account of his excellent historical monograph on the Seljúqs (edited by Houtsma in the recension of al-Bundárí as the second volume of his *Recueil de Textes relatifs à l'Histoire des Seldjoucides*, Leyden, 1889), deserves some mention in this place. Nearly all that is known about him has been set forth by Houtsma in his preface (pp. xi–xxx) to the above-mentioned work, but the following notice, which I found in a manuscript of the *'Uyúnu'l-Akhbár* ("Primary Sources of Historical Data") preserved in the Cambridge University Library (Add. 2,922, *f.* 126[a]), and published at pp. 861–2 of the *Journal of the Royal Asiatic Society* for 1902, has not, I think, hitherto been translated. It occurs under the year A.H. 532 (=A.D. 1137–38), and runs as follows:—

"And in this year died Anúshirwán b. Khálid b. Muḥammad of Káshán [who bore the *kunya*] Abú Naṣr, the *Wazír*. He was born at Ray in A.H. 459 (=A.D. 1066–67), and, after various vicissitudes, became

[1] See p. 5 of de Sacy's edition and commentary thereon; Houtsma's Preface to his edition of al-Bundárí, p. xii; and Brockelmann's *Gesch. d. arab. Litt.*, vol. i, p. 276.

wazír to Sulṭán Maḥmúd [b. Muḥammad b.] Malikshah in A.H. 517 (=A.D. 1123–24), with whom he came to Baghdád, where he took up his abode. He used to live in the Precinct of Ṭáhir[1] in a house on the shore of the Tigris. He was dismissed from, and again restored to, his position of Minister: then the Sulṭán arrested him and cast him into bonds, but subsequently released him. The Caliph al-Mustarshid bi'lláh made him his Minister in the latter part of A.H. 526 (= A.D. 1132), and he continued his administration until he was dismissed in the year A.H. 528 (=A.D. 1134), after which he abode in his house in the Precinct of Ṭáhir, honoured by all,[2] until he died in this year (A.H. 532 = A.D. 1137–38). He was one of the most accomplished of public men, characterised by generosity and nobility, and a friend to men of learning. He summoned to his house Abu'l-Qásim b. al-Ḥuṣayn, in order that his sons might hear from him the *Musnad* of Ibn Ḥanbal according to the reading of Abú Muḥammad ibnu'l-Khashsháb, and granted permission to the general public to be present at these lectures, of which permission great multitudes availed themselves. Ibn Jakíná the poet composed both panegyrics and satires on him, amongst the former, the following:—

"'*They asked me who was the greatest of men in worth:*
I replied, "Their master, Anúshirwán;
And if he shows humility amongst us
That is but one of the signs of him whose rank is high;
For when the stars are reflected on the surface of water
It is not that they are lowly situated."'

"The Qáḍí Náṣiḥu'd-Dín of Arraján wrote to ask him for a tent. Not having one, he sent him a purse containing five hundred *dínárs*, bidding him buy a tent. Al-Arrajání replied as follows:—

"'*Praise God for the bounty of such a man as Abú Khálid,*
Who hath revived generosity for us after that it had departed.
I asked him for a tent wherein I might take shelter,
And he lavished on me a tent-full of gold!'

---

[1] This is no doubt the correct reading, though the MS. has "*adh-Dháhirí*" for "*aṭ-Ṭáhirí.*" See le Strange's *Baghdád during the Abbasid Caliphate* (Oxford, 1900), pp. 118–121, and the map facing p. 107 (site No. 19).

[2] Perhaps, however, for *Makrúm*^{an}, "honoured," we should read *Makrúh*^{an}, "in disgrace"

"He it was who caused the *Maqámát* of al-Ḥarírí to be composed, and to him does al-Ḥarírí allude at the beginning of his *Maqámát* where he says: 'Then suggested to me one whose suggestion is as a decree, and obedience to whom is as a prize' . . . And Anúshirwán was a Shí'ite—may God deal gently with him!"

A few words may be devoted to the great Mu'tazilite commentator and philologist Abu'l-Qásim Maḥmúd b. 'Umar az-Zamakhsharí, who was born at Khwárazm (the modern Khiva) in A.D. 1074, and died near the same place in A.D. 1143. He lived for some time at Mecca, whence he is often entitled *Járu'lláh* ("God's neighbour"). Though a strong opponent of the Shu'úbiyya, who held the Persians to be superior to the Arabs, he composed an Arabic-Persian lexicon for the use of his countrymen, which was published at Leipzig by Wetzstein in A.D. 1844. The *Kashsháf*, his great commentary on the Qur'án; the *Mufaṣṣal*, a very notable work on Arabic grammar; his geographical dictionary, entitled *Kitábu'l-Amkina wa'l-Jibál wa'l-Miyáh*; and his "Collars of Gold" (*Aṭwáqu'dh-Dhahab*), all written in Arabic, are his most important and celebrated works.

az-Zamakhsharí.

Of Abu'l-Fatḥ Muḥammad b. Abi'l-Qásim b. 'Abdu'l-Karím b. Abí Bakr Aḥmad of Shahristán in Khurásán little need be said save that he was born in A.D. 1086; visited Baghdád, where he resided for three years, in A.D. 1116–17; died in his native city in A.D. 1153; and, besides two or three less celebrated works, composed about A.D. 1127 his admirable Book of Sects, of which the Arabic text was published by Cureton in A.D. 1846, and a German translation with notes by Dr. Theodor Haarbrücker in A.D. 1850. For long this has been the only accessible Arabic work dealing with this important subject, but now at last the earlier, fuller, and almost homonymous work of the Andalusian Dháhirite theologian Ibn Ḥazm (b. A.D. 994, d. 1064) has been

ash-Shahristání.

published at Cairo (A.H. 1317–21 = A.D. 1899–1903). For a copy of this fine edition of a most important book of reference hitherto absolutely inaccessible to all save a favoured few, I am indebted to my lamented friend and master, the late Grand Muftí of Egypt, Shaykh Muḥammad ʻAbduh, the greatest man, the most able teacher, and the profoundest thinker produced by Islám in our days.

CHAPTER VI

THE FOUR GREAT POETS OF THE LATE TWELFTH CENTURY, ANWARÍ, KHÁQÁNÍ, NIDHÁMÍ OF GANJA, AND DHAHÍR OF FÁRYÁB

In this chapter I propose to depart from the chronological sequence of events which I have hitherto striven to observe, and to consider together four poets of the later Seljúq period, who are, by the general consent of their countrymen, amongst the greatest masters of verse whom Persia has produced. They were not strictly contemporary, and only one of them can be called a Seljúq poet, but they may conveniently be discussed and contrasted in a single chapter, since they are all figures in the literary world of Persia too important to be summarily dismissed. These four poets are Anwarí of Kháwarán in Khurásán, who, though he survived Sanjar some thirty or forty years, achieved his reputation in that monarch's reign; Kháqání, the poet of Shirwánsháh, born at Ganja (now Elizavetpol) in A.H. 500 (A.D. 1106–7); Nidhámí, also born at Ganja some thirty-five years later; and Dhahíru 'd-Dín Fáryábí, born at Fáryáb near Balkh, who, during the latter part of the twelfth century, frequented in turn the Courts of Ṭughánsháh of Níshápúr, Ḥusámu'd-Dawla Ardashír of Mázandarán, and the Atábeks of Ádharbayján, and finally died at Tabríz about the beginning of the thirteenth century.

Of these four poets Anwarí is at once the most ancient and the most celebrated, and in the following well-known verse is even ranked as one of the three greatest poets whom Persia has produced:—

Anwarí.

Dar shi'r si tan payambarán-and,
Qawlíst ki jumlagí bar án-and:
Firdawsí u Anwarí u Sa'dí,
Har chand ki 'Lá nabiyya ba'dí.'[1]

It is difficult for an European student of Persian, however anxious he may be to give due weight to the opinion of native critics, to think of Anwarí as the equal of Firdawsí and Sa'dí, or as the superior of Náṣir-i-Khusraw or Nidhámí, but this is partly because, as I have already pointed out, the panegyric—and most of Anwarí's *qaṣídas* were panegyrics—however skilfully constructed, can seldom arouse much enthusiasm, save in the heart of him whose praises it celebrates. A friend of mine, Mírzá Muḥammad, one of the most learned and scholarly Persians whom it has ever been my good fortune to meet, is of opinion that Anwarí's reputation rests mainly on the comparatively small number of his *qaṣídas* which are not panegyrics, and this view is probably the true one. In most other forms of verse, such as the *ghazal* and quatrain, Anwarí is not specially distinguished, though his fragments (*muqaṭṭa'át*) often reveal a strong individuality.

Concerning the circumstances of Anwarí's life we possess but little authentic information, though a careful and critical examination of his poems would doubtless furnish us with some hitherto unremarked and trustworthy data for his biography. From other sources we learn but little on which reliance can be placed. 'Awfí in his *Lubábu'l-Albáb* (vol. ii, pp. 125–138 of my edition) as usual tells us practically nothing, save that the poet was skilled in Astronomy, Geometry, and Logic, a fact known to us from other sources, especially from

[1] For the translation of this verse see p. 116 *supra*.

one of Anwarí's own poems cited in the *Ta'ríkh-i-Guzída*,[1] wherein he adds to these accomplishments Music, Metaphysics, Natural Science, and Judicial Astrology, and even declares himself proficient "in every science, pure or applied, known to any of his contemporaries." According to Dawlatsháh (pp. 83–86 of my edition) he was born in Abíward at a village near Mihna in the Dasht-i-Kháwarán, on which account he at first wrote under the pen-name of Kháwarí, which he afterwards changed to Anwarí. He is said to have studied at the Manṣúriyya College of Ṭús, where he lived the cramped and straitened life of a needy student. One day—so runs the tale—there passed by the gate of the College a man gorgeously apparelled, mounted on a superb horse, and surrounded by servants and attendants. Anwarí, struck by his magnificence, inquired who he was,[2] and on learning that he was a poet exclaimed, "Good heavens! Am I so poor when the rank of Science is so high, and is he so rich when the grade of Poetry stands so low? By the glory and splendour of the Lord of Glory, from to-day onwards I will busy myself with Poetry, which is the lowest of my accomplishments!" And that very night, it is said, he composed the celebrated *qaṣída* beginning—

Gar dil u dast baḥr u kán báshad,
Dil u dast-i-Khudáyagán báshad.

"If Heart and Hand can rank as Sea and Mine,[3]
It is this Heart and Hand, O Sire, of thine!"

In the morning he presented himself at Sulṭán Sanjar's reception, and, having recited his poem, was asked whether he

[1] For both text and translation see pp. 7–8 of my *Biographies of Persian Poets contained in the Ta'ríkh-i-Guzída* (*J.R.A.S.* for October, 1900), in the separate reprint. The text will also be found at pp. 704–5 of the Lucknow lithographed edition of A.H. 1297 (= A.D. 1880).

[2] M. Ferté, in the notice on Anwarí which he published in the *Journal Asiatique* for March-April, 1895, suggests (p. 244) that Amír Mu'izzí was the gorgeously-arrayed poet in question.

[3] *I.e.*, in profundity and liberality.

desired a present of money or a position at the Court; to which he replied :—

"Save at thy threshold in the world no resting-place have I;
Except this gate no place is found whereon my head would lie."

Thereupon Sanjar made him an allowance and took him with him to Merv.

According to a very well-known verse cited by Dawlatsháh (p. 84), Kháwarán produced, besides Anwarí, three incomparable geniuses, namely, Abú 'Alí Aḥmad Shádán, who was for a time Prime Minister to Ṭughril Beg; Ustád As'ad of Mihna, a doctor of Theology and Law contemporary with al-Ghazálí, with whom he disputed; and the celebrated Ṣúfí Abú Sa'íd ibn Abi'l-Khayr, whose life and work have already been considered (pp. 261–269 *supra*).

Although Anwarí is said to have been one of the greatest astrologers of his time, he ventured on a forecast which, owing to the notoriety which it attained and its conspicuous non-fulfilment, considerably damaged his prestige. It happened that during Sanjar's reign all the seven planets were at one period in the Sign of the Balance,[1] and Anwarí declared that this conjunction portended gales of such severity that buildings and trees would be overthrown and cities destroyed. Many people were so alarmed by these predictions that they dug cellars in which to take refuge from the impending calamity. But when the fateful night arrived there was so little wind that a naked light burned unwaveringly on the top of a minaret; nor was Anwarí's plea that the effects of such a conjunction did not appear at once, but took time to develop, more successful, for during the whole of that year there was so little wind that it did not suffice for the winnowing of the harvests[2] about Merv, which consequently lay on the ground

[1] See Ibnu'l-Athír, who places the conjunction in A.H. 582 on the 29th of Jumádá II (= September 16, A.D. 1186), and speaks only of *five* planets.
[2] This detail is also mentioned by Ibnu'l-Athír, *loc. cit.*

till the following spring. On this Faríd-*i-Kátib* composed a verse which may be thus paraphrased:—

> "Said Anwarí, 'Such fearful gales shall blow
> As houses, nay, e'en hills, shall overthrow.'
> The day proved breathless; Anwarí, I ween you
> And Æolus must settle it between you!"[1]

This conjunction of the planets is generally considered to have taken place in Rajab, A.H. 581 (=October, A.D. 1185), or possibly, as hinted by Ethé, nearly a year later;[2] so that Anwarí's death, the dates assigned to which by different biographers (and even by the same biographer in different passages of the same work) vary between A.H. 545 and 656 (=A.D. 1150–1258), must have taken place after (probably soon after) this event.

Zhukovski's Memoir on Anwarí.

By far the fullest and best critical monograph on Anwarí is that published at St. Petersburg in 1883 by Professor Valentin Zhukovski, under the title of '*Alí Awḥadu'd-Dín Anwarí: Materials for a Biography and Characteristic-Sketch.* It is unfortunately written in Russian, and is therefore inaccessible to the majority of Orientalists; but we owe to Dr. W. Pertsch an excellent epitome of the biographical portion, published in vol. ii of the *Literatur-Blatt für Orientalische Philologie* (Leipzig, 1884–5). The Russian work comprises xxiv + 146 pages, followed by 90 pages of Persian text, and consists of:—

[1] W. Pertsch gives the following rendering in German (*Literatur-Blatt für Orientalische Philologie*, vol. ii, p. 16):—

> "Ein Wetter kündete uns Anwarí voraus,
> Das Berge stürzen sollt' und Länder tilgen aus;
> Der Tag erschien, allein es blieb so still wie nie:
> Warum, weiss niemand sonst, als Gott—und Anwarí."

[2] Ibnu'l-Athír, who affords contemporary evidence, favours the later date, for he places the conjunction of the five (not seven) planets on the 29th of Jumáda II, A.H. 582 (= September 16, 1186), and alludes both to the predictions of the astrologers and their complete falsification.

A Preface (pp. i–vii);
An Introduction (pp. viii–xxiv);
Chapter i (pp. 1–30). Biography of Anwarí;
Chapter ii (pp. 31–78). Literary activity and characteristics of Anwarí;
Chapter iii (pp. 79–97). The commentaries on Anwarí's poems in general, and that of Abu'l-Ḥasan Faráhání in particular;
Chapter iv (pp. 98–102). The language of Anwarí and the Bibliography of his works;
Translations of *qaṣídas* (pp. 103–135);
Translations of *ghazals* (pp. 135–137);
A Table of the Muhammadan years mentioned in the course of the work, from A.H. 225 to A.H. 1273, with their Christian equivalents (pp. 138–141);
Alphabetical index of proper names (pp. 141–146).

The Persian texts at the end of the volume comprise:—

Selected *qaṣídas* (six in number), the first with full and the remainder with occasional commentary (pp. 2–72);
Selected *ghazals*, four in number (pp. 73–76);
Biography of Anwarí from the *Tadhkira*, or Memoirs, of Dawlatsháh (pp. 78–83);
Biography of Anwarí from the *Mirátu'l-Khayál* of Shír Khán Lúdí (pp. 83–85);
Biography of Anwarí from the *Átash-Kada* of Luṭf 'Alí Beg (pp. 85–88);
Biography of Anwarí from the *Haft Iqlím* of Amín Aḥmad-i-Rází (pp. 88–90).

Amongst the mass of interesting matter collected by Zhukovski, attention may be especially directed to his table (on p. 29) of the various dates assigned to Anwarí's death by different authorities, and his list of the very numerous Arabic and Persian works (over sixty in number) to which Abu'l-Hasan Faráhání refers in his Commentary (pp. 89–96). As regards the former, the date of Anwarí's death is given:—

In the *Átash-Kada* of Luṭf 'Alí Beg (composed in A.H. 1180 = A.D. 1766–77) as A.H. 545 (= A.D. 1150–51) in Zhukovski's text, but as

A.H. 656 (=A.D. 1258) or A.H. 659 (=A.D. 1261) in the Bombay lithographed edition of A.H. 1277 (=A.D. 1860–61);[1]

In the *Taqwímu'l-Tawáríkh* of Ḥájji Khalífa (composed in A.H. 1058=A.D. 1648) as A.H. 547 (=A.D. 1152–53);

In the *Tadhkira* of Dawlatsháh (p. 86 of my edition) as A.H. 547 (=A.D. 1152–53), but some MSS. give other dates, such as A.H. 548 and 556;

In the *Mirátu'l-Khayál* of Shír Khán-i-Lúdí (composed in A.H. 1102 =A.D. 1690–91) as A.H. 549 (=A.D. 1154–55);

In the *Haft Iqlím* of Amín Aḥmad-i-Rází (composed in A.H. 1002 =A.D. 1593–94) as A.H. 580 (=A.D. 1184–85);

In the *Mujmal* of Aḥmad b. Muḥammad b. Yaḥyá Faṣíḥ of Khwáf (composed in A.H. 845=A.D. 1441–42) as A.H. 585 (=A.D. 1189–90);

In the *Khulásatu'l-Ash'ár* of Taqí Khán of Káshán (composed, so far as this earlier portion is concerned, in A.H. 985=A.D. 1577–78) as A.H. 587 (=A.D. 1191);

In the *Mirátu'l-'Álam* of Muḥammad Bakhtáwar Khán (composed in A.H. 1078=A.D. 1667–68) as A.H. 592 (=A.D. 1196);

While, lastly, the date A.H. 597 (=A.D. 1200–1) is given by d'Herbelot and Stewart.

As will be seen, most of these works are comparatively modern, only two, the *Mujmal* and Dawlatsháh's *Tadhkira*, reaching back even as far as the ninth century of the *hijra* (latter half of the fifteenth of our era). Of the older works from which information might be expected, the *Chahár Maqála* makes no mention whatever of Anwarí, while the *Ta'ríkh-i-Guzída* of Ḥamdu'lláh Mustawfí (composed A.H. 730=A.D. 1330) and the *Lubábu'l-Albáb* of 'Awfí (early thirteenth century of our era), though they both consecrate articles to him, omit to mention the date of his death, as does the Arabic *Átháru'l-Bilád* of al-Qazwíní (ed. Wüstenfeld, p. 242, *s.v.* Kháwarán), which merely describes his poetry as "more subtle than water," and says that it is in Persian what that of Abu'l-'Atáhiya is in Arabic—a comparison which seems to me singularly inapt. At present, therefore, no data are

[1] Unfortunately, no trustworthy text of the *Átash-Kada* is available, so that little reliance can be placed on the dates given in the lithographed edition or in the generality of manuscripts, especially when they are not written out fully in words.

available for determining accurately when Anwarí was born or when he died, but, for the reasons given above, his death must have taken place subsequently to A.H. 581, and probably, as assumed by Zhukovski and Ethé, between A.H. 585 and 587 (= A.D. 1189–91).

Before proceeding to a fuller examination of Zhukovski's admirable work, allusion should be made to another monograph on Anwarí by M. Ferté, published in the *Journal Asiatique* for March-April, 1895 (series ix, vol. 5, pp. 235–268). This need not detain us, for it is quite uncritical; the author seems to have had no knowledge of Zhukovski's or Pertsch's work, and contents himself with translating a few of Anwarí's most celebrated poems and reproducing some of the best known, but probably in many cases apocryphal, anecdotes of the biographers.

Zhukovski begins his book with a brief Preface, in which he describes the materials which he had at his disposal, and explains the reasons which led him to select the six *qaṣídas* whereof the text is published at the end of the volume. The first of these, which is also the first in the Lucknow edition, begins:—

Báz ín chi juwání u jamál-ast jahán-rá?

and is chosen because it is at once one of the most celebrated and one of the most difficult and complex of Anwarí's *qaṣídas*, and because Abu'l-Ḥasan Faráhání's commentary on it, which Zhukovski prints with the text of the poem, is particularly full.

The second, beginning:—

Agar muḥawwil-i-ḥál-i-jaháníyán na Qaḍá'st,
Chirá majáriy-i-aḥwál bar khiláf-i-riḍá'st?

is chosen because, in Zhukovski's opinion, Nicolas, who translated it, has misunderstood it, and misrepresented Anwarí on the strength of it.

The third, already mentioned, which begins :—

Gar dil u dast baḥr u kán báshad,
Dil u dast-i-Khudáyagán báshad,

is chosen because it is generally considered to be alike the earliest and one of the most beautiful of Anwarí's *qaṣídas*.

The fourth, published by Kirkpatrick with an English translation, entitled "The Tears of Khurásán," in the first volume of the *Asiatic Miscellany*, p. 286 *et seqq.* (Calcutta, A.D. 1785), is chosen on account of its historic interest, its human feeling, and its celebrity. It begins :—

Bar Samarqand agar bug'zarí, ay bád-i-saḥar,
Náma-i-ahl-i-Khurásán bi-bar-i-Sulṭán bar.

The fifth, beginning :—

Ay birádar, bishnaw ín ramzí zi shi'r u shá'irí,

is interesting as containing Anwarí's confession as a poet.

The sixth and last, beginning :—

Ay Musulmánán, fighán az jawr-i-charkh-i-chanbarí!

is chosen as one of the last and finest of Anwarí's poems (his "swan-song," as Zhukovski terms it), and because of its biographical interest.

Of the *ghazals* only four are given, and Zhukovski has admittedly taken these more or less at random, considering that all of them are about equal in point of merit and interest.

The Preface is followed by an Introduction, dealing with the peculiar position of the professional poet in Persia, especially at this epoch, and emphasizing the necessity under which he laboured, if he wished to make money, of devoting his attention chiefly to political and panegyric verse, varied by satire, the natural counterpart of eulogy. Rhetoric in verse rather than true poetry was generally, as Zhukovski well says, the output of these Court-poets, who fulfilled to a certain extent the functions proper to the journalist in modern times, as well as the more intimate duties of the boon-companion and sycophant. The Court-poet frankly wanted and wrote for money. "If thou wilt give me a thousandth part of what Rúdagí obtained from the bounty of kings, I will produce poetry a thousand times as good," said Shaykh Abú Zarrá'a al-Ma'marí of Gurgán to his patron.[1] The poet was expected to show himself equal to every occasion, whether of joy or grief; to congratulate, as we have seen, the royal eye which first detected the new moon heralding the conclusion of the month of fasting, or to console for a fall from a restive horse, or a bad throw at backgammon, or even a defeat in the field of battle;[2] even to offer condolence to a friend afflicted with toothache.

Another curious point which Zhukovski brings out is that every poet of note had his *ráwí*, or rhapsodist, to whom he entrusted the task of declaiming the poetry which he had composed. Firdawsí mentions Abú Dulaf as his *ráwí*;[3] Abu'l-Faraj-i-Rúní says in a verse cited by Zhukovski: "My *ráwí* has recited in [your] audience-chamber the conquest of Merv and Níshápur"; while Mas'úd-i-Sa'd-i-Salmán, in a verse also cited by Zhukovski, bids his *ráwí*, Khwája Abu'l-Fatḥ, not to find fault with his verse, but remove by his heart-moving and wonderful voice such defects as mar its beauty. The obscurity of much of this high-flown, rhetorical, panegyric verse is such that copious commentary is needed to render it intelligible, and without this aid one is compelled

[1] See p. 10 of my edition of 'Awfí's *Lubáb*, vol. ii.

[2] See the quatrain addressed to Sulṭán Sanjar by Faríd-i-Kátib on the occasion of his defeat by the army of Qará-Khitá (*Ta'ríkh-i-Guzída*, ed. Jules Gantin, vol. i, pp. 260–263).

[3] See Nöldeke's *Iranisches Nationalepos*, p. 24 of the *tirage-à-part*.

to say, "the meaning of the verse is in the poet's belly" (*Ma'na 'sh-shi'r fí baṭni 'sh-shá'ir*).

Zhukovski ends his introduction by an endeavour to distinguish three periods of development in Persian poetry down to the earlier Seljúq period, namely, the epic which accompanied the revival of Persian national feeling under the Sámánids, and which culminated in Firdawsí; the venal panegyric, against which Náṣir-i-Khusraw and 'Umar Khayyám revolted; and the mystic verse to which the disappointed and disillusioned panegyrist (such as Saná'í, and, though too late for practical results, Anwarí also) so often turned at last.

The materials for Anwarí's biography are far less copious than we could wish, but from the eight biographical works enumerated on pp. 369–370 *supra*, in conjunction with what can be gleaned from the poet's own works, Zhukovski has put together in the first chapter of his book nearly as full a notice of his life as it is at present within our power to construct. Of Anwarí's birth and early life we know practically nothing. That he was, as his biographers assert, a diligent student, and well versed in most of the sciences of his age, is proved not only by the varied learning which he is so prone to display in his verse, but by his own explicit declaration in a rather celebrated fragment to which allusion has been already made, and which begins:—

Garchi dar bastam dar-i-madḥ u ghazal yakbáragí,
Ẓan ma-bar k'az nadhm-i-alfádh u ma'ání qáṣir-am.[1]

[1] This fragment, consisting of nineteen verses, will be found in its entirety on p. 307 of the Tabríz edition of A.H. 1266, and, with some difference in the arrangement of the verses, on pp. 704–5 of the Lucknow edition of A.H. 1297 (A.D. 1880). Six verses of it are given in the *Ta'ríkh-i-Guzída* (see my notice of the Biographies of Poets contained in that work published in the *J.R.A.S.* for October, 1900, and January, 1901, pp. 7–8 of the *tirage-à-part*), and at pp. 6–7 of Zhukovski's monograph. In another verse (p. 87, l. 3 of the Lucknow edition) Anwarí says: "In whatever accomplishment you examine me, you will think that therein lies my perfection."

In another fragment quoted by Zhukovski (p. 7), Anwarí similarly boasts of his more frivolous accomplishments, such as his skill in calligraphy, chess, and backgammon; his knowledge of verse, both his own and that of the older poets; and his powers of satire, wit, and invective; so that, as he remarks to his patron, "You need have no fear of being bored."

It is also clear that the biographers are right in their opinion that Anwarí, while little disposed to underrate his own merits as a poet, was not inclined to rate poetry very high. In a verse whereof the correct text (which materially differs in sense from the version contained in the lithographed editions at my disposal [1]) is, I think, that given by 'Awfí (*Lubáb*, vol. ii, p. 117 of my edition), Anwarí says:—

"*After all, I am like Saná'í, even though I be not like Ṣábir,*"

Saná'í being, as we have seen, admittedly a poet of the first class, and far more celebrated than Adíb Ṣábir, whom, however, since he sang Sanjar's praises and died in rendering him a service, Anwarí probably deemed it improper to belittle. In the same poem he says:—

"*Talent is, indeed, a disgrace in our time, else this verse*
Declares that I am not [merely] a poet, but a magician!"

Again he says in another place (p. 694 of the Lucknow edition of 1880):—

"*I have a soul ardent as fire and a tongue fluent as water,*
A mind sharpened by intelligence, and verse devoid of flaw.
Alas! There is no patron worthy of my eulogies!
Alas! There is no sweetheart worthy of my odes!"

He likewise declares (p. 688) that his poetry goes all over

[1] The rendering of this other version is: "*After all I am not like Saná'í nor like Ṣábir.*"

the world, like carrier pigeons, and (p. 34, l. 5) that his style is, by common consent, the best amongst all contemporary work.

On the other hand, speaking of the art of poetry he says (p. 730) :—

> "*O Anwari, dost thou know what poetry and covetousness are?*
> *The former is the child and the latter the nurse!* . . .
> *Like the cock thou hast a crest of Science;*
> *Why dost thou lay eggs like a hen?*"

And he concludes by bidding himself no longer "fling the filth of poetry to the winds." Another interesting fragment, which bears out, so far as it goes, the account given by the biographers of the motives which induced Anwarí to abandon learning for poetry, begins at the bottom of p. 629 of the Lucknow edition. He says :—

> "*Since my consideration may be increased by panegyric and ode,*
> *Why should I consume my soul in the fire of thought?*
> *I have thrown away twenty years in 'perhaps' and 'it may be';*
> *God hath not given me the life of Noah!*
> *Henceforth I will rein in my natural disposition,*
> *If I see the door of acceptance and success open before me;*
> *And if they vouchsafe me no gift, I will, after essaying praise,*
> *Destroy with words of satire the head of such a patron!*"

"Begging," says Anwarí in another place (bottom of p. 41), "is the Law of the poets"; and he is ready enough with threats of satire—and that, generally, of the coarsest kind—when begging avails not. Yet he is keenly alive to the hatefulness of a courtier's life, while recognising, with anger and resentment against his time, that thus only, and not by the scholar's life which he would fain lead, can wealth be obtained. Thus he says (p. 711, ll. 2–4) :—

> "*It is not fitting, in order to conform to the courtier's code,*
> *Again to impose vexation on my heart and soul;*

To wag my tongue in prose or verse,
And bring forth virgin fancies from my mind,
For the whole business of courtiers comes to this—
To receive blows and give abuse."

As to the spitefulness of Fortune towards men of learning, he says (p. 39, l. 6) :—

"*How can any one realise that this blue-coloured hump-back* [*i.e., the sky*]
Is so passionately fond of annoying men of learning?"

And so poor Anwarí, scholar by taste and poet by profession, is torn asunder between this and that, neither content to share the scholar's poverty, nor able to reconcile himself to the hollow insincerity of the courtier's life; keenly sensitive to the rebuffs to which his vocation exposes him, holding his way of life in bitter contempt, longing to follow in the steps of Avicenna, yet living the life of Abú Nuwás. In spite of his dictum that a poet ought not to write verses after he has reached the age of fifty (p. 725, l. 1), he himself practised the art of poetry for at least forty years; since two of his poems (pp. 636 and 651) mention A.H. 540 (= A.D. 1145–46) as the date of the current year, while he continued to write verses after his astrological fiasco, which, as we have seen, took place in or about the year A.H. 581 (= A.D. 1185–86). Yet at the end of his life, after he had, without fault on his part, as it would appear, incurred the resentment of the people of Balkh, he appears to have forsworn courts and the service of kings and nobles, and to have returned to the quiet, secluded, scholarly life which he loved. To this some of his poems bear evidence, notably the fragment printed, with English rendering, at pp. 8–10 of the *tirage-à-part* of the Biographies of Persian Poets which I translated from the *Ta'ríkh-i-Guzída* in the *J.R.A.S.* for 1900–1. Herein he speaks enthusiastically of the peace and quiet which he enjoys in his humble cottage, where dry bread with some simple relish is his fare, and the ink-bottle and the pen take the place of the wine-cup and the rebeck. In the same sense he says in another place (Lucknow edition of 1880, p. 733, ll. 15–16) :—

> "*O Lord, give me, in exchange for that luxury which was of yore,*
> *The contentment of Truth and an innocent livelihood,*
> *Security, health, and acceptable devotion,*
> *A loaf of bread, a ragged cloak, and to sit apart in some corner.*"

Although Sayyid Nuru'lláh Shushtarí, the author of that great biography of eminent Shí'ites entitled the *Majálisu'l-Mú'minín*, or "Assemblies of True Believers," written about A.D. 1586, reckons Anwarí amongst the poets who belonged to the Shí'a sect, the following eulogies of 'Umar on pp. 53, 74, and 720 of the Lucknow edition of his poems, if genuine, would seem to prove conclusively that this was not the case, apart from the fact that a Court-poet of the Seljúqs, who were fanatical Sunnís, could hardly profess in public the heterodox doctrine. In the first of the verses referred to Anwarí speaks of "*the chosen one of the Church of Islám, the chief of God's religion 'Umar,*[1] *who inherits the justice and firmness of* [the Caliph] *'Umar.*" In the second he says that "*the Holy Law was made manifest by 'Umar*"; while in the third he says :—

> "*Through Muḥammad and 'Umar paganism was annulled and religion strengthened;*
> *Thy days naturally restored those days to life again.*"

Nor, at least while he remained a Court-poet, was Anwarí inclined to observe at all strictly the Muḥammadan prohibition of wine. "Dost thou know any way," he says (p. 688, ll. 4–5 of the Lucknow edition), "in which I can excuse my having got drunk and been sick?" And in another fragment (*op cit.*, p. 698, ll. 12–14), he says :—

[1] *I.e.*, Ṣafiyyu'd-Dín 'Umar, the Muftí of Balkh.

"O noble sir, thou knowest that, being afflicted with the gout,
I, thy servant, abstain from everything which is sour.
I asked for wine, and thou didst give me stale vinegar,
Such that, should I drink it, I should rise up at the Resurrection like pickled meat.
Where is thy butler, then, so that I may pour
A cupful of it into the ears and nose of the scoundrel?"

These are the main facts which I have been able to glean from a cursory perusal of Anwarí's collected poems, but there is no doubt that the careful examination of a text more correct than any which we yet possess would supply us with further details of his life and fuller data for judging of his character. Let us now return to the anecdotes related by the biographers, which, though not worthy of much credence, ought not to be passed over without notice.

One of the most celebrated of these, taken from the *Ḥabíbu's-Siyar* (vol. ii, part 4, pp. 103–104 of the Bombay edition of A.D. 1857) gives another account of Anwarí's first appearance at the Court of Sanjar. According to this story, Mu'izzí, the Poet-Laureate, to whom was entrusted the duty of interviewing poets who desired to submit their verses to the King, and of keeping back all those whose merit was not sufficient to entitle them to an audience, had devised an infamous trick to discourage and turn away all applicants of whose talents he was jealous. His memory was so good that he could remember and repeat any poem which he had heard recited once; his son could repeat any poem which he had heard twice, and his servant any poem which he had heard three times. So when any poet desiring audience of the King came before him and recited his poem, he would hear it to the end, and then say, "That is my own poem, and in proof of what I say, hear me recite it." Then, when he had repeated it, he would turn to his son and remark, "My son also knows it"; whereupon the son would also repeat it. Then in like manner he would cause his servant to repeat it, after which he would drive the unfortunate poet from his presence as an unprincipled plagiarist.

For a long while aspirants to poetical honours were in despair of outwitting Mu'izzí's stratagem, until at length Anwarí resolved to see what he could do. Dressing himself in absurd and grotesque apparel, he presented himself before Mu'izzí, and recited certain ludicrous and doggerel verses which aroused the ridicule of all who heard them. Mu'izzí, apprehending no danger from one whom he took for a buffoon, promised to present Anwarí to the King on the following day. When the time came, Anwarí, being called forward, appeared in a dignified and appropriate dress, and, instead of the expected doggerel, recited the first two couplets of the poem :—

Gar dil u dast baḥr u kán báshad,
Dil u dast-i-Khudáyagán báshad.

Then, turning to Mu'izzí, he said, "If you have heard this poem before, then recite the remainder ; if not, admit that it is my own original composition." Mu'izzí was confounded, and was compelled to witness his rival's complete triumph.

As a matter of fact the poem in question itself affords evidence that its author had already for some considerable time been engaged in verse-making, for in it he says :—

Khusrawá, banda-rá chu dah sál-ast
Kash hamí árzúy-i-án báshad,
K'az nadímán-i-majlis ar na-buwad
Az muqímán-i-ástán báshad .

"O Prince, since it is ten years that thy servant
Is possessed by this desire,
That if he may not be one of the intimates of thine assembly,
He may [at least] be one of those who stand at thy threshold . . ."

Be this as it may, Anwarí's own words suffice to prove that he was held in high honour by the King. Thus he says in one place :—

Anwari-rá Khudáyagán-i-jahán
Písh-i-khud khwánd, u dast dád, u nishánd ;
Báda farmúd, u shi'r khwást azú . . .

"The Lord of the world called Anwarí
Before him, gave him his hand, and caused him to be seated;
Called for wine, and asked him for poetry . . ."

Another incident recorded concerning Anwarí in the *Haft Iqlím*, and, in a somewhat different form, in the *Bahāristán*, the *Mujmal* of Faṣíḥ, and the *Lubábu'l-Albáb* of 'Awfí (vol. ii, pp. 138–9) is connected with a warning which he received from a contemporary poet, Khálid b. ar-Rabí', when he was invited by the Ghúrí King 'Alá'u'd-Dín to visit his court. Outwardly this invitation boded no evil; but inwardly the King of Ghúr was filled with rancour against Anwarí, and sought to punish or destroy him, on account of certain satirical verses which he had, or was alleged to have, composed about him. Fakhru'd-Dín Khálid, knowing the true state of the case, wished to warn his friend, but feared to do so openly, lest he himself should incur the wrath of 'Alá'u'd-Dín. He therefore wrote him a letter to which he prefixed three Arabic verses, of which the translation is as follows:—

"Behold the World full-throated cries to thee,
'Beware, beware of my ferocity!
Let not my smiles protracted lull thy fears;
My words cause laughter, but mine actions tears!'
The World to garbage stuffed with musk indeed
I best may liken, or to poisoned mead!"[1]

Anwarí, who was quick enough to take this hint of danger, refused to go, whereupon 'Alá'u'd-Dín sent another messenger, offering Malik Ṭútí, his host for the time being, a thousand sheep in exchange for the poet, who, however, succeeded in prevailing upon his patron not to surrender him to his foe. According to some biographers he also excused himself to the King of Ghúr in the poem beginning:—

[1] In the account given by Zhukovski, the offensive verse is represented as a quatrain, and so is the warning (*op. cit.*, pp. 16–17).

Kulba'ı k'andarán bi-rúz u bı-shab
Jáy-i-árám u khurd u-khwáb-i-man-ast . . .[1]

which, in any case, evidently belongs to the latter part of his life, when he had abandoned the frequenting of Courts.

Anwarí is generally said to have passed the closing days of his life at Balkh, whither he retired after the loss of prestige which he suffered in consequence of the failure of the astrological prediction[2] already mentioned in A.H. 581 (= A.D. 1185–86). Here also misfortune pursued him, for there appeared a satire on the people of Balkh entitled the *Khar-náma*, or "Book of Asses," of which, though it was really from the pen of Súzaní, Anwarí was falsely supposed to be the author. According to other accounts, the offending poem[3] was a fragment of five verses characterising the four chief cities of Khurásán (Balkh, Merv, Níshápúr, and Herát), composed by Futúḥí at the instigation of Súzaní and deliberately ascribed by him to Anwarí, in which Balkh is described as a town "filled with rogues and libertines," and destitute of a single man of sense. In any case Anwarí was roughly handled by the people of Balkh, who, furious at what they considered an unprovoked outrage, paraded him through their streets with a woman's headdress on his head, and would have gone further had they not been dissuaded and pacified by some of the poet's influential friends, such as Sayyid Abú Ṭálib, Ḥamídu'd-Dín the judge, Ṣafi'u'd-Dín 'Umar the *Muftí*, Táju'd-Dín Aḥmad the *Muḥtasib* (or inspector of weights and measures), and Nidhámu'd-Dín Aḥmad the professor, to whom the poet bewails his adventure and offers his thanks in a *qaṣída*

[1] See pp. 593–4 of the 1880 Lucknow lithographed edition, and also the *Biographies of Poets . . . in . . . the Ta'ríkh-i-Guzída*, pp. 8–10 of the separate reprint of my article in the *J.R.A.S.* for October, 1900.

[2] Some of Anwarí's defenders have striven to justify his warning by making it refer not to physical but to political storms, for it was about this time that Chingíz Khán succeeded in establishing his power over the Mongols.

[3] The text is given at p. 27 of Zhukovski's book.

(No. 6 of Zhukovski, pp. 58–72 of the texts) of a hundred verses, beginning :—

> *Ay Musulmánán, fighán az jawr-i-charkh-i-chanbarí,*
> *Wa'z nifáq-i-Tír, u qaṣd-i-Máh, u kayd-i-Mushtarí!*

This *qaṣída*, I may remark, is the original of the piece called "*Palinodia*" which occupies pp. 63–80 of the late Professor E. H. Palmer's *Song of the Reed* (Trübner, 1877); a rendering so free that it can at most be described as a paraphrase, of which the first two verses, corresponding to the first three *bayts* of the original, are as follows :—

> "Ah! the spheres are incessantly rolling,
> And the Archer is shifting his ground,
> And the moon is for ever patrolling,
> And Jupiter going his round.
> The water that tastes to another
> Refreshing and cool on the lip,
> Is as fire that no efforts can smother
> In the cup which I sip.
>
> "The dust that all quiet is lying
> When others recline on the ground,
> Around me in volumes is flying,
> Like a desert where whirlwinds abound;
> And Fate, in the ship of my being,
> In happiness hurries me past,
> But if ever from sorrow I'm fleeing,
> It anchors me fast."

Here, for comparison, is a literal translation of the original three *bayts* which the above stanzas represent :—

> "O Muslims, alas for the tyranny of hoop-like heaven,
> And the treachery of Mercury, the ill-intent of the Moon, and the guile of Jupiter!
> The action of the beneficent water on my palate is fire,
> The state of the quiet earth in my abode is tempestuous!
> With the boat of my life heaven ever deals in [one of] two ways,
> Urging it onward in time of gladness, anchoring it in time of grief."

Perhaps the most celebrated of all Anwarí's poems, at any rate in Europe, is that first translated into English verse by Captain William Kirkpatrick, under the title of "The Tears of Khorassan," in vol. i of the *Asiatick Miscellany*, published at Calcutta in A.D. 1785, pp. 286–310; and again by Professor E. H. Palmer in his *Song of the Reed*, pp. 55–62.

"This poem," says Kirkpatrick, "is one of the most beautiful in the Persian language. The sentiments are throughout natural, and not unfrequently sublime; the images are for the most part striking and just; the diction is at once nervous and elegant, animated and chaste; and the versification, although not everywhere equally smooth and flowing, seems, notwithstanding, to be happily adapted to the subject, the measure being, as I believe, the most slow and solemn that is used in Persian poetry."

It has also a considerable historical interest, as giving a graphic description of the deplorable ravages wrought in what was previously one of the most flourishing parts of Persia by the barbarous Turcoman tribe of the Ghuzz, about the end of the year A.H. 548 (beginning of A.D. 1154). This tribe, whose pasture-grounds lay round about Khatlán, a dependency of Balkh, paid a yearly tribute of 24,000 sheep to the kitchen of King Sanjar. The harshness and greed of his steward (*khwánsálár*) having led to disputes and bloodshed, Qumáj, the Governor of Balkh, wrote to Sanjar to complain of the growing power and insolence of the Ghuzz, and asking to be appointed commissioner (*shaḥna*) over them, promising speedily to reduce them to obedience, and to raise their tribute to 30,000 sheep. Qumáj, however, failed to make good his promise, for he was defeated by them and driven out of their territories, and his son 'Alá'u'd-Dín was slain. Thereupon Sanjar was persuaded by his nobles to take the field in person, and to reject the apologies and indemnity of 100,000 *dínárs* and 1,000 Turkish slaves which the frightened Ghuzz now offered. When he drew near to their encampment they came out to meet him as suppliants, accompanied by their women and children, praying for forgiveness, and offering seven maunds of silver from each household. Again Sanjar was prevented by his *amírs*, Mu'ayyid, Yarunqush, and 'Umar-i-'Ajamí, from listening to their proposals; battle was joined, and the Ghuzz, now desperate, fought with such fury that they utterly routed Sanjar's army, took him prisoner, and brought him captive to Merv, his own capital, which they looted for three days, torturing the unfortunate inhabitants to make them disclose their hidden treasures. Thence, reinforced by thrice their number of disbanded soldiers and other rogues, they pushed on to Níshápúr, where, meeting with some resistance, in which several of their number were killed, they wrought so terrible a massacre in the Great Mosque that "the slain could not be seen for the blood wherein they lay." They also burned the Muṭarriz Mosque, a building capable of holding 2,000 persons, and by the light of the conflagration continued their ravages. They camped outside the city, visiting it daily to kill, torture, plunder, and destroy. Amongst the victims of their cruelty, who numbered several thousand persons, were many eminent and godly men, such as Shaykh Muḥammad Akkáf and Muḥammad b. Yaḥyá, of whom the latter was mourned by the poet Kháqání in at least three different poems.[1] So complete was the desolation of this once flourishing city that, says the author of the unique history of the Seljúqs entitled the *Ráḥatu'ṣ-ṣudúr*, Mu'izzí might have been thinking of it when he wrote:—

"Where once my charmer might be found in gardens fair with friends around,
The owls and vultures now abound, the foxes, wolves, and jackals stray:
Where stood the cups and bowls, the fleet wild-ass now tramples with its feet;
In place of flute and fruit so sweet now crows and ravens wing their way.

---

[1] See *J.R.A.S.* for 1902, p. 854; and the *Kulliyyát* of Kháqání (Lucknow lithographed edition of A.H. 1293), vol. i, pp. 587–590.

26

So utterly the dark-blue Sphere hath swept away those traces dear
That no explorer now, I fear, could guess where once I wooed my may."

Throughout all Khurásán, with the exception of Herát, which successfully held out against them, the Ghuzz acted in the same way and for two years Sanjar was a captive in their hands. Then at length he succeeded, by bribing some of the Ghuzz chiefs, in effecting his escape from Balkh to Merv, where he began to collect an army; but grief at the ruin and desolation of his domains brought on an illness which proved fatal to him in A.H. 552 (= A.D. 1157). He was buried in the Dawlat-Khána at Merv.

The "Tears of Khurásán" was written during Sanjar's captivity, probably about A.H. 550 (= A.D. 1155), and, according to Kirkpatrick, is addressed to Muḥammad b. Sulaymán, Prince of Samarqand, though this is not certain. It is, unfortunately, too long to quote in full, for it comprises seventy-three couplets, but I subjoin a few of the finest passages in the renderings of Kirkpatrick and Palmer. Here are the first three stanzas of the former, corresponding to the first fourteen lines of the latter and the first five couplets of the original:—

I.

"Waft, gentle gale, oh waft to Samarcand,
When next thou visitest that blissful land,
The plaint of Khorassania plunged in woe:
Bear to Turania's King our piteous scroll,
Whose opening breathes forth all the anguished soul,
And close denotes what all the tortur'd know.

II.

"Whose red-tinged folds rich patriot blood enclose,
The mortal fine impos'd by ruthless foes,
And misshap'd letters prove our trembling fears:
Whose every word reveals a pungent grief,
Whose every line implores a prompt relief,
While every page is moistened with our tears.

III.

"Soon as loud Fame our wretched fate shall sound,
The ear of Pity shall receive a wound,
And feel th'extreme of intellectual pain:
Soon as our dismal tale shall meet the view,
The melting orbs shall catch a purple hue,
And sanguine drops the mournful verse distain."

Here, for comparison, is the corresponding portion of Palmer's rendering:—

"O gentle Zephyr! if o'er Samarcand
Some dewy morning thou shouldst chance to blow,
Then waft this letter to our monarch's hand,
Wherein Khorassan tells her tale of woe;
Wherein the words that for the heading stand
Are present danger and destruction nigh;
Wherein the words that are inscribed below
Are grief, and wretchedness, and misery;
On every fold a martyr's blood appears,
From every letter breathes a mourner's sigh;
Its lines are blotted with the orphan's tears,
Its ink the widow's burning anguish dries!
Its bare recital wounds the listener's ears,
Its bare perusal scathes the reader's eyes."

Here, lastly, is the literal rendering of the original:—

"O morning breeze, if thou passest by Samarqand,
Bear to the Prince (*Kháqán*) the letter of the people of Khurásán;
A letter whose opening is grief of body and affliction of soul,
A letter whose close is sorrow of spirit and burning of heart,
A letter in whose lines the sighs of the miserable are manifest,
A letter in whose folds the blood of the martyrs is concealed,
The characters of its script dry as the bosoms of the oppressed,
The lines of its address moist from the eyes of the sorrowful;
Whereby the auditory channel is wounded at the time of hearing,
Whereby the pupil of the eye is turned to blood at the time of looking!"

One more series of parallel passages, arranged in the same order, may be taken before we bid farewell to this remarkable poem :—

XIII.

" Here upstart slaves, to fame and worth unknown,
Rear their proud crests, and in imperious tone,
  Command, whom distant nations still revere :
Here Avarice scoffs at virtue in distress,
And spurns whose bounty grateful thousands bless—
  Oh hard reverse ! and fate too, too severe !

XIV.

" View where sage elders, prostrate at the door
Of some low wretch, in vain relief implore ;
  In vain their anguish and their wrongs disclose :
Behold the sons of rank debauchery bind
Yon holy anchorite, by Heav'n resigned,
  A prey to dungeons and to sharpest woes !

XV.

" Is there, where Ruin reigns in dreadful state,
Whom Fortune smiles on, or whom joys await ?—
  'Tis yonder corpse descending to the tomb :
Is there a spotless female to be found,
Where deeds of diabolic lust abound ?—
  'Tis yonder infant issuing from the womb !

XVI.

" The mosque no more admits the pious race ;
Constrain'd, they yield to beasts the holy place,
  A stable now, where dome nor porch is found :
Nor can the savage foe proclaim his reign,
For Khorassania's criers all are slain,
  And all her pulpits levelled with the ground !

Palmer's translation of this passage runs as follows :—

"Good men to bad men are compelled to stoop
  The noble are subjected to the vile,
The priest is pressed to fill the drunkard's stoup.
  No man therein is ever seen to smile,

Save at the blow that brings release—and doom
  No maiden lives whom they do not defile,
Except the maid within her mother's womb!
  In every town the mosque and house of prayer—
To give their horses and their cattle room—
  Is left all roofless, desolate, and bare.
'Prayer for our Tartar rulers' there is none
  In all Khorassan, it is true—for where,
Where are the preachers and the pulpits gone?"

Here, lastly, is the literal translation :—

"O'er the great ones of the age the small are lords,
O'er the nobles of the world the mean are chiefs;
At the doors of the ignoble the well-born stand sad and bewildered,
In the hands of libertines the virtuous are captive and constrained.
Thou seest no man glad save at the door of Death,
Thou seest no girl a maiden save in her mother's womb.
The chief mosque of each city for their beasts
Is a resting-place, whereof neither roof nor door is visible.
Nowhere [it is true] do they read the *khuṭba* in the name of the Ghuzz,
For in all Khurásán there is neither preacher nor pulpit."

We now pass to the second chapter of Zhukovski's book, in which he treats of the literary activity and characteristics of Anwarí. As regards the models whom he imitated, the following Arabic and Persian poets and men of letters are mentioned in different passages of his poems: al-Akhṭal, Jarír, A'shá, Ḥassán [b. Thábit], al-Buḥturí, Abu'l-Firás, Badí'u'z-Zamán al-Hamadhání, al-Ḥarírí, 'Unṣurí, Firdawsí, Farrukhí, Abu'l-Faraj, Amír Mu'izzí, Saná'í, Adíb Ṣábir, Rashídí, Ḥamídu'd-Dín, Rashídu'd-Dín Waṭwáṭ, Shujá'í and Kamálu'd-Dín Isma'íl; a list which, as Zhukovski observes, shows that he was equally familiar with the old classical poets and with his contemporaries. Amongst the latter he was, as we have already seen, on very friendly terms with Ḥamídu'd-

Dín, the author of the *Maqámát*, with whom he exchanged letters in verse. Of these some graceful specimens are given by Zhukovski (pp. 34–37), including the well-known verse :—

"This grasshopper's foot to the Court of Sulaymán
It shames me to send, and I ask for his pardon;
I fear to imagine the scorn of the basils
For this thorn of acanthus I send to their garden."

Amongst the poets he seems, according to the *Ta'ríkh-i-Guzída* and the *Haft Iqlím*, to have especially admired and imitated Abu'l-Faraj-i-Rúní, who was a native of Lahore and the panegyrist of the Kings of Ghazna, and whose death took place not earlier than A.H. 492 (= A.D. 1099). The princes, rulers, and men of note most frequently mentioned by Anwarí include Sulṭán Sanjar, Abu'l-Fatḥ Ṭáhir b. Fakhru'l-Mulk, the grandson of the Nidhámu'l-Mulk, Sulṭán Ṭughril-tigín, 'Imádu'd-Dín Fírúzsháh, the Governor of Balkh, *Khwája-i-jahán* Majdu'd-Dín Abu'l-Ḥasan 'Imrání, Sayyid Abú Ṭálib, and the above-mentioned Ḥamídu'd-Dín. Zhukovski concludes this chapter with a discussion of Anwarí's different styles, as exemplified in the *qaṣída*, the *ghazal*, the quatrain, the satire, and the fragment; a selection of his verses illustrating the contempt which he felt for the art of poetry; and the metrical criticisms composed by Majdu'd-Dín Hamgar, Imámí[1] and another poet in reply to a question propounded to them as to the respective merits of Anwarí and Dhahír of Fáryáb, whereof it need only be said that all agree in preferring the former to the latter.

The third chapter of Zhukovski's book discusses the difficulty of Anwarí's verse and the aids for its comprehension, especially two commentaries thereon by Muḥammad b. Dá'úd-

[1] The texts of these two poems, with English translations, are given on pp. 60–64 of the *tirage-à-part* of my *Biographies of the Persian Poets from the Ta'ríkh-i-Guzída*. Majdu'd-Dín gives the date of his poem as Rajab, A.H. 674 (= January, A.D. 1276).

i-'Alawí of Shádábád (who also commentated Kháqání's poems), and Abu'l-Ḥasan Faráhání, who flourished in the latter part of the seventeenth century. Of the latter, who used oral as well as written sources (whereof sixty-eight different works are enumerated), Zhukovski expresses a very high opinion.

The fourth and last chapter, which deals with Anwarí's style and language, and with the various European contributions to our knowledge of his work, does not appear to me to need any special remark.

It is now time for us to leave Anwarí, and turn to the consideration of Kháqání, a poet notorious for the difficulty and obscurity of his verse, which, like that of Anwarí, chiefly consists of *qaṣídas*, though he has one long *mathnawí* poem, the *Tuḥfatu'l-'Iráqayn*, or "Gift of the two 'Iráqs," which describes his pilgrimage to Mecca, and supplies us with a good deal of material for his biography. Here again we have an excellent monograph to guide us, the *Mémoire sur Khâcâni, poëte persan du XII*^e^ *siècle*, published both in the *Journal Asiatique* and as a separate reprint (the form in which alone I here cite it) in 1864–65 by Monsieur N. de Khanikof, who truly observes that this poet, "one of the most brilliant figures of the Persian Parnassus," has transmitted to us an exact portrait of several intimate scenes of the life of his epoch.

Kháqání.

From a verse in his celebrated ode to Iṣfahán, it appears that Afḍalu'd-Dín Ibráhím b. 'Alí of Shirwán, originally known as Ḥaqá'iqí but later as Kháqání, was born in A.H. 500 (= A.D. 1106–7), at Ganja, the modern Elizavetpol.[1] His father 'Alí was a carpenter, and his mother a Nestorian Christian converted to Islám (*Tuḥfa*, p. 199, l. 6), who appears to have been a cook by profession. His grandfather, as he informs us

[1] So says Khanikof, but Kháqání's own statement in the *Tuḥfatu'l-'Iráqayn* (lithographed edition of A.D. 1877), p. 35, would seem to imply that he was born at Shirwán.

(*Tuḥfa*, p. 189, l. 9) with his usual frank prolixity, was a weaver, while his paternal uncle, Mírzá Káfí b. 'Uthmán, to whom he chiefly owed his education, was a medical practitioner. At an early age he was left, whether by the desertion or the death of his father, entirely to the care of his uncle, who for seven years acted "both as nurse and tutor," and taught him, beyond the rudiments of learning, Arabic, Medicine, Astronomy, and Metaphysics, but not, as we learn, without tears, for his relative, though actuated by the most kindly motives, was, after the fashion of his time and country, little disposed to spoil the child by sparing the rod. When Kháqání was twenty-five years of age his uncle died, being then only in his fortieth year, and thereupon the poet's general education came to an end.

Abu'l-'Alá of Ganja.

His skill in the art of verse-making, however, he owed to another tutor, to wit, the old poet Abu'l-'Alá of Ganja, one of the Court-poets of Minúchihr Shirwánsháh, to whom in due course he presented his brilliant pupil, who received permission to change his pen-name from Ḥaqá'iqí to the more royal style and title of Kháqání. He also gave Kháqání his daughter in marriage, a mark of favour which caused some annoyance to another of his pupils, the young poet Falakí of Shirwán, who was, however, finally pacified by a gift of 20,000 *dirhams*, "the price," as Abu'l-'Alá remarked, "of fifty Turkish handmaidens infinitely more beautiful than" Kháqání's bride. Shortly after this, however, Abu'l-'Alá, being annoyed, apparently, at certain signs of growing arrogance on Kháqání's part, addressed to him the following insulting verse :—

> "My dear Kháqání, skilful though you be
> In verse, one little hint I give you free:
> Mock not with satire any older poet;
> Perhaps he is your sire, though you don't know it!"[1]

[1] Khanikof very appositely compares the following verse of Heine's in the *Tambour-major* :—

Kháqání, furious, demanded explanations and apologies, whereupon Abu'l-'Alá renewed his attack in the following lines[1] :—

"O Afḍalu'd-Dín, if the truth I should tell thee,
By thy soul, with thy conduct I'm terribly pained;
They called thee in Shirwán 'the son of the joiner,'
The name of Kháqání through me hast thou gained.
Much good have I wrought thee, I trained thee and taught thee,
Enriched thee, and gave thee my daughter to wife:
Why wilt thou neglect me, and fail to respect me,
Who called thee my Master, my son, and my Life?
How often this slander wilt lay to my credit—
Black slander, of which I no memory keep?
What matter if I or another one said it?
What matter if thou wert awake or asleep?"

To this Kháqání replied with a satire of inconceivable coarseness, for which Khanikof, who publishes it with a translation (pp. 16–22), offers an apology, reminding his readers that "it is a cry of anger uttered by a Persian of the twelfth century, an epoch at which, even in Europe, language was not always remarkably chaste." Not content with accusing his former friend and master of the vilest crimes, Kháqání does not hesitate to bring against him a charge incomparably more dangerous than any suspicion of moral delinquency, declaring roundly that he is a follower of Ḥasan-i-Ṣabbáḥ and a confederate of the Assassins of Alamút. Khanikof is of opinion that this satire was composed, for reasons into which he fully enters, between A.H. 532 and 540 (A.D. 1138–46), and that it was about this time that

"Du solltest mit Pietät, mich däucht,
Behandeln solche Leute;
Der Alte ist dein Vater, vielleicht,
Von mütterlicher Seite."

[1] See Khanikof, p. 15; Dawlatsháh, pp. 70–71 of my edition; and a very different version in my *Biographies of Persian Poets from the Ta'ríkh-i-Guzída*, pp. 21–22.

Kháqání left his native town and betook himself to the Court of the then reigning Shirwánsháh, Akhtisán b. Minúchihr, who had transferred his capital from Garshásp, in Ádharbayján, to Bákú. At the Court, however, things did not go altogether well with him, for Shirwánsháh appears to have been exacting, suspicious, and hard to please. That he was very ready to take offence is shown by the following well-known anecdote.[1] Kháqání had on one occasion addressed to him this verse :—

Washaqí dih ki dar bar-am girad,
Yá wisháqí ki dar bar-ash giram.

"Give me a mantle to embrace me,
Or a fair young slave whom I may embrace."

The Kháqán thereupon ordered the poet to be put to death ; but he, divining the cause of his master's anger, took a fly, cut off its wings, and sent it to the offended prince, saying, "This is the real criminal ; I wrote *bá* ('with'), not *yá* ('or'), but this fly alighted on the single dot of the *b* while the ink was still wet and converted it into the two-dotted *y*." "Such," adds Dawlatsháh admiringly, "was the magnanimity of the nobles of that time, and such the wit of its poets and men of letters ; but now if a poet should ask for two hundred-weight of turnips from his patron men would see nothing despicable therein, but would rather be thankful that he should give so little trouble !"

At length Kháqání succeeded in obtaining permission to undertake the pilgrimage to Mecca, which he had already performed as a youth (presumably with his uncle) thirty years before, and we have poems describing his departure from Shirwán, his passage of the Safíd Rúd, and his view of the snow-clad mountain of Sabálán. At this time, as Khanikof shows, he seems to have entertained the idea of visiting

[1] Dawlatsháh, p. 80 of my edition.

Khurásán, attracted, no doubt, by what he had heard of Sanjar's liberality towards poets, but there is no evidence that he ever succeeded in carrying out this plan. On this subject he has several *qaṣídas*, one of which (*Kulliyyát*, vol. i, pp. 440–443) begins :—

Chi sabab súy-i-Khurásán shudan-am na-g'zárand?
'Andalíb-am, bi-gulistán shudan-am na-g'zárand?

"For what reason will they not suffer me to go to Khurásán?
I am a nightingale, yet they will not suffer me to visit the rose-garden." [1]

Another (*loc. cit.*, pp. 443–445) begins :—

Bi-Khurásán shawam, in sha'a'lláh;
Az rah ásán shawam, in sha'a'lláh.

"I will go to Khurásán, if God will;
I will go easily by the road, if God will."

A third (*loc. cit.*, pp. 526–535) begins :—

Rah rawam, maqṣad-i-imkán bi-Khurásán yábam,
Tishna-am, mashrab-i-iḥsán bi-Khurásán yábam.

"I will go my way, I will find the goal of this world in Khurásán;
I am thirsty, I will find the source of benefits in Khurásán."

Kháqání seems, however, to have got as far eastwards as Ray, where he appears for some reason to have been forbidden to proceed further, for he says in a poem entirely addressed to that city (*loc. cit.*, pp. 940–941) :—

Chún nist rukhṣa súy-i-Khurásán shudan mará
Ham báz-pas shawam; na-kasham man balá-yi-Ray.
Gar báz raftan-am súy-i-Tabríz ijázat ast,
Shukrána gúyam az karam-i-pádishá-yi-Ray.

---

[1] See p. 30 of Khanikof's *Mémoire*, where a very corrupt text has resulted in a very incorrect translation.

"Since I have not permission to proceed to Khurásán
I will even turn back; I will not endure the affliction of Ray.
If leave be granted me to go back to Tabríz,
I will give thanks for the favour of the King of Ray."

He seems to have imagined that in Khurásán he would meet with greater appreciation, for he says in a verse from the *qaṣída* cited above :—

Chún zi man ahl-i-Khurásán hama 'anqá bínand,
Man Sulaymán-i-jahán-bán bi-Khurásán yábam.

"Since the people of Khurásán see in me a complete phœnix (*'anqá*),
I may find in Khurásán the Solomon who rules the world."

The last reference is evidently to Sanjar, who is, indeed, explicitly mentioned a little further on; and this poem was evidently written before the disastrous invasion of the Ghuzz (A.D. 1154), one of the victims of which, as already mentioned, was the learned and pious doctor Muḥammad b. Yaḥyá, with whom Kháqání corresponded during his life,[1] and whom he mourned in several fine verses after his violent and cruel death.[2] That he was also in relation with the Court of Khwárazm is proved by several panegyrics addressed to Khwárazmsháh, and a laudatory poem (*loc. cit.*, pp. 469–472) on his laureate Rashídu'd-Dín Waṭwáṭ, who had sent Kháqání some complimentary verses. But after the death of Sanjar and the desolation wrought by the Ghuzz it is unlikely that Kháqání any longer cherished the desire of visiting Khurásán.

Of Kháqání's second pilgrimage, as already remarked, we possess a singularly full account in the rather prosaic *Tuḥfatu'l-'Iráqayn*, of which a lithographed edition was published in

[1] At pp. 1532–1536 of the Lucknow edition of the *Kulliyyát* will be found, amongst Kháqání's Arabic compositions, a prose epistle and a poem addressed to this great doctor.

[2] See the *Kulliyyát*, pp. 587, 877, and 878.

Lucknow in A.H. 1294. This poem is divided into five *maqálas*, or discourses, of which the first consists chiefly of doxologies, the second is for the most part autobiographical, the third describes Hamadán, 'Iráq, and Baghdád, the fourth Mecca, and the fifth and last al-Madína. Khanikof has given (pp. 37–41) some account of the contents (including a list of the persons mentioned), which, therefore, I will not further describe. Besides the *Tuḥfat*, several of Kháqání's finest *qaṣídas* were inspired by this journey, including one, justly admired, which begins (*Kulliyyát*, pp. 319–321) :—

Sar-ḥadd-i-bádiya 'st: rawán básh bar sar-ash;
Tiryák-i-rúḥ kun zi sumúm-i-mu'aṭṭar-ash!

"Here are the confines of the Desert: advance upon it;
And draw from its fragrant breeze healing for the spirit!"

It was on his return from the pilgrimage that Kháqání visited Iṣfahán, where a mischance befell him very similar to that which befell Anwarí at Balkh. He was at first well received, but a satirical verse on the people of Iṣfahán, composed by his pupil, Mujíru'd-Dín of Baylaqán, somewhat injured his popularity, and called forth from the Iṣfahání poet, Jamálu'd-Dín 'Abdu'r-Razzáq, a most abusive reply.[1] In order to exculpate himself from his pupil's indiscretion and restore the Iṣfahánís to good humour, Kháqání composed a long and celebrated *qaṣída* in praise of that city, in the course of which he says, after describing the tributes of praise which he had already paid it :—

"All this I did without hope of recompense, not for greed,
Nor hoping to receive crown or gold from the bounty of Iṣfahán.
That stone-smitten (*rajím*[2]) devil who stole my eloquence

[1] For these verses see pp. 41–42 of Khanikof's *Mémoire*.

[2] For the text and translation of this *qaṣída*, see Khanikof, pp. 93–108, and for these verses the bottom of p. 97 and top of p. 98. *Rajím*, a common epithet of the devil, is an anagram of *Mujír*, to whom allusion is here made.

Rebelled against me if he dared to satirize Iṣfahán.
He will not rise with a white face in the Resurrection,
Because he strove to blacken the neck of Iṣfahán.
Why do the people of Iṣfahán speak ill of me?
What fault have I committed in respect to Iṣfahán?"

This poem, as internal evidence proves, was composed after A.H. 551 (A.D. 1156–57), probably, as Khanikof conjectures, in the following year.

On his return to Shirwán shortly after this, Kháqání, whether on account of his greatly increased self-esteem (a quality in which he was at no time deficient), or because he was accused by his detractors of seeking another patron, incurred the displeasure of Akhtisán Shirwánsháh, and was by him imprisoned in the fortress of Shábirán, where he wrote his celebrated *ḥabsiyya*, or "prison-poem," given by Khanikof at pp. 113–128 of his *Mèmoire*. As to the length of his imprisonment and his subsequent adventures until his death at Tabríz in A.H. 582 (= A.D. 1185)[1] we have but scanty information, but we learn from his poems that he survived his patron Akhtisán, and that he lost his wife and one of his sons named Rashíd, a child not ten years of age. Concerning the elegy in which he bewailed the loss of his wife, Khanikof speaks (p. 49) as follows:—

"Of all Kháqání's poems this is, in my opinion, perhaps the only one wherein he appears as one likes to imagine him, that is to say, as a good and sensible man. Grief causes him to forget his erudition; his verse does not glitter with expressions hard to interpret or grammatical artifices, but goes straight to the heart of the reader, and interests him in a domestic misfortune from which seven centuries separate us."

Kháqání was buried in the "Poets' Corner" at Surkháb,

[1] This date is given both in 'Awfí's *Lubábu'l-Albáb* and the *Ta'ríkh-i-Guzída*, and also by Dawlatsháh. For other dates, ranging up to A.H. 595 (= A.D. 1198–99), see Khanikof's *Mémoire*, p. 55. Khanikof observes that as Akhtisán was alive in A.H. 583, and as Kháqání survived him, the later dates are preferable.

near Tabríz, between Dhahíru'd-Dín Faryábí and Sháhfúr-i-Ashharí, and in 1855 Khanikof was informed by two old men of Tabríz that they remembered his tomb as still standing before the great earthquake which laid most of the monuments of this cemetery in ruins. Excavations which he instituted in the following year failed, however, to produce any sign of it. Amongst the men of letters with whom Kháqání corresponded, besides those already mentioned, were the philosopher Afḍalu'd-Dín of Sáwa and the poet Athíru'd-Dín of Akhsíkat. Other poets whom he mentions, generally in order to boast his superiority over them, are Mu'izzí (p. 702), al-Jáḥidh (*Ibid.*, but the lithographed text absurdly reads Ḥáfidh, and reiterates this gross anachronism in a marginal note thoroughly characteristic of Indian criticism), Abú Rashíd and 'Abdak of Shirwán (p. 703), Qaṭrán of Tabríz (p. 759), Saná'í of Ghazna (p. 795), 'Unṣurí and Rúdagí (p. 799).

Like Anwarí, Kháqání is essentially a *qaṣída*-writer, and it is on this form of verse that his reputation rests, though he also has a complete *Díwán* of odes, a large number of quatrains, and the *mathnawí* already mentioned, viz., the *Tuḥfatu'l-'Iráqayn*, besides some poems in Arabic. His style is generally obscure, extremely artificial, and even pedantic. The comparison instituted by von Hammer between him and Pindar is fully discussed and criticised by Khanikof at pp. 61–64 of his *Mémoire*. Kháqání's poems are voluminous, filling 1,582 large pages in the Lucknow lithographed edition. In one very curious *qaṣída* published by Khanikof (*Mémoire*, pp. 71–80; *Kulliyyát*, pp. 271–278) he makes display of all his knowledge of the Christian religion and ritual, and even proposes (though he afterwards asks God's forgiveness for the proposal) to enter the service of the Byzantine Emperor, embrace the Christian faith, and even, should the Qayṣar (Cæsar) so please, "revive the creed of Zoroaster."

Let us now turn to Nidhámí of Ganja, the third great poet

of this period, the acknowledged master of romantic *mathnawí*, whose influence and popularity in Turkey as well as in Persia remain, even to the present day, unsurpassed in his own line. On him also we have a very careful and scholarly monograph by Dr. Wilhelm Bacher, published at Leipzig in 1871, and entitled *Niẓâmî's Leben und Werke und der zweite Theil des Niẓâmîschen Alexanderbuches, mit persischen Texten als Anhang*, on which I shall draw largely in this portion of my work. In this monograph Bacher has followed the only safe method of constructing trustworthy biographies of the Persian poets, that is to say, he has ignored the utterly uncritical statements of Dawlatsháh and other biographers,[1] and has drawn his information almost exclusively from the best of all sources, the poet's own incidental allusions to his life. Thus the dates of Nidhámí's death given by the biographers vary from A.H. 576 (= A.D. 1180–81) by Dawlatsháh (p. 131 of my edition) to A.H. 596–99 (= A.D. 1199–1203) by Ḥájji Khalífa, but Bacher conclusively proves that the latest of these dates is the correct one, and further establishes the following important chronological data in the poet's life. He was born at Ganja (now Elizavetpol) in A.H. 535 (A.D. 1140–41); wrote the first of his five great *mathnawí*-poems (known collectively as the *Khamsa*, or "Quintet," or as the *Panj Ganj*, or "Five Treasures"), to wit, the *Makhzanu'l-Asrár* ("Treasury of Mysteries"), about A.H. 561 (A.D. 1165–66); wrote the second, the Romance of *Khusraw and Shírín*, in A.H. 571 (A.D. 1175–76); wrote the third, the Romance of *Laylá and Majnún*, in A.H. 584 (A.D. 1188–89); wrote the fourth, the Romance of *Alexander the Great*, in A.H. 587 (A.D. 1191); wrote the fifth and last, the *Haft Paykar*, or

Nidhámí of Ganja.

[1] 'Awfí, who was contemporary with Nidhámí and might easily have given us some trustworthy information about him, as usual confines himself in his notice of this poet (vol. ii, pp. 396–97) to a few stupid and tasteless word-plays.

"Seven Effigies," in A.H. 595 (A.D. 1198–99); and died at the age of sixty-three years and a half in A.H. 599 (A.D. 1202–3).

Nidhámí's proper name, as Bacher shows (p. 9), was probably Ilyás (Elias), while his *kunya* was Abú Muḥammad, and his *laqab*, or title (from which his pen-name was derived), was Nidhámu'd-Dín. His father, Yúsuf the son of Zakí Mu'ayyad, died when he was still young, and his mother, who was of a noble Kurdish family, seems not long to have survived her husband. He also alludes to the death of an uncle on the mother's side, who, as Bacher conjectures, very probably took care of him after his father's death. A brother of his named Qiwámí-i-Muṭarrizí (of whose poems a fine old fourteenth-century manuscript, Or. 6464, has been acquired by the British Museum) also achieved considerable reputation as a poet, and is the author of the *qaṣída* illustrating all the artifices of Persian rhetoric which was given in chapter i. It also appears from various passages in his works that Nidhámí was thrice married, and that he had at least one son named Muḥammad, who must have been born about A.H. 570 (A.D. 1174–75), since he was fourteen years of age when the *Laylá and Majnún* was written. Dawlatsháh (p. 129 of my edition) says that Nidhámí was a disciple of the Shaykh Akhú Faraj of Zanján, whose name Bacher gives as Akhú Farrukh Rayḥání.

Of Nidhámí's life, beyond the above facts, we know very little, but it is clear, as Bacher points out (pp. 14–15), that he had a far higher conception of the poet's aims and duty than the countless panegyrists and Court-poets of whom Anwarí is the type, and that, as tradition and internal evidence both show, he eschewed panegyric and avoided Courts, though he so far adhered to the prevailing fashion of his time as to dedicate his poems to contemporary rulers. Thus the *Makhzanu'l-Asrár* is dedicated to Íldigiz the Atábek of Ádharbayján; *Khusraw and Shírín* to his two sons and successors, Muhammad and Qizil Arslán,[1] as well as to the last Seljúq ruler in Persia, Ṭughril b. Arslán; *Laylá and Majnún* to Akhtisán Minúchihr, King of Shirwán, whom we have already met with as the patron of Kháqání; the *Sikandar-náma* to 'Izzu'd-Dín Mas'úd I, the Atábek of Mawṣil (Mosoul), and afterwards the revised edition of it to Nuṣratu'd-Dín Abú Bakr Bísh-kín, who succeeded his uncle Qizil Arslán as Atábek of Ádharbayján in A.H. 587 (A.D. 1191); and the *Haft Paykar* to the same Nuṣratu'd-Dín.

Dawlatsháh says (p. 129 of my edition) that, besides the above-named five poems which constitute the *Khamsa* or "Quintet," Nidhámí's odes and lyrical verses amounted to nearly 20,000 verses, and Bacher (p. 7) cites a verse from the *Laylá and Majnún* which he considers a proof that the poet arranged his *Díwán* about the same time that he wrote this poem, viz., in A.H. 584 (A.D. 1188–89). 'Awfí, on the other hand (vol. ii, p. 397), says:—"Save for these *mathnawí*-poems little poetry has been handed down from him. In Níshápúr, however, I heard the following recited as his by a certain great scholar"; and he then cites three short *ghazals*, each comprising five *bayts*, of which the last bewails the death of his son. Dawlatsháh (pp. 129–130) cites another of eight *bayts*, in the last of which the pen-name Nidhámí is introduced, but it must be remembered that there were several other poets of this name, whom this very inaccurate biographer is quite capable of confusing with the subject of the present notice. If such a *Díwán* ever existed in reality, it appears long ago to have been lost and forgotten.

Nidhámí's high rank as a poet alike original, fruitful, and of rare and noble genius, is admitted by all critics, Persian and non-Persian, including 'Awfí, Qazwíní, Dawlatsháh, and Luṭf 'Alí Beg amongst biographers, and Sa'dí, Ḥáfidh, Jámí

[1] From Qizil Arslán he received as a substantial reward for his labours the village of Ḥamdúniyán. See my edition of Dawlatsháh, p. 129, ll. 12–15, and Bacher, *op. cit.*, p. 27 and p. 11 of the texts.

and 'Iṣmat amongst the poets.[1] And if his genius has few rivals amongst the poets of Persia, his character has even fewer. He was genuinely pious, yet singularly devoid of fanaticism and intolerance; self-respecting and independent, yet gentle and unostentatious; a loving father and husband; and a rigorous abstainer from the wine[2] which, in spite of its unlawfulness, served too many of the poets (especially the mystical poets) of Persia as a source of spurious inspiration. In a word, he may justly be described as combining lofty genius and blameless character in a degree unequalled by any other Persian poet whose life has been the subject of careful and critical study.

A few words must now be said about each of the five poems constituting the *Khamsa* or "Quintet," though it is impossible in a work of the size and scope of the present to give them anything approaching adequate notice. There are several Eastern editions, of which I use the Ṭihrán lithograph of A.H. 1301 (A.D. 1884), a volume of about 600 pages, containing about 50 *bayts* to the page.

The *Makhzanu'l-Asrár*, or "Treasury of Mysteries," is both the shortest and the earliest of the Quintet, and is of quite a different character to the others, being rather a mystical poem with illustrative anecdotes, after the fashion of the *Ḥadíqa* of Saná'í, or the later *Mathnawí* of Jalálu'd-Dín Rúmí, than a romance. It also appears to me inferior in quality, but perhaps this is partly due to the fact that I dislike its metre, which runs:—

The *Makhzanu 'l-Asrár.*

| — ⏑ ⏑ — | — ⏑ ⏑ — | — ⏑ — |
| — ⏑ ⏑ — | — ⏑ ⏑ — | — ⏑ — |

It comprises, besides a good deal of introductory matter and several doxologies, twenty *maqálas*, or "Discourses," each of

[1] See Bacher, *op. cit.*, pp. 57–58.

[2] See his explicit declaration in the *Sikandar-náma* (Bacher, *op. cit.*, p. 38), where he swears solemnly that during his whole life wine has never defiled his lips.

which deals with some theological or ethical topic, which is first discussed in the abstract and then illustrated by an apologue. The following short specimen, which embodies the well-known story of how the wise and courageous Minister of one of the Sásánian Kings rebuked his master for his injustice and neglect of his people's welfare, may suffice to give some idea of the style of this poem (p. 22):—

"Intent on sport, Núshirwán on a day
Suffered his horse to bear him far away
From his retainers. Only his *Wazír*
Rode with him, and no other soul was near.
Crossing the game-stocked plain, he halts and scans
A village ruined as his foeman's plans.
There, close together, sat two owls apart,
Whose dreary hootings chilled the monarch's heart.
'What secrets do these whisper?' asked the King,
Of his *Wazír*; 'what means the song they sing?'
'O Liege,' the Minister replied, 'I pray
Forgive me for repeating what they say.
Not for the sake of song mate calls to mate:
A question of betrothal they debate.
That bird her daughter gave to this, and now
Asks him a proper portion to allow,
Saying: "This ruined village give to me,
And also others like it two or three."
"Let be," the other cries; "our rulers leave
Injustice to pursue, and do not grieve,
For if our worthy monarch should but live,
A hundred thousand ruined homes I'll give."'"

Khusraw and Shírín.

In the romance of *Khusraw and Shírín*, Nidhámí, both as regards matter and style, follows Firdawsí rather than Saná'í; but though the subject of his poem—namely, the adventures of the Sásánian King Khusraw Parwíz, and especially his amours with the beautiful Shírín and the fate of his unhappy rival Farhád—is drawn from the sources used by Firdawsí, or from similar ones, it is handled in a different and much less objective manner, so as to result not in an epic but in a romantic poem. And the heroic *mutaqárib* metre, consecrated by long usage to the epic, is here replaced by the hexameter *hazaj* :—

| ⏑ – – – | ⏑ – – – | ⏑ – – |
| ⏑ – – – | ⏑ – – – | ⏑ – – |

The poem is a long one (pp. 48–192 of the Ṭihrán lithograph), containing about 7,000 couplets. The following passage (p. 129) describes the lamentation and death of Farhád when, at Khusraw's command, false tidings are brought to him of Shírín's death at the time when he has all but completed the task imposed on him of cutting through the mountain of Bísutún,[1] for the accomplishment of which Shírín's hand was to be his recompense.

"When Farhád heard this message, with a groan
From the rock-gulley fell he like a stone.
So deep a sigh he heaved that thou wouldst say
A spear had cleft unto his heart its way.
'Alas, my labour!'—thus his bitter cry—
'My guerdon still unwon, in grief I die!
Alas the wasted labour of my youth!
Alas the hope which vain hath proved in truth!
I tunnelled mountain-walls: behold my prize!
My labour's wasted: here the hardship lies!
I, like a fool, red rubies coveted;
Lo, worthless pebbles fill my hands instead!
What fire is this that thus doth me consume?
What flood is this which hurls me to my doom?
The world is void of sun and moon for me:
My garden lacks its box- and willow-tree.
For the last time my beacon-light hath shone;
Not Shírín, but the sun from me is gone!
The cruel sphere pities no much-tried wight;
On no poor luckless wretch doth grace alight!
Alas for such a sun and such a moon,
Which black eclipse hath swallowed all too soon!
Before the wolf may pass a hundred sheep,
But on the poor man's lamb 'tis sure to leap.

[1] The old Bagastâna or Behistûn, near Kirmánsháh, so famous for its Achæmenian remains and inscriptions.

O'er my sad heart the fowls and fishes weep;
For my life's stream doth into darkness creep.
Why am I parted from my mistress dear?
Now Shírín's gone, why should I tarry here?
Without her face should I desire to thrive
'Twould serve me right if I were boned alive! . . .
Felled to the dust, my cypress quick lies dead:
Shall I remain to cast dust on my head?
My smiling rose is fallen from the tree:
The garden is a prison now to me.
My bird of spring is from the meadow flown,
I, like the thunder-cloud, will weep and groan.
My world-enkindling lamp is quenched for aye:
Shall not my day be turned to night to-day?
My lamp is out, and chilly strikes the gale:
My moon is darkened and my sun is pale.
Beyond Death's portals Shírín shall I greet,
So with one leap I hasten Death to meet!
Thus to the world his mournful tale he cried,
For Shírín kissed the ground, and kissing died."[1]

Laylá and Majnún.

The romance of *Laylá and Majnún*, which forms the third poem of the Quintet, has been since Nidhámí's time one of the most popular, if not the most popular, of all love-stories in the East, not only in Persia but in Turkey, where Fuḍúlí of Baghdád gave the sad tale of the Distraught Lover and the Night-black Beauty a fresh impulse towards the West of Asia.[2] In Arabic also there is current a Díwán of love-poems, many of them of extreme beauty, ascribed to "the possessed" (*Majnún*) Qays al-'Ámirí,[3] "an almost mythical personage," as Brockelmann says, "who is supposed to have died about A.H. 70 (A.D. 689)." In this poem the scene is laid not in Persia but in Arabia, and the hero and heroine are no longer royal personages but simple

[1] Compare the parallel passage from Sheykhí's Turkish version of the romance in vol. i of Gibb's *History of Ottoman Poetry*, pp. 334–5, and for an analysis of the poem pp. 310 *et seqq.*

[2] An account of this Turkish version of the romance, with specimens, will be found in Gibb's work above mentioned, vol. iii, pp. 85 and 100–104.

[3] See Brockelmann's *Geschichte der arabischen Litteratur*, vol. i, p. 48.

Arabs of the desert. The colouring, however, as was to be expected, is almost entirely Persian. The metre chosen by Nidhámí for this poem runs thus :—

— — ⏑ | ⏑ — ⏑ — | ⏑ — — || — — ⏑ | ⏑ — ⏑ — | ⏑ — — |

The poem occupies pp. 194–278 of the Ṭihrán edition, and probably comprises rather more than 4,000 verses. The following passage describes how Zayd in a dream sees Laylá and Majnún in the Gardens of Paradise, and might serve to prove, were proof needed, how false is the European superstition which pretends that the Muhammadans deny immortality to women, or lightly esteem a pure and faithful love.

"Now when once more the Night's ambrosial dusk
Upon the skirts of Day had poured its musk,[1]
In sleep an angel caused him to behold
The heavenly gardens' radiancy untold,
Whose wide expanse, shadowed by lofty trees,
Was cheerful as the heart fulfilled of ease.
Each flow'ret in itself a garden seemed;
Each rosy petal like a lantern gleamed.
Each glade reflects, like some sky-scanning eye,
A heavenly mansion from the azure sky.
Like brightest emeralds its grasses grow,
While its effulgence doth no limit know.
Goblet in hand, each blossom of the dale
Drinks to the music of the nightingale.
Celestial harps melodious songs upraise,
While cooing ring-doves utter hymns of praise.
Beneath the roses, which like sunsets gleam,
A couch was set beside a rippling stream.
With fair brocades and fine this couch was spread,
Lustrous and bright as heaven's azure bed.
Thereon were seated, now at last at rest,
The immortal angels of these lovers blessed,
From head to foot adorned with robes of light,
Like houris fair in heaven's mansions bright.

[1] Musk is used metaphorically for what is black and fragrant, such as the hair of the beloved, or the sweet darkness of night.

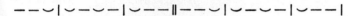

Amidst eternal spring their souls they cheer
With heav'nly wine, and commune mouth to ear.
Now from the goblet ruby wine they sip;
Now interchange their kisses, lip to lip;
Now hidden mysteries of love unfold;
And now in close embrace each other hold.[1]

* * * * *

'Two virgin jewels these, who long did lie
Sealed in a casket of pure constancy.
No joy was theirs within that world of pain,
Nor ever there did they their hopes attain.
Here never shall they suffer grief again,
But as thou seest them shall e'er remain.
Who in that world hath suffered pain and grief,
Thus in this world shall find at last relief.
Who in that world was sorrowful and sad,
His in this world shall be a portion glad.'"

The Haft Paykar.

The *Haft Paykar* or *Bahrám-náma*, though in reality, as we have seen, the last of Nidhámí's poems, comes next in the Ṭihrán edition, in which it occupies pp. 280–394, and comprises rather more than 5,000 verses. It is written in the following metre:—

| — ◡ — — | ◡ — ◡ — | ◡ ◡ — |
| — ◡ — — | ◡ — ◡ — | ◡ ◡ — |

and, like *Khusraw and Shírín*, deals with the legendary history of one of the Sásánian Kings, namely Bahrám Gúr. Many of the episodes related of this monarch, so famous for his knightly deeds and his skill in the chase, have a historical basis, or at least repose on a genuine and ancient tradition, being chronicled by Ṭabarí (whom Nidhámí explicitly names as one of his sources; see Bacher, p. 54); and the title *Bahrám-náma* ("Bahrám-book") better describes the nature and scope of the poem than that of *Haft Paykar* ("Seven Portraits" or "Effigies"), which refers only to one, though the chief,

[1] Zayd in his vision sees an old man of venerable and holy aspect standing by the lovers, and, enquiring of him who they are, receives an answer of which the following passage forms the conclusion.

topic of the romance. The Seven Portraits in question, discovered by Bahrám one day in a secret chamber in his castle of Khawarnaq, represented seven princesses of incomparable beauty, these being respectively the daughters of the Rájá of India, the Kháqán of China, the Sháh of Khwárazm, the King of the Slavs, the Sháh of Persia, the Emperor of Byzantium, and the King of the West, or "Sunset-land." Bahrám falls in love with these portraits, and, succeeding almost immediately afterwards to the throne vacated by the death of his father Yazdigird, he demands and obtains these seven princesses in marriage from their respective fathers. Each one, representing one of the Seven Climes into which the habitable world is divided, is lodged in a separate palace symbolically coloured, and Bahrám visits each of them on seven successive days, beginning on Saturday with the Black Palace assigned to the Princess of India, and ending on Friday with the White Palace in which the Princess of the Seventh Clime is housed. Each of the seven princesses entertains him in turn with stories, somewhat after the scheme of the *Arabian Nights*, and the romance concludes with the story of the unjust Minister, to whose ill deeds Bahrám's attention was directed by the incident of the shepherd and his unfaithful sheep-dog,[1] and is brought to a close with the death of Bahrám.

An interesting episode, illustrating the proverb that "practice makes perfect," occurs in this romance. Bahrám Gúr, it is said, had a favourite handmaiden named Fitna ("Mischief") whom he used to take with him on his hunting expeditions, where she would beguile him, during the intervals of repose, with the strains of the harp, in which she was skilled. One day the King had displayed his prowess in the chase and in archery to the utmost, expecting to win from his favourite some expression of admiration and wonder; but—

[1] This story is given in full in the Nidhámu'l-Mulk's *Siyásat-náma.* See pp. 19–27 of Schefer's edition of the text.

"The maiden, prompted by mere wantonness,
Refused her admiration to express.
The King was patient, till a wild ass broke
Forth from its lair, then thus to her he spoke:
'My skill, O Tartar maid, thy narrow eyes[1]
Behold not, or beholding do despise.
My skill, which knoweth neither bound nor end,
Entereth not thy narrow eyes, O friend!
Behold this beast, and bid my skill impale
What spot thou wilt between its head and tail.'
'Wouldst thou,' said she, 'thy skill to me make clear?
Then with one shaft transfix its hoof and ear.'
The King, when this hard test was offered him,
Prepared to gratify her fancy's whim;
Called for a cross-bow, and forthwith did lay
Within the groove thereof a ball of clay.
Straight to the quarry's ear the pellet shot,
Whereat the beast, to soothe the smarting spot,
And to remove the clay, its foot on high
Did raise, whereon the King at once let fly
An arrow like a lightning-flash, which sped
Straight to the hoof, and nailed it to the head.
Then to the maid of China said the King:
'Success is mine! What think you of this thing?'
'For long,' said she, 'the King this art hath wrought,
In tricks long practised to succeed is naught!
What man hath studied long, he does with ease,
And solves the hardest problems, if he please.
That thus my lord the quarry's hoof should hit
Proves not so much his courage as his wit.'"

The King, infuriated at his favourite's impertinence, handed her over to one of his officers to be put to death; but she by her entreaties, and assurances that her royal lover would repent of his hasty action, induced him to spare her life and to conceal her in his hunting-lodge in the country. In this lodge was a staircase of sixty steps, and she, determined to prove the

[1] There is a double meaning in this epithet, which, besides the literal meaning which it bears as descriptive of the eyes of the beauties of Chinese Tartary, whom the Persian poets never weary of praising, signifies "grudging," "stingy," and "slow to recognise merit."

truth of her assertion that "practice makes perfect," obtained a newly-born calf, and every day carried it on her shoulders up and down these stairs, her strength increasing with its growth. After some time her host, the officer, entertained King Bahrám in this country-house, and Fitna, veiling her face, seized the opportunity of displaying her accomplishment to her former lover, who, filled with admiration at this athletic feat, demanded to see her face, and recognised with joy and forgiveness his sweetheart whom he had supposed to be dead.

The *Iskandar-náma*.

The fifth poem, the *Iskandar-náma* or "Alexander-book," is written in the heroic *mutaqárib* metre proper to epic verse :—

| ⏑ – – | ⏑ – – | ⏑ – – | ⏑ – |
| ⏑ – – | ⏑ – – | ⏑ – – | ⏑ – |

and is divided into two distinct parts, of which the first is properly entitled the *Iqbál-náma*, or "Book of [Alexander's] Fortune," while the second is correctly named the *Khirad-náma*, or "Book of [Alexander's] Wisdom."[1] The former occupies pp. 396–530 and the latter pp. 532–601 of the Ṭihrán edition; together they cannot comprise much fewer than 10,000 verses, of which two-thirds belong to the first part and one-third to the second. Since there exists an English prose translation of the *Iqbál-náma* by Colonel Wilberforce Clarke, and since Dr. E. Wallis Budge has given a very full account of the Alexander Legend in several of the forms which it has assumed in the different literatures of the East, I think it unnecessary to further extend this already lengthy notice of Nidhámí's romantic Quintet.

[1] There is a good deal of confusion about the titles of these two parts, concerning which see Bacher, *op. cit.*, pp. 50–52. In Persian they are often called respectively the *Sharaf-náma* and the *Iqbál-náma*, while in India they are distinguished by the Arabic adverbs *barr*[an] ("on land") and *baḥr*[an] ("by sea"). One English translator has apparently committed the amazing blunder of supposing the first of these two adverbs to be the Hindustání word *baṛá*, and has accordingly translated the title as "The *Great* Book of Alexander"!

Far less known and read than the three poets already discussed in this chapter is D͟hahír (in full D͟hahíru'd-Dín Ṭáhir b. Muḥammad[1]) of Fáryáb, who owes such celebrity as he possesses chiefly to the well-known verse (by whom composed I know not)—

D͟hahíru'd-Dín Fáryábí.

Díwán-i-D͟hahír-i-Fáryábí
Dar Ka'ba bi-duzd, agar bi-yábí.

"Steal the Díwán of D͟hahír of Fáryáb, even if you find it in the Ka'ba."

We have already alluded to the versified judgements of Majdu'd-Dín Hamkar, Imámí and a third poet as to the respective merits of D͟hahír and Anwarí, and though all three decisions are in favour of the latter, the fact that the question could be raised at all clearly shows that, however little D͟hahír's poems are read now, they were once ranked very high. They have been lithographed at Lucknow by Nawal Kashor, but the only text at my disposal has been an undated but good manuscript (Oo. 6. 46) belonging to the University Library of Cambridge, comprising 160 folios, each containing (save for titles and empty spaces) twenty-two couplets, eleven on each side, or in all something over three thousand couplets, forming *qaṣídas*, fragments, *ghazals*, and quatrains.

'Awfí includes a somewhat lengthy notice of D͟hahír in vol. ii of his *Lubáb* (pp. 298–307), in which he rates this poet very high, even declaring that "his verse has a grace which no other verse possesses," and adds that, though born at Fáryáb, in the extreme north-east of Persia, he enjoyed the greatest fame in 'Iráq, where he was especially patronised by the Atábek Nuṣratu'd-Dín Abú Bakr b. Muḥammad "Jahán-Pahlawán" b. Íldigiz of Ádharbayján.

Dawlatsháh also devotes a lengthy article (pp. 109–114 of my edition) to D͟hahír, in which he says that the poet was

[1] So both the *Ta'ríkh-i-Guzída* and Dawlatsháh.

a pupil of Rashídí of Samarqand, that he left Khurásán for 'Iráq and Ádharbayján in the reign of the Atábek Qizil Arslán b. Íldigiz (A.D. 1185–91), having previously been in the service of Ṭughán, the ruler of Níshápúr, and that some critics consider his verse "fresher and more delicate" than that of Anwarí. He was also previously to this, as we learn from Ibn Isfandiyár's *History of Ṭabaristán* (pp. 71–3 of my translation), in the service of the Ispahbad of Mázandarán, Ḥusámu'd-Dawla Ardashír b. Ḥasan (murdered on April 1, A.D. 1210), and to the generosity of this ruler he makes regretful reference in the line:—

Sháyad ki ba'd-i-khidmat-i-dah sál dar 'Iráq
Nán-am hanúz Khusraw-i-Mázandarán dihad.

"Perhaps after ten years' service in 'Iráq
The Prince of Mázandarán may still provide me with bread." [1]

He also visited Iṣfahán, but, being displeased with his reception by the chief judge of that city, Ṣadru'd-Dín 'Abdu'l-Laṭíf of Khujand, he remained there only a short while. Mujíru'd-Dín of Baylaqán, whom we have already met with as the satirist of Iṣfahán and the object of Kháqání's anger, was one of his rivals, of whom he says, alluding to the fine clothes which he affected:—

"If by robes of rich brocades a man may claim to be the best,
Shall we count as man the lizard or the wolf in satin dressed?" [2]

Towards the end of his life Dhahír, like so many other panegyrists, renounced the life of Courts and retired into pious seclusion at Tabríz, where he died at the end of A.D. 1201,[3]

[1] Ibn Isfandiyár adds that when this verse was reported to the Ispahbad by some of his servants who were present when it was recited, he sent the poet a hundred *dínárs*, a horse, a jewelled collar, a cap, and a coat.

[2] Dawlatsháh, p. 114.

[3] The *Ta'ríkh-i-Guzída* and Dawlatsháh both give this date (A.H. 598), and the former adds the month (Rabí' I).

and, as we have seen, was buried in the cemetery of Surkháb by the side of Kháqání and Sháhfúr-i-Ashharí. His poems, however, show no trace of religious feeling, and are conspicuously worldly in their tone, so that, if indeed he repented at the end of his life, we must suppose that his renunciations included the practice of his art.

I have taken the trouble to read through the manuscript of his poems mentioned above, but the result is disappointing, the references to current events or dates being very few, and the verse nearly always of the same polished, graceful, rather insipid kind characteristic of Persian Court-poets, without the occasional outbursts of invective, satire, or deep feeling which redeem the poems of Anwarí and Kháqání. The *qaṣídas* and fragments, with a few *ghazals*, amount to 185, and these are followed by 97 quatrains. The *Díwán* also contains at least one panegyric on Qizil Arslán in *mathnawí* form, but no *mathnawís* proper.

The kings and princes to whom these poems are addressed (so far as they are indicated in the course of the poems, for there are no explanatory titles) are as follows:—

Patrons of Dhahír.

'Aḍudu'd-Dín Ṭughánsháh b. Mu'ayyad,[1] called "King of the East" (*Khusraw-i-Sharq* and *Malik-i-Sharq*), seven or eight poems; Ḥusámu'd-Dín Ardashír b. Ḥasan, King of Mázandarán,[2] three poems; Akhtisán Shirwánsháh (Kháqání's patron), one poem; Qizil Arslán b. Íldigiz, Atábek of Ádharbayján,[3] eleven poems, besides two further allusions to his death; Nuṣratu'd-Dín Abú Bakr Bíshkín b. Muḥammad b. Íldigiz, nephew and successor of Qizil Arslán, thirty-five poems; Ṭughril [b. Arslán], the last ruler of the House of Seljúq in Persia,[4] one poem. Other persons addressed are:—Bahá'u'd-Dín Abú Bakr *Sayyidu'r-Ru'asá*, four poems; Táju'd-Dín Ibráhím, two poems;

[1] He died, according to Ibnu'l-Athír, in A.H. 582 (= A.D. 1186–87).
[2] He died, on the same authority, in A.H. 603 (= A.D. 1206–7).
[3] He was assassinated at Qonya (Iconium) in A.H. 588 (= A.D. 1192).
[4] He was killed at Ray by Khwárazmsháh in April, A.D. 1194.

Majdu'd-Dín Muḥammad b. 'Alí Ash'ath, four poems; Sa'du'd-Dín, two poems; Raḍiyyu'd-Dín, two poems; Iamálu'd-Dín Ḥasan, three poems; Shamsu'd-Dín (*wazír*), five poems; Jalálu'd-Dín, Sharafsháh, 'Imádu'd-Dín (*wazír*), Muḥammad b. Fakhru'l-Mulk (*wazír*), Ṣafiyyu'd-Dín of Ardabíl, 'Izzu'd-Dín Yaḥya of Tabríz, and Niḏhámu'd-Dín (*wazír*), each one poem; and last, but not least, the celebrated Ṣadru'd-Dín Khujandí, one of the most powerful Sháfi'ite doctors of Iṣfahán, who was killed in A.H. 592 (A.D. 1196) by Falaku'd-Dín Sunqur, and to whom eight of these poems are addressed. Concerning Ḏhahír's relations with the Ṣadr of Khujand, whose proper name was 'Abdu'l-Laṭíf, Dawlatsháh (pp. 112-113 of my edition) writes as follows :—

"They say that Ḏhahír went for a tour from Níshápúr to Iṣfahán. At that juncture Ṣadru'd-Dín 'Abdu'l-Laṭíf of Khujand was the chief judge, and one of the most notable men of that country. One day Ḏhahír attended his audience, and observed that the places of honour were occupied by scholars and men of learning. He, having proffered his salutations, seated himself, like a humble stranger, in a [modest] place; but, not receiving such attention as he expected, he was vexed, and handed to the Ṣadr the following fragment of poetry which he had extemporised:—

> 'Riches, Your Eminence, are not so great
> That they with pride your heart should thus inflate.
> Virtue you have, and science: wherefore be
> So proud of adventitious luxury?
> Scholars of talent how can you despise?
> Your own distinction in your talents lies! . . .
> Hear now my counsel, though it hurt your pride,
> And strive to make it in your life a guide.
> Each for the wrongs which he has wrought one day
> Must give redress, and you must cast away
> That shield of self-complacency whereby
> You seek to safeguard your position high,
> Else of all sins for which you will be judged
> You most shall fear for kindly words begrudged!'¹

---

¹ The piece actually occurs in the manuscript I have used, and closely agrees with the text given by Dawlatsháh (p. 113).

"Thereafter, notwithstanding all the attention and civility which the Ṣadr showed him, he would not remain in Iṣfahán, but went to Ádharbayján, where he was generously patronised by the Atábek Mudhaffaru'd-Dín Muḥammad b. Íldigiz."

This story does not altogether agree with the fact that several poems are addressed to the Ṣadr, in one of which the poet speaks of having attended for *two years* at this "fortunate threshold," and begs his patron not to allow him, the possessor of "a thousand treasures of talent," to be in need of the patronage of "a parcel of low fellows." It seems much more probable that the poet, after remaining for two or three years at Iṣfahán, was disgusted at not receiving as much favour as he had expected from the Ṣadr, and therefore determined to seek his fortune in Ádharbayján.

Although we cannot fill in the details, the main outlines of Dhahír's life are clear enough. He began to write poetry while still resident in his native town of Fáryáb, which in one poem he speaks of as his "dwelling-place" (*maskan*). Thence he seems to have gone to Níshápúr, in praise of whose ruler, Ṭughánsháh, the son of Mu'ay-yadá of Ába, he has, as we have seen, several poems. As this prince died in A.D. 1186–87, those poems must have been composed before this date; and as, from one rather obscure line, it appears that the poet was already producing verse at the age of thirty, we may fairly suppose that he was at this period not much above or below this age, and may conjecture that his birth took place about A.D. 1156. As he reached Ádharbayján while Qizil Arslán was still alive, his visits to the Court of Ḥusámu'd-Dín Ardashír b. Ḥasan, King of Mázandarán, and to Iṣfahán would seem to have taken place between A.D. 1187 and 1191, in which year his chief patron, the Atábek Nuṣratu'd-Dín Abú Bakr, succeeded his uncle, Qizil Arslán. If his death really took place in A.D. 1201 (and I know of nothing against this date), we may suppose that for the greater part of the ten remaining years of his life he continued attached to the Court of Abú Bakr, and that his retirement at Tabríz included only the last year or two of his life.

Apart from the persons addressed (several of whom, unfortunately, I am unable to identify), we find here and there more explicit references to the poet's circumstances. Thus in one poem, written, probably, towards the end of his sojourn in Níshápúr, he says:—

Mará bi-muddat-i-shish sál ḥirṣ-i-'ilm u adab
Bi-khákdán-i-Nisbápúr kard zindání;
Bi-har hunar ki kasí nám burd dar 'álam
Chunán shudam ki na-dáram bi-'ahd-i-khud thání.

"For a period of six years desire for science and culture
Has kept me imprisoned in this dust-heap of Níshápúr;
In every accomplishment which any one has mentioned in the world
I have become such that I have no second in my time."

In the same poem I find an allusion which, in conjunction with another passage, inclines me to think that Dhahír was one of those who ridiculed poor Anwarí on account of his unfortunate astrological prediction for September, A.D. 1186, for he mentions:—

Risálatí ki zi inshá-i-khud firistádam
Bi-majlis-i-tu bi-ibṭál-i-ḥukm-i-ṭúfání—

"A tract of my own compilation which I sent
To thy Court, to disprove the predicted storm."

The other passage in which allusion is made to this "storm" contains, if I am not mistaken, a definite reference to Anwarí. It runs:—

An kas ki ḥukm kard bi-ṭúfán-i-bád guft
'Ásíb-i-án 'imárat-i-gítí kunad kharáb':
Tashríf yáft az tu, wa iqbál díd u jáh:
Dar band-i-án na-shud ki khaṭá guft yá ṣawáb.
Man banda chún bi-nukta'í ibṭál karda-am
Bá man chirá zi wajh-i-digar mí-rawad khiṭáb?

"That person who predicted the storm of wind said,
'The hurt thereof will destroy the prosperity of the world.'
He obtained from thee a robe of honour, and gained fortune and rank:
He cared nothing whether he spoke truly or falsely.
Since I, your servant, have falsified [his prediction] with one criticism,
Why am I addressed in a fashion so entirely different?"

Dhahír, then, was probably acquainted with Anwarí, or at least with his verse, and I am much mistaken if Dhahír's poem beginning:—

Ay Falak sar badán dar áwurda
Ki tu gú'í ki khák-i-páy-i-man-ast

be not a 'response' to, or parody of, Anwarí's—

Kulba'í k'andarán bi-rúz u bi-shab
Jáy-i-árám u khurd u khwáb-i-man-ast.

Apart from these indications, I can find no clear reference to any contemporary poet, unless the following be to Nidhámí, whose romance of *Khusraw and Shírín* (or Farhád and Shírín), was, as we have seen, completed in A.H. 571 (=A.D. 1175–76):—

Wa lík bikh-am azín dar 'Iráq thábit níst:
Khushá fasána-i-Shírín u qiṣṣa-i-Farhád!

"But on this account I am not firmly rooted in 'Iráq:
Lucky the story of Shírín and the tale of Farhád!"

And indeed it is likely enough that Dhahír was jealous of his two great contemporaries; for his poems display all the egotism, greed of gain, readiness to take offence and shameless opportunism which, with occasional outbursts of contempt for their own time-serving profession, are so characteristic of these panegyrists. His views in this respect singularly resemble those of Anwarí. To one much earlier poet, namely,

Pindár of Ray, who flourished in the eleventh century of our era, there is the following clear reference, which Dawlatsháh (p. 43, l. 4) both mutilates and misquotes:—

Shi'r-i-Pindár, ki guftí bi-ḥaqíqat waḥy-ast,
Án ḥaqíqat chu bi-bíní buwad az pindárí.
Dar nihán-khána-i-ṭab'am bi-tamáshá bingar,
Tá zi har záwiya'í 'arḍa diham dildárí!

"The verse of Pindár, which thou didst declare to be 'in truth inspired,'
That 'truth,' when thou lookest into it, arises from an illusion.
Glance for delectation through the secret gallery of my genius,
That out of its every corner I may reveal some new charmer!"[1]

Here again, though there is no question of rivalry, we observe the same note of disparagement towards the work of others.

Like most Court-poets in Persia, Dhahír was evidently addicted to wine, and, though apparently professing the Sunní doctrine, was probably entirely careless of religion. Thus in one of his quatrains he says that "it is better to be drunk in Hell than sober in Paradise," while in another (alluding to Alexander's journey, under the guidance of the mysterious immortal Saint Khiḍr, into the Land of Darkness in quest of the Water of Life) he declares himself "the slave of that Khiḍr who brought thee forth from the Darkness of the Grape." That he professed himself a Sunní appears clearly from the manner in which he speaks of the Caliphs 'Umar and 'Uthmán. Of the first he says:—

"How long wilt thou speak of the lily and its 'freedom'?[2]
Art thou then without knowledge of the service of the world's King,
Nuṣratu'd-Dín 'Bú Bakr, the wise and just ruler
Who hath adorned the whole world with the justice of 'Umar?"

[1] Compare pp. 158–159 *supra*.
[2] The epithet *ázád*, which means both "free" and "noble," is habitually applied by the Persian poets both to the lily and the cypress.

Of both he says, in another place:—

"The most great and kingly Atábek, whose justice
Is the restorer of God's Religion and the Prophet's Law,
'Bú Bakr by name, and like 'Uthmán in modesty and clemency,
Who, by virtue of his knowledge and justice, equals Fárúq (*i.e.*, 'Umar) and Ḥaydar (*i.e.* 'Alí)."

To no class, however, does the Arabic proverb *an-Násu 'alá díni Mulúkihim* ("Men follow the creed of their kings") apply more strongly than to Court-poets, and it would be a mistake to attach any great significance to these utterances, which at most show that Dhahír was not a convinced adherent of the Shí'a sect.

Our poet, as we have said, was an importunate beggar, and yet had sense enough to see how bad a use he was making of his talents. The following verses are typical samples of a large portion of his poetry. The first is from a long *qaṣída* addressed to the Ṣadr of Khujand.

"A whole world dances on the waves through thy bounty,
While my bark is thus heavily anchored.
Ask me not of the state in which I am to-day,
For should I tell it thou wouldst not believe.
Trouble lies in ambush round about me,
Poverty unmasks its hosts before me. . . .
Dost thou not desire that, for a little effort [on thy part],
I may spread thy praises through the world?
In [seeking] means of livelihood there cannot be
Love for Abú Bakr or friendship for 'Umar.[1]
There is no jeweller in 'Iráq, so it is natural
That they should not recognise the value of a jewel.
Oh, my heart is pure like a purse of silver,
While my face is sallow like a bag of gold.
I have no fortune beyond this, that I have become
The chief amongst the poets."

---

[1] This line suggests the idea that the poet had been accused before this orthodox doctor of Shí'ite tendencies, for which he seeks to excuse himself. Possibly it was this suspicion which finally drove him from Iṣfahán.

In another *qaṣída* addressed to Bahá'u'd-Dín Abú Bakr *Sayyidu'r-Ru'asá* he says :—

"I have not yet given tongue in thy praise,
Though thy generosity demands an apology from [even] a hundred *qaṣídas.*[1]
My mind has conceived a distaste for poetry,
For it impairs the status of a scholar.
My object is to praise you, else
Where is poetry and where is he![2]
I, whose soul in the arcana of the [Divine] Power
Occupies the station of '[*a bow-shot*] *or even less*,'[3]
How can I take pride in poetry, because
My name is on the roll of the poets?
Not that poetry is bad in itself;
My complaint is of the vileness of my colleagues!"[4]

Again he says in another poem :—

"My talent, indeed, yields me no means of livelihood,
Whether you suppose me at Hamadán or in Baghdád.
Such advantage as I have seen in the world from my scholarship
Was from the harshness of my father and the blows of my tutor.
My poetic talent is my least claim to distinction,
For at its hands I have suffered sundry injustices.
Before whomsoever I recite a line commemorating his praises,
He thenceforth, so far as he is able, remembers me not.
Of poetry the best kind is the ode (*ghazal*), and that, moreover,
Is not a stock-in-trade on which one can found expectations.
The edifice of my life is falling into ruin: how long

---

[1] *I.e.*, "I have not yet composed a single poem in your honour, but had I composed a hundred, an apology would still be due from me for so inadequate a return for your bounty."

[2] *I.e.*, "How far removed is he from poetry, and how far beyond the power of verse is the celebration of his virtues!"

[3] *I.e.*, the nearest point to God reached by the Prophet in his Ascension. See *Qur'án*, liii. 9.

[4] This verse is quoted by Dawlatsháh (p. 10 of my edition), but he erroneously ascribes it to Anwarí.

Shall I decorate the House of Passion with the colour and fragrance of the fair?
What doth it profit me what sweet-lipped loveling dwells in Kashmír?
What doth it avail me what silver-bosomed darling inhabits Nawshád?[1]
Content thee with this much, and say naught of the nature of panegyric,
For I cannot describe the heart-burnings to which it gives rise!
The finest flower which blossoms from it for me is this,
That I call myself a 'slave' and the cypress-tree 'free.'[2]
Now I entitle a fractious negro 'a Houri of Paradise,'
And now address as 'noble' some miserable drunkard!"

Surely no more cynical avowal was ever made by any one practising the trade—for such we must call it—of the panegyrist! And as a trade, indeed, does Dhahír regard his calling, for he says in another poem:—

"I am not a landowner nor a merchant, that I should have
Granaries full of corn, and purses full of silver and gold."

So he must even make money out of his poetry, and to that end must stoop to devices which he despises. He must take what he can get, and then find some pretext for demanding more, as, for instance, when, having received a gift of a fine robe and an ambling mule, he says:—

"I still hope for a saddle and bridle,
Else how can I tell that the mule is good for riding?"

If praise fails to produce money, satire may prove more efficacious; nay, with the rivals and enemies of the victim it may command a better price than panegyric, as the following lines show:—

---

[1] One of those cities, like Yaghmá, Farkhár. Khutan, and Chigil, celebrated for the beauty of their inhabitants.

[2] See p. 419 *supra*, n. 2 *ad calc.*

"O Sire, it is more than a year that I
Drink the wine of thy praises from the goblet of verse.
I have not seen from thee anything which I can mention:
I have not obtained from thee anything which I can put on.
If in any company they question me concerning thy bounty,
I am obliged to stop my ears with cotton.
Be not misled if, in consequence of my virtues,
I remain philosophical, good-tempered, and silent.
When I mount my Pegasus with intent to produce verse,
My colleagues are proud to carry my horse-cloths on their backs.
In praise, like all the rest, on occasions of complaint or thanksgiving,
I shine like the sun or rage like the sea.
If I should recite to a certain person a verse or two of satire on thee,
He would place in my embrace the treasures of the world.
Since, then, they are ready to buy satire of thee for red gold,
It is but right that I should sell at the best market-price."

Often the mere threat of satire seems to have been enough to loose the purse-strings of those who were least susceptible to flattery, for the actual number of satires in the collection is very small. The following, addressed to an ecclesiastic named Muḥiyyu'd-Dín, is of a mildness and delicacy very rare in this kind of poetry:—

"O learned prelate and Muftí of the age, Muḥiyyu'd-Dín,
By knight and castle dost thou excel all creatures![1]
Twice or thrice have I recited *qaṣídas* in thy praise,
But no effort of thine has loosed the knots of my condition.[2]
To-day some fellow stood up in front of thy pulpit,
Crying, 'I repent of my deeds!" Thou didst exclaim, 'Well done!'
Then thou didst demand for him money and clothes from the congregation,

[1] Or, taking the ordinary meaning of the words *asp* and *rukh*, instead of their special significance in the game of chess, "in horses and in face." The double meaning is necessarily lost in English.

[2] *I.e.*, "Thou hast made no effort to solve my difficulties."

Which they gave readily and willingly, without demur or difficulty.
Now since thou hast given me nothing for my verse, at least
Give me something for repenting of that art which thou hast inspired in me!"

It would be easy to multiply instances of the poet's demands for money and complaints of poverty and debt: "Creditors are stationed at my threshold," he says in one place, "as Fortune is stationed at yours." But the above specimens are sufficient, and fairly represent the tone and quality of the whole. Of erudition Dhahír, in spite of his boasts, shows far fewer signs than Anwarí and Kháqání, whose poems, as we have seen, teem with allusions to the most recondite sciences. It is perhaps worth noticing the following verse, which can hardly be regarded otherwise than as a quotation from the Gospels:—

Shutur bi-chashma-i-súzan birún na-khwáhad shud:
Ḥasúd-i-khám-ṭama', gú, darín hawas bi-g'dáz!

"The camel will not go through the eye of a needle:
Bid thine envier with his crude ambitions melt in this vain endeavour!"

I do not know on what principle Dhahír's *Díwán* is arranged, for the order of the poems is neither chronological nor alphabetical. It would seem as though an attempt had been made to put the best poems at the beginning, and it is remarkable that, of the first five, three are chosen as specimens of the poet's work by 'Awfí in his *Lubáb* (vol. ii, pp. 298–307) and a fourth by Dawlatsháh (p. 110). The first poem, which consists of thirty-seven verses, seems to me quite the best in the whole collection, and I will conclude my notice of Dhahír with a few lines from it.[1]

[1] *Lubáb*, vol. ii, p. 299, l. 17 to p. 300, l. 4.

'That thou may'st fill thy belly and clothe thyself withal,
Behold how many a harmless beast to pain and death is thrall!
For thee what grievous burdens insect and reptile bear,
What agonies befall the beasts of earth and birds of air!
Some harmless creature, fearing naught, is grazing on the veldt,
Whilst thou thy knife art sharpening to strip it of its pelt.
With bitter toil poor weakly worms weave for themselves a nest,
That thou of silks and satins fine may'st clothe thee with the best.
Eager thy jaded palate with honey sweet to please,
Thou sittest watching greedily the toiling of the bees.
From the dead worm thou strip'st the shroud to turn it to thy use:
Can any generous soul accept for such a theft excuse?"

I have written thus fully of Dhahír of Fáryáb, not because I would place him on an equality with Anwarí, Kháqání, or Nidhámí, much less with Firdawsí or Náṣir-i-Khusraw, but because he may be taken as a type of the innumerable Court-poets of his time and country, such as Athír of Akhsíkat, Mujír of Baylaqán, Faríd-i-Kátib, Shufurvah of Iṣfahán, and dozens more neither greatly superior nor greatly inferior to himself, of whom it is impossible to give detailed and separate accounts in a work of such scope and character as this.

CHAPTER VII

THE EMPIRE OF KHWÁRAZM AND THE MONGOL INVASION, UNTIL THE FALL OF BAGHDÁD AND THE EXTINCTION OF THE CALIPHATE

We have already spoken, in Chapter V, of the rising power of the Khwárazmsháhs, or Kings of Khiva, who were descended from Anúshtigín, the cup-bearer of Maliksháh. At the period which we have now reached, viz., the beginning of the thirteenth century of the Christian Era, 'Alá'u'd-Dín Muḥammad, the great-grandson of the stiff-necked Atsiz, sat on the throne of Khwárazm, whence he ruled over an empire which, for a few years, rivalled in extent that of the Seljúqs in their most prosperous days. At the time of which we are now speaking, it extended from the Ural Mountains to the Persian Gulf, and from the Indus almost to the Euphrates, and included nearly the whole of Persia except the provinces of Fárs and Khuzistán. That this empire of Khwárazm contained in itself the elements of a stability greater than that of its predecessors and victims, the empires built up by the houses of Ghazna, Seljúq or Ghúr, is in the highest degree improbable; but, in the normal course of events, it might easily have endured for a century or more. The event which annihilated it, amongst many things of far greater value, was a catastrophe which, though probably quite unforeseen, even on the very eve of its incidence, changed the face of the world, set in motion forces which are still effective, and inflicted more suffering on the human race than any other event in the world's history of which records are preserved to us ; I mean the Mongol Invasion.

In its suddenness, its devastating destruction, its appalling ferocity, its passionless and purposeless cruelty, its irresistible though short-lived violence, this outburst of savage nomads, hitherto hardly known by name even to their neighbours, resembles rather some brute cataclysm of the blind forces of nature than a phenomenon of human history.[1] The details of massacre, outrage, spoliation, and destruction wrought by these hateful hordes of barbarians, who, in the space of a few years, swept the world from Japan to Germany,[2] would, as d'Ohsson observes, be incredible were they not confirmed from so many different quarters. How they impressed contemporary writers may be judged by the following extract from that sober and careful historian, Ibnu'l-Athír, who thus opens his account of the matter under the year A.H. 617 (A.D. 1220–21) :

"ACCOUNT OF THE OUTBREAK OF THE TARTARS INTO THE LANDS OF ISLÁM.

"For some years I continued averse from mentioning this event, deeming it so horrible that I shrank from recording it, and ever withdrawing one foot as I advanced the other. To whom, indeed, can it be easy to write the announcement of the death-blow of Islám and the Muslims, or who is he on whom the remembrance thereof can weigh lightly? O would that my mother had not born me, or that I had died and become a forgotten thing ere this befell! Yet withal a number of my friends urged me to set it down in writing, and I hesitated long; but at last came to the conclusion that to omit this matter [from my history] could serve no useful purpose.

"I say, therefore, that this thing involves the description of the greatest catastrophe and the most dire calamity (of the like of which

[1] D'Ohsson's *Histoire des Mongols*, vol. i, p. 387.

[2] The Mongols summoned the Japanese to submit in A.D. 1270, and thrice attacked them, the last time in 1283, but without success. The destruction of the Mongol Armada in 1280 was as complete as that of the Spanish Armada. The worst devastation of the Mongols in Europe happened in the years 1236–41.

days and nights are innocent) which befell all men generally, and the Muslims in particular; so that, should one say that the world, since God Almighty created Adam until now, hath not been afflicted with the like thereof, he would but speak the truth. For indeed history doth not contain aught which approaches or comes nigh unto it. For of the most grievous calamities recorded was what Nebuchadnezzar inflicted on the children of Israel by his slaughter of them and his destruction of Jerusalem; and what was Jerusalem in comparison to the countries which these accursed miscreants destroyed, each city of which was double the size of Jerusalem? Or what were the children of Israel compared to those whom these slew? For verily those whom they massacred in a single city exceeded all the children of Israel. Nay, it is unlikely that mankind will see the like of this calamity, until the world comes to an end and perishes, except the final outbreak of Gog and Magog. For even Antichrist will spare such as follow him, though he destroy those who oppose him; but these [Tartars][1] spared none, slaying women and men and children, ripping open pregnant women and killing unborn babes. Verily to God do we belong, and unto Him do we return, and there is no strength and no power save in God, the High, the Almighty, in face of this catastrophe, whereof the sparks flew far and wide, and the hurt was universal; and which passed over the lands like clouds driven by the wind. For these were a people who emerged from the confines of China, and attacked the cities of Turkistán, like Káshghar and Balásághún, and thence advanced on the cities of Transoxiana, such as Samarqand, Bukhárá and the like, taking possession of them, and treating their inhabitants in such wise as we shall mention; and of them one division then passed on into Khurásán, until they had made an end of taking possession, and destroying, and slaying, and plundering, and thence passing on to Ray, Hamadán and the Highlands, and the cities contained therein, even to the limits of 'Iráq,[2] whence they marched on the towns of Ádharbayján and Arrániyya, destroying them and slaying most of their inhabitants, of whom none escaped save a small remnant; and all this in less than a year; this is a thing whereof the like hath not been heard. And when they had finished with Ádharbayján and Arrániyya, they passed on to Darband-i-Shirwán, and

---

[1] They are properly called *Tatar* (by the Arabs), or *Tátár* (by the Persians). The European form was dictated by a desire to connect them with Tartarus, on account of their hellish deeds and infernal cruelty.

[2] *I.e.*, Mesopotamia, or *'Iráq-i-'Arab* as it is now called, to distinguish it from *'Iráq-i-'Ajam.*

occupied its cities, none of which escaped save the fortress wherein was their King; wherefore they passed by it to the countries of the Lán and the Lakiz and the various nationalities which dwell in that region, and plundered, slew, and destroyed them to the full. And thence they made their way to the lands of Qipcháq, who are the most numerous of the Turks, and slew all such as withstood them, while the survivors fled to the fords and mountain-tops, and abandoned their country, which these Tartars overran. All this they did in the briefest space of time, remaining only for so long as their march required and no more.

"Another division, distinct from that mentioned above, marched on Ghazna and its dependencies, and those parts of India, Sístán and Kirmán which border thereon, and wrought therein deeds like unto the other, nay, yet more grievous. Now this is a thing the like of which ear hath not heard; for Alexander, concerning whom historians agree that he conquered the world, did not do so with such swiftness, but only in the space of about ten years; neither did he slay, but was satisfied that men should be subject to him. But these Tartars conquered most of the habitable globe, and the best, the most flourishing and most populous part thereof, and that whereof the inhabitants were the most advanced in character and conduct, in about a year; nor did any country escape their devastations which did not fearfully expect them and dread their arrival.

"Moreover they need no commissariat, nor the conveyance of supplies, for they have with them sheep, cows, horses, and the like quadrupeds, the flesh of which they eat, [needing] naught else. As for their beasts which they ride, these dig into the earth with their hoofs and eat the roots of plants, knowing naught of barley. And so, when they alight anywhere, they have need of nothing from without. As for their religion, they worship the sun when it arises, and regard nothing as unlawful, for they eat all beasts, even dogs, pigs, and the like; nor do they recognise the marriage-tie, for several men are in marital relations with one woman, and if a child is born, it knows not who is its father.

"Therefore Islám and the Muslims have been afflicted during this period with calamities wherewith no people hath been visited. These Tartars (may God confound them!) came from the East, and wrought deeds which horrify all who hear of them, and which thou shalt, please God, see set forth in full detail in their proper connection. And of these [calamities] was the invasion of Syria by the Franks (may God curse them!) out of the West, and their attack on Egypt, and occupation of the port of Damietta therein, so that Egypt and Syria were like to be conquered by them, but for the grace of God and the help which He vouchsafed us against them, as we have mentioned under the year 614 (A.D. 1217–18). Of these [calamities], moreover, was that the sword was drawn between those [of the Muslims] who escaped from these two foes, and strife was rampant [amongst them], as we have also mentioned: and verily unto God do we belong and unto Him do we return! We ask God to vouchsafe victory to Islám and the Muslims, for there is none other to aid, help, or defend the True Faith. But if God intends evil to any people, naught can avert it, nor have they any ruler save Him. As for these Tartars, their achievements were only rendered possible by the absence of any effective obstacle; and the cause of this absence was that Muḥammad Khwárazmsháh had overrun the [Muslim] lands, slaying and destroying their Kings, so that he remained alone ruling over all these countries; wherefore, when he was defeated by the Tartars, none was left in the lands to check those or protect these, that so God might accomplish a thing which was to be done.

"It is now time for us to describe how they first burst forth into the [Muslim] lands."

Now all this was written nearly thirty years before the crowning catastrophe, to wit, the sack of Baghdád and the extinction of the Caliphate, took place; for this happened in February, A.D. 1258, while Ibnu'l-Athír concludes his chronicle with the year A.H. 628 (A.D. 1230–31), and died two years later. Nor did he witness the horrors of which he writes, but only heard them from terrified fugitives, of whose personal narratives he records several under the year with which his chronicle closes.

"Stories have been related to me," he says, "which the hearer can scarcely credit, as to the terror of them [*i.e.*, the Mongols] which God Almighty cast into men's hearts; so that it is said that a single one of them would enter a village or a quarter wherein were many people, and would continue to slay them one after another, none daring to stretch forth his hand against this horseman. And I have heard that one of them took a man captive, but had not with him any weapon wherewith to kill him; and he said to his prisoner, 'Lay your head on the ground and do not move'; and he did so, and the Tartar went and fetched his sword and slew him therewith. Another man related to me as follows:—'I was going,' said he, 'with seventeen others along a road, and there met us a Tartar horseman, and bade us bind one another's arms. My companions began to do as he bade them, but I said to them, "He is but one man; wherefore, then, should we not kill him and flee?" They replied, "We are afraid." I said, "This man intends to kill you immediately; let us therefore rather kill him, that perhaps God may deliver us." But I swear by God that not one of them dared to do this, so I took a knife and slew him, and we fled and escaped.' And such occurrences were many."[1]

Yáqút al-Ḥamawí the geographer, another eminent contemporary writer (born A.D. 1178 or 1179, died A.D. 1229), and a friend of the great historian above cited, has also left us a picture of the terror inspired by the Mongols, from whose hands he just succeeded in escaping. Besides occasional references in his great Geographical Dictionary, the *Mu'jamu'l-Buldán*, there is preserved in the pages of Ibn Khallikán's Biographies (de Slane's translation, vol. iv, pp. 12–22) the text of a letter which he addressed to al-Qáḍí'l-akram Jamálu'd-Dín Abu'l-Ḥasan 'Alí ash-Shaybání al-Qifṭí, *Wazír* of the King of Aleppo, from Mawṣil, which he had finally, after many hairbreadth escapes, succeeded in reaching in his flight from Merv. This letter, written in A.H. 617 (A.D. 1220–21), describes in glowing language the rich libraries of Merv, which caused him to forget home, friends, and country, and on the contents of which he browsed "with the avidity of a glutton," and the wonderful prosperity of Khurásán, which, says he, "in a word, and without exaggeration, was a copy of Paradise."

"How numerous," he continues, "were its holy men pre-eminent for virtue! How many its doctors whose conduct had for motive the conservation of Islám! The monuments of its science are inscribed on the rolls of Time; the merits of its authors have

---

[1] This passage is translated by d'Ohsson, vol. iii, p. 70, and is noticed by Sir Henry Howorth in vol. i of his *History of the Mongols*, pp. 131–132. Compare also d'Ohsson, vol. i, pp. 387–388.

redounded to the advantage of religion and the world, and their productions have been carried into every country. Not a man of solid science and sound judgement but emerged like the sun from that part of the East; not a man of extraordinary merit but took that country for his settling-place, or longed to go and join its inhabitants. Every quality truly honourable and not factitious was to be found amongst them, and in their sayings I was enabled to cull the roots of every generous impulse. Their children were men, their youths heroes, and their old men saints; the evidences of their merit are clear, and the proofs of their glory manifest; and yet, strange to say, the King who ruled over these provinces (*i.e.*, 'Alá'u'd Dín Muḥammad Khwárazmsháh) abandoned them with unconcern, and said to himself, 'Take to the open country, or else you will encounter perdition!' . . . The people of infidelity and impiety roamed through those abodes; that erring and contumacious race (the Mongols) dominated over the inhabitants, so that those palaces were effaced from off the earth as lines of writing are effaced from paper, and those abodes became a dwelling for the owl and the raven; in those places the screech-owls answer each other's cries, and in those halls the winds moan responsive to the simoom. Old friends who enter there are filled with sadness, and even Iblís himself would bewail this dire catastrophe. . . . Verily to God do we belong and unto Him do we return! It was an event sufficient to break the back, to destroy life, to fracture the arm, to weaken the strength, to redouble sadness, to turn grey the hair of children, to dishearten the bravest, and to stupefy the intelligence! . . . In a word, had not the term of my life been appointed for a later period, it would have been difficult for my friends to have said, 'The unfortunate man is escaped or is arrived!' and they would have struck their hands together like people who are disappointed; while he would have been joined to the millions of millions, or even more, who perished by the hands of the infidels."

The hateful appearance and disgusting habits of the invaders added to the horror inspired by their unscrupulous perfidy and cold-blooded cruelty. The Arab invasion of Persia no doubt wrought much devastation and caused much suffering, but the Arabs were, in the phrase of their Spanish foes, "knights . . . and gentlemen, albeit Moors," and if they destroyed much, they brought much that was noble and admirable in its stead. The Mongols, on the other hand, in the words of d'Ohsson, their admirable historian[1] (pp. vi–vii of vol. i),—

"surpassing in cruelty the most barbarous people, murdered in cold blood, in the conquered countries, men, women, and children; burned towns and villages; transformed flourishing lands into deserts; and yet were animated neither by hate nor vengeance, for indeed they hardly knew the names of the peoples whom they exterminated. One would suppose that history had exaggerated their atrocities, were not the annals of all countries in agreement on this point. After the conquest, one sees the Mongols treat as slaves the feeble remnant of the conquered nations, and cause to groan under a frightful tyranny those whom the sword had spared. Their government was the triumph of depravity; all that was noble and honourable was abased, while the most corrupt men, attaching themselves to the service of these ferocious masters, obtained, as the price of their vile devotion, riches, honours, and the power to oppress their fellow-countrymen. The history of the Mongols, therefore, stamped with their barbarity, offers only hideous pictures, though, being closely connected with that of several empires, it is necessary for a proper understanding of the great events of the thirteenth and fourteenth centuries."

The only virtues which these Mongols or Tartars possessed were those generally called military—to wit, discipline, subordination, and obedience to their superior officers carried to the highest degree. All promotion went by personal merit; failure, disobedience, or incapacity was punished not only by the death of the offender himself, but of his wife and children. The highest officer, if he incurred the anger of his emperor, must submit before all his troops to personal chastisement at the hands of the meanest messenger sent by his master to reprimand him. Yet, though they held life so cheaply, the Mongols rarely had recourse to courage where falsehood and deceit could enable them to gain their ends. If death was the punishment of resistance, it was also in most cases the consequence of surrender. If they spared any of the inhabitants of

[1] *Histoire des Mongols depuis Tchinguiz Khan jusqu'à Timour Bey ou Tamerlan, par M. le Baron C. d'Ohsson;* Paris, 1834–35, 4 vols.

a town which had surrendered to or been reduced by them, it was either to profit by their skill and craftsmanship or to employ them against their countrymen and co-religionists in the vanguard of their next assault. Droves of wretched and outraged captives accompanied the advancing hordes, and, when the next point of resistance was reached, were first employed to erect the engines of the besiegers, then driven forward at the point of the sword to the breaches effected in the city walls to fill with their bodies moat and trench, and were finally, if they still escaped death, put to the sword to give place to a new batch of victims drawn from the prisoners yielded by the fresh conquest. The cruelty of the Mongols was calculated and deliberate, designed to strike with a paralysis of terror those whom they proposed next to attack, while they deemed it safer to leave behind their advancing hosts smoking ruins and a reeking charnel-house rather than risk any movement of revolt on the part of the miserable survivors of their assault.

To trace in detail the history of the Mongols, or even of their doings in Persia, is altogether beyond the scope of this book. Those who desire full information on this matter can find it either in d'Ohsson's great work or in Sir Henry Howorth's *History of the Mongols*. D'Ohsson, in particular, has made admirable use of the Arabic and Persian authorities, which he fully describes and criticises on pp. x–lxviii of the *Exposition* prefixed to the first volume of his work. The five most important Muhammadan sources are: (1) The Arabic Chronicle of Ibnu'l-Athír, already cited; (2) the Arabic Life of Sulṭán Jalálu'd-Dín Mankobirni, written by his private secretary, Shihábu'd-Dín Muḥammad an-Nasawí; (3) the Persian *Ta'ríkh-i-Jahán-gushá*, or History of the World-Conqueror, by 'Alá'u'd-Dín 'Aṭá Malik-i-Juwayní, the secretary of Hulágú Khán; (4) the Persian *Jámi'u't-Tawáríkh*, or Compendium of Histories, of Rashídu'd-Dín Faḍlu'llah; and (5) the Persian *Tajziyatu'l-Amṣár*, better known as the

Ta'ríkh-i-Waṣṣáf. Of the first of these there are two editions, Tornberg's and that of Cairo; of the second, an edition and French translation by M. Houdas (Paris, 1891 and 1895); and of the last (or at least of its first half), an edition and German translation by Hammer Purgstall (Vienna, 1856), and a Persian lithograph. The third and fourth are, unfortunately, at present inaccessible except in manuscript.[1]

Although the disaster of the Mongol Invasion could not probably, have been averted, it was undoubtedly facilitated and' provoked by the greed, treachery, and irresolution of 'Alá'u'd-Dín Muḥammad, King of Khwárazm. By his greed, because, as Ibnu'l-Athír observes, he had weakened or destroyed most of the neighbouring Muhammadan States to build up for himself an unstable and unwieldy empire; so that when he fled before the Mongols, abandoning his people to their fate, no Muhammadan prince was left to unite the forces of Islám against the heathen; by his treachery, because his murder of Mongol merchants and envoys gave Chingíz Khán the best possible excuse for attacking him, and thus learning the weak and defenceless condition of Persia; and by his irresolution, because at the first reverse he passed from arrogant and boastful defiance to the extreme of panic and indecision, until, about two years after his treacherous murder of the Mongol ambassador, he died, a wretched and hunted fugitive, in an island of the Caspian Sea. It needed the gallant deeds of his son Jalálu'd-Dín to save from ignominy the memory of the once mighty Empire of Khwárazm.

[1] Part of the *Jahán-gushá*, describing the first onslaught of the Mongols on the Empire of Khwárazm down to the sack of Níshápúr, has been published by Schefer in vol. ii of his *Chrestomathie Persane*, pp. 106–169; while a portion of the *Jámi'u't-Tawárikh*, comprising the history of Hulágú Khán, was edited by Quatremère, with French translation and notes, in 1836. Another portion of the last-named history has also, I believe, been edited by Bérésine, but it is very scarce, and I have not been able to see a copy. M. Blochet is at present engaged on a continuation of Quatremère's work for the Trustees of the Gibb Memorial Fund, who are also projecting a complete edition of the *Jahán-gushá*.

Another source of weakness to the resisting power of Islám was the quarrel which had arisen between Muḥammad Khwárazmsháh and the 'Abbásid Caliph an-Náṣir, who, suspecting his too powerful vassal of coveting the very metropolis of Baghdád, strove, after the manner of the later Caliphs, to weaken him by intrigues, and even, as hinted by Ibnu'l-Athír and explicitly stated by al-Maqrízí, encouraged the Mongols, at whose hands his posterity was destined to perish and his house to fall, to invade his territories.[1] The mischief appears to have begun with the discovery, on the capture of Ghazna by Khwárazmsháh, of a correspondence between the Caliph and the fallen House of Subuktigín, from which it appeared that the Caliph had been inciting them to revolt against their suzerain. Khwárazmsháh retaliated by denouncing the validity of the 'Abbásid title to be regarded as the pontiffs of Islám, set up a certain Sayyid as a rival claimant to their spiritual authority, and, at a time when he should have been straining every nerve to meet the storm which threatened his north-eastern frontier, undertook a futile campaign against Baghdád, whereof the disastrous issue was precipitated and accentuated by a winter of such severity as was almost unknown in those regions.

Although it appears probable that nothing could long have averted the impending calamity, its actual incidence was due to one of those "pacific missions" of which we hear so much in these days. It seemed good to Chingíz Khán to send to Utrár, an important frontier-town of Khwárazm, a company of merchants laden with the wares of his country. As to the numbers engaged in this mission, considerable difference of opinion exists: according to an-Nasawí there were four merchants only, all Muhammadans and all subjects of Khwárazmsháh; while other writers raise the number to four hundred and fifty.[2] These were barbarously murdered

[1] See d'Ohsson, vol. i, p. 211, and note *ad calc.*
[2] Ibid., pp. 205 *et seqq.*

by the Governor of Utrár, with the connivance of Khwárazmsháh, who affected to believe that they were in reality Mongol spies. Thereupon Chingíz Khán despatched an embassy, consisting of two Mongols and a Turk named Bughrá, to the Court of Khwárazmsháh to protest against this wanton violation of the laws of hospitality and the comity of nations, and to demand that the Governor of Utrár should be given up to them, failing which, they added, Khwárazmsháh must prepare for war. His only answer was to kill Bughrá and send back the two Mongols, whose beards he had shaved off. Thereupon the Mongols held a *quriltáy*, or general assembly, at which it was decided to attack the Empire of Khwárazm.

In spite of a trifling initial success, Muḥammad Khwárazmsháh remained inactive and remote from the point of danger, entrusting the defence of the frontier to the Governors of the threatened towns, and waiting, it is said (though perhaps only to extenuate his cowardice and irresolution) a moment which the astrologers should declare favourable for his enterprise. And while he thus waited, in the autumn of A.D. 1219, the storm burst on Transoxiana. Utrár fell after a siege of five or six months; its Governor, the murderer of the merchants, was taken alive and put to death by having molten silver poured into his eyes and ears; and the survivors of the massacre which ensued were driven to Bukhárá, there to be employed against their co-religionists in the manner already described. After Úzkand and two or three other small towns had been sacked, Jand was reduced after a short siege, and plundered for nine days, but the inhabitants were, for a wonder, spared. Banákat next fell; Khujand was gallantly defended by Tímúr Malik; and in the early part of the year A.D. 1220 the Mongol hosts were masters of Bukhárá, which they plundered and burned, massacring a great number of the inhabitants, and outraging their wives, sisters, and daughters. Amongst those who, preferring death to dishonour, died fighting were the Qáḍi Badru'd-Dín, the Imám Ruknu'd-Dín, and his son. The turn of Samarqand came next; it surrendered on the fourth day of the siege, was plundered in the usual way, and a large number of its inhabitants killed or reduced to slavery.

Meanwhile Muḥammad Khwárazmsháh continued to retreat, warning the inhabitants of the towns through which he passed to do the best they could for themselves, since he could not protect them. Believing that the Mongols would not dare to cross the Oxus, he halted for a while at Níshápúr, but three weeks later, learning that they were already in Khurásán, he fled westwards to Qazwín, whence he turned back into Gílán and Mázandarán. There, being deserted by most of his followers and attacked by pleurisy, he died, a miserable and hunted fugitive, on an island in the Caspian, nominating his son, the brave Jalálu'd-Dín, as his successor. His mother, Turkán Khátún, together with his wives, children, and jewels, fell into the hands of the Mongols. Khwárazm next fell, and, irritated by the stubborn resistance which it had offered, the Mongols put to the sword nearly all the inhabitants except the artisans and craftsmen, who were transported into Mongolia. According to the author of the *Jámi'u't-Tawáríkh*,[1] the besieging army numbered 50,000, and each man of them had twenty-four prisoners to kill! Amongst those who perished was the venerable and pious Najmu'd-Dín Kubrá.[2] The inhabitants of Tirmidh were similarly treated, and in addition, because one old woman was found to have swallowed a pearl, their corpses were eviscerated.

The bloodthirsty ferocity of the Mongols seems to have increased in proportion to their successes, and seldom indeed, from this time onwards, do we hear of any mercy shown by the Tartars to the inhabitants of the towns which they subdued. At Balkh, at Nuṣrat-Kúh, at Nasá, at Níshápúr,

[1] D'Ohsson, vol. i, pp. 262–70, *ad calc.*

[2] See Jámí's *Nafaḥátu'l-Uns*, ed. Lees, pp. 486–87

at Merv, and elsewhere, the same atrocious massacres invariably followed the capture or surrender of the town. Those slain at Merv alone are computed by Ibnu'l-Athír at 700,000, but the author of the *Jahán-gushá* raises their number to the enormous total of 1,300,000, "not counting those whose corpses remained hidden in obscure retreats." At Níshápúr the heads of the slain were cut off, lest any living creature might be overlooked amongst them, and built into pyramids, the heads of men, women, and children being kept apart. Herát fared somewhat better, but Bámiyán, where a Mongol prince was slain in the attack, was utterly destroyed, not even spoils of war being taken, so that for a hundred years it remained a desert void of inhabitants. That nothing might be wanting to complete the ruin which they had wrought, the Mongols frequently destroyed all the grain which they did not need, and often, a few days after they had retired from a town which they had sacked, used to send a detachment to revisit its ruins and kill such poor wretches as had emerged from the hiding-places which had sheltered them from the first massacre. This happened at Merv, where 5,000 survivors of the terrible slaughter mentioned above were thus destroyed. Torture was freely used to make the vanquished disclose hidden treasure, and, as might be expected of those who held human life so cheaply, the treasures of literature and art preserved in these ancient cities were ruthlessly destroyed. Juwayní says that, in the Musulmán lands devastated by the Mongols, not one in a thousand of the inhabitants survived; and declares that even should nothing happen thereafter until the Resurrection to check the increase of population in Khurásán and 'Iráq-i-'Ajam, the population of these two provinces could never attain the tenth part of what it was before the Mongol invasion.[1] It was the terror of the Mongol deeds which lent such deadly meaning to their stereotyped summons to surrender which they addressed to the

[1] D'Ohsson, *op. cit.*, vol. i, pp. 350–51, *ad calc.*

inhabitants of each doomed city:—"If you do not submit, how can we tell what will happen? God only knows what will happen!"[1]

The habits and customs of the Mongols, disgusting in themselves, were in several respects especially repugnant to Muhammadan feeling. They were ready to eat not only things unclean in Islám, but things essentially loathsome, rats, cats, dogs, and even worse: "*Cibi eorum*," says Jean de Plan Carpin, "*sunt omnia quæ mandi possunt; vidimus eos etiam pediculos manducare*."[2] Not only did they dislike washing themselves: they made it a penal offence, nay, even a capital offence, to wash hands or garments in running water. It was also a capital offence with them to kill animals by cutting their throats, the only way in which, according to the Muhammadans, they can be lawfully killed when intended for food; instead of this it was their practice to cut open the body, and, inserting the hand, to squeeze or tear out the heart.[3] In general they were, however, tolerant to the verge of latitudinarianism in matters of religion, and accorded certain privileges, such as exemption from taxes, to the ministers of all creeds, as well as to physicians and certain other classes of men. With Chingíz Khán, indeed, it was a political principle to favour all religions equally, but to give his adhesion to none; and Qubiláy Khán (A.D. 1257–94) was the first of his house to adopt a definite creed, to wit, Buddhism; while Taqúdar (Aḥmad) Khán (A.D. 1282–84) and Gházán Khán (A.D. 1295–1304) were the first to embrace Islám, in which religion the successors of the latter in Persia continued. Thus were the aims of the Christians, who had great hopes of winning the Mongols to their faith and dealing a death-blow to Islám, frustrated; and the most permanent and precious

[1] D'Ohsson, *op. cit.*, vol. i, p. 394.

[2] Ibid., p. 411 *ad calc.*

[3] This statute of the Mongols was revived by Qubiláy Khán under circumstances related by d'Ohsson (vol. ii, pp. 491–92).

fruits of the various Christian missions sent to the Mongol Court of Qaráqorum are the valuable records of their travels and experiences left by Jean de Plan Carpin (Planocarpini), Rubruquis (Guillaume de Ruysbroek), and other monks and priests, who bravely faced a thousand dangers and hardships in the hopes of winning so great a victory for their Church. Yet it was some time before the Christian potentates of Europe realised that the great Khán of the Tartars, who continued from time to time to address to them letters in the Mongol language and Úyghúr script, was no longer to be regarded as a possible convert to Christianity, as clearly appears from a letter addressed to Uljáytú Khudá-banda by Edward II., dated from Northampton on October 16, 1307.[1] Yet, apart from mere political *rapprochements* between the Mongols and the potentates of Europe, which aimed at combined action against the Muslims, the support of the Armenians, and the recovery of the Holy Land from the Muhammadan dominion, certain tribes belonging to the Mongol confederation, such as the Keraites, actually professed Christianity, certain princesses of the blood-royal, such as Úrúk Khátún, were apparently genuinely attached to that religion,[2] and two of the Íl-Kháns of Persia, Taqúdar Aḥmad and Uljáytú Khudá-banda, both in later days vehement professors and supporters of the Muhammadan doctrine, were actually baptized in infancy, in each case under the name of Nicolas.[3]

Infinitely destructive and disastrous as it was to life, learning, and civilisation, and especially to the Arabian culture, which, as we have already seen, maintained itself with such extraordinary vitality in Persia for six centuries,

[1] See d'Ohsson, *op. cit.*, vol. iv, pp. 592–94; and Abel Remusat's *Mémoire sur les relations politiques des Princes chrétiens et particulièrement les Rois de France avec les Empereurs Mongols.*

[2] Ibid., vol. iv, p. 79 *ad calc.*

[3] Ibid., vol. iii, pp. 561–62 *ad calc.*, and vol. iv, p. 79 *ad calc.*

long after the wave of Arab conquest had utterly subsided, the Mongol invasion did, perhaps, contain some quickening elements, and the Mongol character, for all its reckless ferocity, some potentialities of good. One of its few good effects was the extraordinary intermixture of remote peoples, resulting in a refreshing of somewhat stagnant mental reservoirs, which it brought about. In Europe it was a cause, if not the chief cause, of the Renaissance, for it thrust the Ottoman Turks out of the obscurity of Khurásán into the prominence of Constantinople, and was thus ultimately responsible for the destruction of the Byzantine Empire and the dispersion of the Greeks and their treasures into Europe. It also, by the breaking down of a hundred frontiers and the absorption of dozens of States, great and small, enabled travellers like Marco Polo to make known to Europe the wonders, hitherto so jealously guarded, of nearly the whole of Asia. And within Asia it brought together, first in conflict and then in consultation, Persians and Arabs with Chinese and Tibetans,[1] and confronted, on terms of equality which had not existed for five or six centuries, the doctors of Islám with Christian monks, Buddhist lamas, Mongol *bakhshis* or medicine-men, and the representatives of other religions and sects.

Of course, matters were very much improved when Hulágú Khán's successors in Persia abandoned their heathen superstitions and embraced the religion of Islám, which soon resulted in their alienation from their pagan kinsmen of Qaráqorum and their identification with, and final absorption

[1] In A.D. 1272 two Persian engineers, 'Alá'u'd-Dín and Isma'íl, were employed by Qubiláy Khán at the siege of Fanching in China (d'Ohsson, *op. cit.*, vol. ii, p. 389); while Hulágú Khán, when he set out on his campaign against Persia and Baghdád, in A.D. 1252, brought with him a thousand Chinese engineers to construct and work catapults and other artillery (Ibid., vol. iii, p. 135). The celebrated Persian astronomer and philosopher, Nasíru'd-Dín Ṭúsí, was assisted by Chinese astronomers in the compilation of the *Zíj*, or Tables, which he constructed for Hulágú Khán about A.D. 1259 (Ibid., iii, p. 265).

into, the conquered people over which they ruled. But even Hulágú Khán, the destroyer of Baghdád and deadly foe of Islám, was the patron of two of the greatest Persian writers of this period, the astronomer Naṣíru'd-Dín of Ṭús and the historian 'Aṭá Malik of Juwayn, author of the *Ta'ríkh-i-Jahán-gushá*, or "History of the Conqueror of the World," *i.e.*, Chingíz Khán. Two other historians, 'Abdu'lláh b. Faḍlu'lláh of Shíráz, better known as *Waṣṣáf-i-Ḥaḍrat*, and the *Wazír* Rashídu'd-Dín Faḍlu'lláh, both of whom flourished in the reign of Gházán Khán (A.D. 1295–1304), must certainly be ranked amongst the greatest of those who have written in the Persian language on this important branch of knowledge. Persian literature, indeed, in the narrower sense of that term, can hardly be said to have suffered permanently from the Mongol Invasion, since three of the greatest and most famous poets of Persia, Sa'dí of Shíráz, Farídu'd-Dín 'Aṭṭár, and Jalálu'd-Dín Rúmí were contemporary with it, and many other most famous poets were subsequent to it; but the destruction of Baghdád as the metropolis of Islám, and its reduction to the rank of a provincial town, struck a fatal blow at the semblance of unity which had hitherto subsisted amongst the Muhammadan nations, and at the prestige and status in Persia of the Arabic language, which, hitherto the chief vehicle of all culture, henceforth becomes practically the language of the theologians and philosophers only, so that after the close of the thirteenth century we shall relatively seldom have occasion to speak of Arabic works produced in Persia.

We must now proceed to consider, in broad outlines only, the several periods of Mongol ascendancy in Persia, which may be said to extend from the first invasion of that country by Chingíz Khán in A.D. 1219 to the death of Abú Sa'íd Khán in A.D. 1335, to which succeeded half a century of anarchy, culminating in another Tartar invasion, that of Tímúr-i-Lang, or "Lame Tímúr," better known in Europe as Tamerlane

(A.D. 1380–1400). This last event, which forms the transition to what may fairly be called the history of Modern Persia, lies outside the scope of this volume, which only extends to the Mongol period properly so called; and it is only mentioned here as a landmark which the reader should keep in view.

The first period of Mongol ascendancy may be called, in Stanley Lane-Poole's nomenclature, that of the Great Kháns (Chingíz, Ogotáy, Kuyúk, and Mangú, A.D. 1206–57), during which the whole empire conquered by the Mongols was ruled from Qaráqorum by lieutenants or pro-consuls directly appointed from the Mongol metropolis. At the great *quriltáy* held in A.D. 1251, at the beginning of Mangú's reign, two expeditions were resolved on, each of which was entrusted to one of Chingíz Khán's grandsons, both brothers of the reigning emperor Mangú, namely, the expedition against China, directed by Qubiláy Khán; and that against Persia, Mesopotamia, and Asia Minor, directed by Hulágú Khán.

The second period, which may be called that of the heathen Íl-Kháns, or hereditary viceroys of Persia and Western Asia, begins with the arrival of Hulágú Khán on the hither side of the Oxus in January, 1256, and ends with the killing of Baydú on October 5, 1295. During this period Islám was gradually regaining strength, and fighting with ever-increasing success the battle against Buddhism and Christianity, while the bonds uniting the Persian Íl-Kháns with the Mongols of the "mother country" were undergoing gradual dissolution. It is worth noticing, as illustrating the gradual change of religious feeling amongst the Mongol settlers in Persia, that, while the violent death of Aḥmad Taqúdar in August, 1283, was, in part at least, caused by his zeal for Islám,[1] the equally violent death of Baydú twelve years later was largely due to his dislike of that religion and his predilection for Christianity;[2] while the first act of his successor, Ghází́n, was to

[1] D'Ohsson, *op. cit.*, vol. iii, p. 608.

[2] Ibid., vol. iv, p. 141, and note *ad calc.*

make public profession of the Muhammadan faith, and to destroy the Christian churches and Buddhist temples which had been erected in Persia. At a later date (A.D. 1300) he even ordered that all the *bakhshís*, or Mongol priests, resident in Persia should either sincerely embrace Islám or else leave the country, on pain of death.[1] Yet on the accession of Gházán Khán in A.D. 1295 the heathen and anti-Muslim faction of the Mongol nobles and generals, disgusted at his zeal for Islám, formed a conspiracy to dethrone him which was quenched in their blood.[2] Ten years later, when Islám was thoroughly re-established as the dominant religion in Persia, we find some of the Mongol princesses and nobles endeavouring to induce Uljáytú Khudá-banda to renounce the Muhammadan faith and return to the religion of his ancestors, but of course without success;[3] and this appears to be the last manifestation in Persia of Mongol paganism, which in earlier days showed itself in such revolting forms as the sacrifice of girls chosen for their extreme beauty to the *manes* of deceased Mongol emperors, and the wholesale murder of all persons met by the funeral *cortège*, lest the news of the death should become known before it was officially proclaimed.[4]

To return now to the periods of Mongol ascendancy which we have just distinguished. In the first, or purely destructive period, we have to consider two separate waves of invasion, that of Chingíz Khán (A.D. 1219–27), and that of Hulágú Khán (A.D. 1255–65). The first fell chiefly on Khurásán, and extended westwards as far as Ray, Qum, Káshán, and Hamadán. During it were performed those prodigies of valour

[1] D'Ohsson, vol. iv, pp. 281–282.

[2] Ibid., vol. iv, pp. 157 *et seqq.*

[3] Ibid., vol. iv, pp. 538–539.

[4] Forty of the most beautiful maidens were sacrificed by Ogotáy to the spirit of Chingíz Khán (d'Ohsson, vol. ii, p. 13), as well as a number of the finest horses; while the Mongol soldiers who accompanied the corpse of Mangú Khán to its last resting-place in the Altai Mountains declared that on the way thither they had killed no fewer than 20,000 persons! (d'Ohsson, vol. i, p. 384).

wrought by Jalálu'd-Dín Khwárazmsháh and chronicled so fully and graphically by his secretary, Shihábu'd-Dín Muḥammad of Nasá, who accompanied him until he met his death at the hands of a Kurd on August 15, A.D. 1231. The second wave of Hulágú's invasion broke on Khurásán at the beginning of A.D. 1256, engulfed alike the heretical Isma'ílís of Alamút and Kúhistán and the orthodox Caliphate of Baghdád, and was only stemmed by the gallant Mamelukes of Egypt at the battle of 'Ayn Jálút, which was fought on Friday, September 3, A.D. 1260, and resulted in a decisive victory for the Egyptians, notable as the first victory gained by the Muslims over the Mongols since the death of Jalálú'd-Dín Khwárazmsháh thirty years before. Henceforth the spell was broken, and the Muslims, perceiving that their terrible foes were, after all, not invincible, plucked up a fresh courage which showed itself on many a blood-stained field, notably at the battle of 'Ayntáb, on April 16, 1277, when Baybars (al-Malik adh-Dháhir) utterly defeated the Mongol army, of whom 6,770 were left dead on the field. Still greater was the victory obtained at Marju'ṣ-Ṣafar, near Damascus, on April 23, 1303, by the Egyptians under al-Maliku'n-Náṣir, who brought with him on his triumphal entry into Cairo 1,600 Mongol prisoners in chains, each carrying round his neck the head of another Mongol slain in the battle, while in front marched a thousand spearmen, each carrying another Mongol head on his lance.

We have already sufficiently described the savage proceedings of Chingíz Khán's troops in the first invasion, and those who desire to follow in detail the miseries suffered by Utrár, Jand, Banákat, Bukhárá, Níshápúr, Samarqand, Khabúshán, Ṭús, Isfará'in, Dámghán, Simnán, Nakhshab, Urganj (also called Kúrkánj and, by the Arabs, Jurjániyya), Tirmidh, Balkh, Nuṣrat-Kúh, Nasá, Kharandar, Merv, Herát, Kardawán, Bámiyán, Ghazna, Ray, Qum, Marágha, Arbíl, Káshán, Baylaqán, Hamadán, and scores of other Persian towns and hamlets, can find it all set forth in the *Ta'ríkh-i-Jahán-gushá*, the *Jámi'u't-Tawáríkh*, or the works of d'Ohsson or Sir Henry Howorth, from which they may also convince themselves that the sufferings endured by Persia and Asia Minor were almost equalled by those of Central Asia and China, and almost surpassed by those of Eastern Europe. During the reign of Qubiláy Khán (A.D. 1260–94), when Marco Polo was making his memorable journeys through the Mongol Empire, that empire had attained its greatest extent, nay, perhaps a greater extent than any other empire has ever attained; for it included China, Corea, Cochin-China, Tibet, India north of the Ganges, Persia, most of Asia Minor, the Crimea, and a large part of Russia, as far west as the Dnieper.[1] In Persia, as we have seen, their empire practically collapsed on the death of Abú Sa'íd in A.D. 1335, and in China about fifty years later, but in Russia their dominion endured until the close of the fifteenth century.[2] The last remnants of the Mongol Empire, the Khánates of Khiva (*i.e.*, Khwárazm) and Bukhárá, only lost their independent existence some thirty and odd years ago (A.D. 1868 and 1872), while the Khánate of the Crimea was extinguished in 1783, and a lineal descendant of this house, Sulṭán Qirím-Giráy Kattí Giráy, married a Scotch wife and settled in Edinburgh.[3]

Across the dark days of Chingíz Khán's invasion, when the Persian sky was obscured by the smoke of burning towns, and the Persian soil was soaked with the blood of her children, the personality of Jalálu'd-Dín Khwárazmsháh flashes like some brilliant but ineffectual meteor. A more dauntless prince, perhaps, never fought a more desperate fight, and he deserved a better fate than to die at last (in A.D. 1231), helpless and unarmed, at the hands of a Kurdish mountaineer. We have seen how his father, 'Alá'u'd-Dín Muḥammad Khwárazm-

[1] D'Ohsson, vol. ii, pp. 477 *et seqq.*
[2] Ibid., vol. ii, pp. 183–186.
[3] See S. Lane-Poole's *Mohammadan Dynasties*, p. 235.

sháh, changed by the terror of the Mongols from the likeness of a ravening wolf into that of a timid hare, died miserably, a hunted fugitive, on an island in the Caspian Sea, in A.D. 1220; while his proud and cruel grandmother, Turkán Khátún, whose last act before abandoning Khwárazm was to murder in cold blood the helpless princes of the Houses of Seljúq, Ghúr, and other royal lines there detained as hostages,[1] was carried captive by Chingíz to Qaráqorum, in A.D. 1223, and by him bidden to halt and weep a last adieu to her country as she was conducted across the frontiers of Khwárazm.[2] For the moment Jalálu'd-Dín, girt with his father's sword and fortified by his father's blessing, could only fly before the storm towards the Indian frontier;[3] and here it was that one of his most celebrated achievements was performed. He and his little army were overtaken on the banks of the Indus by a Mongol host of greatly superior strength. After offering a desperate resistance, in which he displayed the most conspicuous gallantry, from dawn till mid-day, and finally perceiving that the battle was irretrievably lost, he made a final and desperate charge; then, turning quickly, he stripped off his armour, and, with his horse, plunged into the river and swam across it to the other side, followed by the survivors of his army, many of whom perished by drowning or by the arrows of the Mongols.[4] Rallying the remnants of his army, he first repelled the attack of an Indian prince named Júdí; then, encouraged by this success and strengthened by fresh reinforcements and supplies, threatened Qarája, Prince of Sind, and Íltatmish, Prince of Dihlí, and, in spite of their

[1] D'Ohsson, vol. i, pp. 258–259.

[2] Ibid., vol. i, p. 322.

[3] Ibid., vol. i, p. 255.

[4] Ibid., vol. i, pp. 306 *et seqq.* His mother, wife, and other female relations who were with him, according to the *Jahán-gushá*, fell into the hands of the Mongols; but according to his secretary, an-Nasáwí, Jalálu'd-Dín, being unable to save them, caused them, at their own request, to be drowned in the river, lest they should suffer worse things at the hands of their cruel foes.

alliance against him, maintained himself on their territories until the retreat of the pursuing Mongols permitted him to re-enter Persia and endeavour to regain possession of his father's Empire.

His achievements and adventures during the remaining eight years of his life may be read in detail in the monograph of his secretary, an-Nasáwí, of which not only the Arabic text but an excellent French translation has been published by M. Houdas. His hand was against every man, for he had to contend not only with the Mongols, who were ever on his tracks, but with the faithlessness of his brother, Ghiyáthu'd-Dín, and the disloyalty of Buráq Ḥájib, the ruler of Kirmán. And, as if this was not enough, he must needs attack the Caliph of Baghdád, chastise the Turkmáns and the Assassins, and invade Georgia. In A.D. 1223 we see him storming through Kirmán, Fárs, and Iṣfahán to Ray; in 1225 he defeats and slays the Caliph's general Qushtímúr, pursues his army almost to the gates of Baghdád, takes Tabríz, and successfully attacks the Georgians; in 1226, having reduced Tiflís, he has to hasten back to the south-east of Persia to punish Buráq Ḥájib for a treacherous intrigue with the Mongols; in 1227, having chastised the Turkmáns and the Assassins, he defeats the Mongols at Dámghán, and puts to death four hundred of them who fall into his hands, defends Iṣfahán against them, and again, hearing that the Georgians are forming a confederacy against him, turns back thither, kills four of the greatest champions in single combat, and inflicts on them a crushing defeat; in 1229, while striving to organise a league of Muslim princes against the Mongols, he is surprised and put to flight by an army of 30,000 Mongols under Noyán Chormághún, but succeeds in taking Ganja (now Elizavetpol). But after this his fortune seems to fail and his energy to flag; he takes to drink and grows purposeless, melancholy, and even maudlin, as shown by his exaggerated and unreasoning grief over the death of his favourite, Qilij; and, finally, fleeing from the

30

Mongols, is, as we have seen, murdered in a Kurdish village on August 15, 1231. Much uncertainty prevailed as to his fate, which even the great historian Ibnu'l-Athír declared himself unable to ascertain; and for twenty-two years after his death rumours were constantly arising in Persia that he had reappeared, while several impostors who pretended to be he were arrested, examined, and put to death by the Mongols.[1] This, indeed, is no unique phenomenon in the case of a national hero who is the last hope of a lost cause; the same thing happened, for example, in the case of our English Harold, and the parallel is rendered closer by the fact that popular tradition in both cases represents the hero as withdrawing from the world, living the life of an anchorite, and dying at last, at a ripe old age, in the odour of sanctity.[2]

Reign of Ogotáy.

Chingíz Khán died in China on August 18, 1227, in the twenty-second year of his reign and the sixty-sixth of his age, but two years elapsed ere the Mongol princes and chiefs could be assembled from all parts of the lands they had conquered to the *quriltáy* convened to choose his successor. The actual election of his son Ogotáy, therefore, was approximately synchronous with the death of Jalálu'd-Dín and the extinction of the line of Khwárazmsháhs. The reign of Ogotáy was comparatively short, for he died in December, 1241, his death being accelerated by that passion for strong drink which was one of the many evil characteristics of his race. Its chief events were the foundation of the Mongol capital of Qaráqorum in A.D. 1235, the expedition despatched against Persia under the Noyán Chormághún, and the invasion of Russia and Poland in A.D. 1236–41. This last was characterised by the same horrors which had already been enacted in Persia: Moscow, Rostov, Yaroslav, Tver, Chernigov, Kiev, also Cracow, Pest, and many less celebrated towns, suffered the full

[1] D'Ohsson, vol. iii, pp. 65–66.

[2] See my edition of Dawlatsháh, pp. 147–148.

rigours of Mongol cruelty, and in Poland alone 270,000 ears of victims slain, mostly in cold blood, were collected in sacks by the invaders as evidence of their prowess. All Christendom was deeply moved by the news of these atrocities, and Pope Gregory IX sent a circular letter to all Christian princes wherein he strove to incite them to a crusade against the Tartars. Yet, judged by Mongol standards, Ogotáy had the reputation of being a mild and liberal ruler, and is so described even by the Muhammadan authors of the *Ta'ríkh-i-Jahán-gushá* and the *Ṭabaqát-i-Náṣirí* (ed. Nassau Lees, pp. 380–396), both of whom give instances of his personal clemency and dislike of unnecessary bloodshed, which contrasted strongly with the ferocity of his elder brother, Chaghatáy.[1]

Reign of Kuyúk.

On the death of Ogotáy his widow, Turákína, carried on the government until her eldest son, Kuyúk, could return to Mongolia from the campaign against Russia and Poland in which he was engaged at the time of his father's death. The great *quriltáy* at which he was formally elected was remarkable for the number of representatives of foreign and more or less subject nations who attended it, amongst whom were included representatives of the Caliph of Baghdád, the *Shaykhu'l-Jabal*, or Grand Master of the Assassins of Alamút, and two monks sent by the Pope, one of whom was John of Planocarpini (Jean de Plan Carpin), to whose memoirs we have already alluded. The latter, who presented letters from the Pope dated August, 1245, were well received, for two of Kuyúk's Ministers, Kadak and Chingáj, professed the Christian religion, which their influence caused their master to regard with some favour; but the representatives of the orthodox Caliph and of the heretical *Shaykhu'l-Jabal* were dismissed with menaces which were soon to be made good. The Christians, indeed, were already inclined to overlook the atrocities committed on their co-religionists in

[1] See also my edition of Dawlatsháh, pp. 153–154, where one or two of these anecdotes are cited.

Russia and Poland, and to hail the Mongols as the destroyers of Saracen power;[1] besides the Papal representatives sent to the great *quriltáy*, a Dominican mission was sent to Baydú, in Persia, in A.D. 1247, while a mission headed by Rubruquis (Guillaume de Ruysbroek) was despatched by St. Louis from Nicosia, the capital of Cyprus, on February 10, 1249. This last did not arrive at Qaráqorum until the end of A.D. 1253, when Kuyúk had been succeeded by Mangú.

Reign of Mangú.

Kuyúk died in April, 1248, and was succeeded by his cousin Mangú, the son of Tulúy, the son of Chingíz, who was crowned on July 1, 1251. The grandsons of Ogotáy, greatly incensed at the passing of the supreme power out of their branch of the family, conspired against him, but were captured ere they could effect anything, and put to death. Two great expeditions were resolved on at this same *quriltáy* of 1251, against China and against Persia. The former was entrusted to Qubiláy, the latter to Hulágú, both brothers of the Emperor Mangú. With the arrival of Hulágú in Persia we enter the second of the three periods of Mongol dominion (A.D. 1256–95), that, namely, of the heathen Íl-Kháns, when Persia and Western Asia were assigned to a particular branch of the Mongol royal family, who, though subject to the Great Khán, became practically independent even before their conversion to Islám finally identified them with their subjects and cut them off from their heathen kinsmen in Mongolia and China. We may, therefore, for our purposes, ignore the glories of "Kubla Khan" and the splendours of his capital, "Xanadu" or "Kambalu" (*Khán-báligh—i.e.*, Pekin), made familiar to English readers by Coleridge and Longfellow, and confine our attention to the doings of Hulágú ("the great captain Aläu" of Longfellow) and his descendants, the Íl-Kháns of Persia.

Hulágú started from Qaráqorum in July, 1252, having received special instructions to exterminate the Assassins and

[1] D'Ohsson, vol. ii, p. 240.

to destroy the Caliphate of Baghdád. He was accompanied by a number of Chinese engineers and artillerymen[1] to assist him in his siege operations. He proceeded slowly at first, spent the summer of 1254 in Turkistán, and only reached Samarqand, where he remained for forty days, in September, 1255. At Kesh he was met, in January, 1256, by Arghún, who had been re-appointed Governor-General of Persia by Mangú in A.D. 1253, and who was accompanied by his chief secretary, or *ulúgh-bitikji*, Bahá'u'd-Dín Juwayní, and his son, 'Aṭá Malik Juwayní. The latter was attached to Hulágú in the capacity of secretary, accompanied him through this momentous campaign, was present at the sack of Alamút, the chief stronghold of the Assassins, and was thus in a position to make use of the most authentic and authoritative materials for composing his great history, the *Jahán-gushá*, to which we have repeatedly had occasion to allude.

Hulágú.

Of the earlier history of the Assassins, or Isma'ílís of Alamút, we have already spoken. The first of them was the celebrated Ḥasan-i-Ṣabbáḥ, the contemporary of 'Umar Khayyám and originator of the "New Propaganda," whose power may be said to date from his capture of the fortress of Alamút on Rajab 6, A.H. 483 (= September 4, A.D. 1090), and who died on May 23, A.D. 1124.[2] He was a stern man, and, having put to death both his sons for disobedience to the religious law, he appointed to succeed him his colleague, Kiyá Buzurg-ummíd, from whom the remaining six Grand Masters of the Order were directly descended. This man's son Muḥammad succeeded him on his death on January 20, A.D. 1138, and died on February 21, A.D. 1162. He in turn was followed by his son Ḥasan, called by his

Résumé of the history of the Assassins.

[1] A thousand, according to Juwayní.

[2] These dates are taken from the *Jámi'u't-Tawáríkh*, which gives a much more detailed history of the Isma'ílís than the *Jahán-gushá*, with which, however, it agrees closely, often *verbatim*.

followers *Ḥasan ʿalá dhikrihi's-salám*, or "Ḥasan, on whose mention be peace." This Ḥasan boldly declared himself to be, not the descendant of Kiyá Buzurg-ummíd, but of the Fáṭimid Imám Nizár b. al-Mustanṣir, in whose name the "New Propaganda" had been carried on: in other words, the Imám himself, not merely his representative. He had already in his father's lifetime shown signs of such ambitions, which had been sternly repressed, some two hundred and fifty of his partisans being put to death and an equal number expelled from Alamút. But on his father's death he was in a position to give effect to his designs, and on Ramaḍán 17, A.H. 559 (= August 8, A.D. 1164), he held a great assembly of all the Ismaʿílís, which he called *ʿÍd-i-Qiyámat*, or "The Feast of the Resurrection," and, in a *khuṭba* or homily which he preached, not only declared himself to be the Imám, but announced that the letter of the Law was henceforth abrogated, and that all the prescriptions of Islám were intended not in a literal, but in an allegorical sense. This announcement, being favourably received and generally acted on by his followers, greatly added to the horror with which the orthodox Muslims regarded them, and it was from this time, according to Rashídu'd-Dín Faḍlu'lláh, that they began to be called *Maláḥida*, *i.e.*, the heretics *par excellence*, though Ḥasan chose to name his new abode *Mú'min-ábád*, or "the Believer's Town." He greatly elaborated the Ismaʿílí doctrine in its philosophical aspects, and instituted a fresh propaganda, which he called *Daʿwat-i-Qiyámat*, or "the Propaganda of the Resurrection." Finally he was assassinated by his brother-in-law, Ḥusayn ibn Námáwar, a scion of the once great house of Buwayh or Daylam, at Lamsar, on January 10, A.D. 1166. He was succeeded by his son, Núru'd-Dín Muḥammad, who began by extirpating all the surviving Buwayhids, including his father's murderer, as an act of vengeance. He followed his father's doctrines and practices, and possessed, it is said, considerable literary ability and know-

ledge of philosophy. He it was who converted the great philosopher, Fakhru'd-Dín Rází by "weighty and trenchant arguments"—in other words, gold and the dagger—if not to his doctrines, at least to a decent show of respectfulness towards the formidable organisation of which he was the head, and this was, indeed, the beginning of the philosopher's good fortune, since the handsome allowance which he received from Alamút on condition that he refrained from speaking ill of the Isma'ílís, as had formerly been his wont, enabled him to present himself in a suitable manner to the princes of Ghúr, Shihábu'd-Dín and Ghiyáthu'd-Dín, and even to the great Muḥammad Khwárazmsháh himself.

Muḥammad, the son of *Ḥasan 'alá dhikrihi's-salám*, died on September 1, A.D. 1210, and was succeeded by his son, Jalálu'd-Dín, who utterly reversed the policy of his father and grandfather, abolished all antinomianism, and declared himself an orthodox Muslim, whence he was known as *Naw-Musulmán*, "the New Musulmán," or "Convert to Islám." He made formal profession of his fealty to the 'Abbásid Caliph an-Náṣir li-díni'lláh, entered into friendly relations with the surrounding Muslim princes, sent his mother (in A.D. 1210) to Mecca to perform the Pilgrimage, and, in order to convince the doctors of Qazwín (who, as near neighbours of Alamút, were least inclined to believe in the *boná fide* character of his conversion) of his sincerity, invited them to send a deputation to inspect his libraries and destroy all such books as, in their opinion, savoured of heresy. All were at last convinced of the genuineness of his professions, and the Caliph showed him honours so marked as to arouse the jealousy of Khwárazmsháh, and cause the beginning of that estrangement between Khwárazm and Baghdád which had such fatal results.[1] He also allied himself with the Atábek Mudhaffaru'd-Dín Uzbek (A.D. 1213–15) against Náṣiru'd-Dín Manglí, and—alone of the Grand Masters of Alamút—

[1] See p. 436 *supra*.

resided for a year and a half beyond the shadow of his fastnesses in 'Iráq, Arrán, and Ádharbayján. Later he allied himself with Jalálu'd-Dín Khwárazmsháh, but, on the appearance of Chingíz Khán on the scene, he deemed it prudent to tender his allegiance to him, his ambassadors being the first to do homage to the heathen conqueror when he crossed the Oxus. This act probably put the final touch to the disgust which his actions had inspired in the sect of which he was the supreme pontiff, and very shortly afterwards, on November 2 or 3, A.D. 1220, he died suddenly, poisoned, as it was supposed, by some of his women. He was succeeded by his only son, 'Alá'u'd-Dín, then only nine years of age, whose *wazír* acted at first as his regent, and inaugurated his reign by putting to death, even by burning, a number of the late Grand Master's female relatives whom he suspected, or pretended to suspect, of complicity in the death of Jalálu'd-Dín *Naw-Musulmán*.

According to Rashídu'd-Dín, 'Alá'u'd-Dín, when about fifteen years old, developed a moody melancholia which made it dangerous to approach him with any unwelcome news, or to inform him of any circumstance likely to displease him. During his reign the great astronomer Naṣíru'd-Dín Ṭúsí, author of the well-known treatise on Ethics known as the *Akhláq-i-Náṣirí*, was kidnapped by Náṣiru'd-Dín, the Isma'ílí Governor of Quhistán,[1] and sent to Alamút, where he remained as an honoured, if unwilling, guest until it was captured by the Mongols. This fact has a double importance, literary and historical: literary, because, as already remarked (p. 220 *supra*), it is probable that, by confusion of names, a garbled version of it was incorporated in the pseudo-autobiography of Náṣir-i-Khusraw, who lived more than a

[1] The work in question was named after, and originally dedicated to, this Náṣiru'd-Dín, though in a later recension the author apologises for this dedication and for certain concessions which he made to Isma'ílí sentiments.

century and a half earlier; historical, because it was Naṣíru'd-Dín Ṭúsí who first induced the unfortunate Ruknu'd-Dín Khursháh, of whom we shall speak directly, to surrender himself into the hands of the perfidious Mongols,[1] and afterwards persuaded Hulágú, when he was deliberating on the fate of al-Musta'ṣim bi'lláh, the last 'Abbásid Caliph, that no heavenly vengeance was likely to follow his execution.[2] What irony that this double-dyed traitor should be the author of one of the best-known works on Ethics written in Persian!

'Alá'u'd-Dín married very young, and his eldest son Ruknu'd-Dín Khúrsháh was born when he was only eighteen years of age. Between him and this son, whom he originally nominated as his successor, so great a jealousy gradually grew up that he desired to revoke this nomination; but the Isma'ílís, acting on their old principle, that an explicit nomination to the Imámate by an Imám was irrevocable, refused to allow it, and on the last day of Shawwál, A.H. 653 (= December 1, A.D. 1255), 'Alá'u'd-Dín was found murdered at Shír-kúh. The actual murderer, Ḥasan of Mázandarán, was killed by order of Rúknu'd-Dín, and his body was afterwards burned; but it was believed that Ruknu'd-Dín himself incited Ḥasan to do this deed, in proof of which Rashídu'd-Dín adduces the fact that he caused Ḥasan to be assassinated instead of dealing with him by more regular and legal methods, for fear of the disclosures which he might make under examination. This historian, after remarking that no parricide escapes the swift and condign vengeance of Heaven (in proof of which he cites the cases of Shírúyè the Sásánian and al-Muntaṣir, the 'Abbásid Caliph, both of whom murdered their fathers and lived but a short while to enjoy the fruits of their crime), points to the curious coincidence that Ruknu'd-Dín finally surrendered himself into the hands of his destroyers on the

[1] See my translation of Ibn Isfandiyár's *History of Ṭabaristán*, p. 259.
[2] D'Ohsson, vol. iii, ch. 4 and ch. 5.

last day of Shawwál, A.H. 654 (= Sunday, November 19, A.D. 1256), exactly a year, according to the lunar reckoning of the Muḥammadans, after his father was found murdered.

We must now return to Hulágú's expedition, which we left at Kesh in January, 1256. Tún and Khwáf, two of the strongholds of the Assassins in Quhistán, were the first places to bear the brunt of his attack. Both were taken about the end of March, 1256, and all the inhabitants of the latter over ten years of age were put to death, save a few girls of exceptional beauty, who were reserved for a worse fate. Then began the usual tactics of the Mongols, who, as already said, were wont to gain all they could by lying promises ere they unsheathed the sword which no oath could blunt and no blood satiate. Ruknu'd-Dín, torn by conflicting fears, had neither the courage to resist to the bitter end nor the prudence to seek by a full and instant submission the faint chance of a prolonged though ignominious life. He tried to bargain, but always it was he who gave while the Mongols merely promised, ever tightening their nets upon him. He surrendered some of his strongholds on the understanding that the garrisons and inhabitants should be spared, and sent his brother, Sháhinsháh, with 300 other hostages, to Hulágú; but soon, on some pretext, Sháhinsháh was put to death at Jamál-ábád, near Qazwín (whence, says Juwayní, the Qazwínís were afterwards wont to use the expression "sent to Jamál-ábád" as a euphemism for "executed"), and at a later date all the Isma'ílís who had surrendered, even to the babes in their cradles, were ruthlessly slaughtered. Some of the stalwarts were for a desperate resistance, and, even after Ruknu'd-Dín Khúrsháh had sought and obtained from Hulágú Khán a *yarlígh*, or written guarantee of safety, they repulsed a Mongol attack with great slaughter. But, as already said, the end came on November 19, when Ruknu'd-Dín gave himself up to the Mongols, and Alamút and Maymún-Dizh were pillaged and burned. 'Aṭá Malik-i-Juwayní obtained permission from

his master, Hulágú, to select from the world-renowned library of Alamút such books as he deemed most valuable and free from all taint of heresy, as well as some astronomical instruments which he coveted, and he has also left us a pretty circumstantial account of the strong and cunning workmanship which made the Castle of Alamút so long impregnable. According to a historical work by Fakhru'd-Dawla the Buwayhid which he found in the library, it was originally constructed by one of the princes of Daylam in A.H. 246 (= A.D. 860–61). Of the remaining strongholds of the Assassins in Persia (for the Syrian branch was never extirpated in such fashion, and their remnants still exist in that country), Lamsar was taken on January 4, A.D. 1257, while Gird-i-Kúh was still unsubdued in A.H. 658 (= A.D. 1260), when Minháj-i-Siráj was writing his *Ṭabaqát-i-Náṣirí* (ed. Nassau Lees, p. 418).

As for the unfortunate Ruknu'd-Dín, he was taken to Hamadán, and was at first well treated by his captors. A Mongol girl for whom he had conceived a passion was given him to wife, and he was presented with a hundred dromedary stallions, whom it pleased him to see fight with one another—a taste more degraded, if not less appropriate to his condition and pretensions, than his father's eccentric fancy for pasturing sheep. But on March 19, A.D. 1257 (at his own request, according to Juwayní and Rashídu'd-Dín, though this we may be permitted to doubt), he was sent off under escort to Qaráqorum to appear before Mangú Khán, the Mongol Emperor. On the way thither he was compelled to summon his officers in Quhistán to surrender their castles, of which the inhabitants, in spite of promises of safety, were of course massacred by the Mongols as soon as they had left the shelter of their walls, 12,000 of them being put to death in Quhistán alone. At Bukhárá Ruknu'd-Dín was roughly handled by his warders, and, on his arrival at Qaráqorum, Mangú Khán ordered him to be put to death, observing that it was a pity that the post-horses had been uselessly fatigued by bringing him so far, and issuing instructions that all of his surviving followers were to be ruthlessly destroyed. Vast multitudes must have perished, without doubt, but not all, for remnants of the sect, as I was informed by a very intelligent and observant Bábí dervish of Kirmán, of whom I saw a great deal when I was in Cairo in the early part of the year 1903, still exist in Persia, while in India (under the name of "Khojas" or "Khwájas") and Chitrál (under the name of "Mullás"), as well as in Zanzibar, Syria, and elsewhere, they still enjoy a certain influence and importance, though it requires a great effort of imagination to associate their present pontiff, the genial and polished Ágha Khán, with the once redoubtable Grand Masters of Alamút and the "Old Man of the Mountain"—"Le Vieux" of Marco Polo's quaint narrative.

The extirpation of the Assassins won for Hulágú Khán the applause of the orthodox Muhammadans, but his next procedure was one which only those whose position rendered it impossible for them to speak freely could mention without expressions of the utmost horror. Six months after the unfortunate Ruknu'd-Dín Khúrsháh had been sent to meet his doom at Qaráqorum, Hulágú Khán, having destroyed the Assassins root and branch, sent from Hamadán, which he had made his head-quarters, a summons to the Caliph al-Musta'ṣim bi'lláh to surrender himself and Baghdád, for five centuries the metropolis of Islám, to the Mongols. Two months later, in November, 1257, Hulágú took the field. He was accompanied by several Muhammadan princes, such as Abú Bakr b. Sa'd-i-Zangí, the Atábek of Shíráz, chiefly known as the patron of the great poet and writer, Sa'dí, and Badru'd-Dín Lúlú, the Atábek of Mosul, to whom Ibnu'ṭ-Ṭiqṭiqí so often refers in his charming manual of history, the *Kitábu'l-Fakhrí*; also by his secretary 'Aṭá Malik Juwayní, author of the often-quoted *Ta'ríkh-i-Jahán-gushá*, and Naṣíru'd-Dín Ṭúsí, the astronomer. Already

the Caliph had sent Sharafu'd-Dín 'Abdu'lláh ibnu'l-Jawzí as ambassador to Hulágú while he was still at Hamadán, but his reply to the Mongol ultimatum being, as usual, deemed unsatisfactory and evasive, the main Mongol army under Hulágú advanced directly upon Baghdád from the east, while another army under Báјú Noyán fetched a compass from the north by way of Takrít, near Mosul, so as to approach the doomed city from the west. The former army, according to Ibnu'ṭ-Ṭiqṭiqí,[1] exceeded 30,000 men, while the latter, according to the author of the *Ṭabaqát-i-Náṣirí*[2] (who, however, probably exaggerates) was 80,000 strong. The Caliph's available troops, on the other hand, according to the authority last named, amounted only to 20,000 men.

The first encounter took place at Takrít, where the Caliph's soldiers succeeded in destroying the bridge by which Báјú Noyán intended to cross the Tigris. Their success, however, was of brief duration, and soon the Mongols were swarming into Dujayl, al-Isḥáqí, Nahr Malik, Nahr 'Ísá, and other dependencies of Baghdád, while the panic-stricken inhabitants of these places fled to seek refuge in the metropolis. The ferry-men, as we learn from the *Kitábu'l-Fakhrí*, profited by the panic, exacting from the terrified fugitives for a passage across the river golden bracelets, precious stuffs, or a fee of several *dínárs*. The next encounter took place at Dujayl on or about January 11, 1258. Here again the Caliph's army, commanded by Mujáhidu'd-Dín Aybak, entitled *ad-Dawídár aṣ-Ṣaghír* (the Under-Secretary of State), and Malik 'Izzu'd-Dín b. Fatḥu'd-Dín, achieved a trifling initial success, in spite of the numerical inferiority of their forces; but during the night the Mongols, aided very probably by the Chinese engineers whom they had brought with them, succeeded in flooding the Muslim camp, an achievement which not only materially conduced to the defeat of the Caliph's army, but greatly

[1] *Kitábu'l-Fakhrí* (ed. Cairo, A.H. 1317), p. 300.
[2] Ed. Nassau Lees, p. 426.

aggravated the ensuing slaughter of the fugitives, especially the infantry. Of this battle, *à propos* of the invasion of Persia by the Arabs in the seventh century of our era, and the misplaced contempt of the well-armed and sumptuously equipped Persians for the tattered and half-naked Bedouin, the author of the *Kitábu'l-Fakhrí* (ed. Cairo, p. 72) gives the following personal account from his friend Falaku'd-Dín Muḥammad b. Aydímir.

"I was," says he, "in the army of the Under-Secretary when he went forth to meet the Tartars on the western side of the City of Peace (Baghdád), or the occasion of its supreme disaster in the year A.H. 656 (began January 8, A.D. 1258). We met at Nahr Bashír, one of the dependencies of Dujayl; and there would ride forth from amongst us to offer single combat a knight fully accoutred and mounted on an Arab horse, so that it was as though he and his steed together were [solid as] some great mountain. Then there would come forth to meet him from the Mongols a horseman mounted on a horse like a donkey, and having in his hand a spear like a spindle, wearing neither robe nor armour, so that all who saw him were moved to laughter. Yet ere the day was done the victory was theirs, and they inflicted on us a great defeat, which was the Key of Evil, and thereafter there befell us what befell us."

Most of the fugitives perished in the quagmires produced by the artificial flood already mentioned, except such as succeeded in swimming the river and escaping through the desert into Syria, and a few who, with the Dawídár, succeeded in re-entering Baghdád. The Dawídár and 'Izzu'd-Dín urged the Caliph to escape by boat, whilst there was yet time, to Baṣra, but the *Wazír* Ibnu'l-'Alqamí (according to the author of the *Ṭabaqát-i-Náṣirí*, p. 427) opposed this plan, and, while the Caliph still hesitated, the Mongols encompassed the city on every side. The siege proper seems to have begun on January 22: on the 30th a general assault was made, and on February 4 the Caliph again sent Ibnu'l-Jawzí to Hulágú with costly presents and offers of surrender. A few days later, lured by the usual false and specious promises of clemency, he

gave himself up, and, together with his eldest and second sons, Abu'l-'Abbás Aḥmad and Abu'l-Faḍá'il 'Abdu'r-Raḥmán, was cruelly put to death by order of Hulágú. As to the manner of his death, great uncertainty prevails, but the story that he was starved to death in his treasure-house, popularised by Longfellow in his poem "Kambalu," is less probable than the account given by most of the Muslim historians that he was wrapped in a carpet and beaten to death with clubs. Some such fate certainly befell him, for it was against the Mongol practice to shed royal blood, and when one of their own princes was executed they generally adopted the barbarous method of breaking his back.

The sack of Baghdád began on February 13, 1258, and lasted for a week, during which 800,000 of the inhabitants were put to death, while the treasures, material, literary, and scientific, accumulated during the centuries while Baghdád was the metropolis of the vast empire of the 'Abbásid Caliphs were plundered or destroyed. The loss suffered by Muslim learning, which never again reached its former level, defies description and almost surpasses imagination: not only were thousands of priceless books utterly annihilated, but, owing to the number of men of learning who perished or barely escaped with their lives, the very tradition of accurate scholarship and original research, so conspicuous in Arabic literature before this period, was almost destroyed. Never, probably, was so great and splendid a civilisation so swiftly consumed with fire and quenched with blood. "Then there took place," in the words of the *Kitábu'l-Fakhrí*, where it describes the storming of Baghdád, "such wholesale slaughter and unrestrained looting and excessive torture and mutilation as it is hard to hear spoken of even generally; how think you, then, of its details? There happened what happened of things I like not to mention; therefore imagine what you will, but ask me not of the matter!" And remember that he who wrote these words (in A.D. 1302, only forty-four years after the event of which he speaks) lived under a dominion which, though Muslim, was still Mongol, that, namely, of Ghάzán, the great-grandson of Hulágú.

There is a good deal or doubt as to the part played by the Caliph's *wazír*, Mu'ayyidu'd-Dín Muḥammad ibnu'l-'Alqamí, in the surrender of Baghdád. In the *Ṭabaqát-i-Náṣirí* (pp. 423 *et seqq.*) he is denounced in the bitterest terms as a traitor who deliberately reduced the numbers and strength of the garrison, and afterwards induced the Caliph to surrender, his motive in this being partly ambition, but chiefly a burning desire to avenge certain wrongs done to followers of the Shí'a sect, to which he himself belonged, by the Caliph's eldest son. Ibnu'ṭ-Ṭiqṭiqí, on the other hand, warmly defends him against this charge, which, he says, is disproved by the fact (communicated to him by Ibnu'l-'Alqamí's nephew, Aḥmad ibnu'ḍ-Ḍaḥḥák) that, on the surrender of Baghdád, the *wazír* was presented by Naṣíru'd-Dín Ṭúsí to Hulágú, who, pleased with his appearance and address, took him into his favour and associated him with the Mongol resident, 'Alí Bahádur, in the government of the ruined metropolis, which, he argues, he would not have done if he had known him to have betrayed the master whose favour he had so long enjoyed. It must be borne in mind, however, that these two men, Ibnu'l-'Alqamí, the ex-*wazír* of the Caliph, and Naṣíru'd-Dín Ṭúsí, who, for all his ethical and religious treatises, betrayed his Isma'ílí hosts and fellow-countrymen and helped to compass the Caliph's death to gain the favour of a bloodthirsty and savage heathen like Hulágú, both belonged to the sect of the Shí'a, as did also the worthy author of the *Kitábu'l-Fakhrí*; and for my part, I fear that the fact reported by the latter must probably be interpreted in quite the opposite way to that which he has adopted. It would, at any rate, thoroughly accord with all that we know of the Mongols, and particularly of Hulágú, to suppose that Ibnu'l-'Alqamí, seduced by fair promises and blinded by a religious fanaticism which preferred (as is not unfrequently the

case) a heathen to a heretic, and possibly acting in conjunction with his co-religionist Naşíru'd-Dín Ṭúsí, now exalted to the rank of Hulágú's *wazír*, betrayed Baghdád and the Caliph into the hands of the Mongols, who, as usual, showed him favour until their object was completely achieved and they had made all the use of him they could, and then got rid of him as quickly as possible. This conjecture is, I think, supported by the fact that he died in May, 1258, only three months after his master, whom he is accused of having betrayed. Yet the matter is doubtful, and will, in all probability, never now be certainly cleared up, so let him who will not follow Ibnu'ṭ-Ṭiqṭiqí in praying that God may be merciful to him at least refrain from the curses showered upon him by the author of the *Ṭabaqát-i-Náṣirí*, who shows a far greater fanaticism for the Sunní cause than does Ibnu'ṭ-Ṭiqṭiqí (a historian of extraordinary sense, moderation, and good feeling) for the Shí'a.

The account of the Caliph al-Musta'ṣim's character with which the *Kitábu'l-Fakhrí* concludes leaves us with the impression of an amiable but weak ruler, ill-fitted to grapple with the fearful peril which overshadowed all his days ere it finally overwhelmed him. He was attentive to his religious duties, gentle, continent in word and deed, a good scholar and calligraphist, devoted to his books, and very considerate towards his attendants; but, on the other hand, timid in action, undecided in judgement, and ignorant of statecraft. He refused to follow the evil custom generally followed by his predecessors of keeping his sons and other nearer male relatives in confinement, lest they should conspire against him or seek to usurp his place; and on one occasion, when a young servant had fallen asleep on the ground beside him while he was reading in his library, and in his sleep had rolled on to the carpet specially spread for him, and even put his feet on the cushion against which he was leaning, he signed to the librarian to wait till he had left the room, and then to wake the lad, lest he should be overcome with fear and confusion on account of what he had done. In love of books and encouragement of men of letters the *wazír* Ibnu'l-'Alqamí was not behind his master: his library comprised ten thousand volumes, including many rare and precious works, and many authors and poets dedicated their works to him. He was also, according to Ibnu'ṭ-Ṭiqṭiqí, from whom all these particulars are derived, not only liberal, but quite devoid of the love of wealth.

Like the author of the *Ṭabaqát-i-Náṣirí*, I should have preferred to end this volume of mine, so far as the historical portion of it is concerned, with some event less lamentable than this, the supreme catastrophe of Islám and of the Arabo-Persian civilisation of the 'Abbásid Caliphate. But here is the natural point at which to interrupt my *Literary History of Persia:* a history which I hope some day to continue in another volume, or in other volumes, down to our own times. But, so far as this volume is concerned, it remains only for me to discuss in two concluding chapters the literature of the period which I have just attempted to sketch in outline; a period, roughly speaking, which comprises the first fifty or sixty years of the thirteenth century of our era.

CHAPTER VIII

WRITERS OF THE EARLIER MONGOL PERIOD

(A.H. 600–660 = A.D. 1203–1262)

In this chapter I propose to speak of the principal writers of the period described in the last, leaving only the Persian poets, concerning at least three of whom there is a good deal to be said, for the concluding chapter of this volume. These writers may be divided into three classes, viz. (1) those of Persian birth who wrote exclusively or chiefly in Persian; (2) those of Persian birth who wrote exclusively or chiefly in Arabic; and (3) non-Persian authors who wrote in Arabic, but who, either because of some special connection with Persia or Persian topics, or because of their influence and importance in the world of Islám generally, cannot be altogether passed over even in a book treating primarily of the Literary History of Persia only. Practically, however, it will be more convenient to ignore this distinction, and to consider them together, class by class, according to the subject on which they wrote, without regard to the language which they employed, since at this time the Arabic language was still generally used in Persia as the language of culture, learning, and science, and only fell from this position with the fall of the Caliphate and the destruction of Baghdád, the metropolis of Islám.

Let us begin with the historians, biographers, and geographers, to the most important of whom we have already had frequent occasion to refer. Foremost amongst these, and, indeed, amongst the chroniclers of all time and all lands, is 'Izzu'd-Dín ibnu'l-Athír al-Jazarí (that is, a native of Jazíratu'bni 'Umar, near Mosul), the author of the great chronicle known as *al-Kámil* ("the Perfect" or "Complete"), which contains the history of the world, as known to the Muslims of that period, from the earliest times down to the year A.H. 628 (= A.D. 1230–31). The biographer Ibn Khallikán, who visited him at Aleppo in November, A.D. 1229, speaks of him in the highest terms, praising equally his modesty and his learning. As this biographical notice can be read by all in de Slane's translation (vol. ii, pp. 288–290), I shall refrain from citing it here, and will only add that he was born in May, A.D. 1160, and died in the same month of A.D. 1233. His great work, the "Perfect" Chronicle, was published in its entirety by Tornberg at Leyden in 1851–76 in fourteen volumes, and at Buláq in A.H. 1290–1303 (= A.D. 1873–86), in twelve volumes. Unfortunately the Egyptian edition, which alone can be easily obtained now, has no index, so that its utility is considerably impaired; a serious matter in a book of reference indispensable to the student of Muhammadan history. Besides this great chronicle, Ibnu'l-Athír wrote a history of the most eminent Companions of the Prophet, entitled *Usdu'l-Ghába* ("Lions of the Thicket"), published at Cairo in five volumes in A.H. 1280 (A.D. 1863–64); a revised abridgement of the *Ansáb*, or "Genealogies," of as-Sam'ání, unpublished; and a history of the Atábeks of Mosul, printed in full in vol. ii of the *Recueil des historiens arabes des croisades*.

Historians, biographers, and geographers.

Ibnu'l-Athír.

Another general historian of merit who belongs to this period, and who, like Ibnu'l-Athír, wrote in Arabic, is the Jacobite Christian Yuḥanná Abu'l-Faraj, better known as Barhebræus (*Ibnu'l-'Ibrí*, *i.e.*, "the son of the Jew," his father Ahrún, or Aaron, having been converted from Judaism to

Christianity), or by the name Gregorius, which he assumed in A.D. 1246, when he was made Bishop of Gubos, near Maláṭiyya. He was born at that town in A.D. 1226, fled with his father, who was a physician, from the terror of the advancing Mongols, to Antioch in 1243, and thence visited Tripoli. In 1252 he was promoted to the see of Aleppo, and in 1264 he was elected Mafriyán, or Catholicus, of the Eastern Jacobites, during which period he resided alternately at Mosul and in Ádharbayján (Tabríz and Marágha), in the north-west of Persia. He died at the last-mentioned place on July 30, A.D. 1286. His history, the *Mukhtaṣaru Ta'ríkhi 'd-Duwal* ("Abridgement of the History of Dynasties"), was originally written in Syriac, and the Arabic version was made towards the end of his life at the request of certain Muslims of note. It was published by Pococke with a Latin translation at Oxford in A.D. 1663; a German translation appeared in A.D. 1783; and a new and excellent edition by the Jesuit Ṣáliḥání was printed at Beyrout in A.D. 1890. This last, which comprises 630 pages, contains, besides the text, a short life of the author, a full index of names, and useful chronological tables. The history treats of ten dynasties, viz. (1) the Patriarchs (*al-Awliyá*) from the time of Adam; (2) the Judges of Israel; (3) the Kings of Israel; (4) the Chaldæans; (5) the "Magians," *i.e.* the Persian Kings from the mythical Gayúmarth down to the last Darius, who was defeated and killed by Alexander the Great; (6) the ancient or "idolatrous" Greeks; (7) the Kings of the "Franks," by which term he means the Romans; (8) the Byzantine or "Christian" Greeks; (9) the Muslims; (10) the Mongols, whose history is carried down to the accession of Arghún in A.D. 1284. A very interesting account of Barhebræus and his times is given by Professor Nöldeke in his *Sketches from Eastern History* (pp. 236–256 of the English translation of Mr. John Sutherland Black), and to this we refer such as desire further information about his life and work.

Abu'l-Faraj Barhebræus.

Minháj-i-Siráj.

Of the general historians who wrote in Persian during this period, the most notable is, perhaps, Minháj-i-Siráj of Júzján, near Balkh, the author of the *Ṭabaqát-i-Náṣirí*, which I have several times had occasion to cite in the preceding chapter. He was born about A.D. 1193, and, like his father and grandfather, was originally in the service of the House of Ghúr. In A.D. 1226 he came to India, and attached himself first to Sulṭán Náṣiru'd-Dín Qubácha, but when, about a year later, this prince was overthrown by Shamsu'd-Dín Íltatmish, he passed into the service of the conqueror, to whose son, Náṣiru'd-Dín Maḥmúd Sháh, he dedicated his history, which he completed in September, A.D. 1260. Further particulars of his life are given in Rieu's *Persian Catalogue*, pp. 72–3, and in Sir H. M. Elliot's *History of India*, vol. ii, pp. 260–1. His history is divided into twenty-three sections, beginning with the Patriarchs and Prophets, and ending with the Mongol Invasion, concerning which he gives many interesting particulars not to be found elsewhere. Part of the work has been published by Captain Nassau Lees and translated by Major Raverty in the *Bibliotheca Indica*. The published portion of the text unfortunately comprises only those dynasties which were connected with India, and omits entirely the sections dealing with the Táhirís, Ṣaffárís, Sámánís, Daylamís (House of Buwayh), Seljúqs, Khwárazmsháhs and other dynasties of much greater interest to the student of Persian history. Towards the end of the book is given a very curious Arabic *qaṣída* ascribed to Yaḥyá A'qab, one of the disciples of 'Alí ibn Abí Ṭálib, the Prophet's cousin and son-in-law, foretelling the calamities of the Mongol Invasion. This poem, with a Persian prose translation, occurs on pp. 439–443 of the printed text.

One other general history composed during this period deserves, perhaps, a passing mention from the fact that it was one of the earliest Arabic chronicles published in Europe. This is the *Kitábu'l-Majmú'i'l-Mubárak* of Jirjís (or 'Abdu'lláh)

b. Abi'l-Yásir b. Abi'l-Makárim al-Makín b. al-ʿAmíd, whereof the text, accompanied by a Latin translation, was printed at Leyden in A.D. 1625, by the learned Dutch Orientalist Erpenius (Thomas van Erpe), with the title *Historia Saracenica, arabice olim exarata a Georgio El macino et latine reddita opera Th. Erpenii.* An English translation by Purchas appeared in the following year, and a French translation by Vattier in 1657, so that this book, with the later chronicle of Abu'l-Fidá, Prince of Ḥamát (born A.D. 1273, died A.D. 1331), was for a long while the chief Arabic source for the history of Islám accessible to European scholars. On this ground only is it mentioned here, for the author, who was born in A.D. 1205 and died in A.D. 1273, was an Egyptian Christian, not connected in any way with Persia.

Al-Makín.

We pass now to those historians and biographers who treated of a particular dynasty, monarch, period, province, town, or class, including those who wrote biographical dictionaries. In the chapter treating of the House of Subuktigín or Dynasty of Ghazna, we repeatedly had occasion to refer to al-ʿUtbí's *Ta'ríkhu'l-Yamíní*, or history of Sulṭán Maḥmúd Yamínu'd-Dawla of Ghazna. This book, originally written in Arabic, was in the period now under discussion translated into Persian by Abu'sh-Sharaf Náṣiḥ of Jurbádhaqán, or, to give it its Persian name, Gulpáyagán, a place situated between Iṣfahán and Hamadán. The translation, as shown by Rieu, who gives copious references to the literature bearing on this subject (*Persian Catalogue*, pp. 157–8), was made about A.D. 1205–10, and is represented in the British Museum by a fine old manuscript transcribed in A.D. 1266. A lithographed edition was published at Ṭihrán in A.H. 1272 (= A.D. 1855–56), and this Persian translation of al-ʿUtbí's work has itself been translated into Turkish by Dervísh Ḥasan, and into English by the Rev. James Reynolds. The relation between it and its Arabic original has been carefully studied by Professor Nöldeke

Special historians and biographers.

Al-Jurbádhaqání.

in vol. xxiii of the *Sitzungsberichte der Kaiserlichen Akademie* (Vienna, 1857, pp. 15–102). He points out (p. 76) that the Persian version is, save for the letters, documents, and poems cited in the original Arabic from al-'Utbí's work, of the freest kind, the translator's object being not so much to produce an accurate rendering as a rhetorical imitation of his original; hence he considers himself at liberty to change, omit, and add as much as he pleases.

Of the House of Seljúq, the dynasty which succeeded the House of Ghazna, there also exists an important monograph in Arabic, of which the third and last recension (that now rendered accessible to scholars in Houtsma's excellent edition) dates from this time. The history in question, which has been frequently referred to in the chapters of this book treating of the Seljúq period, was originally composed in Persian by the Minister Anúshirwán b. Khálid, who died, according to the *'Uyúnu'l-Akhbár*,[1] in A.H. 532 (= A.D. 1137–38). It was afterwards translated into Arabic, with considerable amplifications and additions, by 'Imádu'd-Dín al-Kátib al-Iṣfahání in A.D. 1183; and this translation was edited in an abridged and simplified form in A.D. 1226 by al-Fatḥ b. 'Alí b. Muḥammad al-Bundárí. The relations of these recensions to one another are fully discussed by Houtsma in the illuminating Preface which he has prefixed to his edition of the last of them, that of al-Bundárí, which, as he points out, exists in two recensions, a longer one represented by the Oxford MS., and a shorter one represented by the Paris Codex. To al-Bundárí we are also indebted for an Arabic prose epitome of the *Sháhnáma* of Firdawsí, of which an excellent manuscript (Qq. 46 of the Burckhardt Collection) is preserved in the Cambridge University Library. Professor Nöldeke, on p. 77 of his *Iranisches Nationalepos*, has called attention to the possible importance of this work as an

Al-Fatḥ al-Bundárí.

[1] F. 126^a of the Cambridge manuscript marked Add. 2,922.

aid to the reconstitution of a more correct text of the *Sháhnáma.*

Amongst the histories of particular dynasties composed in this period, a very high place must be assigned to one which has been largely used in the last chapter, I mean the Persian *Ta'ríkh-i-Jahán-gushá*, or "History of the World-Conqueror" (*i.e.*, Chingíz Khán), of 'Aṭá Malik-i-Juwayní. The importance of this book has been sufficiently emphasised, and the circumstances of its author have been sufficiently described already. That no edition of this work has ever been published, in spite of the excellent materials for such which exist, especially in the Bibliothèque Nationale at Paris,[1] is nothing less than a scandal which it is one of my chief ambitions to remedy. It consists of three volumes or parts, of which the first treats of the origin and history of the Mongols and the conquests of Chingíz Khán; the second of the Khwárazmsháhs; and the third of the Assassins, or Isma'ílís of Alamút and Kúhistán, and of Hulágú's campaign against them. D'Ohsson, who made large use of this book in compiling his *Histoire des Mongols*, is, I think, unduly severe on the author, whose circumstances compelled him to speak with civility of the barbarians whom it was his misfortune to serve.

'Aṭá Malik-i-Juwayní.

Shibábu'd-Dín Muḥammad b. Aḥmad an-Nasawí (*i.e.*, of Nasá, in Khurásán), the secretary and biographer of the gallant Jalálu'd-Dín Khwárazmsháh, next claims our attention. His memoirs of this ill-fated prince, like the work last mentioned, have been repeatedly referred to in the last chapter, and are accessible in the Arabic text and French translation published by M. Houdas (Paris, 1891, 1895). They were written in A.H. 639 (= A.D. 1241–42), some ten years after the death of Jalálu'd-Dín, with whom the author was closely associated throughout the greater part of

An-Nasawí.

[1] See my article on the contents of this history and the materials for an edition in the *J.R.A.S.* for January, 1904.

his adventurous career, and their interest and importance are well indicated by M. Houdas in the Preface which he has prefixed to his translation, from which we may cite a few of the most salient paragraphs.

"Aussi, sauf de rares moments qu'il consacra à remplir des missions de confiance, En-Nesawi ne quitta point Djelâl ed-Dîn pendant la plus grande partie de son règne, et il était encore auprès de lui la veille du jour où ce prince allait dans sa fuite succomber sous le poignard d'un Kurde sauvage. Non seulement il a assisté à la plupart des événements qu'il raconte, mais le plus souvent il y a pris personellement une part plus ou moins active, aussi peut-on dire jusqu'à un certain point que sa 'Vie de Mankobirti' constitue de véritables mémoires.

"Grâce à la confiance dont l'honorait le sultan, grâce aussi à ses relations intimes avec les plus hauts personnages de l'empire, En-Nesawi a pu voir les choses autrement qu'un spectateur ordinaire; il lui a été loisible d'en pénétrer les causes ou d'en démêler les origines. Et, comme il ne composa son ouvrage que dix ans après la mort de son maître, on comprend qu'il ait pu parler en toute franchise sur tous les sujets qu'il traitait. On sent du reste dans son récit que, si parfois il exprime ses critiques avec une certaine réserve, c'est qu'il ne veut pas être accusé d'ingratitude envers celui à qui il dut toute sa fortune. Peut-être aussi avait-il encore à cette époque à ménager la réputation de quelques-uns de ses amis quoique, sous ce rapport, il ne semble pas cacher ses vrais sentiments. Dans tous les cas la modération même dont il use est un gage de sa sincérité.

"Non content de décrire ce qu'il a vu ou de rapporter ce qu'il a entendu dire, En-Nesawi apprécie les événements dont il parle: il en recherche les causes et en tire des renseignements souvent curieux si on se reporte à ces époques lointaines. Il semble que, tout en admirant le Kámil *d'Ibn El-Athîr, il sente la sécheresse un peu trop marquée de cette chronique et qu'il ait voulu montrer, pour sa part, qu'on pouvait employer une forme plus attachante, où la curiosité de l'esprit trouvait sa satisfaction et où la raison rencontrait un aliment qui lui convenait.*

"En-Nesawi manie la langue arabe avec beaucoup d'élégance; néanmoins on sent dans son style l'influence persane. . . ."

To this excellent appreciation of the man and his book it is unnecessary to add anything more in this place.

We come now to biographers, amongst whom Ibn Khallikán

holds the highest place, not only amongst his contemporaries, but amongst all Muslim writers. His celebrated work the *Wafayátu'l-A'yán* ("Obituaries of Men of Note"), begun at Cairo in A.D. 1256 and completed on January 4, 1274, is one of the first books of reference which the young Orientalist should seek to acquire. The text was lithographed by Wüstenfeld in 1835–43, and has since been printed at least twice in Egypt, while it is accessible to the English reader in the Baron MacGuckin de Slane's translation (4 vols., London, 1843–71). The author, a scion of the great Barmecides, or House of Barmak, was born at Arbela in September, 1211, but from the age of eighteen onwards resided chiefly in Aleppo, Damascus, Cairo, and Alexandria, where he held several important scholastic and judicial posts, and finally died in October, 1282. Later supplements to his great biographical dictionary were written by al-Muwaffaq Faḍlu'-lláh aṣ-Ṣaqá'í (down to A.D. 1325), and Ibn Shákir (died A.D. 1362), and it was translated into Persian by Yúsuf b. Aḥmad b. Muḥammad b. 'Uthmán in A.D. 1490, and again by Kabír b. Uways b. Muḥammad al-Laṭífí in the reign of the Ottoman Sulṭán Selím (A.D. 1512–19).

Ibn Khallikán.

Coming now to biographers of special classes or professions, we have to mention two important works in Arabic and one in Persian which belong to this period, to wit, al-Qifṭí's *Notices of the Philosophers*, Ibn Abí Uṣaybi'a's *Lives of the Physicians* and 'Awfí's Biographies of Persian Poets entitled "The Marrow of Understandings" (*Lubábu'l-Albáb*). All these either have been published or are in process of publication, al-Qifṭí by Dr. Julius Lippert (Leipzig, 1903), Ibn Abí Uṣaybi'a by A. Müller (Königsberg, 1884), and the *Lubáb*, of which one volume was published in 1903, while the other is still in the press, by myself. Let us consider them in the above order.

Biographers of special classes.

Jamálu'd-Dín Abu'l-Ḥasan 'Alí b. Yúsuf al-Qifṭí was born at Qifṭ, in Upper Egypt, in A.D. 1172. His paternal ancestors came originally from Kúfa, while his mother belonged to the great Arab tribe of Quḍá'a. He studied with ardour in Cairo and

Al-Qifṭí.

Qifṭ till he reached the age of fifteen, when his father Yúsuf was appointed by Saladin (Ṣaláḥu'd-Dín) to a high judicial post in Jerusalem, whither the family transferred their residence. About A.D. 1201 our author's father, Yúsuf, went to Ḥarrán, celebrated even in the early 'Abbásid period as the centre of Greek philosophic culture in Asia, and hence called Hellenopolis, where he became *wazír* to al-Malik al-Ashraf. Thence, after performing the pilgrimage to Mecca, he retired to Yemen, where he ultimately died in A.D. 1227. His son, our author, meanwhile had gone to Aleppo, where he was placed in charge of the Ministry of Finance, and received the title of al-Qáḍí'l-Akram. He seems to have been not only an upright and capable servant of the State and a diligent seeker after knowledge, but a ready helper and patron of men of learning, the geographer Yáqút, driven westwards from Khurásán, as we have seen, before the Mongol Invasion, being one of those to whom he extended hospitality and protection. Though desiring above all things leisure to pursue his studies, he was obliged in A.D. 1236 to accept office for the third time, and it was as Wazír to al-Malik al-'Azíz that he died twelve years later, in December, 1248. Fuller details of his life, mostly derived from Yáqút's *Mu'jamu'l-Udabá* (of which an edition is now being prepared by Professor Margoliouth, of Oxford, for publication in the E. J. W. Gibb Memorial Series), will be found in the interesting and sympathetic Introduction which Dr. Lippert has prefixed to his edition of the *Ta'ríkhu'l-Ḥukamá*, and in which he is summed up as "an Arabian Wilhelm von Humboldt." He wrote much, and Yáqút, who predeceased him by nearly twenty years, enumerates the titles of about a score of his works, nearly all of which, unfortunately, appear to be lost, destroyed, as A. Müller supposes, by the Mongols when they sacked Aleppo in A.D. 1260. Even the *Ta'ríkhu'l-Ḥukamá*, in the form wherein it now exists, is, in the opinion of its learned editor, Dr. Lippert, only an abridgement of the original. The book, in the recension which we possess, contains 414 biographies of philosophers, physicians, mathematicians, and astronomers belonging to all periods of the world's history from the earliest times down to the author's own days, and is rich in materials of great importance for the study of the history of Philosophy. It has been freely used by several contemporary and later writers, notably Ibn Abí Uṣaybi'a, Barhebræus, and Abu'l-Fidá. The arrangement of the biographies is alphabetical, not chronological.

Ibn Abí Uṣaybi'a.

Ibn Abí Uṣaybi'a, the author of the *Ṭabaqátu'l-Ḥukamá*, or "Classes of Physicians," was born at Damascus in A.D. 1203, studied medicine there and at Cairo, and died in his native city in January, 1270. His father, like himself, practised the healing art, being, to speak more precisely, an oculist. The son numbered amongst his teachers the celebrated physician and botanist Ibn Bayṭâr, and was for a time director of a hospital founded at Cairo by the great Saladin (Ṣaláḥu'd-Dín). His book was published by A. Müller at Königsberg in A.D. 1884, and at Cairo in 1882, and a fine old manuscript of it, transcribed in A.H. 690 (= A.D. 1291), is included amongst the Schefer MSS. now preserved in the Bibliothèque Nationale at Paris. Wüstenfeld's useful little *Geschichte der Arabischen Aerzte und Naturforscher* (Göttingen, 1840) is chiefly founded upon the work of Ibn Abí Uṣaybi'a.

Muḥammad 'Awfí.

Muḥammad 'Awfí, the author of the often-cited *Lubábu'l-Albáb*, and also of an immense collection of anecdotes entitled *Jawámi'u'l-Ḥikáyát wa Lawámi'u'r-Riwáyát*, next claims our attention. He derived his *nisba* of 'Awfí, as he himself tells us in a passage which occurs in vol. i of the latter work, from 'Abdu'r-Raḥmán b. 'Awf, one of the most eminent of the Companions of the Prophet, from whom he professed to be descended. His earlier life was chiefly passed in Khurásán and Transoxiana, especially in Bukhárá, whence he presently made his way to India, and attached himself to the court of Sulṭán Náṣiru'd-Dín Qubácha, to whose *Wazír*, 'Aynu'l-Mulk Ḥusayn al-Ash'arí, he dedicated his biography of Persian poets, the *Lubábu'l-Albáb*. When in April, 1228, the above-mentioned prince lost his kingdom and his life at the fall of the fortress of Bhakar, 'Awfí, like the historian Minháj-i-Siráj, of whom we have already spoken, passed into the service of the conqueror, Shamsu'd-Dín Iltatmish, to whom he dedicated his *Jawámi'u'l-Ḥikáyát*. This, with a few additional particulars as to the dates when he visited different towns and the eminent poets and other persons with whom he was acquainted, is practically all that is known of his life. As to his works, the *Jawámi'u'l-Ḥikáyát* still remains unpublished, though manuscripts of it are not rare, a particularly fine old copy which formerly belonged to Sir William Jones and is now in the Library of the India Office (W. 79) being specially deserving of mention. This vast compilation of anecdotes of very unequal worth is divided into four parts, each comprising twenty-five chapters, each of which in turn contains a number of stories illustrating the subject to which the chapter is devoted. The style is very simple and straightforward, in which particular it offers a forcible contrast to 'Awfí's earlier and more important work, the *Lubábu'l-Albáb*. This latter—"the oldest Biography of Persian Poets," as Nathaniel Bland called it in his classical description of one of the only two manuscripts of it known to exist in Europe[1]—was largely used by Ethé in the compila-

[1] Bland's article appeared in vol. ix of the *J.R.A.S.* in 1848. The MS. which he described was lent to him by his friend, John Bardon Elliott, and on his death was sold amongst his own books to Lord Crawford of Balcarres, whose son, the present Lord Crawford, sold it in 1901, together with his other Oriental MSS., to Mrs. Rylands of Manchester, by whom it was placed in the John Rylands Library in that city. The other manuscript known to exist in Europe forms part of the Sprenger Collection in the Berlin Library, and belonged formerly to the King of Oude. Both of these MSS. I used in preparing my edition, of which

tion of numerous and excellent monographs on the early Persian poets, but has otherwise been almost inaccessible to scholars until the publication of my edition, of which one volume appeared in 1903, while the other is nearly complete and should appear in the course of 1906. It is, on account of its antiquity, and the large number of otherwise unknown or almost unknown poets whose biographies it gives, a work of capital importance for the history of Persian Literature, but in many ways it is disappointing, since the notices of most of the poets are as devoid of any precise dates or details of interest as they are inflated with turgid rhetoric and silly word-plays, the selection of poems is often bad and tasteless, and, while several poets of great merit, such as Náṣir-i-Khusraw and 'Umar Khayyám, are entirely omitted, many mediocrities, especially towards the end of vol. i, where the author treats of his contemporaries at the Court of Sulṭán Náṣiru'd-Dín Qubácha, are noticed in exaggerated terms of praise in articles of quite unnecessary length. Yet, in spite of these defects, the work, containing as it does notices of nearly three hundred Persian poets who flourished before Sa'dí had made his reputation, is of the very first importance, and, when properly exploited, will add enormously to our knowledge of this early period of Persian Literature. Yet it is hard to avoid a certain feeling of annoyance and irritation when one reflects how easily the author, with the means at his disposal, could have made it far more interesting and valuable.

Local histories. **Ibn Isfandiyár.** We come now to local histories, of which the most important composed in Persian during this period is the History of Ṭabaristán of Muḥammad b. al-Ḥasan b. Isfandiyár. We know little of the author save what he himself incidentally tells us in the pages of his book,

vol. ii was published first in 1903, while vol. i is now (April, 1906) nearly completed. At least one other MS. must exist in Persia, for the work was largely used by the late Riḍá-qulí Khán in the compilation of his *Majma'u'l-Fusaḥá*, lithographed at Ṭihrán in A.D. 1878.

which represents him as returning from Baghdád to Ray in A.H. 606 (= A.D. 1209–1210), and finding there in the Library of King Rustam b. Shahriyár the Arabic history of Ṭabaristán composed by al-Yazdádí in the time of Qábús b. Washmgír (A.D. 976–1012); on this he based his own Persian work. Shortly afterwards he was obliged to return to Ámul, whence he went to Khwárazm, at that time, as he says, a most flourishing city and a meeting-place of men of learning. Here he remained at least five years, and discovered other materials germane to his subject which he incorporated in his book, on which he was still engaged in A.H. 613 (= A.D. 1216–17). His subsequent history is unknown, and we cannot say whether or no he perished in the sack of Khwárazm by the Mongols in A.D. 1220, or whether he had previously returned to his home in Mázandarán. Of his book not much need be said, since its value can be judged from the abridged translation of it which I published as the second volume of the E. J. W. Gibb Memorial Series. It contains a great deal of legendary matter in the earlier part, but much historical, biographical, and geographical information of value in the Muhammadan period, and in particular many details concerning persons of local celebrity, but of considerable general interest, notably poets who wrote verses in the dialect of Ṭabaristán, which seems at that time to have been extensively cultivated as a literary vehicle. Ibn Isfandiyár's chronicle is naturally brought to an end with the death of Rustam b. Ardashír in A.H. 606 (= A.D. 1209–10), but a later hand has carried on the record as far as A.H. 750 (= A.D. 1349–50).

ad-Dubaythí.

Local histories of the type of Ibn Isfandiyár's work are numerous, and constitute a well-defined division of Persian Literature. We have, for example, such local histories of Iṣfahán, Shíráz, Yazd, Qum, Herát, Sístán, Shushtar, &c., besides several others of Ṭabaristán. Of these last several were published by Dorn, but in general this class of works exists only in manuscript, though a few have been lithographed in the East. But there is another kind of local history which may more accurately be described as a local Dictionary of Biography, treating, generally in alphabetical order, of the eminent men produced by a particular town or province. Such a book was composed on the learned men of Baghdád by Ibnu'l-Khaṭíb (b. A.D. 1002, d. 1071) in Arabic in fourteen volumes, and at the period of which we are now speaking a Supplement to this, also in Arabic, was written by Abú 'Abdi'lláh Muḥammad ad-Dubaythí, who died in A.D. 1239. This book does not, so far as is known, exist in its entirety; there is a portion of it at Paris, and what I believe to be another portion in the Cambridge Library. This last is on the cover ascribed to Ibnu'l-Khaṭíb, but as he died, as stated above, in A.D. 1071, and as the volume contains matter referring to the year A.H. 615 (= A.D. 1218–19), it evidently cannot be his work, but rather the Supplement. As this volume, which is of considerable size, contains only a portion of one letter (*'ayn*) of the alphabet, the work must have been of a very extensive character.

Geographies and Travels.

Yáqút.

We next come to books of Geography and Travel, of which I will here mention only three, all written in Arabic. The most important of these, to which I have already referred in the last chapter, is the great Geographical Dictionary of Yáqút, entitled *Mu'jamu'l-Buldán*, published by Wüstenfeld in six volumes (1866–71). Yáqút b. 'Abdu'lláh, born in A.D. 1179 of Greek parents, and hence called "ar-Rúmí," was enslaved in boyhood, and passed into the possession of a merchant of Ḥamát, whence he took the *nisba* of al-Ḥamawí. He received an excellent education and travelled widely, his journeys extending south-east as far as the Island of Kísh in the Persian Gulf, and north-east to Khurásán and Merv, where, as we have seen, he was busily at work in the splendid libraries which then graced that city when the terrible Mongol Invasion drove him in headlong flight to Mosul. There, in the spring of A.D. 1224, he completed his great work, the *Mu'jamu'l-Buldán*, a most precious book of reference for all that concerns the geography and much that touches the history of Western Asia, accessible, so far as the Persian part is concerned, to non-Orientalists in M. Barbier de Meynard's *Dictionnaire Géographique, historique et littéraire de la Perse et des contrées adjacentes* (Paris, 1871). He is also the author of two other geographical works, the *Marásidu'l-Ittilá'* (edited by Juynboll at Leyden, 1850–64), and the *Mushtarik*, which treats of different places having the same name, edited by the indefatigable Wüstenfeld at Göttingen in 1846. Besides these he composed a Dictionary of Learned Men, entitled *Mu'jamu'l-Udabá*, of which a portion is to be edited by Professor D. S. Margoliouth in the E. J. W. Gibb Memorial Series; and a work on Genealogies. A good and sympathetic appreciation of Yáqút is given by Von Kremer in his charming *Culturgeschichte des Orients*, vol. ii, pp. 433–6.

al-Qazwíní.

Another geographer and cosmographer of a less scientific type is Zakariyyá b. Muḥammad b. Maḥmúd al-Qazwíní, the author of two works (both published by Wüstenfeld in 1848–49). One of these is entitled *'Ajá'ibu'l-Makhlúqát* ("The Marvels of Creation," or, rather, "of created things"), and treats of the solar system, the stars and other heavenly bodies, and the animal, vegetable, and mineral kingdoms, and also contains a section on monsters and bogies of various kinds. The other is entitled *Athárul-Bilád* ("Monuments of the Lands"), and is a more or less systematic description of the chief towns and countries known to the Muhammadans at that period, arranged alphabetically under the Seven Climes, beginning with the First, which lies next the Equator, and ending with the Seventh, which includes the most northerly lands. The former of these two books is by far the more popular in the East, and manuscripts, often with miniatures, both of the original and still more of the Persian translation, are common. The latter, however, is in reality by far the more important and interesting, for not only does it contain a great deal of useful geographical information, but also much valuable biographical material, including, under the towns to which they belonged, a great number of the Persian poets, such as Anwarí, 'Asjadí, Awḥadu'd-Dín of Kirmán, Fakhrí of Gurgán, Farrukhí, Firdawsí, Jalál-i-Ṭabíb, Jalál-i-Khwárí, Kháqání, Abú Ṭáhir al-Khátúní, Mujír of Baylaqán, Náṣir-i-Khusraw, Nidhámí of Ganja, 'Umar-i-Khayyám, Abú Sa'íd b. Abi'l-Khayr, Saná'í, Shams-i-Ṭabasí, 'Unsurí, and Rashídu'd-Dín Waṭwáṭ. The geographical information, too, though inferior in point of accuracy to that given by Yáqút and the earlier geographers, is full of interesting and entertaining matter. It is rather curious that though there is no mention made of England, the account of the Sixth Clime includes an article on Ireland, with some account of whale-fishing, while a long notice is devoted to Rome. Under the Seventh Clime we find accounts of the ordeals by fire, by water, and by battle in vogue amongst the Franks; of witchcraft, witch-finding, and witch-burning; and of the Varangian Fiord. Indeed, I know few more readable and entertaining works in Arabic than this. Strictly speaking, it falls just outside the period with which this volume concludes, for the first edition was written in A.D. 1263, and the second, considerably enlarged and modified, in A.D. 1276. The author was born at Qazwín, in Persia, in A.D. 1203, lived for a while at Damascus about A.D. 1232, was Qáḍi (Judge) of Wásiṭ and Ḥilla under the last Caliph al-Musta'ṣim, and died in A.D. 1283. His *'Ajá'ibu'l-Makhlúqát* is dedicated to 'Aṭá Malik-i-Juwayní, the author of the *Ta'ríkh-i-Jahán-gushá*.

Ibn Jubayr.

A few words should be said about the traveller Ibn Jubayr, whose travels were published by the late Professor W. Wright at Leyden in 1852. He was a native of Granada, and enjoyed a considerable reputation not only as a scientific writer, but as a poet. He made three journeys to the East, performing on each occasion the Pilgrimage to

Mecca. He started on his first journey on February 4, 1183, and returned towards the end of April, 1185. His second journey, to which he was moved by the news of the capture of Jerusalem by Saladin (Ṣaláḥu'd-Dín), began in April, 1189, and ended in the middle of September, 1190. His third journey was prompted by the death of his wife, to whom he was greatly attached, and led him first from Ceuta to Mecca, where he remained for some time, and thence to Jerusalem, Cairo, and Alexandria, at which last place he died on November 29, 1217. His first journey is that whereof he has left us a record.

Passing now to the Philosophers, the two chief ones of this period, of whom something has been already said in the last chapter, are Fakhru'd-Dín Rází and Naṣíru'd-Dín Ṭúsí. The former was born on February 7, 1149, studied in his native town, Ray, and at Marágha, journeyed to Khwárazm and Transoxiana, and finally died at Herát in A.D. 1209. His literary activity was prodigious: he wrote on the Exegesis of the Qur'án, Dogma, Jurisprudence, Philosophy, Astrology, History, and Rhetoric, and to all this added an Encyclopædia of the Sciences. Brockelmann (*Gesch. d. arab. Litt.*, vol. i, pp. 506–08) enumerates thirty-three of his works of which the whole or a portion still exists. One of his latest works is probably a treatise which he composed at Herát in A.D. 1207 in reprobation of the pleasures of this world. One of his works on Astrology, dedicated to 'Alá'u'd-Dín Khwárazmsháh, and hence entitled *al-Ikhtiyárátu'l-'Alá'iyya*, was originally composed in Persian, as was his Encyclopædia, composed for the same monarch in A.H. 574 (= A.D. 1178–79).

Philosophers.

Fakhru'd-Dín Rází.

Of Nasíru'd-Dín Ṭúsí also mention has been made in the preceding chapter. He was born, as his *nisba* implies, at Ṭús in A.D. 1200[1]; was for some while, as we have seen, though

[1] So Ibn Shákir. Brockelmann (vol. i, p. 508) says 1210, I know not on what authority.

much against his will, associated with the Assassins; and, on the surrender of Alamút and Maymún-Dizh, passed into the service of Hulágú the Mongol, by whom he was held in high honour. Accompanying the Mongol army which destroyed Baghdád, he profited by the plunder of many libraries to enrich his own, which finally came to comprise, according to Ibn Shákir (*Fawátu'l-Wafayát*, vol. ii, p. 149), more than 400,000 volumes. He enjoyed enormous influence with his savage master Hulágú, who, before undertaking any enterprise, used to consult him as to whether or no the stars were favourable. On one occasion he saved the life of 'Alá'u'd-Dín al-Juwayní, the *Ṣáḥib-Díwán*, and a number of other persons under sentence of death, by playing on Hulágú's superstitions. In the building of the celebrated observatory at Marágha, begun in A.D. 1259, he was assisted by a number of men of learning, whose names he enumerates in the *Zíj-i-Ílkhání*. He died at Baghdád in June, 1274. He was a most productive writer on religious, philosophical, mathematical, physical, and astronomical subjects, and no fewer than fifty-six of his works are enumerated by Brockelmann (vol. ii, pp. 508–512). Most of them are, of course, in Arabic, which was still in his time the Latin of the Muhammadan East, and the language of science, but he also wrote a number of books in Persian, and even, as Ibn Shákir twice remarks in his biography in the *Fawátu'l-Wafayát* (vol. ii, p. 151), composed a great deal of poetry in that language. His prose works in Persian include the celebrated treatise on Ethics (the *Akhláq-i-Náṣirí*); the *Bíst Báb dar ma'rifat-i-Usturláb* ("Twenty Chapters on the Science of the Astrolabe"); the *Risála-i-Sí Faṣl* ("Treatise in Thirty Chapters") on Astronomy and the Calendar; the celebrated *Zíj-i-Ílkhání*, or almanac and astronomical tables composed for Hulágú Khán; a treatise on Mineralogy and precious stones, entitled *Tansúq-náma-i-Ílkhání*; and several other tracts on Philosophy, Astronomy, and Mathematics,

Naṣíru'd-Dín Ṭúsí.

besides a treatise on Ṣúfí ethics entitled *Awṣáfu'l-Ashráf*, and another on Geomancy. Of his Arabic works the *Tajrídu'l-'Aqá'id* (on scholastic or religious Philosophy) is probably the most celebrated. For a fuller account of his works, see Brockelmann, the *Fawátu'l-Wafayát* of Ibn Shákir, and the *Majálisu'l-Mú'minín*, &c. The last-mentioned work quotes from Shahrazúrí's *History of the Philosophers* a very severe criticism of him, which declares, amongst other damaging statements, that his scientific reputation was less due to his actual attainments than to his violent temper and impatience of contradiction, which, taken in conjunction with the high favour he enjoyed at the Court of Hulágú, made it imprudent to criticise or disparage him. Of his Persian poems little seems to have survived to our time, and Riḍá-qulí Khán in his immense Anthology, the *Majma'u'l-Fuṣaḥá* (vol. i, pp. 633–34), only cites of his verses six quatrains and a fragment of two couplets. It may be added that at p. 374 of the same volume he gives five quatrains of the earlier philosopher, Fakhru'd-Dín Rází, of whom we have already spoken. Another astronomer whose name should at least be mentioned is al-Jaghmíní of Khwárazm, who is generally believed to have died in A.D. 1221, though considerable uncertainty exists as to the period at which he flourished, and only one of his works, the *Mulakhkhaṣ*, seems to be preserved.

Of a few other Arabic-writing authors of this period it is sufficient to mention the names. The Jewish philosopher and physician Maimonides (Abú 'Imrán Músá b. Maymún) of Cordova, who in later life was physician to Saladin (Ṣaláḥu'd-Dín), and who died in A.D. 1204, is too great a name to be omitted, though he has no connection with Persia. Also from the Maghrib, or Western lands of Islám, was the Shaykh Muḥiyyu'd-Dín al-Búní († A.D. 1225), one of the most celebrated and most prolific writers

Maimonides.

Shaykh al-Búní.

on the Occult Sciences. From the West also (Malaga) came the botanist Ibnu'l-Bayṭár, who died at Damascus in A.D. 1248. Mention may also be made of al-Tífáshí, who wrote on Mineralogy, precious stones, and others matters connected with Natural Philosophy. Amongst the philologists of this period mention should be made of 'Izzu'd-Dín Zanjání, who died at Baghdád in A.D. 1257, and who was the author of a work on Arabic grammar, of which copies are extraordinarily common; Jamál al-Qurashí, who translated into Persian the *Saḥáḥ*, the celebrated Arabic lexicon of al-Jawharí; Ibnu'l-Ḥájib (d. A.D. 1248), the author of the *Káfiya* and the *Sháfiya*, two very well known Arabic grammars; al-Muṭarrizí, born in A.D. 1143, the year of az-Zamakhsharí's death, and known as "*Khalífatu'z-Zamakhsharí*" ("the Lieutenant of az-Zamakhsharí); and Ḍiyá'u'd-Dín ibnu'l-Athír, the brother of the great historian so often cited in these pages, who died at Baghdád in A.D. 1239, and wrote several works on Arabic philology, of which the *Kitábu'l-mathali's-sá'ir* is perhaps the best known. A third brother, Majdu'd-Dín ibnu'l-Athír (b. A.D. 1149, d. 1209), was a traditionist and theologian of some repute. Of greater importance is 'Abdu'llah b. 'Umar al-Bayḍáwí, a native of Fárs, who was for some time Qáḍí, or Judge, of Shirwáz, and who composed what is still the best known and most widely used commentary on the Qur'án, as well as a rather dull little manual of history, in Persian, entitled *Niḏhámu't-Tawáríkh*. To this period also belongs one of the greatest calligraphers the East has ever produced, namely, Yáqút, called al-Musta'ṣimí because he was in the service of the unhappy Caliph whose fate was described in the last chapter. In the

Ibnu'l-Bayṭár.

al-Tífáshí.

'Izzu'd-Dín Zanjání.

Jamál al-Qurashí.

Ibnu'l-Ḥájib.

al-Muṭarrizí.

Ḍiyá'u'd-Dín ibnu'l-Athír.

Majdu'd-Dín ibnu'l-Athír.

al-Bayḍáwí.

Yáqút al-Musta'ṣimí.

notice consecrated to him in Mírzá Ḥabíb's excellent *Khaṭṭ u Khaṭṭáṭán* ("Calligraphy and Calligraphers," Constantinople, A.H. 1306, pp. 51–53) mention is made of three copies of the Qur'án in his handwriting preserved in the Ottoman capital; one, dated A.H. 584 (= A.D. 1188–89), in the Mausoleum of Sulṭán Selím; another, dated A.H. 654 (= A.D. 1256), in Saint Sophia; and a third, dated A.H. 662 (= A.D. 1263–64), in the Ḥamídiyya Mausoleum. For a copy of the *Shifá* of Avicenna made, it is stated, for Muḥammad Tughluq, King of Delhi (but this seems to involve an anachronism), he is said to have received 200,000 *mithqáls* of gold. He died A.H. 667 (= A.D. 1268–69), according to a chronogram in verse given by Mírzá Ḥabíb, but according to Brockelmann (vol. i, p. 353) in A.H. 698 (= A.D. 1298–99). He and his predecessors Ibn Muqla and Ibnu'l-Bawwáb are reckoned the three calligraphers to whom the Arabic script is most deeply indebted. Another writer unpleasantly familiar to Persian school-children is Abú Naṣr-i-Faráhí, the author of a rhymed Arabic-Persian vocabulary still widely used in Persian schools, and of a rhymed treatise in Arabic on Ḥanafite Jurisprudence. He died in A.D. 1242. Much more important is the very rare treatise on Persian Prosody known as the *Mu'ajjam fí Ma'áyíri Ash'ári'l-'Ajam*, composed by Shams-i-Qays in Shíráz for the Atábek Abú Bakr b. Sa'd-i-Zangí (A.D. 1226–60), chiefly celebrated as the patron of the great poet Sa'dí. This valuable work, represented in Europe, so far as I know, only by the British Museum MS. Or. 2,814 (though Dr. Paul Horn discovered the existence of two manuscripts at Constantinople), is now being printed at Beyrout for the E. J. W. Gibb Memorial Series. The book is remarkable for the large number of citations from early and sometimes almost unknown Persian poets (including many *Fahlawiyyát* or dialect-poems) which it contains. Of the author little is known beyond what Rieu

Abú Naṣr-i-Faráhí.

Shams-i-Qays.

(*Persian Supplement*, pp. 123–25) has gleaned from this work. He was probably a native of Khurásán or Transoxiana, and was involved in the rout of the troops of Khwárazm by the Mongols before the fortress of Farzín in the summer of A.D. 1220. Another book of this period which ought not to be passed over in silence is the Persian translation of the *Marzubán-náma*, originally written in the dialect of Ṭabaristán by Marzubán-i-Rustam-i-Sharwín, author of a poem called the *Níkí-náma* in the same dialect, and dedicated to Shamsu'l-Ma'álí Qábús b. Washmgír (A.D. 976–1012), and turned into the ordinary literary language of Persia about A.D. 1210–15 by Sa'd of Waráwín.[1]

Marzubán-náma.

We come now to a much more important group of writers, the great Ṣúfís and Mystics of this period, amongst whom are included some of the most celebrated names in this branch of thought and literature, including two of Arabian race, whose singular eminence makes it very doubtful whether the once popular view, that Ṣúfíism is essentially an Aryan reaction against the cold formalism of a Semitic religion, can be regarded as tenable. These two are 'Umar ibnu'l-Fáriḍ, the Egyptian mystical poet, and Shaykh Muḥiyyu'd-Dín ibnu'l-'Arabí, the illustrious theosophist of Andalusia. Besides these we have to speak of the two Najmu'd-Díns, called respectively *Kubrá* and *Dáya*; Shaykh Rúzbihán; and Shaykh Shíhábu'd-Dín 'Umar Suhrawardí. A few words may also be devoted to Ṣadru'd-Dín of Qonya (Iconium), the most notable of Shaykh Muḥiyyu'd-Dín's disciples, and perhaps one or two other contemporary Mystics, excluding the two great mystical poets, Shaykh Farídu'd-Dín 'Aṭṭár and Mawláná Jalálu'd-Dín Rúmí, who will be discussed at some length in the next chapter.

Ṣúfís and Mystics.

[1] See Ethé's *Neupersische Litteratur* in vol. ii of the *Grundriss der Iranischen Philologie*, p. 328; Schefer's *Chrestomathie Persane*, vol. ii, pp. 171–199 of the texts and pp. 194–211 of the notes; and my *Abridged Translation of Ibn Isfandiyár's History of Ṭabaristán*, p. 86.

Rúzbihán.

In point of time Shaykh Abú Muḥammad Rúzbihán b. Abí Nasr al-Baqlí, nicknamed *Shaṭṭáḥ-i-Fárs* ("the Braggart of Fárs"),[1] was the earliest of the Mystics above mentioned, for he died in Muḥarram, A.H. 606 (= July, A.D. 1209) at his native place, Shíráz. His tomb is mentioned in the Arabic work (British Museum MS. Or. 3,395, f. 110^b) correctly entitled *Shaddu'l-Azár*, but commonly known as the *Hazár Mazár* ("The Thousand Shrines"), which was composed about A.D. 1389 by Mu'ínu'd-Dín Abu'l-Qásim Junayd of Shíráz on the saints of his native town. It is there stated that Shaykh Rúzbihán in his youth travelled widely, after the customary fashion of these Ṣúfí dervishes, visiting 'Iráq, Kirmán, the Ḥijáz, and Syria; and that he composed a great number of works, of which some thirty, according to the Persian *Shíráz-náma* (composed in A.D. 1343 by a grandson of the eminent mystic, Shaykh Zarkúb), were celebrated, including a mystical commentary on the Qur'án, entitled *Laṭá'ifu'l-Bayán*, or "Subtleties of Enunciation"; the *Mashrabu'l-Arwáḥ*, or "Fount of Inspiration of Souls"; the *Manṭiqu'l-Asrár*, or "Language of Mysteries," &c. He also wrote verses in Persian, of which the following are specimens:—

"*That which the eyes of Time have never seen,*
And which no tongue to earthly ears hath told,
Its tint hath now displayed in this our day:
Arise, and in our day this thing behold!"

* * * *

"*From Farthest East to Threshold of the West*
I in this age am guide to God's Straight Road.
How can the Gnostic pilgrims me behold?
Beyond the Far Beyond's my soul's abode!"

He preached regularly in the *Jámi'-i-'Atíq*, or Old Mosque, for fifty years, and died at the age of eighty-four, so that his

[1] For the technical meaning of *Shaṭṭáḥ*, see Flügel's edition of the *Ta'rífát* ("Definitions"), pp. 132, 285.

birth must be placed about A.D. 1128. The Atábek Abú Bakr b. Sa'd, the patron of the poet Sa'dí, was his friend and admirer, and he had studied with Shaykh Abu'n-Najíb Suhrawardí (died A.D. 1167–68) in Alexandria. A few further particulars, and several marvellous stories of the kind so common in hagiological works, may be gleaned from the notice of him which Jámí has inserted in his *Nafaḥátu'l-Uns* (ed. Nassau Lees, pp. 288–290).

Najmu'd-Dín Kubrá.

Abu'l-Jannáb Aḥmad b. 'Umar al-Khíwaqí (of Khiva or Khwárazm), commonly known as Shaykh Najmu'd-Dín "Kubrá," next demands notice. His title *Kubrá* (whereby he is distinguished from the other celebrated Najmu'd-Dín called *Dáya*), is, according to the most authoritative and plausible explanation, an abbreviation of the nickname *aṭ-Ṭámmatu'l-Kubrá* ("the Supreme Calamity"), given to him by his companions on account of his great vigour and skill in debate and discussion. He was also nicknamed *Walí-tirásh* ("the Saint-carver"), because it was supposed that any one on whom his glance fell in moments of divine ecstasy and exaltation attained to the degree of saintship; and Jámí (*Nafaḥát*, p. 481) has some wonderful anecdotes to show that this beneficent influence was not limited to human beings, but extended to dogs and sparrows. His title, *Abu'l-Jannáb*, is said to have been given to him by the Prophet in a dream, its interpretation being that he was sedulously to avoid the world.

That Najmu'd-Dín Kubrá was one of the many victims who perished in the sack of Khwárazm by the Mongols in A.H. 618 (= A.D. 1221) is certain, and it is a proof of the high esteem in which he was held that out of some 600,000 slain on that fatal day he alone is mentioned by name in the *Jámi'u't-Tawáríkh*. "Since Chingíz Khán," says the author of that work (India Office MS. No. 3,524 = Ethé, 2,828, f. 499[b]), "had heard of that Shaykh of Shaykhs and Pole-star of Saints Najmu'd-Dín Kubrá (on whom be God's mercy), and knew somewhat of his character, he sent him a message to say that he intended to sack Khwárazm and massacre its inhabitants, and that one who was the greatest man of his age should come out from it and join him, now that the moment had arrived for the incidence of the catastrophe. 'That I should come forth from amongst them,' replied the Shaykh, 'would be an action remote from the way of virtue and magnanimity.' And afterwards he was found amongst the slain." Still further evidence is afforded by a poem on his death composed by al-Mu'ayyad b. Yúsuf aṣ-Ṣaláḥí, and quoted by al-Yáfi'í in his *Mirátu'z-Zamán*, or "Mirror of Time" (British Museum MS. Or. 1,511, f. 341), of which the two following verses :—

> "*Who hath seen an Ocean of Learning [drowned] in Oceans of Blood?*"

and—

> "*O Day of Disaster of Khwárazm, which hath been described,*
> *Thou hast filled us with dread, and we have lost Faith and Renown!*"

suffice to confirm the place, occasion, and manner of his death. On this historical foundation several less credible stories have been raised; these are given by Jámí (*Nafaḥátu'l-Uns*, pp. 486–7) in the following form :—

"When the Tartar heathen reached Khwárazm, the Shaykh [Najmu'd-Dín Kubrá] assembled his disciples, whose number exceeded sixty. Sulṭán Muḥammad Khwárazmsháh had fled, but the Tartar heathen supposed him to be still in Khwárazm, whither consequently they marched. The Shaykh summoned certain of his disciples, such as Shaykh Sa'du'd-Dín Ḥamawí, Raḍiyyu'd-Dín 'Alí Lálá and others, and said, 'Arise quickly and depart to your own countries, for a Fire is kindled from the East which consumes nearly to the West. This is a grievous mischief, the like of which hath never heretofore happened to this people' (the Muslims). Some of his disciples said, 'How would it be if your Holiness were to pray, that perhaps this [catastrophe] may be averted from the lands of

Islám?' 'Nay,' replied the Shaykh, 'this is a thing irrevocably predetermined which prayer cannot avert.' Then his disciples besought him, saying, 'The beasts are ready prepared for the journey: if your Holiness also would join us and depart into Khurásán, it would not be amiss.' 'Nay,' replied the Shaykh; 'here shall I die a martyr, for it is not permitted to me to go forth.' So his disciples departed into Khurásán.

"So when the heathen entered the city, the Shaykh called together such of his disciples as remained, and said, 'Arise in God's Name, and let us fight in God's Cause.' Then he entered his house, put on his *Khirqa* (dervish robe), girded up his loins, filled the upper part of his *Khirqa*, which was open in front, with stones on both sides, took a spear in his hand, and came forth. And when he came face to face with the heathen, he continued to cast stones at them till he had no stones left. The heathen fired volleys of arrows at him, and an arrow pierced his breast. He plucked it out and cast it away, and therewith passed away his spirit. They say that at the moment of his martyrdom he had grasped the pigtail of one of the heathen, which after his death could not be removed from his hand, until at last they were obliged to cut it off. Some say that our Master Jalálu'd-Dín Rúmí refers to this story, and to his own connection with the Shaykh, in the following passage from his odes:—

> '*Má az án muḥtashamán-im ki sághar gírand;*
> *Na az án muflisakán ki buz-i-lághar gírand!*
> *Bi-yakí dast may-i-kháṣṣ-i-Ímán núshand:*
> *Bi-yakí dast-i-digar parcham-i-káfar gírand!*'

> 'O we are of the noble band who grasp the Cup of Wine,
> Not of the wretched beggar-crew who for lean kids do pine:
> Who with one hand the Wine unmixed of fiery Faith do drain,
> While in the other hand we grasp the heathen's locks amain!'

"His martyrdom (may God sanctify his spirit!) took place in the year A.H. 618 (= A.D. 1221). His disciples were many, but several of them were peerless in the world and the exemplars of their time. Such were Shaykh Majdu'd-Dín of Baghdád, Shaykh Sa'du'd-Dín of Ḥamát, Bábá Kamál of Jand, Shaykh Raḍiyyu'd-Dín 'Alí Lálá, Shaykh Sayfu'd-Dín Bákharzí, Shaykh Najmu'd-Dín of Ray, Shaykh Jamálu'd-Dín of Gílán, and, as some assert, our Master Bahá'u'd-Dín Walad, the father of our Master Jalálu'd-Dín Rúmí, was also of their number."

Of Shaykh Najmu'd-Dín Kubrá's works two at least are

preserved in the British Museum. One, a short tract in Arabic of two or three pages only, has as its text the well known aphorism of the Mystics, "The ways unto God are as the number of the breaths of His creatures": the other, in Persian, is entitled *Ṣifatu'l-Ádáb*, and treats of the rules of conduct which should be observed by the Ṣúfí neophyte. The great Mystic poet, Farídu'd-Dín 'Aṭṭár, as pointed out by Mírzá Muḥammad in his Introduction to Mr. R. A. Nicholson's edition of the *Tadhkiratu'l-Awliyá* (vol. i, p. 17), alludes in terms of the greatest respect to Najmu'd-Dín Kubrá in his *Maḏhharu'l-'Ajá'ib*, or "Display of Marvels," and was himself, according to Jámí's *Nafaḥát* (p. 697), a disciple of his disciple Majdu'd-Dín of Baghdád, of whom in this connection we may say a few words.

Majdu'd-Dín al-Baghdádí.

Shaykh Abú Sa'íd Majdu'd-Dín Sharaf b. al-Mu'ayyad b. Abi'l-Fatḥ al-Baghdádí is said by Jámí to have come to Khwárazm originally as a physician to attend on Khwárazmsháh, though from references to other accounts this appears very doubtful. In any case he seems to have attached himself to Najmu'd-Dín Kubrá as one of his disciples, but gradually, as it would appear, he came to regard himself as greater than his master, until one day he observed, "We were a duck's egg on the sea-shore, and Shaykh Najmu'd-Dín a hen who cherished us under his protecting wing, until finally we were hatched, and, being ducklings, plunged into the sea, while the Shaykh remained on the shore." Najmu'd-Dín Kubrá, hearing this, was greatly angered, and cursed Majdu'd-Dín, saying, "May he perish in the water!" This saying was reported to Majdu'd-Dín, who was greatly alarmed, and sought by the most humble apologies and acts of penance to induce his master to revoke the curse, but in vain; and shortly afterwards Khwárazmsháh, under the combined influence of jealousy and drink, caused him to be drowned in the river. Najmu'd-Dín (somewhat illogically, as we may venture to think), was greatly incensed at this act, which, according to the story, was but the fulfilment of his own prayer, and prayed God to take vengeance on the King, who, greatly perturbed, sought in vain to induce the Shaykh to withdraw his curse. "This is recorded in the Book," was the Shaykh's answer: "his blood shall be atoned for by all thy kingdom: thou shalt lose thy life, along with very many others, including myself." As to the date of Majdu'd-Dín's death there is some doubt, the alternative dates A.H. 606 and 616 (= A.D. 1209–10 or 1219–20) being given by Jámí.

Sa'du'd-Dín Ḥamawí.

Sa'du'd-Dín Ḥamawí was another of the disciples of Najmu'd-Dín Kubrá who attained some celebrity, and is said by Jámí (*Nafaḥát*, p. 492) to have composed a number of works, of which only the *Kitáb-i-Maḥbúb*, or "Book of the Beloved," and the *Sajanjalu'l-Arwáḥ*, or "Mirror of Spirits," are mentioned by name. These books are described by Jámí as full of "enigmatical sayings, cyphers, figures, and circles, which the eye of understanding and thought is unable to discover or solve." He seems to have been subject to prolonged trances or cataleptic seizures, one of which lasted thirteen days. Specimens of his verses, both Arabic and Persian, are given in the *Nafaḥát*, according to which his death took place about the end of A.H. 650 (= February, 1253), at the age of sixty-three. He was acquainted with Ṣadru'd-Dín al-Qúnyawí, of whom we shall speak further on in connection with Shaykh Muḥiyyu'd-Dín ibnu'l-'Arabí.

Najmu'd-Dín Dáya.

We now come to the other Najmu'd-Dín, known as "*Dáya*," who was, according to Jámí, the disciple both of Najmu'd-Dín Kubrá and of Majdu'd-Dín. In his most important work, the *Mirṣádu'l-'Ibád*, or "Watch-tower of [God's] Servants," of which a fine old MS. (Or. 3,242) transcribed in A.H. 779 (= A.D. 1377–78) is preserved in the British Museum, he gives his full name (f. 130ᵃ) as Abú Bakr 'Abdu'lláh b. Muḥammad Sháháwar, and explicitly speaks (f. 17ᵃ) of Majdu'd-Dín Baghdádí—"the

King of his time"—as his spiritual director. Of his other works, the *Baḥru'l-Ḥaqá'iq*, or "Ocean of Truths," written at Síván in Asia Minor, whither he had fled from the advancing Mongols, in A.H. 620 (= A.D. 1223), is the most celebrated. In Asia Minor he foregathered, according to Jámí, with Ṣadru'd-Dín of Qonya and the celebrated Jalálu'd-Dín Rúmí. He died in A.H. 654 (= A.D. 1256).

Shihábu'd-Dín Suhrawardí.

Shaykh Shihábu'd-Dín Abú Ḥafṣ 'Umar b. Muḥammad al-Bakrí as-Suhrawardí was another eminent mystic of this period, who was born in Rajab, A.H. 539 (=January, 1145), and died in A.H. 632 (= A.D. 1234–5). Of the older Shaykhs who guided his first footsteps in the mystic path were his paternal uncle, Abu'n-Najíb as-Suhrawardí, who died in A.H. 563 (= A.D. 1167–68), and the great Shaykh 'Abdu'l-Qádir of Gílán, who died about two years earlier. Of his works the most famous are the *'Awárifu'l-Ma'árif*, or "Gifts of [Divine] Knowledge," and *Rashfu'n-Naṣá'iḥ*, or "Draughts of Counsel." The former is common enough in manuscript, and has been printed at least once (in A.H. 1306 = A.D. 1888–89) in the margins of an edition of al-Ghazálí's *Iḥyá'u'l-'Ulúm* published at Cairo. Ibn Khallikán, in the article which he devotes to him (de Slane's translation, vol. ii, pp. 382–4), quotes some of his Arabic verses, and speaks of the "ecstasies" and "strange sensations" which his exhortations evoked in his hearers. "I had not the advantage of seeing him," says this writer, "as I was then too young." Sa'dí of Shíráz, who was one of his disciples, has a short anecdote about him in the *Bústán* (ed. Graf, p. 150), in which he is represented as praying that "Hell might be filled with him if perchance others might thereby obtain salvation." He was for some time the chief Shaykh of the Ṣúfís at Baghdád, and seems to have been a man of sound sense; for when a certain Ṣúfí wrote to him: "My lord, if I cease to work I shall remain in idleness, while if I work I am filled with self-satisfaction: which is best?" he replied,

"Work, and ask Almighty God to pardon thy self-satisfaction." He must not be confused with the earlier Shaykh Shihábu'd-Dín Yaḥyá b. Ḥabsh as-Suhrawardí, author of the *Ḥikmatu'l-Ishráq*, or "Philosophy of Illumination," a celebrated theosophist and thaumaturgist, who was put to death at Aleppo for alleged heretical tendencies by Saladin's son, al-Maliku'dh-Dháhir, in the year A.H. 587 or 588 (= A.D. 1191 or 1192) at the early age of thirty-six or thirty-eight, and who is, in consequence, generally distinguished by the title of *al-Maqtúl*, "the slain." This latter seems to have been a much more original and abler, if not better, man, and his "Philosophy of Illumination," still unpublished, impressed me on a cursory examination as a remarkable work deserving careful study.

Shihábu'd-Dín "al-Maqtúl."

We now come to one who is universally admitted to have been amongst the greatest, if not the greatest, of the many mystics produced in Muslim lands—to wit, Shaykh Muḥiyyu'd-Dín ibnu'l-'Arabí, who was born at Murcia, in Spain, on July 28, A.D. 1165, began his theological studies at Seville in A.D. 1172, and in A.D. 1201 went to the East, living in turn in Egypt, the Ḥijáz, Baghdád, Mosul, and Asia Minor, and finally died at Damascus on November 16, A.D. 1240. As a writer he is correctly described by Brockelmann (vol. i, pp. 441 *et seqq.*) as of "colossal fecundity," 150 of his extant works being enumerated.[1] Of these the most celebrated are the *Fuṣúṣu'l-Ḥikam* ("Bezels of Wisdom") and the *Futúḥátu'l-Makkiyya* ("Meccan Victories" or "Disclosures"), of which the first, written at Damascus in A.D. 1230, has been repeatedly lithographed, printed, translated, and annotated in the various lands of Islám, while the second, a work of enormous extent, has also been printed in Egypt. The fullest account of

Shaykh Muḥiyyu'd-Dín ibnu'l-'Arabí.

[1] He himself, in a memorandum drawn up in A.D. 1234, enumerated the titles of 289 of his writings. Jámí says (*Nafaḥát*, p. 634) that he wrote more than five hundred books.

his life with which I am acquainted occurs in al-Maqqarí's *Nafḥu'ṭ-Ṭíb min Ghuṣni'l-Andalusi'r-Raṭíb* ("the Breath of Fragrance from the fresh branch of Andalusia," Cairo ed. of A.H. 1302 = A.D. 1884–85, vol. i, pp. 397–409), and a very full biography is also given by Jámí in the *Nafaḥátu'l-Uns* (ed. Nassau Lees, pp. 633–45). He was, like most of the mystics, a poet; many of his verses are quoted in the *Naf'u'ṭ-Ṭíb*, and his *Díwán* has been lithographed by Mírzá Muḥammad Shírází, of Bombay, in a volume of 244 pages. His poems are described by Jámí as "strange and precious." By many doctors of theology he was looked at askance as a heretic, and in Egypt several attempts were made to kill him, but his admirers were both numerous and enthusiastic, and at the present day, even in Shí'ite Persia, he still exercises a great influence, greater, perhaps, than any other mystagogue. He claimed to hold converse with the Prophet in dreams; to have received his *khirqa*, or dervish-cloak, from Khiḍr; and to know the science of alchemy and the "Most Great Name" of God. He was acquainted with the mystical poet, 'Umar ibnu'l-Fáriḍ, and asked his permission to write a commentary on his *Tá'iyya*, or *T-qaṣída*, to which request the other replied, "Your book entitled *al-Futúḥátu'l-Makkiyya* is a commentary on it." He believed in the value of dreams, and in man's power to render them by his will veridical: "It behoves God's servant," he said, "to employ his will to produce concentration in his dreams, so that he may obtain control over his imagination, and direct it intelligently in sleep as he would control it when awake. And when this concentration has accrued to a man and become natural to him, he discovers the fruit thereof in the Intermediate World (*al-Barzakh*), and profits greatly thereby; wherefore let man exert himself to acquire this state, for, by God's permission, it profiteth greatly." His style is obscure, probably of set purpose, after the fashion of the Muslim Theosophists and mystics, whose unorthodox ideas must always be clad in words which are susceptible of a more or less orthodox interpretation, if they would not share the fate of Ḥusayn b. Manṣúr al-Ḥalláj or Shaykh Shihábu'd-Dín "*al-Maqtúl.*" Thus on one occasion Shaykh Muḥiyyu'd-Dín was taken to task for the following verse which he had composed :—

"*O Thou who seest me, while I see not Thee,*
How oft I see Him, while He sees not me!"

He at once repeated it again with the following additions, which rendered it perfectly unexceptionable :—

"*O Thou who seest me* ever prone to sin,
While Thee I see not willing to upbraid:
How oft I see Him grant His grace's aid
While me He sees not seeking grace to win."

In this connection I cannot do better than quote what Gobineau,[1] with his usual insight into the mind of the East, says of a much later philosopher, Mullá Sadrá, for his words are equally true of Shaykh Muḥiyyu'd-Dín and his congeners. "*Le soin qu'il prenait de déguiser ses discours, il était nécessaire qu'il le prît surtout de déguiser ses livres ; c'est ce qu'il a fait, et à les lire on se ferait l'idée la plus imparfaite de son enseignement. Je dis à les lire sans un maître qui possède la tradition. Autrement on y pénètre sans peine. De génération en génération, ses élèves ont hérité sa pensée véritable, et ils ont la clef des expressions dont il se sert pour ne pas exprimer mais pour leur indiquer à eux sa pensée. C'est avec ce correctif oral que les nombreux traités du maître sont aujourd'hui tenus en si grande considération, et que, de son temps, ils ont fait les délices d'une société ivre de dialectique, âpre à l'opposition religieuse, amoureuses de hardiesses secrètes, enthousiaste de tromperies habiles.*" The *Fuṣúṣu'l-Ḥikam* is seldom met with unaccompanied by a commentary, and it is doubtful

[1] *Les Religions et les Philosophies dans l'Asie Centrale* (Paris, 1866), p. 88.

if even with such commentary its ideas can be fully apprehended without assistance from those who move in those realms of speculation in which their author lived and from which he drew his intellectual energy. No mystic of Islám, perhaps, with the possible exception of Jalálu'd-Dín Rúmí, has surpassed Shaykh Muḥiyyu'd-Dín in influence, fecundity, or abstruseness, yet, so far as I am aware, no adequate study of his works and doctrines has yet been made in Europe, though few fields of greater promise offer themselves to the aspiring Arabist who is interested in this characteristic aspect of Eastern thought.

In a book dealing primarily with Persian literature it would, perhaps, be out of place to speak at much greater length of a writer whose only connection with Persia was the influence exerted by him, even to the present day, through his writings. One of the Persian mystic poets and writers of note who came most directly under his influence was Fakhru'd-Dín 'Iráqí, who attended Ṣadru'd-Dín Qúnyawí's lectures on the *Fuṣuṣu'l-Ḥikam*, his master's *magnum opus*, and was thereby inspired to write his remarkable *Lama'át*, which long afterwards (in the latter part of the fifteenth century of our era) formed the text of an excellent and elaborate commentary by Mullá Núru'd-Dín 'Abdu'r-Raḥmán Jámí, entitled *Ashi'atu'l-Lama'át*. Awḥadu'd-Dín of Kirmán, another eminent mystic poet of Persia, actually met and associated with Shaykh Muḥiyyu'd-Dín ibnu'l-'Arabí, and was doubtless influenced by him; and I am inclined to think that a careful study of the antecedents and ideas of the generation of Persian mystics whom we shall have to consider early in the next volume will show that no single individual (except, perhaps, Jalálu'd-Dín Rúmí) produced a greater effect on the thought of his successors than the *Shaykh-i-Akbar* ("Most Great Shaykh") of Andalusia.

The following is a specimen of his verse, of which the Arabic original will be found in al-Maqqarí's *Nafḥu't-Ṭíb* (ed. Cairo, A.H. 1302), vol. i, p. 400.

"My Soul is much concerned with Her,
Although Her Face I cannot see:
Could I behold Her Face, indeed,
Slain by Her blackened Brows I'd be.
And when my sight upon Her fell,
I fell a captive to my sight,
And passed the night bewitched by Her,
And still did rave when Dawn grew bright.
Alas for my resolve so high!
Did high resolve avail, I say,
The Beauty of that Charmer shy
Would not have made me thus to stray.
In Beauty as a tender Fawn,
Whose pastures the Wild Asses ken;
Whose coy regard and half-turned head
Make captives of the Souls of Men!
Her breath so sweet, as it would seem,
As fragrant Musk doth yield delight:
She's radiant as the mid-day Sun:
She's as the Moon's Effulgence bright.
If She appear, Her doth reveal
The Splendour of the Morning fair;
If She Her tresses loose, the Moon
Is hidden by Her night-black Hair.
Take thou my Heart, but leave, I pray,
O Moon athwart the darkest Night,
Mine Eyes, that I may gaze on Thee.
For all my Joy is in my sight!"

'Umar ibnu'l-Fáriḍ.

Ibnu'l-Fáriḍ whose full name was Sharafu'd-Dín Abú Ḥafṣ 'Umar, must next be noticed, for though, like Ibnu'l-'Arabí, he had no direct connection with Persia, he was one of the most remarkable and talented of the mystical poets of Islám; a fact which it is important to emphasise because of the tendency which still exists in Europe to regard Ṣúfíism as an essentially Persian or Aryan manifestation, a view which, in my opinion, cannot be maintained. Ibnu'l-Fáriḍ, according to different statements, was born at Cairo in A.H. 556 (= A.D. 1161), or A.H. 566 (A.D. 1170–71), or (according to Ibn Khallikán) on Dhu'l-

Qa'dasi, A.H. 576 (= March 22, 1181). His family was originally from Ḥamát, in Syria, whence he is generally given the *nisba* of *al-Ḥamawí* as well as *al-Miṣrí* ("the Egyptian"). His life was not outwardly very eventful, most of the incidents recorded by his biographers being of a semi-miraculous character, and resting on the authority of his son Kamálu'd-Dín Muḥammad. In his youth he spent long periods in retirement and meditation in the mountain of al-Muqaṭṭam by Cairo, which periods became more frequent and protracted after the death of his father, who, towards the end of his life, abandoned the Government service and retired into the learned seclusion of the Jámi'u'l-Azhar. Acting on the monition of an old grocer in whom he recognised one of the "Saints of God," Ibnu'l-Fáriḍ left Cairo for Mecca, where he abode for some time, chiefly in the wild valleys and mountains surrounding that city, and constantly attended by a mysterious beast which continually but vainly besought him to ride upon it in his journeyings. After fifteen years of this life, according to Jámí (*Nafaḥát*, p. 627) he was commanded by a telepathic message to return to Cairo to be present at the death-bed of the grocer-saint, in connection with whose obsequies strange stories of the green birds of Paradise whose bodies are inhabited by the souls of the martyrs are narrated. From this time onwards he appears to have remained in Egypt, where he died on the second of Jumáda I, A.H. 632 (= January 23, A.D. 1235).

Unlike Ibnu'l-'Arabí, he was by no means a voluminous writer, for his literary work (at any rate so far as it is preserved) is all verse, "of which the collection," as Ibn Khallikán says (vol. ii, p. 388, of de Slane's translation), "forms a thin volume." His verses are further described by this writer (*loc. cit.*) as displaying "a cast of style and thought which charms the reader by its grace and beauty, whilst their whole tenour is in accordance with the mystic ideas of the Ṣúfís." Besides his strictly classical verses, he wrote some more popular poetry of the kind entitled *Mawáliyát*. Of these Ibn Khallikán gives some specimens, one of which, on a young butcher, is remarkable not only for its *bizarre* character, but as being almost identical in sense with a quatrain ascribed in the *Ta'ríkh-i-Guzída* to the Persian poetess Mahsatí (or Mahastí, or Mihastí).[1]

Like Shaykh Muḥiyyu'd-Dín, Ibnu'l-Fáriḍ saw the Prophet in dreams, and received instructions from him as to his literary work.[2] He never, it is said, wrote without inspiration; sometimes, as Jámí relates,[2] he would remain for a week or ten days in a kind of trance or ecstasy, insensible to external objects, and would then come to himself and dictate thirty, forty, or fifty couplets—"whatever God had disclosed to him in that trance." The longest and most celebrated of his poems is the *Tá'iyya*, or *T-qaṣída*, which comprises seven hundred and fifty couplets. "He excels," says al-Yáfi'í, "in his description of the Wine of Love, in his *Díwán*, which comprises the subtleties of gnosticism, the Path, Love, Yearning, Union, and other technical terms and real sciences recognised in the books of the Ṣúfí Shaykhs."[3] In personal appearance he was, according to his son Shaykh Kamálu'd-Dín Muḥammad, "of well-proportioned frame, of comely, pleasing, and somewhat ruddy countenance; and when moved to ecstasy by listening [to devotional recitations and chants] his face would increase in beauty and radiance, while the perspiration dripped from all his body until it ran under his feet into the ground." "Never," adds Kamálu'd-Dín, "have I seen one like unto him in beauty of form either amongst the Arabs or the Persians, and I of all men most closely resemble him in appearance."

The best edition of Ibnu'l-Fáriḍ's *Díwán* with which I am

[1] See, for Ibnu'l-Fáriḍ's verse, Ibn Khallikán, *loc. cit.*; and for Mahsatí's the *tirage-à-part* of my translation of this portion of the *Ta'ríkh-i-Guzída* (from the *J.R.A.S.* for October, 1900, and January, 1901, pp. 71–72).

[2] *Nafaḥát*, p. 628.

[3] Ibid., p. 629.

acquainted is that published by the Shaykh Rushayd b. Shálib ad-Daḥdáḥ al-Lubnání at Paris in 1855, with a French preface by the Abbé Bargès, Professor of Hebrew at the Sorbonne. Besides the text of the poems, it contains two commentaries, one by Shaykh Ḥasan al-Búríní, purely philological, the other, by Shaykh 'Abdu'l-Ghaní an-Nábalúsí, explaining the esoteric meaning.

The following is a rather free translation of a poem in the *Díwán* of Ibnu'l-Fáriḍ (edition of ad-Daḥdáḥ, pp. 263–268) which has always seemed to me both typical and beautiful :—

"Where the Lote-tree at the bending of the glade
Casts its shade,
There the Lover, led by passion, went astray,
And even in the straying found his way.

In that southerly ravine his heart is stirred
By a hope in its fulfilment long deferred:
'Tis the Valley of 'Aqíq;[1] *O comrade, halt!*
Feign amazement, if amazement makes default!
Look for me, for blinding tears mine eyes do fill,
And the power to see it lags behind the will.
Ask, I pray, the Fawn who haunts it if he knows
Of my heart, and how it loves him, and its woes.
Nay, my passionate abasement can he know
While the glory of his beauty fills him so?
May my heart, my wasted heart, his ransom be!
His own to yield no merit is in me!
What think'st thou? Doth he deem me then content,
While I crave for him, with this my banishment?
In sleepless nights his form I vainly try
To paint upon the canvas of the eye.
If I lend an ear to what my mentors say
May I ne'er escape their torments for a day!
By the sweetness of my friend and his desire,
Though he tire of me, my heart shall never tire!
O would that from al-'Udhayb's limpid pool
With a draught I might my burning vitals cool!
Nay, far beyond my craving is that stream:
Alas, my thirst and that mirage's gleam!"

[1] "The Valley of Cornelians," a valley in Arabia, near al-Madína.

Since in this book Arabic literature necessarily occupies a secondary place, it is impossible to discuss more fully the work of this remarkable poet, who, while strongly recalling in many passages the ideas and imagery of the Persian mystical poets, excels the majority of them in boldness, variety, and wealth of expression. Too many of those who have written on Ṣúfíism have treated it as an essentially Aryan movement, and for this reason it is particularly necessary to emphasise the fact that two of the greatest mystics of Islám (and perhaps a third, namely Dhu'n-Nún of Egypt, who, in the opinion of my friend Mr. R. A. Nicholson, first gave to the earlier asceticism the definitely pantheistic bent and quasi-erotic expression which we recognise as the chief characteristics of Ṣúfíism) were of non-Aryan origin.

CHAPTER IX

FARÍDU'D-DÍN 'AṬṬÁR, JALÁLU'D-DÍN RÚMÍ, AND SA'DÍ, AND SOME LESSER POETS OF THIS PERIOD

The three great mystical poets of Persia.

IF Ibnu'l-Fáriḍ, of whom we spoke at the conclusion of the preceding chapter, be without doubt the greatest mystical poet of the Arabs, that distinction amongst the Persians unquestionably belongs to Jalálu'd-Dín Rúmí, the author of the great mystical *Mathnawí*, and of the collection of lyric poems known as the Díwán of Shams-i-Tabríz. Now Jalálu'd-Dín, as we have already observed, regards Saná'í, of whose work we have spoken at pp. 317–322 *supra*, and Farídu'd-Dín 'Aṭṭár, of whom we shall immediately speak, as his most illustrious predecessors and masters in mystical verse, and we are therefore justified in taking these three singers as the most eminent exponents of the Ṣúfí doctrine amongst the Persian poets. For in all these matters, as it seems to me, native taste must be taken as the supreme criterion, since it is hardly possible for a foreigner to judge with the same authority as a critic of the poet's own blood and speech; and, though I personally may derive greater pleasure from the poems of 'Iráqí than from those of Saná'í, I have no right to elevate such personal preference into a general dogma.

Farídu'd-Dín 'Aṭṭár, like so many other Eastern poets, would be much more known and read if he had written very much less. The number of his works, it is often stated (*e.g.*, by Qáḍí Núru'lláh of Shushtar in his *Majálisu'l-Mú'minín*), is equal to the number of *Súras* in the Qur'án, viz., one hundred and fourteen; but this is probably a great exaggeration, since only about thirty are actually preserved, or mentioned by name in his own writings. Of these the best known are the *Pand-náma*, or "Book of Counsels," a dull little book, filled with maxims of conduct, which has been often published in the East; the *Manṭiqu'ṭ-Ṭayr*, or "Language of the Birds," a mystical allegory in verse, which was published with a French translation by Garcin de Tassy (Paris, 1857, 1863); and the *Tadhkiratu'l-Awliyá*, or "Memoirs of the Saints," of which vol. i has been already published in my "Persian Historical Texts" by Mr. R. A. Nicholson, and vol. ii is now in the press. To the first volume is prefixed a critical Persian Preface by my learned friend Mírzá Muḥammad b. 'Abdu'l-Wahháb of Qazwín, who constructed it almost entirely out of the only materials which can be regarded as trustworthy, namely, the information which can be gleaned from the poet's own works. As this preface is untranslated, and is, moreover, the best and most critical account of 'Aṭṭár which we yet possess, I shall in what here follows make almost exclusive use of it.

Farídu'd-Dín 'Aṭṭár.

The poet's full name was Abú Ṭálib (or, according to others, Abú Ḥámid) Muḥammad, son of Abú Bakr Ibráhím, son of Muṣṭafá, son of Sha'bán, generally known as Farídu'd-Dín 'Aṭṭár. This last word, generally translated "the Druggist," means exactly one who deals in *'iṭr*, or otto of roses, and other perfumes; but, as Mírzá Muḥammad shows by citations from the *Khusraw-náma* and the *Asrár-náma*, it indicates in this case something more, namely, that he kept a sort of pharmacy, where he was consulted by patients for whom he prescribed, and whose prescriptions he himself made up. Speaking of his poems, the *Muṣíbát-náma* ("the Book of Affliction") and the *Iláhí-náma* ("the Divine Book"), the poet says that he composed them both in his *Dárú-khána*, or Drug-store, which was at that time

Biography of Shaykh 'Aṭṭár.

frequented by five hundred patients, whose pulses he daily felt. Riḍá-qulí Khán (without giving his authority) says in the *Riyáḍu'l-'Árifín* ("Gardens of the Gnostics") that his teacher in the healing art was Shaykh Majdu'd-Dín of Baghdád, probably the same whom we mentioned in the last chapter as one of the disciples of Najmu'd-Dín Kubrá.

Concerning the particulars of Shaykh 'Aṭṭár's life, little accurate information is to be gleaned from the biographers. The oldest of these, 'Awfí, whose *Lubábu'l-Albáb* contains a singularly jejune article on him (vol. ii, pp. 337–9), places him amongst the poets who flourished after the time of Sanjar, *i.e.*, after A.H. 552 (= A.D. 1157), and the fact that 'Aṭṭár in his poems frequently speaks of Sanjar as of one no longer alive points in the same direction. Moreover, the *Lubáb*, which was certainly composed about the year A.H. 617 (= A.D. 1220–21), speaks of 'Aṭṭár as of a poet still living. He was born, as appears from a passage in the *Lisánu'l-Ghayb* ("Tongue of the Unseen"), in the city of Níshápúr, spent thirteen years of his childhood by the shrine of the Imám Riḍá, travelled extensively, visiting Ray, Kúfa, Egypt, Damascus, Mecca, India, and Turkistán, and finally settled once more in his native town. For thirty-nine years he busied himself in collecting the verses and sayings of Ṣúfí saints, and never in his life, he tells us, did he prostitute his poetic talent to panegyric. He too, as he relates in the *Ushtur-náma*, or "Book of the Camel," like Ibnu'l-'Arabí and Ibnu'l-Fáriḍ, saw the Prophet in a dream, and received his direct and special blessing.

One of the latest of his works is the *Maḏhharu'l-'Ajá'ib*, or "Manifestation of Wonders" (a title given to 'Alí ibn Abí Ṭálib, to whose praises this poem is consecrated), which, according to Mírzá Muḥammad (for I have no access to the book), is remarkable both for its strong Shí'ite tendencies and for the marked inferiority of its style to his previous works. The publication of this poem appears to have aroused the anger and stirred up the persecuting spirit of a certain orthodox theologian of Samarqand, who caused the book to be burned and denounced the author as a heretic deserving of death. Not content with this, he charged him before Buráq the Turkmán [1] with heresy, caused him to be driven into banishment, and incited the common people to destroy his house and plunder his property. After this 'Aṭṭár seems to have retired to Mecca, where, apparently, he composed his last work, the *Lisánu'l-Ghayb*, a poem which bears the same traces of failing power and extreme age as that last mentioned. It is worth noting that in it he compares himself to Náṣir-i-Khusraw, who, like himself, "in order that he might not look on the accursed faces" of his persecutors, retired from the world and "hid himself like a ruby in Badakhshán."

Date of 'Aṭṭár's death.

As to the date of Shaykh 'Aṭṭár's death, there is an extraordinary diversity of opinion amongst the biographers. Thus the Qáḍí Núru'lláh of Shushtar places it in A.H. 589 (= A.D. 1193), and the old British Museum Catalogue of Arabic MSS. (p. 84) in A.H. 597 (= A.D. 1200–1), on the authority of Dawlatsháh (see p. 192 of my edition), who gives A.H. 602 (=A.D. 1205–6) as an alternative date, though both these dates are in direct conflict with the story which he gives on the preceding page or 'Aṭṭár's death at the hands of the Mongols during the sack of Níshápúr in A.H. 627 (= A.D. 1229–30). Dawlatsháh also gives yet a fourth date, A.H. 619 (= A.D. 1222), which is likewise the date given by Taqiyyu'd-Dín Káshí, while Ḥajji Khalífa and Amín Aḥmad-i-Rází mention both A.H. 619 and 627. This latter date, indeed, seems to be the favourite one, having eight authorities (mostly comparatively modern) in its favour,[2] while a still later date, A.H. 632 (=A.D. 1234–35), is also mentioned by Ḥájji Khalífa.

[1] One of the descendants of the Gúr Khán and *amírs* of Khwárazmsháh, who conquered Kirmán in A.H. 619=A.D. 1222.

[2] All these, however, as Mírzá Muḥammad points out, draw their information from one source, viz., Jámí's *Nafaḥátu'l-Uns*.

It will thus be seen that the difference between the earliest and the latest date assigned to 'Aṭṭár's death is no less than forty-three lunar years, and, in fact, that no reliance can be placed on these late biographers. For more trustworthy evidence we must consider the data yielded by the poet's own works, which will enable us to fix the date at any rate within somewhat closer limits. Though it is hardly credible that, as some of his biographers assert, 'Aṭṭár lived to the age of one hundred and fourteen, a verse in one of his own poems clearly shows that his age at least reached "seventy and odd years," but how much beyond this period he survived we have no means of ascertaining. In one of his *Mathnawís* he alludes to the revolt of the Ghuzz Turks, which took place in A.H. 548 (=A.D. 1153–54), while a copy of the *Manṭiqu'ṭ-Ṭayr* in the British Museum (Or. 1,227, last page) and another in the India Office contain a colophon in verse giving "Tuesday, the Twentieth Day of the Month of God, A.H. 573" (= A.D. 1177–78) as the date on which the poem was completed. Moreover, 'Aṭṭár was a contemporary of Shaykh Majdu'd-Dín Baghdádí (or Khwárazmí), and, according to Jámí's *Nafaḥát* (p. 697), his disciple, which latter statement seems to be borne out by what 'Aṭṭár himself says in the Preface to the *Tadhkiratu'l-Awliyá* (ed. Nicholson, vol. i, p. 6, l. 21); and Shaykh Majdu'd-Dín died either in A.H. 606 (= A.D. 1209–10) or A.H. 616 (= A.D. 1219–20). The most decisive indication, however, is afforded by a passage in the *Madhharu'l-'Ajá'ib*, wherein Shaykh Najmu'd-Dín Kubrá, who, as we saw in the last chapter, was killed by the Mongols when they took and sacked Khwárazm in A.H. 618 (= A.D. 1221), is spoken of in a manner implying that he was no longer alive. We may, therefore, certainly conclude that 'Aṭṭár survived that year, and that his birth was probably antecedent to the year A.H. 545 or 550 (A.D. 1150–55), while there is, so far as I know, no weighty evidence in support of Jámí's statement (*Nafaḥát*, p. 699) that

Legends concerning 'Aṭṭár.

he was killed by the Mongols in A.H. 627 (= A.D. 1229–30), still less for the detailed account of the manner of his death given by Dawlatsháh (p. 191 of my edition), who seeks to give an air of verisimilitude to his improbable story by a great precision as to the date of the event, which he fixes as the 10th of Jumáda II, A.H. 627 (= April 26, A.D. 1230). Other constantly recurring features in most of the later biographies of Shaykh 'Aṭṭár are the account of his conversion, the account of his blessing the infant Jalálu'd-Dín, afterwards the author of the great mystical *Mathnawí*, and the miracle whereby his holiness was demonstrated after his death to an unbelieving father. These stories are in my opinion mere phantasies of Dawlatsháh and his congeners, unworthy of serious attention, but they may be found by such as desire them in Sir Gore Ouseley's *Biographical Notices of Persian Poets* (London, 1846, pp. 236–243).

Limited scope of the present notice.

Most of 'Aṭṭár's copious works remain, as I have said, unpublished, except in the Lucknow lithographed edition of 1872, which, unfortunately, I do not possess. An immense amount of pioneer work remains to be done ere this great mystic's work can be described even in broad outlines, and I, writing at a distance from the few libraries in this country where manuscripts of all his important works are preserved, am obliged to content myself here (since nothing more need be said about the *Tadhkiratu'l-Awliyá* or the *Pand-náma*) with a few observations on the most celebrated of his mystical *Mathnawís*, the *Manṭiqu'ṭ-Ṭayr*, or "Speech of the Birds," accessible, as already stated, in the excellent edition of Garcin de Tassy. This scholar gives in his preface to the translation a poem of twenty-four couplets copied from the monument erected over the poet's tomb in Níshápúr; but since the monument in question was only erected about the end of the fifteenth century, by order of Sulṭán Abu'l-Ghází Ḥusayn, who reigned over Khurásán from A.D. 1468–1506, it is of no great authority, and it is hardly worth trying to explain the inconsistencies which it presents.

The *Manṭiqu'ṭ-Ṭayr* is an allegorical poem of something over 4,600 couplets. Its subject is the quest of the birds for the mythical Símurgh, the birds typifying the Ṣúfí pilgrims, and the Símurgh God "the Truth."

The *Manṭiqu 'ṭ-Ṭayr.*

The book begins with the usual doxologies, including the praise of God, of the Prophet, and of the Four Caliphs, the latter clearly showing that at this period Shaykh 'Aṭṭár was a convinced Sunní. The narrative portion of the poem begins at verse 593, and is comprised in 45 "Discourses" (*Maqála*) and a "Conclusion" (*Khátima*). It opens with an account of the assembling of the birds, some thirteen species of whom are separately apostrophised. They decide that for the successful pursuit of their quest they must put themselves under the guidance of a leader, and proceed to elect to this position the Hoopoe (*Hudhud*), so celebrated amongst the Muslims for the part which it played as Solomon's emissary to Bilqís, the Queen of Sheba. The Hoopoe harangues them in a long discourse, which concludes with the following account of the first Manifestation of the mysterious Símurgh.

"*When first the Símurgh, radiant in the night,*
Passed o'er the land of China in its flight,
A feather from its wing on Chinese soil
Fell, and the world in tumult did embroil,
Each one did strive that feather to pourtray;
Who saw these sketches, fell to work straightway.
In China's Picture-hall that feather is:
'Seek knowledge e'en in China'[1] *points to this.*
Had not mankind the feather's portrait seen,
Such strife throughout the world would ne'er have been.
Its praise hath neither end nor origin:
Unto what end its praise shall we begin?"

---

[1] This is a well-known traditional saying of the Prophet.

No sooner, however, has the quest been decided upon than the birds "begin with one accord to make excuse." The nightingale pleads its love for the rose; the parrot excuses itself on the ground that it is imprisoned for its beauty in a cage; the peacock affects diffidence of its worthiness because of its connection with Adam's expulsion from Paradise; the duck cannot dispense with water; the partridge is too much attached to the mountains, the heron to the lagoons, and the owl to the ruins which these birds respectively frequent; the *Humá* loves its power of conferring royalty; the falcon will not relinquish its place of honour on the King's hand; while the wagtail pleads its weakness. All these excuses, typical of the excuses made by men for not pursuing the things of the Spirit, are answered in turn by the wise hoopoe, which illustrates its arguments by a series of anecdotes.

Excuses of the birds.

The hoopoe next describes to the other birds the perilous road which they must traverse to arrive at the Símurgh's presence, and relates to them the long story of Shaykh Ṣan'án, who fell in love with a Christian girl, and was constrained by his love and her tyranny to feed swine, thus exposing himself to the censure of all his former friends and disciples. The birds then decide to set out under the guidance of the hoopoe to look for the Símurgh, but they shortly begin again to make excuses or raise difficulties, which the hoopoe answers, illustrating his replies by numerous anecdotes. The objections of twenty-two birds, with the hoopoe's answers to each, are given in detail. The remaining birds then continue their quest, and, passing in succession through the seven valleys of Search, Love, Knowledge, Independence, Unification, Amazement, and Destitution and Annihilation, ultimately, purged of all self and purified by their trials, find the Símurgh, and in finding it, find themselves. The passage which describes this (ll. 4,201–4,221) is so curious, and so well illustrates the Ṣúfí

Pilgrimage of the birds.

conception of "Annihilation in God" (*Fanà fi'lláh*) that I think it well to give here a literal prose rendering of these twenty verses :—

"*Through trouble and shame the souls of these birds were reduced to utter Annihilation, while their bodies became dust.*[1]

Being thus utterly purified of all, they all received Life from the Light of the [*Divine*] *Presence.*

Once again they became servants with souls renewed; once again in another way were they overwhelmed with astonishment.

Their ancient deeds and undeeds[2] *were cleansed away and annihilated from their bosoms.*

The Sun of Propinquity shone forth from them; the souls of all of them were illuminated by its rays.

Through the reflection of the faces of these thirty birds (sí murgh) *of the world they then beheld the countenance of the* Símurgh.

When they looked, that was the Símurgh : *without doubt that* Símurgh *was those thirty birds* (sí murgh).

All were bewildered with amazement, not knowing whether they were this or that.

They perceived themselves to be naught else but the Símurgh, *while the* Símurgh *was naught else than the thirty birds* (sí murgh).

When they looked towards the Símurgh, *it was indeed the* Símurgh *which was there;*

While, when they looked towards themselves, they were sí murgh (*thirty birds*), *and that was the* Símurgh ;

And if they looked at both together, both were the Símurgh, *neither more nor less.*

This one was that, and that one this; the like of this hath no one heard in the world.

All of them were plunged in amazement, and continued thinking without thought.

Since they understood naught of any matter, without speech they made enquiry of that Presence.

They besought the disclosure of this deep mystery, and demanded the solution of 'we-ness' and 'thou-ness.'

Without speech came the answer from that Presence, saying: 'This Sun-like Presence is a Mirror.

---

[1] *Tútiyá* ("tutty")—*i.e.*, mummified.

[2] *I.e.*, sins of commission and omission.

Whosoever enters It sees himself in It; in It he sees body and soul, soul and body.
Since ye came hither thirty birds (sí murgh), *ye appeared as thirty in this Mirror.*
Should forty or fifty birds come, they too would discover themselves.
Though many more had been added to your numbers, ye yourselves see, and it is yourself you have looked on.'"

Jalálu'd-Dín Rúmí.

Jalálu'd-Dín Muḥammad, better known by his later title of Mawláná ("our Master") Jalálu'd-Dín-i-Rúmí (*i.e.*, "of Rúm," or Asia Minor, where the greater part of his life was spent), is without doubt the most eminent Ṣúfí poet whom Persia has produced, while his mystical *Mathnawí* deserves to rank amongst the great poems of all time. He was born at Balkh in the autumn of A.D. 1207, but soon after that date the jealousy of 'Alá'u'd-Dín Muḥammad Khwárazmsháh compelled his father, Muḥammad b. Ḥusayn al-Khaṭíbí al-Bakrí, commonly known as Bahá'u'd-Dín Walad, to leave his home and migrate westwards. He passed through Níshápúr, according to the well-known story, in A.D. 1212, and visited Shaykh Farídu'd-Dín 'Aṭṭár, who, it is said, took the little Jalálu'd-Dín in his arms, predicted his greatness, and gave him his blessing and a copy of his poem, the *Iláhí-náma*. From Níshápúr the exiles went to Baghdád and Mecca, thence to Maláṭiyya, where they remained four years, and thence to Lárinda (now Qaramán), where they abode seven years. At the end of this period they transferred their residence to Qonya (Iconium), then the capital of 'Alá'u'd-Dín Kay-qubád the Seljúq, and here Jalálu'd-Dín's father, Bahá'u'd-Dín, died in February, 1231.

His family.

Jalálu'd-Dín married at Lárinda, when about twenty-one years of age, a lady named Gawhar ("Pearl"), the daughter of Lálá Sharafu'd-Dín of Samarqand. She bore him two sons, 'Alá'u'd-Dín and Bahá'u'd-Dín Sulṭán Walad. The former was killed at Qonya in a riot, which also resulted in the death of Jalálu'd-Dín's spiritual director, Shamsu'd-Dín of Tabríz (Shams-i-Tabríz), while the latter, born in A.D. 1226, is remarkable as being the author of "the earliest important specimen of West-Turkish poetry that we possess"—to wit, 156 couplets in the *Rabáb-náma*, or "Book of the Rebeck," a *mathnawí* poem composed in A.D. 1301. The late Mr. E. J. W. Gibb, who gives further particulars about this poem, as well as other interesting facts about its author and his father, has translated a considerable portion of it into English verse, as well as some *ghazals* by the same author.[1] At a later date Jalálu'd-Dín (having apparently lost his first wife) married again, and by this second marriage had two more children, a son and a daughter. He died in A.D. 1273, and was buried in the mausoleum erected over his father's remains in A.D. 1231 by 'Alá'u'd-Dín Kay-qubád, the Seljúq Sulṭán of Qonya.[2]

Jalálu'd-Dín seems to have studied the exoteric sciences chiefly with his father until the death of the latter in A.D. 1231, when he went for a time to Aleppo and Damascus to seek further instruction. About this time he came under the influence of one of his father's former pupils, Shaykh Burhánu'd-Dín of Tirmidh, who instructed him in the mystic lore of "the Path," and after the death of this eminent saint

Shams-i-Tabríz.

he received further esoteric teaching from the above-mentioned Shams-i-Tabríz, a "weird figure," as Mr. Nicholson calls him,[3] "wrapped in coarse black felt, who flits across the stage for a moment and disappears tragically enough." This strange personage, said to have been the son of that Jalálu'd-Dín "*Naw-Musulmán*," whose

[1] See Gibb's *History of Ottoman Poetry*, vol. i, pp. 141–163.

[2] For some account of the mausoleum, see M. Cl. Huart's *Konia, la ville des Derviches Tourneurs* (Paris, 1897), pp. 194–211, ch. xi: "Les philosophes mystiques du xiie siècle, Chems-eddin Tebrizi, Djelál-eddin Roûmi.—Les derviches tourneurs."

[3] *Selected Odes from the Díwán-i-Shams-i-Tabríz*, p. xviii of the Introduction.

zeal for Islám and aversion from the tenets of the Assassins whose pontiff he was supposed to be has been already described (pp. 455–456 *supra*), had earned by his extensive and flighty wanderings the nickname of *Paranda* ("the Flier"). Redhouse[1] describes him as of an "exceedingly aggressive and domineering manner," and Sprenger[2] as "a most disgusting cynic," but Nicholson[3] has best summed up his characteristics in the following words: "He was comparatively illiterate, but his tremendous spiritual enthusiasm, based on the conviction that he was a chosen organ and mouthpiece of Deity, cast a spell over all who entered the enchanted circle of his power. In this respect, as in many others, for example, in his strong passions, his poverty, and his violent death, Shams-i-Tabríz curiously resembles Socrates; both imposed themselves upon men of genius, who gave their crude ideas artistic expression; both proclaim the futility of external knowledge, the need of illumination, the value of love; but wild raptures and arrogant defiance of every human law can ill atone for the lack of that 'sweet reasonableness' and moral grandeur which distinguish the sage from the devotee."

According to Shamsu'd-Dín Aḥmad al-Aflákí's *Manáqibu'l-'Arifín* (of which a considerable portion, translated into English, is prefixed, under the title of "Acts of the Adepts," to Sir James Redhouse's versified translation of the First Book of the *Mathnawí*),[4] Jalálu'd-Dín's acquaintance with this mysterious personage (whom he had previously seen, but not spoken with, at Damascus) began at Qonya in December, 1244,[5] lasted with ever-increasing intimacy for some fifteen months, and was brought to an abrupt close in March, 1246, by the violent

[1] Translation of Book I of the *Mesneví (Mathnawí)*, p. x of the Translator's Preface.

[2] *Catalogue of the Oudh MSS.*, p. 490.

[3] *Selected Odes, &c.*, p. xx of the Introduction.

[4] Published by Trübner, London, 1881. See p. 23.

[5] Ibid., and also p. 99.

death of Shams-i-Tabríz to which reference has already been made. The tall, drab-coloured felt hat and wide cloak still worn by members of the Mevleví Dervish order, as well as the peculiar gyrations which have earned for them amongst Europeans the name of "Dancing Dervishes," are said by al-Aflákí to have been instituted at this time by Jalálu'd-Dín in memory of his lost friend, though a few pages further on (pp. 27–28) he adds other reasons for the introduction of the chanting and dancing practised by his disciples.

The *Mevleví* or "dancing" Dervishes.

It is uncertain at what date the great mystical Mathnawí was begun. It comprises six books,[1] containing in all, according to al-Aflákí's statement, 26,660 couplets.[2] The second book was begun in A.D. 1263, two years after the completion of the first, when the work was interrupted by the death of the wife of Ḥasan Ḥusámu'd-Dín, the author's favourite pupil and amanuensis. The first book, therefore, was ended in A.D. 1261, but we have no means of knowing how long it was in the writing. In any case it was probably begun some considerable time after the death of Shams-i-Tabríz, and was completed before the end of A.D. 1273, when the death of Jalálu'd-Dín took place.[3] Its composition, therefore, probably extended over a period of some ten years. Each book except the first begins with an exhortation to Ḥasan Ḥusámu'd-Dín ibn Akhí Turk, who is likewise spoken of in the Arabic preface of Book I as having inspired that portion also. As he became Jalálu'd-Dín's assistant and amanuensis on the death of his predecessor, Saláḥu'd-Dín Ferídún *Zar-kúb* ("the Gold-beater"), in A.D. 1258, it is probable that the *Mathnawí* was begun after this period.

[1] A seventh book, sometimes met with, which has been lithographed in the East, is certainly spurious.

[2] Redhouse's *Mesneví*, pp. xi and 104.

[3] He died at sunset on Sunday, 5 Jumáda II, A.H. 672=16 December, A.D. 1273. See the work above cited, p. 96.

It is unnecessary to say more about Jalálu'd-Dín's life, of which the most detailed and authentic account is that given by al-Aflákí in his "Acts of the Adepts," partly translated by Redhouse. It is true that many of the miraculous achievements of Jalálu'd-Dín and his predecessors and successors which are recorded in this work are quite incredible, and that it is, moreover, marred by not a few anachronisms and other inconsistencies, but it was begun only forty-five years after the Master's death (viz., in A.D. 1318) and finished in 1353; and was, moreover, compiled by a disciple living on the spot from the most authoritative information obtainable, at the express command of Jalálu'd-Dín's grandson, Chelebí Amír 'Árif, the son of Bahá'u'd-Dín Sulṭán Walad.

Miracles attributed to Jalálu'd-Dín.

As regards the lyrical poems which form the so-called *Díwán* of Shams-i-Tabríz, it is, as Nicholson points out (*op. cit.*, p. xxv and n. 2 *ad calc.*), implied by Dawlatsháh that they were chiefly composed during the absence of Shams-i-Tabríz at Damascus, while Riḍá-qulí Khán regards them rather as having been written *in memoriam*; but Nicholson's own view, which is probably correct, is "that part of the Díwán was composed while Shams-i-Tabríz was still living, but probably the bulk of it belongs to a later period." He adds that Jalálu'd-Dín "was also the author of a treatise in prose, entitled *Fíhi má fíhi*, which runs to 3,000 *bayts*, and is addressed to Mu'ínu'd-Dín, the *Parwána* of Rúm." This work is very rare, and I cannot remember ever to have seen a copy.

The *Díwán* of Shams-i-Tabríz.

Both the *Mathnawí* and the *Díwán* are poetry of a very high order. Of the former it is commonly said in Persia that it is "the Qur'án in the Pahlawí (*i.e.*, Persian) language," while its author describes it, in the Arabic Preface to Book I, as containing "the Roots of the Roots of the Roots of the Religion, and the Discovery of the Mysteries of Reunion and Sure Know-

Rank and worth of the *Mathnawí*.

ledge." "It is," he continues, "the supreme Science of God, the most resplendent Law of God, and the most evident Proof of God. The like of its Light is 'as a lantern wherein is a lamp,'[1] shining with an effulgence brighter than the Morning. It is the Paradise of the Heart, abounding in fountains and foliage; of which fountains is one called by the Pilgrims of this Path *Salsabíl*,[2] but by the possessors of [supernatural] Stations and God-given powers 'good as a Station,'[3] and 'Best as a noon-day halting-place.'[4] Therein shall the righteous eat and drink, and therein shall the virtuous rejoice and be glad. Like the Nile of Egypt, it is a drink for the patient, but a sorrow to the House of Pharaoh and the unbelievers: even as God saith,[5] 'Thereby He leadeth many astray, and thereby He guideth many aright; but He misleadeth not thereby any save the wicked.'" It is written throughout in the apocopated hexameter Ramal metre, *i.e.*, the foot *Fá'ilátun* (— ◡ — —) six times repeated in each *bayt* (verse), but shortened or "apocopated" to *Fá'ilát* (— ◡ —) at the end of each half-verse, and, as its name implies, rhymes in doublets. It contains a great number of rambling anecdotes of the most various character, some sublime and dignified, others grotesque and even (to our ideas) disgusting, interspersed with mystical and theosophical digressions, often of the most abstruse character, in sharp contrast with the narrative portions, which, though presenting some peculiarities of diction, are as a rule couched in very simple and plain language. The book is further remarkable as beginning abruptly, without any formal doxology, with the well-known and beautiful passage translated by the late Professor E. H. Palmer, under the title of the "Song of the Reed"; a little book less widely known than it deserves, and containing, with other translations and original verses of less value, a paraphrase, not only of the opening canto of the *Mathnawí*, or "Song of the Reed" proper, but of

[1] *Qur'án*, xxiv, 35. [2] Ibid., lxxvi, 18. [3] Ibid., xix, 74. [4] Ibid., xxv, 26. [5] Ibid., ii, 24.

several of the stories from the beginning of Book I. These, though rather freely translated, are both graceful and thoroughly imbued with the spirit of the poem, and I regard them as one of the most successful attempts with which I am acquainted at rendering Persian verse into English.

Jalálu'd-Dín's English translators.

Indeed, amongst the Persian poets Jalálu'd-Dín Rúmí has been singularly fortunate in his English interpreters. Besides the "Song of the Reed" mentioned above, there is the complete versified translation of Book I made by Sir James Redhouse and published by Messrs. Trübner in their "Oriental Series," which also contains in another later volume an abridgement, with selected extracts rendered in prose, of the whole poem, by Mr. E. H. Whinfield, who, both here and in his edition and translation of the *Gulshan-i-Ráz*, or "Mystic Rose Garden," of Shaykh Maḥmúd Shabistarí, has done such excellent work in investigating and interpreting the pantheistic mysticism of Persia. Nor has the *Díwán* been overlooked, for Mr. R. A. Nicholson's *Selected Poems from the Díwán-i-Shams-i-Tabríz, edited and translated with an Introduction, Notes, and Appendices* (Cambridge, 1898) is, in my opinion, one of the most original and masterly studies of the subject yet produced. In particular his classical scholarship enabled him carefully to examine and demonstrate the close relation which, as both he and I believe, exists between the doctrines of the Ṣúfís of Islám and the Neo-Platonists of Alexandria; a thesis treated in a masterly manner in the introduction to the *Selected Poems*, and one on which he is still working. His edition of Shaykh Farídu'd-Dín 'Aṭṭár's *Tadhkiratu'l-Awliyá*, or "Biography of the Saints," of which vol. i has been already published and vol. ii will shortly appear in my "Persian Historical Texts Series," has furnished him with much fresh material, and he tells me that he is now inclined to ascribe the definite eclectic system of philosophical Ṣúfiism more to Dhu'n-Nún of Egypt than to any other single individual; a fact which, if confirmed, is of the utmost importance, as supplying the final link connecting the Ṣúfís with the School of Alexandria.

The existence of the translations mentioned above renders it unnecessary for me to quote largely from the works of Jalálu'd-Dín, and I shall content myself with presenting to the reader one short but typical passage from the *Mathnawí*, and two odes from the *Díwán*. The former is taken from the *Story of the Jewish Wazír* in Book I, and my rendering may be compared with those of Palmer in the "Song of the Reed" (pp. 24–25) and Redhouse (p. 29, l. 25—p. 31, l. 12).

Translation from the *Mathnawí*.

"*Nightly the souls of men thou lettest fly*
From out the trap wherein they captive lie.
Nightly from out its cage each soul doth wing
Its upward way, no longer slave or king.
Heedless by night the captive of his fate;
Heedless by night the Sultan of his State.
Gone thought of gain or loss, gone grief and woe;
No thought of this, or that, or So-and-so.
Such, even when awake, the Gnostic's[1] *plight:*
God saith: 'They sleep':[2] *recoil not in affright!*
Asleep from worldly things by night and day,
Like to the Pen moved by God's Hand are they.
Who in the writing fails the Hand to see,
Thinks that the Pen is in its movements free.
Some trace of this the Gnostic doth display:
E'en common men in sleep are caught away.
Into the Why-less Plains the spirit goes,
The while the body and the mind repose.
Then with a whistle dost Thou them recall,
And once again in toil and moil they fall;
For when once more the morning light doth break;
And the Gold Eagle of the Sky[3] *doth shake*

---

[1] "Gnostic" is the literal translation of *árif*, and both terms probably come from the same source, and refer to the supra-intellectual cognition of Divine Verities recognised by the Neo-Platonists and their successors.

[2] *Qur'án*, xviii, 17. The verse is from the *Súratu'l-Kahf*, or "Chapter of the Cave," and refers to the "People of the Cave," or, as we call them, "The Seven Sleepers."

[3] *I.e.*, the Sun.

Its wings, then Isráfíl[1]*-like from that bourn*
The 'Cleaver of the Dawn'[2] *bids them return.*
The disembodied souls He doth recall,
And makes their bodies pregnant one and all.

Yet for a while each night the Spirit's steed
Is from the harness of the body freed:
'Sleep is Death's brother': *come, this riddle rede!*
But lest at day-break they should lag behind,
Each soul He doth with a long tether bind,[3]
That from those groves and plains He may revoke
Those errant spirits to their daily yoke.

O would that, like the 'Seven Sleepers,' we
As in the Ark of Noah kept might be,
That mind, and eye, and ear might cease from stress
Of this fierce Flood of waking consciousness!
How many 'Seven Sleepers' by thy side,
Before thee, round about thee, do abide!
Each in his care the Loved One's whisper hears:
What boots it? Sealéd are thine eyes and ears!"

The *Díwán-i-Shams-i-Tabríz.*

In the East the *Díwán* is much less read and studied than the *Mathnawí*, though by some European scholars it is placed far above it in poetic merit and originality. And, if we are to credit one of al-Aflákí's anecdotes (No. 14, pp. 28–30 of Redhouse's translation), this was the opinion of some of Jalálu'd-Dín's most illustrious contemporaries, including the great Sa'dí himself, who, being requested by the Prince of Shíráz to select and send to him "the best ode, with the most sublime thoughts, that he knew of as existing in Persian," chose out one from the *Díwán* in question, saying: "Never have more beautiful words been uttered, nor ever will be. Would that I could go to Rúm

[1] Isráfíl is the angel of the Resurrection, whose trumpet-blast shall raise the dead to life.
[2] This title is given to God in the Qur'án, vi, 96.
[3] Compare Ch. Huart's *Livre de la Création et de l'Histoire* (*Kitábu'l-Bad' wa 't-Ta'ríkh*), vol. ii, p. 103.

(Asia Minor), and rub my face in the dust at his feet!"[1] Of these odes Mr. Nicholson has treated with so much learning and taste in the monograph to which I have already referred that for me, who have made no special study of the *Díwán*, to add anything to what he has said would be superfluous. I cannot, however, forego the pleasure of quoting two of the beautiful verse-translations (portions of Odes xxxi and xxxvi of his selection) which he has included in the second Appendix to his monograph. This is the first:—

Nicholson's renderings of two odes from the *Díwán*.

"Lo, for I to myself am unknown, now in God's name what must I do?
I adore not the Cross nor the Crescent, I am not a Giaour or a Jew.
East nor West, land nor sea is my home, I have kin nor with angel nor gnome,
I am wrought not of fire nor of foam, I am shaped not of dust nor of dew.
I was born not of China afar, not in Saqsín and not in Bulghár;
Not in India, where five rivers are, nor 'Iráq nor Khurásán I grew.
Not in this world nor that world I dwell, not in Paradise neither in Hell;
Not from Eden and Riḍwán[2] I fell, not from Adam my lineage I drew.
In a place beyond uttermost Place, in a tract without shadow of trace,
Soul and body transcending I live in the soul of my Loved One anew!"

This is the second:—

"Up, O ye lovers, and away! 'Tis time to leave the world for aye.
Hark, loud and clear from heaven the drum of parting calls—let none delay!

---

[1] It is stated by al-Aflákí that this desire of Sa'dí's was afterwards fulfilled, but I know of no other authority for this alleged meeting of these two great poets.

[2] Riḍwán is the Guardian of Paradise.

The cameleer hath risen amain, made ready all the camel-train,
And quittance now desires to gain: why sleep ye, travellers, I pray?
Behind us and before there swells the din of parting and of bells;
To shoreless Space each moment sails a disembodied spirit away.
From yonder starry lights and through those curtain-awnings darkly blue
Mysterious figures float in view, all strange and secret things display.
From this orb, wheeling round its pole, a wondrous slumber o'er thee stole:
O weary life that weighest naught, O sleep that on my soul dost weigh!
O heart, towards thy heart's love wend, and O friend, fly toward the Friend,
Be wakeful, watchman, to the end: drowse seemingly no watchman may."

I can recall but few English verse-renderings of Eastern poetry which seem to me at once so adequate and so beautiful as these of Mr. Nicholson; and I only regret that the drudgery of editing, proof-correcting, attending futile meetings, and restating ascertained facts for a public apparently insatiably greedy of Encyclopædias, hinder him, as they hinder so many of us, from pursuing with more assiduity the paths which we are alike most fitted and most eager to tread.

Sa'di of Shíráz.

We come now to Sa'dí of Shíráz, the third of the great poets of this epoch, and, according to a well-known rhyme previously quoted, one of the three "Prophets of Poetry," the other two being Firdawsí and Anwarí. No Persian writer enjoys to this day, not only in his own country, but wherever his language is cultivated, a wider celebrity or a greater reputation. His *Gulistán*, or "Rose-garden," and his *Bústán*, or "Orchard," are generally the first classics to which the student of Persian is introduced, while his *ghazals*, or odes, enjoy a popularity second only to those of his fellow-townsman Ḥáfidh. He is a poet of quite a different type from the two already discussed in this chapter, and represents on the whole the astute, half-pious, half-worldly side of the Persian character, as the other two represent the passionately devout and mystical. Mysticism was at this time so much in the air, and its phraseology was—as it still is—so much a part of ordinary speech, that the traces of it in Sa'dí's writings are neither few nor uncertain; but in the main it may be said without hesitation that worldly wisdom rather than mysticism is his chief characteristic, and that the *Gulistán* in particular is one of the most Macchiavellian works in the Persian language. Pious sentiments and aspirations, indeed, abound; but they are, as a rule, eminently practical, and almost devoid of that visionary quality which is so characteristic of the essentially mystical writers.

Particulars of Sa'dí's life.

The poet's full name appears, from the oldest known manuscript of his works (No. 876 of the India Office, transcribed in A.D. 1328, only thirty-seven years after his death) to have been, not, as generally stated, Muṣliḥu'd-Dín, but Musharrifu'd-Dín b. Muṣliḥu'd-Dín 'Abdu'lláh. He is generally said to have been born at Shíráz about A.D. 1184, and to have died more than a centenarian in A.D. 1291. That he lost his father at an early age is proved by the following passage in the *Búslán*:—

"Protect thou the orphan whose father is dead;
Brush the mud from his dress, ward all hurt from his head.
Thou know'st not how hard his condition must be:
When the root has been cut, is there life in the tree?
Caress not and kiss not a child of thine own
In the sight of an orphan neglected and lone.
If the orphan sheds tears, who his grief will assuage?
If his temper should fail him, who cares for his rage?
O see that he weep not, for surely God's throne
Doth quake at the orphan's most pitiful moan!
With infinite pity, with tenderest care,
Wipe the tears from his eyes, brush the dust from his hair.
No shield of parental protection his head
Now shelters: be thou his protector instead!

When the arms of a father my neck could enfold
Then, then was I crowned like a monarch with gold.
If even a fly should upon me alight
Not one heart but many were filled with affright,
While now should men make me a captive and thrall,
No friend would assist me or come to my call.
The sorrows of orphans full well can I share,
Since I tasted in childhood the orphan's despair."

Sa'dí's education and travels.

On his father's death, according to Dr. Ethé, whose article on *Persian Literature* in vol. ii (pp. 212–368) of the *Grundriss der Iranischen Philologie* contains (on pp. 292–296) the best account of Sa'dí with which I am acquainted, he was taken under the protection of the Atábek of Fárs, Sa'd b. Zangí, whose accession took place in A.D. 1195, and in honour of whom the poet took the pen-name of "Sa'dí" as his *nom de guerre;* and shortly afterwards he was sent to pursue his studies at the celebrated Nidhámiyya College of Baghdád. This marks the beginning of the first of the three periods into which Dr. Ethé divides his life, viz., the period of study, which lasted until A.D. 1226, and was spent chiefly at Baghdád. Yet even during this period he made, as appears from a story in Book v of the *Gulistán*, the long journey to Káshghar, which, as he tells us, he entered "in the year when Sulṭán Muḥammad Khwárazmsháh elected, on grounds of policy, to make peace with Cathay" (*Khaṭá*), which happened about the year A.D. 1210. Even then, as we learn from the same anecdote, his fame had preceded him to this remote outpost of Islám in the north-east, a fact notable not merely as showing that he had succeeded in establishing his reputation at the early age of twenty-six, but as confirming what I have already endeavoured to emphasise as to the rapidity with which knowledge and news were at this time transmitted throughout the realms of Islám.

The first period of his life.

While at Baghdád he came under the influence of the eminent Ṣúfí Shaykh Shihábu'd-Dín Suhrawardí (died in

A.D. 1234), of whose deep piety and unselfish love of his fellow-creatures Sa'dí speaks in one of the anecdotes in the *Búştán*. Shamsu'd-Dín Abu'l-Faraj ibnu'l-Jawzí, as we learn from an anecdote in Book ii of the *Gulistán*, was another of the eminent men by whose instruction he profited in his youth.

The second period of Sa'dí's life, that of his more extensive travels, begins, according to Dr. Ethé, in A.D. 1226, in which year the disturbed condition of Fárs led him to quit Shíráz (whither he had returned from Baghdád), and, for some thirty years (until A.D. 1256) to wander hither and thither in the lands of Islám, from India on the East to Syria and the Ḥijáz on the West. To his departure from Shíráz he alludes in the following verses in the Preface to the *Gulistán* :—

The second period.

"O knowest thou not why, an outcast and exile,
In lands of the stranger a refuge I sought?
Disarranged was the world like the hair of a negro
When I fled from the Turks and the terror they brought.
Though outwardly human, no wolf could surpass them
In bloodthirsty rage or in sharpness of claw;
Though within was a man with the mien of an angel,
Without was a host of the lions of war.
At peace was the land when again I beheld it;
E'en lions and leopards were wild but in name.
Like that was my country what time I forsook it,
Fulfilled with confusion and terror and shame:
Like this in the time of 'Bú Bakr the Atábek
I found it when back from my exile I came."

Sa'dí's return to his native town of Shíráz, to which he alludes in the last couplet of the above poem, took place in A.D. 1256, which marks the beginning of the third period of his life, that, namely, in which his literary activity chiefly fell. A year after his return, in A.D. 1257, he published his celebrated *mathnawí* poem the *Búştán*, and a year later the *Gulistán*, a collection of

The third period.

anecdotes, drawn from the rich stores of his observation and experience, with ethical reflections and maxims of worldly wisdom based thereon, written in prose in which are embedded numerous verses. Both these books are so well known, and have been translated so often into so many languages, that it is unnecessary to discuss them at length in this place.[1]

We have already said that Sa'dí's travels were very extensive. In the course of them he visited Balkh, Ghazna, the Panjáb, Somnáth, Gujerat, Yemen, the Ḥijáz and other parts of Arabia, Abyssinia, Syria, especially Damascus and Baalbekk (*Ba'labakk*), North Africa, and Asia Minor. He travelled, in true dervish-fashion, in all sorts of ways, and mixed with all sorts of people : in his own writings (especially the *Gulistán*) he appears now painfully stumbling after the Pilgrim Caravan through the burning deserts of Arabia, now bandying jests with a fine technical flavour of grammatical terminology with schoolboys at Káshghar, now a prisoner in the hands of the Franks, condemned to hard labour in the company of Jews in the Syrian town of Tripoli, now engaged in investigating the mechanism of a wonder-working Hindoo idol in the Temple of Somnáth, and saving his life by killing the custodian who discovered him engaged in this pursuit.[2] This last achievement he narrates with the utmost *sang froid* as follows :—

"*The door of the Temple I fastened one night,*
Then ran like a scorpion to left and to right;
Next the platform above and below to explore
I began, till a gold-broidered curtain I saw,
And behind it a priest of the Fire-cult[3] *did stand*
With the end of a string firmly held in his hand.

---

[1] Ethé (*loc. cit.*, pp. 295–6) gives a copious and excellent bibliography.

[2] This story is told by Sa'dí at the end of ch. viii of the *Búslán*.

[3] It is astonishing how little even well-educated Muslims know about other religions. Sa'dí, for all his wide reading and extensive travels, cannot tell a story about a Hindoo idol-temple without mixing up with it references to Zoroastrian and even Christian observances.

As iron to David grew pliant as wax,
So to me were made patent his tricks and his tracks,
And I knew that 'twas he who was pulling the string
When the Idol its arm in the Temple did swing.

When the Brahmin beheld me, most deep was his shame,
For 'tis shame to be caught at so shabby a game.
He fled from before me, but I did pursue
And into a well him head-foremost I threw,
For I knew that, if he should effect his escape,
I should find myself soon in some perilous scrape,
And that he would most gladly use poison or steel
Lest I his nefarious deed should reveal.

You too, should you chance to discover such trick,
Make away with the trickster: don't spare him! Be quick!
For, if you should suffer the scoundrel to live,
Be sure that to you he no quarter will give,
And that though on your threshold his head should be bowed
He will cut off your head, if the chance be allowed.
Then track not the charlatan's tortuous way,
Or else, having tracked him, smite swiftly and slay!

So I finished the rogue, notwithstanding his wails,
With stones; for dead men, as you know, tell no tales."

Sa'dí as an "ethical" teacher.

When Saʿdí is described (as he often is) as essentially an ethical poet, it must be borne in mind that, correct as this view in a certain sense undoubtedly is, his ethics are somewhat different from the theories commonly professed in Western Europe. The moral of the very first story in the *Gulistán* is that "an expedient falsehood is preferable to a mischievous truth." The fourth story is an elaborate attempt to show that the best education is powerless to amend inherited criminal tendencies. The eighth counsels princes to destroy without mercy those who are afraid of them, because "when the cat is cornered, it will scratch out the eyes of the leopard." The ninth emphasises the disagreeable truth that a man's worst foes are often the heirs to his estate. The fourteenth is a defence of a soldier who deserted at a critical moment because his pay was in arrears. The fifteenth is delightfully and typically Persian. A certain minister, being dismissed from office, joined the ranks of the dervishes. After a while the King wished to reinstate him in office, but he firmly declined the honour. "But," said the King, "I need one competent and wise to direct the affairs of the State." "Then," retorted the ex-minister, "you will not get him, for the proof of his possessing these qualities is that he will refuse to surrender himself to such employment." The next story labours this point still further: "Wise men," says Sa'dí, "have said that one ought to be much on one's guard against the fickle nature of kings, who will at one time take offence at a salutation, and at another bestow honours in return for abuse." And, to make a long story short, how very sensible and how very unethical is the following (Book i, Story 22):—

"It is related of a certain tormentor of men that he struck on the head with a stone a certain pious man. The dervish dared not avenge himself [at the time], but kept the stone by him till such time as the King, being angered against his assailant, imprisoned him in a dungeon. Thereupon the dervish came and smote him on the head with the stone. 'Who art thou,' cried the other, 'and why dost thou strike me with this stone?' 'I am that same man,' replied the dervish, 'on whose head thou didst, at such-and-such a date, strike this same stone.' 'Where wert thou all this time?' inquired the other. 'I was afraid of thy position,' answered the dervish, 'but now, seeing thee in this durance, I seized my opportunity; for it has been said:—

"When Fortune favours the tyrant vile,
The wise will forego their desire a while.
If your claws are not sharp, then turn away
From a fearsome foe and a fruitless fray.
'Tis the silver wrist that the pain will feel
If it seeks to restrain the arm of steel.
Wait rather till Fortune blunts his claws:
Then pluck out his brains amidst friends' applause!"'"

Indeed, the real charm of Sa'dí and the secret of his popularity lies not in his consistency but in his catholicity; in his works is matter for every taste, the highest and the lowest, the most refined and the most coarse, and from his pages sentiments may be culled worthy on the one hand of Eckhardt or Thomas à Kempis, or on the other of Cæsar Borgia and Heliogabalus. His writings are a microcosm of the East, alike in its best and its most ignoble aspects, and it is not without good reason that, wherever the Persian language is studied, they are, and have been for six centuries and a half, the first books placed in the learner's hands.

Catholicity of Sa'dí.

Hitherto I have spoken almost exclusively of Sa'dí's most celebrated and most popular works, the *Gulistán* and the *Bústán*, but besides these his *Kulliyyát*, or Collected Works, comprise Arabic and Persian *qaṣídas*, threnodies (*maráthí*), poems partly in Persian and partly in Arabic (*mulamma'át*), poems of the kind called *tarjí'-band*, *ghazals*, or odes, arranged in four groups, viz., early poems (*ghazaliyyát-i-qadíma*), *ṭayyibát* (fine odes), *badáyi'* (cunning odes), and *khawátím* ("signet-rings" or, as we might say, "gems"), besides quatrains, fragments, isolated verses, obscene poems (*hazaliyyát*), and some prose treatises, including three mock-homilies of incredible coarseness (*khabíthát*), several epistles addressed to the *Ṣáḥib-Díwán*, or first prime minister of Ḥulágú Khán the Mongol, and his successor, Shamsu'd-Dín Muḥammad Juwayní, some amusing but not elevating anecdotes labelled *Muḍḥikát* (Facetiæ), a *Pand-náma*, or Book of Counsels, on the model of 'Aṭṭár's, and others.

Sa'dí's works.

It would evidently be impossible to discuss in detail or give specimens of each of these many forms in which the activity of Sa'dí manifested itself. Nor is the above list quite exhaustive, for Sa'dí has the reputation ot being the first to compose verse in the Hindustání or Urdú language, something of which he apparently acquired during his Indian travels, and specimens of these verses I have

Sa'dí as a linguist.

met with in a manuscript belonging to the Royal Asiatic Society, though as to their genuineness I do not venture to express an opinion. He also composed some *Fahlawiyyát*, or poems in dialect, specimens of which I published in the *J.R.A.S.* for October, 1895, in a paper entitled "Notes on the Poetry of the Persian Dialects" (see especially pp. 792–802). There is one poem of his not mentioned in this article, and on which I cannot now lay my hand, which contains couplets in a considerable number of languages and dialects. Until, however, we have both a better text of Sa'dí's works and a fuller knowledge of these mediæval dialects of Persian, a doubt must always remain as to the poet's real knowledge of them. It is quite possible that they were very "impressionist," and that he really knew no more about them than do some of those who write books about Ireland, to which they endeavour to give an air of verisimilitude by spelling English words in a grotesque manner, and peppering the pages with distorted or ill-comprehended Irish words like "musha," "acushla machree," and "mavourneen."

Sa'dí's *qaṣídas*.

In Persia and India it is commonly stated that Sa'dí's Arabic *qaṣídas* are very fine, but scholars of Arabic speech regard them as very mediocre performances. His Persian *qaṣídas* are, on the other hand, very fine, especially one beginning :—

> "*Set not thy heart exclusively on any land or friend,*
> *For lands and seas are countless, and sweethearts without end.*"

Another celebrated *qaṣída* is the one in which he laments the destruction of Baghdád by the Mongols and the violent death of the Caliph al-Musta'ṣim in A.D. 1258. Of this a specimen has been already given at pp. 29–30 *supra*.

In his *ghazals*, or odes, as already said, Sa'dí is considered as inferior to no Persian poet, not even Ḥáfiḏh. The number of these *ghazals* (which, as already explained, are divided into four classes, *Ṭayyibát*, *Badáyi'*, *Khawátím*, and "Early Poems"), is considerable, and they fill 153 pages of the Bombay lithographed edition of the *Kulliyyát* published in A.H. 1301 (= A.D. 1883–84). I give here translations of two, which may serve as samples of the rest. The first is as follows:—

Sa'di's *ghazals*.

"*Precious are these heart-burning sighs, for lo,*
This way or that, they help the days to go.
All night I wait for one whose dawn-like face
Lendeth fresh radiance to the morning's grace.
My Friend's sweet face if I again might see
I'd thank my lucky star eternally.
Shall I then fear man's blame? The brave man's heart
Serves as his shield to counter slander's dart.
Who wins success hath many a failure tholed.
The New Year's Day[1] *is reached through Winter's cold.*
For Laylá many a prudent lover yearns,
But Majnún wins her, who his harvest burns.
I am thy slave: pursue some wilder game:
No tether's needed for the bird that's tame.
A strength is his who casts both worlds aside
Which is to worldly anchorites denied.
To-morrow is not: yesterday is spent:
To-day, O Sa'di, take thy heart's content!"

The second is a great favourite with the Shírázís, by reason of the well-deserved compliment paid to their city.

"*O Fortune suffers me not to clasp my sweetheart to my breast,*
Nor lets me forget my exile long in a kiss on her sweet lips pressed,
The noose wherewith she is wont to snare her victims far and wide
I will steal away, that so one day I may lure her to my side.

[1] The Persian New Year's Day (*Nawrúz*) falls at the Vernal Equinox (about March 21st), and coincides with the outburst of flowers and verdure which makes even the deserts of Persia so beautiful in the season of spring.

Yet I shall not dare caress her hair with a hand that is over-bold,
For snared therein, like birds in a gin, are the hearts of lovers untold.
A slave am I to that gracious form, which, as I picture it,
Is clothed in grace with a measuring-rod, as tailors a garment fit.
O cypress-tree, with silver limbs, this colour and scent of thine
Have shamed the scent of the myrtle-plant and the bloom of the eglantine.
Judge with thine eyes, and set thy foot in the garden fair and free,
And tread the jasmine under thy foot, and the flowers of the Judas-tree.
O joyous and gay is the New Year's Day, and in Shíráz most of all;
Even the stranger forgets his home, and becomes its willing thrall.
O'er the garden's Egypt, Joseph-like, the fair red rose is King,
And the Zephyr, e'en to the heart of the town, doth the scent of his raiment bring.
O wonder not if in time of Spring thou dost rouse such jealousy,
That the cloud doth weep while the flowrets smile, and all on account of thee!
If o'er the dead thy feet should tread, those feet so fair and fleet,
No wonder it were if thou should'st hear a voice from his winding-sheet.
Distraction is banned from this our land in the time of our lord the King,
Save that I am distracted with love of thee, and men with the songs I sing."

Not much biographical material is to be gleaned from these odes, though in one (Bombay lithograph of A.H. 1301, p. 58), Sa'dí speaks of himself as being in danger, through love, of losing in five days the reputation for wisdom and prudence which he had built up in fifty years, while there are a good many allusions to his patron the *Ṣáḥib-Díwán*, one of which occurs in an ode written, apparently, just as Sa'dí was about to leave Shíráz for Baghdád. In this he says (p. 117):—

Dilam az ṣuḥbat-i-Shíráz bi-kullí bi-g'rift:
Waqt-i-án-ast ki pursí khabar az Baghdád-am.

Hích shak níst ki faryád-i-man ánjá bi-rasad—
'Ajab ar Ṣáḥib-i-Díwán na-rasad faryád-am!
Sa'diyá, ḥubb-i-waṭan garchi ḥadíthíst ṣaḥíḥ,
Na-tuwán murd bi-sakhtí ki man ínjá zádam!

"My soul is weary of Shíráz, utterly sick and sad:
If you seek for news of my doings, you will have to ask at Baghdád.
I have no doubt that the Premier there will give me the help I need;
Should he help refuse to one like me, I should deem it strange indeed!
Sa'dí, that love of one's native land is a true tradition is clear![1]
But I cannot afford to die of want because my birth was here!"

Another point worth noticing is that a considerable number of verses from Sa'dí's *Díwán* occur not only (which is natural enough) in his *Gulistán*, but (which is more curious) in the *Díwán* of his equally famous but more modern fellow-townsman Ḥáfiḏh. In a cursory reading I have found eight examples of the former class, and three of the latter, and probably a careful search would reveal more. To begin with the first class, on p. 37 of the *Ṭayyibát* in the Bombay lithographed edition of A.H. 1301 (No. clxiii) we find the verse:—

Verses of Sa'dí's odes cited in the *Gulistán* and by Ḥáfiḏh.

Na ánchunán bi-tú mashghúl-am, az bihishtí rú,
Ki yád-i-khwíshtan-am dar ḍamír mí-áyad.

"O thou whose face is of Paradise, my preoccupation with thee is not such that thought of myself can enter my mind."

This verse is quoted in chap. v of the *Gulistán*.

Again, in the *Badáyi'* (p. 93), occurs the verse:—

Án-rá ki jáy níst, hama shahr jáyi-úst,
Darwísh har kujá ki shab ámad saráyi-úst.

"The whole town is the home of him who has no home:
The poor man's house is wherever night overtakes him."

[1] The tradition in question is very well known, and runs: *Ḥubbu'l-waṭan mina'l-Ímán*—"Patriotism is a part of Faith."

In chap. iii of the *Gulistán* this verse occurs, with the following modification of the first hemistich :—

> "*Shab har tuwángarí bi-sará'í hamí ravad.*"
>
> "*At night every rich man goes to a house.*"

Again, on p. 99 of the *Badáyi'* occurs the hemistich :—

> "*Banda chi da'wa kunad? Ḥukm khudáwand-rást!*"
>
> "What objection can a servant raise? It is for the master to command!"

This, also with the addition of a new hemistich to match it, likewise occurs in chap. i of the *Gulistán*, in the story of 'Amr ibn Layth and his slave. The other verses in the *Díwán* which also occur in the *Gulistán* are the following. Two couplets from the *ghazal* on p. 100 beginning :—

> *Mu'allim-at hama shúkhí u dilbarí ámúkht;*
> *Jafá u náz u 'itáb u sitamgarí ámúkht.*

> "Thy master taught thee all [the arts of] coquetry and heart-stealing;
> He taught thee cruelty, coyness, recrimination and tyranny."

The couplet (on p. 115 of the *Badáyi'*) :—

> *'Ajab az kushta na-báshad bi-dar-i-khayma-i-Dúst:*
> *'Ajab az zinda, ki chún ján bi-dar áwurd salím!*"

> "There is no wonder at him who is slain at the door of the Beloved's tent:
> The wonder is at the survivor, in what way he saved his soul alive."

The couplet (on p. 144 of the *Khawátím*) :—

> *Dídár mí-numá'í, u parhíz mí-kuní:*
> *Bázár-i-khwísh u átash-i-má tíz mí-kuní.*

> "Thou showest thy face and withdrawest:
> Thou makest brisk thine own market and the fire which consumes us."

And lastly (on p. 145 of the *Khawátím*), a modification of the verses from the Preface of the *Gulistán* already translated on p. 528 *supra*.

In the chapter at the beginning of this work treating of the Poetry and Rhetoric of the Persians, mention was made of the figure called *tadmín*, or the inclusion by a poet in his verse of a hemistich, a couplet, or more, from the works of another poet; and it was observed that, in order to avoid incurring a charge of plagiarism (*sirqat*), it was incumbent on the poet making use of this figure either to cite only verses so well known to every educated person that no one could suppose he intended to ascribe them to himself, or, if he quoted from a less-known poet, to make formal mention of that poet's name. The fact that Ḥáfidh, in the following passages where he introduces verses by his predecessor Saʿdí, makes no such acknowledgement of their provenance is another proof (were any needed) of the great popularity of Saʿdí's lyric poetry.

In one of his most celebrated odes Ḥáfidh says :—

> *Bad-am guftí u khursand-am : ʻafáka'llah, nikú guftí:*
> *Jawáb-i-talkh mí-zíbad lab-i-laʻl-i-shakar-khá-rá !"*

"Thou didst speak me ill, and I am content: God pardon thee, thou didst speak well :
A bitter answer befits a ruby lip which feeds on sugar !"

The first half of this verse occurs in Saʿdí's *Ṭayyibát* (p. 86, No. ccclxxxiii), as follows :—

> *Bad-am guftí u khursand-am : ʻafáka'llah, nikú guftí :*
> *Sag-am khwándi u khushnúd-am : jazáka'lláh, karam kardí !*

The hemistich with which it is here joined means :—

Thou didst call me a dog, and I acquiesced : God reward thee thou didst confer on me a favour !"

Again in the *Badáyiʻ* (p. 107, No. lxxvii) Saʿdí says :—

Juz in-qadar na-tuwán guft dar jamál-i-tu 'ayb,
Ki mihrabáni az án tab' u khú na-mí áyad.

"One can mention no defect in thy beauty save this,
That love comes not forth from that nature and disposition."

Ḥáfidh has taken the first hemistich of this verse, and joined it with the following one of his own :—

Ki khál-i-mihr u wafá nist rú-yi-zíbá-rá.

"That the beauty-spot of love and fidelity is not on that fair face."

Again in the *Ṭayyibát* (p. 80, No. ccclix) Sa'dí says :—

Zawqí chunán na-dárad bí dúst zindagání :
Dúd-am bi-sar bar ámad zín átash-i-nihání.

"Life without the Friend has no great attraction :
My head is enveloped in smoke [of the heart, *i.e.*, sighs] by reason of this hidden fire."

Ḥáfidh has taken the first hemistich of this, and has supplemented it by the "complete anagram" of itself :—

Bí-dúst zindagání zawqí chunán na-dárad.

I am not aware that attention has hitherto been called to this indebtedness of Ḥáfidh to his predecessor, and on this account I have discussed the matter with what some may be tempted to regard as unnecessary elaboration.

Lesser poets of this period.

The lesser poets of this epoch are many, and from 'Awfí's *Lubábu'l-Albáb* alone a list of at least fourscore who were more or less contemporary with the three great poets to whom this chapter is specially devoted might, I should think, be compiled. Lack of space, however, compels me to confine myself to the brief mention of two of the most notable, viz., Sharafu'd-Dín Muḥammad Shufurvah and Kamálu'd-Dín Isma'íl, called *Khalláqu'l-Ma'ání*, "the Creator of Ideas," both of Iṣfahán. A third poet, Amír Khusraw of Dihlí (Delhi), whose reputation might appear to entitle him to notice, is omitted on the principle already laid down that India is wholly excluded from the scope of this book, and I will therefore only say that he was born at Patiyálí in A.D. 1253, died at Dihlí in A.D. 1325, and worked chiefly on the lines of Nidhámí of Ganja.

Sharafu'd-Dín Shufurvah and Jamálu'd-Dín 'Abdu'r-Razzaq (the father of Kamálu'd-Dín Ismaíl) were both panegyrists of the *Ṣadr-i-Khujand*, the Chief Judge (*Qáḍí'l-quḍát*) of Iṣfahán, and belong to a somewhat older generation than the poets of whom we have just been speaking, for the latter died in A.D. 1192 and the former in A.D. 1204. Both of them came into conflict, under circumstances to which reference has been made in a previous chapter (pp. 397–398 *supra*), with Kháqání's pupil Mujíru'd-Dín-i-Baylaqání, who satirised them with bitterness, and is said to have forfeited his life in consequence. They also satirised one another in the intervals of praising their common patron. I have met with nothing of Jamálu'd-Dín's which specially impressed me, but Sharafu'd-Dín Shufurvah has a remarkably fine poem describing the past splendour and actual devastation of Iṣfahán, of which I published the text in my *Account of a Rare Manuscript History of Iṣfahán*, published in the *J.R.A.S.* for 1901 (pp. 53–55 of the *tirage-à-part*).

Sharafu'd-Dín Shufurvah.

Kamálu'd-Dín Isma'íl, "the Creator of Ideas," son of the above Jamálu'd-Dín 'Abdu'r-Ruzzáq, was, like his father, essentially a panegyrist. Amongst those whose praises he sung were Ruknu'd-Dín Ṣá'id b. Mas'úd; several of the Khwárazmsháhs, including Tukush, Quṭbu'd-Dín Muḥammad and Jalálu'd-Dín; Ḥusámu'd-Dín Ardashír, King of Mázandarán; and

Kamálu'd-Dín Isma'íl.

the Atábeks of Fárs, Sa'd b. Zangí and his son and successor, Abú Bakr b. Sa'd, both of whom we have already met with as patrons of Sa'dí. Kamálu'd-Dín was one of the many illustrious victims who perished at the hands of the Mongols. According to Dawlatsháh (pp. 152–3 of my edition) he was both rich and liberal; but, meeting with ingratitude from some of the recipients of his favours, he reviled and cursed the people of Iṣfahán in verses whereof this is the purport:—

"*O Lord of the Seven Planets, send some bloodthirsty pagan*
To make Dar-i-Dasht like a [*bare*] *plain* (dasht), *and to cause streams* (jú) *of blood to flow from Júpára!*[1]
May he increase the number of their inhabitants by cutting each one into a hundred pieces!"

His malign wish was soon only too completely fulfilled, for the Mongol army under Ogotáy entered Iṣfahán in or about A.D. 1237, and proceeded to torture, plunder, and massacre in its usual fashion. At this time, according to Dawlatsháh (who, as has been already pointed out, is of little weight as an authority, and much addicted to romance), Kamálu'd-Dín Isma'íl had adopted the ascetic life and habit of the Ṣúfís, and had retired to an hermitage situated outside the town, in consequence of which he was not for some time molested. The Iṣfahánís took advantage of this to deposit in his custody some of their treasures and valuables, which he concealed in a well in the courtyard of his hermitage. One day, however, a Mongol boy armed with a crossbow fired at a bird in this courtyard, and in doing so dropped his "drawing-ring" (*zih-gír*),[2] which rolled into the well wherein the treasure was

[1] These are two districts of Iṣfahan, introduced on account of the word-play to which each of them is here made to lend itself. See Le Strange's *Lands of the Eastern Caliphate*, p. 205.

[2] On the "Mongolian loose" and "drawing-ring" in shooting with the bow, see the volume on Archery in the Badminton Library (London, 1894), pp. 79–81.

hidden. Search for the ring led to the discovery of the treasure; the Mongol greed was aroused, and poor Kamál was put to the torture to make him reveal other hoards of treasure which they supposed him to possess. In his death-agony he is said to have written with his life-blood the following quatrain:—

> "*When life dissolves, fierce anguish racks the soul;*
> *Before His Face this is the least we thole;*
> *And yet withal no word I dare to breathe:*
> *This is his prize who renders service whole!*"

Conclusion.

In the history of a nation—and still more in its intellectual history—there comes no point where we can say with perfect satisfaction and confidence, "Here ends a period." Yet, for practical convenience, such dividing-lines must needs be made; and, as has already been pointed out, in the history of Persia, and, indeed, of Islám, no sharper dividing-line between ancient and comparatively recent times can be found than the catastrophe of the Mongol Invasion. From this awful catastrophe Islám has never recovered, especially in its intellectual aspects. The Mongols as a world-power, or even as a political factor of importance, have long disappeared from the scene, but they changed the face of a continent, and wrought havoc which can never be repaired. The volume which I now at last bring to a conclusion covers a period of only about two centuries and a half; but I think that, should health and leisure be vouchsafed to me to bring the history down through the remaining six centuries and a half to our own times, it will be easier in a volume of this size to give adequate treatment to the later and longer period than to the earlier and shorter, whereof I now close the account—an account which, however prolix and detailed it may seem to the casual reader, is in reality, as I acutely realise, lamentably sketchy and inadequate. Yet had I waited until I could see my way to making it adequate, I should never have finished this volume at all; and in literature as in love there is deep truth in the Turkish proverb:—

"Yár-sız qalir kimesnè 'ayb-siz yar isteyan"—

which, rendered into English, means:—

"Surely he remaineth friendless who requires a faultless friend."

INDEX

In the following Index the prefixes *Abu* ("Father of ..."), and *Ibn* ("Son of ...") are disregarded in the arrangement of Muhammadan names into which they enter: thus, for example, such names as *Abu Tahir* and *Ibn Sina* are to be sought under T and S respectively. A hyphen prefixed to a name indicates that it is properly preceded by the Arabic definite article *al-*; the letter *b.* between two names stands for *ibn*, "son of ..." Names of books, both Oriental and European, are printed in italics.

For typographical reasons, it has been found necessary to omit in the Index the accents indicating the long vowels and the dots and dashes distinguishing the hard letters in the Arabic and Persian names and words which it comprises. The correct transliteration of such words must therefore be sought in the text.

36

H

J

Murajjaz (variety of prose), 20, 21
Murassa' (variety of ornate prose), 24
Murcia (Spain), 497
Musa, Imam —, 182, 194
Musa Arslan b. Seljuq, 167, 170, 172
Musabba' ("Sevensome"), 43
Musaddas ("Sixsome"), 24, 25, 43
Musajja' (variety of ornate prose), 20, 21
Musalla ("the Oratory," near Shiraz), 27, 76–77
Musammat (variety of poem), 23, 24, 39, 41, 42, 45
Musaylima (the False Prophet), 122
Mush u Gurba ("Mouse and Cat," a poem by 'Ubayd-i-Zakani), 78
Mushtarik (by Yaqut), 482
Musibat-nama (by 'Attar), 506
Musk (metaphor for hair), 407
Abu Muslim (organiser of 'Abbasid Propaganda), 9
Abu Muslim (Governor of Ray), 203, 300
Musnad (of Ibn Hanbal), 361
-Mustadhhir ('Abbasid Caliph), 304
Mustafa, 347. See *Muhammad*
-Musta'li (Fatimid Caliph), 199, 201, 203, 204
-Mutansir (Fatimid Caliph), 162, 168, 198, 200, 201, 203, 204, 206, 210, 222, 229, 231, 253, 311
-Mustarshid('Abbasid Caliph), 11, 192, 304, 305, 312, 361
-Musta'sim (last 'Abbasid Caliph), 12, 29, 457, 460, 465, 533
Mustazad ("complemented" or "increment poems"), 23, 39, 43, 44
-Mustawfi (work ascribed to Nasir-i-Khusraw), 244
Mutadadd (antithesis), 62
Mutalawwin (variety of verse), 63
-Mu'tamid ('Abbasid Caliph), 217
-Mutanabbi (Arabic poet), 88, 115, 124, 144
Mutaqarib (metre), 144, 276
Mutarraf (variety of prose), 21, 59
Mutarriz Mosque of Nishapur, massacre in —, 385
-Mutarrizi (Arabic philologist), 487
-Mu'tasim ('Abbasid Caliph), 279
-Mutawakkil ('Abbasid Caliph), 279, 281
Mutawazi (variety of prose), 21, 59
Mutawazin (variety of prose), 21, 59
Mutazalzil (rhetorical figure), 73
Mu'tazili sect, 134, 160, 354, 362
Ibnu'l-Mu'tazz, 87
Muthamman (octameter), 24, 25
Muwaffaq, Abu Mansur — (author of Pharmacology), 115
Muwaffaq, Fadlu'llah -Saqa'i (author of Supplement to Ibn Khallikan's *Biographies*), 475
Muwaffaq of Nishapur, Khwaja —, 174, 221–222
Muwashshah (variety of verse), 23, 24, 41, 44, 45, 66
Muwassal (rhetorical figure), 67
Muzdawaj (rhyme), 63. See *Mathnawi*
"Mysteries" (*asrar*, name of Indian hemp), 205

N

-Nabalusi, Shaykh 'Abdu'l-Ghani —, 504
-Nabigha (ancient Arabian poet), 228
Ibnu'n-Nabih, 87
Nabil, of Zarand, Babi poet, 70
Abu Nadhar 'Abdu'l-'Aziz b. Mansur. See *'Asjadi*
Nadhim of Herat (Persian poet), 146
Nadhira ("parallel"), 45, 82
Nadir Shah, 5
Nafahatu'l-Uns (by Jami), 263, 438, 491–493, 494, 495, 497, 498, 502, 503, 509, 510
Nafhu't Tib min Ghusni'l-Andalusi'r-Ratib (by -Maqqari), 498, 500
Nahawand, 186, 188
Nahhas, Abu'l-Ma'ali — (author of satirical verses), 186
Nahr Bashir, 462
Nahr 'Isa, 461
Nahr Malik, 461
Na'im, Hajji — (executed by Qabus b. Washmgir), 104
Na'in, 224
Abu'n-Najib Suhrawardi, 491, 496
Najjar-i-Sagharchi (Persian poet), 335
Abu'n Najm Ahmad b. Qus, 153. See *Minuchihri*
Abu Najm-i-Sarraj (Isma'ili da'i), 202
Najmu'd-Din, 337 (= Nidhami-i-'Arudi, *q.v.*)
Najmu'd-Din Abu Bakr Muhammad -Rawandi, 117
Najmu'd-Din Abu Hafs 'Umar of Nasaf (theologian and jurisconsult), 355
Najmu'd-Din Daya of Ray, 249, 250, 252, 256, 489, 493, 495–496
Najmu'd-Din Kubra, 438, 489, 491–495, 508, 510
Nakhshab, 446. See *Nasaf*
Nama-i-Khusrawan (by Prince Jalal), 6
Napoleon I, 60
Naqib, 197
Naqibu'l 'Alawiyyin, 114
Narshakhi (author of History of Bukhara), 114
Nasa, 107, 138, 170, 438, 446, 473
Nasaf (= Nakhshab), 342, 355, 446
-Nasawi, Shihabu'd-Din Muhammad — (author of Memoirs of Jalalu'd-Din Mankoburni), 434, 436, 446, 473–474
Nasibis, 229. See *Sunnis*
Nasihat (of 'Abdu'llah Ansari), 270
Nasihu'd-Din of Arrajan, Qadi —, 361
-Nasir ('Abbasid Caliph), 436, 455
Nasir-i-Khusraw, 160, 162, 169, 189, 200–201, 211, 218–246; 224 *et seqq.* (dualistic theory); 271, 274, 289, 365, 374, 425, 456, 479, 483, 509
Nasiru'd-Din of Tus (philosopher), 220, 243, 256, 257, 442, 443, 456, 457, 460, 462, 465, 484–486
Nasiru'd-Din 'Abdu'r-Rahim b. Abi Mansur, Isma'ili Governor of Quhistan, 220, 456
Nasiru'd-Din Mahmud Shah b. Shamsu'd-Din Iltatmish, 470
Nasiru'd-Din Mangli, 455
Nasiru'd-Din Qubacha, 470, 478, 479
Nasiru'd-Din Shah Qajar, 181, 187
Nasr II (Samani), 202
Nasr b. Ahmad (Samani), 15, 16, 202, 215
Abu Nasr Ahmad b. Mansur of Tus, called Asadi, 148, 272. See *Asadi, the Elder*
Abu Nasr 'Arraq (mathematician), 96, 97
Abu Nasr-i-Farahi (author of *Nisab*), 488
Abu Nasr -Isma'ili, 294
Abu Nasr Khalil b. Ahmad 152
Nasr b. Mansur -Tamimi, 279
Nasr b. Subuktigin, Abu'l-Mudhaffar — (brother of Sultan Mahmud of Ghazna), 100, 101, 121, 122
Abu Nasr -'Utbi. See *'Utbi*
Nasru'llah b. 'Abdu'l-Hamid, Abu'l-Ma'ali — (translator of *Kalila and Dimna* into Persian), 299, 346, 349, 351

U

V

W